Hitler

Diagnosis of a Destructive Prophet

Fritz Redlich, M.D.

OXFORD
UNIVERSITY PRESS

OXFORD

UNIVERSITY PRESS

Oxford   New York

Athens   Auckland   Bangkok   Bogotá   Buenos Aires   Calcutta
Cape Town   Chennai   Dar es Salaam   Delhi   Florence   Hong Kong
Istanbul   Karachi   Kuala Lumpur   Madrid   Melbourne   Mexico City
Mumbai   Nairobi   Paris   São Paulo   Singapore   Taipei   Tokyo
Toronto   Warsaw

and associated companies in
Berlin   Ibadan

First published by Oxford University Press, Inc., 1998
198 Madison Avenue, New York, New York 10016

First issued as an Oxford University Press paperback, 2000

Oxford is a registered trademark of Oxford University Press

Library of Congress Cataloging-in-Publication Data
Redlich, Fritz, 1910–
Hitler : diagnosis of a destructive prophet / Fritz Redlich.
p. cm.   Includes bibliographical references and index.
ISBN 0-19-505782-1 (cloth)
ISBN 0-19-513631-4 (Pbk.)
1. Hitler, Adolf, 1889–1945—Psychology.
2. Hitler, Adolf, 1889–1945—Mental health.
3. Heads of state—Germany—Psychology.
4. Austria—Social conditions
5. National socialism—Psychological aspects.
6. Heads of state—Germany—Biography.
I. Title.   DD247.H5R384   1998
943.086'092—dc21   [B]   97-48888

1 3 5 7 9 10 8 6 4 2

Printed in the United States of America
on acid-free paper

To Herta

Er nennt's Vernunft und braucht's allein um tierischer als jedes Tier zu sein. [He calls it reason and employs it resolute to be more brutish than is any brute.]

Johann Wolfgang von Goethe, Faust,
*Part I, Mephisto's Prologue in Heaven
(Translated by Walter Kaufmann,
New York, 1963)*

Contents

Preface

ADOLF HITLER—a nameless man as he called himself before he became the leader of Germany[1]—with the help of fanatic disciples and gullible masses profoundly changed Germany and the political face of Europe. He unleashed a terrible war and unprecedented genocide in which fifty million people died. This is why he horrifies and fascinates so many. This is why people want to know more about him, and why hundreds of thousands of books and articles—ranging in quality from eminent scholarship to trash—have been written about him. Yet many burning questions remain unanswered. One of the largely unresolved questions is whether physical illness or mental disorder could contribute to an understanding of his behavior. That is the topic of this book, the only topic to which I—not a historian by profession—could make a contribution.

My scholarly interest in Hitler started late, fifteen years ago, at the time of my retirement from a position as a university psychiatrist in the mid-1980s. I lived at the time in greater Los Angeles, close to the community of Torrance, the world capitol of so-called revisionism, and began to study the literature on the denial of the Holocaust and related propositions that Hitler would have been a great and benign leader had it not been for the wicked Jews and, amongst other things, the manipulations of his malignant physician, Dr. Theodor Morell. The politically motivated effort to rehabilitate Hitler is not a new endeavor. Gordon A. Craig, an eminent student of modern German history, recognized it more than fifteen years ago.[2] The endeavor has gained momentum, less through the action of skinheads and other crazies than through the writings of some scholars. The medical

aspects of revisionism—the so-called medical stab-in-the-back thesis—
interested me and fell into my field of competence as a specialist in psychiatry
and neurology. My personal interest in Hitler goes back to my youth.
As a young socialist, I was deeply opposed to National Socialism. I discovered as an adult that I had Jewish ancestors and was forced to leave my native
Austria when it became part of the Third Reich. I emigrated to the United
States, where I was able to continue my academic work, and also participated
in World War II as a medical officer in the U.S. Army in the fight against
National Socialism. Seven unfortunate family members died during the war,
six in concentration camps and one as a member of the German air force.
Undoubtedly, these personal experiences had a profound impact on me and
this book. As a physician I am accustomed to thinking in terms of prevention. My hope is that this book will, if only to the slightest degree, aid prevention through knowledge. Prevention might be of the utmost importance
because a future dictator like Hitler would possess nuclear and biological
weapons, information about genetic engineering, and have access to cyberspace.[3]

During the course of my research, I discovered that only a small number
of publications about Hitler's medical illnesses exist. Scanning the literature
taught me that there were enough problems to warrant a new treatise on the
subject. In contrast to the scant medical literature,[4] psychological comments
abound. Obviously, everybody feels entitled to opinions about psychological
matters. Such comments are contained in the great biographies, but also in
monographs and books written by psychiatrists, psychologists, and psychoanalysts.[5] I asked myself whether I could add new observations and conclusions and decided to try.

Thus, this book is a short pathography, in contrast to the existing
biographies of Adolf Hitler. The word pathography is defined in *The Greater
Oxford Dictionary* as the study of the life and character of an individual, as
influenced by disease. Questions that are posed in this book include the following: What were Hitler's illnesses? How severe were they? Did they interfere with his work? Was he mentally impaired? If so, what kind of
impairment was it? Did Hitler abuse drugs, and what were the consequences
of such abuse? Was Hitler's criminal behavior caused by psychological
impairment or drug abuse? Was Hitler competently treated?

I have been very concerned that my statements are as objective as
humanly possible. A friend, the political scientist Irving Bernstein, told me
that political scientists and historians are inclined to regard the question of
objectivity as a dead horse that one should stop beating, and maintained that
it is not the scholar but the lay person who has problems with objectivity.[6]
Yet in scanning the medical literature it is my impression that the objectivity
problem is not obsolete. A controversy among German historians, the so-
called "Historikerstreit," raged for years and has barely reached a sub-acute
stage. During Hitler's lifetime, the dictator was viewed by large numbers of
people, his close associates, and also scholars as either a superman or a devil.
It may take another hundred or more years to be able to discuss Hitler *sine*

ira cum studio (exploring without anger), and much will be lost because a distant view is not the same as a close view. In a spirited article, Ron Rosebaum cited the views of Jewish intellectuals—notably Claude Lanzmann, director of the remarkable Holocaust film *Shoah*—who are opposed to any attempt to explain Hitler, because explaining inevitably leads to empathy.[7] There is a kernel of truth in this. However, empathy is not sympathy. Intellectuals are expected to contribute to enlightenment. One danger is identification with the aggressor, and only knowledge is likely to reduce or prevent that danger. Total objectivity is unrealistic, but an attempt to attain it must be made.

A pathography offers an opportunity—and also a constraint—in tackling the problem. Physicians are trained to study problems with some detachment (at times too much of it). It is not an insurmountable problem to explore Hitler's somatic complaints with some degree of objectivity and equanimity. Greater discrepancies of opinion, however, and more heat than enlightenment are expressed when Hitler's behavior, and particularly his monstrous crimes, are being explored. To a certain extent, differences of opinion can be related to ethnic differences among the observers. Populations who were victims of the National Socialist regime—such as Jews, Gypsies, and Slavs (Russians, Poles, Czechs, and Serbs), and also Germans, who were both victims and perpetrators—hold different beliefs about Hitler than those who were not directly touched by his fury. Among leading scholars, however, ethnic differences are smaller than in the general population.

The most vexing cause of a lack of objectivity can be traced to personal reactions. Some of these responses are conscious, and hence can be the subject of discussion and scrutiny, while others are preconscious and unconscious, which means that they are not directly available for discourse. Freud developed the concept of countertransference in his case studies.[8] It designates unconscious reactions, on the part of the analyst toward the patient, that interfere with therapeutic work. According to analytic doctrine, such responses must be analyzed in the joint work of therapist and patient to set the therapy back on the right track. In the newer view of some psychoanalysts, countertransference also can provide important cues for the observer. Analogous to the therapeutic situation, a historical investigation also generates unconscious responses to the subject of the investigation on the part of the investigator that may help or hinder the process. Unfortunately, it is very difficult to identify such responses and their origin. I have been quite frustrated by my inability to pinpoint countertransference and make a succinct statement about what I have learned from it. Awareness of countertransference, however, makes the investigator more alert, and also more prudent. Some self-analysis of countertransference may help reduce anxious and angry feelings that interfere with the work. As a Hitler investigator, one should not feel like a herpetologist who fears snakes—or at least if one does, one should try to analyze one's fears.

The primary sources I have used are the written and oral statements made by Hitler,[9] and selected published statements by contemporaries who

were in prolonged contact with him.[10] I found that evaluating Hitler's statements calls for extraordinary wariness. As a physician, I am used to hearing
deliberately or preconsciously false statements from patients. While Hitler's
lies to his doctor did not surprise me, still I was dumbfounded by Hitler's
political distortions. To make matters more complicated, Hitler at times was
extraordinarily candid. Distinguishing truth from lie in Hitler's case is a taxing endeavor for historians and pathographers. A different problem is
encountered in many of the statements made by Hitler's contemporaries
who became memoirists. Many of them were fighting for their lives, property, and reputations in court, and thus their reports need to be scrutinized
with great care. The same guardedness I encountered in the few interviews
with contemporaries who had been in close contact with Hitler.[11]

With respect to psychiatric methods, my approach to the case study of
Adolf Hitler is eclectic, derived from my lifelong work as a psychiatrist. The
clinical practice of psychiatry is based on the triad of biological sciences,
behavioral sciences (including psychology, sociology, and cultural anthropology), and psychoanalysis (the interpretative science of the unconscious).
Somewhat to my surprise, I found the value of the psychoanalytic method
more limited in understanding Hitler than I had expected. The analysis of
transference (the patient's repetition of earlier behavior within the context of
the psychoanalytic situation), which leads in the joint work of analyst and
patient to the discovery of unconscious processes, is not applicable to the
study of historical personalities. Hitler did not describe for posterity a single
dream—perhaps he had heard about Freud's remark that dreams are the
royal road to the unconscious and did not want "Jewish brain parasites" to
penetrate his psyche. There are hardly any significant parapraxias (slips of the
tongue, forgetting, etc.—what Peter Loewenberg called the byways to the
unconscious[12]) on Hitler's part. I believe that most psychoanalysts investi-
gating Hitler have speculated more than the facts permit. I attempted to
analyze some of Hitler's irrational and impulsive acts, metaphors, and
imagery, but the yield was modest. After expressing such skepticism about
application of the psychoanalytic method, however, I would like to state that
my psychological profile of Hitler would not have been possible without the
general insights that Sigmund Freud, Anna Freud, Carl G. Jung, Alfred
Adler, Erik Erikson, Alexander and Margarete Mitscherlich, and many of
their students have given the world.

Two other specific methodologies warrant description. The presentation
of data and conclusions follows the principle of operationalism, an approach
described by the American physicist Percy W. Bridgman, and also by the
philosophers of the Viennese school of logical positivism.[13] In essence,
Bridgman postulated that concepts and theories are determined by the operations of the investigation—such as observations, measurements, and tests—
which yield data. In the case of this opus, these are observations of Hitler's
transactions. From this derives the simple division of this book into Part I
(Chapters 1 to 7), a description of Hitler's developmental and political years,
and Part II (Chapters 8 and 9), a review, analysis, and synthesis of the data

presented in Part I. Part II also contains a critique of the opinions set forth
by other Hitler authors. The division, in my opinion, enhances objectivity,
and also provides scholars with the opportunity to arrive at independent
conclusions about Hitler's behavior and health. Of course, it does not guarantee objectivity, because the data presented in Part I are my choice. The
appendices contain a glossary of medical terms, a chart of Hitler's extended
family, a table of significant medications, a chronology of Hitler's illnesses,
and the report of the Russian autopsy. The glossary should help the medically uneducated reader to understand the medical terms used throughout
this work. By necessity, the study is Hitler-centered, or what historians call
intentionalist, but it recognizes the importance of social and political forces
that shaped Hitler and National Socialism. I have no intention of trying to
demonstrate that psychological factors are the most important factors in an
appraisal of Hitler; however, they are important in light of Hitler's highly
personal point of view about history and his role in it. It is my goal to high-
light a segment of the Hitler portrait that historians, if they care to use it,
ultimately may integrate into a comprehensive picture.

Another significant feature of the book is the recognition that assertions
in the biological and social sciences, and in clinical medicine, are rarely certain, but in varying degrees probable. I have many times referred to events
and to inferences about events as very likely, likely, unlikely, or very unlikely.
I deliberately chose the words "likely" and "unlikely," and in most cases
avoided the word "probable," a term used in mathematical probability theory. Very likely or very unlikely roughly refer to near certainty, and likely
simply means that an event or assumption is more likely than unlikely. In
meteorology and clinical medicine, such subjective estimates (guesstimates
in clinical jargon) are common, and of course at times wrong.

This book is written for an intelligent general reader interested in
Hitler's personality and illnesses. The medical assessment and psychological
profile merits the attention of behavioral scientists, physicians, and, especially, psychiatrists. I hope that the book will be of some interest to historians, as well, because it contains some new and rarely mentioned views and
data, such as: (1) the presence of psychotic and mentally retarded members
in Hitler's extended family, and of real and self-assumed developmental
anomalies in Hitler; (2) new data about amphetamine abuse; (3) the tentative diagnosis of giant cell arteritis, an autoimmune disease; (4) the degeneration hypothesis, or the significance of Hitler's irrational views about
syphilis as a Jewish hereditary disease causing degenerative changes and his
mission to destroy the evil and sick Jews and thus to redeem and cure the
Germans and, ultimately, the world; and, finally, (5) an interpretation of
Hitler as a charismatic, paranoid, destructive leader and prophet.[14]

Of course, I have asked myself whether I have come a tiny bit closer
during twelve years of work to an understanding of this enigmatic and terrible person. Perhaps it is an impossible task, as the architect and later armament minister Albert Speer[15] and General Alfred Jodl[16]—two of Hitler's
close collaborators and admirers—admitted. Perhaps one should not write

about a person one loathes, as my friend the late Peter Ostwald, a psychiatrist and biographer of composers, once advised me. Certainly, if this policy were carried out faithfully, it would result in a vast paper reduction, but how would we then become informed about Hitler? Finally, I tell myself that one can never completely explain or understand another person, or even oneself. We are only able to look through windows of behavior and hope that gifted persons will open new windows.

Acknowledgments

MANY HELPED ME with this book, and I am grateful to them. Four friends—two historians, Professor Peter Loewenberg of the University of California, Los Angeles, and Professor Norbert Frei of the University of Bochum, Germany, and two psychiatrists Eugene Bliss, M.D., of the University of Utah and Garrett O'Connor, M.D., of the University of California, Los Angeles—read the entire manuscript. Thomas Detre, M.D., of the University of Pittsburgh, Lawrence Friedman, M.D., and Edwin Shneidman, Ph.D., of the University of California, Los Angeles, read individual chapters. To Professor Loewenberg I could turn at any time for advice, not only about historical questions but about psychoanalytic problems. Professor Frei I met through a gratuitous incident—in the summer of 1986 I had an appointment with the late Professor Martin Broszat of the Institut für Zeitgeschichte in Munich, and the busy man referred me to his associate, Norbert Frei. Since that time, Professor Frei has given me many days of counsel and advice; furthermore, a warm friendship has developed from this collaboration. He, more than anyone else, helped me navigate and find my way through territory that was new for me. I greatly benefited from discussing Hitler's intricate psychiatric problems with Eugene Bliss, M.D., and Garrett O'Connor. The latter in particular encouraged me not to give up, no matter how tough it was to understand these problems. Richard Pasternak, M.D., Medizinalrat Dr. Lotte Slama-Klepsch, and Kevin R. Frawley, D.D.S., provided significant help with certain medical and dental questions. Professor Ernst Günther Schenck helped not only with medical information provided in his classic text, *Patient Hitler*, but also provided authentic information about the Third

Reich. It was very gratifying for me when, during such cooperation, a collegial friendship developed between two former enemies. I am grateful to Ottmar Katz for helping me to orient myself in Hitler's weird medical and political world. From a dear friend, the late professor Karl Deutsch, I learned much about Hitler's nationalism. To attend the lectures of Professor Michael R. Marrus, while he was guest professor at UCLA, was invaluable.

In spring 1986, about a year after I started to work on this opus, I met Professor Shlomo Aronson, professor of political science at Hebrew University in Jerusalem and a highly regarded expert in the politics of the Third Reich, then guest professor at the University of California, Los Angeles. We concluded that our skills in writing a pathography of Adolf Hitler would complement each other and decided to collaborate. During weekly conferences extending over a year, I learned a great deal from Professor Aronson and his publications. Just about when we started to write jointly—in the spring of 1987—Professor Aronson decided to return to Hebrew University. We agreed to discontinue our work, because collaboration—which is never easy—would have been very cumbersome at a distance of more than 8000 miles. By mutual consent, we agreed that I, by myself, would continue to work on this project.

The assistance of John Taylor of the National Archives in Washington, D.C., has been invaluable. I received much help from Stephen Novak, an intellectual companion, and also from Annette Moore, who shaped the manuscript with intelligence, sensitivity, and patience. I gratefully acknowledge the discretionary grants I received from the former president of the Carnegie Foundation, Dr. David Hamburg, and from Dr. Gardner Lindsey, former director of the Center for Advanced Study in the Behavioral Sciences at Stanford. Last but not least, I want to thank senior editor Nancy Lane, her successor, Thomas LeBien, and the production editor Helen Mules of Oxford University Press for their encouragement and constructive assistance in producing this opus. I particularly appreciate Mr. LeBien's gentle effort to keep me focused on the principal task of the book.

An important and relevant work by Wolfgang Wippermann, *Der Kosequente Wahn Ideologie und Politik Adolf Hitler*, München, 1989, came to my attention while my opus was already in the printer's hands. Some of Wippermann's ideas about syphilis are similar to mine.

HITLER

I

HITLER'S LIFE
FROM BIRTH TO DEATH

1

Family and Childhood

ADOLF HITLER was born on 20 April 1889 in the Austro-Bavarian border town of Braunau on the river Inn. On the main square stands a statue of the town's patron saint, Johannes Palm, a German nationalist and hater of the French who was executed by Napoleonic soldiers. Thirty-five years later, Hitler created his own legend of his birthplace.[1] In the first sentence of *Mein Kampf*, Hitler pontificated in the language of a prophet: "Today, it seems to me providential that fate should have chosen Braunau on the Inn as my birthplace. . . . this little town on the boundary between two German states, which we at least have made it our life's work to reunite by every means at our disposal."[2] This passage is both an expression of the self-made Hitler myth and the blueprint for a gigantic program that Hitler tried to accomplish about fifteen years later. In reality, the Hitler family stayed in Braunau for only three years, and the town had little or no impact on the boy. What shaped Hitler was not Providence, but unique political, economic, and biopsychosocial facts that set the stage on which he played out one of mankind's greatest tragedies. The exploration of the biopsychosocial factors appropriately begins with a description of Hitler's family.[3]

The Hitler Family

The story begins with Hitler's parents: Adolf Hitler's father, Alois Hitler, the illegitimate son of Anna Maria Schickelgruber and an unknown father; and his mother, Clara Hitler, daughter of Johann Baptist Pölzl and Johanna Pölzl, *née* Hüttler.[4] The Hitlers and the Schickelgrubers came from the Waldviertel in Lower Austria, then a backward region of somber forests only a short distance from the lively and glittering capital of the Austro-Hungarian Empire. In spite of its proximity to Vienna, no greater contrast could be imagined than that which existed between the Viennese and the peasants who were Hitler's ancestors, who lived in hamlets and tilled the meager soil in small farms. Illiteracy, illegitimacy, and inbreeding were common in the region, and occurred within the Hitler family.[5] (See Appendix 2 for Hitler's extended family tree.)

Hitler's Father: Alois Hitler (Schickelgruber)

Hitler's father, Alois, the son of an unmarried forty-two-year-old peasant woman named Anna Maria Schickelgruber, was born on 7 June 1837 in the village of Strones in Lower Austria. Rumor had it that Anna Maria Schickelgruber had gone to Graz or Vienna before her pregnancy to find employment as a domestic worker, like many peasant girls from the Waldviertel; however, it is quite possible that she never left. She did not reveal the father's name at the time of her child's baptism, nor at any later date. At the time of delivery, she lived with the family of a peasant, Johann Trummelschläger, and his wife. Shortly thereafter she moved into her father's house and five years later married a journeyman mill worker, Johann Georg Hiedler. Anna Maria died on 7 January 1847, when the child was nine years old. After her death, even though Johann Georg remained alive until 1857, Alois lived with Johann Georg's brother, a prosperous peasant named Johann Nepomuk Hiedler. Nineteen years later, in 1876, Johann Nepomuk Hiedler requested from the village priest in Döllersheim that Alois Schickelgruber's name on his certificate of baptism be changed to Alois Hitler, and that Johann Georg Hiedler be recognized as the father. He brought three witnesses with him—one of them his son-in-law Josef Romeder—who testified that Johann Georg Hiedler had told them he was Alois's father and signed a statement with three X's. Although the delayed procedure was open to question, it was recognized by State and Church. By then, Johann Georg had been dead for almost twenty years, and Alois was thirty-nine. Historians have speculated as to why such a request was made and who Adolf Hitler's paternal grandfather was. Maser maintains that Johann Nepomuk was the father: He induced his vagrant brother to marry Anna Maria, he took great interest in Alois, but would not have been able to raise him as a foster son if his wife had known about his paternity.[6] According to the official Nazi version, Johann Georg was the father. The discrepancy would be of little interest if not for the fact that Adolf Hitler was uncertain about who his paternal grandfather was, and about whether he might have been a Jew.

Almost nothing is known about the first five years of Alois's life, when he lived with his mother. It is likely that those first few years were harsh. After his mother's death, when Alois moved into the house of his uncle, he was well accepted. He attended the village school and became the apprentice to a local cobbler. At the age of sixteen, he moved to Vienna and continued to practice his trade. At the age of eighteen, he joined the Imperial Customs

Service as a frontier guard. With discipline and industry, he was able to rise rapidly in the ranks of the service. He was assigned to numerous stations of the Customs Service in upper Austria until he reached the highest possible rank for anyone with only elementary schooling. He was a robust and restless man—a good provider for his family—who attained lower middle-class status through his work. Alois was known as a reliable public servant, loyal to the Emperor, obedient to those above him, and demanding strict obedience from those below him. It seems he was not popular with his colleagues. One of them described him as zealous and compulsively punctual. Yet he was considered a fair person, though rough and insensitive at times. One characteristic trait was his independence from others, both colleagues and townspeople. He cast off his early background but retained some peasant shrewdness that showed in the sound management of his finances. At work, in the family, and toward his sons, he was an authoritarian personality, a petty tyrant. He was pleased with his achievements, being the only one in his peasant clan to rise to a middle-class position. One can discern from photographs that he carried his uniform with pride and pomposity. Hitler was eager to describe Alois Sr. as a liberal[7] and a cosmopolitan to show how he had distanced himself from his father's views and to demonstrate his independence. Although marked anti-Semitism was prevalent in Alois's milieu, he was not a radical ethnocentric or an anti-Semite. The family physician, Dr. Eduard Bloch, was a Jew. Alois's best friend was a Czech named Wessely. Alois had no use for the Catholic Church but wanted his wife to attend and to bring the children up as Catholics. It is possible that he sympathized with Georg von Schönerer's anti-Semitic, anti-clerical, and anti-Habsburg German Nationalist Party, which, as a loyal public servant, he could not openly express. Rumors existed that he drank a lot. If so, he kept his drinking well hidden while he was on active duty. He was critical of uncontrolled drinking in a letter and reportedly believed that excessive drinking was not compatible with duty in the Customs Service[8]—many alcoholics, however, are critical of fellow alcoholics.

Hitler's father was married three times and had an illegitimate child before he was married. His first wife was Anna Glassl, whom he married in 1873, the daughter of a customs official who was Alois's superior. Anna was ten years older than Alois, and, in all likelihood, this union brought monetary advantages and helped his career. After he started an affair with Franziska (Fanny) Matzelsberger, a servant in the inn where Alois and his wife resided, Anna divorced him. When Anna died in 1885, Alois married Franziska. At that time his young niece, Clara Pölzl, who later became Adolf Hitler's mother, worked as a servant in Alois's household. Franziska, well aware of Alois Sr.'s wandering eye, insisted that Clara return to her family. The first child of Alois Sr. and Franziska, Alois Jr., was born out of wedlock. Later, the couple had a second child, Angela. When Fanny became ill with tuberculosis, Clara was called back to the household to take care of the children. She became not only a nursemaid, but also Alois's mistress while Fanny was still alive. Six months after Fanny's death, Alois married Clara. Before the wedding could take place, Alois had to obtain a papal dispensation because he and Clara were considered cousins since he had been recognized as Johann Georg Hiedler's "legitimate" son. The letter he wrote was both correct and devious, stating the merits of marrying a poor girl who otherwise might not find a husband, but not admitting that she was pregnant by him.[9]

At the age of fifty-eight, after forty years of service with the rank of Customs Officer First Class, Alois Sr. retired in 1895 for unstated health reasons. He hoped to devote himself to an agreeable life spent with friends and to enjoy his avocation of beekeeping, but the restless man kept moving from one small upper Austrian town to another. Within a year he bought a small farm in Hafeld, sold it, moved to Lambach, and finally relocated to a house with nine acres of land in Leonding. Some of the money for these purchases came from his inheritance from Johann Nepomuk and other small legacies in the family;[10] the origin of the rest is unclear. He missed his work and found little pleasure in retirement and domestic life. Although he begat eight children in his marriages, he did not enjoy them, with the possible exception of the youngest—Paula. To escape from domestic friction and boredom, he spent more time in the local pub. It is likely that, at the time of his retirement, the "old gentleman" was a clinical alcoholic who tyrannized his family. Alois Sr. died suddenly on 3 January 1903, in the village inn, after coughing up some blood. On the death certificate, the cause of death was described as a pulmonary hemorrhage. Hitler stated that the cause of his father's death was a "stroke of apoplexy."[11] In his obituary, Alois Sr. was described as

> a progressive man and a warm friend of the Free School [a school without religious instruction]. From time to time he would utter a harsh word, but under a rough shell there was a good heart. He always committed himself energetically to what was just and right.[12]

As obituaries are usually eulogies, the reference to his roughness seems significant.

Hitler's Mother: Clara Hitler *née* Pölzl

Clara was born on 12 August 1860 in Spital, another village in the Waldviertel. She was the daughter of Johann Baptist Pölzl and Johanna, *née* Hüttler. After minimal schooling, she gladly followed the invitation of Alois Sr. to work in his household after Fanny became ill with tuberculosis. She became first his servant and nursemaid, then his mistress, and finally his wife. The attractive young woman, twenty-three years younger than her husband, was the most sympathetic member of the Hitler clan. Her husband completely dominated her, and for a long time she called him Uncle.[13] The autodidact Alois was far superior to Clara in terms of education, and he did not hesitate to express this. Whereas his handwriting was calligraphic and he composed letters and documents in an Austrian bureaucratic style, she was barely able to write her name.[14] In the monologues Hitler stated with black humor:

The Internal Ministry of the Reich issued a questionnaire to find out whether a person should be sterilized. If my mother had been asked, "Why does an iron ship swim?" Three-quarters of such questions my dear mother could never have answered! I would never have been born.[15] [Yet these questions determined life or death or sterilization for tens of thousands of people.]

Clara adjusted to her status, had some appreciation for culture, arranged for Adolf to have piano lessons, and encouraged him to learn. Her view of her husband as a towering authority extended beyond his death. She kept a rack with his pipes in the kitchen and pointed at them when she wanted to emphasize her authority.[16] By most authors, she has been described as a warm and docile person who devoted herself to her family. She came to the Hitler household as a buoyant and optimistic young woman, then gradually became depressed. It happened with good reason: It was no fun being married to Alois and taking care of his children, and, most important, three of her children died in early childhood. Clara's painful illness and death from carcinoma of the breast was the final stroke of ill fortune. In *Mein Kampf* Hitler made the rather simplistic statement: "I honored my father, but I loved my mother."[17] Later, he stated repeatedly that he feared his father. As the story unfolds, it will become evident that Hitler was deeply ambivalent, mostly loving but not quite trusting his mother, and mostly hating his father but also yearning for his love.

The Siblings

Of Hitler's siblings, Otto died shortly after birth, Gustav and Ida died of diphtheria in early childhood, and Edmund died of diphtheria in 1900, at age five, when Adolf was eleven. Adolf had an ambivalent attitude toward his living siblings. He avoided and disliked his half-brother, Alois Jr., son of Alois Sr. and Franziska Matzelsberger, who remained in the Hitler household until he was thirteen and then either left of his own will or was kicked out by his irate father, who reduced his inheritance to the legal minimum. Alois Jr. attended elementary school for eight years, worked as a common laborer, and later became a waiter. In 1900 and 1902, he served short prison sentences for theft. During his wanderings through Europe and the British Isles, he married an Irish woman, Brigid, in 1909 and had a son named Patrick with her but abandoned them after a short period of marriage. After the First World War he returned to Germany and in 1924 was sentenced to another prison term of six months for bigamy. During the thirties Alois Jr. acquired a bar, and later a restaurant in Berlin. Hitler resented the way Alois Jr. and Patrick gossiped about the Hitler family. Articles appeared in *Paris Soir*[18] and in American newspapers. Patrick complained that his uncle did not help him find a suitable job, and Uncle Adolf felt that no one should profit from carrying the name of Hitler. Adolf Hitler disliked and ignored both Alois Jr. and Patrick, but he took no punitive action against them. He rarely talked about them and did not want to be reminded of them. His attending surgeon,

Hanskarl von Hasselbach, learned of Alois Jr.'s existence only after 1945.[19] However, Hitler allotted 60,000 marks to Alois Jr. in his first will in 1938.[20] John Toland reported that Patrick Hitler became an American citizen, changed his name, served in the United States Navy, lived an anonymous life somewhere in the New York metropolitan area, and had a son with the name of Adolf.[21]

Hitler's half-sister, Angela, five years older, and his sister, Paula, six years younger, were inconspicuous people. In her youth, Angela was an attractive girl. Before her marriage, Adolf had a closer relationship with her than with Paula. Angela finished elementary school and then helped out in the Hitler household until she married Leo Raubal, a tax collector, in 1903. She had two daughters, Angela (known as Geli) and Friedericke (Friedl). Antagonism developed between Adolf and the Raubals when Leo criticized the idling Adolf and suggested that he become a postal clerk. Leo died in 1910, and Angela Sr. had to fend for herself and her daughters, as well as for Paula. She intimated that she might go to court for a share of Adolf's inheritance allotment, which Adolf received under false pretenses that he was a student. However, Adolf "voluntarily" gave her that share.[22] In 1930, Adolf asked Angela to manage his household in Berchtesgaden. From 1928 until the time of her suicide in 1931, Geli lived in a room in Hitler's large apartment in Munich, an arrangement to which her mother did not object. After Geli's death, Angela stayed on in Adolf's employ. A year later he abruptly asked her to leave, presumably because she was critical of Hitler's relationship with Eva Braun. At the age of fifty-two, Angela married Professor Martin Hammitzsch, director of an architectural school, and Adolf frostily referred to her as Frau Hammitzsch.[23] She died in 1949 at the age of sixty-six. Paula Hitler attended elementary school, later a secretarial school, and worked in various Austrian government agencies as a clerk. Paula was not a shining light but rumors that she was mentally retarded are false. When she lost her job in 1930, Adolf supported her. She assumed Adolf's pet name Wolf because she did not want to be in the limelight as the Führer's sister, and lived a quiet, anonymous life. Paula professed affection for her brother and believed he liked her, but there is no evidence of any real closeness on his side. During her interrogation in 1945, she made the remark that she wished Adolf would have become a builder.[24] Clearly, Hitler had a low opinion of his sisters' intelligence. In a conversation with Christa Schroeder he called them stupid geese.[25] In spite of his ambivalence, however, he remembered all of his siblings in his personal will.

Other Relatives

Hitler's mother Clara had two sisters: Theresa, who married a shrewd and prosperous peasant named Johann Schmidt; and the hunchbacked spinster Johanna, who was considered a difficult person. Theresa and her husband hosted the Hitler family many times during Adolf's childhood and adolescence. One housekeeper—Maria Hörl—quit work in the Hitler household because she considered Johanna crazy.[26] According to rumor, Dr. Kriechbaum, a general practitioner in Braunau, diagnosed her as schizophrenic, but is it not known how he arrived at this diagnosis, nor even whether he examined her. In any case, she was an odd woman. It also has been said that Adolf was frightened of Johanna and that she was unkind to him as a child, but this did not prevent him from asking for her support when he ran out of money in Vienna in 1909. Johanna also helped out in the Hitler household when Clara was ill. In 1944, statements came to the attention of Heinrich Himmler and Martin Bormann indicating that a cousin of Alois Sr., Josef Veit (the son of a peasant named Josef Veit and Josefa Schickelgruber, a sister of Hitler's grandmother, Anna Maria Schickelgruber), had relatives who were mentally retarded and psychotic.[27] It is likely that this was known to Hitler (in spite of his denials, he was well informed about his family tree), and, with his great concern about degeneration, it would have worried him. In the official table of ancestors by Rudolph Koppensteiner, the Veits were not mentioned.[28] One additional putative "relative" must be noted. Werner Maser became convinced that, during the First World War, Hitler fathered an illegitimate son, Jean Marie Loret, born 25 March 1918, with a French peasant woman.[29] Anthropological examination by the Institute of Anthropology at the University of Heidelberg, however, could not confirm this assumption.[30]

After the war, Adolf Hitler distanced himself from his family. Christa Schroeder summed it up: "He has no feelings for the family."[31] It was more than that—Hitler had little in common with his cousins in the country or with his siblings. He had outgrown them. He was rightly wary of Alois Jr. and his son Patrick, although they actually never harmed him. Perhaps they knew too much, but what they revealed in French and American papers was innocuous. Hitler was opposed to nepotism and criticized Napoleon for it. His feelings about his relatives were truly mixed. Though he remembered them in his will, he also gave orders to make the countryside around Döllersheim, one of the villages in his ancestral region (Ahnengau), into an artillery range. The historian Robert Waite assumed that he did this to wipe out birth records,[32] but the records were transported to Vienna before the destruction;[33] nevertheless, the leveling of the village was a hostile act. Certainly, Hitler believed that the private life of a leader and his origin should remain unknown, even mysterious. There is no reason to assume that he had fantasies about his ultimate descent from a very exalted person, although such fantasies are common (psychoanalysts refer to such fantasies as the family romance).

The Jewish Grandfather

Hitler had another concern about his lineage—namely, that his maternal grandfather was a Jew. He expressed this concern during World War I to an officer in his regiment, a Captain Schuh.[34] Hitler reassured himself against such doubts by ordering investigations of the Hitler family by the race office (Rassenamt) of the Schutzstaffel (SS), with the predictable outcome that he was a pure Aryan.[35] Apparently this was not enough, and Hitler asked Hans Frank, his private lawyer (and later governor of the General Government for the annexed area of Poland), to conduct a private investigation of his family tree. Frank dutifully carried out the examination and reported his findings to Hitler. The original report has not been found. In his book, *Im Angesicht des Galgens*, written shortly before his execution, Frank made some garbled statements about a putative Jewish grandfather that became the main source for assumptions that Hitler's grandfather might have been a Jew.[36] The main reasons for the investigation were "insinuations and repulsive blackmail" by Hitler's nephew to the effect that Hitler's paternal grandfather was a Jew. In fact, no such insinuations were ever proven. According to Frank's investigation, Hitler's grandmother, Anna Maria Schickelgruber, from Leonding, worked as a cook in the house of a Jew named Frankenberger or Frankenreithner and was impregnated by his son. After the birth of the child—Hitler's father—Anna Maria went back to the Waldviertel but received alimony and corresponded with young Frankenberger or Frankenreithner. In addition, according to Frank, Adolf Hitler knew about all of this from his father and grandmother. Frank later reversed himself and stated that all of this was not true, that the story had been maintained only to enable Anna Maria to obtain money from the Jew. The fact that Adolf Hitler definitely had no Jewish blood in his veins appeared so self-evident to Frank, reflecting on the man's basic nature, that not another word on the matter might be warranted. Frank reversed himself once more and concluded:

> Then I must concede that it is not completely out of the question that, consequently, Hitler was a half Jew, the product of extramarital relations between Schickelgruber and the Jew from Graz. Accordingly, Hitler himself would have been one-quarter Jewish. If this were the case, his hatred of Jews could be seen as psychotic rage against his relatives. But who can make sense of that?

Perhaps one can; however, Frank's statement is confused and riddled with errors. Anna Maria Schickelgruber was not from Leonding. It is uncertain whether she ever worked in Graz. Hitler could not have heard from his grandmother that Johann Georg was his grandfather, because she had been dead for nearly forty years when he was born. Furthermore, it is unlikely that Alois Sr. discussed his origin with Adolf, who was thirteen at most. At the time of Alois Sr.'s birth, alimonies in the modern sense did not exist, and Anna Maria could not have been engaged in any correspondence because she was illiterate. Decisive is the work of Nikolaus Preradowicz, a historian at the University of Graz, who proved that no Jews resided in Styria at the time of Alois Sr.'s birth. They began to settle in Styria only after 1856.[37]

Frank's statement was made shortly before his execution, when he was in great distress. It is very likely, however, that Hitler commissioned a private report about his genealogy, that Frank's statement is not a fabrication, and that Hitler received a report from him. Hitler seemed unsatisfied and continued to ruminate about the "Jewish grandfather." Albert Speer told Cornelius Schnauber about Hitler's worry over his descent.[38] The story took hold. In 1950, in his book about Hitler's youth, Franz Jetzinger even produced a photograph of Hitler's father, commenting on his Jewish features.[39] Bradley F. Smith, however, established that it was a portrait of a different man.[40] More startling are remarks that Hitler made about ancestry in the monologues:

> Of family and history I have no idea. In this respect I am completely ignorant. Before I did not know that I had relatives. Only when I became Reichs Chancellor I learned this. I am a totally unfamilial creature. That does not suit me. I belong only to my people. . . .
>
> Pfeffer [his SA chief] once told me what he learned about his family. I said to him this does not interest me. He was absolutely stunned. Everybody had ancestors. There is no living person who has no ancestors. . . . It's just an incident, for one the books were burnt, the other one has them. . . .[41]

What a statement from a man who was responsible for the deaths of millions of Jews! Another reason to assume that Hitler might have been preoccupied with the possible existence of a "Jewish grandfather" is an important segment of the so-called Racial Laws (Gesetze zum Schutz des Deutschen Blutes) of Nuremberg in 1935. One portion of the law stated that Aryan women under the age of forty-five were not permitted to work as servants in houses of male Jewish householders. It is known that Hitler took a strong personal interest in the creation of these laws.[42] It is probable that he was motivated by his fear that his grandmother had been impregnated by a Jew.

Thus, no evidence exists to indicate that Hitler's father was half-Jewish. However, Hitler was concerned that his paternal grandfather might have been a Jew. The fact also emerges that Hitler could not document his descent, yet this was a demand that was imposed on every citizen of the Third Reich.

Infancy and Early Childhood

Assisted by a midwife, Clara delivered Adolf in the family quarters of the Pommer Inn in Braunau on 20 April 1889. The newborn was described as a weakly, frail child, but no data about birth weight or early growth have been preserved. The well-known baby picture shows a well-fed, angelic little boy—negating the frailty story. Looking at this portrait, nobody would even think of Adolf Hitler's future development into a murderous tyrant. The picture perhaps demonstrates our difficulty in discerning elements at this early age that would be meaningful for adult life, and also serves to caution us against drawing sweeping conclusions on the basis of photographs. No abnormalities were recorded concerning Hitler's birth; however, to discover developmental abnormalities such as monorchism or hypospadia* would have required a careful examination by a physician or midwife. It is not known whether Hitler was breast- or bottle-fed, or whether he had serious feeding problems or suffered major oral frustrations in infancy and childhood. No

---

* Definitions of medical terms can be found in Appendix 3.

data on toilet training, bed-wetting, or severe neurotic traits exist. Nothing is known about rage attacks in infancy and early childhood, but it is likely that they occurred. Kubizek reported rage attacks during Hitler's puberty. Most probably, Hitler was a very active, "difficult," disobedient, argumentative child, but no data about persistent serious antisocial or extremely aggressive acts during his childhood are known.

Until Adolf was about five, he received a lot of tender maternal care. It is highly probable that Clara was quite indulgent and spoiled him, and perhaps Hitler's adult craving for sweets—which went beyond the customary Austrian liking for cake and whipped cream—could be traced to such indulgence. His father was absent from the family home for long periods due to his duties as a customs official, which meant that life at home in his infancy was peaceful. In the mid-nineties, however, paradise was lost; Adolf's brother Edmund was born in 1894 and sister Paula in 1896, making it necessary for Adolf to be moved out of the parental bedroom to accommodate the younger children. Hitler's great interest in his parents' bedroom is illustrated by a drawing he made of it at the age of ten, calling it "our room"—not a bad drawing, incidentally.[43] Some of Adolf's care was taken over by his six-year-old half-sister Angela and the domestic help the Hitler family employed. The decrease in maternal care must have been painful, but at the same time it eliminated the common trauma of witnessing parental sexual intercourse in the shared bedroom. Between ages five and eight Adolf referred to himself as a little gang leader and recounted with pleasure some of the games he played.[44] They were mostly war games—borrowing scenarios from events such as the Boer War, when he sided with the Boers against the British. His favorite was the Indian and trapper game. Later Adolf read with enthusiasm the popular and puerile writings of Karl May, an author who wrote extensively but without any first-hand knowledge about North America, the Wild West, and the adventures of a noble Indian chief, Winnetou, and his trapper friend, Old Shatterhand. Hitler's interest in Karl May's stories persisted into his adult life, which could be considered unusual and primitive.[45]

Adolf's life definitely became less pleasant when his father retired in 1893 and spent more time at home. Alois Sr. was better at producing than rearing children. With the exception of Paula, the youngsters irritated him. According to Paula, Adolf and Alois Jr. were provocative and disobedient and received frequent thrashings—which, however, did not change their behavior.[46] Controversy exists concerning facts and interpretations surrounding these punishments. Some have viewed Hitler's father as brutal and cruel, while others (like Hitler's later godfather, Josef Mayrhofer) have maintained that Alois Sr.'s bark was worse than his bite.[47] (Both were pretty bad.) One must also consider the reality that, in Germany at the end of the century, physical punishment of children was the rule and not the exception. It is reasonably certain, however, that Hitler felt shamed and humiliated. Alice Miller considered such punishment and, more significant, the humiliation associated with it to be the causes of Hitler's later cruelty and inclination to seek vengeance.[48] The "toga boy" story, told to Toland by Mrs. Hanfstaengl, illustrates the point: In a show of rebellion, Adolf decided to run away from home. Somehow, father Alois learned of these plans and locked the boy in an upstairs room. During the night, Adolf tried to squeeze through the barred window. He couldn't quite make it, so he took off his clothes. As he wriggled his way to freedom, he heard his father's footsteps on the stairs and hastily withdrew, draping his nakedness with a tablecloth. This time, Alois did not punish with a whipping. Instead, he burst into laughter and shouted to Clara that she should come up and look at the "toga boy." The ridicule hurt Adolf more than any switch, and it took him, he confided, a long time to get over the episode.[49] What Hitler resented and feared was his father's scorn. He even felt that his mother could not be trusted and was on his father's side. The likelihood of considerable turmoil in childhood, between three and six, is hinted at by some passages in the second chapter of *Mein Kampf* that in all likelihood refer to observations of parental intercourse. This will be cited in detail in the section about *Mein Kampf* in Chapter 5, and discussed in Chapter 9.

Failure in Middle School

Adolf Hitler received very good grades in the country elementary schools. It was an obvious decision by his father to enroll Adolf in a secondary school that provided his son the opportunity for a higher career that had been denied himself. Two types of secondary schools existed to choose from: the *Gymnasium*, where classical languages and the humanities were taught; and the *Realschule*, which offered a curriculum of mathematics, geometry, drawing, sciences, and modern languages. Hitler's father, a practical man, considered the modern *Realschule* preferable.[50] According to Hitler, his father was influenced in this choice by his son's ability to draw.[51] A governmental career would have been open to graduates from either school. The typical Austrian secondary school was not demanding. Students with average intelligence could pass, and Adolf's superior intelligence should have enabled him to pass easily, yet he was a dismal under-performer. In his later accounts about his school performance, he was less than honest.[52] Jetzinger provided an accurate account of Hitler's school record, listing the following marks at the Linz *Realschule*:[53] In first grade Hitler failed mathematics and natural history, earned marks of 3 in conduct and 4 in diligence—abysmally low—and had to repeat the class.* In second grade he again flunked mathematics and earned a 3 in conduct and a 4 in diligence. In third grade, he again had a 3 in conduct and a 4 in diligence, and in French he earned a 5 (a failing mark). Later he passed the make-up examination in French. The 3 in conduct, an unusually bad mark, is noteworthy. Adolf must have been very troublesome for his teachers. Like many failing students, he was very critical of the curriculum and of his instructors. The teachers were "nuts" (*hatten einen Klaps*) and had

---

* The grades in Austrian middle schools ranged from a high of 1 to a failing grade of 5. In conduct and diligence, any grade below 1 was an indication that the child posed definite behavior problems. A 3 would point to serious misbehavior.

"dirty collars".[54] The only exception was the professor of history, Leopold Poetsch, who gave Adolf a 2 (commendable) and was highly praised by his student. Hitler gave Poetsch credit for teaching him to appreciate history with real understanding. His number-one enemy was the school priest, Father Salo Schwartz, whom he ridiculed and engaged in discussion about inconsistencies in the Bible. A significant comment on Hitler's school performance was furnished by his principal teacher, Eduard Huemer, who gave the following explanation in his testimony at Hitler's putsch trial in 1924:

> Hitler was gifted, one-sided, uncontrolled, and was known to be stubborn, inconsiderate, righteous, and irate; it was difficult for him to fit into the school milieu. He also was not diligent, because otherwise, with his talent, he would have been more successful; he could draw well, could do well in the sciences, but his desire to work always disappeared rapidly. Instructions and admonitions were received with undisguised irritation; from his schoolmates he demanded unconditional submission, liked the Führer role, and was inclined to pranks, which, in an immature youngster, is not rare.[55]

After Hitler became chancellor, however, Huemer praised him to high heaven. He must have been in a cold sweat that his old report might be discovered and that he would be held accountable for it.

In *Mein Kampf*, Hitler minimized his failure but presented whatever went wrong as the result of bad teaching and a protest against his father, who wanted to force him into a bureaucratic career, although this view is negated by the fact that Hitler's poor school performance continued after his father's death. The old man's anger and dissatisfaction with the boys mounted; he kicked Alois Jr. out, and it is possible that Adolf's fate might have been the same had it not been for Alois Sr.'s sudden death in 1903. Adolf's childhood friend, August Kubizek, reported that Hitler cried bitterly at his father's grave,[56] but this is hearsay because Kubizek did not know Adolf during the time when his father was alive. After Alois Sr.'s death, Clara had to take over and was no match for her unmanageable son. Hitler's poor school performance continued. After Adolf's failure in the third grade, the teachers advised his mother to transfer him to another *Realschule* in nearby Steyr. In 1904, at a considerable financial sacrifice, she placed him with a family in Steyr as a boarder and enrolled him at the local *Realschule*. Again, Adolf did not pass. In the summer of 1905, at the end of the school year, his marks were: conduct 3, diligence 4, religion 4, German 5 (failing), geography and history 4, mathematics 5 (failing), chemistry 4, physics 5 (failing), stenography 5 (failing), and, amazingly, drawing 2 and gymnastics 1.[57] However, he had one more chance—a make-up examination in the fall of 1905, which he passed, although he did not return to school. In the monologues, with mock shame, Hitler chatted about how he got drunk after his final examination, tore up his credentials, and used the pieces as toilet paper. When the credentials were found and shown to him by the school director, he was remorseful and vowed never to drink again.[58] This is an unlikely story, if for no other reason than school credentials (made of a parchment-like paper) are not a substitute for newspaper, which was commonly used as toilet paper at that time—yet it definitely indicates how Hitler felt about school.

The Spurious Pulmonary Disease

In *Mein Kampf*, Hitler told the story of how he succeeded in quitting the hated secondary school:

> . . . Then suddenly an illness came to my aid and in a few weeks decided my future and ended the eternal domestic quarrel. As a result of my serious lung ailment, a physician advised my mother, in most urgent terms, never to send me into an office. My attendance at the *Realschule* had, furthermore, to be interrupted for at least a year [author's note: a false statement]. The goal for which I had so long silently yearned, for which I had always fought, had— through this event—suddenly become almost reality of its own accord.[59]

During a visit with his family in the Waldviertel, Hitler's uncle Johann Schmidt in Weitra talked about Adolf's illness and consulted with Dr. Keiss, a local practitioner, who allegedly made statements to the effect that Adolf would not live long, implying that he suffered from advanced tuberculosis. Schmidt also reported that Adolf "recovered" through fresh air, warm cow's milk, and fresh vegetables (!).[60] Adolf at that time had the appearance of an asthenic youngster, if one can trust the sketch by his school comrade Sturm-lechner. Yet no record of weight loss, fever, expectoration, or bacteriological evidence exists. No chest X-rays were available at that time, and it would have been unlikely for a country practitioner to carry out a bacteriological sputum examination. Furthermore, if Hitler had been that seriously ill, he would not have returned for the make-up examination in Steyr. It is possible that he suffered from an upper respiratory viral infection, but a precise diagnosis cannot be reconstructed. In my opinion, it is more likely that Hitler achieved his goal (avoiding school attendance) by exaggerated complaints, and a combination of malingering and hysterical play-acting. He had learned at an early age to use real and imaginary illnesses for his purposes. Years later in *Mein Kampf*, however, Hitler claimed that a physician advised his mother in most urgent terms that, with such an illness, it would be inadvisable for Adolf to do office work.[61] Such a medical opinion is also unlikely because, if anything, a quiet, sedentary occupation would have been indicated. Whatever ailed him, Dr. Eduard Bloch, the family physician, stated that he never heard of such an illness or diagnosis.[62] However, Adolf was able to persuade his mother to let him stay out of school and study painting in preparation for the entrance examination at the Vienna Academy of Fine Arts.

A Difficult Puberty and Adolescence

Hitler's explanation of consciously failing in school to force his father to let him become an artist is, at best, a partial explanation. The price of not advancing through grades and repeating grades in school is high: ostracism and humiliation—to which Hitler was highly sensitive. Any child who falls behind his classmates becomes the subject of scorn by his new classmates. The story, however, helped Hitler avoid facing his adolescent turmoil. And turmoil it was. Hitler considered his puberty and adolescence an especially painful period.[63] Puberty is always a difficult period for the subject and his environment, but Hitler's puberty might have been particularly tough, because of the following issues. The ambivalent relationship with his father became more strained. Adolf was rebellious and angry, and his father was unable or unwilling to love, respect, or understand his son. This was reinforced by the mother, who, in the boy's eyes, became the father's ally. Hitler experienced sexual turmoil. The boy was tempted but also severely inhibited and threatened to give in to his sexual temptations. In all probability, he became painfully aware of a congenital defect of the genitalia at the onset of puberty.

A different set of explanations for Hitler's school failures and related characterological changes has been offered by the neuropsychiatrist Johann Recktenwald.[64] He asserted that, when Hitler's brother Edmund died of measles in 1900, Hitler contracted measles encephalitis followed by severe personality changes. However, no record of measles encephalitis, a lethal disease that could hardly be overlooked, exists. Recktenwald also assumed that Hitler afterward developed a condition that in older German psychiatric terminology was called an "*Unhold*" syndrome (*Unhold* is best translated as monster) and had been observed in some juvenile patients with encephalitis lethargica (von Economo's disease). Parkinson's syndrome and, in some patients, antisocial personality changes many years after the acute episode of illness have been described. Yet in Hitler's case no evidence of severe antisocial behavior in his youth exists. The only known incident of cruelty to animals during Hitler's youth is the Leonding billy goat story reported by D. Güstrow (a pen name), a former defender in the notorious People's Court.[65] The storyteller, whom Güstrow defended in a military court, was a soldier, Stefan Wasner, who served in the German army in World War II and had been a schoolmate of Hitler's in Leonding. Wasner often amused his comrades with tall stories about the Führer's childhood. One story got the raconteur into lethal difficulties. According to Wasner, Adolf and his playmates caught a billy goat in a pasture, wedged a piece of wood into its mouth, and Adolf pissed into it; the animal closed its jaws and Adolf screamed. The soldiers listened uneasily to the tale and reported it to their officers. Wasner was promptly arrested and interrogated. A psychiatric expert witness did not save the soldier, who stuck to his story to the bitter end and was sentenced to death and executed. Güstrow, Wasner's public defender, vouched for the veracity of the story. If true, it is a grim story of everyday life in the Third Reich, the title of Güstrow's book.

"*The Hollowness of a Comfortable Life*"[66]

Adolf had won his battle about not attending school. In modern times, he might have come to the attention of a school psychologist, but such an institution came into existence only decades later. Between 1905 and 1908, with the exception of two short trips to Vienna, Hitler stayed home, ostensibly to prepare himself for the entrance examination of the Academy of Fine Arts in Vienna. In characterizing the period, he spoke of the hollowness of a comfortable life, yet the period was not comfortable. His family groaned about the boy who had no better plans for his future than to pursue an uncertain career as an artist. They thought he was lazy and obstreperous. Hitler deeply resented the advice of his brother-in-law, Leo Raubal, to enter the postal service, and the counsel of his godfather, Josef Mayrhofer, to consider the baker's trade. Not only the family, but Adolf, too, was disgusted. He actually was busy all the time: He read a lot, wrote poems and plays, took long walks into the surroundings of Linz, and attended the theater and opera—yet the activities were unfocused and erratic. With more shame than pride, he had to admit that he had no income-producing job.[67] With typical hubris, he criticized his friend August Kubizek for not studying hard enough in school.[68] He developed intriguing fantasy projects: rebuilding Linz and later Vienna,[69] providing workers with better housing,[70] and creating a Reich orchestra that would travel to different cities and perform where no orchestras existed.[71]

August (Gustl) Kubizek

In 1905, Adolf met August (Gustl) Kubizek. Gustl was the son of an upholsterer and wall paperer, and worked as an apprentice in his father's shop. In 1908, his father permitted Gustl, who had developed an occupational bronchitis, to pursue his real interest—the study of music. According to Kubizek, it was Adolf who persuaded Gustl's father to permit his son to study music at the Vienna Academy of Music.[72] Gustl was nine months older than Adolf and became Hitler's only friend. Kubizek called it a peculiar friendship,[73] yet at times it resembled the romantic friendship that so often develops between boys in early adolescence. Perhaps this friendship resembled the relationship between Don Quixote and Sancho Panza more than an ordinary boyhood friendship. Kubizek wrote that Hitler was sensitive to his needs and at times helped him. More likely, the truth is that the boys needed each other and complemented each other for a while. Most of all, Hitler needed a person who would listen to his discourses and harangues without protest or criticism, and who would express admiration when Hitler spoke of his plans to establish a traveling Reich orchestra that would perform in localities that had no orchestras of their own. A strong tie between Hitler and Kubizek was their common interest in music. Like many other provincial central European cities, Linz had a fairly good theater with a respectable opera repertory. Tickets were cheap and gave the boys a chance to enjoy a lot of theater and opera. The undisputed idol for both boys was Richard Wagner. One night after a performance of Wagner's *Rienzi*, the boys went for a stroll to the Pöstelberg, a hill within Linz. Adolf was excited and talked about future tasks that he would perform like Rienzi. (In the opera, Rienzi dies in the flames of a burning Rome.)

Kubizek reported some relevant observations about Hitler's behavior.

Adolf was extremely tense, excitable, given to rages without any particular reason, restless, and, in his relationship with Gustl, demanding, jealous, and impatient. Yet he fascinated Gustl endlessly, which made it possible for the boys to remain close for three years. Posterity also has learned from Kubizek about some aspects of Hitler's erotic and political behaviors in Linz. Kubizek described Adolf's passion for a young lady, Stefanie Jansten, daughter of an Army officer, usually referred to just as Stefanie. From his sixteenth to his eighteenth year, Adolf had a crush on Stefanie, with whom he never talked.[74] He waited for the young maiden on street corners, watched her on promenades with her mother, and got angry when he saw her in the company of young officers. Like many other teenagers, Hitler wrote letters and poems that were never mailed. He felt certain that she would wait for him and that eventually he would marry her. When Gustl once said to Adolf that he should introduce himself to her and her mother, Adolf sadly rejected the idea because he felt Stefanie's mother would inquire about his job, and he had none. Romantic infatuations are the rule and not the exception during puberty and adolescence. However, Hitler's infatuation was not the ordinary romance. The distant romance with "Besieker," a code name for Stefanie that was actually the name of a schoolmate, lasted three years and supports the thesis of a youth with passionate feelings and strong sexual inhibitions. The infatuation persisted while Hitler was in Vienna in 1907. Kubizek stated that Hitler was more interested in receiving news about Stefanie than about his mother's illness.

Little is known about Hitler's sex life during adolescence and childhood. One can only assume that young Adolf, after the death of his father, found himself the only male in a household with three females and might have been both aroused by his young and rather attractive half-sister, Angela. Twenty years later, according to all reports, Angela's daughter Geli became Hitler's only true love. Hitler's little sister, Paula, mentioned that he was shy and avoided being kissed by her.[75] Hitler also reported that he once went to a peep show where he noticed that one of his professors was present, too.

Hitler's Political Views in Linz

Beyond any doubt, in Linz and later in Vienna Hitler was an ardent German nationalist. Like many others at that time, he became interested in Pan-Germanism, stipulating the superiority of Germans over other nationalities in the Austro-Hungarian Empire and the concept of a union of the German Reich and German Austria, which was the credo of the Nationalist Party and of many Pan-Germanic organizations such as the Deutscher Schulverein (an educational organization) and the Deutscher Turnverein (a gymnastic club). It is likely that Hitler supported the political activities of these organizations in spirit, but there is no record of his having belonged to any of them. One can safely assume that Hitler was not politically active in Linz, although he may have talked about political issues because he liked to talk about everything under the sun. He asserted that he was not an anti-Semite; his father would not have tolerated any anti-Semitic views.[76] In *Mein Kampf*,

Hitler stated:

> There were few Jews in Linz. In the course of the centuries, their outward appearance had become Europeanized and had taken on a human look [!]; in fact, I had even taken them for Germans. The absurdity of this idea did not draw upon me, because I saw no distinguishing features but the strange religion. The fact that they had, as I believed, been persecuted on this account sometimes . . . almost turned my distaste at unfavorable remarks about them into horror. Thus far, I did not so much suspect the existence of an organized opposition to the Jews.[77]

At best, this statement is a half-truth. Considerable anti-Semitism existed in Linz, particularly amongst professors and students at the *Realschule*. Kubizek was convinced that young Hitler was already an anti-Semite during his time in Linz and reported one remark made as they passed a synagogue: "This does not belong."[78] Kubizek also stated that, in Vienna, Hitler later became a member of the Antisemitenbund,[79] which cannot be correct because this organization did not exist during Hitler's youth.[80] Probably, Hitler just shared the general social anti-Semitism without any great intensity or commitment to action. He harbored anti-Czech sentiments—which were strong in provincial Austria. Kubizek, although he had a Czech name, considered himself and was considered by others to be an Austrian of German nationality. It is very likely that, while in Linz, Hitler had mild to moderate ethnocentric sentiments.

The Death of Hitler's Mother

In the winter of 1906/7, Hitler's mother became very ill. The course of the illness can be reconstructed on the basis of office notes and an article written by Clara's physician, Dr. Eduard Bloch, after he emigrated to the United States.[81] In January 1907, Clara consulted Dr. Bloch, a respected Jewish general practitioner. He diagnosed a malignant tumor of the breast and admitted her to a local hospital where she was operated on by a well-known surgeon, Dr. Karl Urban. The pathological diagnosis was sarcoma of the breast. As no histological examination was reported, it is about certain that the tumor was a carcinoma. Because sarcomas are very rare, Clara was discharged after nineteen days of hospitalization and returned for her after-care to Dr. Bloch. After 3 April, she saw Dr. Bloch regularly until early summer, and then again in September. It seems that she improved temporarily during the spring and summer of 1907, but got worse again in the fall, when Dr. Bloch made frequent house calls. At the end of September 1907, Dr. Bloch treated the purulent chest wound with iodoform to disinfect it, a treatment still used to deodorize wounds. From the medical notes, one can deduce that Dr. Bloch applied iodoform gauze to her chest wound, possibly occasionally also crystalline iodoform. It is not possible to determine how much iodoform gauze was used, nor how often applications were made. It is unlikely that Clara received morphine injections, as injections at that time were not administered by general practitioners.[82] During the late fall, Clara's condition deteriorated rapidly. She suffered greatly and died on 21 December 1907. The cause of death was listed on Dr. Bloch's death certificate as a malignant tumor of the breast, identical with the discharge diagnosis from the hospital where she had been operated. The total cost of treatment was moderate, about 500 to 600 kronen.[83]

Rudolph Binion concluded that Hitler's anti-Semitism was the result of mistreatment and death of Hitler's mother by iodoform poisoning and further asserted that Dr. Bloch overcharged and exploited the Hitler family.[84] These assertions are based on Binion's painstaking analysis of the notes found by officials of the Hauptarchiv and the Gestapo in Dr. Bloch's office.[85] He assumed that these notes constituted a medical record. Dr. Bloch's daughter, Mrs. Gertrud Kren, maintained that the medical record, the so-called "journal," disappeared; it did not become part of the Hauptarchiv.[86] A comparison of handwriting samples by Dr. Bloch and his wife Lily Bloch shows that the notes were written by her.[87] According to Mrs. Kren, Dr. Bloch did not dictate his medical records to her but gave information to his wife that enabled her to bill patients for services. The notes in question were billing notes, from which only a limited reconstruction of Clara Hitler's case is possible. It is certain that Clara suffered and died from breast cancer and did not, as Binion maintained, die from iodoform poisoning.[88] She was treated by Dr. Bloch according to the state of the art at the beginning of the century, and Adolf Hitler recognized his services gratefully and remembered them without rancor in 1938. As an expression of gratitude, Hitler sent Dr. Bloch a self-painted postcard in 1906. In *Mein Kampf* Hitler stated, "It [his mother's death] was the conclusion of a long and painful illness that from the beginning left little hope of recovery. Yet it was a dreadful blow, particularly for me."[89] Binion developed an elaborate hypothesis that Hitler's anti-Semitism and resolution to gas the Jews thirty-five years later was vengeance against Dr. Bloch, who "killed" his mother. Binion's hypothesis will be taken up and critiqued again in Chapter 9.

The Failed Entrance Examination

At the end of September 1907, Hitler traveled to Vienna to take the entrance examination for the Vienna Academy of Fine Arts. He passed the preliminary screening test but failed in the final, decisive test. The report of the Academy stated tersely, "Adolf Hitler, born Braunau, 20 April 1889, German, Catholic, Father: Civil Servant. Four classes in *Realschule*. Drawing test: Unsatisfactory. Not enough heads."[90] It was a bitter disappointment. Hitler stated: "I was so convinced I would be admitted that when I received my rejection it struck me as a bolt from the blue."[91] The professors who made the decision felt something was missing from Hitler's portfolio—a human touch—because the pictures over-emphasized landscapes and buildings. What seemingly struck the professors was that the pictures were not alive. Some experts have agreed with the professors, while others have felt Hitler had enough talent to be admitted. Actually, the orientation of the Academy professors was conservative, although amongst the candidates admitted during that year was Egon Schiele, an avant-garde painter. As in all Austrian institutions of higher education at the turn of the century, hardly any Jews were on the faculty and few Jewish students were admitted, so Hitler could not claim that "Jewish influence" was responsible for his rejection. Many have pondered how the professors on the admissions committee influenced history by rejecting Hitler! Hitler requested an interview with the president of the Academy, Professor Siegmund L'Allemand, who advised him to become an architect. This made sense to Hitler, who realized that his talent as a painter was modest. After that, Hitler said, ". . . in a few days I myself knew that I should someday become an architect."[92] He also knew that to be admitted to a school of architecture, he would have to graduate from the *Oberrealschule* (the upper classes of the *Realschule*), and although he talked about such a plan, he never entertained the idea seriously or mastered the discipline of going back to school. In Munich, a more realistic opportunity presented itself to Hitler—becoming a builder or a draftsman—which he did not pursue. Beyond any doubt, however, the rejection by the Academy was a major blow, and Hitler did not tell Clara about it because he did not want to disappoint his sick mother. Later, Hitler rationalized his failure by stating he had failed because his parents did not have the money to pay for his education.[93]

The Dissolution of the Hitler Household

During the spring of 1907, Hitler stayed with the family, who had moved to the northern suburb of Urfahr. According to Kubizek and neighbors, Hitler helped out in the household when his mother was seriously ill.[94] He went away for his examination in the fall; statements about when he returned are contradictory. Dr. Bloch, Kubizek, and Paula testified that he was present at his mother's funeral and before. In his analysis of the billing notes, Binion established from an annotation on the doctor's bill that Hitler was in Linz during the fall.[95] The question still remains as to why he was away for a relatively long time when his mother was so ill. At most, the absence for the examination at the academy would have taken a few days. Was it callous indifference, or Hitler's inability to witness his mother's suffering? It is probable that, at the time when Clara was failing rapidly, a change in Adolf's attitude toward his mother occurred. For years, he had been annoyed with her criticisms and admonitions, but, according to several witnesses, when she was seriously ill he took care of her in an exemplary fashion.[96] Bloch stated that Hitler was inconsolable at his mother's death.[97]

It did not take long to settle the Hitler estate. Probably about 3000 kronen remained from the 5000 kronen that Clara cleared after the sale of the Leonding property. Adolf thus received 750 to 1000 kronen. In addition to this sum, he inherited money from his mother and later from his Aunt Johanna in 1911 or 1912. Furthermore, Adolf and Paula received orphan pensions of 25 kronen per month. Their guardian, Josef Mayrhofer, decided on equal allowances because he erroneously considered Adolf a student. Later, when Angela complained that this was unfair because she had to take care of Paula as well as her own daughters, Adolf turned over his part of the orphan's support without any court action. When he departed for Vienna on 18 February 1908, he had no financial worries. Leaving the remaining members of the household was easy and permitted Adolf more than ever to pursue his dreams and fantasies. He was glad to return to Vienna and had enough resilience and reality sense to plan for another entrance examination at the Academy.

2

Vienna

IN *Mein Kampf* Hitler stressed the misery and deprivation of his stay in Vienna:

> Today this city can arouse in me nothing but the most dismal thoughts. For me the name . . . represents five years of hardship and misery. . . . Hunger was my faithful bodyguard; he never left me for a moment and partook all I had, share and share alike. . . . And during this time I studied as never before—aside from my architecture and my rare visits to the opera, paid for in hunger, I had but one pleasure: my books.[1]

However, Hitler's real life during his first year in Vienna differed markedly from this account. His orphan's pension of 25 kronen, supplemented by his share of money from the family inheritance, enabled him to live a very modest but carefree life at the beginning of his Viennese stay. In his first year there, he probably spent 80 kronen a month, which corresponds roughly to the income of a young middle school teacher. Hitler's problem was that, in contrast to his friend Kubizek, he spent more money than he owned and was totally broke by the winter of 1909/10. He then had to depend on the monies he earned as a day laborer until he received more money from Aunt Johanna and began to paint again.

After Hitler's arrival in Vienna he rented a small room in the back tract of Stumpergasse 29 from an old Czech woman, Frau Zakreys.[2] Like most cheap rentals in Vienna at that time, it was small, poorly heated, lit by a kerosene lamp, and infested with bed bugs. Hitler recalled it in the monologues and demanded that Vienna first would have to be cleaned up.[3] Such quarters, however, were not different from those of many other poor students. Hitler made a special point that he starved in Vienna, but this is true only for the winter of 1909/10, when he stayed in the Meidling shelter for the homeless. He spoke of rare visits to the opera, but during "the good days" he went to the opera almost daily. Kubizek believed Hitler ate his main meal at some nearby restaurant or, at times, at the University dining hall, which Hitler disliked because foreign students ate there. Kubizek recalled with some amusement that Hitler faced the wall while munching his strudel so he would not have to look at these students.[4]

In 1908 Hitler admired the grandiosity of the city. Kubizek recounted how he was met upon his arrival at the western railroad station by Hitler, elegantly dressed with a hat and cane.[5] After feasting on the provisions Gustl's mother had packed, Adolf insisted on a long nocturnal walk to show his tired friend the splendid buildings of Vienna's inner city. On the following day, the youngsters went room-hunting. They met on this excursion a scantily dressed landlady, and after a hasty retreat Hitler muttered to his friend, ". . . what a Potiphar," leaving posterity to wonder about the chaste Joseph.[6] When the boys could not find anything, Frau Zakreys consented to put them up in one of her own rooms, which was just large enough for a rented piano and two beds.

Hitler was socially isolated in Vienna, which did not bother him, as he thought of himself as a loner. He spent much time in cafés, which was customary in Vienna. The cafés were cozy, newspapers could be read, and, for the price of one beverage, a person could spend the whole day there. In such cafés one could easily make superficial contact with other guests, which rarely matured into lasting relationships and suited Hitler well. On one occasion the boys bought a lottery ticket, and Hitler was certain that they would win the jackpot; when this did not happen, he was furious. One entry in the Hauptarchiv, the "good heart story," deserves attention. The owner of a small coffee house in Vienna's proletarian 15th District recounted that Hitler protested against the unjust treatment of an employee and concluded the account by asserting, "You could not imagine what a good heart Adi has."[7] The experience of blatant social injustice in Vienna contributed to Hitler's self-understanding as a fighter for social justice. Hitler was keenly aware of the gross social injustice in Vienna. Once, in silence, he watched a hunger demonstration.[8]

The Enjoyment of Culture

Visits to Vienna's Imperial Opera House were the highlights of Hitler's and Kubizek's existence. Their admiration for Richard Wagner continued to be unbounded. Hitler adored not only Wagner's music, but also the symbolic and mystical quality of his poetry. At the Imperial Opera and Vienna's second opera house, the Volksoper, he heard most of Wagner's operas and was particularly impressed by *Parsifal* and *Tristan and Isolde*, which he saw forty times.[9] He was lukewarm about other works, such as Verdi's operas, and had little use for the work of French, Russian, and Czech composers. He had less interest in orchestral works, with the exception of the music of Anton Bruckner, a native son of upper Austria. He also liked "lighter" composers, such as Johann Strauss and Lehar. He appreciated the compositions of Felix Mendelssohn, particularly his violin concerto, and of Gustav Mahler, who at that time was director of the Imperial Opera.[10] (In the Third Reich, the "Jewish" music of Mendelssohn and Mahler was forbidden.) Often, the boys could hear only a part of the long operas they attended because they had to rush home to avoid paying the janitor his gratuity for opening the gate of the tenement house after ten o'clock. Kubizek reported an amazing episode that illustrates Hitler's dominance and disregard for realistic limitations. On one occasion, he mentioned to his friend the existence of a concept for an opera that had been considered by Richard Wagner but never composed: *Wieland der Schmied*. The plot was based on a Nordic saga of cruelty, murder, and incest. As Hitler knew nothing about composition, harmony, or instrumentation, Hitler persuaded the reluctant Kubizek to write down the score that he dictated to him. After an initial burst of activity, the effort was abandoned.[11]

At that time, Hitler was engaged in writing other plays, but posterity has never learned what they were. Beyond any doubt, Hitler read a lot of books, pamphlets, and daily papers,[12] both in his room and in the poorly stocked district libraries, also sitting for hours on park benches in the nearby Imperial Gardens, reading and dreaming. Kubizek mentioned Hitler's early interest in German hero mythology and military topics, such as the Boer War.[13] Hitler also made a point of exhibiting his familiarity with Nietzsche and Schopenhauer. It is unlikely that he acquired any in-depth knowledge of these philosophers, as this would have required very thorough reading. In fact, Hitler claimed just that,[14] but it is more likely that much of his rather broad but superficial knowledge had been gained from abbreviated publications or pamphlets, amongst them pamphlets by Jörg L. von Liebenfels (his real name was Josef Lanz), a strange philosopher and former novitiate of the Monastery of Heiligenkreuz. Lanz, a charismatic person who impressed, amongst others, the eminent Swedish dramatist August Strindberg, viewed world history as a struggle between superior blonde, blue-eyed beings and inferior ape-like creatures. Hitler bought issues of *Ostara*, the periodical in which Lanz published his obtuse articles. It probably contributed to Hitler's racism to a degree, but certainly not as much as Daim, Wilfred Lanz's biographer, claimed.[15] Later, Hitler distanced himself completely from Lanz, whose publications were forbidden in the Third Reich. There is no doubt that, with his excellent memory, Hitler absorbed at that time a good deal of knowledge in his autodidactic style, but as he did not accept guidance and was disinclined to listen to critique or to other opinions, his knowledge remained one-sided and superficial. He remained uninfluenced by the great minds of Vienna at the turn of the century (against whom he later became hostile), such as Freud, Wittgenstein, the writers Schnitzler and Hofmannsthal, the architect Adolf Loos. Hitler was aware of the works of Sigmund Freud and Alfred Adler but, as one would expect, did not appreciate them. Curiously, he mentioned their chief concepts—the inferiority complex and the unconscious—a number of times. He fiercely demanded that Germans must overcome any feelings of inferiority: "Whether the others love us is irrelevant if they only respect us. If they hate us it does not matter as long as they fear us."[16]

The Art Student

In 1908 and the first half of 1909, Hitler saw himself as an aspiring art student. His description of the Vienna years as a "dog life of an art enthusiast" is quite apt.[17] In his fantasy, after rebuilding Linz, Hitler was rebuilding Vienna. He had great ideas, such as building an underground railroad terminal and pedestrian zones in the inner city. Whether these were his own ideas or whether he read about them cannot be established. Finally, Hitler had to admit to Kubizek that he flunked the entrance examination and that he was not attending classes, in the course of an argument in which he cursed the professors who turned him down: "All old spastic pedantic civil servants, limited bureaucrats, stupid officials. The whole Academy should be blown up."[18] When Kubizek inquired about what Hitler would do next, at first he did not reply. Later, Hitler told him, "You need teachers, I don't."[19] He talked about "snares" that prevented his ascent.[20] Yet he continued to prepare himself to try for another entrance examination. In October 1908, Hitler tried for the second time and once again failed. This time, he was not even admitted to test drawing, a devastating blow. He never talked about the second failure, and did not mention it in *Mein Kampf* or in the monologues. It demolished any chance for an academic artistic career and virtually destroyed even a pretense to view himself or present himself to the world as an academic artist. Hitler had not finished his middle school, nor had he any training in trade or business school. He still had one realistic alternative: He remembered that the Director of the Academy, Professor Siegmund L'Allemand, advised him after the first failure to become an architect rather than a painter.[21] To pursue such a career, he would have to return to the *Realschule* and graduate before he could enter the Technical University for the study of architecture. However, Hitler could not muster the discipline to do this, and the idea of becoming a contractor, which would have been possible without the prerequisite of a higher education, was unacceptable to him. He was too devastated and too conceited to consider such an option. All he could do was dream about a future of great architectural achievements. Undoubtedly, he was a stubborn dreamer, and eventually his goal of constructing immense buildings was achieved, at great cost to humanity. His failure coincided with the depletion of his finances. During the summer of 1908, Kubizek returned to Linz and Hitler remained at Stumpergasse 29. When Kubizek returned, he found the rent paid but an empty room, and not even a message from his friend. Hitler moved to a room in Felberstraße 22 on 18 November 1908, shortly after his second rejection by the Academy of Fine Arts. It is quite

likely that he did not want to face his disciplined friend. It reflects on the
character of their friendship that he simply disappeared. Kubizek, on the
other hand, did not attempt to find him, which would have been easy given
Vienna's system of registration. One can safely assume that the close relationship between the two boys had become difficult. The patient and disciplined Kubizek became fed up with Hitler's depression and his arrogant
allures of superiority. Kubizek wrote: "He was at odds with the whole
world."[22]

The next contact between the two occurred after Hitler had become
Chancellor. Kubizek sent him a note of congratulations, and Hitler sent a
short reply dated 4 April 1933:

> My dear Kubizek:
>   Only today your letter of 2 February was brought to my attention.
> Considering the hundreds of thousands of letters I have received since Janu-
> ary, this is not surprising. My joy was great to receive news from you about
> your life and your address. I would like—when the time of my most difficult
> struggles is over—to reawaken the most beautiful years of my life. Perhaps it
> is possible that you might visit me. Wishing you and your mother the best, I
> am remembering our old friendship.
>   Yours,
>   Adolf Hitler (signed in his absence)[23]

(In their letters, Kubizek and Hitler still used the familiar German form of
address, "*Du.*") Kubizek was surprised that Hitler referred to "the most beautiful years" in Vienna. They met for the first time after Hitler "liberated"
Linz. Hitler was condescending but friendly and used the formal *Sie* in speaking with his old friend. He was appalled that Kubizek had become a city
clerk, and promised to help with the education of Kubizek's sons—a promise
he kept. Kubizek twice followed Hitler's invitation to come to Bayreuth. In
one of these encounters, Kubizek reminded Hitler of the performance of
Rienzi, after which Hitler had felt so inspired that he vowed to liberate Germany.[24] True or not, Hitler liked the story and remarked, "This was the
beginning." It might have been more appropriate to speak of "the end" rather
than the beginning: The people's tribune Rienzi is pursued by enemies, abandoned by followers, and killed when Rome burns.

Some Interest in Politics

Hitler was impressed with two major political figures. One was Georg
von Schönerer, the leader of the Deutschnationale Partei. Hitler liked von
Schönerer's pan-German and anti-Semitic ideas but criticized him for his
erratic style and his feuding with other folkish politicians, such as Franz Stein
and Karl Hermann Wolf. Hitler also objected to von Schönerer's support of
the Away from Rome movement. Later, in *Mein Kampf,* Hitler had harsh
words for the "folkish comedians" dressed in bear skins, holding their bull-

horns over their bearded heads, and brandishing scholarly words.[25] While he admired Vienna's mayor, the able populist Karl Lueger, head of the Catholic Party (Christlich-Soziale Partei), he could not accept Lueger's Catholic orientation or his devotion to the house of Habsburg. Lueger secured the following of small businessmen and craftsmen who were threatened by the influx of Jewish traders from Eastern Europe and by Jewish capitalists in Vienna. Yet Lueger had many rich Jewish friends and supporters. One of his slogans was, "I determine who is a Jew." Clearly, Hitler did not appreciate this kind of anti-Semitism.

One incident that occurred when he was a construction worker helps explain his antagonism toward Marxism:

> Our discussions at work were often very heated. I argued back, from day to day better informed than the antagonists, until one day they made use of the weapon which most readily conquers reason: terror and violence. A few of the spokesmen on the opposing side forced me either to leave the building at once, or be thrown off the scaffolding.[26]

Hitler never forgot this humiliation at the hands of "people who are not worthy to belong to a great nation."[27] In *Mein Kampf* he stated that the socialist trade unions were manipulated by Jews. Later, his anger was directed not against his fellow workers but against the Jewish "wire-pullers" who, in his opinion, seduced the workers.[28] It is possible that Hitler's encounter with the construction workers was a lesson in terror and counter-terror, in which he later became a master. Another significant experience was watching a mass demonstration of Viennese workers. For nearly two hours, with baited breath, Hitler watched the "gigantic human dragon."[29] Over the years, Hitler developed an amazing practical knowledge of mass psychology. The experience in Vienna was only the beginning. In *Mein Kampf* he wrote at length about a visit to the Austrian Parliament, where he was appalled by what appeared to him as laziness, apathy, and indifference on the part of the deputies who were absent from conferences, slept through sessions, and engaged in meaningless debate. It can be assumed that his fierce opposition to democracy and a parliamentary system was related to this experience.[30]

Anti-Semitism

In *Mein Kampf* Hitler emphasized that he developed from a weak-kneed cosmopolitan into a radical anti-Semite while he was in Vienna. "Once, as I was strolling through the Inner City I suddenly encountered an apparition in a black caftan and black hair locks. Is this a Jew? was my first thought. . . . Is this a German?"[31]

> The cleanliness of this people, moral or otherwise, I must say, is a point in itself. By their very exterior you could tell that these were no lovers of water, and, to your distress, you often knew it with your eyes closed. Later I often

grew sick to my stomach from the smell of these caftan wearers. Added to
this was their unclean dress and their general unheroic appearance. . . . [32]

A few lines later:

> Was there any form of filth or profligacy, particularly in cultural life, without
> at least one Jew involved in it? If you cut even cautiously into such an
> abscess, you found, like a maggot in a rotting body, often dazzled by the
> sudden light—a kike.[33] . . . The relation of the Jews to prostitution and,
> even more, to the white slave traffic, could be studied in Vienna as perhaps
> in no other city of Western Europe, with the possible exception of southern
> French ports.[34]

Hitler tried to create the impression that his political anti-Semitism originated in Vienna. However, there is reason to assume that his anti-Semitism
in Vienna was not as fierce as he claimed in *Mein Kampf,* and, most of all, he
was not a politically active anti-Semite. Despite all of his expressions of gutter
anti-Semitism in *Mein Kampf,* Hitler's radical, racist anti-Semitism did not
start in Vienna, but in the summer of 1919, after Germany's defeat in World
War I. It is proven that Hitler had numerous contacts with Jewish art dealers
and frame makers (Josef Neumann and Samuel Morgenstern), as well as Jewish clients. Hamann described in convincing detail Hitler's contacts with
Jewish art dealers and other Jews who helped him, as well as a visit with
Kubizek to the distinguished Jewish Jahoda family, a sponsor of the arts.[35]
Reinhold Hanisch, whom he met in the Meidling flophouse, reported that
Hitler ranted and raved more about the Social Democrats, the Czechs, and
the Habsburg dynasty than about Jews.[36] Nobody has been able to discover
a specific traumatic experience with Jews during the years in Vienna. All one
can find is tremendous sexual frustration, envy, and bitterness over his lack of
professional success. Whatever anti-Semitism Hitler exhibited then was
different from the political anti-Semitic system he developed later. It was
an anti-Semitism of envy, of a man who had failed in his sexuality and
in his occupation. Hitler's statements—written down fifteen years later—
about his experiences with Jews and Marxists are to be viewed with caution.
These experiences did not constitute the granite foundation he claimed; they
were experiences and fantasies that he fitted, both deliberately and preconsciously, into his political system that emerged gradually between the end of
World War I and the time when he was a prisoner in Landsberg. One can
only speculate as to why Hitler put the origin of his political beliefs so point-
edly into the years in Vienna. Possibly, he wanted to minimize what he
learned after the end of World War I. He was never a person who acknowledged sources or persons from whom he learned, with the exception of the
contributions by his middle-school teacher, Professor Poetzsch, and his principal mentor, Dietrich Eckart, to whom he dedicated *Mein Kampf.* Hitler's
anti-Semitism in Vienna was not the consistent political anti-Semitism that
developed at the end of World War I. Brigitte Hamann reached the same

conclusion.[37] Already before Vienna, however, in Linz, Hitler was an ardent German nationalist with strong ethnophobic beliefs—anything that was non-German (particularly Czech or Jewish) was rejected by him. He spoke of the non-Germans in the multiethnic monarchy as "guest people."

A Deprived Sex Life

Clearly, Hitler's sexual life already was deprived in Linz; it did not improve in Vienna.[38] The crush on Stefanie began to fade. Hitler did not have the courage to make contacts with girls of his own class—as a matter of fact, he avoided them in theaters, opera houses, and cafés where such contact could be easily established. In the opera, for instance, he preferred the more expensive *promenoir*, where girls were not admitted. He also shunned sexual and social contact with women of the lower classes, domestics, and factory workers. Kubizek reported Adolf's indignation, perhaps jealousy, when a female student visited Gustl. On another occasion, Hitler angrily rejected an invitation for a rendezvous with a lady in the opera.[39] His fear of prostitution and syphilis was so strong that he later devoted ten pages to it in *Mein Kampf*, describing it as a major scourge of humanity. No evidence exists to indicate that Hitler had sexual intercourse with a prostitute or any casual acquaintance in Vienna, and no record of infection with any venereal disease has been found. Hitler and Kubizek made one visit to a lower-class red light district in the Spittelberggasse, the "den of iniquity," where the boys observed prostitutes beckoning to men from behind windows, about which Hitler erupted in moral indignation, saying that Jew-infested Vienna extinguished the "flame of life."[40] Kubizek also recounted that the two boys met a homosexual and that Adolf, in contrast to Gustl, was quite informed about this variant of sexual behavior.[41]

The Social Descent

Little is known about the short period Hitler spent in the Felberstraße, but it marked the beginning of a steep social descent. To eat, he had to work in various lowly jobs as a manual laborer. This was the period during which he had the best opportunity to observe Vienna's social and economic problems.[42] On 22 August 1909 Hitler moved to another miserable room in the Sechshauserstraße 58. He stayed briefly without paying the rent but left some of his belongings behind on 16 September 1909.[43] In these rapid moves, he registered as a student, writer, and painter. Obviously, he could not use the more common title of "academic painter," which would have been fraudulent because he never attended an academic institution to study painting. One motive for the frequent moves was Hitler's disinclination to serve in the Austro-Hungarian Army. He was adamantly opposed to being a soldier of the Emperor and even tried to dissuade Kubizek from registering.[44] Too much has been made of anti-military remarks Hitler made, such as objecting to arming the newly invented airplanes.[45] To the annoyance and frustration of historians, Hitler contradicted himself quite frequently. At times he did it deliberately to confuse his listeners. The only possibility for arriving at sound interpretations is to count how often he made his statements. In the case of a love of war, one can establish that Hitler never was a pacifist.

The fall and winter of 1909/10 were tough. Unable to afford other quarters, Hitler slept on park benches at "Mother Green's" as long as the fall weather remained mild, like many other homeless persons in an over-populated city that was inhospitable to its poor. He reached the nadir of his existence seeking admission at a shelter, the Meidlinger Obdachlosenheim, maintained in part by Jewish philanthropists under the auspices of the Emperor.[46] After a process of disinfection of the guests and their clothing, including an obligatory bath, the lodgers were fed soup and bread, could spend the night in a crowded dormitory for the period of a week, with the possibility of renewal of the shelter. In the morning lodgers had to leave the premises; some found occasional work as day laborers shoveling snow or carrying packages at the railroad stations. They spent long hours trudging from one soup kitchen to another. They spoke of "calling on Kathi" when they received bread and soup at the nearby convent of St. Katharina. For Hitler, with his dislike of physical closeness and dirt, this must have been a very bitter and demoralizing period.

During the Meidling flophouse period Hitler met Reinhold Hanisch, a vagabond who worked erratically. Hanisch, an illustrator, was an experienced tramp who taught Hitler some survival techniques, but his motivations were not entirely charitable. He quickly discovered Hitler's ability to draw and paint and offered himself as a salesman, to split the receivables with Hitler. Hitler painted mostly buildings and landscapes in picture postcard style, as well as an occasional commercial advertisement. Hanisch also convinced Hitler to ask Aunt Johanna for money to buy decent clothing. The venture was successful and enabled Hitler and Hanisch to move from the dump in Meidling to the Männerheim in the Meldemannstraße in the Brigittenau, a district populated largely by proletarians, amongst them many poor Jews and Czechs, on 9 February 1910. Compared with the shelter, the abode at Meldemannstraße was luxurious. It was a cheap, nonprofit hotel for working men who flocked to Vienna from the provinces and could neither find nor afford private lodgings. The private sleeping cells each contained a cot, a night stand, and a chest for clothes, and could not be used during the daytime. Bathrooms, laundry and cooking facilities, and spacious day-rooms for study and recreation were available. Hitler used the day-rooms to paint, or rather to copy paintings, which provided income for him and Hanisch. Josef Greiner maintained that Hitler also produced sketches for decorations to be used on the back rests of divans and, occasionally, paintings and drawings for advertisements, such as mouth wash and hair tonic.[47] At first Hanisch was Hitler's only agent, but later he used others after he lodged a complaint against Hanisch for cheating him on the sale of a picture. The disputed amount was small—about 12 kronen—but Hanisch was sentenced to one week in jail, not only for fraud but also for registering under a false name. After Hitler became Chancellor of the Reich, Hanisch, then living in Austria, forged and sold pictures that he claimed had been painted by Hitler. In November 1936, he was arrested by the Austrian police and died in prison, allegedly from pneumonia according to one report and from suicide according to another, on 4 February 1937. Evidence exists that he was badly beaten, and it is likely that he was murdered by the Viennese police, which at that time had been infiltrated by Austrian National Socialists.[48] Hitler's life at the Männerheim was much better than it had been at the shelter in Meidling, yet he had no friends, no affectionate bonds. From a clinical point of view, he still would have been considered a depressed person, though at this time the depression had become lighter and he was able to earn a living. He spent considerable time in lengthy discussions and at times made long speeches to indifferent audiences at the Männerheim. He was virtually out of contact with the remaining members of his family.

Leaving Vienna in Disgust

In 1912 Hitler inherited some money from his Aunt Johanna, enough to refurbish his clothing and contemplate a move. He came to the conclusion that the existence as a small-time freelance illustrator living in a cheap hotel inhabited by impecunious newcomers and drifters showed little promise. Hitler's later denigration of Vienna can be seen as an angry revenge for the suffering and unjust treatment, but also as a deliberate endeavor to create the myth of a man who overcame tremendous odds, rose to great heights, and finally returned triumphantly to the place of his humiliation. Hitler described his having arrived while he was in Vienna at a major and consistent *Weltanschauung*. This is not the case; it was not until the early twenties that a relatively coherent system emerged. What he gained in Vienna, however, was a wide variety of experiences. A beginning awareness of mass movements, for example, may have emerged as Hitler watched the powerful May Day parades of the Social Democratic Party. His disgust of parliamentary procedures may have had its origins in visits to the Parliament, where he watched the sleeping deputies. These experiences shaped his disrespect for the masses of voters who accepted such a system, but also his resolve to influence masses to achieve his goals.

After a sheltered childhood and adolescence, Hitler became acquainted with the misery of the lower classes. Ideas of social justice emerged, but already in Vienna he strongly opposed the Marxist solution to arrive at a just system through a class struggle among proletarians and capitalists. Hitler felt uncomfortable with the upper-class bourgeoisie, aristocracy, and royalty, and he detested and even feared the lower lower-class (*Lumpenproletariat*). Later he developed deep contempt for the "cowardly" bourgeoisie. He had a fine sense for decay, and behind the glamorous front and an exciting, artistic, and intellectual world, Vienna was the decaying capital of a moribund empire. Hitler hated and feared decay and degeneration. Vienna made him vigilant, angry, hard, and revengeful. In June 1913 Hitler left Vienna and moved to Munich. A major motivation was to escape the draft into the Austro-Hungarian Army.

Both in Vienna and in Munich before the First World War, Hitler saw himself as an aspiring and frustrated young artist, a true bohemian, and not a politician. Nobody has described this better than Thomas Mann in "Bruder Hitler":

> Must we not, even against our will, recognize in this phenomenon an aspect of the artist's character? We are ashamed to admit it, but the whole pattern is there: the recalcitrance, sluggishness, and miserable indefiniteness of his youth; the dimness of purpose, the what-do-you-really-want-to-be, the vegetating like a semi-idiot in the lowest social and psychological bohemianism, the arrogant rejection of any sensible and honorable occupation because of the basic feeling that he is too good for that sort of thing. . . . Along with that, the uneasy conscience, the sense of guilt, the rage at the world, the revolutionary instinct, the subconscious storing up of explosive cravings for compensation, the churning determination to justify oneself, to prove oneself.[49]

3

To Munich and World War I

AS MUCH AS he disliked Vienna, Hitler loved Munich—where he arrived in March 1913 and not, as he stated, in 1912.[1] His happiness was clearly expressed in *Mein Kampf*. Munich was:

> . . . a German city! What a difference from Vienna. . . . I grew sick to my stomach when I even thought back on this Babylon of races. In addition the dialect was much closer to me, which, particularly in my contact with Lower Bavarians, reminded me of my former childhood. There were a thousand things which were or became inwardly dear and precious to me. But most of all, I was attracted by this wonderful marriage of primordial power and fine artistic mood. . . . I even achieved the happiness of a truly inner content-ment. This period was the happiest and by far the most contented of my life.[2]

It was a quiet period for Hitler. He rented a small room in a lower middle-class district from Josef Popp, a tailor,[3] and registered as an art-painter. Popp and his wife, however, believed that Hitler was an academic painter. The Popps and their children liked Hitler, calling him an Austrian charmer who kept a certain distance. They were not aware of any friends, male or female, and Hitler did not receive visitors. He spent considerable time in his room, reading books and pamphlets. The Popps did not know what Hitler read but mentioned that he often quoted military literature. They also reported that Hitler was withdrawn. Another tenant, Rudolf Häusler, who shared Hitler's room, moved out because he could not stand Hitler's perorations. As far as they were political, Hitler's discussions dealt with the decline of the Austro-Hungarian Empire and his dislike of the Habsburgs. He repeatedly stated that he would fight for the Reich but not for the Habsburgs.[4] At times Hitler went out to cafés to read papers, eat, and sell his paintings. He would spend two to three hours at a time painting, mostly copying Munich's buildings and Bavarian landscapes from picture postcards. According to Maser, this was not fraudulence, but laziness.[5] More likely, it was Hitler's endeavor to save time and energy, because Hitler was not lazy. Yet this type of painting was simply a livelihood for Hitler. While in Munich, he made about 1200 marks a year, a fairly good income, comparable to that of a clerk or a teacher, yet in a letter to the Magistrate of Linz he stressed his poverty.[6]

Draft Dodger

An upsetting incident interrupted Hitler's routine on Sunday, 18 January 1914. Prior to this, the Magistrate in Linz had noted on 11 August 1913 that Hitler had not reported to the Austro-Hungarian draft board in 1909 and had not notified the Austrian authorities of his whereabouts after leaving the Männerheim and the country—a crime according to the law of the Austro-Hungarian monarchy. When the Magistrate began to make inquiries as to his whereabouts, neither Hitler's half-sister, Angela Raubal, nor his former guardian, Joseph Mayrhofer, were able or willing to provide information about him. It was not until 10 January 1914 that the Magistrate learned from the Munich police that Hitler had moved to Munich and registered at the Popp residence. On 12 January 1914, the Linz authorities requested through the Austro-Hungarian Consulate in Munich that Hitler appear for a draft examination in Linz. The Consul asked the Munich police to bring Hitler to him, but as this happened on a weekend, when the Consulate was closed, Hitler was arrested and spent a weekend in jail. The Austrian Consul did not think Hitler was a criminal, but a poor devil, possibly a sick man who had been wronged. When the Linz Magistrate abruptly denied Hitler's telegram requesting a postponement of the examination due to insufficient time, the Austrian Consul wrote a letter asking for consideration of Hitler's request.[7] At the same time, Hitler wrote his "poor devil letter" to the Linz authorities,[8] stating that he was the son of a public servant, an art-painter who had studied to become an architectural painter. He denied any intention to avoid the draft. Though he admitted to "a sin of omission" in not having responded to a request in 1909, he said that he had responded by letter in 1910 but received no answer from the government. He stated:

> . . . it was an unbelievably bitter time for me. I was an inexperienced young man without any financial support, too proud to accept support or to ask for it. Without support, completely on my own, the few crowns, or rather pennies, I received for my paintings were just enough to pay for my sleeping cot. For two years I had no other friend than sorrow and misery, no other companion than unremitting hunger. I have never known the beautiful

word youth. Today I have memories of frostbite on fingers, hands, and feet.
Yet I remember that time with a certain joy, now that . . . the worst is over.
In spite of the greatest misery, dubious company, I have kept my name and
my conscience pure, and I am innocent before the law except for my sin of
omission in not responding to the draft in 1909. . . .

Hitler also declared his willingness to pay a small fine. The facts were different: Hitler did not want to serve in the Austro-Hungarian army. Later, he
described his sentiments: "Austria had long ceased to be a German state and,
in the second place, the internal conditions of the Empire were moving closer
to disintegration from hour to hour."[9] Clearly, he didn't share such thoughts
with the Austrian Consul, who interceded on his behalf. It is certain that
Hitler sought to avoid the Austrian military service by rapidly moving from
one place to another in Vienna, and finally when, during the period at the
Männerheim, he believed further moves in Vienna would not help him avoid
the draft, he moved to Munich without informing the Austrian authorities.
Altogether, he avoided three draft calls. But finally he was forced to appear
before the Austro-Hungarian Imperial-Royal draft board in Salzburg.

On 5 February 1914, the draft board commission in Salzburg found
Hitler "unfit for full or limited duty, too weak, unfit to bear arms."[10] The
statement was signed by Hitler, in pencil. The draft board commission's decision must have pleased Hitler (for not having to serve), but it also must have
been devastating for him, as he was so concerned about fitness and the ability
to bear arms. No wonder he ordered the Gestapo to search everywhere for
his military papers. One does not know how the commission arrived at this
judgment. Hitler was a skillful actor who was quite capable of "playing sick"
and repeating the old tale about tuberculosis, but the commission consisted
of hard-nosed men who would not have been inclined to excuse him lightly.
(Shortly before World War 1, only one-third of draftees were inducted.)
Hitler was not decrepit or malnourished. A candid photo taken on 1 August
1914, when Germany entered the war, showed him well-nourished and with a
happy expression (welcoming the declaration of war). It is not likely but possible that the medical examiners detected the alleged genital deformation.
Whatever happened during the draft board examination, six months later
Hitler enthusiastically enlisted with the Bavarian regiment known as the List
Regiment of the Reserve Infantry.

No Pacifist

About the declaration of war between Germany and the Austro-Hungarian
monarchy, Hitler stated, "overpowered by stormy enthusiasm, I fell down on
my knees and thanked Heaven from an overflowing heart for granting me the
good fortune of being permitted to live at this time."[11] It should be recognized that some of the greatest minds of the time, such as Thomas Mann and
Sigmund Freud, and many intellectuals and artists from all nations, joined the
hurrah at the outbreak of war with enthusiasm. They quickly changed their

minds, however, while Hitler did not. For Hitler war was also the end of a depressed, dreary, and boring existence, permitting him to join the millions who felt as he did. Any reservations about becoming part of a highly regulated and disciplined cadre vanished. It was an enthusiastic, voluntary act. A few days after volunteering he stated:

> With trembling hands I opened the document; my request had been approved and I was summoned to a Bavarian regiment. My joy and gratitude knew no bounds. For me as for every German, there now began the greatest and most unforgettable time of my earthly existence.[12]

On 16 August 1914 Hitler became a private in the Sixth Reserve Battalion of the Bavarian Infantry Regiment Number 16 (the List Regiment). After rather cursory training, the battalion was moved to the West Front on 21 October and engaged in the battle at Yser on 19 October and in the fierce fighting of the major battle of Ypern from 30 October to 24 November 1914. Altogether, Hitler participated in seventeen major battles, amongst them the fierce fighting at Sommes, Arras, and Reims. His regiment was involved in almost continuous mobile and trench warfare throughout the war. Hitler was assigned to the dangerous position of dispatch runner and regimental ordinance. However, this position also had the advantage of greater sleeping comfort and frequent meals at Regimental Headquarters, which he did not mention in his accounts. Hitler was a passionate soldier, and, according to many officers and soldiers with whom he served, he was fearless and conscientious.[13] He considered bravery and defiance of danger and death great virtues. It is of interest to note that in his defiance of death in the First World War, and also during the first two years of the Second World War, Hitler showed considerable disregard for his own safety.

Although officers as well as enlisted men described Hitler as a courageous and devoted soldier and a good comrade, he also was viewed as aloof, brooding, eccentric, and restless, reading pocket editions of philosophical works, wandering around at night, and shooting rats.[14] His comrades thought he was a screwball. He showed no interest in women and did not participate in the soldiers' rough talk about sex. His fellow soldiers derided Hitler for his prudishness and called him a monk. However, gossipy tales about contacts with French women also were reported.[15] Hitler had little contact with his family, received no mail and no gifts, and spent only one furlough in the Waldviertel. The List Regiment was his home.[16] Indeed, it was the first time the homeless man had a "home" since he left Linz. He never complained about hardships or dangers, nor did he express wishes that the war would end.

Until the surrender of the German army, Hitler and most Germans believed in victory. He often lectured to his comrades—whether they were interested or not—and expressed his fervent patriotism and his views on the conduct of the war. To the combat-weary soldiers, this was annoying. One of Hitler's superiors, Captain Fritz Wiedemann, later an adjutant of Hitler, stated that Hitler discussed philosophical and political problems in the manner of small folk.[17] Hans Mend, another dispatch runner, held unfavorable opinions about Hitler. In contradictory statements he first described Hitler as a good soldier and later belittled him. Mend died in 1934, in a concentration camp. (In the Third Reich, the chances of longevity for those who denigrated the Führer were low.) During his time with the List Regiment, Hitler hinted to his comrades that someday he would be a very important person. After Hitler had become Chancellor, Wiedemann asked one of Hitler's buddies, Weiss Jackl, whether he ever thought such a thing could happen, and Jackl replied, "perhaps a deputy in the Bavarian Diet, but not more."[18]

Hitler described some of his war experiences in letters to Popp and Hepp, as well as in many of his monologues.[19] With the exception of one passage in a letter to Hepp, where he wrote that whoever did not surrender would get killed, there is no record of any cruel behavior on Hitler's part during World War I.[20] Hitler also recognized how:

> . . . initial enthusiasm cooled and the exuberant joy was stifled by fear. The time came when every man had to struggle between the instinct of self-preservation and the admonitions of duty. . . . At last my will was undisputed master. In the first few days I went over the top with rejoicing and laughter. I was now calm and determined. And this was enduring. Now Fate could bring on the ultimate tests without my nerves shattering or my reason failing. The young volunteer had become an old soldier.[21]

Hitler received several decorations for bravery and being wounded in battle. On 4 August 1918 he received the Iron Cross First Class (abbreviated EKI) for bravery in the battle of Wytschaete. It was uncommon for an enlisted man to receive this high decoration. Hitler valued the medal and always pinned it to his uniform, although later he falsely stated that he did not wear the decoration because it had been given to him by the Regimental Adjutant Captain Heinrich Guttman, a "cowardly Jew," who also wore the Iron Cross First Class.[22] After he became Commander in Chief, in a gesture of reverse modesty, Hitler distanced himself from his bemedaled general staff officers and diplomats and wore only the EKI.

The assignment as dispatch runner for Regimental Headquarters not only gave Hitler unusual autonomy, but also provided the opportunity for him to learn more about military strategy and tactics than the ordinary infantryman. When he later became the Supreme Commander of the German armed forces in World War II, Hitler often pointed to his World War I experiences, setting himself up as a military expert with experience. Some of his convictions, such as his aversion to stationary warfare and his unwillingness to retreat or accept defeat, can be traced to his experience as a common soldier. Hitler was deeply impressed by British propaganda and psychological warfare and later shaped much of his own propaganda after what he had learned during World War I and later from the Bolsheviks.[23]

There is no doubt about Hitler's brave performance in combat, but historians have been puzzled as to why he was not promoted to a higher rank than lance corporal. Although a definitive explanation is wanting, according to Captain Wiedemann this might have happened because Hitler was considered by many to be an odd and sloppy person with poor posture. Later, Wiedemann surprised and amused the prosecuting attorney of the Nuremberg Military Trials, Robert W. M. Kempner, when he stated that the regimental authorities thought Hitler lacked leadership talent.[24] More important was the fact that Hitler stated that he did not want a promotion. Perhaps he was not ready for it internally, as he was still too depressed and lacked self-confidence. Another explanation for his reluctance may have been his need for autonomy, his need to stay out of the chain of command as far as this was possible. It is correct that Hitler did not exhibit leadership qualities at that time, nor did he view himself as a leader. In his later career, the story of his ascent from the unknown soldier to the Führer served Hitler well. It was the only way to bypass national heroes such as Generals Ludendorff and Hindenburg.

The Combat Gas Injury

On 5 October, Hitler was wounded by a shrapnel splinter in his left thigh and hospitalized from 9 October to 1 December at Beelen. For this wound he received a service medal for combat injuries. On 5 March 1917, at his request, he was reassigned to his old regiment. A more alarming injury occurred on 14 October 1918, shortly before the end of the war. Hitler and several hundred soldiers were surprised by a British attack with combat gas. Hitler suffered from a mild case of mustard gas poisoning, affecting his eyes. He was evacuated first to the field hospital at Oudenarde and then, on 19 October, was sent to the reserve hospital at Pasewalk. The symptoms were conjunctivitis with blepharospasm, excessive secretion from the conjunctivitis, and severe pain ("My eyes had turned into glowing coals"[25]). It can be assumed that no keratitis or iritis was present. No corneal scars or other sequelae were ever found. Hitler was unable to open his eyes, which he called blindness. Martin Dresse, a judge, later stated that he had seen Hitler's medical record and remembered that Hitler was not blind, but rather suffered from severe burning of the eyes.[26] Only the eyes were affected, and Hitler did not suffer from any significant burns of the airways. Combat gas injuries were dreaded, and, like others with similar injuries, Hitler undoubtedly suffered great anxiety. With his interest in painting and architecture, this was a very threatening injury. He maintained that, as a blind painter, he was 100 percent invalid—to which the presiding judge at the Putsch trial remarked that he was reassigned for full duty.[27] The hospital records from Pasewalk disappeared. According to later rumors, they were in the possession of Heinrich Himmler and General Wilhelm Canaris, but this has never been substantiated. Himmler later mentioned to his masseur, Felix Kersten, that Hitler had syphilis when he was at Pasewalk, another unsubstantiated statement. Hitler probably received the standard symptomatic therapy for combat gas injuries, consisting of compresses soaked with mildly anti-inflammatory solutions. He recovered quickly. He stated that his eyesight returned until he had a relapse on 10 November, when a regimental chaplain informed the soldier patients that Germany had surrendered and the Emperor abdicated. In *Mein Kampf*, Hitler described his reaction:

> I could stand it no longer. It became impossible for me to sit still one minute more. Again, everything went black before my eyes; I tottered and groped my way back to the dormitory, threw myself on my back and dug my burning head in my blanket and pillow.[28]

One day later, he calmed down and could see again. This episode was a psychogenic (more specifically, hysterical) reaction, but it also provides evidence of Hitler's intense feelings and despair over the defeat. Professor Karl Wilmans, a psychiatrist at the University of Heidelberg, talked quite openly to students about Hitler's hysterical blindness;[29] Wilmans lost his job after the National Socialists seized power.

Hitler's episode of hysterical blindness was the topic of a novel, *The Eye Witness*, by Ernst Weiss, an émigré, published after Weiss's suicide.[30] Weiss described a hospitalized German soldier, an odd and rather disagreeable person, who claimed he lost his eyesight after a mustard gas attack on the Western Front. A military psychiatrist diagnosed the blindness as a hysterical symptom and treated the soldier with hypnosis. The main hypnotic command was for the soldier to overcome everything through his tremendous willpower. He responded, regained his eyesight, and became convinced that he could achieve anything he set out to do. The soldier in the roman à clef is Adolf Hitler; the hypnotist, a psychiatrist, is modeled after Professor Edmund Forster, who allegedly supplied the bits of information that enabled Weiss to write the story. The information on which the novel is based was first given to an emigrated journalist who did not see fit to publish a factual article based on what Forster had told him, but supplied the authors Ernst Weiss and Joseph Roth with material that Weiss used to write his novel.

Dr. Forster was head of the psychiatric service at Pasewalk military hospital at the end of the war. Because no medical records could be found, it cannot be established whether Forster treated Hitler or even saw him as a consultant.[31] Individual psychotherapy was virtually unknown during the First World War, and particularly during the disintegration of the German army it would have been most unlikely to occur. Hitler commented defensively during the putsch trial in 1924 that the situation in Pasewalk was chaotic, stating before the court that there had been no treatment for the individual soldier.[32] At the trial, he was quite concerned about establishing the "blind cripple" myth.[33] Because Forster left the Pasewalk hospital on 14 November 1918, he would have had little time to treat Hitler between 9 and

14 November. Furthermore, Professor Forster looked askance at hypnosis and preferred coercive and punitive methods for treating patients who were diagnosed as hysterics, malingerers, and, in particular, "war tremblers."

In any case, Hitler recovered quickly from his hysterical episode. What happened to Professor Forster is not central to Hitler's trauma but is of some interest. Forster was known to make critical remarks about the National Socialist regime. In 1933 he was "persuaded" to retire from his university chair. In all likelihood, this retirement was not the result of unacceptable scientific views, but rather due to his critical remarks about National Socialism. Shortly after his "retirement," on 28 August 1933, Forster committed suicide by shooting himself. He feared that the National Socialist regime was after him. Actually, Forster's retirement was handled administratively, and he was not apprehended by the Gestapo or prevented from traveling to France and Switzerland.[34] Can this relative leniency be explained by concern on the part of the regime that Forster really knew something or that any publicity about Pasewalk, right or wrong, could be damaging to Hitler? No definitive answer to this question exists.

Germany's Defeat

Hitler liked to refer to himself as a blind cripple—which he never was. He dated his resolution to become a politician to the time of his "blindness," hinting at a vision that told him to save Germany. Whether Hitler had a vision is very uncertain and actually unimportant. Visions are stock-in-trade for prophets and would-be prophets. Later, he maintained the posture of a prophet and savior but realistically distanced himself from the vision. However, Hitler stated many times that he was guided by Providence and/or the Almighty, depending on the audience, and gradually came to believe the "mission" legend. His decision to enter politics probably came in bits and pieces. It was based on his belief that Germany had been not defeated but betrayed, and that it must be restored to even greater glory. General Ludendorff had asked for an armistice because he saw no hope of fighting against the overwhelming manpower and logistical superiority of the Entente, but Hitler and many other Germans could not accept this because German troops were still fighting on foreign soil. Hitler and many Germans did not believe that German leadership and German soldiers were responsible for the surrender. Then as well as later during World War II, Hitler remained convinced that Germany had never been defeated, but rather betrayed by inner enemies. He was critical of the German Emperor Wilhelm II but held the top generals von Hindenburg and von Ludendorff in high regard for many years, until his opinions about them changed, too. The inner enemies were Marxists and Jews. Against them Hitler resolved to fight. At the end of the war, these thoughts were dim and not yet publicly expressed. He made a point about having been a soldier during the war and having no time for politics.[35] The first ideas about becoming a political speaker occurred during the war, but actual steps were taken almost a year later. Hitler's ruminations are reflected in passages from *Mein Kampf*:

> . . . and now the first ideas came to me of later engaging in political activity. Precisely this was what caused me often to assure the small circle of my friends that, after the war, I meant to be a speaker in addition to my profession. I *believe* that I was very serious about this. . . .[36]

A little later, in the summer or early fall of 1919—one cannot be sure when, because Hitler was never precise about dates—he wrote:

> In these days endless plans chased one another through my head. For days I wondered what could be done, but at the end of every meditation was the sober realization that I, nameless as I was, I did not possess the least basis for any useful action. . . . I could not decide to join any of the existing parties.[37]

In contrast to millions of German soldiers who happily returned to their homes at the end of the war, Hitler had no home to return to. He stayed in the army, which had become the Army of the Weimar Republic. Again he felt bewildered, but the war had hardened him. It had been a moratorium for Hitler. He had recovered from his dysphoria. He had performed well as a soldier, and his feeling of worth had increased. War was collective aggression for an accepted cause, a notion that was not lost on Hitler. He was proud to have participated in the task of fighting for a greater Germany. The passive civilian had turned into an aggressive fighter, more resentful than ever. He also realized that this was a time of major change in the world.

4

Entry into Politics

DEFEATED GERMANY was in a chaotic state.[1] Emperor Wilhelm II had fled, and Friedrich Ebert, a moderate socialist, became the first President of the newly established Weimar Republic. Nowhere in the nation was the turmoil greater than in Munich. After King Ludwig of Bavaria abdicated, Kurt Eisner, a socialist and former theater critic, became Bavaria's Minister-President. Eisner was a naïve and inexperienced administrator without any support from the bureaucracy, police, or army. Only a few weeks after he took office, he was assassinated by Count Arco-Valley, a right-wing fanatic. Eisner's successor was a socialist teacher, Johannes Hoffmann, whose reign lasted until March 1920, when Communist members of the so-called Spartakusbund established the *Räterepublik*, a proletarian dictatorship. Some of the leaders were Bolsheviks and Jews—Paul Axelrod, Max Lewin, Eugen Levin, the author Ernst Toller, and the poet Erich Mühsam—which fueled anti-Semitic, xenophobic, and anti-intellectual sentiments among the populace. After a few turbulent weeks of expropriations and executions, the *Räterepublik* was toppled in bloody and cruel fighting by army units and free corps militia recruited from nationalist political groups. Army units were sent, at Hoffmann's request, by the socialist Reich Defense Minister, Gustav Noske. After a short, uneasy rule, Hoffmann resigned under pressure from right-wing groups in March 1920, and was followed by Gustaf Ritter von Kahr, a conservative Catholic and Bavarian monarchist. From its birth, the Weimar Republic was despised by many and rightly called the Unloved Republic. Hitler, too, condemned the revolution and the Republic, though without it his own rise would have been unthinkable.

At the end of the war, Hitler's primary concern, like that of millions of other Germans, was survival. After his discharge from the Pasewalk hospital, he was stationed first at the Maximilian Barracks in Munich and later transferred to a camp for returned prisoners-of-war in Traunstein, where he earned extra pay by sorting military clothing. Hitler was lying low and watching events. At one time, he was allegedly arrested by Spartakus troops and forced to wear a red arm band, but soon released. During the early spring of 1919, he was assigned to the Press and Propaganda Unit of the Second Infantry Regiment, with the task of providing patriotic reeducation for soldiers of the Reichswehr who were returning to civilian life. The appointment was a major break for Hitler.[2] He was designated as an educational officer but also functioned as a *V-Mann, Vertrauensmann* (literally a trusted person), a title in bad repute because V-men had the task of spying on comrades. Hitler reported to Captain Karl Mayr, who soon became aware of the exceptional oratorical talents of his *V-Mann*. In preparation for his assignment, Hitler had received some training from scholars, amongst them Professor Alexander Georg von Müller, who taught a course in patriotic history, and Gottfried Feder, an engineer and self-styled economist who lectured on his pet theory about international loan capitalism that was enslaving the German people. It is unknown what Hitler learned in these lectures—probably little, because he never learned much in formal courses. He informed himself more through personal discourse and reading, but it is not clear what he read and what he absorbed. Captain Mayr—to whom Hitler owed so much—later left the nationalist movement and became a Social Democrat. After Hitler's seizure of power, he was sent to the Buchenwald concentration camp, where he died in May 1945.[3]

The Anti-Semitic Banner

During the summer of 1919, Hitler developed an extremely anti-Semitic world view. Many Germans were eager to blame Jews, the eternal scapegoat, for their plight, humiliations, and impoverishment. Hitler understood this very well and, within a short time, used it for his own political purposes, radicalizing German anti-Semitism to a degree heretofore unknown in modern Europe. Hitler's anti-Semitism cannot be explained by conscious motivation alone. Exploration of the inner fires that fed this anti-Semitism will be pursued throughout this study. The person who influenced Hitler profoundly, and the only one he mentioned specifically as a mentor, was Dietrich Eckart, a journalist and author twenty years Hitler's senior, whom Hitler met in Munich in 1919. Eckart was known in literary circles for his translation of Ibsen's *Peer Gynt*. He also published a vitriolic anti-Semitic weekly, *Auf gut Deutsch*. Eckart became the first chief editor of the *Beobachter* (later the *Völkischer Beobachter*), the party paper. Hitler was critical of his alcoholism, and his tenure as editor was short. Although Hitler dedicated *Mein Kampf* to Eckart, Hitler paid little attention to him during the last years of Eckart's life.

Before the relationship between Hitler and Eckart cooled off, the two men had dialogues about anti-Semitism that were published under the title *Der Bolshewismus von Moses bis Lenin*.[4] Citations from the Old Testament, which both Eckart and Hitler knew fairly well, abound, to demonstrate the wickedness of Jews and their intent to destroy the Aryan race. Eckart also drew Hitler's attention to Otto Weininger, a Viennese Jewish philosopher with strong anti-Semitic and anti-feminist views. To Hitler, such self-confessions by Jews were proof of their badness and destructiveness.[5]

Amongst the anti-Semitic pamphlets and books that Hitler read, one vicious work stands out. It was a fraudulent, malicious publication by the Tsar's Secret Police, called the *Protocols of the Wise Men of Zion*, describing a Jewish world conspiracy.[6] It had been concocted by reactionary anti-Semitic Russians and was brought to Hitler's attention by the party philosopher Alfred Rosenberg, a Baltic Russian and fierce anti-Semite. Some of Hitler's lectures about the Jewish world conspiracy were very similar to passages in the *Protocols*. Hitler maintained that the *Protocols* were valid and used many of their statements.[7] Hitler was less impressed with Rosenberg's philosophy, presented in the confused and unreadable *Der Mythos des zwanzigsten Jahrhunderts*.[8] Already in Vienna, Hitler had been familiar with Richard Wagner's anti-Semitic writings,[9] although, with all his admiration for the Master, he never referred to them. It is certain that Hitler was well acquainted with the anti-Semitic tome by Houston Stewart Chamberlain, Wagner's son-in-law, *The Foundations of the Twentieth Century*.[10] Hitler's racist mentors also drew his attention to Henry Ford's anti-Semitic writings in Ford's newspaper, *The Dearborn Independent*. Ford maintained that the international Jew had been responsible for World War I—one of Hitler's favorite topics.

On 16 September 1919, at the request of Captain Mayr, Hitler wrote a resume for Alfred Gemlich,[11] another *V-Mann*, explaining his views on anti-Semitism. It was Hitler's first political document, and it contains the essential elements of his new racist-destructive anti-Semitism. In abstract, the lengthy letter states the following:

> Anti-Semitism must not be based on emotions, but on recognition of facts. Above all, Jews are a race and not a religious community. Through incest they have greater racial purity than others. The thinking and feelings of Jews are determined by their craving for money and power. They have corrupted princes through byzantine flattery and sapped national pride, the strength of the people, through derision and vice. All higher striving—be it religion, socialism, democracy—is only a means to satisfy their need for money and power. The work of Jews results in a racial tuberculosis of nations. [The term "racial tuberculosis" is one of Hitler's neologisms. He believed that he and other family members suffered from the "white plague." More frequently, he spoke of syphilis as destructive.] Whereas emotional anti-Semitism finds its ultimate expression in pogroms, rational anti-Semitism is

expressed in planned legislative measures and the elimination of privileges that Jews hold in contrast to other foreigners. The last goal will be the definitive removal of Jews. Only a strong national government can accomplish this.

Hitler accused the government of the Weimar Republic of preventing the cheated German people from fighting against the cheaters, the Jews.

During the summer and fall of 1919, Hitler addressed soldiers about the topics he considered of vital importance: the betrayal of Germany by its inner enemies, the shame of Versailles, the threat of Bolshevism, and the role of the Jew. After one of these lectures he said to himself, "I could speak."[12] Just when this occurred is unclear, but it was a turning point. Hitler developed a new feeling of self-worth. He knew he could deliver a message to which many Germans would listen, and he was confident they would be willing to follow the messenger. Based on a vulgar social Darwinism, Hitler's message was that the Germanic–Nordic race—its best representatives being, in Hitler's view, the Germans—should rule the world and must eliminate the Jew, the eternal enemy who wanted to destroy, defile, and poison all other races. Fest commented: "That moment signified—if any specific moment did—the breakthrough to himself, the 'hammer stroke' of fate, that shattered the shell of everyday life."[13] Hitler developed a sense of mission that, in time, enabled him to become a charismatic leader, a fanatic prophet. A comprehensive hypothesis about this crucial metamorphosis will be developed in Chapter 9.

It was in the fall of 1919, and not in November 1918, that Hitler had become a politician. He was thirty years old. In *Mein Kampf* he later expressed his conviction that:

> a man should not engage in public political activity before his thirtieth year. He should not do so, because at that time, as a rule, he is engaged in molding a general platform on the basis of which he proceeds to examine the various political problems and finally establish his own position on them.[14]

Hitler believed he had done just that.

The German Workers Party

One of the small groups Hitler was ordered to reconnoiter was the German Workers Party (Deutsche Arbeiterpartei, or DAP). Anton Drexler, a locksmith who worked for the German State Railroads, a naïve man, founded the party and chaired its Munich section. Karl Harrer, a sports journalist, headed the national organization. The number of party members was small; two-thirds belonged to the middle class and were young professionals, students, employers, and independent businessmen. One-third were skilled workers, mostly from the German State Railroads, and 13 percent of the total group were discharged soldiers. The organization was run by an executive committee of six, from which women were excluded. Notwithstanding this bias, large numbers of women flocked to the meetings after Hitler became a speaker. The DAP program envisioned a unified German state without classes and without class struggle. It favored the socialization of large trusts, abolition of exploitation through dividends and interests, and improvement of social conditions for skilled workers. It was radically anti-Semitic and did not recognize Jews as German citizens. With the slogan "common good above individual good," the DAP promoted a program that had a utopian socialist flavor. It adhered to parliamentary procedures; its executive committee was elected by the membership and served at its pleasure.

The Munich section of the DAP met in a back room of the Sterneckerbräu, one of Munich's small beer halls. Most of the early meetings, big or small, were held in beer halls. At one of the meetings, Hitler listened to speeches by Gottfried Feder and a "professor" who presented views about a fusion of Bavaria and Austria. The latter speech provoked Hitler to such a violent verbal attack that the speaker fled the room. Drexler, a man not known for his talents as a speaker, welcomed the orator Hitler, saying to another member in Bavarian dialect, "He has a big mouth. We could use him."[15] In the meantime, Hitler read Drexler's book, *Mein politisches Erwachen*,[16] and concluded that Drexler's views were similar to his own. Hitler wrote that his decision to join was made during a sleepless night while he was watching some mice playing on the floor of his barracks room.[17] The association of the mice with the humble members of the club was not far-fetched. Hitler considered neither the civilian Drexler nor anyone else in the DAP his equal. He stated that the group sent him a membership card without his asking for it, which amazed him. It was not a membership card, however, but rather an application, because Hitler formally applied for membership. After careful deliberation, he made another "most difficult decision of his life" and decided to join, in spite of his contempt for this "club of the worst manner."[18] He realized that, as an obscure person, he would be more successful in a small party he could shape than in any established political organization. Furthermore, he sensed that the time was ripe for major changes that would have been impossible in the old order before the war. Although decisions were difficult for Hitler, his professed hesitation to join the DAP is contradicted by two letters. In the first, dated 4 October 1919, he asked Captain Mayr, to whom he reported about his visit, for permission to join the group. In the second letter, dated 19 October 1919, he wrote to the DAP and expressed his eagerness to become a member.[19] In another letter, he stated that he was a businessman but wanted to become a political speaker.[20] Hitler realized that his chances of entering politics without money, title, reputation, or education were slim.[21] Obviously, he realized that this small-time group of modest and clumsy burghers would provide a good point of entry for him. Hitler clearly felt superior to them. He was assigned membership number 555,[22] but he lied that his membership number was seven, which was his number on the executive committee to which he had been assigned as chairman of the propaganda committee.[23]

Chairman of Propaganda and Public Orator

No task pleased Hitler more than becoming chairman of propaganda. To his satisfaction, within two years he mastered the art of political speaking before large masses,[24] with the goal of attracting listeners and converting them into fanatic disciples. Earlier, he said he hadn't been able to speak a single sentence before an audience of more than four strangers.[25] Bullock called him the greatest demagogue in history.[26] Hitler viewed his oratorical ability as the gift of a great artist.[27] In *Mein Kampf* he presented his views on mass psychology, political speaking, and propaganda, which he acquired between 1923 and 1929.[28] He believed that men were won over less by the written than by the spoken word, and that every great movement on the earth owed its growth to great orators, and not to great writers. Hitler undoubtedly realized that he was not a talented writer. Another assumption that guided him was his conviction that masses were inferior. He considered them emotional, fickle, forgetful, and in need of guidance. According to Hitler, they were like women, but he also asserted that major changes were not possible without the masses.[29] The political leader must be sensitive to them if he wishes to overcome their prejudices, which are not based on reason, but for the most part are unconsciously supported only by sentiment.[30] The speaker gets a continuous amendment of his speech from the crowd he is addressing, since he can always see in the faces of his followers the extent to which they are able to follow his arguments.[31] The speaker must assure that the weakest member of the audience is not left behind, and, if necessary, he must repeat the argument over and over again.[32] Professors of public speaking and literature might have flunked Hitler in their courses, but he contemptuously stated that he did not speak for professors.[33] "One does not measure the speech of a statesman by the impression it leaves on a university professor, but by the effect it exerts on the people."[34] At all times, the speaker must remain the master and not the slave of the masses. Hitler claimed—and rightly, too—that he was one in a thousand, who could speak today before a public consisting of street cleaners, locksmiths, and sewer workers, and tomorrow hold forth a lecture in an auditorium full of university professors and students.[35]

Based on these principles, Hitler developed a very effective technique of public speaking. He stated that it was preferable to speak in the evening, rather than in the morning, when listeners were tired, and that after leaving work people were happy to join a crowd of persons with sentiments similar to their own.[36] Under such conditions, individuals succumbed to the "magic" influence of Hitler. He called it mass suggestion and intended to produce a conversion, whereby the man who entered the meeting doubting and wavering became a link in the national community.[37] He also paid careful attention to spatial and temporal arrangements for his speeches. The lecture hall had to be the right size. The speaker's entrance was preceded by a display of flags and martial music, and by torch parades. The demonstrations were carefully staged, and the huge meetings at the Reichsparteitag and on other solemn occasions were spectacular. Before the speech, there was an air of great expectation. Hitler started his lectures slowly, usually reciting the stereotyped and repetitious tale of his own and the party's ascent—what Domarus called the party story.[38] The audience was both expectant and drowsy, almost hypnotized—exactly what Hitler wanted.[39] Then Hitler's voice rose, gradually and intermittently, in passionate outbursts in which his tone became high-pitched with anger and fanaticism. At the conclusion Hitler was exhausted, bathed in sweat, and almost in a state of altered consciousness. One could almost describe some of the speeches as orgiastic experiences—not only for Hitler, but for the audience as well. Men and women alike yelled, groaned, and fainted. Paul Devrient, an opera singer and voice teacher, claimed to have helped Hitler vocalize in 1932, a time when Hitler faced rhetorical disaster because he had abused his voice.[40] According to Devrient, Hitler had no choice but to become his student. Devrient's exaggerated description and claim that he helped Hitler overcome these difficulties has remained a well-kept secret, however, and nobody in Hitler's environment ever became aware of a voice teacher. Only much later, in 1935, after the removal of a laryngeal polyp, Hitler obtained help from a speech therapist.

Hitler taught himself to speak. His preparation for the early speeches consisted of making notes about salient points. Usually, he spoke freely, without referring to his notes. Later, he dictated his speeches, using the dictation as a rehearsal and at times displaying the same intense emotion during dictation that he exhibited during the lecture itself.[41] He rehearsed in front of a mirror. A picture taken of such a rehearsal by his photographer, Heinrich Hoffmann, was not permitted to be shown in public. Early models for Hitler's oratory were Vienna's mayor, Karl Lueger, and famous Catholic preachers. Influencing others through the spoken word was the powerful instrument Hitler used throughout his political career. Only in the last war year did his speeches become tired and listless. The content of Hitler's early speeches encompassed a few basic themes presented with variation but unchanging vulgarity that his audiences appreciated. It was the shame of Versailles, the treachery of the Bolsheviks, the cowardice of the aristocracy and bourgeoisie, and—most of all—the vices, crimes, and diseases of the ultimate culprit, the Jew.

The impact of Hitler's speeches on his audiences—with the exception of persons who were immune for racial or political reasons and had well-established oppositional political, philosophical, or religious views—was overwhelming. Yet many opponents, particularly intellectuals, found his speaking obnoxious and repulsive. Eitner stated that Hitler had the voice of a cheap actor in a sideshow.[42] It is more appropriate to compare his speeches to the acts of today's rock stars and television evangelists. The ratings during his successful years would have been very high. Among many who commented on the power of Hitler's oratory, only two are cited here: André Francois-Poncet, the French Ambassador in Berlin; and the businessman Kurt W. Lüdecke, a follower who later became an opponent. François-Poncet compared Hitler to a great orator in the Latin tradition (what praise from a critical Frenchman!), who instinctively employed all the figures of rhetoric. He was the virtuoso, playing upon all the chords of eloquence, excelling in caustic irony and invective.[43] François-Poncet was well aware of the extraordinary mutual identification of the masses with Hitler when they yelled in response to his orations: "Hitler is Germany, and Germany is Hitler." Lüdecke commented:

> Presently my critical faculty was swept away. . . . I do not know how to describe the emotion that swept over me as I heard this man. His words were like a scourge. When he spoke of the disgrace of Germany, I felt ready to spring on any enemy. His appeal to German manhood was like a call to arms, the gospel he preached the sacred truth. He seemed another Luther. I forgot everything but the man. Then glancing around, I saw this magnetism was holding these thousands as one.
>
> Of course I was ripe for this experience. I was a man of thirty-two, weary of disgust and disillusionment, a wanderer seeking a course, a patriot without a channel for his patriotism, a yearner for the heroic without a hero. The intense will of the man, the passion of his sincerity seemed to flow from him into me. I experienced an exaltation that could be likened only to a religious experience.[44]

Although he belittled the importance of the written word, Hitler valued written propaganda. One of his first political acts on behalf of the party was to acquire a newspaper. The *Münchner Beobachter*, owned by Rudolf Freiherr von Sebottendorf, the founder of the right-wing, semi-secret Thule Society, became the party organ, the *Völkischer Beobachter*. Hitler used mass media — film as well as broadcasts — with great skill and conviction. What he might have done in the era of cyberspace is unthinkable. Along with his gifted propagandist, Joseph Goebbels, Hitler was ahead of his time in using propaganda unscrupulously, without concern about its truthfulness. Beyond any doubt Hitler had exceptional talent and a strong interest in effective propaganda. He was both original and imitative, borrowing techniques from the Marxist parties and Catholicism. Before Hitler's major speeches, bands and orchestras played martial music. Impressive lighting effects (a forerunner of "light and sound"), including torch parades before the meetings, created a receptive atmosphere. The giant meetings at the national party conventions — the first of which was held as early as 1921 — and particularly the meetings after the seizure of power were spectacular. They were staged in grandiose, overpowering settings, designed by Hitler's architects as well as by himself to be uplifting and awe-inspiring. One expression of Hitler's extraordinary flair for propaganda was the development of the new party flag, displayed already in midsummer 1920. Hitler had been familiar with the swastika, an ancient sun symbol that had been used for centuries in Asia and the Americas, since his childhood, when he saw it in the coat of arms of the Abbott of Lambach. Around 1910, at the suggestion of anti-Semite Guido List, it was used as a symbol by anti-Semitic organizations. Hitler was credited for the swastika design on the national flag and the party insignia, assisted by another party member, the dentist Friedrich Krohn. He used the colors of Wilhelminian Germany but gave them a new interpretation. Red he viewed as symbolizing the social ideal of the Party, white as the nationalistic ideal, and the swastika overall as the mission, the struggle for victory of the Aryan race. The Nobel Prize laureate Elias Canetti experienced it as a cruel symbol, like a wheel of torture.[45] Indeed, the swastika had the effect of a torch,[46] inspiring Hitler's followers and frightening his enemies.

The Drummer

Hitler's own statement about his sudden transition from a rather passive and unpolitical person to an active, fanatic leader is misleading. It was not a quick, satori-like experience in 1919. It took time, perhaps years, for him to achieve this. In a number of statements Hitler presented himself as a forerunner or drummer for the movement. Others called him Führer before he saw himself in that role. He loved the address of *"mein Führer,"* which came into use quite early, although Hitler maintained he was not aware when it occurred.[47] The drummer metaphor signifies the great importance Hitler attributed to propaganda and recruitment, and his talent in these endeavors. It is this author's impression, however, that he used the designation primarily when he felt the need to defend himself, such as during the putsch trial, or when he wanted to appear inoffensive or harmless. The term drummer also has a self-derogatory connotation, and Hitler was rarely self-derogatory. More significant was his self-understanding as a *Wegbereiter* (literally, preparer of the path), a trailblazer or scout before the real leader arrives. He allegedly made reference to Saint John the Baptist in a private conversation with an early party member, Georg Schott, when he stated, "We are all small Saint Johns. I wait for Christ."[48] Several other statements confirm that Hitler saw himself at the beginning of his political career as such a forerunner, scout, or prophet. In his speech to the National Klub on 29 May 1922, he stressed to the industrialists that he wanted nothing personal, but viewed himself as the drummer of the national freedom movement. When challenged by a discussant, Hitler added, "When the national front is so strong that it can reach for power, then the Führer will be here, too."[49] Four years later, during the putsch trial, he still referred to his task as that of the drummer: "[It was not] out of modesty [that] I wanted to be the drummer; this is the highest, everything else is a bagatelle."[50]

Hitler's struggle to define and justify his Führer role can be well discerned in a note he jotted down on 26 August 1921, outlining the qualities of a leadership. Paraphrased, he stated that the first chairman must have the best head and the right disposition; he must have a good sense of timing, must be responsible to himself and the cause, and must be granted freedom of action.[51] He added also that those who are able should have free rein, not crediting the American source of the phrase. Even after Hitler had been acclaimed as the greatest leader, the greatest general, the greatest German, however, some inner doubts remained. It took more than three years after the seizure of power for him to state in the annual Bürgerbräu speech on 11 November 1936, "You have heard the voice of a man, and it went to your heart. I awakened you, and you followed this voice."[52] On 13 November, two days after seeing himself as Führer, Hitler continued, "This is the miracle of our time: That you found me among so many millions and that I found you is Germany's good fortune."[53] His reference to himself as being a forerunner (a Saint John the Baptist) raises the question as to whether Hitler had anyone in mind to play the role of savior. It is possible that, for a short time, he considered General Erich Ludendorff, with whom he had entered a strange and uneasy alliance. The cooperation of the powerful World War I general with the former corporal in itself was amazing. The general, like other conservative politicians such as von Kahr and, later, Papen and Hugenberg, sought Hitler's help because he realized Hitler was a leader of masses. General Ludendorff also knew that without these masses he could never achieve his goal of establishing a conservative regime, or possibly a restoration of the monarchy. Initially, Hitler felt flattered by the attention of General Ludendorff, who, like himself, was a bitter enemy of the Weimar Republic. Slowly, however, Hitler recognized that the general was an inept politician and began to criticize him for his odd religious beliefs, which Ludendorff shared with his second wife, Doctor Matilde von Kemnitz. Hitler proceeded to downgrade the couple step by step. During the putsch, and particularly during the ensuing trial, Ludendorff played a secondary role. In 1925, Ludendorff was induced by Hitler to run against General Hindenburg and lost the election. When President Hindenburg appointed Hitler Chancellor, Ludendorff sent Hindenburg a bitter letter, stating:

> By your nomination of Hitler as Chancellor of the Reich, you have delivered our fatherland to one of the greatest demagogues of all time. I solemnly prophesy that this unholy man will throw the Reich into a precipice and bring our nation into unspeakable misery. Future generations will curse you in your grave for your deed.[54]

There was no open éclat between Hitler and Ludendorff. The two talked privately before the General's death, and Ludendorff was buried with great honors.

The Need for Dominance

Even though Hitler lacked sufficient self-assurance to view himself as leader in the early 1920s, he had a strong need to be dominant—to have not only the last word, but the only word, and preferably without opposition or objection. At an early point in his career, Hitler had forced the ousting of the national chairman of the DAP, Karl Harrer, and shortly afterward of Anton Drexler. The leadership of the DAP, which became the NSDAP (Nationalsozialistische Deutsche Arbeiterpartei), knew that a revolutionary overthrow of the German or Bavarian government was, considering their small numbers, impossible. (In 1922, the NSDAP had 2000 members; in 1923, some 50,000 members.) Harrer and Drexler favored mergers with other "patriotic" splinter groups to amass the necessary strength for action. Hitler insisted that these groups give up their identity and submit to NSDAP dominance. In the spring, Hitler and Eckart went to Berlin to establish contact with members of the Kapp Putsch (organized by the ultraright-wing politician Wolfgang Kapp). After the putsch was crushed by the Reichswehr, they learned on their return that Drexler and Harrer, behind Hitler's back, had negotiated with Free Corps leaders, in particular Otto Dickel, who favored reconciliation among all national combat groups. On 17 June 1921, in a fit of rage, Hitler resigned from the party. Drexler knew that, without Hitler, the little party would remain an insignificant splinter party, and he persuaded Hitler to return. Hitler insisted on becoming chairman, with far-reaching powers, and the members obliged. He also insisted on a structure that he called a "German democracy," in which the leader was elected and then became the sole authority. He could be impeached if he performed badly (but who would impeach him?). With this dictum, Hitler established his authority once and for all—and became the virtually undisputed leader of the movement. He insisted that other groups join the NSDAP but did not permit mergers. His strategy turned out to be correct. On 10 October 1922, Julius Streicher—head of the extreme anti-Semitic German Socialist Party—submitted to Hitler unconditionally. Shortly afterward some of the patriotic combat organizations, including Reichsflagge and Oberland, joined, too. These were critical early successes. Hitler continued to recruit, but he wanted new members only if they could be organized under an active leader. He found such men of action who, under his leadership, determined what happened in the party and, later, in Germany.

The Old Guard

It is important to understand Hitler's relationship with the persons who became members of his early cadre. He dominated them, but they also exerted considerable influence on him. Within the context of this work, it is possible to provide only a very cursory description of these men. Most important is their extraordinary aggression and, with rare exceptions (e.g., latecomers Albert Speer and Lutz Graf von Schwerin-Krosigh), their self-righteousness and brutality. Without these men, Hitler would not have become the leader he was. Their impact on him was almost as great as his impact on them. A number of the future leaders of the Third Reich were among the old guard who helped Hitler during the early days of the party. It was an all-male group; the many female admirers and followers were not admitted to the inner circle—indeed, Hitler stated that a German girl was a subject and became a citizen only upon marrying a German citizen.[55] Many of the old guard were young ex-soldiers and officers—angry and disgruntled men, aggressive adventurers with a passionate hatred for the Weimar Republic and a wartime morality that permitted them to break existing laws and rules if this served their cause. Amongst them were men who could boast remarkable achievements and abilities, like the World War I flying ace Hermann Göring and the ex-diplomat and capable businessman Max Erwin von Scheubner-Richter. With some exceptions, they were capable and intelligent. Some of Hitler's early buddies were outright criminals, such as Julius Streicher and the bouncer and horse-trader Christian Weber. All admired Hitler as a fanatic, determined man of great ability. What made them so submissive to Hitler has remained a puzzle. They believed in him and were, for the most part, absolutely loyal to him. To Hitler, such loyalty was more important than ability. One gains the impression that, from the beginning of his political activity, Hitler was dogmatic and insisted that only his opinion counted. He expected more than loyalty. He asked for total belief. It was not the ordinary flattery potentates demand and expect, but a profound conviction about his messianic message.

Few of Hitler's early associates remained in their prominent positions until the end of the regime. The relationship with Eckart, Hitler's most influential early mentor, and the lesser ideologue Rosenberg have been noted before. Hitler used his prize catch, Hermann Göring, in very important assignments, as leader of the parliamentary National Socialist faction, executor of the Four-Year Plan, and, later, Reichsmarschal of the Armed Forces. Göring was a powerful, iron-fisted man whose bonhomie was superficial. Hitler was quite forgiving in tolerating Göring's absurd vanity and, later, even his inefficiency, probably caused by his morphine addiction. Only at the very end of the regime Hitler expelled Göring from all of his posts and from Party membership, based on the false assumption that Göring had betrayed him. Even before the Nuremberg Military Tribunal, Göring, as the leader of the accused, staunchly defended Hitler. Another early follower, Rudolf Hess, was designated Führer deputy, but the likely successor was Göring, although Hitler believed that nobody could replace him. Hess had an almost canine devotion to Hitler, who affectionately called him *"mein Hesserl"* and the "conscience of the Party." He served Hitler more with his heart than his brain. After his flight to Scotland as an "angel of peace," allegedly against Hitler's will, he was depicted as a psychotic criminal. One of the most important early associates was Captain Ernst Röhm, a rough trooper who, at two different times, became Supreme Chief of the Sturmabteilung (SA)—an organization he helped build. Röhm opposed Hitler not only in defining the function of the SA, but also in never fully accepting Hitler's role as a messianic leader. Eventually, he paid for his opposition to the Führer with his life. Another very capable early helper was the staunch National Socialist Gregor Strasser, who retained a degree of independence from Hitler by disagreeing with some of his political decisions and not fully accepting Hitler's absolute authority. Gregor Strasser also was murdered. His brother, Otto Strasser, attacked Hitler for his "capitalist" views but was able to escape from Germany. Ernst (Putzi) Hanfstaengl, scion of an affluent and cultured Munich family, whose mother was American, was disliked and even despised by most of Hitler's companions and decided to flee Germany after he was subjected to some rough practical jokes. The other court jester, Heinrich Hoffmann, was able to survive the intrigues of the Hitler court and amassed a fortune by becoming Hitler's exclusive photographer. A prominent fanatic follower, Robert Ley, organized the German Labor Front and survived until the end of the regime, although Hitler was personally critical of his excessive drinking. The men who had the greatest staying power were second-string players, such as the bureaucrats who helped Hitler avoid the clerical tasks that he detested: the lawyer Wilhelm Frick, who became Minister of the Interior; Hitler's personal lawyer, Hans Frank; and Hitler's sergeant in World War I, Max Amann, who became czar of the National Socialist press. Amongst the early followers, Hitler particularly valued Max Erwin von Scheubner-Richter, who was German Vice Consul in Turkey at the time of the Armenian genocide and told Hitler how one Asian nation destroyed another. At the beginning of his ascent, Hitler felt secure and comfortable with his chauffeurs and bodyguards, whom Hanfstaengl called the *"Chauffeureska."* Only later Hitler detached himself from this group, as well as from the old guard who had marched with him to the Feldherrenhalle during the Hitler putsch. Hitler used the familiar form of address (*"Du"*) with only Eckart, Röhm, the bodyguard Emil Maurice, and the criminal roughneck Christian Weber.

Contacts with the Munich Bourgeoisie

As early as in 1919, Hitler became acquainted with members of the Thule Society, a semi-secret lodge dedicated to ultraright-wing politics and anti-Semitism with the explicit intention to topple the Weimar Republic. The society was founded by an adventurer, Rudolf Glauer, who after adoption became rich and acquired the name Rudolf Freiherr von Sebottendorf. Members were prominent men in business, industry, and academic circles, amongst them Eckart, Hess, and Frank, as well as several Free Corps leaders. To become a member one had to prove Aryan descent; one of the proofs was a footprint! Hitler never joined and later distanced himself from the society. Thule members, however—particularly Eckart and Hess—were useful to him by introducing Hitler to Munich high society. Through these contacts he met Ernst Hanfstaengl, industrialist Hugo Bruckmann, locomotive manufacturer Ernst von Borsig, publisher Julius Lehmann, and piano manufacturer Carl Bechstein. It was the wives of these tycoons, particularly Mrs. Bruckmann (née Princess Cantacuzene), who took Hitler (whom they called Wolf) under their wings. They were fascinated with the odd, fanatic man who appeared at their apartments in a dyed blue suit made from a uniform, wearing a quasi-military trench coat and carrying a holster with a gun and horsewhip. Hitler's favorite garb at that time was lederhosen, leather shorts customarily worn in the Alpine provinces of Germany and Austria. He never felt comfortable among members of society and always felt contempt—as well as a touch of awe—for the haute bourgeoisie; however, he held his nose because they were useful to him. Frau Hanfstaengl, Frau Bechstein, and Frau Bruckmann helped him with further connections, support, and gifts. In addition, more humble creatures, such as the widow of a middle school professor, Karola Hofmann—the "Hitler Mommy" (*Hitler Mutti*)—looked after his comfort. He enjoyed free meals at his favorite restaurant, the Osteria, or was taken to lunch by party members. He lived in a modest, two-room apartment with linoleum floors in a lower middle-class district of Munich. He remembered these days as a happy period ("The sky was full of violins").[56] Most of all, Hitler was enormously busy, driven by his lectures and his provocative politics. Gossip had it that party members saw him driving through the streets in an open automobile surrounded by smoking women, yet one of Hitler's consistent traits was his dislike for smokers. The mock title attributed to him— "King of Munich"—referred more to his domination of the streets and assembly halls than to any hedonism.

Hitler's Income

The subject of the origins of Party funds and Hitler's personal income has been controversial, if for no other reason than that Hitler did not talk about it. Ever since his youth, he had been both careless and secretive about money matters. Generally speaking, he was inclined to spend more than he had and did not mind debts. He delegated the management of his financial affairs to Hess and, later, to Bormann. He insisted that the sources of the Party's and Hitler's personal income would be considered separately. A separation of personal and party income also coincided with Hitler's wish not to be involved in audits of Party finances. Marxist scholars maintained that big business, in its desire to support fascism against communism, heavily supported the National Socialists. Exploring the subject not theoretically but empirically, H. A. Turner, Jr., summarily concluded that, before the seizure of power, big business supported the NSDAP ambivalently, with relatively small amounts.[57] Both before and after the seizure of power, the Party was substantially supported by membership fees. One large contribution of 100,000 Goldmark was given to Göring for the Party by the industrialist Fritz Thyssen, who later became an adversary. The finance minister Walther Funk repeatedly received small donations. Both Göring and Funk used these funds in part for private purposes. Hitler was informed but not deeply involved in the financial management of the Party. At one time when the Party could not pay its debts, Hitler became very upset and even threatened to commit suicide. He did not like to solicit funds and left this job to others. Occasionally, however, he engaged in some fund-raising. From all one knows, he did not obtain funds in exchange for specific promises or services. His self-image as a leader who would condemn corruption and punish it harshly did not permit this. There were exceptions when it came to persons who were loyal supporters, such as Streicher and Göring. Once during the war, in the monologues Hitler expressed anger about food being taken from officers and smuggled out, exclaiming, "What else could these men take but food, as Russia has no art treasures."[58] The remark is indicative of Hitler's conviction that he determined what was moral and immoral. What was helpful to National Socialism was defined as moral.

Little is known about Hitler's private funds. He did not receive a salary from the Party, but rather unspecified remunerations for his services. What these funds were and how he used them was never disclosed. The German tax office before the seizure of power was very interested in this question but never got to the bottom of it. During the twenties, Hitler's earned income was obtained in the form of fees for lectures not organized by the Party and royalties for articles he published in the *Illustrierter Beobachter*. Yet the picture changed radically in 1930, when Hitler moved from his modest quarters in the Thierschstraße to an expensive nine-room apartment in the swank Prinzregentenstraße and bought his first mountain retreat, Haus Wachenfeld near Berchtesgaden, also acquiring a chauffeur-driven Mercedes. He was never an elegant dresser, but his clothing was neat and appropriate—no more Lederhosen. At this same time, the Party financed the purchase of the Palais Barlow (which became the Braunes Haus) and its expensive renovation and refurbishing. These developments coincided with the increase in sales of *Mein Kampf* in 1930 (for more detailed royalty figures, see Chapter 5), but who financed the loans that were necessary for these acquisitions remains unknown. The figures from his tax returns reflect a rising income during the years from 1925 to 1933:

1925	19,843 Reichsmark
1926	15,903 RM
1927	11,494 RM
1928	11,818 RM
1929	15,448 RM
1930	48,472 RM
1931	55,132 RM
1932	54,639 RM
1933	1,232,235 RM

Still, these amounts would not have been sufficient to cover his expenses. After extensive wrangling with the tax office concerning how he could afford and finance these extravagant purchases, Hitler was charged back taxes. Oren Hale described Hitler as an unscrupulous tax evader.[59] Yet tax evasion was a common practice—almost an indoor sport—in Europe at the time. Hitler considered the Weimar Republic a bitter enemy and had no scruples about his tax swindle. After he became ruler of the Third Reich, all back taxes and penalties were forgiven and no agency would have dared accuse Hitler of tax fraud. He was a wealthy man following the seizure of power. He received a salary as President of the Reich, and all official expenses were paid by the state. He continued to receive large royalties from sales of *Mein Kampf* and other writings, including articles in the *Völkischer Beobachter* and the weekly *Illustrierter Beobachter*, to which he made regular contributions. Large amounts also accrued to him as royalties for a postal stamp depicting his head. Data concerning a perennial Hitler gift from industry have never been proven. In any case, Hitler had enough money to buy expensive art—often it was confiscated art—at ridiculously low prices. Some of the confiscated "degenerate" art was bartered for useful commodities and "good art" in foreign markets.

Increasing Violence

Hitler's speeches became ever more aggressive, and in particular his statements about Jews were extremely vulgar and threatening, barely surpassed by the slanderous expletives of Streicher's publications in *Der Stürmer*. Attempts at discussion or protest by dissenters led to bloody fights. The Hall Guard (*Saalschutz*) was established to protect meetings in beer halls. Later, these troops were organized into sport and gymnastic units that in a short time became the SA. One of the early commanders was Hermann Göring. The moving spirit, however, was Ernst Röhm. After its reorganization in 1925, the SA grew into a formidable armed organization. Hitler never clearly defined its function, viewing it as a political-educational body, whereas Röhm defined the group as a paramilitary organization, which in time led to a serious and deadly conflict. One SA unit served as Hitler's personal guard (*Stoßtrupp Hitler*), the germ cell of the SS (*Schutzstaffel*). Hitler relished the battles in the meeting halls but engaged in personal violence only once, when he and his associate Herman Esser beat up an opponent, another patriotic splinter party politician, Otto Ballerstedt. Hitler received a three-month prison sentence, which bothered him less than the possibility that he, still an Austrian citizen, could be deported. Good connections with the Munich police and officials in the Bavarian Ministry of the Interior, however, prevented this. Ballerstedt was one of the opponents Hitler remembered; he was murdered on 30 June 1934. The atmosphere of terror led to serious political crimes throughout the Reich. After the murder of Foreign Minister Walter Rathenau on 24 June 1922, the government issued the Law for Protection of the Republic. It had little impact on Bavaria, however, and Hitler provoked a bloody street battle in Coburg on 14/15 October 1922 after which the Nazi victims were celebrated as heroes.

The Crisis Year 1923

In 1923 the economic and political situation in Germany became extremely unstable. Unemployment, strikes, and riots plagued the nation. The violent fights in streets and assembly halls were at their worst in Bavaria, because in many other German states the NSDAP was forbidden. A galloping inflation upset all social classes: A liter of milk and a loaf of bread cost 500,000 paper mark on one day and a million on the next day. The occupation of the Ruhr by the French army on 23 January 1923 prevented German payment of hefty reparations. The French occupation caused national resistance on the part of all parties but the NSDAP. Hitler maintained that it was not in Germany's best interest to unify against France, but rather to destroy the inner enemy. It was a risky move that showed the strength and conviction of the NSDAP's fanatic leader.

On 23/24 January 1923, Hitler convened the first Parteitag. The Bavarian government had forbidden the meetings, but Hitler managed to influence the ambivalent government and police officials to rescind the order, a major political victory that resulted in even greater popularity for Hitler, but most of all in the readiness of other nationalist splinter parties to join the NSDAP under Hitler's unconditional leadership. It also emboldened Hitler to risk a major test of strength. On 1 May, when the socialists staged a major demonstration on the Theresienwiese in Munich, he organized a meeting of armed SA members and patriotic combat league troops on nearby parade grounds. He first asked for arms from the Bavarian Reichswehr, and on refusal flew into a rage and had the arms stolen from an army depot by Captain Röhm. A resolute General Otto von Lossow of the Reichswehr asked for a return of the weapons, and Hitler gave in. This was a painful defeat for Hitler. He withdrew to a villa in Berchtesgaden and sulked. It took some doing by his followers, particularly Röhm and Eckart, to bring him back for action. Hitler realized that he had lost ground. The conservatives in the Bavarian government had become more powerful, and Hitler felt under pressure from his own lieutenants to move. His real worry, however, was that the trio of minister Franz von Kahr, General Otto von Lossow, and Hans Ritter von Seisser, the Chief of the Bavarian State Police, would beat him to the punch—or, more concretely, the putsch.

At that moment, while Hitler's prestige had declined, General Ludendorff occupied center stage. The political situation in Bavaria had become so explosive that Bavarian Minister-President Eugen von Knilling asked von Kahr to return from retirement and become State Commissioner, with dictatory powers to reestablish order. Von Kahr wanted to establish order in cooperation with von Lossow and the chief of the Bavarian gendarmerie, von Seisser, but he also was eager to reestablish the Bavarian monarchy and separate from the "Jewish–Bolshevik" Berlin government. To achieve this, he would need Hitler's help. What Hitler feared was that he would be used by von Kahr or—even worse—that von Kahr and his associates would carry out the move against Berlin before Hitler had a chance to do so. Undoubtedly, Hitler also felt pressured by Röhm and other followers to act on his own.

The Putsch

When he learned about the commemorative meeting that von Kahr planned to hold on 8 November 1923 at the Bürgerbräu to announce his own plan, the aroused and suspicious Hitler, pushed by his own lieutenants and their followers in the Kampfbund, decided to use the occasion of the memorial at the Bürgerbräu to force Kahr, Lossow, Seisser, and other key players to join him in a putsch against the government of the Reich. Rarely has the truism been more correct than in the Hitler putsch, that military or political victory is achieved by the party that makes fewer mistakes. A putsch around the anniversary of the founding of the Weimar Republic had been predicted, but there were so many predictions of a putsch that the Bavarian government ignored them, and von Kahr's meeting at the Bürgerbräu on the evening of 8 November proceeded with inadequate security. Hitler was even able to induce police to clear the street of spectators so he could move his military units to the Bürgerbräu and enter it while von Kahr delivered a formal speech. Accompanied by a few vassals, a very excited Hitler fought his way to the rostrum of speakers at the Bürgerbräu amid shouts of "Theatre, Mexico" from the audience. To get attention, he fired a shot at the ceiling, then told the surprised triumvirate of von Kahr, Lossow, and von Seisser that the national revolution had broken out and that he had four shots in his revolver, three for the triumvirate and one for himself, in case the revolution was not successful. At the same time, he asked forgiveness for his manner and informed the triumvirate and the audience about the composition of the new government. He would be head of the government, von Kahr would be Reichsverweser (prime minister), and von Lossow, von Seisser, and Ernst Pohner, the former Police President of Munich and a staunch Hitler supporter, would occupy key positions in the new government. Von Kahr, Lossow, and von Seisser showed no inclination to consent and were hustled into a side room to confer with Hitler. Hitler assured the assembly that the three men agreed to join him under his leadership. In the meantime, General Ludendorff arrived, irritated because he had not been sufficiently informed about plans and also because Hitler assigned to him only the leadership of the army (over which neither Hitler nor Ludendorff had control). When Hitler was called out of the room, he charged General Ludendorff with guarding the triumvirate. The general made the mistake of letting the three men leave when they gave their word of honor to cooperate with the putschists. After their escape the three rightly maintained that their word of honor was obtained under pressure and organized units of the Reichswehr and *Landespolizei* to fight Hitler and his putschists. Another profound mistake on the part of the putschists was to remain inactive until the next morning, when the chance for a revolutionary takeover had passed. The Kampfbund achieved little more than the temporary occupation of the War Ministry and Police Headquarters, and the destruction of the offices of the Social Democratic daily, the *Münchner Post*. As the day went on and Hitler, von Ludendorff, and their lieutenants at the Bürgerbräu did not hear from the escaped triumvirate, they began to realize that their revolution had failed. After heated debates, they decided to stage a march on the Government headquarters near the Feldherrenhalle. It remained uncertain whether the fateful march was an attempt to free the besieged putschists in the inner city, the action favored by von Ludendorff, or a "parade" for propaganda purposes to enlist the sympathies of the Munich population before all was lost. A marching column with Hitler, Scheubner-Richter, and Ludendorff in the first

row overran one police unit at the Ludwig Bridge after Göring threatened to
kill the captured government hostages, an order that Hitler countermanded
out of concern that the government must have no martyrs. At the second
police cordon, a shot was fired. It remained unknown who fired this first
shot, but shooting broke out from both sides, leaving sixteen putschists and
three policemen dead. Hitler was injured when Scheubner-Richter, with
whom he had marched arm-in-arm, was shot and fell dead, pulling Hitler to
the ground and injuring his left shoulder joint. Ludendorff marched on, convinced that German soldiers and policemen would not shoot at their legendary hero of World War I.

After his injury, Hitler made his way to the rear, was hustled into a car by
an SA surgeon, Dr. Walter Schultze, and was brought to Hanfstaengl's country house. Dr. Schultze had to treat Hitler's dislocated shoulder on the spot
without the benefit of a radiological examination. He performed the simple
manipulation, relocating the humerus head in the shoulder joint. Either during the fall or during the treatment, some damage to the brachial plexus
might have occurred, which caused Hitler considerable pain for years, inducing him for some time to use his left arm sparingly. Later it was maintained
that Hitler suffered from a fracture of the humerus and the clavicle.[60] In great
pain, Hitler was deeply dejected and talked of suicide.[61] He had good reason
to be dejected: His leadership and personal behavior during the putsch had
been dismal. Helen Hanfstaengl stated that she had to wrestle Hitler's
revolver out of his hand in order to prevent him from killing himself. Erna,
Ernst Hanfstaengl's sister, however, maintained that Hitler was not suicidal.
By the time he was arrested by Police Lieutenant Rudolf Belleville, Hitler was
calm. Frau Hanfstaengl and Belleville helped him dress and pinned the Iron
Cross First Class on his coat before he was transported in a police car to
Landsberg Prison.[62] Of the other leaders of the putsch, Röhm and the Free
Corps leaders, Friedrich Weber and Hermann Kriebel, were arrested, Göring
fled to Austria, and Rosenberg fled too. Indictments were issued against
Ernst Hanfstaengl and Julius Streicher but later dropped. Ludendorff, to his
dismay, was also arrested when he walked "hero style" across the Odeonplatz,
in contrast to the fugitive Hitler. It seemed to be the end of the NSDAP, but
actually it was a new beginning.

5

Ascent to Power

Hitler in Landsberg Prison

HITLER ARRIVED at the prison of Landsberg dressed in pajamas and a raincoat to which the Iron Cross was pinned, and was admitted to the prison infirmary because of his shoulder injury. Dejected over his role in the failed putsch, he threatened to commit suicide by a hunger strike. It is quite possible that the attempt to march to Berlin and overthrow the government might have succeeded with better planning and leadership; it was one of the rare moments when Hitler reproached himself. Ernst Hanfstaengl, Anton Drexler, the widow of Max Erwin Scheubner-Richter, and a prison pedagogue, Alois Ott, tried to console him. In the ensuing trial, he stated:

> In this moment I did not want to know anything about this mendacious and calumnious world. And when in the course of the next few days, in the second week, the campaign of denunciation continued and people of whom I knew that they were innocent, and their only guilt was that they belonged to our movement, who knew nothing of the matter, were arrested only because they shared our conviction, and one feared that this conviction would be expressed, I resolved to defend myself to the last breath. That's why I entered the court, not to deny anything or to decline any responsibility. . . .[1]

Hitler felt he had been treated unjustly—an old and pervasive feeling. Most of all, however, he sensed that the upcoming trial would provide an extraordinary and dramatic opportunity to present himself and his views to the world, as well as to adopt a very effective strategy of self-defense.

On 8 January 1924 the prison physician, Dr. Josef Brinsteiner, reported on Hitler's physical and mental condition. It is the only statement about Hitler's mental status that was made while he was alive, but the task demanded more than Doctor Brinsteiner had to offer.

Administration of the Prison Landsberg
RE: Expert examination of the mental status of prisoner Adolf Hitler

In the examination of the psychological status and behavior of Adolf Hitler, it was found that he is not tainted through heredity or upbringing. His putsch of 8 November 1923, which often is called folly or madness, could easily give rise to the opinion that Hitler undertook or prepared the putsch because of pathological mental state. If one hears the motivations and explanations about this from Hitler, one comes to the definite view that Hitler was always master of his actions and will and that his mind was not under pathological influence, even though the preconditions and motivations for the putsch were faulty. The inner and outer influences which had impact on Hitler were undoubtedly responsible to a high degree for his behavior, but certainly did not cause any pathological coercion on his will. Also the strong pathological reaction with a transient pathological emotional depression which occurred for a short time after the putsch does not permit any conclusion about a pathological disposition of Hitler.

Hitler is motivated by great enthusiasm for the thought of a greater unified Germany, also he has a very lively temperament. He has an outstanding rhetorical talent and far above average political and historical knowledge. . . . Through his fascinating personality and his convincing rhetorical talent, he impressed single individuals and large masses and prepared what led to the putsch of 8 November. Such events are, like other important events (awakening of enthusiasm for war), founded in the normal psyche of individuals and, especially, of large masses. Before an unprejudiced judgment after the event, such thinking and acting, partly based on suggestion and autosuggestion, cannot stand up, but need not be pathological. Whether and to what extent Hitler is responsible for his acts may not be the subject matter of the physician. Since the putsch of 8 November, Hitler had a dislocation of the left shoulder [joint] with a fracture of the humerus head and a subsequent very painful traumatic neurosis.* Hitler is still in constant medical therapy and will probably suffer from a partial ankylosis (*Versteifung*) and painful affliction of the left shoulder. His ability to stand trial is not affected by this.

Signed: *Obermedizinalrat* Dr. Brinsteiner
General Practitioner and District Physician
Landsberg, 8 January 1924[2]

---

* "Neurosis" in this context seems to refer to a somatic disorder of the nerves, not a personality disorder—clearly an unaccepted definition.

It must be kept in mind that the prison doctor was a general practitioner with little knowledge of psychiatry and neurology. All he wanted to establish was Hitler's fitness to stand trial. Dr. Brinsteiner's medical report about the shoulder injury was confused. During the first few weeks, Hitler suffered from pain and limitation of movement after dislocation and relocation of his left shoulder joint. At the time of the trial, he did not wear a shoulder sling, and pain was not mentioned. Dr. Brinsteiner mentioned a fracture of the humerus head; however, this is quite unlikely, because in the event of such a fracture the upper arm and shoulder joint would have been X-rayed. Furthermore, a plaster cast would have been routinely applied. The report meant only that Hitler suffered from pain, a so-called brachialgia, resulting from injury of the brachial plexus after dislocation. If any tremor would have existed, it would have been noted and recorded, because medical personnel as well as lay persons were quite alert to so-called war tremblers (*Kriegszitterer*) — a post-traumatic hysterical reaction. The term neurosis as used in this report was inappropriate. Dr. Brinsteiner did not mention any mental illness. Apparently, Hitler was well and vigorous. The "nervous stomach," for which he at times swallowed plenty of pills, either did not bother him or was not mentioned by Dr. Brinsteiner or Hitler.

Before Hitler's discharge, on 15 September 1924, Otto Leybold, the director of the prison, wrote the following letter to the State Attorney's office in Munich, supporting Hitler's early release:

> Hitler has shown himself a man of order, of discipline, not only in respect to himself, but also in respect to his fellow inmates. He is easily content, modest, and desirous to please. Makes no demands, is quiet and sensible, serious and quite without aggressiveness, and tries painstakingly to abide by the prison rules. He is a man without personal vanity, is satisfied with the institution's food, does not smoke or drink, and though comradely is able to exert a certain amount of authority over his fellow inmates. . . . Hitler will attempt to revitalize the national movement according to his own principles, but no longer as in the past by violent methods, which of necessity may be directed against the government; instead, he will work in league with the concerned governmental agency. . . . In the ten months of his imprisonment, he undoubtedly has become more mature and quieter. . . . He will not be an agitator against the government. . . . He emphasizes that a state without a solid inner structure and firm government cannot survive. . . . Beyond any doubt, Hitler has a politically independent head with extraordinary willpower and decent thoughts. Considering all this, I consider him worthy to be discharged on probation. . . .[3]

The Hitler Trial

Hitler entered the trial, which lasted from 26 February to 1 April 1924, not as the accused but as the accuser.[4] He accused President Friedrich Ebert, Minister Phillipp Scheidemann, and other high government officers of treason,

and declared the Weimar Republic unconstitutional. The trial was supposed
to have been held at the Supreme Court in Leipzig but took place on home
territory in Munich. It was presided over by a superior court judge, Dr.
George Neihardt, a co-judge, and two lay judges. Judge Neihardt was very
permissive and let Hitler interrupt, shout, cross-examine, and hold lengthy
political monologues. The prosecuting attorney, Dr. Erhardt Stenglein,
found it difficult to make his points in this atmosphere. Compared with
Hitler, the nine co-defendants played minor roles in the trial. Hitler's aggressive stance was in sharp contrast to the petulant attitude of General Ludendorff, who felt offended when he was cast in a secondary role and, to his dismay, acquitted. Hitler was still sensitive to charges that he had behaved in a
cowardly manner when he was injured and fled, while General Ludendorff,
the legendary hero of World War I, had proudly marched on. The proceedings established Hitler as the most important figure in the trial as well as the
putsch.

Hitler's tactics during the trial were simple and powerful. First, he did
not deny his intent to overthrow the Berlin government of traitors and
angrily discounted the role of his co-defendants. Second, he claimed that he
did not want anything other than what his accusers—Kahr, Seisser, and Lossow—wanted. Kahr and Seisser were unable or unwilling to defend themselves against these accusations, possibly because of their own obscure plot-
ting. Only Lossow made some counterattacks, accusing Hitler of vacillation
and shifting strategies. Altogether, the three gentleman played a rather passive role in the trial, helping Hitler turn a lost cause into a dramatic victory.
Third, Hitler falsely dramatized his own background, particularly with
respect to his activities in the war and his combat gas injury. He maintained
that he did not view himself as the leader of any new government, but rather
as the leader of a fight for a new government. In endless speeches, tolerated
by the court, he declared that he was not a traitor but rather a patriotic German who wanted to do his best for his country. In an eloquent hyperbole at
the end of the trial, he declared:

> From the first day, my aim was a thousand times higher than to be minister.
> Thousands can become ministers. What I wanted was to be the destroyer of
> Marxism. This is my task, and I know I will accomplish it. . . . Then the title
> of minister is ridiculous. . . . It was not out of modesty that I wanted to be
> the drummer, but because it is the highest. Everything else is a bagatelle.[5]

He declared that his army would grow, and that the goddess of the "eternal
court of history"—and not the gentlemen of the court—would acquit him.[6]
Hitler's defense was effective. The judgment was lenient: for Hitler, five years
of prison with the assurance of an early pardon and, according to the constitution, deportation to Austria—what Hitler feared most. He emerged from
the trial as a hero and a martyr—exactly what he wanted.

For Hitler, the fortress of Landsberg to which the sentenced prisoner
returned was more a retreat than a prison. He called it a "university education

at the state's expense," and also the "first Brown House."[7] He was the single occupant of a room, not a prison cell, which was superior to his quarters in Vienna, and he was treated respectfully by prison personnel. Criminal prisoners cleaned his and the other political prisoners' rooms. He had ample time to think, read, take care of his correspondence, and receive visitors. On his birthday Hitler received an abundance of congratulations and so many presents of food that the room almost looked like a gourmet food store. He did not participate in the physical exercises of his fellow political prisoners, because he thought he would look ridiculous as an active sportsman.[8] As their undisputed leader, he distanced himself from his fellow prisoners. During his imprisonment, Hitler made a giant stride forward in establishing his identity as a leader, relying on a devoted cadre; learned from past mistakes; resolved to renew his political efforts and gave much thought to a strategy for the future; and wrote *Mein Kampf*.

Mein Kampf

Mein Kampf*, Hitler's most important publication, is a book of historical significance that cannot be dismissed lightly.[9] It is most revealing about Hitler's program and personality. Together with the monologues and, ultimately, the political testament, *Mein Kampf* provides a meaningful, but not truthful, account of his personal and political development. The first volume was written entirely while Hitler was in prison. It was dictated in part to Rudolf Hess, although Hess's wife, Ilse, denied this and maintained that Hitler did some of his own typing, using two fingers.[10] Some of the typing was done by Emil Maurice, one of Hitler's bodyguards. The prison director, Otto Leybold, stated that one could hear the clatter of the typewriter from Hitler's room all day long. The second volume was dictated to secretaries. *Mein Kampf* was entirely Hitler's work. There were neither ghostwriters nor contributors. Hess's editorial contribution consisted only of minor corrections, which can be deduced from style and content. The fierce and crude writing in *Mein Kampf* was quite different from Hess's style. Minor editorial contributions also were rendered by Pater Bernhard Stempfle, an ex-priest and anti-Semitic editor of the *Miesbacher Anzeiger*; Ernst Hanfstaengl and personnel from the editorial offices of the *Völkischer Beobachter*; the music critic Max Czerny; and Max Amann of the Eher publishing house.[11]

Hitler claimed to write about his own development, as far as this was necessary for an understanding of his political achievements and goals, and to counteract the "legends" of the "Jewish Press" regarding his life. He wished to address his followers, who "belong to the movement, side with him heart and soul, and whose minds are desirous of greater enlightenment."[12] Somewhat defensively, he also stated in the foreword that each great movement owes its growth to great orators and not to great writers. The original titles proposed by Hitler were "A Reckoning" (*Eine Abrechnung*) and "Four and a

---

* The word *Kampf* could be translated as fight, struggle, or battle.

Half Years of Fighting against Lies, Stupidity, and Cowardice." The motive of correcting an injustice was obvious and very strong. It explains, in part, the angry, contentious tone of the work.

Part I of *Mein Kampf* was published in the summer of 1925, Part II at the end of 1926. Hitler hoped that the book would provide a source of revenue for him, to cover expenses that he incurred during his political activity and trial. During the first four years, however, sales were slow. By 1930, 23,000 copies of the first volume had sold and 13,000 of the second. When Books I and II were published in a single volume in 1930, some 287,000 copies were sold. After Hitler's assumption of power, when the sale of the book as a gift to newlyweds at the expense of communities became compulsory, the total sales rose dramatically. Altogether, ten million German copies were sold. The book was translated into sixteen languages. It netted Hitler eight million marks. In spite of such gigantic sales, the book was not widely read. Using a small random sample, Karl Lange calculated that, before 1933, of 120 persons who owned the book, only 11 had read it completely, 16 had read it partially, and 84 had not read it at all; after 1933, of 120 people, only two had read the entire book, and 59 had read parts of it. The book remained an unread bestseller.[13] More important, many leading politicians of the period did not read it, at least not in its entirety.

Goebbels wrote on 10 June 1931 (and why so many years after the book's publication?), "I have read *Mein Kampf* in the afternoon and evening. The book is honest and brave. Only the style is insignificant. One has to be magnanimous. Hitler writes as he talks. This appears spontaneous but unskilled."[14] Intellectuals, as well as the masses for whom the writing was intended, found it difficult and obnoxious to follow Hitler's tortuous thinking, his redundancies, and his convoluted, crude language. Many politically neutral readers, and even sympathizers, were stunned by the unmitigated hatred. Outside the Third Reich, the book was widely depicted as a piece of propaganda produced by a sick mind, rather than as the work of a major statesman. Because readers were shocked by Hitler's style, some of his remarks on nationalism and socialism and his critical and constructive comments about the social and political evils of the period were minimized and overlooked. If the book had been carefully studied, the probability of underestimating Hitler during his ascent as a major political figure might have been smaller. After the war, the German editions were banned in the Federal Republic of Germany, a misguided act of censorship. Reading *Mein Kampf* is a good preventive.

Critics have commented on Hitler's illiterate and vulgar style during the *Kampfjahre* (a term widely and proudly used by Nazis to refer to the years between 1919, Hitler's entry into politics, and 1933, the seizure of power). Hitler's venomous rhetoric during that time was raw material for his book. As examples of its crude and convoluted style, *Mein Kampf* referred to Marxist soldiers at the end of World War I as "orientals who came out of a gonorrhea hospital (*Tripperlazarett*)"[15] and stated that "the Goddess of Suffering took me in her arms, often threatening to crush me, my will to resistance grew, and in the end this will was victorious."[16] Hitler's style and syntax are offensive, but, more than anything else, it is the unbridled hatred that is upsetting. Yet Hitler's loaded words also had a powerful impact on the receptive and uncritical reader. In essence, Hitler presented himself as a prophet who had been chosen by fate to deliver his people from misery and lead them to the glory of a Reich of a thousand years—a theme he pursued relentlessly from the first sentence of the book to the last page, which concludes ". . . that the best racial elements must someday become lords of the earth."[17] Three major components of the work can be distinguished: (1) Hitler's ideology, essentially a statement of a vulgar social Darwinism extolling the rule of the strong and the suppression of the weak, with the practical consequences of conquest and genocide; (2) the history of the National Socialist movement, the repetitious accounts that Domarus called the "party history";[18] and (3) Hitler's autobiography, obviously of special interest for students of Hitler's behavior. It is of interest to note the falsifications regarding his own life history. One can distinguish three different types: errors that can be ascribed to sloppiness; deliberate, conscious falsifications (Hitler clearly told his audience only what he wanted them to know); and errors and distortions of which Hitler was not conscious. Sometimes it is difficult to distinguish between the last two categories because Hitler often operated at the border of deliberate and preconscious falsification.

Among the glaring distortions, abundant evidence exists that Hitler's childhood was not as idyllic as he described it in *Mein Kampf*. He was more honest about his painful adolescence. Hitler's explanation for his failure in school—to spite his father—is, at least in part, wrong. The "severe pulmonary illness" did not occur. The abysmal poverty he described in Vienna lasted only a short time (from late fall 1909 to early winter 1910), and not for the "five most miserable years" he described in *Mein Kampf*. Moreover, the assertion that he was a manual laborer is exaggerated, because he performed manual work only for a very limited period of time in 1909. Hitler misrepresented his ideological evolution. What he learned about history in his middle school years was not important. His anti-Semitism in Vienna was highly personal, not political. Obviously, his evasion of Austrian military service is not mentioned. The combat gas injury is exaggerated, not only in *Mein Kampf*, but also at the putsch trial and on other occasions. On 29 November 1921, Hitler wrote a short biography that contains gross distortions, albeit different from those in *Mein Kampf*.[19] This document was written in the form of a letter written to an unknown person at the request of Dietrich Eckart. The most amazing error in the short biography is so striking that one might assume Hitler had another person write the letter without correcting it. He described his father's occupation as a postal clerk. He stated that his aim was always to become a builder and made no mention of his desire to become a painter and architect. He falsely stated that he had only 80 kronen when he went to Vienna at the age of seventeen and was forced to work as a day laborer in construction—in fact, he performed such work only for a short time when he was nineteen. He falsely stated that he moved to Munich in 1912 (it was 1913).[20]

In *Mein Kampf*, certain unconscious passages, probably resulting from unconscious memories or fantasies, have been interpreted by psychohistorians as significant autobiographical preconscious experiences,[21] while other historians who have not shared this point of view have regarded the statements as valid but insignificant observations.[22] The author's interpretations will be presented in Chapter 9. Here only the raw data are reported, offering an opportunity for readers to draw their own conclusions. The first passage is cited in its entirety:

> In a basement apartment consisting of two stuffy rooms, dwells a worker's family of seven. Among the five children there is a boy of, let us assume, three years. This is the age at which the first impressions are made upon the consciousness of the child. Talented persons retain traces of memory from this period down to advanced old age. The very narrowness and overcrowding of the room do not lead to favorable conditions. Quarreling and wrangling will very frequently arise as a result. In these circumstances, people do not live with one another, they press against one another. Every argument, even the most trifling, which in a spacious apartment can be reconciled by a mild segregation, thus solving itself, here leads to loathsome wrangling without end. Among the children, of course, this is still bearable; they always fight under such circumstances, and among themselves they quickly and thoroughly forget about it. But if this battle is carried on between the parents themselves, and almost every day in forms which for vulgarity often leave nothing to be desired, then, if only very gradually, the results of such visual instruction must ultimately become apparent in the children. The character they will inevitably assume if this mutual quarrel takes the form of brutal attacks of the father against the mother, of drunken beatings, is hard for anyone who does not know this milieu to imagine. At the age of six the pitiable little boy suspects the existence of things that can inspire even an adult with nothing but horror. Morally poisoned, physically undernourished, his poor little head full of lice, the young "citizen" goes off to public school. After a great struggle he may learn to read and write, but that is about all. His doing any homework is out of the question. On the contrary, the very mother and father, even in the presence of the children, talk about his teachers in school in terms that are not fit to be repeated and are more inclined to curse the latter to their face than to take their little offspring on their knees and teach him some sense. All the other things that the little fellow bears at home do not tend to increase his respect for his dear fellow men. Nothing good remains of humanity, no institution remains unassailed, beginning with his teacher and up to the head of the government; whether it is a question of religion or of morality as such, of state or society, it is all the same; everything is reviled in the most obscene terms and dragged into the filth of the basest possible outlook. When at the age of fourteen the

young man is discharged from school, it is hard to decide what is stronger in him: his incredible stupidity as far as any real knowledge and ability are concerned, or the corrosive insolence of his behavior, combined with an immorality, even at this age, that would make your hair stand on end.

What position can this man—to whom even now hardly anything is holy—who, just as he has encountered no greatness, conversely suspects and knows all the sordidness of life, occupy the life into which he is now preparing to emerge?[23]

In a second passage, similar to the first, Hitler described a married couple that is fighting and quarreling. "As the man becomes estranged from his wife, he becomes more intimate with alcohol, and the woman has to fight to get a few pennies. . . . When he comes home on Saturdays and Sundays, scenes occur that God have mercy."[24] In a third example, Hitler wrote about a peasant boy who seeks his fortune in the city: He first has money and "does not have to lose heart, but after he loses his job it is impossible to find a new job, and his misery is very great. . . . The man in time forgets all ideas of order and discipline."[25] Hitler claimed to have observed such situations a hundred times. Some of the most irrational statements in *Mein Kampf* occur in the thirteen pages dedicated to the dangers of syphilis, a "Jewish disease" and one of the most important problems faced by mankind.[26] Hitler thundered against the indifference of the political leadership about this terrible poisoning of the health of the national body. For Hitler, syphilis was not just an infectious disease transmitted by sexual intercourse with infected partners (particularly prostitutes), but a disease that is transmitted from one generation to the next. He mistook "congenital" syphilis for "hereditary" syphilis. He seemed particularly concerned that sexually experienced husbands ("horned Siegfrieds") would infect their innocent wives, who wouldn't dare report their husbands to the health authorities. Hitler believed that available therapies were inadequate. He proposed early marriage and education, as well as measures directed against the "stifling perfume of eroticism." Ultimately, he recommended preventing the propagation of defective people (victims of syphilis as well as other diseases) as an act of reason and humanity. If necessary, he wrote in 1925, the incurably ill would be pitilessly segregated—"a barbaric measure in the view of the individual struck by it, but a blessing for his fellow men and posterity. The passing pain of a century will and can redeem millennia of suffering."[27] Seemingly, Hitler was later embarrassed by these assertions—they were too revealing—he remarked that they were fantasies behind bars, and stated that he would have omitted the remarks about syphilis from *Mein Kampf*,[28] although ten years later he still considered syphilis and Christianity—the offspring of Judaism—humankind's two greatest plagues.[29]

Besides *Mein Kampf*, Hitler authored numerous weekly articles in the *Illustrierter Beobachter*. The themes and conclusions were mostly a rehash of statements made previously in lectures. Before the seizure of power, the articles provided a source of income for Hitler. In contrast to these rather insignificant articles, another major Hitler opus was found by Gerard Weinberg in the National Archives. This tome, of approximately 200 pages, is the most succinct expression of Hitler's vulgar Darwinism. It includes a concise outline of his desire for a pact with Italy and Great Britain and his goal of conquering living space in the East. Last but not least, it contains a merciless attack addressing the destruction of the Jews. Even the topic of "syphilization" is not forgotten.[30]

Reentry into Politics

Hitler was discharged from prison on 20 December 1924, after serving only nine months of his five-year sentence. The early release came as a surprise for many, but not for Hitler, who was ready to apply what he had learned during his stay at Landsberg. In prison he took a giant step toward establishing his authority over his fellow prisoners by distancing himself from them and feeling superior to them. He emerged with an identity as a leader of a revolutionary movement. He began to sense more strongly his identity not only as that of a prophet who had undergone a period of martyrdom, but also as a leader of his party. He no longer saw himself solely as "the drummer." Now he believed he was more than an agitator and propagandist. A perceptive follower, Werner Best, later called him a suasive prophet.[31]

The Party was in disarray, which suited Hitler well. Von Scheubner-Richter, whom Hitler valued highly, was dead; Göring had fled the country; Rosenberg was an inadequate caretaker for the Party; and Hitler relied at the time, uncritically, on two of the worst elements in the Party: Julius Streicher and Hermann Esser. Furthermore, he had to deal with difficult personalities such as General Ludendorff, Captain Röhm, and the upcoming Strasser brothers. This time, Hitler did not repeat the mistake of letting the command slip from his hands or being pushed by his followers. At the first Party meeting on 26 February 1925, he told a challenger:

> Little friend, wait a while what conditions I will set for you. I am not wooing the big crowd. After a year, my fellow party members, you can judge whether I did well. If not I will resign; but until then I alone will lead the movement, and nobody sets conditions for me as long as I personally carry the responsibility, and I carry the responsibility absolutely for everything in the movement.[32]

The other lesson he had learned was that the time was not ripe for a putsch or a revolution by the NSDAP. Hitler resolved to pursue a course of legality to persuade the masses, high and low, rich and poor, and, most of all, the workers, to vote for the National Socialist German Workers' Party (NSDAP), which was reconstituted on 26 February 1926.

Hitler expressed his real feelings to his early admirer Carl Luedecke:

> . . . instead of working to achieve power by an armed coup, we shall have to hold our noses and enter the *Reichstag* against the Catholic and Marxist

deputies. If out-voting takes longer than out-shooting them, at least the results will be guaranteed by their own constitution. Any lawful process is slow. . . . Sooner or later we shall have a majority—and, after that, Germany.[33]

One of the reasons for the legality course was Hitler's fear of being deported. According to German law, he should have been deported to Austria after serving his sentence. The conservative Catholic Austrian government certainly was not eager to see him return, and German friends, the Minister of Justice Franz Gürtner and the Munich Police President Ernst Pöhner, worked hard to prevent deportation. The threat of exile remained alive until Hitler became a German citizen on 30 April 1932, in order to qualify as a candidate in the presidential election. To make this possible, the State of Braunschweig offered him a governmental post as a land surveyor, and even considered a phony university appointment as a professor of political pedagogy.

Through the intervention of Pöhner and Gürtner, Hitler was received by the Bavarian Minister President Heinrich Held, which gave him a measure of respectability. He was able to reassure Held about his peaceful and legal intentions. Held advised, "The lion is tamed, one can loosen the fetters." With such assurances of legality, Hitler lectured again, and the *Völkischer Beobachter* appeared again on 27 February 1925. However, Hitler found it very difficult to restrain his aggressive style of writing and speaking. Remarks such as "either the enemy goes over our corpses or we over theirs"[34] did not escape the attention of the governments in Bavaria and other German states, and an edict was issued to forbid Hitler to speak in public. The *Sprechverbot* was rescinded only in 1926, in Prussia in 1927. Robbed of his most important weapon, Hitler felt frustrated and handicapped. He was forced to be less active than he wanted to be, not only in fighting his political enemies, but in asserting his control over his associates in the party. To Hitler legality, or rather pseudo-legality, meant that he would gain parliamentary seats in order to abolish the Parliament and the democratic state. In the trial of three National Socialist officers accused of treason, he declared under oath before Germany's supreme court that if party regulations were to conflict with the law they would not be carried out, but he added with amazing frankness the exact opposite: "I can assure you that when the Nazi movement struggle is successful, then there will be a Nazi court of justice, the November 1918 revolution will be avenged, and heads will roll."[35]

Feuds in the Party

Almost from the beginning, Hitler clashed with Röhm concerning the role of the SA and its control. Röhm saw the SA, largely his creation, as a military unit equal to the armed forces and not under the authority of the party. In practice, this meant that it would not be under Hitler's direct control. Hitler was wary of paramilitary units and saw the SA as a political organization answering to him, not as an independent organization. During the putsch he had learned not to fight against the Reichswehr. Hitler replaced Röhm with Pfeffer von Salomon, an arrogant Prussian officer who was hardly more cooperative than Röhm and did not last long, forcing Hitler to recall Röhm from Bolivia. The seizure of power, however, was not the end of Hitler's troubles.

Hitler fought with the Strasser brothers over economic policy and over the primacy of nationalist versus socialist issues. The Strasser brothers expressed sympathies for the Soviet Union years before Hitler concluded his pact with the Bolsheviks. Gregor Strasser, a pharmacist, was an able organizer, a good speaker, and a great help to Hitler as Gauleiter (district leader) in Lower Bavaria and as a troubleshooter with the dissident northern German National Socialists. Politically, Gregor and Otto Strasser were to the left of Hitler, favoring nationalization of heavy industry and some cooperation with the Soviet Union, which Hitler vigorously opposed. Hitler wanted to preserve private ownership and a spirit of competition, and, while he was politically weak, he preferred not to antagonize the wealthy bankers and industrialists whose support he needed. The differences between Hitler and the Strassers became quite acute when Hitler favored compensation to the high aristocracy that had lost its fortunes and landholdings after the war. Hitler favored private ownership but believed that the Party ultimately must control national production. While he was not the pawn of German industry,[36] it cannot be denied that German industry worked in close alliance with Hitler to their mutual benefit. Otto Strasser was particularly aggressive in his criticism of Hitler in word and print. On Hitler's orders, he was expelled from the Party by Gregor's ex-secretary, Joseph Goebbels, who, in the meantime, had become Gauleiter of Berlin. After this, Otto left Germany and continued his opposition from Czechoslovakia and, later, Canada. Gregor yielded, and Hitler offered his hand in conciliation. In 1934, however, a serious new feud erupted between Hitler and Gregor Strasser, ending with Hitler's victory and Strasser's murder in 1936.

Rising Stars in the Party

Hitler was soon impressed with a rising star, Doctor Paul Joseph Goebbels, the young assistant of his antagonist, Gregor Strasser, and set out to win Goebbels over. Goebbels came from a middle-class Catholic family and had been expected to become a priest, but studied German literature instead. Rather unsuccessful as a journalist and writer, he blamed Jewish publishers for his lack of success and became a fanatic National Socialist. Goebbels's first impression of Hitler was negative. On 15 February 1926 he wrote in his diary about Hitler and the Bamberg meeting:

A reactionary? Unbelievably clumsy and uncertain. Russian question: absolutely wrong. England and Italy natural allies . . . terrible. Our task is the destruction of Bolshevism. Bolshevism is a Jewish trick. We must inherit Russia's 180 millions. Compensation of the princes. Right is right. Also for the princes. Don't touch question of private property. Terrible. Progress is enough, content with it. Feder nods, Ley nods, Streicher nods. God, we are not up to these swine from the south. Half an hour's discussion after a speech of four hours. I can't say a word, as if somebody hit me on the head.[37]

It did not take more than a few months for Goebbels to change his mind. Goebbels became one of Hitler's most fanatic aides and admirers. As Minister of Propaganda, Goebbels almost equaled his master's skills in propaganda and manipulation of the masses, but at times he sounded more shrill and vicious. He presented himself as a man of absolute integrity and the highest ethical standards. It was well-known in the highest Nazi circles, however, that although he constantly professed his love for his "sweet" wife Magda (a well-known actress much admired by Hitler), Goebbels forced many female employees in his Ministry to have sexual relations with him, and Hitler did nothing about it. Only once Hitler persuaded Goebbels to end a love affair with the actress Lydia Baarova and preserve his marriage. In time, Goebbels dominated the media, press, theater, and film, as well as the cultural life of the Third Reich. He used the media in a masterful fashion in the service of National Socialist propaganda. In collaboration with Hitler, Goebbels shaped his master's political propaganda—the glamour and power of mass meetings, parades, memorials, and, most of all, the overpowering and seductive ritual of the colossal national party meetings. Goebbels outdid Hitler in his venomous hatred of opponents, which permitted Hitler to be more "moderate." In his relationship with the little man with the club foot, Hitler was always the master, and Goebbels the disciple.[38]

A valuable member of the inner circle was Richard Walter Darré, the son of a German businessman living in Argentina. Hitler had limited understanding of peasants (his forebears), and he appreciated Darré's skillful propaganda for winning the rural electorate under such powerful slogans as "blood and soil." One of Hitler's most important collaborators continued to be Robert Ley, a fierce National Socialist and anti-Semite, who became the principal organizer of German workers (the Deutsche Arbeitsfront), a mission very close to Hitler's heart. Hitler became quite upset about Ley's alcoholism when Ley's wife, whom Hitler liked very much, committed suicide. Inge Ley was not the only wife of a prominent associate to whom Hitler felt attracted; others were the spouses of Hanfstaengl, Goebbels, and von Schirach. A leader for the National Socialist League of Women, Gertrud Scholtz Klink, who never changed her National Socialist views, was appointed relatively late and had little influence amongst the great of the Third Reich.

Opportunistic Alliances

On 28 February 1925, Germany's president, Friedrich Ebert, died. In the elections that followed, the World War I hero Paul Ludwig Hans Anton von Beneckendorff and von Hindenburg (1847–1934), Prussian aristocrat and landowner, at heart always a monarchist though he was not disloyal to the Weimar Republic (to which he had sworn an oath of allegiance), became the candidate supported by an alliance of right-wing parties and was elected to the German presidency in March 1925. During the early period of his regime, von Hindenburg's tremendous prestige and political talents contributed to a calming of the political waters. He was opposed to civil disobedience and for a while succeeded in restraining Hitler. One fringe benefit accrued to Hitler after von Hindenburg's victory. A person who had remained a thorn in Hitler's side since the time of the putsch and trial, General Ludendorff, was disposed of in a particularly tricky manner. Promising electoral support, Hitler encouraged Ludendorff to run for the German presidency against the other World War I hero, von Hindenburg. However, no support for the campaign was forthcoming from Hitler, and Ludendorff suffered a disastrous defeat, receiving only 1 percent of the vote.

During the late twenties, the Party remained small. In 1924, the Nazis had only twelve deputies in the Reichstag. The most important reason for this slow growth was Germany's recovery. Germany had become able to compete on world markets, and the most stringent and humiliating conditions of the Treaty of Versailles had been eliminated, largely through the efforts of the outstanding politician Gustav Stresemann, who died early at the age of sixty-one in 1929. Hitler, however, remained convinced of his ultimate victory and looked for alliances that would help the Party become nationally significant. One such alliance was his cooperation with the conceited and pompous media tycoon Alfred Hugenberg, an ultraconservative member of the German National People's Party (Deutschnationale Volkspartei). The reason for this alliance, for which Hitler was criticized by his own party members, was to oppose the so-called Young Plan, redefining Germany's obligations to pay war reparations. In plebiscites regarding the Young Plan, its sponsors were defeated, but Hitler gained from his cooperation with Hugenberg. He received badly needed financial support and massive publicity in the Hugenberg press. The affiliation helped him become known as a national leader, rather than a provincial politician. After the defeat, Hitler coldly detached himself from Hugenberg, who approached him again after the NSDAP scored impressive electoral successes.

Hitler's Health

Except for frequent colds that he always dreaded, Hitler's health during the *Kampfjahre* was good. At one time, according to information from Hermann Esser,[39] he consulted an older woman physician, Dr. Babette Steininger. It is puzzling why Hitler, with his prejudices about the professional competence of women, would have gone to a female physician. The reason for this medical consultation is unknown, and it is not even certain whether it occurred, but it might have been the indigestion and episodic stomach pains that had troubled him since adolescence, according to a statement by Johannes von Müllern-Schönhausen.[40] Hitler was always concerned about illness, though, and his chauffeurs and bodyguards always had to carry a suitcase of medications for him when they were traveling.

Several Hitler associates, amongst them Otto Wagener, reported that Hitler became a vegetarian after the death of his niece Angela (Geli) Raubal in 1931.[41] As a teenager and young man, Hitler certainly ate meat.[42] He also ate meat during his service in World War I and probably before his imprisonment at Landsberg. Hitler's vegetarianism was quite strict. He praised raw food but did not adhere to a diet of uncooked foods, which was a fad at the time. He avoided any kind of meat, with the exception of an Austrian dish he loved, *Leberknödl* (liver dumpling). For a while he ate cooked and canned fish, but later the only animal products he consumed were milk, butter, and cottage cheese. He liked leguminous vegetables but gave them up when they caused intestinal pain. For the same reason he also restricted his eating of salads and most kinds of breads (which he ate without crust). His indulgences in rich Austrian desserts never changed.[43] As usually is the case with over-concerned and hypochondriacal eaters, there was a lot of fuss and aggravation in preparing Hitler's meals. With rare exceptions after the early thirties Hitler did not consume alcoholic beverages; just occasionally a glass of beer or wine. He found wine too sour and beer too bitter. He was critical of some of his alcoholic associates such as the "Reichs-Drunkard" Ley.

Hitler's opposition to smoking was absolute. He considered smoking a dangerous habit and thought ahead of his time that smoking caused cancer. It is not known when he stopped smoking. Nobody in his presence was permitted to smoke. He entertained plans to take stringent steps against smoking after victory.

Hitler's schedule was taxing, but he was a hard worker and had no trouble pursuing it. Just as in prison, he did not exercise except for using an expander to assure his ability to respond for hours with a raised arm to the *"Heil Hitler"* greeting during large meetings.

Women

Certainly, from the mid-thirties on, Hitler was able to engage in enjoyable leisure activities. During the *Sprechverbot* he had time to visit operas, concerts, and theaters, and to enjoy as much of a social life as he liked. Hitler told Ward Price, a Hitler-friendly journalist, that he was happy in his political life but unhappy in his private life, unhappier than any person he had ever known.[44] In all likelihood, he was referring to the unhappiness in his relationships with women. Yet in the monologues as well as in a conversation with Leni Riefenstahl,[45] Hitler bragged that he "knew" many women. The women he met were a mixed lot: the sister of the leader of the British fascists, Valkyrie Mitford; the daughter of the famous tenor Walter Slezak, Gretl Slezak (a second-degree non-Aryan, according to National Socialist laws); the daughter of the American ambassador, Martha Dodd; secretaries and salesgirls Susi Liptauer and Maria (Miezl) Reiter; the sister of one of his chauffeurs Jenny Haug; and others. Just what sexual or erotic experiences Hitler had with these women is a matter of conjecture. What is known is that one of them, Angela (Geli) Raubal, died a violent death and that at least four—Eva Braun, Valkyrie Mitford, Susi Liptauer, and Maria Reiter—made suicidal attempts, by any measure an extraordinary record. Hitler wanted contact with women, and love letters from German women that were recently discovered (somewhat reminiscent of the fan mail received by modern rock stars) prove that many German women would have loved to have had relationships with their Führer. What Hitler engaged in was contact at arm's length—with older maternal types as well as with young actresses, singers, and dancers he invited to his receptions. He entertained more serious personal relationships with what he called *"Paradefrauen,"* a term he used to refer to the exceptional women he held in high regard and to whom he pointed when he felt accused of discrimination.[46] Three of these were artists: the film director and actress Leni Riefenstahl; Gerdy Troost, the widow of Hitler's favorite architect; and Winifred Wagner, the wife of Richard Wagner's son Siegfried. All of them were ardent National Socialists. Winifred Wagner's views about National Socialism never changed—when asked what she thought about the Holocaust, she reported that Hitler's dark side did not interest her.[47] The only politician amongst the parade-women was Gertrud Scholtz Klink. Hitler detested "political" women and did not allow them to hold elected office.[48] Riefenstahl denied any sexual contact with Hitler and stated only once that Hitler might have been sexually interested in her. She described her first encounter with Hitler using unmistakenly sexual symbolism. She had attended a rally, was too far away to see his face, but heard his voice:

> That very same instant, I had an almost apocalyptic vision that I was never able to forget. It seemed as if the earth's surface were spreading out in front of me, like a hemisphere that suddenly splits apart in the middle, spewing out an enormous jet of water, so powerful that it touched the sky and shook the earth. I felt as if I were paralyzed. Although there was a great deal in his speech that I didn't understand, I was still fascinated and I sensed that the audience was in bondage to this man.[49]

Only a few women got close: Geli Raubal, Eva Braun, and Maria Reiter. About others one cannot be certain, but in any case they were not significant persons in Hitler's life. Reiter was the only woman who explicitly described sexual intercourse with Hitler—in contrast to Eva Braun, who only hinted at it in her diary.[50] Hitler met Maria Reiter when she was nineteen years old. She declined an initial proposal to become his mistress, but later, after she had married and separated from her husband, she reported an alleged sexual encounter with Hitler.[51] She recalled: "He pressed me to his body and kissed me. It was well past midnight. He leaned back more and more on his sofa. Wolf grabbed me even more firmly. I let anything happen with me. I was never as happy as during that night."[52] Based on this description, it is difficult to know what happened, or even whether the account is valid.

The Unsolved Death of Angela (Geli) Raubal

Angela (Geli) Raubal, born in 1909 in Linz, was the daughter of Hitler's half-sister, Angela. After finishing middle school and a short stay in Vienna, she moved to Munich and considered enrolling at the University of Munich as a medical student. She also took singing lessons and vaguely considered a career as an opera singer. She was a lively and flirtatious young lady whose interest in neither music nor medicine was overwhelming. Several contemporary witnesses—such as Robert Wagener,[53] Henriette Hoffmann von Schirach[54] and her father, Hitler's photographer,[55] and, most of all, Hitler—considered her a radiant person. According to all witnesses, Hitler was in love with his half-niece. Ernst Hanfstaengl, a more critical observer, viewed Geli as a dull, provincial maiden who was good for Hitler, however, because she might cure his alleged impotence.[56] According to Hanfstaengl, Hitler behaved like a "mooncalf" in Geli's presence. In contrast to Hanfstaengl, the Hoffmanns did not believe that Hitler had sexual relations with Geli. Henriette Hoffmann von Schirach also denied any intimate contact with Hitler herself.[57] The good relationship between Geli and her uncle deteriorated when it became obvious that Hitler would never marry her, but resented and prevented her contacts with other men, one of them Hitler's bodyguard Emil (Moisl) Maurice.[58] At the same time, Hitler consorted with other women, amongst them Eva Braun. It is likely that Geli knew of Eva but did not meet her. Hitler's avuncular jealousy must have made Geli feel like a bird in a gilded cage. Clearly, the relationship soured. On 18 September 1931, when Hitler was in the middle of a strenuous campaign, Geli and Hitler allegedly had an argument about permission for her to go to Vienna to visit her singing teacher. Afterward, Hitler departed for Nuremberg and Hamburg on a campaign trip. According to Heinrich Hoffmann, Hitler left in an apprehensive mood.[59] After his departure, Geli retired to her room and told Hitler's housekeeper, Frau Winter, that she would go to the movies later. When Geli did not appear the next morning, Frau Winter and her husband broke into the locked room and allegedly found Geli dead on the floor in a puddle of blood, shot in the breast with Hitler's 6-35 Walter revolver; her nose was broken, and an unfinished letter to a friend in Vienna was found in the room. Frau Winter notified the Party leadership at the Braunes Haus. Hess and Gregor Strasser rushed to the scene; the police came later. Hitler allegedly was flagged down in his car on the way to a meeting in Hamburg by a hotel page with the urgent request to call Hess. After getting the news from Hess, Hitler raced back to Munich; his driver received a speeding ticket. According to Hoffmann, Hitler spent the next few days in a state of suicidal depression in the mountain retreat of Adolf Müller.[60]

A police report, which was never found, communicated to the newspapers that the medical student Angela Raubal had committed suicide by a shot into the lungs, and several other articles appeared.[61] Hitler was enraged by the press reports of Geli's death in the Munich papers, which were actually quite restrained (even in the social democratic daily, the *Post*). He denied any involvement, swore to punish the journalists, and published a démenti in the *Post*. It read as follows:

1. It is untrue that I repeatedly quarreled with my niece or that a violent argument occurred on Friday, 18 September.
2. It is true that I had no quarrel, or argument, whatsoever.

3. It is untrue that I was opposed to a trip by my niece to Vienna.
4. It is true that I was not opposed to the planned trip by my niece to Vienna.
5. It is untrue that my niece wanted to be engaged in Vienna or that I had any objection to such engagement.
6. It is true that my niece was troubled by the prospect of a public appearance, as she did not seem to possess the necessary talent, and that she wanted to go to Vienna in order to have her voice tested by a singing teacher.
7. It is untrue that I left my apartment on 18 September, 1931, after a severe argument.
8. It is true that no quarrel and no upset occurred when I left my apartment on that day.

The riposte was awkward damage control and only increased suspicion of foul play.

According to Robert Wagener, an autopsy of Geli's body was performed.[62] Ottmar Spann, Professor of Forensic Medicine in Munich, could not establish that such an autopsy was performed; Wagener also claimed that Hitler attended the autopsy—which would be a highly unusual act—and afterward became a vegetarian.[63] On 21 September, Geli's remains were quickly transported in a sealed coffin to Vienna's Central Cemetery. She was buried by Father Pant, a friend of the Raubal family. Otto Strasser—in an Office of Strategic Services (OSS: Washington, D.C.) interview report—maintained that Father Pant told his brother Paul, a Benedictine monk, that he would never bury a victim of suicide in a Catholic ceremony, but that his rights obliged him not to say more. The insinuation by Strasser was that Geli had been murdered.[64]

After a week of vehement grief, Hitler had recovered, continued his campaign, and delivered a major speech in Hamburg. On 26 September 1931, by special permission of the Austrian government, Hitler briefly visited Geli's grave in Vienna. He commissioned Professor Adolf Ziegler to paint her portrait and Professor Liebermann to sculpt her head. Geli's room, with all her belongings, became a shrine and remained locked to all but him. Shortly before the end of the war, Hitler ordered her belongings and memorabilia destroyed by his adjutant Schaub. More comments about this event, unfortunately without a definite resolution, can be found in Chapter 9.

Hitler's Alleged Perversion

Geli's mysterious death has been linked with the account of a severe perversion, an assumption that can be traced to an OSS interview by Otto Strasser. One morning, Strasser claimed, Geli came to his apartment in Munich and was very upset about her uncle. According to the story:

> Hitler was very generous with her [Geli] in some respects and very harsh with her in others, and frequently locked her up for long periods of time because she refused to accede to his wishes. Strasser tried to make light of

the matter and said to Geli: "Well, why don't you sleep with him. What difference does it make if he is your uncle?" Geli responded that she would be very glad to sleep with him if that was all he wanted, but she just couldn't go through with the other performance again. After much urging concerning the nature of this performance, she finally told Strasser that Hitler made her undress and that he would lie down on the floor. Then she would have to squat down over his face where he could examine her at close range, and this would make him very excited. When the excitement reached its peak, he demanded that she urinate on him, and that gave him his sexual pleasure. Geli said the whole performance was extremely disgusting to her and that, although it was sexually stimulating, it gave her no gratification. Since Hitler refused to let her have any contact with other men, she was in the position of being continually stimulated without any adequate outlet, and that couldn't possibly continue. It was shortly after this visit that Geli was killed, and Strasser was satisfied in his own mind that Hitler had demanded that Geli go through with this performance again and that she had refused, and that Hitler thereupon became enraged and murdered her. His brother Gregor also believed this to be the case, and it was from this time that his relations with Hitler became strained. Gregor was one of the few people who was called to the house shortly after Geli's death and saw her before the funeral. Otto Strasser believed that it was this knowledge that led to Gregor's murder during the Blood Purge in 1934.[65]

Otto Strasser changed his story, however, in his book, *Hitler und Ich*, when he spoke of Hitler as an ascetic with a perverse fantasy.[66] Whatever Otto's brother, Gregor Stasser, knew about this affair, he spoke about Hitler with wry amusement as a strange person who did not touch women; yet Gregor Strasser at no time referred to Hitler as a pervert.[67] Waite also cited a story suggesting that party treasurer Franz Xaver Schwarz was forced to buy back pornographic pictures Hitler had painted of Geli. No such pictures were ever found. Some thirty years later, nude pictures of Geli were in circulation, but turned out to be fraudulent.[68] Furthermore, Gregor Strasser's murder in 1934, three years later, was politically motivated. Until 1932, he held important and highly esteemed positions. Another witness, the gossipy Ernst Hanfstaengl, stated that he heard from a girlfriend that Geli called her uncle a monster.[69] Whether or not this is true, and what it might refer to, remains unknown. Clearly, it is third-party gossip. In any case, perverse behavior and a perverse fantasy are not identical. Otto Strasser also claimed without any proof that Hitler had perverse relations with Henriette Hoffmann, to which her father consented in order to retain Hitler as a client.[70]

One more account of a perversion was supplied to OSS investigators by A. Zeissler, an American movie director who worked in Germany during the thirties.[71] One of his actresses, Renate Müller, reportedly told him that she once went to Hitler's room, expecting to have sexual relations, but was asked instead to undress and kick Hitler while he lay on the floor until he obtained an orgasm. Renate Müller, a severe alcoholic who later committed suicide, is not what might be called a reliable witness. Insinuations about murder, suicide, and perversion will be discussed in Chapter 9.

Eva Braun

Eva Braun was born in Munich in 1912, the second of three daughters of Fritz Braun, a middle school teacher of draftsmanship, and his wife, Franziska. After finishing public school, Eva was sent to a business school run by nuns. At seventeen, she became a receptionist at Heinrich Hoffmann's photo shop, where she also occasionally modeled for commercial products.[72] Probably in 1929, Hitler first met the attractive, slim brunette in Hoffmann's shop and occasionally invited her to dinner. After Geli's death, this relationship became closer but had to be kept secret because her father would not tolerate a love relationship without the prospect of marriage. Hitler's half-sister, Angela Sr., also looked at the relationship with disapproval—Hitler later fired her because of her unkind feelings toward Eva. Through a Czech newspaper, Eva's father heard about the relationship and confronted Hitler about his intentions.[73] Soon, however, Eva's father accepted the fact that his daughter was having an affair with Germany's most powerful politician, and even joined the Party. Hitler never forgave him for his opposition; in his first personal will, he bequeathed money to Eva's mother but not to Fritz Braun. Hitler first installed Eva in an apartment, then in 1932 bought a villa for her, making it possible for her to quit her job. He eventually housed Eva at the Berghof, where she had an apartment with a bedroom adjoining Hitler's. While Eva considered her relationship with Hitler a love affair, for him she was a mistress. Hitler referred to Eva as *"Tschapperl,"* a Viennese expression denoting a helpless and unsophisticated but rather dear person. Eva Braun had no specific functions on the Berghof and spent her days as a lady of leisure, but never became the first lady. Much time was spent on dressing (quite tastefully), body care, sports (she liked gymnastics, skiing, and swimming), dancing, filming or photographing others or being photographed, and socializing with girl friends. Eva smoked, but never in Hitler's presence. She read mostly light literature, with the exceptions of publications by Oscar Wilde and Pearl S. Buck. She could watch movies endlessly, double and triple features. Two Scotch terriers and a tomcat alleviated her obvious loneliness. She never talked about politics or showed any interest in the subject—actually a prerequisite for her relationship with Hitler. She refused to relieve the plight of the nuns who had been her teachers and did not make any serious effort to save her brother-in-law, SS General Fegelein, from the firing squad. The world inside and outside of Germany hardly knew Eva existed; only the intimates in Hitler's court met with her, along with some of her friends and family members. At times she was consumed by jealousy, especially when Hitler neglected her to spend time with the buxom Valkyrie Mitford or attractive actresses and dancers.

Hitler had neither the time nor the inclination to provide the emotional support Eva wanted. In her self-pity, she made a suicide attempt on 1 September 1932, inflicting a light bullet wound on her neck. A physician and friend of the Hoffmanns, Dr. Platen, hospitalized her briefly. Hitler sent flowers but did not visit her in the hospital. Afterward, the relationship continued unchanged, but following her second suicide attempt (using sleeping pills), Hitler was alarmed and became more considerate of her. Gradually, according to Eva's sister Ilse, Hitler's *Tschapperl* evolved into a rather demanding mistress. In the later part of the war, the relationship between Hitler and Eva Braun became closer when he began to feel lonely, let down by his misfortunes in the war, and in need of support. After the attempt on his life on 20 July 1944, he sent his torn and bloody clothes to Eva. According to Ilse, Eva became harder, more assertive with his adjutants and courtiers, who disliked her. One exception was Speer, who held her in high regard and felt sorry for her.[74] In March 1945 she left the Berghof and joined Hitler in the Reichskanzlei, where they married one day before their suicide.

From fragments of a diary written by her, one gets some vivid impressions of the relationship between Eva Braun and Adolf Hitler in 1935. The diary fragments have been published by other authors, such as Gun and Maser,[75] and therefore are not reproduced in this volume. The complete diary allegedly was found and retained by an American counterintelligence officer, Captain Robert A. Gutierrez.[76] The preserved fragment, covering the period from 25 or 26 February 1935 to 28 May 1935, vividly conveys the picture of a twenty-five-year-old, unhappy, frustrated, and childish mistress. In her naive way, Eva loved Hitler and depended entirely on his mood and timetable. She felt neglected and complained about it bitterly. Hitler had other thoughts, which he expressed much later when he explained to his slightly shocked secretaries that marriages create obligations, and hence great men are better off with mistresses.[77] Eva felt that Hitler for a long time was not sensitive to her wishes. Indicating that she did not receive a present from him (she wanted a puppy), she reported that she bought herself some costume jewelry and gorged herself with food. In another statement, she indicates with some resentment, "When he left he gave me, like once before, a small envelope with money. How nice it would have been if he had added a greeting or a kind word." From the diary fragments, one can conclude that Hitler and Eva Braun had a sexual relationship: "He uses me only for certain purposes; nothing else is possible. . . . Nonsense . . . when he says he loves me it is just in that moment. Like his promises that he never keeps. Why does he torture me but does not finish right now?" What the specific nature of the sexual relationship was cannot be determined from this remark.

No definitive knowledge about Eva Braun's sexual relationship with Hitler exists. Speer wrote that Hitler, when he was fifty, told him that he would soon free Eva—"What should she do with an old man?"[78] Eva's hairdresser allegedly stated under oath that Eva told him no coital activity took place.[79] The same opinion was expressed by a Dr. Scholten, a gynecologist who allegedly operated on Eva for a "narrow vagina,"[80] causing pain in sexual intercourse. Also, according to Gun, Eva Braun once remarked about a couch in Hitler's living room, on which Chamberlain sat, "If this couch could talk!" But the couch did not talk, and we have no definitive knowledge about any intimate relationship between the two allegedly impaired partners. Hitler's manservant, Linge, maintained that he eavesdropped at the door of Hitler's bedroom and heard noises associated with sexual activity. But Linge is not to be believed. As evidence of Hitler's genital normalcy, Linge maintained that he had seen Hitler's testicles when once they both urinated against a tree, which is of course a near impossibility and almost certainly an apocryphal tale.[81]

The Great Depression

Hitler benefited from a worldwide economic crisis. The precipitating event, with consequences of catastrophic proportion, was the crash of the New York Stock Market on Black Friday, 29 October 1929. No country was more affected than Germany, hit by a very serious withdrawal of credit and inability to export. Banks, industrial corporations, and business firms went bankrupt, which affected large and small investors, and most of all middle-class savers. Workers faced a devastating increase in unemployment. In 1928 the number of unemployed was 1.4 million; in 1932, at the height of unemployment, it was 5.6 million.[82] An agricultural crisis resulting from bad crops further aggravated the grim situation, and small as well as large landowners in Germany were affected as much as city dwellers. In this period of national embitterment (from 1929 to 1932), the Germans directed their anger and despair against the Weimar Republic. Hitler clearly recognized the significance of the events, and welcomed them. According to Shirer, he stated, "Never in my life have I been so well disposed and inwardly contented than in these days."[83] Hitler had a keen eye for opportunities offered by catastrophic constellations. He could not offer a solution, but he pointed to the future and promised work after the assumption of power. One aggravating facet in the crisis was the objection of a chauvinistic French government to a German–Austrian customs union, which led to the closure of large German and Austrian banks and increased the feeling of humiliation and resentment, all water on Hitler's mills.

Hitler's response to the crisis was an all-out effort, unheard-of in Germany, to attract members and voters in the upcoming electoral campaign. Until the depression of 1929, Hitler declared himself in favor of a small, tightly organized, compact party. In 1930 he decided in favor of a mass party, and only in 1933 were admissions to the party restricted. The election of 14 September 1930 was a stunning victory that surpassed the hopes of the National Socialist leadership. The National Socialist German Worker's Party (NSDAP) won 107 seats and 18.3 percent of the total vote. In the Reichstag election of 31 July 1932, the NSDAP increased to 230 seats, or 37.3 percent of the total vote.[84] The NSDAP had become the strongest party of the German parliament. In his electioneering, Hitler imaginatively used new methods of propaganda. It was the real beginning of the Hitler myth. Nobody before had used radio and public address systems as effectively. He initiated impressive "Deutschland Flüge" (Germany flights) to meetings all over Germany. In a single day, Hitler would fly to several cities where thousands of enthusiastic followers waited for the charismatic Führer to descend from the sky. In 1930, a significant number of Germans outside the party were ready to believe his messages and promises. Hitler was well on his way to becoming the new savior for a large number of Germans. In turn, this expectation and admiration had a profound effect on Hitler. The masses confirmed his own belief that he was a messianic leader. This confirmation helped him overcome some of his inherent passivity and self-doubt, and enabled him to present himself as a rigorous and resolute leader with a vision. In the early thirties, Hitler gained greatly in inner security and had become a powerful leader who could not be ignored by any German politician, left or right.

The End of the Weimar Republic

The events that led to the collapse of the Weimar Republic are exceedingly complex and not completely understood and documented to this day. Turner made the case that events might have taken a different course if General von Schleicher had been more resolute.[85] Yet it is undeniable that Hitler showed exceptional political skill during this period. Only a brief sketch of the events, highlighting Hitler's thoughts and decisions, is presented in this text. The support of a large number of Germans gave Hitler a feeling of confidence, yet he realized that a majority would be unlikely and his Party was not strong enough for a revolutionary takeover. Right-wing and Zentrum Party leaders recognized his strength. Each one of the last three Weimar Chancellors asked Hitler to serve as their Vice-Chancellor. However, against the advice of Gregor Strasser, Hitler turned them down. He was convinced that he would someday be leader of Germany and refused to enter any coalition or compromise.

Hitler was wooed not only by chancellors, but by politicians from right-wing political groups as well. The so-called Harzburg Front—named after their first meeting place in Bad Harzburg—invited Hitler to join them. The group consisted of ultra-conservative politicians, amongst them the press tycoon Alfred Hugenberg, bankers, businessmen, industrialists, retired generals, and leaders of the *Stahlhelm*. The Front's aim was to destroy the Weimar Republic and eventually reestablish the monarchy. Hitler attended a meeting but left quickly, feeling contempt for the self-serving reactionary group, which simply desired to turn the clock back and had no understanding or concern for the needs of the masses. A short time later, Hitler met with industrial and business leaders in the Industrie Klub, and promised to retain the capitalist system.

The last three Chancellors of the Weimar Republic ruled by presidential emergency order based on Article 48 of the Constitution. They could be overruled by the Reichstag, which time and time again was prevented from taking such an action by being disbanded or by a vote of no confidence in the cabinet. This meant that Germany was ruled not by legislation but by decree, a big step toward dictatorship. At the same time, the Social Democrats and the liberal bourgeoisie became weaker and more resigned. The communists remained militant in the streets, but also increasingly unpopular with a large part of the German population. The next two Chancellors were recommended to President von Hindenburg by General Kurt von Schleicher, who occupied the second highest post in the Ministry of the Army. General von Schleicher, called the Field Grey Eminence, was a highly intelligent officer who took a greater interest in politics than military matters. He preferred making and breaking Chancellors rather than assuming responsibility himself. He stood for a powerful Germany with a strong army rather than a strong party. He thought little of Hitler and did not hesitate to express his opinion: Hitler was a figure on his chess board; at times he wanted to use him, at other times to bypass him. Hitler was convinced that von Schleicher had intrigued against him and put him on his black list for future reckoning. Von Schleicher and his wife were killed in the SA massacre on 30 June 1934.

In the escalating crisis, General von Schleicher suggested that President von Hindenburg appoint Heinrich Brüning as the next Chancellor. Brüning, whom President von Hindenburg initially liked because he had been a machine gunner in World War I, scored successes on the foreign affairs front (the Treaty of Versailles was virtually abolished) but was resented for his stringent domestic programs. His enemies—amongst them the government employees whose salaries were severely cut—referred to the able man as the "Hunger Chancellor." When violent acts by the SA and SS became intolerable, Brüning and his Army Minister, General Wilhelm Gröner, reluctantly decided to ban the SA and the SS. This, in turn, upset General Schleicher's schemes, as he had negotiated with Röhm to establish a closer relationship between the Army and the SA. Another nail in Brüning's coffin was the protest of the East Elbian big landowners, close to President von Hindenburg, who called him an "agrarian Bolshevik" because some of their lands were turned over to small farmers who had served in World War I. Schleicher found it easy to persuade the President to dismiss Chancellor Brüning and his Army Minister Gröner, even though Gröner was a paternal friend who had been largely responsible for Schleicher's rise. The man who finally undermined Brüning, however, was Hitler. When von Hindenburg's term of office neared its end, the eighty-three-year-old President—whom Brüning considered his most important supporter—did not want to run for reelection. Brüning sought a change in the constitution to permit von Hindenburg to remain in office until he could finalize his foreign and domestic reconstruction program. Hitler, all of a sudden a protector of the constitution, refused to cooperate. For Hitler and his party in their march to power, it was more important to destabilize Brüning and, ultimately, the Weimar Republic. Hitler's refusal necessitated a new presidential election, in which a tired von Hindenburg and an eager Hitler were the main contenders.

President von Hindenburg was a tremendous figure of respect for many Germans, also for Hitler during his military and early political years. The old President was aptly called the "wooden Titan," not only because wooden statues of him were erected to celebrate his victory over the Russians in the woods of Tannenberg.[86] Yet the hero of Tannenberg also had considerable political talent. An avowed monarchist who disliked civilian government and parliamentary procedures, as President he obeyed the laws of the Weimar Republic, to which he had sworn allegiance. During the early years of his reign, the *"Ersatz Kaiser"* provided a certain stability for the German ship of state as it sailed through turbulent waters. Von Hindenburg recognized Hitler's successes as a politician, but it is certain that he did not like the loquacious former lance corporal. Whether he actually referred to Hitler as the "Bohemian corporal" to whom he would not even offer the Ministry of Postal Services is not documented, but is quite possible. It is known, however, that von Hindenburg repeatedly scolded and even humiliated Hitler — for example, by not asking him to sit down during a meeting with him. Hitler's reaction was not angry or rebellious, but meek and actually rather mature. He knew that an unbridgeable gap in upbringing separated the two men. At times, Hitler was outright deferential, but he also knew that he would outlast the old President. Like many Germans, Hitler was aware that von Hindenburg suffered from a mild cerebral deterioration in the thirties and increasingly depended on his son Oskar, his secretary Otto Meissner (an experienced bureaucrat who later worked for Hitler), the master intriguant General Schleicher, and Franz von Papen. During the campaign Hitler left the attacks to Goebbels, who at times praised von Hindenburg and at other times viciously attacked him, calling him the head of a party of traitors and a faithless old man who had dropped his own chancellor (i.e., Brüning). Through his intransigence Hitler forced von Hindenburg to run in an election against — of all people — himself. The campaign was short; after a long period of hesitation, Hitler participated in it wholeheartedly. To his and his party members' disappointment, he lost. On 13 March 1932, von Hindenburg, however, did not win a majority (he had 49.6 percent of the vote), and had to face Hitler again. The results of the run-off election on 10 April 1932 were: von Hindenburg 53 percent, Hitler 36.8 percent, and the communist Thälman 10.2 percent. Hitler vowed to fight on. As Party leader, he was stronger than ever, and far ahead of the other parties. The National Socialist party had become the strongest and most dynamic, that is, aggressive, party. Von Hindenburg felt dismayed because he disliked winning as the candidate of the Social Democratic and Catholic parties. Under the influence of Schleicher and von Papen, the president asked Brüning to resign.

At Schleicher's suggestion, Franz von Papen became Brüning's successor. Von Papen was a conservative opportunist, well connected with the captains of German industry through his marriage to a wealthy heiress. Until his nomination, von Papen, a member of the exclusive Herrenklub, was better known for his equestrian than his political skills and was dubbed the "gentleman rider." General Schleicher picked von Papen because he viewed him as a political and intellectual lightweight who could easily be manipulated. He was that indeed, but also a wily politician; yet he was wrong in his assumption that Hitler could be tamed. He later alternated between being a critic of

Hitler and being an obedient servant. After the seizure of power, von Papen performed valuable services for Hitler in preparing the Anschluss in Austria, later in preventing Turkey from fighting on the side of the Allies and helping as a conservative Catholic to establish and maintain the Concordat, and, most of all, in aiding Hitler to become Chancellor. He was shrewd enough to gain an acquittal from the international military tribunal, although a court of the Federal Republic of Germany sentenced him to eight years in prison. Only once Von Papen had the courage to attack Hitler, in his Marburg speech of 17 June 1934, for his dictatorial style. The speech was written by von Papen's associate, the writer Edgar Jung, who was executed for this service in the massacre of 30 June 1934. Von Papen was spared because he was von Hindenburg's protégé and had learned his lesson—not to oppose or criticize the dictator.

Von Papen's Cabinet (the "Cabinet of Barons") consisted mostly of members of the aristocracy and plutocracy who showed no concern and understanding for the problems of the average German. In contrast to Hitler with his fanatic ideology, they were mostly interested in securing priorities of their own class and, eventually, restoring the monarchy. Furthermore, their political skills were grossly inferior to Hitler's. To please Hitler, von Papen lifted the ban on the SA and SS, which virtually led to civil war in the streets of German cities. On the bloody Sunday of Altona on 17 July 1932 alone, eighteen persons, two of them SA men, were killed. On 24 March 1932, von Papen ordered the dismissal of the Social Democratic government of Prussia, the last remaining bastion of the Weimar Republic. In spite of all enticements, Hitler again declined the offer to become Vice-Chancellor, demanding the chancellorship. After von Hindenburg—with von Papen's and Schleicher's counsel—decided to reject Hitler's demand, Hitler was lured into the President's office, on 13 August 1932, with the promise that negotiations were still in order. A stern President received Hitler standing and told him that it was incompatible with his conscience and his duty to grant Hitler the total power he requested. Von Hindenburg expressed his regret that Hitler felt unable to support a national government, and he admonished Hitler to be chivalrous in the conduct of his opposition. Hitler felt angry and humiliated, which may have contributed to his determination to topple the von Papen government. In a tricky move, Göring, then President of the Reichstag, inflicted a devastating vote of non-confidence on von Papen, which forced a new election. When von Papen could not find a coalition, civil unrest increased and the old President was forced to let von Papen, his favorite politician, go. Hitler again refused to participate in government unless he obtained the chancellorship, and von Hindenburg reluctantly asked General Schleicher to form a new government. It was the first time Schleicher was forced to assume direct responsibility.

Schleicher's plan in this extremely difficult situation called for the Social Democratic and Catholic trade unions to cooperate in a program of work procurement by the state, but the unions did not trust the wily general and refused to cooperate. Schleicher again tried his luck in negotiating with

Hitler to participate in his government, but Hitler—on the advice of Goebbels and Göring—turned him down. Only Gregor Strasser saw merit in the participation of the NSDAP in the government. Without Hitler's knowledge, Schleicher asked Strasser to become Vice-Chancellor, which Strasser considered a reasonable course. Goebbels and other party stalwarts screamed treason. Hitler became increasingly anxious about the possibility of a split in the party and hysterically declared, "If the Party splits, I will finish my life in three minutes." Strasser did not want to fight Hitler, resigned from all of his posts, and left quietly for a family vacation in Italy. Following his departure, Hitler stripped Strasser of all his offices and pronounced him a traitor. His vengeance reached Strasser sixteen months later, when he was murdered in the SA massacre.

Schleicher's situation looked dismal, but the Nazis suffered a serious setback as well. They lost votes in the Reichstag election of November 1932. The Germans were clearly tired and disgusted with unemployment and civil war-like conditions. Hitler and particularly Goebbels believed that another success was essential. The chance of recovering from recent losses presented itself in elections in the state of Lippe. After an all-out effort in the tiny state, the Nazis once again gained votes. This success—they gained 12.5 percent over a 1931 election—buoyed Hitler sufficiently to begin vigorous negotiations with von Papen to topple Schleicher and establish a new government, which pleased von Papen, who wanted to repay Schleicher in his own coin and who also felt certain that, this time, he could "tame" Hitler.[87] Influenced by von Papen and his son Oscar, President Hindenburg forced Schleicher to resign. In secret negotiations at the home of the banker Kurt von Schroeder, von Papen first proposed a split chancellorship, but then yielded and accepted Hitler's proposal to be appointed Chancellor with only two National Socialists—Frick as Minister of the Interior and Göring as Minister of Aviation and Commissioner of Prussia—in the cabinet. The remaining eight ministry positions would be held by members of the German National People's Party or individuals from von Papen's former cabinet without party affiliations. Hitler reassured Oskar von Hindenburg about his benevolence but probably also hinted at the self-serving behavior of the von Hindenburgs in their acquisition of a large estate in Prussia. Oskar von Hindenburg, in turn, finally convinced the old President to accept Hitler as Chancellor after von Hindenburg's protégé, General Werner von Blomberg, was designated War Minister. Hitler also insisted on new elections, which Hugenberg opposed even after Hitler assured him that the cabinet would remain unchanged—an empty promise and outright lie. The parties were still arguing in the antechambers of the President's office until von Hindenburg's secretary admonished them that it was improper to keep the President waiting. At noon on 30 January 1933, Hitler became Chancellor according to the constitution and laws of the Weimar Republic. Until the very last days, Hitler and his cohorts were not certain that this would happen. Finally, the day of triumph had come. The appointment was the result of a complex power play in which Hitler, through laying in wait, sudden aggressive forays, and tremendous determination and belief in his cause, achieved his goal. In the evening, Goebbels arranged a huge torch parade, which Hitler and his men watched with enormous satisfaction. Hitler talked until the early hours of the next morning about the Party's past and the future of the Reich of a Thousand Years. No record of the discussion was kept, but the world soon learned about Hitler's plans.

6

Führer and Chancellor

The Seizure of Power

ON 30 JANUARY 1933, Goebbels wrote in his diary, "It is almost like a dream." He described the enthusiasm the Germans showed as they marched by the old President and the young Chancellor in an endless torch parade. He concluded on a more sober note: "To work. Prepare the election. It will be the last, and it will be won by a sky-high majority."[1] Indeed, for Hitler it was like a dream. He was elated and stunned. Yet in spite of the public applause, he realized that he was not yet Germany's Führer but rather the head of a conservative cabinet with a minority of two National Socialist ministers—a cabinet in which von Papen and Hugenberg, possibly with the help of President von Hindenburg and his camarilla, would try to do him in to pursue their own aims of reestablishing the monarchy. One of his first tasks was to get rid of this cabinet. Hitler believed that the coming election would give him the power and means to pursue his own far-reaching plans. It would be only a short waiting period.

His first proclamation as Chancellor reads like a campaign platform. Like politicians before and after him, he made promises, invoking the name of the Almighty in whose service he acted. To employers he promised an improved economy, to workers employment, to peasants an end to a marginal existence and a recognition of their importance, and to all except the Jews a unity of spirit and goodwill. Christianity would promote morality, and the family would provide the seed of statehood. In four years unemployment would be eliminated.[2] Hitler made far-reaching promises to the top generals in a secret

meeting two days after the seizure of power. Rather timid and almost deferential in the presence of the top brass, Hitler promised to break the fetters of
the Versailles treaty (most had already been eliminated), reestablish general
military service, vastly enlarge the army and navy, create a new air force, and,
most of all, eventually fulfill his old dream of an expansion to the east in
order to procure living space, food, and raw materials.[3] Hitler sought to present himself as a strong and reasonable man. His statement to the Associated
Press on 3 February 1933 was defensive:

> Remember that I am persistent and have strong nerves. If I did not possess
> great decisiveness I would not be standing before you today. I was described
> as a bloodthirsty and inflammatory speaker, talking against foreign power. I
> never made an inflammatory speech. Nobody wants peace and quiet more
> than I. . . .[4]

In many speeches, but particularly in his major peace speech of 18 May 1933,
Hitler praised peace:

> If I talk this moment as a German National Socialist, I want to state in the
> name of the national government and the national rise that our young Ger-
> many is inspired by the deepest understanding of similar sentiments and
> convictions and of the justified demands of other peoples. The generation of
> young Germans that knew in its life only deprivation, misery, and the woe
> of its people has suffered too much through the insanity of war and inflicted
> the same on others. As we are bound by unlimited love and fidelity for our
> people, we respect the national rights of other peoples with equal under-
> standing and want to live with them from the bottom of our heart in peace
> and friendship. We do not know the concept of Germanization. The mental-
> ity of the past century, that one could make Germans out of the Poles, or
> perhaps the French, is just as alien to us as we would passionately resist the
> opposite attempt. We see the neighboring European nations as a given fact.
> The French, the Poles are our neighbors, and we know that no conceivable
> historical event can change this reality.[5]

Actually, the speech was a prelude to Germany's withdrawal from the League
of Nations, because Hitler believed that "peaceful Germany" had not been
treated well by the neighbors in the League. In a secret* speech on 10
November 1938, Hitler reversed himself completely:

> Circumstances have forced me for decades always to speak of peace. Only
> under such continuous emphasis was it possible for me to acquire, piece by
> piece, freedom for the German people and to give them the armament that
> always has been necessary as a prerequisite for the next step. It is evident that

---

* "Secret" meant only that the statement was made before a restricted audience and was not
published in government publications or the National Socialist press.

such a decade's propaganda (for peace) has its precarious aspects, because it can, in the brains of many persons, fit the view that the present regime identifies itself with the status quo. . . . Necessity was the reason that I talked of peace for years. It was particularly necessary, therefore, to change the people psychologically and to make it clear to anybody that there are things which cannot be resolved peacefully. The mass of our people began to call slowly for a violent solution. This lasted many months. The problem had to be solved "so or so" [a frequent expression of Hitler's].[6]

Hitler planned to secretly build up German military power, which meant that the buildup could not be sudden, and to negotiate if necessary, such as in the case of a fleet agreement with Great Britain. From the very beginning, Hitler figured a war was necessary to reach his goal of political and economic domination of Continental Europe and, most of all, Eastern Europe.

The Election

The election campaign was short and intense. It used the powers and means of the state and relied to an unprecedented degree on radio broadcasts. The campaign was interrupted by an alarming event. On 27 February 1933 the Reichstag was set on fire by an anarchist, Marinus van der Lübbe, also a member of the Dutch Communist Party. Hitler, Goebbels, and Göring rushed to the spot and concluded that the arson was the work of Communists, the signal for a general strike and Communist takeover. With the consent of von Hindenburg, Hitler issued the Law for the Protection of State and People, which drastically reduced the civil rights of individuals and parties. It abolished the right of assembly, freedom of the press, privacy of communication, habeas corpus, and opened the way for arrest and incarceration without warrant or trial. This was the law that made Germany a police state and also eliminated the power of Hitler's conservative cabinet members, who voted for it.

The Reichstag Fire

The Reichstag fire dominated the rest of the electoral campaign. All Communist deputies were arrested. Van der Lübbe was convicted as the lone arsonist, and, after a special law was enacted—the Lex van der Lübbe—the German Supreme Court sentenced him to death. To Hitler's dismay, the others accused, the Bulgarian communist Georgi Dimitroff and the German Communist Deputy Leader Ernst Torgler, were acquitted. According to Hans Mommsen, the events have not been completely clarified.[7] It is possible that the Nazis "used" the crazed van der Lübbe to commit the act. What is clear is that Hitler used the Reichstag fire to the utmost to introduce and reinforce repressive measures. Certainly the Communist Party had no reason to commit such an act. Ten days before the election, the Nazis pursued Communists and Social Democrats with unchecked fury. The relentless persecution was accepted without major protest by the majority of the German people. Hitler knew that the Communists were unpopular with many Germans, and both the Communists and the Social Democrats were weak. Yet the result of the election was a disappointment to Hitler and the Party. The Nazis increased their number of deputies but obtained only 43.9 percent of the vote. However, a mere plurality did not deter Hitler from pursuing his radical policy of building the new Germany. Elections or plebiscites were significant only in that they suited the aim of the dictator. Actually, Hitler had a "majority," because all of the Communist and twenty-eight Social Democratic deputies were in jails or concentration camps.

Political Gleichschaltung

The time for political *Gleichschaltung*—an electrician's term designating the reduction to one current—had arrived. On 21 March 1933, the day of the opening of the new Reichstag, the Day of Awakening, a solemn celebration took place in Potsdam. In the presence of the government's high brass, Party officials, and the diplomatic corps, von Hindenburg and Hitler resolved to work together to build a new Germany. It was not easy for Hitler to appear in a top hat on this solemn occasion, because he did not like his appearance in such garb and it alienated the radical elements within the Party, but the act of playing along with von Hindenburg and the conservative forces paid off. With the cooperation of the German Nationalist Party during the first session of the new Reichstag, Hitler was able to push through the Reichstag one of his most important pieces of legislation, the Enabling Act. It eliminated most legislative functions of the Reichstag and gave Hitler and his cabinet far-reaching power of legislation and unrestricted power to conduct foreign policy. Although it stipulated the end of all parties but the NSDAP, only the Social Democrats voted against it. When Otto Wels, chairman of the Social Democratic Party, stated that his party would oppose the law, Hitler haughtily told him, "I don't want you to vote for it; Germany shall be free, but not through you."[8] It took only three months further to abolish all of the other parties. By midsummer 1933 the National Socialist German Workers Party was the only party. The Reichstag became, as opponents whispered, a glee club in which members could vote for Hitler's laws and intone the national anthem and the NS battle song, the Horst Wessel *Lied*. The second step of political *Gleichschaltung* was busting the powerful social democratic and Christian unions and, after confiscating their assets, establishing the German Workers Front (Deutsche Arbeitsfront) under Robert Ley. Hitler was eager to win over the workers from the Communist, Social Democratic, and Zentrum parties, who joined in droves. Bringing workers into his camp was important to Hitler, who saw himself as "a worker of the fist and head," and fit his ideology to overcome class struggle and have the workers unite behind him, giving up their allegiance to international communism and socialism. The third aspect of political *Gleichschaltung* was a transfer of the power of government from the state to the central government. Although Hitler's Minister of the Interior, Wilhelm Frick, was anxious to bring this about, Hitler was ambivalent. The Gauleiter and the Reichsstatthalter, the mighty rulers of *Gaue* and states, were reluctant to give up their power; they were aided by Hitler's inclination to side with loyal party stalwarts. Conflicts between governing bodies in the NSDAP were present at all levels. The redundancy of offices created a bureaucratic chaos in a country that before had an orderly bureaucracy.

The Concordat and the Fight against the Church

Hitler feared the threat the churches posed for political *Gleichschaltung*. He tried to preempt these problems through the Concordat with the Vatican and establishment of a Church of the Reich. He considered the Concordat one of his important achievements, one that no German statesman before him had accomplished. Pope Pius XI and his Secretary of State, Cardinal Eugenio Pacelli (later Pope Pius XII), were eager to establish the Concordat to strengthen Germany as a bulwark against Bolshevism. The Concordat provided a clear division between political activities belonging to the Reich and religious activities of the Church. It sanctioned the abolition of the Catholic Zentrum party and its sister party, the Bavarian People's Party. It was well received by the majority of the German bishops and clergy, and the Catholic population. The bishops and clergy were generally anti-Semitic, and the majority of practicing German Catholics did not object to what became known as the Aryan Rule and closed their eyes to the sterilization laws even though they were incompatible with Christian doctrine. Hitler was viewed as a moderate in matters of religion, as opposed to the radicals in his party—such as Bormann, Rosenberg, and Himmler—who pleaded for the quick and total destruction of the Church. Yet even the inner circle did not know exactly where he stood. Bormann once wistfully chided Hitler for being "very religious."[9] After the *Machtergreifung* (seizure of power) and before the war, he presented himself as a moderating force in the fight against the Church, but he did not stop the ongoing harassment of the Catholic Church by the Party or the campaign to discredit the Church through accusations against members of religious orders of violations of currency laws and sexual crimes, including homosexual and heterosexual relations with minors. The claim was later made by Hitler's Church Minister, Hanns Kerrl, that 7000 such cases had occurred. In reality, however, about seventy priests and members of religious orders were convicted. The harassment of the Church and breaking of the rules of the Concordat finally induced Pope Pius XI to protest in his encyclical *Divini redemptoris* on 14 July 1937 against both National Socialist and Bolshevik persecution of the Church. Although it was read from German pulpits, the encyclic had little effect on National Socialist church policy. Friedländer compared Pius XI to Chamberlain, who initially believed that a dialogue with Hitler was possible but then changed his mind.[10] Pope Pius XI died on 10 February 1939 and was succeeded by the Germanophile Cardinal Eugenio Pacelli. The new Pope Pius XII was obsessed with the Bolshevik world danger and unwilling to protest Nazi crimes against the Jews until 1944, when it was too late.

The Protestant religions were foreign to Hitler. A unified Church of the Reich seemed a solution, a religious body that would further his goals. He appointed a mediocrity, Ludwig Müller, as Reich's Bishop, but the members of the synod elected Parson Friedrich von Bodelschwingh, a humane man who was the head of an institution for the mentally disabled. Under Hitler's pressure, von Bodelschwingh was forced to yield to the Reichsbischof, but he became one of the founders of the Confessing Church, a movement of ministers and lay persons who were opposed to the *Gleichschaltung* of the Church and the Aryan Rule. Reichsbischof Müller was later unseated, and a serious opposition evolved under the leadership of the intrepid Pastor Martin Niemöller, a former World War I U-boat captain who before had voted for the NSDAP for many years. Following a personal confrontation with the Führer, Niemöller was sentenced to a prison term of seven months and subsequently sent to the concentration camp at Sachsenhausen, where he remained until the end of the war. Annoyed with the feuds among the Protestant churches, Hitler appointed another weak leader, Hanns Kerrl, as church minister who also was unable to unite the various factions. When Germany started the Second World War, a cessation of the strife was proposed, but the euthanasia project, implemented at that same time, provided new fuel for the clerical opposition. However, with rare exceptions such as Bishop Theophilus Wurm, neither Catholic nor Protestant bishops effectively opposed the genocide of the Jews. Hitler's anticlerical and antireligious beliefs—though not his actions—steadily increased, particularly during the late phases of the war.

Hitler and Röhm

When Röhm returned from Bolivia as supreme leader to reestablish order in the ranks of the turbulent SA, Hitler extended far-reaching concessions that did not become public. At the time of the *Machtergreifung*, 600,000 to 700,000 SA troops dwarfed the standing army of 100,000. Among the SA were many unemployed, frustrated, and angry individuals, as well as some outright criminals who were hard to discipline. After the NSDAP seized power, Röhm and the SA wanted their reward—power, jobs, and a move to the left. Hitler resisted the SA pressure because it restricted his power and endangered his relationships with the generals and the industrialists, whose support he needed to accomplish his plans. Hitler and the Party found control over the SA difficult to maintain; to Hitler's annoyance, Röhm had not made Party membership a condition of admission to the SA. Under pressure, Hitler made Röhm a member of his cabinet, but he was opposed to making him Minister of War—a post occupied by General Blomberg, who had Hitler's as well as President von Hindenburg's confidence. Hitler also opposed Röhm's request that the Reichswehr provide military training for the SA and viewed the role of the SA men as political soldiers, a rather vague definition. Hitler was opposed to the concept of a militia and wanted only the army to carry arms. Röhm's ambitions were strongly opposed by Army

High Command and by bitter and powerful enemies in the Party (particularly Göring, Hess, and Goebbels). The SS leaders, Himmler and Heydrich, strove for independence from the SA.

Hitler felt threatened, unappreciated, and, most of all, ridiculed by Röhm, who did not appropriately recognize the Führer's messianic authority. After sending him a cordial and appreciative letter on 1 January 1934, Hitler condemned Röhm's slogan about carrying out a second revolution. Amongst the SA leadership as well as the rank and file were many who wanted to eliminate the aristocratic and bourgeois cliques, although no concrete plans existed. After Hitler opposed such a course, Röhm overtly yielded but kept on criticizing Hitler personally for his conservative bent. Such derogatory remarks were promptly reported to Hitler, who was alarmed by them. He might have continued to defer a solution if not for rumors — planted by Goebbels, Göring, and Himmler — that opponents such as Schleicher, Gregor Strasser, and von Papen had tried to influence President von Hindenburg to restore the monarchy by means of an army coup. On 17 March 1933, von Papen, angered by his own loss of power and worried that Hitler would succeed von Hindenburg, delivered a protest lecture at Marburg University, ghost-written by his associate Edgar Jung. The speech was immediately suppressed by Goebbels, but it fueled Hitler's suspicion of a plot against him and triggered plans for brutal action. Hitler ordered police investigations of Röhm's and other high SA leaders' homosexuality, which until then he had ignored.

In June 1934, in cooperation with the army leadership — which stood to benefit from it — Hitler decided to use the SS to destroy the leadership of the SA. Actually, Röhm had agreed to a cooling-off period, sent his chiefs on summer vacation, and himself went to Bad Wiessee, a Bavarian spa, for a cure and rest. Hitler issued an original hit list of seven that was later expanded by Göring with the Führer's consent. Planning an ambush, Hitler asked for a meeting with SA leaders in Bad Wiessee, on 30 June. After he flew to Munich and motored to the spa in the early morning hours before the SA leaders arrived, he stormed into the bedroom of a sleepy and surprised Röhm and yelled, "Röhm, you are under arrest!" After initial hesitation, he issued the order to execute Röhm. Hess eagerly volunteered for the job, but the "honor" went to Theodor Eicke, later the first Kommandant of the Dachau concentration camp. The highest SA leaders on the original list were arrested throughout Germany and summarily executed without trial. Many were completely unsuspecting as they started on their vacations — one of them, Karl Ernst, was on his honeymoon. The executioners were SS men under Himmler and Heydrich, with the army providing arms and tactical support. The murders were not limited to Party comrades. A number of Hitler's old enemies were on the hit list and were rubbed out gangland style — including Gregor Strasser, the ex-Bavarian Minister-President von Kahr, General von Schleicher and his wife, Edgar Jung, and another von Papen associate, Herbert von Bose. Mistake killings occurred: the murder of Willi Schmid, a music critic, was a mistake, but not that of Pater Stempfle, who had aided Hitler in writing *Mein Kampf* and was a confidant of Hitler's beloved niece Geli. Hitler ordered a few of the eager executioners punished, which helped to clear him of the suspicion of politically and personally motivated assassination. Altogether, about 300 people were killed. The SA became a politically insignificant force under a new leader, Victor Lutze, a critic of Röhm and clearly subservient to Hitler. The willingness of the army generals to become accomplices to murder without due process—murdering not only the SA leaders but of two of their own, General Schleicher and General von Bredow—forfeited their honor in Hitler's view. The contempt he developed for "the generals" might have had its origins at that time.

Politically, Hitler emerged from the crisis with flying colors. On 1 July, while executions were still going on in the neighborhood of the Reichskanzlei, he cheerfully attended a garden party. Yet, according to witnesses, the massacre of his old comrades upset him. His preoccupation with the matter lasted for months, perhaps even years. In a statement to his cabinet on 6 July 1934, and in a very long speech before the Reichstag on 13 July, Hitler claimed that he had been forced to suppress a revolution against the Third Reich and to decimate the culprits.[11] He painted a picture of his opponents as traitors and personally immoral men. Much was made of the homosexuality of Röhm and members of the SA leadership, but in reality only one SA leader, Edmund Heines, had been found in bed with a lover. Hitler had known about Röhm's bisexuality for a long time and tolerated it until the massacre on 30 June. The German public not only approved, but even applauded the resolute action that had been taken by their Führer, who spared no one, regardless of rank. President von Hindenburg nodded approval. General Blomberg expressed his deep appreciation and admiration for Hitler's act. Although the army was pleased about the elimination of the SA, they did not realize at the time that in a few years, under Himmler's leadership, the SS would become a serious rival. Hitler explained his actions as being necessary for the benefit of the country. Although the murder of the SA leadership was prompted by Hitler's need for control and authority, it was characteristic of the regime. In a democracy, the defeated rebels would have been arrested and tried for high treason. In the Third Reich, the accused were lynched. Hitler's massacre—even though it was accepted by President von Hindenburg, the army, and the majority of the people—was a major deviation from the morality of the Western world.

One reason the German population acquiesced was their relief that no major upheaval occurred. In several speeches, Hitler boasted that his revolution was tempered and disciplined, that no windows had been broken—though such vandalism would occur during the *Kristallnacht*, five years later. Hitler emerged from the massacre of 30 June with tremendous power. His authority was increased further when he managed to succeed President von Hindenburg as Chancellor and Führer. While von Hindenburg was still alive, Hitler's cabinet, at his request, appointed him as von Hindenburg's successor. Hitler saw von Hindenburg shortly before his death. What they discussed is not known, but it hardly matters because the old President was demented and confused. Although von Hindenburg was more responsible than any other person for Hitler's appointment as Chancellor, he had a restraining influence on him. After his death, the last restraint was gone.

The Economic Miracle

Taking power in the depths of the Great Depression, Hitler knew that the Germans expected him to eliminate unemployment and promptly establish a sound economy. The year 1934, however, was difficult for Hitler and the Nazis. It was referred to as a year of crisis. Norbert Frei spoke of a "hangover" mood among the population.[12] Big business and industry were concerned about trade deficit and currency problems, and about possible socialist leanings by the new regime. The middle class felt little had changed. The grand promises had not been fulfilled. Jewish department stores had not been closed. The buying power of the population remained low and prices were high. Peasants, farmers, and large estate owners complained that their plight had worsened. Their income had not risen, and initial attempts by the State to regulate food distribution were clumsy and met with resentment among the agricultural providers. Even the workers, Hitler's favorite social class, though enjoying a decline in unemployment, still waited for higher wages and were forced to accept the loss of collective bargaining and the right to strike.

The politician Hitler knew that rapid changes were essential. Most of all, he wanted to eliminate unemployment, and, indeed, it disappeared in Germany at a time when other industrialized nations, particularly the United States, were suffering heavily from it. Increasing employment was one of Hitler's most remarkable achievements, for which he was given due credit by the population. The economic recovery induced many Germans to believe that Hitler was a man who kept his promises. He increased production to support rearmament and, to a lesser degree, to increase consumer goods. People joked about "cannons and margarine" but found the program acceptable. The hidden cost was that the armament program overheated the German economy, which Hitler later tried to remedy by the takeover of Austria and the Sudetenland, the invasion of Czechoslovakia, and, ultimately, the invasion of Russia.

Hitler's economic czar was Hjalmar Schacht, an imaginative financier who became president of the Reichsbank and Minister of Finance. Schacht favored the gold standard, while Hitler rejected it, adhering instead to the concept that the wealth of a nation is its productivity. Schacht devised an ingenious program of deficit financing through the so-called Mefo-discounts. These were discounted drafts on a fictitious company—the Metallurgische Forschungsanstalt—underwritten by the largest German steel producers and honored by the government to finance the rearmament program without producing inflation, increased indebtedness, or a negative foreign trade balance. Under Schacht's influence, in the mid-thirties Hitler followed principles similar to views of John Maynard Keynes, the outstanding economist of his time, who proposed deficit financing and public works employment for military and civil projects. The prototype was the Autobahn. Hitler never mentioned Keynes's name, and what Hitler learned about Keynes is unknown. It is likely that Hitler had some knowledge of Keynes, because Keynes was a severe critic of the Treaty of Versailles. In 1934, 4 percent of the gross national product in Germany went to armament; in 1939, this rose to 50 percent. For Hitler, this was not fast enough, and Schacht was demoted to Minister without Portfolio. As Schacht's successor and head of the four-year plan, Hitler appointed Göring, perhaps because he was ignorant of economics but willing to follow the Führer's wishes. In 1944, Schacht was accused of contacts with the Resistance and imprisoned at the concentration camp of Ravensbruck. In his trial at the International Military Court he was acquitted.

Hitler frequently discussed such economic issues as production and consumption, but in essence he viewed them as political, psychological, and social phenomena. He believed in the primacy of politics over economics. Unemployment and inflation, which he dreaded, he considered political problems. By "political" he meant action overcoming fear and greed. He boasted to Schacht, "The primary remedy for the stabilization of our currency is the concentration camp."[13] For Hitler, the discipline of economics had a materialistic, actually a Marxist–Jewish flavor, and thus could not unify the nation, which Hitler considered all-important. His most significant economic–political goal was autarky, and he emphasized this in many speeches and monologues. Hitler wanted to achieve autarky not only by means of technical innovations—such as the production of synthetic rubber and motor fuels—but foremost through the conquest of European Russia, which would provide Germany with both agricultural products and raw materials. Ultimately, autarky was both an economic and a military goal. The Allies' blockade of Germany in the First World War had undermined German material and morale, and Hitler was determined to prevent this from happening again. Psychologically, autarky expressed Hitler's passion for inviolacy.

The question of whether Hitler favored a capitalist or a socialist order has been amply discussed in the literature. Henry A. Turner, Jr., disproved the view that he was a stooge of capitalism.[14] According to Rainer Zitelmann, Hitler had anticapitalist views.[15] However, Hitler was inconsistent in his economic and political views. In many statements he called the bourgeoisie weak, selfish, and cowardly, and, in contrast, praised the working class.[16] On 19 November 1920, he declared that his Party fought neither right nor left, but took the most valuable from both sides.[17] In the early twenties he paid attention to Feder's anticapitalist concept of the "slavery of interest," but later discarded it. In the late twenties Hitler distanced himself from the socialist views of Otto Strasser and Robert Wagener, but after the assumption of power he supported Ley and his pro-labor sentiments. Yet in his last major speech to industrial, military, and Party leaders on 4 July 1944, he stated, "When this war is concluded with our victory, the private initiative of the German economy will experience its greatest epoch."[18] During the war, industrial corporations remained in charge, although their power—like in the Western Allied nations—was curtailed. In a speech to the Gauleiter in February 1945, Hitler complained, "We have liquidated the fighters of the left, but unfortunately forgot to destroy the right. This is our big sin of omission."[19] Only a few large state-owned corporations, such as the Göring industries and the Volkswagen Werke, came into being. No expropriations occurred except in the case of Jewish enterprises and the plunder in occupied countries. As Hitler valued both initiative and control, he opted for a mixture of free market and planned economy.

Workers received only slightly higher wages than they had earned in the best years of the Weimar Republic, but considerable social benefits: better pensions, more vacation time, improvement of the work place, better health and recreational facilities. The organization Strength through Joy (Kraft durch Freude, abbreviated KDF), patterned after the Italian *Dopo Lavore* organization, contributed much to the leisure activities of the German masses. It was the first organization of mass tourism, taking workers on low-cost vacations from Norway to the Azores. With some pleasure, Hitler participated on one of the steamship trips. Premarital loans, construction of three- to four-room low-rent apartments, and assistance for exceptional needs in winter were additional benefits planned for workers. Of equal importance was a feeling of equality and the opportunity for upward social mobility. A large number of Germans enjoyed the psychic as well as material benefits of these conditions and appreciated Hitler for creating them. While the benefits for farmers were not spectacular, all types of landowners enjoyed being called the guardians of "blood and soil."

Hitler intended to do more for industrial and agricultural workers, but the preparations for war and the war itself prevented this. He made plans for further social reforms after the victory. Whatever he had in mind, Hitler believed he could control the economy. It was a question of will, not economic laws. According to his dictum, the state was not the servant of capital, but capital the servant of the state. He was convinced that the leadership ultimately decided on production and consumption, and on sacrifices—which, however, always remained modest. If one considers the twin concepts implied in the name of the Party—national and socialist—which Hitler viewed as unique, one must consider the socialist twin as rather atrophic.

Führerstaat *and Führer Principle*

After the political *Gleichschaltung*, the elimination of Röhm and his lieutenants, initial economic success, and beginning rearmament, Hitler was ready to create a political structure—based on ideas expressed in *Mein Kampf*, in the Second Book, and in numerous speeches and articles—that would enable him to carry out his radical programs and establish the Führerstaat, also called the Third Reich, a term the Nazis eventually rejected because it insinuated a limited duration, while the National Socialist Reich was to last for a thousand years and more.[20] The following remarks are limited to some psychosocial aspects of the Führerstaat as Hitler visualized it. Its most important characteristic is the supreme position of the Führer. In *Mein Kampf*, Hitler rejected the democratic mass idea and pronounced that the earth belonged to an elite. In place of the idea of majority, he offered personality. His philosophy harks back to the early days of the Party, when Hitler's followers, "the best people,"[21] picked him—the best mind amongst them—as their leader. All further struggles, elections, Hitler's appointment as Chancellor and, finally, as Führer, after Chancellor Hindenburg's death, were only extensions of the initial act. It was the complete denial of the rule of the majority, which Hitler considered the rule of the stupid and incapable masses and their representatives. According to Hitler, the ideas of democracy and equality were promoted by Jews in order to destroy a nation.[22] "There must be no majority decisions," he said, "but only responsible persons, and the word 'council' must be restored to its original meaning. Surely, every man will have advisors by his side, but the decisions will be made by one man."[23] His model was the military command structure. "The principle that made the Prussian army in its time into the most wonderful instrument of the German people must someday . . . become the principle of the construction of our whole state conception: authority of every leader downward and responsibility upward."[24] Hitler's goal was a military command structure without any checks or balances.

Hitler held enormous power in the Führerstaat, greater than that of any other European ruler, perhaps even Stalin's, whom he ambivalently admired and hated.[25] As Chancellor, Hitler headed the civilian government. He initiated or approved legislation. As Commander in Chief, he headed Germany's armed forces. He was the ultimate authority in judiciary matters, often reversing sentences (usually to the detriment of the accused). As Führer of the National Socialist Party, he led the cadre that was designated to lead the government. He held these powers in a government that had no constitution, no laws about election or appointment of its leader, personal but no legal designations for a successor, and no laws governing impeachment. Through his deputies, he had total control of the press and other news media. Ernst Fraenkel described the National Socialist state as a double state: One part followed laws as they existed in democratic countries, another part had no laws.[26] The latter dealt with enemies of the state. Who the enemies were, however, with the exception of the Jews, remained vague. Anybody could be declared an enemy at any time. Initially, the Jews, prototypical enemies, were considered foreigners (*Ausländer*), but gradually they lost all rights, including the right to live. Hitler divided German nationals into citizens and subjects:

> The German citizen is the lord of the Reich. The man without honor or character, the common criminal, the traitor to the fatherland, etc., can at

any time be divested of this honor. He thus again becomes a subject. Furthermore, the German girl is a subject and only becomes a citizen when she marries. But the right of citizenship can also be granted to female German subjects active in economic life.[27]

Hitler ruled a huge and complex hierarchy. In fact, he was on top of two hierarchies: the hierarchy of the government of the Reich and states and the hierarchy of the Party. The relationship between these hierarchies was ill-defined. Overlap in functions and appointments was frequent. The vertical chain of command was relatively clear. Hitler issued orders to a kitchen cabinet, and the members of the cabinet issued orders to the next echelon—ministers and high Party functionaries—who, in turn, issued orders to the lower echelon, down to the myriad of "little Hitlers." Party functionaries vastly multiplied the number of functionaries in the regular government. Spoilsmanship remained a problem even after Hitler decided to stop admitting new members into the Party after 1933, because, theoretically, he was opposed to a large party. During the war years, 700,000 "little Hitlers" could be counted.[28] Many historians have commented on the redundancy of organizations and functions, competing competencies, and the administrative jungle in the Third Reich. This situation was aggravated by the fact that the functionaries were an aggressive lot—believing in Hitler's thesis of life as an eternal struggle, justifying the term "bureaucratic Darwinism." Although little disobedience or sabotage occurred until late in the war, end-running was common, often resulting in Hitler's making decisions on the basis of whomever he saw last. Even the tough Martin Bormann, who functioned as Hitler's powerful ranking administrator, could reduce but not prevent this.

Hitler's close associates never opposed him effectively. Hess stated that Adolf Hitler was his conscience, and Göring remarked to Schacht that "I often make up my mind to say something to him, but when I come face to face with him my heart sinks into my pants."[29] The other members of the inner circle were just as submissive. In all units of the armed forces, discipline was harsh, and disobedience was drastically punished during the war—for example, the generals who disobeyed Hitler's orders not to retreat in the Russian winter of 1941/42 were quickly and drastically disciplined. Hitler's tough minions also demanded obedience from their subordinates. Why these men recognized Hitler's authority so readily can be explained only by the charismatic character of his role. Hitler demanded absolute loyalty, which induced him to tolerate and even protect outright inferior members such as Streicher. He was not adverse to advice—he actually needed and accepted it if it was offered in a respectful manner—but he had a low tolerance for critique.[30] Admirer Hans S. Ziegler, Intendant of the National Theater in Weimar, stated that Hitler was opposed to art criticism in particular,[31] but he personally was extremely critical of art he disliked.

In an examination of the limits of Hitler's power, Edward N. Peterson concluded that Hitler's main difficulty was not due to a limitation of power but the fact that Hitler often did not know what he wanted and felt helpless.[32] This thesis needs to be qualified by Zitelmann's observation that Hitler saw the "big lines and the smallest details" but neglected the important mid-range decisions.[33] He had some sense for strategic considerations, but, on the other hand, he concerned himself with details (e.g., during the war, the demolition of bridges). Many commentators have assumed that Hitler consciously employed the Machiavellian principle of rule and divide to control his aggressive associates, but it seems more likely that this was accomplished by default rather than intentionally.

Hitler disliked and resented many administrative tasks that a leader of a country must perform. His resentment of bureaucrats and bureaucracies can be traced to his own youth, when he thought of the office in which his father worked: "I yawned and grew sick to my stomach at the thought of sitting in an office, deprived of my liberty; ceasing to be master of my own time and being compelled to force the content of my whole life into blanks that had to be filled out."[34] In the monologues, Hitler stated, "One always asks me to praise the bureaucracy. I can't do it."[35] Hitler not only avoided but neglected administration. He delegated freely, but unpredictably. His four chancellories were headed up by capable administrators—most important, from 1941 to the end of the regime, by Martin Bormann. Hitler's dream was to rule Germany, and indeed later the world, with a small elite force. But in reality, the huge competing and antagonistic bureaucracies of state and Party became an administrative nightmare. The ordinary Germans did not like these bureaucracies and called the bemedaled bureaucrats "gold pheasants." The great charismatic leader was never blamed for these conditions, and in fact the Germans would say, "if the Führer only knew," referring to the inefficient bureaucracies and their misdeeds. On one occasion, Christa Schroeder brought the saying to Hitler's attention, but he brushed it aside and declared, "I know everything."[36]

Hitler's administrative weaknesses were quite obvious. Unlike other German leaders, such as Bismarck and Metternich, he was unwilling to study documents carefully before he reached decisions. He prided himself on operating with the ease of a somnambulist,[37] which proved to be a rather unreliable approach. Basically, Hitler thought little of written agreements. His contempt for documents and his inclination to break a very large number of political contracts created a climate of distrust in the international scene and eventually played a role in Hitler's downfall. He did not decide easily, notwithstanding his reputation for being a decisive man with an iron will. Once a decision was made, Hitler was unwilling to alter it, fearing a change of will could harm his reputation. He explained, perhaps apologetically, that an order would take only a very short time, but thinking prior to the decision was an arduous and time-consuming job.[38] In some cases, the delays in making major decisions, such as before the German army marched into Austria or when he pondered the question of withdrawal from the Norwegian outpost at Narvik, were caused by a high level of anxiety. Hitler had a strong disinclination to commit himself and a pronounced tendency to keep things in flux. In spite of his admiration, Goebbels frequently felt uneasy about Hitler's propensity to delay and hesitate. Historians have noted Hitler's aversion to commit himself and to "being pinned down." Even though there was a certain tendency toward procrastination and vacillation, however, many examples of firm and even precipitous decisions can be given.

In numerous statements Hitler expressed his conviction that the masses of Germans—not to mention those of conquered or dominated nations—needed to be ruled by elites, because in themselves the masses, even the German masses, were not capable of rational or creative action. The ruler had to press individuals into a highly organized or structured system. The leader must be sensitive to the needs of the masses and able to understand them but not be guided by them. He maintained that the masses were emotional and needed to be molded—not in a half-hearted manner, but through the utmost will and strength. The leader must convey his fanatic conviction to the people. Hitler did not consider all masses equal, of course. Germanic masses, according to Hitler, were superior to Slavic masses, also to African Negroes and to "negroized" Americans. The German masses would be indoctrinated with National Socialist ideology, while the eastern Slavic peoples would be deprived of virtually any education.[39]

Hitler's Police

Frei correctly commented that enthusiasm for the Führer and not fear or resistance was the important sentiment in the mid-thirties.[40] Yet a powerful police force was an intrinsic feature of the system. In a short time Germany became a police state as formidable in its terrorist practices as Stalin's Soviet Union. Hitler wanted a strong and brutal police. During the *Kampfjahre* he commented on how he valued the bullies who protected him and his meetings.[41] His expectation about the military leadership was similar—he wanted his generals to be "cold dog-snouts, disagreeable people such as I have in the Party."[42] In the occupied territories he wanted the police to have their revolvers secured loosely in their holsters.[43] Typically, Hitler wanted his subordinates to show brutality and harshness but did not want to dirty his own hands. Hitler left little doubt about what he wanted when he sensed potential threats: "I have instructed the Reichsführer SS in case of inner upheaval to exterminate everything in the concentration camps. With this, the leadership of the masses will be removed."[44]

Hitler's emphasis on police power was reinforced by his distrust and dislike of the judiciary. After the Reichstag fire trial, Hitler's anger with the criminal justice system became virtually uncontrolled. He wanted a radical purging of the legal profession. Most of all, lawyers had to learn to put the common good above the individual good. He was opposed to juries and wanted judges who would pass harsh sentences that would serve the interests of the nation. He established new courts, the Special Courts and the People's Court, which in time became instruments of terror. Absurdly, he wanted Nordic judges rather than judges of other races.[45] Hitler was particularly angered by the procedural slowness of civil law and the mild sentences passed by the criminal courts. This is in stark contrast to the 32,000 death sentences passed in civilian and military courts during the twelve years of the regime.

Göring and the Minister of the Interior, Wilhelm Frick, set out to create a bureaucracy and a police force on which Hitler could depend. The first move the regime made was the massive purge of the higher bureaucracy, and particularly the upper echelon of the police. All Jews, social democrats, communists, and persons who were suspect of opposing the regime were removed. Göring established the first political secret police in Prussia (the Gestapa, which later became incorporated into the Gestapo). The Law for the Protection of the Reich enabled Göring to use brutal methods with little restraining control. The SA and the SS cooperated with Göring's Prussian police and set up wild concentration camps in which many political prisoners were murdered or treated with extreme cruelty. At the time Göring seized control of the Prussian police, Heinrich Himmler became Police President of Munich. Göring's police force remained part of the State Executive, but Himmler's was a special police force organized under his command as the Reichsführer SS—which meant outside the still prevailing laws of the state. His second-in-command was the cold technocrat Reinhard Heydrich, in charge of the security service (Sicherheitsdienst, or SD) of the SS, later in the Reich Security Main Office. At first Himmler was accountable to both Göring and Röhm, Supreme Leader of the SA. After the elimination of the SA as a potent force, for a short time Himmler remained still accountable to Göring, but soon all criminal, and political security forces—as well as a vast surveillance service extending into every organization, town, village, and virtually every household—were under Himmler's command. Himmler and Heydrich provided Hitler with a formidable instrument of control and power.

Heinrich Himmler grew up in a conservative Catholic family. His father was a middle school teacher, and much of the schoolmaster in Himmler can be traced to an identification with his father. Himmler volunteered to serve in World War I but saw no front service. After his discharge, he studied agriculture and operated a chicken farm; later this interest in breeding and killing chickens was transferred to the breeding and killing of humans. On the basis of a diary that Himmler kept during adolescence, Loewenberg concluded that Himmler was schizoid and compulsive, inclined to deny feelings.[46] He became a member of the free corps Reichsflagge, but had no close contact with Hitler until the mid-twenties. After he became Reichsführer SS in 1929, he organized Hitler's elite bodyguards into the SS according to strict racial principles. The bespectacled man with a receding chin differed markedly from the ideal Aryans he recruited into the SS. Himmler was superstitious, believed in astrology, and maintained mythical ideas about the old *Germanen*, which Hitler belittled. He was hypochondriacal, and tried to cure his stomach pains through medicinal herbs and the employment of a Finnish masseur, Felix Kersten. Yet Himmler was an indefatigable, capable, and ambitious organizer who in time developed the SS into a very powerful organization. He created an industrial empire under SS control within the concentration camps and formed the Waffen SS, against the wishes of army leadership, as an integral part of Germany's armed forces. With Hitler as the ultimate authority, Himmler and Heydrich were the principal organizers of the genocide of the Jews, Gypsies, and Slavs. In 1943, Himmler developed doubts about Hitler, not only about his chances of winning the war, but also about his qualities as a leader. He told his masseur he had learned that Hitler suffered from a syphilitic brain disease, general paresis.[47] Data to substantiate this have never been found, and the assumption that Hitler had general paresis can be dismissed (see Chapter 8). Until April 1945, weeks before his death, Hitler considered Himmler an absolutely faithful vassal, living by the motto of the SS, "Our honor is fidelity." Hitler had a high opinion of Himmler's ability, even though he did not consider him a potential successor because he was not an artistic person.[48] Two weeks before Germany's surrender, without Hitler's knowledge, Himmler contacted a Swedish emissary, Count Bernadotte, in a completely unrealistic peace feeler. In a fit of rage, Hitler expelled him from the Party and stripped him of all offices. Himmler committed suicide after he was captured by British troops.

Propaganda and the Führer Myth

Hans Ulrich Thamer has aptly given his Hitler biography the subtitle "Seduction and Force" (*Verführung und Gewalt*).[49] Hitler's keen interest in political propaganda was a continuation of his interest in propaganda during World War I, and National Socialist propaganda became the prototype of the big lie. Hitler put his best men in charge of propaganda, first Gregor Strasser and later Strasser's assistant, Joseph Goebbels, who developed into a genius of vicious propaganda. There has been controversy as to whether Hitler or Goebbels was the true spirit of National Socialist propaganda. Hitler concerned himself with propaganda a long time before the unsuccessful writer Joseph Goebbels had even thought about it. When Hitler made Goebbels Minister of Propaganda, he provided him with a huge budget but retained ultimate control. Goebbels had to contend with other powerful personalities within the Third Reich who controlled propaganda within their various domains: von Ribbentrop in foreign affairs and Otto Dietrich in the press. When it came to conflict, Hitler was the ultimate authority, particularly when he rejected Goebbels's attempt to extend his propaganda activities into the Wehrmacht. Goebbels, however, was very useful to Hitler with his broad grasp of propaganda and effective use of film, theater, radio, art, the liturgy and rituals of the National Socialist state, and, last but not least, seductive and powerful slogans. Goebbels was inventive in altering language, inventing powerfully seductive slogans, and replacing negative connotations with positive connotations—for example, the word "relocation" (*Umsiedlung*) became the term designating deportation to death camps.

Hitler's power was enhanced by what became known as the Hitler myth.[50] It is a variant of the cult of personality that has been associated with leaders throughout the history of mankind, during modern times particularly with Mao, Mussolini, and Stalin, but also with democratic leaders—Charles de Gaulle, Winston Churchill, Franklin D. Roosevelt, John F. Kennedy, and Ronald Reagan, to name a few—not to forget Pope John XXIII and Pope John Paul. In democracies, critical counter-forces help to correct the myth. Essentially, it is an unrealistic, in some cases pseudo-religious glorification of a beloved or feared leader by his subjects. It involves a gross overestimation of the leader's qualities—in the minds of his subjects the leader becomes omnipotent and omniscient, all-loving or able to destroy his and his country's enemies. The leader becomes a prophet, a hero, a savior, a destroyer. In many statements, Hitler eagerly emphasized his heroic qualities as a leader. He considered courage a sublime virtue and cowardice a despicable trait. He portrayed himself and was viewed by others as a man who lived only for his country, who sacrificed himself for it. Hitler believed that a leader must be different from the masses.[51] While many of his associates (e.g. Göring) were showing off their uniforms and decorations, Hitler remained deliberately simple in dress—which, however, served to enhance his stature. Another part of the Führer myth was a falsification and aggrandizement of life data. Hitler supplied such legends about his life in *Mein Kampf* and other publications, as well as in the monologues, thus contributing to the legend. The process of self-glorification began at the onset of his political career and was enhanced during his trial and prison sentence (many revolutionary leaders boast about a crucial period of imprisonment),[52] but the real beginning of the Hitler cult can be traced to his successful campaigns in 1930 and 1932, when thousands waited for their Führer—God-like—descending from the sky during his electioneering flights.[53]

A significant number of Germans not only respected and admired but loved him as well, and this constituted the basis of the Hitler cult. It was truly the overestimation of the love object, an apt Freudian term, that enabled Hitler to view himself and present himself as a superman and a charismatic leader. The Führer myth increased with each major expansion, each foreign policy success. The annexation of Austria and the Sudetenland produced an enormous increase in Hitler's prestige and reputation. In contrast to the dismay the Western world began to feel about Hitler, the Germans' enthusiasm for the Führer was expressed in a gigantic celebration on Hitler's fiftieth birthday. The outbreak of the war, according to Kershaw, created more anxiety than enthusiasm. A last high was attained after the defeat of France on 16 July 1940. It was the day of Hitler's famous jig—actually trick photography—at Compiègne. The Führer myth began to wane after the disastrous winter campaign of 1941/42, and particularly after the destruction of Hitler's Sixth Army at Stalingrad. But, it never disappeared entirely.

The effect of the Führer myth on the Germans and on Hitler cannot be overestimated, even though he expressed annoyance at overt flattery. As the years went by, Hitler himself believed more and more in the myth that he and his followers had created. He needed the myth to counter his own feelings of inadequacy and inferiority, as much as he denied such feelings. Essentially, Hitler believed he fulfilled the wishes and desires of his people—which to a certain degree was correct. He had an uncanny sensitivity for the needs of Germans in times of national distress. But he went even further, viewing himself as an instrument of history, of fate, and ultimately of a divine creator whose wishes he fulfilled—in short, as a charismatic leader destined to lead the masses who believed in him. As he was never sure of such a role of absolute greatness, he felt compelled to move on to ever riskier tasks to prove himself and his worth.

The outstanding pictorial document of the Führer myth is a film called *Triumph of the Will*, produced by Leni Riefenstahl.[54] Hitler is the central person in this picture. The film begins with the descent of the Führer's airplane from the clouds, a union of the Führer with hundreds of thousands of participants and their absolute devotion to him. It is a fascinating depiction of the power of the movement. Naturally, it omits all negative aspects of Hitler and his regime. When the film was shown over and over again in the movie houses of Germany, it greatly enhanced the myth of National Socialist Germany and its Führer.

Hitler's Mission

Hitler's goals and ideas were extreme, and ultimately utopian, millenary. They were expressed before him, but in their synthesis they were novel. The supreme concept for Hitler was race. He considered the Germans to have the optimal, predominantly Nordic mixture of races. Therefore, the Germans should establish European hegemony and ultimately rule the world. A popular Nazi slogan was, "Today Germany, tomorrow the world." Hitler's economic achievements, such as the abolition of unemployment, the military buildup, and elimination of the last vestiges of the Treaty of Versailles, were just preliminary steps on the way to his real goal. In the National Socialist society, the individual had to subordinate his needs to the collective need. National Socialist society was to be run by an elite group of the best (i.e., the strongest) men, above whom stood the best (the strongest) of all, the Führer. With rare exceptions, only men of the Germanic races and married women could obtain full citizenship. Citizens were expected to be competitive in their endeavors for the benefit of society, to be loyal to the Führer, and to develop a spirit of cooperation. Allied nations with people of Nordic–Germanic blood were expected to develop a similar philosophy and programs, although Hitler remarked that National Socialism was not for export.[55] Because the Germans did not possess the resources necessary for their survival, they would have to obtain these resources from other nations, and if the other nations were not willing to give up resources, the Germans would acquire them through war. Inferior races in Eastern Europe and Africa would have to be subjugated to a slave-like existence. To enable the Germans to improve their racial qualities, they would be subjected to educational and legal measures to refrain from mixing with inferior races. Improvement of the race would also be achieved through proper breeding and sterilization or killing of undesirable, weak or sick members. Many might die through wars or racial hygienic measures, but it would be in the service of a good cause. There was, however, as Sebastian Haffner, put it, one race that was the spoiler in this merry game: the international, capitalist, and communist Jew.[56] Although the Jewish race or nation also wanted to rule the world, it lacked the creative ability to build a state and would eventually destroy the state as well as itself. To avert this danger, Jews had to be prevented from mixing with members of the Nordic–Germanic race and had to be removed by forced emigration or expulsion or, if this was opportune or necessary, eliminated by murder. According to Hitler, this was all based on insights derived from history and the natural sciences.

The Sterilization Law

The significance of the sterilization law for Hitler's program can be deduced from the fact that it was one of the earliest acts. Hitler considered the sterilization law and the euthanasia activities (the latter never became legal) to be extremely important measures. On 14 July 1933, the Law for the Prevention of the Generation of the Genetically Ill, in short, the sterilization law, was established. According to the leader of the medical profession, Dr. Gerhard Wagner, it formed the basis of the "purpose of the state" for National Socialism.[57] The law stipulated compulsory sterilization by surgical procedure for genetically ill persons in cases when, according to medical science, it was highly probable that any offspring would suffer from severe genetic mental and physical illness. The qualifying diagnostic categories were congenital mental deficiency, schizophrenia, manic-depressive psychosis, hereditary epilepsy, hereditary blindness or deafness, Huntington's chorea, chronic alcoholism, mental impairment due to late syphilis (even though therapies already existed to treat such impairment), and various congenital and hereditary malformations. The sterilization of habitual criminals—particularly those convicted of sexual crimes—was included, and in some of these cases the medical procedure was castration rather than sterilization. Physicians were required to report cases warranting sterilization, whereupon a genetic advisory board, after examining the patient and medical records, decided whether sterilization should occur. If so, the procedure was carried out within a period of two weeks. Sterilization was practiced in other nations as well, but nowhere on the scale it occurred in Nazi Germany. Altogether between 1933 and 1939, approximately 350,000 persons were sterilized—0.5 percent of the population, compared with 11,000 sterilized in the United states between 1907 and 1930.[58]

Another law serving the genetic prevention of mental illness was the Law for the Protection of the Genetic Health of the German People, a marital health statute establishing that only healthy people would be permitted to get married. Apart from the negative measures undertaken within the sterilization law, National Socialism emphasized "positive" measures such as requiring every married SS man to have at least four children and promoting *Operation Lebensborn* (translated "source of life"), which "facilitated" the breeding of healthy offspring by healthy German men and unmarried women. (Some 11,000 births resulted.) Hitler was strictly opposed to having children of his own, pointing to monarchs and noblemen with degenerate offspring.[59] Bormann's recommendation of polygamy to produce more children was followed by Bormann himself but "officially" by few others. During the war, the "Germanization" of racially desirable orphans from the Eastern territories was carried out by bringing them to Germany for "adoption." A vast system of genetic education and genetic research was created, with the purpose of furthering the development of the Germanic superman and the prevention of genetic degeneration. None ever became genetically significant.[60] Yet sterilization was greeted by the majority of lawyers and physicians as a desirable measure. Only weak spiritual opposition was expressed by the Protestant and Catholic churches. Originally, sterilization was a racially neutral procedure, but during the war German scientists carried out research on mass sterilization of undesirable races—that is, Jews and Gypsies.

Eugenics and racial hygiene were not the invention of the Nazis. A vast literature had developed beginning in the middle of the nineteenth century, based on the work of stellar scientists Charles Darwin, Jean Baptiste Lamarck, and Gregor Mendel, as well as lesser luminaries such as Cesare Lombroso. Until the second half of the current century, more heat than light has been produced by a host of investigators, and the general controversy regarding nature versus nurture in man remained undecided. In Germany, biologist Alfred Ploetz took a strong anti-environmental view that was followed by his students who wrote a widely read book on human genetics that became the bible of Nazi geneticists.[61] The basic psychiatric contributions leading to the law on sterilization procedures were supplied by Ernst Rüdin. At present, it can be said with certainty that the sterilization program of 1933 with respect to schizophrenia, manic-depressive psychosis, epilepsy, chronic alcoholism, and many genetic illnesses was not justified on scientific grounds. The only exceptions would have been voluntary sterilization procedures or cases of rare diseases with a homozygotic form of transmission, such as Huntington's chorea. Hitler was eager to get support for his racist ideas from scientists. One supporter of the sterilization program was the eminent ethologist Konrad Lorenz, who after the war received the Nobel Prize. Lorenz, who was not an anti-Semite, held strong convictions about the degeneration of modern man, particularly within urban environments. As natural selection does not work, according to Lorenz, selection by the state was justified. Lorenz also believed that racial mixtures lead to decline.[62] After the fall of the Third Reich, Lorenz considered his earlier views naive.[63] The support of scientists such as Lenz and Lorenz, however, helped Hitler and his men tout the phrase, "National Socialism is nothing but applied biology."[64] Much earlier, in *Mein Kampf*, Hitler had written:

> It is a half measure to let incurably sick people steadily contaminate the remaining healthy ones. This is in keeping with the humanitarianism which, to avoid hurting one individual, lets a hundred others perish. The demand

that defective people be prevented from propagating equally defective off-spring is a demand of the clearest reason and, systematically executed, it represents the most humane act of mankind. It will spare millions of unfortunates undeserved suffering and consequently will lead to a rising improvement of health as a whole. The determination to proceed in this direction will oppose [sic; should be "pose"] a dam to the further spread of venereal diseases. For if necessary the incurably sick will be pitilessly segregated—a barbaric measure for the unfortunate who is struck by it, but a blessing for his fellow men and posterity. The passing pains of a century can and will redeem millenniums from suffering.[65]

Hitler also assumed links between defects and the mixture of races:

[it was necessary] . . . to see to it that the blood is preserved pure, and by preserving the best humanity to create the possibility of a nobler development of that being. . . . Therefore, a folkish state must begin by elevating marriage and giving it the consecration of an institution that is called upon to produce images of the Lord and not monstrosities between man and ape.[66]

Two pages later:

Those who are physically and mentally unhealthy and unworthy must not perpetuate their suffering in the body of their children. In this the folkish state must perform the most gigantic educational task. And some day this will seem to be a greater deed than the most victorious wars of our present bourgeois era. By education it must teach the individual that it is no disgrace, but only a misfortune deserving of pity, to be sick and weakly, but that it is a crime and hence at the same time a disgrace to dishonor one's misfortune by one's own egotism in burdening innocent creatures with it; that by comparison it bespeaks a nobility of highest idealism and the most admirable humanity if the innocently sick, renouncing a child of his own, bestows his love and tenderness upon a poor, unknown young scion of his own nationality, who with his health promises to become some day a powerful member of a powerful community. And in this educational work the state must perform the purely intellectual complement of its practical activity. It must act in this sense without regard to understanding or lack of understanding, approval or disapproval.[67]

On 30 January 1934, when Hitler reviewed the achievements of the first year of the regime, he talked about the importance of sterilization for the health of the nation, emphasizing the economic factor with regard to unwarranted expenses for the nation, already anticipating step one of the euthanasia program:

It is a great merit of the National Socialist movement that already in the past year by legislation the first attack on the threatening slow decline of the people was made. When, especially from the clerical side, concerns over such legislation were expressed, the legislation was opposed, I want to say the following: It would be more useful, honest, and most of all Christian in the past centuries not to side with those who deliberately destroyed healthy life than to mutiny against those who want nothing else except to prevent illness.

Furthermore, the permissiveness in this matter is not only cruelty against the individual innocent victims, but cruelty against the totality of the people. If this development would continue, like in the last hundred years, the number of those requiring public care would threaten to reach the number of the ones who are the only providers for the community.

It is not the churches who feed these unfortunates, but the people. If the churches are ready to take the genetically ill under their care and protection, we are glad to dispense with sterilization. As long as the state is damned to supply from its citizens yearly increasing sums—which in Germany already surpass the sum of 350 million Reichsmark—for the maintenance of the regrettably genetically ill of the nation, then it is forced to provide in such remedy which prevents in the future undeserved suffering, but also prevents that millions of healthy persons are deprived of essentials in order to artificially keep millions of unhealthy alive.[68]

In 1937, the number of sterilizations began to decline. It is likely that Hitler and the regime lost interest because they were in a hurry to show results, and any tangible effects of the program (even in homozygotic genetic diseases) would not be discernible for a long time. Many of the clinicians and geneticists who recommended the procedures knew this. Another possibility is that Hitler's interest shifted to a more radical program: the euthanasia program, or the elimination of genetically defective persons and other undesirables. In 1935 Hitler informed the leader of the German physicians, Dr. Gerhard Wagner, that the euthanasia program could be carried out only in case of war.[69] A war would make it plausible to stipulate that scarce resources (i.e., food and medical facilities) be preserved, and that "useless eaters" be killed and medical facilities emptied and used in the service of the war.[70]

Hitler and the Jews in the Third Reich before World War II

The establishment of the Führerstaat created the conditions for gradually realizing the anti-Semitic programs Hitler proposed in *Mein Kampf*, the second book, and many speeches and articles. The persecution of the Jews started shortly after the empowerment law. On 30 March 1933, Hitler supported a "spontaneous" boycott against Jewish stores. The party called it a protest and a warning to Jews in foreign countries because of their hostility against Germany. It was followed only half-heartedly by the German population. Schacht, charged with the program for economic recovery, objected to the measure because a foreign boycott would interfere with his economic recovery plan. Hitler relented, and the boycott was called off. The first anti-Jewish act of legislation was the Law for the Restoration of Public Employees on 7 April 1933. It introduced the *"Arierparagraph,"* stipulating that Jews could not be employed as public servants. The law pertained only to the Reich but was quickly adhered to by the states and municipalities. Victims, who were discharged or pensioned, included not only lawyers and administrative personnel, but also teachers in all institutions of learning, physicians, dentists, and performing artists. President von Hindenburg objected that the law covered veterans of the First World War, as well as children or parents of veterans, but Hitler paid no attention to the old man's objections. After von Hindenburg's death, no Jew remained in public office except for those who were aryanised. Later, even Jews with combat service and decorations rarely benefited from any privileges, and some were exterminated.*

Two factions of anti-Semites existed within the NSDAP leadership. The more radical faction—including Goebbels, Himmler, and Heydrich—wanted to eliminate and restrict Jews without being hampered by legislation. The second faction favored legislation and a slower course. Schacht and some of the jurists in the ministries (e.g., Bernhard Loesener) belonged to the second group. Because Hitler did not want to be hampered by any restraining regulations, it was a surprise that he put regulation of the Jewish question on the agenda for the "Party Congress of Honor" in the fall of 1935. It is possible that he did it at that time because the congress program was meager. It contained only one other legislative item, the Reich Flag Law, and needed to be fattened up. Bureaucrats from the ministries were hastily called in and worked long hours to present Hitler and his advisors from the party with acceptable solutions. One of them, Dr. Bernhard Loesener from the Ministry of the Interior, felt some sympathy for the threatened group but quickly realized that nothing could be done on behalf of full Jews and attempted to alleviate the lot of half- and quarter-Jews. Among Hitler's advisors, the Reichsärzteführer, Gerhard Wagner favored treating all Jews and persons of Jewish descent alike, barring them from marriage with Aryans and sterilizing their offspring. After frantically working on the question of half- and quarter-Jews, Loesener, through his Minister of the Interior, Wilhelm Frick, presented Hitler with several proposals. Hitler first accepted the more lenient version, but later reversed himself.[71]

According to the Law for the Protection of German Blood, established on 14 November 1936, Jews were defined as descendants from three or four Jewish grandparents, or from two Jewish grandparents if they belonged to the Jewish religion or were married to Jews. A person of mixed racial (Aryan and Jewish) origin (*Mischling* of the first degree) was defined as a person with one Jewish grandparent, a *Mischling* of the second degree from two Jewish grandparents. These definitions were quite unsatisfactory from a racial

---

* One exception was Dr. Edouard Bloch, physician of Hitler's mother, who was permitted to emigrate without severe molestation. The opposite example comes from the author's own family. His cousin, Robert Eisner, who had been a captain in the Austro-Hungarian army and was decorated for bravery, died in Auschwitz. A black joke circulated about Jews wearing their war medals at that time: Goldberg asked Grünbaum, "Why do you wear the decoration for bravery?" Grünbaum replied, "Because I am scared."

point of view because they ultimately relied on the concept of religion and not race. The new law considered extramarital sexual intercourse between Aryans and Jews a crime. One sub-section forbade any Aryan woman under the age of forty-five to work in a Jewish household, a relatively minor point in which Hitler was particularly interested. Hitler also expressed the opinion that women who engaged in intercourse with Jews should not be prosecuted as drastically as males,[72] but Heydrich, who disagreed with his Führer on this point, sent them to concentration camps anyway. Besides the Law for the Protection of German Blood and Honor, the Reich Citizenship Law (*Reichsbürgergesetz*) was established concurrently. Through this legislation a Jew could be not a *Reichsbürger*, but a *Staatsbürger* (a second-class citizen), unable to vote or to display the German flag. When these two laws were established, many Jews believed that they provided a new and stable order under which they could live, in preference to an uncertain fate in emigration. During 1936, the year of the Olympic Games in Berlin, anti-Semitism was put on a back burner because the Third Reich wanted to impress visitors from all over the world with its vitality and not its brutality. Behind the scenes, however, anti-Semitism increased, and Jews were subjected to ever-increasing harassment.

The anti-Semitic excesses in Austria after Hitler's occupation in 1938 exceeded anything that had happened before in Germany. Rare exceptions occurred, including the aryanization of Jews who were considered useful to the regime and a few cases when high officials intervened. An event that triggered a vicious pogrom on 9/10 November 1938 was the murder of a German diplomat, Ernst von Rath, by Herschel Grynszpan, a Jew whose parents had been deported from Germany to Poland. Von Rath was shot in Paris on 7 November 1938 and died on the 9th. That night, ninety-one Jews were murdered, most of the synagogues went up in flames, thousands of Jewish stores were destroyed and looted, and innumerable windowpanes were broken—earning the pogrom the name *Kristallnacht* or "Crystal Night."[73] Hitler and the Nazi leadership were assembled in Munich to celebrate the anniversary of the putsch when they learned from Goebbels about the incident and the "spontaneous" retaliatory actions that had been taken against Jews in some communities. Otto Dietrich, Hitler's press chief, stated that he had been present when the Führer told Goebbels to let things take their course.[74] Goebbels spoke in Hitler's place and told the Gauleiter who were present that the party should neither organize nor prevent retaliatory actions. This was a clear signal to stage a "wild" pogrom. Himmler criticized the power-hungry Goebbels for his "empty-headedness" in initiating such an action at a politically sensitive moment (the Czech crisis). The enormous material damage represented a serious insurance problem. The pogrom was carried out by members of the SA, first in uniform, then in civilian clothes, and by the criminal fringe population that always participates in lootings. The foreign press was severely critical. Hitler had a private discussion with Göring and Goebbels, followed by a session with the ministers on 12 November 1938 under the chairmanship of Göring, to establish damage control. It is not known whether Göring or Goebbels advanced the idea of letting the Jews take care of the cost for the insurance and pay 1.2 billion Reichsmark—confiscating one-fifth of their income—as a fine for Rath's murder. In the boisterous session of the ministers (during which participants delighted in the humiliation inflicted on the Jews), it was resolved to saddle the Jews with further severe restrictions: They were not to use public swimming pools or parks, their travel on railroads was restricted, and their ability to make a living was severely curtailed. The SS detained 20,000 Jews in concentration camps to "motivate" them to emigrate. Only a few had the desire to stay, but it became difficult to find countries where they would be received, a fact that Hitler did not fail to notice. In February 1939, the party court, chaired by Walter Buch, Bormann's father-in-law, stated in a secret memorandum that the oral instructions of the Reich Propaganda Minister had, in all likelihood, been understood by all present party leaders as implying that the Party must not be perceived on the outside as the organizer of the demonstration. The Party court acquitted all murderers and punished only a few rapists for *Rassenschande* (sexual relations between Aryans and Jews). It has been established that Hitler did not direct the pogrom or the following degradation but gave Goebbels and the party the green light to proceed with it. Hitler never tried to prevent it and agreed with the decision not to punish the criminals. Goebbels had the gall to say in his diary on 12 November 1938 that the Jews ought to be grateful to him.[75]

On 30 January 1939, a little over two months after the *Kristallnacht*, while preparations for the invasion of the crippled Czech republic were on Hitler's mind, as part of a long speech before the Reichstag Hitler threatened the Jews with extinction if they started a war:

> I have been a prophet many times in my life, and usually people laughed about me. In the days of struggle for power, it was primarily the Jewish people who laughed about my prophesies that someday I would assume leadership of the state and people and then also, amongst other things, would solve the Jewish problem. I believe that the once loud laughter of the German Jews has ended with a croak in their throats. [Hitler became extremely angered when he was not taken seriously or was made the target of derision.]
>
> Today I want to be a prophet again: If international finance Jewry in and outside of Europe should again succeed in pushing the peoples into a world war, the result will not be the Bolshevization of the earth and hence a victory for Jewry, but rather the destruction of the Jewish race in Europe.[76]

Gleichschaltung *of Education*

National Socialism was a movement of the young. At the time Hitler seized power, he was forty-four, Goebbels thirty-six, Göring forty, Hess thirty-nine, and Himmler thirty-three. Gregor Strasser's statement, "Make room you oldies, (*Macht Platz ihr Alten*)," well reflected Hitler's ideas.[77] Hitler strongly believed only the young can be educated to become "good national social-ists." To Hitler, education meant first and foremost indoctrination in the spirit of National Socialism. He put training in physical education first, char-acter training second, and general education third.[78] Physical training was important, first, because it was a prerequisite for military training and, sec-ond, because it would restore beauty and help two beautiful bodies find each other, thus preventing the seduction of hundreds of thousands of girls by repulsive Jewish bastards.[79] Hitler worried that "excessive emphasis upon purely intellectual development . . . leads to the premature onset of sexual imaginings, which might lead young men to prostitutes and contracting syphilis."[80]

It is interesting that Hitler stressed physical education so strongly, because he himself was disinclined to engage in active sports. At no time can one detect any active interest in physical exercise on Hitler's part, except as a middle school student, when Hitler earned high marks in gymnastics. After entering politics, he no longer engaged in active sports. He claimed he had been a good skier in his youth. This is unlikely, but he might have skied on a hillock in Steyr in 1905. At that time, skiing was an exclusive sport. Later, he opposed skiing for adults in responsible positions, as in the case of Furtwan-gler or Speer, because it was too dangerous.[81] Nobody ever saw him swim as an adult, and he expressed criticism of Mussolini, who was seen in swimming trunks on a beach. Hitler never got on a horse and never stepped into row-boats. He remained disinterested in team sports, even soccer, Germany's most popular sport, but he had an interest in boxing and received Schmeling, the German heavy-weight champion, even after he was knocked out—to Hitler's great dismay—by the black American champion Joe Louis. Hitler's only physical workouts were expander exercises that enabled him to endure taking the German greeting with an outstretched arm during the endless parades.[82] His interest in spectator sports, particularly martial sports, was politically motivated. He used the Olympic games as a forum for demon-strating himself to the visitors as a benign leader and Nazi Germany as a civi-lized country. According to Hitler, the most important goals of character education were the soldierly virtues of loyalty, obedience, courage, and will-ingness to bring sacrifices for the common good. A household saying described the Nazis' ideal qualities for a German boy: fast as a grayhound, tough as leather, and hard as Krupp steel. In contrast to the ideal of the mar-tial superman that was applied for males, for women the goals remained tra-ditional: to become a mother and care for the family.[83] Hitler's ultimate edu-cational goal was far-reaching and extraordinarily ambitious: He wanted to create a new man, a National Socialist German, and he believed that this was possible, although not through the schools.

Hitler's ideas about the deficiencies of traditional education were shaped by his own experiences with schools and teachers. He never lived down his dismal performance in middle school and blamed the system and the teachers for this experience. As an adult, Hitler continued to berate and belittle teach-ers and their methods with scathing irony, yet a generation of teachers comprised his greatest admirers. On 29 August 1942, maintaining that the majority of his own teachers had been mentally disturbed, Hitler let go about teachers and made the following statement:

> The professors are "buttock-drummers" and will always be that. A real person does not start for 30 years with the abc's. With a woman that's possible. Whenever she has a child it starts all over. There never has been one professor who was creative except Felix Dahn.[84] Imagine a man who teaches French for 30 years. It used to be that the stupid credentials were decisive throughout the whole life. Read my credentials. I had bad grades in German. This idiot of a professor spoiled the German language for me, this ignoramus, this little dwarf. I would never be able to write a letter. Imagine with a five [the lowest grade] given to me by this cretin, I could never have become an engineer. Now, thank God, we have the Hitler Youth, and the other side of the boys can be judged. There one can judge the capacity for leadership. A boy must have the opportunity for that.[85]

Some of Hitler's ideas about education were common-sense ideas, such as building a more specific education on the basis of a broad general education. He considered the teaching in public schools to be stultifying, opposed overloading the young brain with rote data, and recommended the teaching of broad principles. This is in curious contrast to the fact that he himself crammed data about gun calibers and ship tonnages just to impress his audiences during staff conferences and monologues. He accepted the importance of teaching mathematics, physics, and chemistry because these were important in a technical society. For Hitler, history was a most important subject.[86] In history, he demanded that the principles of racial struggles be taught, not social and economic conflicts.[87] The study of history must help the student learn to understand German greatness and superiority. The study of history must set the purity of race in the center of all life.[88] Hitler insisted that only those who had talent should be educated. It was "criminal lunacy to keep on drilling a half-born ape until people think they have made a lawyer out of him.[89]" In keeping with his xenophobia, he was opposed to the teaching of foreign languages: It would overload the brain. The classical *Gymnasium* was downgraded, although Hitler recognized the value of teaching Latin to understand the structure of European languages. He never had the opportunity to study Latin or Greek; they were not taught in the *Realschule*. To Hitler's frustration, except for the downgrading of the classical *Gymnasium*, elementary and middle schools had only small changes in their basic curricula during the Third Reich. He blamed this on his own Minister of Education, Dr. Bernhard Rust, a bitter foe of Baldur von Schirach, head of the Hitler Youth. Most important, after 1933 "racial science" was a compulsory subject in the schools.

Changes in the universities and institutions of higher learning were massive. One-third of university teachers, including an appreciable number of Aryans, were dismissed.[90] Hitler professed that National Socialism was based on science.[91] In reality, however, he did not appreciate the scientific method and its slow, critical testing of hypotheses. He was interested in results that would promote German technology, particularly in its preparation for and conduct of the war. He was also eager to receive confirmation for his ideas about eugenics, racial hygiene, sterilization, euthanasia, and, ultimately, genocide—which he received, to an appalling degree, from National Socialist scientists in newly established and lavishly supported departments of anthropology and genetics. In the sciences and humanities, whenever no conflict with National Socialist doctrine existed, the level of German education remained high because much talent remained in Germany. In some fields, however, particularly in physics, the loss was serious. Many of the most eminent physicists from fascist countries—including Albert Einstein, Edward J. Teller, and Enrico Fermi—emigrated to the United States and Great Britain. One victim of Nazi intolerance was psychoanalysis. Most German and Austrian analysts were Jews and emigrated, but a few remained and were able to revive psychoanalysis in Germany after the war. Oddly, they received some protection from a cousin of Hermann Göring, the Commissioner of Psychotherapy, Dr. Matthias Göring.

Hitler's antidote to the stultifying school system was the Hitler Youth, along with the League of German Girls. For Hitler these were the organizations that would fulfill what he hoped and struggled for, more than just the vindication of old resentments against school and parental authority. In May 1935 the number of Hitler Youth members was 70,000; in 1939 it was 7,000,000. This growth was partly due to the outlawing of most rival youth groups.[92] The slogan was "The young should be led by the young." This was the organization where "reeducation" (*Umerziehung*) would take place, where a new human being would be created. Hitler Youth was more than an organization; it was a movement in which many members were proudly aware of their identification with Hitler, not in name only, and Hitler identified with them. It was the organization that supplied leaders and teachers and future leaders for the SS as well as the cannon fodder for the *Waffen* SS. In one of his last photographs, a sick Hitler honored some Hitler Youth, almost children, for their willingness to die for him. An elite of the Hitler Youth was destined to be trained in the NAPOLA (*Nationalpolitische Erziehungsanstalten* or National Socialist political schools) and the *Ordensburgen* (the universities of National Socialism). As Hitler cynically described:

> This youth does not learn anything but to think German, act German, and when these boys and girls enter our organization at ten and for the first time breathe fresh air, they enter the Hitler Youth four years later and we keep them for four years. And then, we don't return them to the old class and status ideologists, but we take them into the Party, the Arbeitsfront, the SA, or SS, into NSKK, etc. And after they are there for two years or a year and a half, they come to the labor service and will be polished by their symbol, the German spade. And what is present of class consciousness or status arrogance the *Wehrmacht* will continue to treat for two years and when they

return after two, three, or four years, in order to prevent relapses, again into the SA, SS, etc., and they won't be free for the rest of their lives.[93]

These National Socialist institutions never became what their chief proponents, Hitler, Himmler, von Schirach, and Ley, had in mind. The ultimate defeat, and an element in youth itself, a craving for independence, prevented this goal.

Baldur von Schirach (1907–1974) was the first leader of the Hitler Youth. His father was theater director in Weimar, his mother an American. Von Schirach became a National Socialist in 1925 and attracted Hitler's attention after he organized the National Socialist student movement with phenomenal success and, later, the Hitler Youth. He can be described as a fanatic-romantic Nazi. He understood the need of youth for romantic ideals, composing odes and even prayers to Hitler as well as slogans such as "Leader, we follow" and "Your will is our creed." Although von Schirach called the Hitler Youth the soldiers of the future, he was less interested in the military functions of the organization than Hitler. The stalwart Nazi leaders ridiculed von Schirach for his effeminate traits, and in 1940 he was replaced by the more militant Arthur Axmann and became Gauleiter of Vienna. As Gauleiter, Hitler believed, von Schirach became intrigued with the Viennese.[94] While Hitler had been infatuated with von Schirach at first, he turned harshly against him, undoubtedly influenced by Schirach's enemy Bormann. The story of von Schirach and his wife, Henriette (daughter of Hitler's photographer Heinrich Hoffmann), protesting against atrocities committed against Jews, which irritated Hitler and caused him to ban the Schirachs from his court, is probably overdrawn. Von Schirach was an anti-Semite who cooperated in the removal of 150,000 Jews from Vienna and knew about their fate. The Nuremberg High Military Court sentenced him to twenty years in prison.

Art and Architecture

Art meant a lot to Hitler. He saw himself as an artist and stated many times that he would rather have been an artist than a politician and military leader. He valued art, but it was German art alone Hitler wanted to further; he had little use for any other kind. Classical Greek and Roman art, which he appreciated, he considered variants of Germanic art. It was his strong and genuine concern with the arts that made his intolerance so devastating. The shameful book-burning that took place at many German universities on 10 May 1933 and the picture-burning on 20 March 1939 could not have happened without his nod of approval. It is mind-boggling to read Hitler's words of protest against the destruction of the libraries in antiquity by the Church.[95] Hitler believed he brought about a flowering of German art and literature. In fact, the opposite occurred, because art flowers only if it is free. German art, theater, film, and music withered during the Third Reich. They became, to varying degrees, provincial and mediocre. Hitler's taste in music and the fine arts was exceedingly conservative and intolerant.

Hitler's strongest artistic interest was architecture. Architects who worked with him—such as Paul Troost, Hermann Giesler, and Speer—recognized his talent and knowledge, not only of aesthetics but also of the technology of architecture. Hitler originally was deeply impressed by the neo-Baroque style of the pompous nineteenth-century buildings of the Viennese Ringstraße, but later, under the influence of Troost, he favored a neoclassical style that became the official style of the National Socialist buildings. This style, according to Hitler, symbolized the eternal character of National Socialism. This was also expressed by the nature of the materials that were used to construct the buildings: granite, limestone, and steel. Materials such as glass, concrete, and synthetics were considered foreign and degenerate. Modern trends in design such as those of the Bauhaus school were rejected. Hitler wanted to make Berlin the capital of the world, and its architecture was to symbolize that aim. To the end of his life, Hitler drew sketches of architectural projects. What characterized Hitler's architectural aims more than anything else was the megalomanic, monumental character of his building plans. For example, he planned to build a cupola of 300 meters for a congressional hall—much higher than the basilica of St. Peter, a church tower in Linz, higher than St. Stephen's in Vienna—and to construct buildings in Berlin larger than anywhere else in the world. Hitler wanted to erect "sacral–political" buildings, not banks and department stores. Of the gigantic buildings he planned, only the new Reichstag, the Reichskanzlei, and the building on the vast terrain in Nuremberg for the annual Party Congresses were completed. Innumerable other edifices, however, were constructed during the building mania between 1933 and 1939. More attractive work places and factories were built under the slogan of "Beauty of Work," but little was done about another Hitler project—building three- and four-room apartments for workers.

Hitler promoted monumental sculptures that were intended to complement the gigantic architectural achievements. The style was borrowed from the sculptures of Greco–Roman antiquity. One of Hitler's treasured possessions was a gift from Mussolini, a copy of the antique disc-thrower sculpture by Myron of Eleuthra from 450 B.C. As in architecture, the emphasis was on super-dimensional art. Sculptors such as Arno Breker and Josef Thorak were commissioned to produce oversized, muscular men, fertile and gracious women, heroic soldiers, peasants, and workers—similar to productions in the Soviet Union. Hitler himself acquired the conservative, super-dimensional, muscular sculptures of Josef Thorak and Arno Breker. Internationally recognized German sculptors like Georg Kolbe fell into line and produced objects that pleased the regime. Busts of Hitler, but not of other Nazi luminaries, became wholesale articles for adorning buildings and households.

In general, Hitler collected and appreciated paintings that were realistic and displayed good technique. His interest focused on Romantic German paintings of the nineteenth and early twentieth century, such as a favorite picture by Hans Makart, *The Plague in Florence*. Hitler loved the drawings of Adolf Menzel, a painter with an exquisite technique. Other favorites were the genre pictures of Rudolf von Alt, Eduard Grützner, and Carl Spitzweg. Among contemporaries, he appreciated the robust peasant types of Sepp Hilz and the voluptuous nudes of Franz von Stuck, with snakes coiling around them. According to Hanfstaengl, von Stuck was Hitler's favorite contemporary painter. Hitler had no use for modern abstract painting or sculpture, and vehemently rejected and forbade German expressionist painting, which he considered decadent. He viewed cubist art as an expression of insanity.[96] According to Henry Picker, Hitler bought the following paintings for the gallery he planned to establish in Linz: 8 Spitzweg, 4 Lenbach, 3 Stuck, 2 Feuerbach, 1 Cranach, 1 Canaletto, 1 Schwind, 1 Kaulbach [?], 1 Breughel, 1 Böcklin, 1 Defregger.[97] Buying often meant confiscating pictures owned by Jews or trading "degenerate" art for paintings he liked on the international art market. In France it was outright confiscation; the justification was the Nazi claim that Napoleon robbed Germany and such art had to be returned. The German plunder, however, by far exceeded what Napoleon stole.[98]

To call Hitler a prolific reader would be an understatement. He devoured books. He regularly read at night before falling asleep. His valet Linge described how Hitler opened his bedroom door a crack, appearing in a long white nightgown, and was handed a bundle of newspapers, resumes, and SD reports.[99] Hitler described how he read: He always read a book by looking first at the end, then a few passages in the middle, and only after he had gained a positive impression did he work through an entire book.[100] What he did not tell was which books he read in the original texts, and which he read in newspaper articles and as digests. His tastes were conventional. In the monologues, he listed a number of well-known international works: *Don Quixote, Robinson Crusoe, Uncle Tom's Cabin, Gulliver's Travels,* and also the work of Felix Dahn, not exactly a world-class author. He said he barely read German novels anymore except for Karl May.[101] May's books were loved by German children and adolescents, with his descriptions of brave native American Indians and trappers. Hitler claimed that he learned much about America and its geography from May's work. Hitler was fairly well acquainted with the Old and New Testaments. He read the scriptures systematically and hunted, together with his mentor Eckart, for citations that corroborated his anti-Semitic beliefs. It is likely that Hitler's reading from 1933 to 1945 was mostly confined to political and military texts.

Music comforted and inspired Hitler. He preferred operatic music and, most of all, ever since his youth, the operas of Richard Wagner. He supported the Wagner shrine at Bayreuth with large donations. He discounted Wagner's effeminacy and love of luxury. Possibly the appreciation of such effeminate traits made it possible for Hitler to accept his own passive needs. He continued making visits to Bayreuth and spoke of its sparkling beauty until it closed during the war, later than other theaters. Among the Wagner family, Hitler behaved in a more relaxed fashion than anywhere else. He liked Siegfried and felt close to Winifred, Siegfried's wife. However, for months he avoided the Wagners because Siegfried had fallen into the "hands of the Jews" and the Jewish baritone Friedrich Schorr was permitted to sing Wotan, to Hitler's annoyance.[102] Hitler also appreciated the music of Beethoven and Weber, and preferred the Upper Austrian Bruckner to Brahms, whom he considered a protégé of Jews. It seems Hitler had little appreciation of chamber music. About Richard Strauss, Germany's most eminent contemporary composer, Hitler and particularly Goebbels had negative feelings, because Strauss had refused to give shelter to displaced persons in his villa, yet Hitler refrained from attacking the ranking German musician. Hitler did not hesitate to assert his often trivial opinions about music. He remarked in the monologues, for instance, that the Mozart family was German, not Austrian, because they came from Augsburg.[103] Beethoven's compositions had an admixture of Slavic music, but Bach's was pure German. According to Hanfstaengl, Hitler had little understanding of Bach and Mozart.[104] Hitler also appreciated lighter musical fare. He liked Johann Strauss, but not his "effeminate" waltzes. Lehar's *Merry Widow* he saw as often as some Wagner operas. It is not certain whether Hitler was musical. He took piano lessons as a child and auditioned as a youngster for a choir in Vienna. Von Hasselbach, however, stated that he whistled melodies off-key.[105] His judgment about conductors was uninformed. He called Bruno Walter an absolute zero and maintained that he was praised by critics only because he was a Jew.[106]

In his youth, Hitler was an ardent theater-goer, but as Chancellor he found little time to attend performances. He became an avid movie fan. He watched movies privately, and together with Eva Braun often viewed double features. After the emigration of eminent film directors such as Fritz Lange, Max Reinhardt, Billy Wilder, and Josef von Sternberg, German movies had become less interesting, in spite of a reservoir of good actors. Hitler liked such internationally recognized German actors as Hans Albers, Gustaf Gründgens, and Emil Jannings, and the Swedish actress Greta Garbo. The elite of the Berghof preferred watching American movies rather than the less-than-mediocre German propaganda pictures such as *Hitler Junge Quex* or the anti-Semitic film *Jud Süß*. Hitler was attracted to movies with heroic themes, like *Lives of a Bengal Lancer* and *Viva Villa*, in which Wallace Beery portrayed the cruel Mexican revolutionary leader Pancho Villa.[107] Hitler liked local comedians such as Munich's celebrated Karl Valentin, whom he even permitted certain liberties in his jokes.[108] Hitler probably never saw Charlie Chaplin—whom his theater expert Ziegler described as a boring clown[109]—in *The Great Dictator* (one of Chaplin's great films, produced in 1940).

Hitler a Revolutionary Leader?

In several speeches Hitler expressed his belief that the National Socialist revolution was one of the most important revolutions in world history. At the annual Party Convention (Reichsparteitag) in September 1933, he stated that, except for the fascist revolution in Italy, no revolution had been carried out with greater inner discipline. Again on 14 October 1933, in a radio talk, he stressed the unbloody, disciplined character of his revolution as compared with the French revolution of 1789, and the Hungarian and Bavarian revolutions after World War I. Hitler was proud to point out that no windows had been broken.[110] (This had to wait until the *Kristallnacht* of November 1938.) Hitler took particular pride in noting that only 27 persons had died and 150 were injured. The truth, however, is that millions of people were killed by Nazis, not counting those who were casualties of war.

Hitler vacillated in his sentiments about the desirability of a revolution. He favored it before the putsch of November 1923, which he introduced with the awkward announcement, "I inform the audience that the German revolution has broken out." During the pseudo-legal phase after the putsch, Hitler warned of a revolution because the state had been too strong before the seizure of power. On 13 July 1934, after the massacre of the SA leadership and other opponents, Hitler declared, "The revolution for us is not a permanent condition. If in the natural evolution of a people, a lethal inhibition is forcefully imposed, then the artificially interrupted evolution may be restored by a violent act. However, there is no state of a permanent revolution, or a beneficial development through periodic recurrent revolts."[111] Obviously, Hitler's remark was opportunistic and designed to reassure the German people and, particularly, the circle around Hindenburg that no revolution would occur.

What Hitler called the German revolution was not the work of undisciplined masses but of his "enlightened leadership." It was not a social revolution with a change in the distribution of wealth, but a racial revolution, ultimately the creation of a new Germanic superman. He clearly stated this in the opening of the Reichsparteitag on 7 September 1937:

> Germany experienced the greatest revolution in our land by planned national, hence racial, hygiene. The consequences of such German racial hygiene are more decisive for the future of our nation than the effect of all other laws. Because we create new human beings. . . . They will protect our nation, like so many historical sad precedents of other races, from extinction on this earth forever. . . . What sense would our work and our efforts make, if we would not be in the service of the preservation of Germans? . . . What is the sense of any service for such a German, if we omit the most important, to keep him pure in his blood and uncontaminated? . . . All other mistakes can be corrected, all other errors undone, only an omission in this matter can never be remedied. Whether our work in racial hygienic matters was fertile, you can evaluate in these days yourself. Because what you encounter in the German human being. Come and see for yourself whether under National Socialist leadership it has become better or worse. Measure not only the increased number of births, but most of all the appearance of our youth. . . . How beautiful are our boys and our girls, bright their eyes, how healthy and vigorous their posture, how wonderful the bodies of hundreds of thousands and millions that have been trained and cared for by our organizations. . . . Where are better men than you see here? It is really the rebirth of a nation as the result of conscious breeding of a new man.[112]

In one area of major change in the modern world—the emancipation of women—Hitler was definitely reactionary and defensive, although German women, particularly during the war, experienced a degree of liberation not planned by Hitler. In the monologues, he defended his thesis:

> In no local organizations of the Party could a woman occupy the smallest position. One always said the Party was hostile to women, that we just see in a woman a machine of procreation or an object of gratification of lust. This is not the case. In social work for juveniles and charity work I gave them much latitude. In 1924 the political women appeared: Frau von Treuenfels, Mathilde von Kemnitz. They wanted to become deputies of the *Reichstag* in order to improve the mores. I told them 99 percent of the matters under discussion are masculine topics, which they can't judge. The women wanted to protest but were unable to protest when I maintained that they knew men as well as I knew women. A man who screams that's not nice, but it's much worse in women. Her voice becomes more shrill, the more she screams. They begin to scratch and to prick with hair pins. The more courteous one is, the more one is able to detain women from matters for which they are not suited. Anything associated with blood or battle is entirely man's business. In many things, one has to engage women, because their mind is more practical. For instance, in furnishing an apartment. Professor Troost understands the matching of colors in interior decoration like hardly a man.[113]

Related to Hitler's ambivalence about revolutionary changes was his attitude toward modernity. Turner[114] focused on Hitler's intent to colonize conquered eastern territories with German peasants, his use of slogans such as "Blood and Soil," his presentation of the peasant as an antidote to intellectualism, industrialization, and the asphalt mentality. In sharp contrast was Hitler's acceptance of a high-tech society. He advocated technical change, foremost in automotive transportation, but also in modern city planning, protection of the environment (where he was far ahead of his time), and even modernization of household equipment to improve the lot of the *Hausfrau*.

Hitler's love for automobiles had far-reaching military and civil implications. His high-powered Mercedes cars were prize possessions. He bought his first Mercedes as soon as he was discharged from prison in December 1925.[115] Hitler promoted the German automobile industry and considered the director of the Mercedes company, Karl Porsche, Germany's greatest technical genius.[116] He was the moving spirit behind the production of a car for everyman—the Volkswagen. No evidence exists that he invented or suggested the beetle-like shape of the Volkswagen, but he favored it, as well as the air-cooled motor. The Volkswagen indeed gained worldwide popularity, but it was produced on a mass basis only after the war. He cherished a six-seater Mercedes compressor that he owned since 1929. He felt a childlike joy when his chauffeur was able to pass big American cars, but did not recommend fast cars for everyone's use. He instructed his drivers to drive slowly on dusty roads lest pedestrians be molested.[117] He was never publicly seen driving a car. He had several chauffeurs—Emil Maurice, Julius Schreck, Erich Kempka—with whom he was on unusually intimate terms. Hitler claimed an associate, Adolf Müller, taught him how to drive.[118] This is possible, although in Germany in the twenties, one had to take lessons in a driving school and pass an elaborate examination before one could obtain a driver's license. Hitler offered the explanation that he did not drive because if an accident had occurred when he was on probation after the putsch it could have led to his expulsion from Germany.[119] This explanation certainly would not be valid after he became a German citizen in 1931. Nobody would expect a head of state to drive his car, but it is of interest that Hitler was never seen or photographed while driving. In one picture, presumably taken between 1928 and 1931, "Uncle Adolf" is instructing his niece Geli on how to drive![120] Of greater importance, however, was Hitler's firm conviction about the superiority and necessity of motorized warfaroe over traditional warfare. Some of his ideas came from his tank generals, such as Heinz Guderian and Erwin Rommel, and some from General Charles de Gaulle; however, it was Hitler who ordered the implementation of such ideas.

Clearly, Hitler was ambivalent about modernization—which is not unreasonable. He pined for the past, when the "sky was full of violins,"[121] for the Wagnerian world and the epoch of the German Romanticists. Judged by his deeds rather than by ambivalent statements, Hitler was in favor of industrial modernization and clearly wanted Germany to be a technically advanced state, concomitant with his longing for a vanishing romantic world, but most of all, he wanted to create a Germanic superman.

The Chancellor's Private Life

Being a ruler and administrator was less to Hitler's liking than being an agitator and Party leader. As he became more powerful, Hitler became isolated, lonely, and angry. Werner Best, an astute observer, commented during the mid-thirties that Hitler had become an angry leader.[122] Apart from his contact with Eva Braun, the hidden mistress, Hitler's life was devoid of intimacy. He spent much of his leisure time at the Berghof near Berchtesgaden, where he enjoyed the grandeur of the mountain scenery. The Berghof was a place of both relaxation and work. Important conferences took place there, and it provided an opportunity for the hard-working Hitler at times to shift gears into an inactive lifestyle and to rest and dream. The loneliness of the charismatic leader is reflected in the strange remark, "In my youth I was an odd loner and did not need company. Now I can't be alone anymore. I find it most beautiful to dine with a woman, and I would rather be at the Osteria [a Munich restaurant] than to eat alone at home."[123] Hitler liked small dinners that he often arranged himself. He disliked the fanciness of international chefs, and he intensely disliked state dinners, particularly at the highly formal Italian court where he complained about being forced to sit next to dried-out gray old hags with deep décolletés and crucifixes between shriveled breasts.[124] He enjoyed large receptions where he could surround himself with beautiful actresses, singers, and dancers, while keeping them at a safe distance.

While Hitler stuck to his rather tasteless vegetarian diet, he offered his guests simple, well-prepared German *Hausmannskost*. He asked his major domo Artur Kannenburg to serve his guests meals that were similar to his own meatless fare. He had the good sense not to recommend a vegetarian diet for his troops, although he told Goebbels in April 1942 that he would tackle the vegetarian problem after the war.[125] Privately, however, Hitler scorned meat eaters, calling them corpse eaters, and extolled the virtues of vegetarianism. He postulated that carnivorous animals were inferior to herbivorous animals, that elephants were stronger and hardier than lions, and that the strongest men on earth were vegetarians—Japanese wrestlers and Turkish porters.[126] From his own experience, he reported that when he ate meat he had to drink four liters of beer and six bottles of water, and sweated profusely. Since he had become a vegetarian he needed a swallow of water only once in a while.[127] He reflected that, if a child was offered meat or fruit and cakes, it invariably would choose fruit and cakes.[128] He praised a polenta diet,[129] yet the unbalanced polenta diet of poor peasants in the Po Valley causes pellagra. Hitler reflected on the possible role of meat in the etiology of cancer[130] before any scientific knowledge on the subject existed.

One gains the impression that Hitler's social life gradually had become empty. He had moved away from the old guard and *Chauffeureska* but had not established any close, intimate contact with the high military or civilian personnel who worked closely with him. Speer once claimed wistfully, "If Hitler had a friend, it would be me."[131] Until the end of his life, he found some consolation in a friendly, superficial relationship with secretaries and dieticians.

Early Illnesses

In the mid-thirties some health problems began. In encounters and photographs Hitler appeared vigorous—although, of course, pictures taken for propaganda purposes would hardly portray illness. The public firmly believed that their Führer was in excellent health. Hitler reportedly consulted an otolaryngologist, Wilhelm Guberlet, but for the orator Hitler, inclined to misuse his voice, this type of consultation would not have been unusual.[132] Another physician, mentioned by Henriette Hoffmann, was professor of urology L. Kielleuthner.[133] Hoffmann reported that after the war while she was sitting in a Munich park reading a book about famous residents of Schwabing, in which Hitler was mentioned, she was joined by Professor Kielleuthner, who was taking a walk in the park. Upon noting the book, he volunteered the information that Hitler had been one of his patients, although he said that he had not been able to help him because he had seen him too late. What Hitler suffered from was not mentioned.[134] The assertions of Kurt Krueger, who claimed that he was Hitler's psychiatrist, are sheer fiction.[135] Hitler discounted his early health problems. When Dr. Morell tried to obtain a case history as to illnesses before 1936, Hitler asserted that he "was never ill." Morell stated in his diary on 31 March 1945:

> I reminded him about the fracture of his left clavicle and the injury to his upper arm before the beginning of his imprisonment, about which I learned only recently and by chance. . . . "There is nothing to record about this, because it is unimportant, and I have full mobility at present."[136]

The story of the "severe pulmonary illness" and the findings of "weakness" by the Austrian draft board were forgotten, repressed, or simply not admitted; even the combat wounds to his thigh and the mustard gas injury went unmentioned. During his campaign against the very old von Hindenburg, Hitler emphasized his youth, health, and vigor.

While it is not certain whom he consulted during the twenties and early thirties, it is known that Hitler was a self-medicator. Amongst the unprescribed medications he took were Dallmann cola tablets, which contained very small amounts of caffeine and extracts of the coca plant. In 1929, probably at the advice of his adjutant, Wilhelm Bruckner, Hitler took Balistol, a substance used to clean gun barrels that also was believed to relieve gastrointestinal symptoms. Balistol contained mineral oil, sodium salts, and 8.5 percent amyl alcohol. In contrast to the dangerous methyl alcohol, which causes blindness and death, amyl alcohol in small doses produces only headaches and nausea. Hitler developed these symptoms, stopped taking the substance at the advice of Dr. Ernst Robert Grawitz, chief physician of the SA, and promptly recovered. A third medication, also available without prescription, was Koester's anti-gas pills. Hitler took these pills to relieve flatulence that was annoying and embarrassing to him. The anti-gas pills contained extracts of strychnine, belladonna, and gentian. Extract of strychnine contains 1 to 2 percent strychnine, which means that each pill contained approximately 0.04 milligram of the substance. The dose recommended by the manufacturer of Koester's anti-gas pill was two to four pills three times per day. Twelve to sixteen pills—the maximum amount Hitler occasionally took—were harmless. The amount of atropine in the extract of belladonna contained in one pill is even smaller, completely innocuous.[137]

After 1936 Hitler required the services of several physicians, even though at that time he was objectively not seriously ill. In the mid-thirties, he was bothered by colds, tinnitus, gastrointestinal symptoms, and an itching skin irritation (later diagnosed as eczema) of the left calf. Whether Hitler's colds occurred more frequently or were any more severe than those experienced by the average person remains unknown, but Hitler took them seriously and considered them to be the result of bacterial infections, which he dreaded. He demanded careful attention to these colds on the part of his attending physician and expected drastic treatment with sulfonamides once they became available. Besides colds, he complained of occasional dizziness and a metallic ringing in his ears (tinnitus). Whether the dizziness was just a feeling of uncomfortable unsteadiness or a rotary dizziness (vertigo) remains unknown. Professor Karl von Eicken, Hitler's otologist, could find no definitive otological, neurological, or vascular causes and did not take the symptoms very seriously. He observed that the tinnitus occurred after Hitler had Röhm murdered and considered it psychogenic. His advice to treat it with a good night's rest, daily exercise, and alternating hot and cold baths was not followed. Instead, at the suggestion of Winifred Wagner, Hitler treated the tinnitus with the lipid lecithin, available without prescription, and believed that it benefited him.[138]

In the spring of 1935, Hitler complained of increasing hoarseness, which naturally upset the orator. When Professor von Eicken diagnosed a small vocal cord tumor, Hitler's anxiety increased and he became worried about carcinoma of the larynx, a disease from which the German Emperor Friedrich, father of Emperor Wilhelm II, had suffered and died. Professor von Eicken operated on Hitler on 21 May 1935 and removed a tumor of one millimeter in size. The pathological diagnosis was papilloma of the larynx, a benign tumor, and Hitler recovered quickly, regaining his voice within a few weeks. It is possible that the pathologist, Professor Robert Rössle, chose the term papilloma rather than applying the "undignified" terms of singer's or screamer's node. The episode was kept secret from the public. At the time, Hitler was involved in difficult negotiations with the British over a fleet agreement. Meetings had to be canceled, and the rumors ranged from a lethal to a diplomatic illness. Von Eicken operated again on 10 November 1944 for a second bout of hoarseness, once more followed by the patient's prompt vocal recovery. This time, the pathologist reported not a papilloma, but rather a detachment and thickening of the vocal cord caused by inflammation and strain on the mucous membrane—such as that seen in the early stages of a so-called singer's node. As the histological differential diagnosis of such tumors and pseudo-tumors is difficult, it is likely that Hitler suffered in both incidents from singer's nodes.

The Attending Surgeons

On 15 August 1934, Hitler's adjutant Wilhelm Bruckner was seriously injured in a car accident near Reit im Winkl in Upper Bavaria. A young surgeon, Dr. Karl Brandt, brought him to the nearest hospital and stayed with him until he recovered. Bruckner recommended to Hitler that he retain Dr. Brandt as attending surgeon for himself. Hitler was sufficiently worried about the possibility of being in an accident and appointed not only Dr. Brandt but a second surgeon, Dr. Werner Haase. When Dr. Haase became ill with tuberculosis, he was replaced by Brandt's friend Dr. Hanskarl von Hasselbach.

Dr. Karl Brandt (1904–1948) was a well-trained young surgeon embarked on an academic career. An ardent National Socialist, he became a member of the NSDAP in 1932 and joined the SS in 1934. Brandt never rendered any surgical services to Hitler. He believed that Hitler's gastrointestinal and neurological symptoms were psychogenic.[139] In 1940 Hitler bestowed a professorship on him, and Brandt rapidly became involved in administrative health issues, in inspecting medical facilities and devising health policies. After the outbreak of the war, these activities occupied him full-time. In 1943, he was appointed Reich's Commissioner for all German medical services. He played a key role in the National Socialist euthanasia program and later became involved in the human experimentation program in concentration camps. Following the Doctors' Feud in the fall of 1944 (see Chapter 7), Hitler dismissed both Brandt and von Hasselbach abruptly. A few months later, Brandt was arrested on the accusation that he had allowed his family to move to the part of Germany most likely to be occupied by American troops. With Hitler's nod of approval, Brandt was sentenced to death. Eventually, with Himmler's help, Brandt's friend Speer persuaded Hitler to stay the execution. Lifton classified Brandt as an idealist, the "decent Nazi" type.[140] Brandt was convinced that his views about "euthanasia" were ethical and, furthermore, that he was carrying out Hitler's orders, which he found reasonable and moral. Only after the end of the war did he change his mind about Hitler. What Brandt failed to understand was that, through his personal ambition, he had lost track of the physician's ethical standards on the slippery slope of National Socialist medicine. In the so-called "doctors' trials" in Nuremberg, Brandt was sentenced to death for his roles in the euthanasia project and in human experimentation in concentration camps.

Dr. Hanskarl von Hasselbach (1903–1988), a well-trained academic surgeon, treated Hitler once for injuries sustained in the assassination attempt on 20 July 1944. Dr. Hasselbach also was given the title of professor by Hitler in 1943. The officers of the Allied interrogation considered von Hasselbach the most honorable and sympathetic of Hitler's physicians. He was never accused of any war crimes. During his interrogation as a prisoner of war, von Hasselbach dodged questions about Hitler's crimes and mistakes. He described Hitler as highly intelligent, possessing an enviable memory and an immense thirst for knowledge. However, von Hasselbach believed that Hitler lacked practical knowledge of mankind. He noted that Hitler aged rapidly after 1943, whereas before then he had appeared younger than his age.[141]

Hitler's Search for a Personal Physician

During the mid-thirties, Hitler's gastrointestinal troubles got worse. He complained about recurrent epigastric postprandial pains, belching, vague discomfort in the cardiac region, flatulence, and constipation. With considerable self-pity, he talked to Speer about his troubles. He complained that food made his condition worse. Pointing to his plate, he said:

> . . . a man is supposed to keep alive with that, look at it. It's easy for the doctors to say that people ought to eat what they have an appetite for. Hardly anything is good for me nowadays. After every meal the pain begins. Leave out even more? Then how am I going to exist?[142]

Hitler told Speer about his starvation diet: a little soup, salad, small quantities of the lightest foods. He no longer ate anything substantial. Hitler's account is contradicted by the fact that his weight was rather stable. Except for one episode in the fall of 1944 when he lost ten kilograms in ten days, actually Hitler was worried about gaining weight because of his indulgence in pastries. However, Speer noted that, at times, Hitler had to absent himself from conferences, presumably because of gastric discomfort. Notwithstanding Hitler's complaints, the gastrointestinal symptoms in the mid-thirties were relatively mild as compared with the symptomatology in 1943. He ate hastily, did not chew his food well, and talked while he ate, resulting in aerophagia, or the swallowing of air. This, in turn, caused belching and flatulence. Moreover, Hitler's gastrointestinal symptoms undoubtedly were aggravated by his dental problems, which required the pureeing of food. Hitler's teeth were in miserable condition and needed continuous attention. He had fourteen natural teeth left, four on the upper jaw and ten on the lower. He had three bridges, all of which were somewhat unusual. His upper teeth were all connected in one bridge of nine teeth supported by four natural teeth. On the lower left, he had a six-tooth bridge supported by three natural teeth. On the lower right, his most distinctive feature was a three-tooth bridge supported by two natural teeth, with a lingual arm connecting the two teeth by skipping one in the middle.[143] Hitler was in continuous treatment with Professor Hugo Blaschke. In contrast to the majority of German dentists, Proffessor Blaschke was not a physician but held a doctor of dental surgery degree from an American college of dentistry at the University of Pennsylvania, followed by postgraduate work in London. He reported that Hitler endured pain stoically, in contrast to Goebbels, who did not and was a difficult patient.

In addition to the troublesome gastrointestinal symptoms, Hitler complained about an itching skin affliction of his calves that bothered him greatly. Only intimates, amongst them his photographer Hoffmann and, to some extent, Speer, knew about Hitler's complaints. In 1936 Hitler was sufficiently worried about his physical well-being to search for a personal physician. He asked his surgeons for advice, but they were not eager to get involved with non-surgical illnesses and, least of all, with any potentially psychosomatic or personality problems on Hitler's part. Drs. Brandt and von Hasselbach advised Hitler to seek the advice of an academic physician. Rumors existed to the effect that Hitler was referred to the two most eminent German physicians, Professor Gustav von Bergmann in Berlin and Professor Hans Eppinger in Vienna, but no such consultation ever took place. Hitler did not like famous and overbearing academic physicians; he also did not want a physician who was a high-ranking Party member. He preferred an experienced, discreet practitioner who would take complaints seriously and consider his wishes and demands.[144] It was very important to Hitler that nobody know anything about him that he did not wish to reveal. He did not follow his surgeons' advice to choose an academic physician, but picked a general practitioner.

In 1936 Heinrich Hoffmann, Hitler's photographer and confidante, recommended and introduced Hitler to a medical practitioner, Dr. Theodor
Morell, who previously had treated him successfully for pyelitis. During the
initial encounter in Hoffmann's garden in May 1936, Morell undoubtedly
told Hitler about his holistic approach and, particularly, about the Mutaflor
cure that helped many of his patients.[145] The essence of the cure was to culture and detoxify sick coli-bacilli from the patient's feces and ingest the invig-
orated bacilli. The healthy bacilli would kill the sick bacilli in the patient's
gut. Hitler must have been impressed with a treatment in which strong,
healthy bacilli kill sick, weak ones. Morell promised Hitler he would cure
him within a year. When, after the treatment—presumably after several
Mutaflor cures—the eczema disappeared and the gastrointestinal symptoms
improved, Morell was employed as Hitler's personal physician (*Leibarzt*). He
stayed with him almost to the last days of Hitler's life.

Morell was born on 18 July 1886, in Traisa, Hessen, and died on 20 May
1948 in the hospital of Tegernsee in Bavaria. The Morell family had emigrated from France during the Huguenot persecution, hence the French
name. Morell's father was a school teacher, and Morell attended a teacher's
college before he decided to study medicine. He attended several medical
schools at the Universities of Munich, Giessen, Heidelberg, Grenoble, and
Paris (not unusual at that time), and graduated from the University of
Munich in 1912. Afterward, he was a ship's doctor, worked in a rural practice
for a short time, and served as a medical officer in World War I. In 1917 he
married an actress, Johanna Moeller, who took a great interest in the financial aspects of his practice. In 1918 he established an office in suburban
Berlin, later moved to the swank Kurfürstendamm.

Morell was a general practitioner who called himself a specialist in male
urological diseases (predominantly gonorrhea) and electrotherapy—an odd
combination. He never performed any urological surgery—as a matter of
fact, he was trained neither in nonsurgical urology nor in physical therapy.
He also was wrongly called a specialist in venereal and skin diseases, although
many of his patients sought consultation for venereal diseases. Since the mid-
thirties he ran an elaborate practice with two assistant physicians, Dr. Wolfgang Wohlgemuth and, later, Dr. Richard Weber. Morell also employed tech-
nicians to handle the impressive apparatus for electrical and hydrotherapy, an
X-ray machine, and a laboratory—quite unusual for a general practitioner at
the time. Morell made money from this odd combination of activities. His
clientele consisted of the worried well: businessmen, members of the aristocracy (amongst them Crown Prince August Wilhelm), and many actors and
singers (such as the famous Jewish tenor Richard Tauber). The great majority
of his patients felt that Morell helped them and expressed their gratitude. His
reputation and prestige grew, and he allegedly was offered positions (which
he declined) at the courts of the Shah of Persia and the Rumanian king. After
Hitler retained him, Morell became extremely busy treating not only higher-
and lower-level persons within the Hitler court, but also dignitaries from
satellite governments. As a salary for his service, Hitler paid Morell an annual

fee of 60,000 Reichsmark—about four times as much as a general would receive. In addition, Hitler gave Morell generous gifts, and financed the renovation of his house on the swank Schwaneninsel after it was bombed, including construction of a bomb shelter. Hitler also supported Morell's "research," putting Germany's only electron microscope at his disposal. Most of all, being Hitler's personal physician enabled Morell to engage in lucrative pharmaceutical enterprises. His large income derived mostly from the large profits he obtained as owner and shareholder of a string of pharmaceutical firms. Until the summer of 1941, shortly after the attack on Russia, Hitler required little medical attention, but Morell and his wife loved Hitler's hospitality and were frequent guests at the Berghof. A detailed account of Dr. Morell's treatment of Hitler during the war is presented in Chapter 7, and a critical appraisal of his medical regimen from a contemporary view in Chapter 8.

The Shift to Foreign and Military Affairs

The year 1936 saw a distinct shift from domestic to foreign matters and preparations for war. The foreign interests were not new; they had been expressed in *Mein Kampf* and the second book more than a decade before, but Hitler now deemed the time right—after internal consolidation and secret rearmament—for his new ventures. Hitler had no use for conventional diplomacy. He distrusted the upper class, cautious traditionalists of the German Foreign Office. What he could not achieve by persuasion, bullying, bluster, and bluff, Hitler would acquire by military means. The military buildup could no longer be hidden, and Hitler began to openly express what he had felt all along in his heart: that a war to accomplish his goals was necessary and justified. Major steps were leaving the League of Nations on 14 October 1933 and the introduction of general military service on 16 March 1935. Both were popular measures among the Germans. The introduction of a general draft was openly announced because the buildup of the German armed forces could no longer be hidden. In many speeches, Hitler declared that it was impossible for the Germans, a defeated people, to remain in the Völkerbund. He used the themes of humiliation and defamation to explain his posture, although in fact little of the "shame of Versailles" still remained. The Western democracies and Russia protested Hitler's aggressive behavior but took no punitive or preventive action, which Hitler interpreted as a sign of weakness. He had an uncanny sense for weakness, and any lack of countermeasures further reinforced his aggressive pursuit.

No risks were involved in the reunion of the Saar region with Germany on 15 January 1935. For Hitler, it provided an opportunity to let his propaganda machine run on high tours. He was even able to get the Zentrum party in the Saar on his side. Repeatedly he stated categorically that he had no other territorial claims against France. The next foreign coup, the occupation of the demilitarized zone of the Rhineland, was a more aggressive and risky venture, because Hitler's small military force could easily have been crushed by the French. Hitler was extremely anxious about this venture, which could have ended in a catastrophe for him. It would have been an occasion for international resistance, but none occurred. The Germans approved the venture retroactively with a 98.3 percent vote, and even if this figure was exaggerated, the successful action impressed the German population. It gave a strong hint to Hungary, Rumania, Bulgaria, and Poland about the new order, and provided tremendous reassurance for Hitler. An expression of the confidence the Germans had in Hitler was his ability to negotiate a nonaggression pact with Poland already on 18 November 1933. No other German politician would have gotten away with it.

The Anglo–German naval agreement of 18 June 1935, which fixed the strength of both fleets in a ratio of 35 to 100 after he had secretly achieved parity of the German and British air forces, was a major political success. One of Hitler's major goals was to forge an alliance among Germany, Italy, and Great Britain against Russia. A secondary goal was to undermine the relationship between Great Britain and France. The task proved difficult after Italy invaded Ethiopia, threatening Great Britain's African and Mediterranean interests. For a while, however, Hitler was able to support Mussolini's war without alienating the British. He was eager to convince the British to support his foreign policies and was quite successful in achieving this until Winston Churchill became prime minister. The man who helped Hitler conclude the naval agreement was Joachim von Ribbentrop (1893–1946), a nouveau riche through marriage to the heiress of the German champagne firm of Henkell. Von Ribbentrop was devoted to Hitler and an ardent Nazi and anti-Semite (which he hotly denied during the proceedings of the International Military Tribunal of Nuremberg). At first Hitler referred to him as the new Bismarck.[146] The British did not share this opinion and disliked the arrogant and aggressive man. Hitler soon recognized von Ribbentrop's limitations but kept him probably because he wanted a servant in foreign affairs rather than a foreign minister. Von Ribbentrop was sentenced by the International Military Tribunal to die on the gallows.

In a conference on 5 November 1937 with Field Marshall Werner von Blomberg, Colonel General Werner von Fritsch, General Admiral Erich Raeder, Göring, and Foreign Minister Konstantin von Neurath, Hitler argued for military action, at the earliest in 1938 and latest in 1943. The minutes for this meeting were taken by Colonel Friedrich Hoßbach and were duly considered in the deliberations of the International Military Court, because they clearly described Hitler's intentions to annex Austria, destroy the Czechoslovakian state, and wage war. In a confused statement, Hitler expressed his view that autarky could not be obtained through peaceful means and weighed the possibility of a war with England and France. He believed that the *Duce* would not object to an occupation of Czechoslovakia. Poland would stay out of the conflict, as in all likelihood would Russia, as well, because it feared Japan. Hitler's rambling statement left his listeners bewildered and skeptical. Shortly afterward the skeptics, Generals von Blomberg and Fritsch and Minister von Neurath, were relieved of their positions. The program was a clear expression of Hitler's *Zeitangst*, or fear that he would not have time to carry out his plans. The fact that he made his first personal will in 1939, when he was just about fifty years old, may provide another bit of corroborating evidence that Hitler was worried about an early death. Foreign visitors and journalists, however, gained the impression that he was in good health and good form. Britain's Foreign Minister, Anthony Eden, particularly during his first visit, was favorably impressed, as was the British ex-King George (an admirer of Hitler). Mme. Titayna, a correspondent for the Paris *Soir*, visited on 23 January 1936 and wrote, "Hitler's face was full of intelligence and energy. It lights up when he speaks. I understand in a moment why this leader of men exerts such influence over the masses. There was no hint of illness, . . . although Hitler at that time did not feel well."[147]

General Blomberg provided Hitler with a good excuse for changing the military leadership. The divorced general married a woman who had a police record of secret prostitution. Upon discovering this, after he had attended the wedding, Hitler was outraged and used the incident to fire Blomberg. Colonel General von Fritsch would have been the rightful successor but was accused of having a sexual relationship with a male prostitute, which Göring promptly brought to Hitler's attention. Hitler believed or pretended to believe the story and forced von Fritsch to resign, even though it was proved that not von Fritsch but another officer was the culprit. The prostitute was sentenced to death. When a court rehabilitated General von Fritsch, Hitler did not reinstate him. In his place he appointed Walther von Brauchitsch as Chief Commander of the Army and himself as Commander in Chief of the Armed Forces. The high brass, clearly cognizant of the intrigue and injustice, did not protest—which again did not go unnoticed by Hitler, whose contempt for his generals began to mount.

Hitler's Relationship with Benito Mussolini

In the mid-thirties, Hitler had gained such status that Mussolini could not afford to ignore Hitler and the Third Reich, and a fateful relationship between the two dictators ensued. Over the years, Hitler maintained a closer relationship with the Italian dictator Benito Mussolini than with any other foreign leader. Interesting parallels and differences in the facts and legends pertaining to the two dictators exist. Mussolini admired his father, a blacksmith and socialist politician. Like Hitler, Mussolini always maintained that he loved his mother, a schoolteacher. Rather than real love and regard for her, however, it is more likely that he had ambivalent feelings, which he later transferred to his wife, Rachelle, and probably also the many women he seduced and exploited. Young Benito was a difficult child and was thrown out of two schools for unruly behavior. Unlike Hitler, he graduated from middle school and worked in different jobs as a teacher and laborer in both Italy and Switzerland, where he learned to speak French and German. Hitler made a point of explaining his closeness to Mussolini on the grounds that both men had worked in construction jobs.[148] Eventually, the revolutionary young socialist Mussolini, who served several prison sentences for his political activities, became a journalist and, in 1912, editor of the Socialist daily *Avanti*. He parted with the Socialist Party because he was in favor of entering the First World War on the side of the Allies. After the war, he founded fascist combat units and, finally, the Italian Fascist Party. The political turmoil created by weak, constantly changing governments, economic distress, crippling strikes, and the support of the bourgeoisie and aristocracy out of fear of communism enabled Mussolini to become Minister-President of a coalition government. After his March on Rome, he became Italy's leader—the *Duce*—as head of a fascist party. Mussolini was a major and internationally recognized leader when Hitler was the leader of a small party and virtually unknown outside of Germany. In *Mein Kampf*, Hitler wrote:

> I conceived the most profound admiration for the great man south of the Alps, who, full of ardent love for his people, made no pacts with the enemies of Italy, but strove for their annihilation by all ways and means. What will rank Mussolini among the great of this earth is his determination not to share Italy with the Marxists, but to destroy internationalism and save the fatherland from it.[149]

Mussolini was cognizant of Hitler's willingness to abandon the Germans in South Tyrol for the price of a political alliance. Hitler copied much of the organization of the militia, the leisure organization Dopo Lavore, and even the fascist greeting with the outstretched arm. Italians called Hitler "*Il Imitatore*" (the Imitator). The title of the leader, Duce e Capo di Governimiento, was taken over by the Germans as *Führer und Reichskanzler*. Hitler admitted that there would have been no brown shirts without black shirts.

Similarities between German and Italian fascism were greater than the subtle or profound differences historians perceive.[150] Both systems emphasized fierce nationalism and militarism. Both were authoritarian and opposed parliamentary and democratic procedures. Both dictators wanted above all to expand their territories. One essential difference, however, was that for Mussolini the supreme concept was the state, while for Hitler it was nation and race and, specifically, the dominance of the "Nordic–Germanic" race. For Hitler, the state was the means to an end. Mussolini was not a fanatic anti-Semite, and, although Italy was not free of anti-Semitic discrimination, cruel persecution of Jews in Italy started only under German pressure. Hitler wanted to eliminate Jews, whereas Mussolini wanted to restrict them. Amongst such restrictions, Jewish children in Italy were barred from public schools. Mussolini's anti-Semitism was not murderous—Hitler actually was irritated that the Italian dictator was not anti-Semitic enough. Mussolini liked to invoke philosophers of power (Friedrich Nietzsche, Vilfredo Pareto) to legitimize his policies. In contrast, Hitler adhered to a theory of vulgar Darwinism without even mentioning Darwin's name. In a frank statement about the doctrine of fascism, Mussolini dispensed with all theory and stated,

"Our program is simple. We wish to govern Italy. They ask me for programs, but there are already too many. It is not programs that are wanting for the salvation of Italy, but men and willpower."[151]

Similarities and also differences existed in the personalities of the two dictators. Both men were convinced that they had a historic mission. Both were vainglorious, exhibitionistic, and dramatic. Hitler and Mussolini were able to impress their associates and, even more, their peoples as strong leaders, while often they were vacillating and indecisive. Both impressed the masses through their oratory. Both loved to talk, but, as Ciano observed, Hitler out-talked Mussolini, much to the latter's distress. Himself a brutal man, Mussolini criticized Hitler for his brutality, particularly for the murder of the SA leadership. Overall, though, Mussolini was a more rounded person than Hitler. He had a family and seemed to care for his five children. He loved sports, rode horses, drove cars, and—to Hitler's dismay—swam on public beaches and piloted airplanes. Quite different from the inhibited Hitler, Mussolini had one love affair after the other, exceeding what might be considered the Italian norm. Notwithstanding the prowess both men displayed, they were hypochondriacal and overly concerned with illness and treatment. In contrast to Hitler, Mussolini was quite superstitious, believing in "*malochio*," the evil eye.

Throughout their relationship, Hitler praised Mussolini: "He is a very great man. . . ."[152] Hitler's was not the only foreign voice praising him. The Italian dictator received laudatory comments from the conservative British statesmen Eden, Halifax, and Churchill, even after the Abyssinian War, before Italy declared war on the Allies. Amongst the admirers were Mahatma Gandhi, who visited Mussolini accompanied by his goat,[153] and, oddly, Sigmund Freud, who sent Mussolini his book, *Culture and Its Discontent*, with a personal inscription, "To the hero of our culture, from an old man, Sigmund Freud."[154]

Hitler was critical of Mussolini's relationship with the Italian King, Victor Emanuel III (King Nutcracker, as Hitler called the little King) and his court, whom Hitler detested. Hitler criticized Mussolini's relationship with the Catholic Church and even recommended the occupation of the Vatican during the war.[155] Whenever Hitler was annoyed with Mussolini—and he had reasons to be after Mussolini's Greek and North African adventures—Hitler displaced his anger on the Italians, and particularly the Southern Italians.[156] Mussolini's views about Hitler were more negative, notwithstanding laudatory toasts during their meetings. Prince Starhemberg reported a remark indicating Mussolini's irritation: "Instead of speaking to me about current problems, he recited me *Mein Kampf*, that boring book which I have never been able to read."[157] Count Ciano also stated that Mussolini disliked Hitler and said, "the Germans are dirty dogs . . . personally I had my fill of Hitler."[158] Yet Mussolini ordered the execution of Count Ciano, his son-in-law.

During the first meeting between the two dictators, on 14 June 1934, Hitler made a poor impression on Mussolini and his entourage. Hitler was ill at ease, dressed in inconspicuous civilian garb (at the advice of his Foreign

Minister von Neurath, for which Hitler never forgave him), while Mussolini was decked out in the fascist uniform. Mussolini was clearly the dominant party. His criticism of Hitler increased over Hitler's role in the assassination of the Austrian Chancellor Dollfuss on 25 July 1934. Mussolini felt closer to the ideology and practices of Austrofascism than National Socialism. Relations between the dictators improved during the Spanish Civil War (1936–39). A decisive change came during the Abyssinian War. Hitler skillfully managed to aid Mussolini without antagonizing the British. When Mussolini visited Germany in 1937, he was impressed with Hitler's power. More about the changes in this relationship, when Hitler became the dominant partner, and finally Mussolini's fall and his murder, will be taken up in forthcoming sections of this book.

The Annexation of Austria

When Mme. Titayna asked Hitler what he thought about the annexation of Austria, he replied, "This is a question about which nobody gets excited here. It is needed in Vienna for inner political reasons. The question of annexation is not acute in Berlin."[159] On 30 January 1937, he asserted, "The time of surprises is over"[160]—which was radically different from what he stated in the first paragraph of *Mein Kampf*: "One blood demands one Reich,"[161] which later became the effective slogan, "One People, one Reich, one Führer." Annexing Austria was essential and would assure that the domination of Europe would be more than a dream. The nationalist ideological goal of reuniting all Germans in one Reich was important, but Göring, who did not do well with his Four-Year Plan, had his eye on Austria's raw materials, manpower, and territory.

Troubles between Nazi Germany and the Austrian regime were not new. On 12 February 1934, Austrian Chancellor Engelbert Dollfuss brutally crushed a socialist uprising and established a reactionary dictatorship—Austrofascism. The leaders were Dollfuss and Ernst Rüdiger, Prince of Starhemberg, the commander of the paramilitary Heimwehr. In many respects, the philosophies of Austrofascism, Italian fascism, and National Socialism were similar, but the measure of political and racist suppression in Austria, compared with Germany's, was mild. On 16 July 1934, a second uprising occurred in which National Socialists occupied government buildings and the Austrian radio station in Vienna. Dollfuss was shot and bled to death without receiving any medical attention. The putsch was crushed. It is inconceivable that Hitler did not know about plans for the coup, which had been substantially aided by his ambassador. However, he denied any knowledge of it, criticized Austrian National Socialists, recalled his ambassador, and replaced him with von Papen. Dollfuss's successor, his Minister of Justice, Kurt von Schuschnigg, had to bank on the support of Mussolini, who at that time preferred an independent but weak Austria to a strong Germany on its northern border. Hitler was annoyed over the continued suppression of National Socialists by a regime that he considered illegitimate and ineffective. During the Abyssinian

War, Mussolini had to make concessions in return for Hitler's help, and Austria was forced to yield to Hitler's demands for economic and political cooperation with Germany. Yet Hitler still complained that the Austrians were not fulfilling their obligations to the Germans. With Mussolini's knowledge, on 2 February 1938, Hitler summoned the Austrian Chancellor Schuschnigg to his mountain retreat.[162] For hours he berated Schuschnigg for resisting National Socialism, threatened to invade, and warned that no nation would defend Austria. To emphasize his threat, in a theatrical gesture he yelled for General Keitel, who was summoned to the conference just for the purpose of bluff. At lunch, Hitler again was a charming host. During the afternoon, Schuschnigg was presented with Hitler's demands by von Ribbentrop and von Papen: He was to appoint Arthur Seyss Inquart, an Austrian National Socialist, as Minister of the Interior, with control over the police, and another National Socialist as Minister of Finance. Further, he was to permit an exchange of officers of the two armies and close cooperation in economic matters as dictated by Germany. When Schuschnigg asked for further discussion, he was brusquely told that there would be none and that he had three days' time to accept Hitler's demands. Seyss Inquart was appointed, and an Austrian National Socialist regime seemed imminent. This was what Hitler hoped for, because he was still uncertain about Mussolini's attitude and believed that *Gleichschaltung* in Austria—short of a German takeover—would give him what he needed. The hard-pressed Schuschnigg felt the only way he could resist Hitler was to unilaterally announce on 8 March that the Austrians would vote on 13 March whether Austria should remain independent or be annexed by Germany. When Hitler learned about this, he flew into a rage and ordered the invasion. Mussolini was informed about events by Hitler's envoy, Prince Phillip von Hessen, and, to Hitler's relief, did not object. Hitler's telephone message to Mussolini, via Prince Phillip, read: "Then please tell Mussolini I will never forget this, never, never."[163] On 11 March, units of the German army crossed the Austro-German border. Before this decision was reached, Hitler had been in a state of great excitement. An eyewitness, the Austrian Nazi Edmund Glaise Horstenau, described it in the following way:

> It was terrible. The Führer did not come to rest, and he did not let anybody else in his environment sleep. Like mad he ran from one room to another, issued orders and canceled orders, asked for advice, did not heed advice, sweated profusely, and drove everybody crazy. I don't think I could stand to be in the Führer's company without becoming hysterical.[164]

Schuschnigg gave orders not to resist in order to avoid bloodshed. Without the support of the Social Democrats, who had been demolished by the Austrofascist regime, no resistance was possible. Hitler definitively decided in favor of an annexation in Linz, his home town, after he experienced an enthusiastic reception from the populace. On 13 March 1938 he entered Vienna. To gain six and a half million people, badly needed resources, and beyond this to return as a liberator to the city where he had had to endure years of humiliation was an incredible triumph. On 14 March, in a mass meeting of 200,000 people on the Heldenplatz, Hitler declared that Austria had become a part of the German Reich. Standing at attention, as if reporting to an invisible superior, he reported before history the execution of the biggest mission of his life: "As Führer and Reich Chancellor I report the entrance of my home country into the Reich."[165]

The Nazis proceeded with a rapid and efficient *Gleichschaltung* of Austria. Schuschnigg, his cabinet officers, and thousands of people who were suspected of resistance were arrested. Schuschnigg spent the next seven years in VIP sections of German concentration camps; after some solitary confinement, Schuschnigg's wife was permitted to join him. Austrian Jews were humiliated and disenfranchised to an unprecedented degree. Great Britain and France launched paper protests that only reinforced Hitler's plans for further conquests. On 10 April, 99.7 percent (including such dignitaries as Vienna's Cardinal Theodor Innitzer and the nestor of the Social Democratic Party, Karl Renner) voted for the reunion, though it is likely that the actual percentage of yes votes was lower. Nevertheless, a substantial Austrian majority was in favor of the Anschluss. This was perhaps Hitler's greatest unopposed successful achievement. He had assessed the weakness of his opponents correctly and used bluff and aggressive play-acting effectively. The new Nazi mayor of Vienna was told that the city would remain a pearl amongst Germany cities of the Reich.[166] In fact, it declined and became a provincial city. The negative aspects of Hitler's ambivalent feelings toward Vienna prevailed. In the monologues he stated that he remembered the bedbugs rather than the beauty of the city.[167] Austria was a rich prize. With its raw materials, it saved Göring's Four-Year Plan from bankruptcy.

The Destruction of Czechoslovakia

On 21 April 1938, ten days after the plebiscite in Austria, Hitler gave secret orders to General Keitel to prepare for the invasion of Czechoslovakia under the code name "Green." From the very beginning, Hitler's goal was not only the unification of the Germans of the Sudetenland with the Reich, but the destruction of an independent Czechoslovakia. In his general directive, he stated that such an invasion must not occur out of the blue but must follow a political incident and provocations, which the leader of the Sudeten Germans, Konrad Henlein, fully obeyed.[168] Henlein made escalating demands, assuming that they would not be fulfilled, and engaged in provocative actions. When such terrorist tactics were met by Czech counter-measures, Hitler complained of terror. After Henlein had to flee Czechoslovakia, he continued his activities from Bavaria through raids in the Sudeten-German regions of Eger and Asch. British opinion was on the side of the suppressed, and Hitler cleverly took advantage of these sentiments. His aim was clear: The elimination of an independent Czechoslovakia would give him absolute reign in central and southeastern Europe. The bordering states of Hungary, Poland, Russia, Yugoslavia, Bulgaria, and Rumania understood this, but Great Britain and

France did not seem to appreciate the situation when they began to yield to Hitler's demands. The agricultural and industrial riches of the Czech provinces were vast. In addition to the promise of this bounty, Hitler had been motivated since his Vienna days by an old contempt for the Czechs, whom he considered an inferior nation hostile to Germans: "Czechs were not destined to be rulers."[169] The tactics were clear: He wanted to create turmoil in Czechoslovakia internally by military threats from Germany, win over Great Britain and France through diplomacy, and turn them against Russia and its "Bolshevist satellite," Czechoslovakia. It was not clear, however, whether Hitler would start a war over the Sudetenland. His advisors were divided over the question. Von Ribbentrop favored the risk of invasion; Göring and General von Brauchitsch, Chief of the Army, cautioned against it. General Ludwig Beck, Chief of the General Staff, who was opposed to Hitler's expansionist plans, together with Carl Friedrich Goerdeler, the mayor of Leipzig, had plans to overthrow the regime in case of an invasion into Czechoslovakia. They hoped for British cooperation in this, a hope that vanished completely after the Munich Conference. These plans became known to Hitler and his intelligence agencies only after the assassination attempt of 20 July 1944.

On 20 May, Czechoslovakia's President Beneš learned of plan "Green" and ordered a partial mobilization. Hitler was stunned when Great Britain and France were sympathetic. He accelerated his military preparations against Czechoslovakia and also stepped up construction of the Westwall fortifications. At this point, he correctly assessed France as weak and torn by internal strife. The Britons puzzled him; he could not figure out why they yielded at one time and were stubborn another. Hitler pursued the idea of a deal with Great Britain regarding Czechoslovakia, and later Poland, probably encouraged in his thinking by gestures from British sympathizers, Great Britain's ex-Prime Minister, Lloyd George, and the Duke of Windsor, the former King George.[170] On 12 September 1938, Hitler angrily announced the imminent invasion of Czechoslovakia. In response, the alarmed British Premier Neville Chamberlain, at the suggestion of the French Premier Daladier, surprised Hitler by asking for a meeting on 14 September. Hitler let Chamberlain travel to his mountain resort in the farthest southeastern corner of Germany, figuring he would then be dealing with an exhausted old man who had just had his first airplane ride. Chamberlain's motivation came from his assessment that his hard-pressed Empire would only stand to lose in the event of an armed conflict, hardly from any ethical concern for the rights of "a far away people." Hitler understood Neville Chamberlain's point of view all too well; he belittled Chamberlain as sclerotic and corrupt, and maintained that his real interest was in profiting from the British armament industry.[171] He referred to British diplomats as little worms. At the summit meeting Chamberlain, in spite of his increasing irritation with Hitler, remained calm and patient, pursuing his goal of peace. The Führer's tactics were alternately friendly and accommodating, then aggressive and intransigent. When Hitler insisted on his schedule of invasion for 1 October, Chamberlain threatened to leave. At that moment Hitler agreed to a pause, and Chamberlain left to discuss the matter with his Cabinet, and also to soften up the Czechs. He arrived for a second conference with Hitler in Bad Godesberg on 22 September 1939, with very far-reaching concessions from the Czechs to cede territories where the German populations exceeded 50 percent, and to agree to a plebiscite under international supervision. To Chamberlain's surprise, Hitler, who had become increasingly aggressive and insisted on military occupation of the Sudetenland, refused the offer. Two days after the disappointed Chamberlain departed, Hitler threatened again to wage war against Czechoslovakia in a mass meeting at the Sports Palace in Berlin. In great agitation, he cited wildly exaggerated reports of atrocities and terror, stating that thousands of Germans had been massacred, hundreds of thousands had been forced to flee. "The Czech state began with a lie and the father of the lie was called Beneš. Germany cannot stand such affront and humiliation."[172] The annexation of the Sudetenland would be Germany's last territorial demand, he promised. Hitler begged the Germans to stand behind him as their first soldier. The eminent American journalist William Shirer made an interesting observation about the end of Hitler's speech:

> For the first time in all the years I have observed him, he seemed tonight to have completely lost control of himself. When he sat down Goebbels sprang up and shouted into the microphone, "One thing is sure: 1918 will never be repeated!" Hitler looked up to him, a wild eager expression in his eyes, as if those were the words which he had been searching for all evening and hadn't quite found. He leaped to his feet and with a fanatical fire in his eyes that I shall never forget, brought his right hand, after a grand sweep, pounding down on the table and yelled with all the power in his mighty lungs, "*Ja.*" Then he slumped to his chair exhausted.[173]

Chances for a peaceful solution seemed to have vanished. Although the masses at the Sports Palace pledged that they would stand behind the Führer, the general German population was not enthusiastic about a strategy that might possibly lead to war. At this point, a renewed and final effort for a peaceful solution was made by British statesmen, with the concurrence of the French. They sought the intervention of Mussolini, who was interested in avoiding a European war. On 28 September 1938, Mussolini sent Ambassador Cattolico to urge a reluctant Hitler to agree to a conference that would decide the fate of the Sudetenland. Mussolini assured Hitler that he would back his demands, and Hitler agreed, provided no Czechoslovakian, Hungarian, or Polish delegation be invited.

At Mussolini's request, the conference was held in Munich on 29 September, because Hitler was adamant about occupying the Sudetenland on 1 October. There was no time to prepare carefully for the event. Minister Neurath and State Secretary Ernst von Weizsäcker drew up loose agendas, bypassing von Ribbentrop, and delivered them to Mussolini, who presented them officially as his own. Hitler met Mussolini in Kufstein, south of

Munich, for a briefing before the conference. Chamberlain and Daladier and their delegations went directly to Munich. The conference, lasting from 12:30 p.m. until midnight, was poorly organized and desultory. Mussolini, who spoke all the languages of the participating statesmen, played an important role. Chamberlain was eager to appease and preserve peace. Daladier was in the difficult position of selling out his ally Czechoslovakia and remained rather quiet. Hitler, the central figure in the group, was disgruntled and irritable, although all of his demands concerning the Sudetenland were fulfilled.

The Munich agreement specified the occupation of the Sudetenland and territories next to the Austrian border between 1 October and 10 October in four stages: transfer and exchanges of population along ethnic lines, transfer of Czechoslovakian military installations, transfer of equipment, and transfer of industrial enterprises. The plebiscites in the mixed ethnic districts were never held. Poland received the area around Tešin. Hungary had to wait for a while for its spoils. Great Britain, France, Italy, and Germany guaranteed the new borders, and the residual Czechoslovakian Republic, contemptuously referred to by Hitler as the "*Resttschechei*" (the residual Czech land), did Hitler's bidding. The right to an extraterritorial road from Germany to Austria was granted by the Czechs. The alliance with Russia was canceled. The Czechoslovakian government began to pass anti-Semitic legislation. President Beneš fled into exile. Chamberlain was still happy with the results: The dismemberment of Czechoslovakia did not seem to concern him, considering that peace had been preserved. The German people also appreciated the preservation of peace, the new bloodless conquest of 28,000 km² and a population of 3.6 million Sudeten-Germans, and Chamberlain was celebrated by Germans as a peace-maker. The leader of the opposition, Winston Churchill, expressed a different opinion about the German occupation:

> At Berchtesgaden one pound was demanded at pistol's point. When it was given, at Godesberg two pounds were demanded at pistol's point. Finally the dictator consented to take one pound, seventeen shillings, and six pence, and the rest in promises of goodwill for the future. . . . We are in the presence of a disaster of the first magnitude.[174]

Hitler was not satisfied. Gaining valuable territory and crippling Czechoslovakia and its military might were not enough. He would have preferred to totally conquer Czechoslovakia as he had planned in the Parteitag speech on 12 September 1938.[175] Schacht reported overhearing Hitler's remark, "That guy Chamberlain has spoiled my entrance into Prague."[176] In fact, his entry was only postponed. Hitler's displeasure probably increased during a separate private conference with Chamberlain on 30 September, in which they agreed to consultation before taking any military action. Hitler felt uneasy about such restrictions and canceled the agreement. He also felt annoyed with the relief of the German population over the Peace of Munich. He explicitly stated in the spring of 1945 that he considered it a mistake that he did not conquer Czechoslovakia at the time he annexed the Sudetenland.[177]

The German military preparations for an invasion of the Czech Republic were preceded by reports of atrocities by the Czechs similar to those that the German press had reported in the Sudeten crisis. At most, there were individual incidents involving protests of humiliated Czechs against Germans, but no organized resistance existed at the time. The most important German political move was to induce some disgruntled and ambitious Slovak politicians, through threat and persuasion, to secede from the Czechs and establish an independent Slovakian state headed by the collaboror Josef Tiso, a Catholic priest. After such dismemberment of Czechoslovakia, the German government declared that the agreements made in Munich with respect to the new Czechoslovakian boundaries were not valid anymore, giving Hitler a flimsy excuse to threaten a military invasion of the unhappy Czech Republic. He ordered the Czech president, Emil Hacha, to report to him in Berlin on 14 March 1939. Hacha was to be given military honors as head of state, but he did not learn of Hitler's agenda until the actual confrontation—for which Hacha had to wait five hours until midnight. Hitler showered the timid Hacha and his subservient foreign minister Frantisek Chvalkovski with abuse, telling them that the world would not give a damn about the fate of the Czech state. Hacha fainted during the tirade and was promptly treated by Dr. Morell. He recovered quickly after the doctor gave him an injection. It is not certain what the medication was, whether it was glucose—a placebo—or a sedative. Hitler believed the latter, stating, "On the next day, he [Hacha] asked what it was that made him into another human being. The injection by Professor Morell did it."[178] Hitler requested that Hacha immediately telephone his government in Prague and tell them not to resist the invading army. Having ordered German troops into Czech lands, Hitler speciously offered to take the Czech people under the protection of Germany and guarantee them an autonomous existence suited to their ethnic peculiarities, and Hacha placed the fate of the Czech people in the hands of the Führer. When Hitler emerged from the meeting—he referred to his bullying as "Hachaising"—he told the waiting secretaries, "Children, this is the greatest day in my life. I shall go down in history as the greatest German."[179]

In the morning, German troops entered the Czech lands at many points. Quickly advancing toward Prague, they did not observe any resistance by a grieving and sullen population. Hitler followed them to take up his quarters in Prague's ancient fortress, the Hradšin, where a swastika flew from its tower. The Czech lands were absurdly called a Reich Protectorate. Von Neurath was appointed its first "protector." By gambling Hitler had gained additional formidable industrial resources and clearly established leadership in central Europe, with serious implications for the Balkan countries, Hungary, and Poland. The Western powers and the United States could not overlook the fact that Hitler had subjugated a foreign people in spite of his assurances that he would not conquer any territories, and specifically that he "did not want any Czechs." Even Mussolini was annoyed and was reported to have said, "The Italians will laugh at me; every time he invades a county he sends me a telegram."[180] In childish spite, to keep up with his fellow dictator, he invaded Albania on 17 April 1939. Hitler did not care; he asserted that he had acted according to the principle that the victor would not be asked any questions.[181]

Pressuring Poland

Annexing the Czech Republic was Hitler's first major foreign policy misjudgment. In a speech on 17 March 1939 in the British Parliament, Prime Minister Chamberlain was applauded for announcing that England would not tolerate another act of German aggression against any nation.[182] He raised the rhetorical question as to whether an old venture was at an end or a new one was beginning. He did not have to wait more than a few days for the answer, when Hitler started a risky new forage. On 21 March, German Foreign Minister von Ribbentrop informed the Polish Ambassador Lipsky that Germany had requested that the Free City of Danzig become a German city and that an extraterritorial route for cars and rail traffic be established, the so called Polish corridor, to connect East and West Prussia. In return, Germany would provide access to the sea for Poland. Until 1939, the fate of German nationals in Poland did not concern Hitler any more than the fate of the Germans in South Tyrol. The Poles actually profited from the destruction of Czechoslovakia by acquiring part of the Tešin territory. In light of subsequent developments, it can be assumed that Hitler wanted Poland to become Germany's satellite for a future German war against Russia. The German request was foremost a trial balloon to test Polish readiness to cooperate with Hitler. The Poles agreed to examine nationality problems in Danzig, without its incorporation, but rejected the idea of a German corridor. They were aware that Hitler had requested and received extraterritorial roads through Bohemia and Moravia—which, however, had not stopped him from invading. Poland feared a similar fate and considered the German request an untrustworthy proposal, a dictate and not a point of negotiation. Encouraged by British and French assurances, the Poles undoubtedly overestimated their own strength and the instant assistance they could receive from the Western powers. Another reason for Polish resistance and suspiciousness was the return of Memel by Lithuania under German pressure on 23 March 1939. Even within the German Foreign Secretary's office, Ernst von Weizsäcker, number-two man after von Ribbentrop, jotted down in his diary that after the Czech coup the Allies were ignited for action and that Germany's political credibility had reached the zero point.[183]

Indeed, Chamberlain offered Poland formal military assistance in case of attack and strengthened Poland's resistance. Hitler was enraged at Chamberlain's interference. In his speech at Wilhelmshaven on 1 April 1939, on the occasion of the launching of the battleship *Tirpitz*, Hitler furiously attacked Great Britain and Poland, repeating old clichés about the injustice at Versailles, the policy of encirclement, and Great Britain's hypocrisy in granting itself the right to be a world power and denying such a role for Germany.[184] He canceled the Polish–German treaty, the Anglo–German naval treaty, and ordered "White," the plan to attack Poland. In another rambling speech before his military top command on 23 Mary 1939, Hitler weighed the possibility of a war against either Poland or Great Britain and France. He believed that France would not interfere. A victorious war in Poland would enable him to wage war against both England and France when the circumstances warranted it, but he also considered attacking them first. He told his generals, who listened in bewilderment, that the real task was not Danzig or the destruction of Poland, but rather the conquest of living space in the East. He also told the High Commissioner of Danzig, Professor S. Burckhart, that his real aim was to attack the Soviet Union: "Everything I undertake is directed against Russia. If the West is too dumb and blind to understand this, I will be forced to ally myself with the Russians to defeat the West; and after its defeat, I will—with my united forces—turn against the Soviet Union."[185] To his interpreter Schmidt, he stated that he "needed an alibi, most of all for the German people, to show that I have done everything to secure peace. That's why I made this magnanimous proposal about the settlement of Danzig and the Corridor question."[186]

From the end of April, Hitler's aggression increased, which was manifesting itself in his reply to a letter from President Roosevelt on 14 April requesting nonaggression pacts with thirty-one countries. Hitler's response, in his Reichstag speech on 28 April 1939, was a long, tortuous account of his previous moves (into Austria, the Sudetenland, Czechoslovakia, and Memel), which, according to him, had enhanced peace. With bitter sarcasm, Hitler answered Roosevelt point by point, accusing him of meddling in European affairs, while he (Hitler) did not meddle in American affairs, or in the British problem of Palestine. The speech was received by the German deputies with guffaws and laughter. Hitler neither considered nor cared that his speech might offend Roosevelt and the Americans or might make it easier for the American President, in spite of rampant U.S. isolationism, to reinforce ties between Great Britain and the United States. Hitler described Germany as a country that was surrounded by enemies and constantly attacked. He portrayed himself as a former unknown soldier and worker who only wanted to serve his country, while Roosevelt, the President of an enormously wealthy country, saw fit to worry about the problems of the world.

The Nazi–Soviet Nonaggression Pact

In August 1939, when the German–Polish conflict became acute, an event occurred that shook the world: the Soviet–German nonaggression pact. On 23 August 1939 Hitler, the arch enemy of the "Bolshevist–Jewish World Plague" (an expression he had used only three months before), and Stalin, the champion against fascist brutes, concluded a ten-year nonaggression pact and trade agreement. With great concern, for some time Hitler had watched English and French attempts to improve their relations with the Soviet Union. Hitler was aware that these negotiations were slow, difficult, and inept because of mutual dislikes and suspicions. At this time he decided to try to beat the Allies to the punch and establish a better relationship of his own with Russia. The Russians seemed interested, and Hitler viewed the replacement of

Russia's Jewish Foreign Minister, Maxim M. Litvinov, with Vyacheslav M. Molotov as a good omen.

The Anglophobe von Ribbentrop was most anxious to conclude such an agreement for his master.[187] First, a trade agreement was negotiated between the two nations. Stalin badly needed credits and wanted to industrialize the Soviet Union. The trade agreement, signed on 19 August 1939 after some difficult negotiations, established German credits of 200 million Reichsmark for Russia and the exchange of agricultural products for Germany and industrial goods for Russia. As soon as it was accomplished, Hitler urged Stalin to receive von Ribbentrop as Hitler's plenipotentiary to negotiate a political treaty. Both Stalin and Hitler had no illusions that, sooner or later, they would attack each other, but in 1939 Stalin had no such intentions, especially because the pact would help him industrialize his country and possibly permit him to move his frontiers to the west without a war. He peremptorily dismissed some warnings from his generals that Germany might attack. Hitler had no intention of sticking to a treaty with the Soviet Union any longer than it suited his purposes; clearly his goal always was to gain Russian space. To General Halder Hitler stated defensively that "the Soviet Pact is misunderstood by many Party members. It is a pact with Satan in order to drive out the Devil."[188] Cheating the devil is a common theme in German literature and folklore.

In response to a telegram from Hitler requesting that Stalin receive the German Foreign Minister von Ribbentrop immediately, the Russian dictator, after letting an anxious Hitler wait for two days, invited von Ribbentrop to come to Moscow. Hitler also sent his photographer Heinrich Hoffmann to the Kremlin, with instructions to observe Stalin's appearance, demeanor, and relationships with people—as well as with a specific request to discover whether Stalin had attached ear lobes. These, according to Nazi racist folklore, occurred frequently in Jews.[189] Hitler was triumphant when von Ribbentrop returned with a ten-year nonaggression treaty with a cancellation period. A secret addendum determined the division (after victory) of Poland and the Baltic states to satisfy Germany and Russia. Both Hitler and Stalin were pleased, and Stalin drank to Hitler's good health. Hitler's statement of 30 January 1937, that the Soviets were an unbearable danger to the world was forgotten or repressed. Hitler felt that the British now surely would give up backing the Poles.

Forging Alliances

Shortly before the outbreak of the Second World War, Hitler signed major treaties with Japan and, later, with Italy. He claimed that his liking for Japan extended back to the Russo–Japanese War in 1905, when he rooted for Japan's victory[190]—certainly not an adequate political explanation. In 1936, Germany had signed the Anti-Comintern Pact with Japan, in which each nation pledged to stand firm against the spread of Russian Communism. The Tripartite Pact of September 1940 carved the Eastern Hemisphere into spheres of influence controlled by Germany, Italy, and Japan, and in good time the satellite countries. Later, however, Hitler mused about the danger Japan posed for the white race.[191] The treaty with Italy, the so-called Pact of Steel, was signed on 22 May 1939 and stipulated that the German and Italian nations were determined to act side by side and with united forces to secure their living space and maintenance. It provided for political, economic, and military assistance in case one of the partners became "involved in a war." Misgivings about the pact existed on both sides. The leading German statesmen, in spite of all diplomatic pomp and politeness, looked down on their Italian partners. Count Ciano, for his part, had strong reservations about Germany's military ventures and expressed concern that an alliance with the "barbarians to the North" could lead to catastrophic consequences for his country, but was unable to convince his father-in-law, Mussolini. As a first test of the Pact of Steel, however, Mussolini felt obliged to tell Hitler in August 1939 that he was not ready to provide military assistance; if Hitler was upset, he did not express it in public.

The Outbreak of War

After his speech to his military commanders on 23 August 1939,[192] Hitler seemed quite determined to invade Poland: The time to attack was now. Only he or Mussolini could be leaders in a war, and the time was ripe because a criminal or an idiot could assassinate him at any moment. There would be no repetition of any delay such as that which occurred during the Czechoslovakian coup. No dirty dog (*Schweinehund*)—i.e., Chamberlain—could interfere. He dismissed the likelihood that Great Britain and France would stand by their treaties with Poland. If England had intended to help, it would have given Poland money. France would remain neutral. In England no person of stature existed, no masters, no personalities. Germany could only gain. It had nothing to lose, but because of restrictions the Germans could carry on only for a few years. He then analyzed the world situation and concluded that favorable conditions would not exist in a few years. The proposals concerning Danzig and the corridor were eliminated by the meddling of England. "We face harsh alternatives. . . . It is a great risk. Iron nerves, iron determination. . . ." A blockade by England would be ineffective. An attack on Germany in the West would be impossible. In another protocol of the same speech, he stated that Poland must be destroyed quickly. One had to close one's heart against pity, take a brutal approach. Eighty million Germans must receive their due. The stronger has the right. Greatest hardness and quickness of decision were necessary.[193]

In two conferences about Poland with the British Ambassador Neville Henderson on 23 and 24 August 1939, Hitler appeared impetuous and unstable, and complained that no progress was made. Hitler screamed about the terrible atrocities that had been inflicted on Germans by the Poles and claimed that the English were indifferent to such treatment and wanted war. At that point, the correct English diplomat deliberately started to scream, and Hitler became quiet.[194] It is quite possible that Hitler's anger was play-acted, because, after the conference, he laughingly slapped his thighs and predicted that Chamberlain and his cabinet would fall because of the German pact with Russia. To Hitler's amazement, however, the British stood fast in their military alliance with Poland. Neither Britain's firm attitude nor Mussolini's message that Italy was not ready for war unless it were to receive very large amounts of steel, coal, oil, and weapons seemed to change Hitler's mind about the invasion of Poland. Hitler was unable to furnish these materials for Mussolini but replied in a rather restrained manner that, under the circumstances, he would count on Mussolini's neutrality and some help in manpower. Hitler postponed the attack on Poland until 1 September. His advisors differed in their views. Von Ribbentrop, whom von Weizsäcker considered to be insane, favored war, whereas Göring opposed it. Hitler permitted Göring to use a Swedish businessman, Birger Dahlerus, who had good contacts in London, to act as a go-between. Dahlerus considered Hitler's behavior in two meetings on 27 August and on 1 September abnormal and incomprehensible. The author's interpretation will be offered in chapter 9. The first meeting took place on 26 August:

> . . . Suddenly he [Hitler] stopped in the middle of the room and stood there staring. His voice was blurred and his behaviour that of a completely abnormal person. He spoke in staccato phrases and it was clear that his thoughts were concentrated on the tasks which awaited him in the case of war. "If there should be war, he said, then I will build U boats, build U boats, U boats." His voice became more indistinct and finally one could not follow him at all. Then he pulled himself together, raised his voice as though addressing a large audience and shrieked: "I will build airplanes, build airplanes, airplanes, build airplanes, airplanes and will destroy my enemies." He seemed more like a phantom from a storybook (Swedish: in a saga) than a real person. . . . Hitler continued as though in a trance: "War does not frighten me, encirclement of Germany is an impossibility, my people admire and follow me faithfully. If privations lie ahead I shall be the first to starve and set my people a good example. I will spur them to superhuman efforts." His eyes were glassy, his voice unnatural as he went on: "If there should be no butter I shall be the first to stop eating butter, eating butter. My German people will loyally and gladly do the same." He paused, his glance wandered and he said "If the enemy can hold out for several years, I, with my will power over the German people, can hold out one year longer. Thereby I know that I am superior to all the others."
>
> In the second meeting Hitler declared that he was determined to crush Polish resistance and annihilate the Polish nation. . . . He grew more and more excited and began to waive his arms as he shouted in my face, "If England wants to fight for a year, I shall fight for a year, if England wants to fight for two years, I shall fight two years. . . . He paused then yelled, his voice rising to shrill scream and his arms milling wildly: "If England wants to fight for three years, I shall fight for three years . . ." The movements of his body now followed those of his arms and when he finally bellowed "and if necessary I will fight for ten years," brandished his fist and bent down so it nearly touched the floor.[195]

When Dahlerus reported Hitler's strange behavior, it reinforced the wariness of the British statesmen.

A similar observation had been made one year earlier by Shirer,[196] and interpreter Schmidt also noted that, in his meeting with the French Ambassador Coulondre on 25 August, Hitler at times exhibited an absence of mind and repeated the arguments he used with Henderson in a mechanical fashion. His thoughts seemed to be elsewhere, and he was obviously in a hurry to terminate the discussion.[197]

Once more, Hitler formulated sixteen points for a settlement between Germany and Poland. These were the same points that had been presented before, except for an internationally supervised plebiscite in the Polish corridor that would enable the Germans and the Slavs (Poles and Kashubes) to determine the state of their territory. The sixteen points, however, were communicated officially to neither the British nor the Poles. The British learned about them when Göring, against Hitler's explicit wishes, read the points to Dahlerus, who communicated them from memory to the British Foreign Office. Hitler also demanded that a plenipotentiary for the Poles appear within one day to discuss the sixteen points. The plenipotentiary did not come and the Polish Ambassador Lipsky who saw von Ribbentrop on 31 August was told that it was too late. With hindsight one can conclude that the Poles backed by the British–French guarantee of assistance were unrealistic about their strength and instant help from their allies. The only man, however, who wanted a war was Hitler. A dismal trick by Heydrich was a fake occupation of the Gleiwitz radio station by inmates from a concentration camp wearing Polish uniforms. The radio station was "liberated," and the "Poles" were left behind, dead. With no further negotiations, Hitler stuck to his schedule. On 1 September 1939, at 4:45 a.m., the German battleship *Schleswig-Holstein* shelled a Polish ammunitions depot in the harbor of Danzig, and German troops crossed the border into Poland without a declaration of war.

In a major address before the Reichstag on that same date, Hitler informed the Germans that their country was at war. He spoke about his love of peace and his infinite patience, saying, however, that he now would put on the gray coat that was the holiest and dearest to him, and "not take it off until victory, or I will not survive the end. . . . The word capitulation I do not know."[198] The British demanded again on 1 September that hostilities end and that German troops withdraw to their own borders. Mussolini offered once more to intervene diplomatically, but Hitler continued his rapid advance into Poland. On 3 September 1939, Great Britain and France declared war on Germany. Hitler was shocked that they fulfilled their obligations to Poland. Hitler did not bumble into a war, as the British historian A. J. P. Taylor's main thesis would have it.[199] Rather, he caused an immense catastrophe by being a reckless gambler.

7

Warlord

Section I: Political, Military, and Personal Events

HITLER'S INEXORABLE MARCH to doom and destruction during World War II is a straightforward story that can be described with confidence. Conversely, the multiple and moderately severe illnesses that Hitler developed during the war are complex and to this day not completely understood. To make them more comprehensible for the reader, this chapter is subdivided into Section I, describing political, military, and personal events; and Section II, citing medical events. To interdigitate them would add unnecessarily to the complexity of the medical history.

The Annihilation of Poland

On 1 September 1939, fifty-seven German divisions invaded Poland. Hitler was thoroughly aware that he attacked a weak opponent. He did not declare war; he considered it counterproductive and old-fashioned, although with respect to some military customs, such as the display of the national flag, he stuck to military etiquette. Great Britain and France waited three days before they declared war against Germany, in agreement with their treaties with Poland. Their reluctance was not lost on Hitler. He knew about French public opinion, expressed in the question, "To die for Danzig?" Thus, he was all the more surprised when the actual declaration of war arrived. Schmidt described the moment when Hitler received the British ultimatum:

Hitler sat there as if he had turned to stone, and stared ahead. He was not disconcerted or enraged, as it was told. He just sat quietly and without any emotion. After a while, which seemed like an eternity, he turned to Ribbentrop, who stood petrified at the window. "What now?" he asked his Foreign Minister with a furious expression, as if he would express that von Ribbentrop had given him the wrong information about the reaction of the British. Ribbentrop answered with a soft voice, "I assume the French will render an identical ultimatum within the next hour."[1]

When Great Britain and France declared war on 3 September 1939, Hitler pretended, declared, and possibly even half-believed it meant that they were responsible for the war. His own deeds he forgot, denied, or suppressed. He claimed that all he had done was to undo the "Shame of Versailles." He stated: "I have shown my friendship for England many times . . . my politics were always based on the thought of mutual understanding. I have always been rejected with hypocritical explanations and ever new pretenses to restrict the German living space and, although we never threatened British interests, to make our life more difficult or impossible."[2] The fact that he wanted to destroy Poland after it refused to give in to his demands and ally itself with him in a future assault on Russia was never mentioned in public. Hitler knew from SD (Security Service) reports that the German population was not enthusiastic about the war, in contrast to their attitude at the beginning of World War I. Neither Goebbels's attempt to whip up enthusiasm nor Hitler's martial assertions changed their view. The Germans at that time preferred Hitler in the role of an "unbloody" general.

The greater numerical strength and superior quality of the German army enabled Hitler to defeat the Polish army in six weeks. The Polish soldiers fought gallantly, but tanks could not be fought by horse cavalry with lances. The Russian army entered Poland on 17 September 1939, and in mid-October Poland was defeated and divided. The western part was annexed by Germany, the eastern part by Russia. The remainder of Poland, the so-called General Government, was under German control, a dumping ground for Polish slave labor and Jews concentrated in ghettoes. A vigorous and confident Hitler viewed the rapid advance of his army in visits to the front, at times with considerable neglect of his own safety. Later, front visits became very rare, when Hitler conducted his war from headquarters and maps.

Clearly, Hitler was incensed with the Poles because they had no desire to join him as cannon fodder in a war against Russia. He felt contempt for their aristocracy, whom he considered arrogant and incompetent, though only a few years before he had concluded a friendship treaty with them. During occasional front inspections, Hitler watched Jews in their orthodox garb fleeing from burning towns and villages. Goebbels poured oil on the flames of Hitler's hatred: "I told him of my trip [to the front]. He listened carefully and shared my opinion about the Jewish and Polish problem. The Jewish danger must be banned. But it will surface again in a few generations. A total cure for it does not exist. The Polish aristocracy deserves their demise. It is without any rapport with the people, who are nothing but a burden."[3]

Hitler did what he always did when a dirty job needed to be done: He delegated it to his most reliable executioners—Himmler and Heydrich. The army leadership was glad to learn that they would be spared the dirtiest job. Although some, like General Walter Reichenau, participated gladly, others looked the other way. Very few protested—such an exception was General Johannes Blaskowitz, a devout Catholic, who objected to the atrocities and, at Hitler's request, was promptly transferred to the Western front. One week after the beginning of the hostilities, Hitler appointed Himmler Reichskommissar for strengthening the German nationhood. The intent was to kill the Polish aristocracy and intellectuals, use Polish workers as slave labor, and deport Jews to ghettos and concentration camps and transplant Germans in their place. The destructive phase of the plan was carried out with great brutality, while the resettlement of Polish land by German peasants never amounted to much. Himmler enunciated Hitler's intent that the education of the Poles should be limited to elementary reading and writing, just enabling them to perform unskilled labor. This was clearly Hitler's view, and later he recommended the same treatment for the Russians.[4] At the end of the Polish campaign, Heydrich reported that 90 percent of the Polish aristocracy, higher priesthood, and intelligentsia had been eliminated.[5]

The Euthanasia Program

On 18 October 1939, Hitler signed a secret decree:

> *Reichsleiter* Bouhler and Dr. Brandt are charged with the responsibility of enlarging the authority of certain physicians to be designated by name, in such a manner that persons who, according to human judgment, are incurable, can, upon a most careful diagnosis of their position of sickness, be accorded a mercy death.[6]

During the next eighteen months, 70,000 to 80,000 patients, most of whom suffered from psychiatric diseases, were killed.[7] In the early phase of the program, children were killed, later adults with mental illness, and finally persons with medical illnesses such as tuberculosis and cancer. Most of the children who were killed suffered from significant congenital mental retardation, epilepsy, or severe malformations. The majority of adults were schizophrenics, manic depressives, mentally retarded persons, epileptics, chronic alcoholics, or geriatric patients. Further, Hitler's decree was back-dated to 1 September 1939, the beginning of the Polish campaign, to cover earlier killings.[8] Hitler's signing of the secret decree on his private stationery was supposed to circumvent the process of changing the law to enable physicians to kill patients; however, it had sufficient authoritative force to convince physicians to participate in the program. The euthanasia program was meant to succeed the program of compulsory sterilization.

Gerhard Wagner (Reichsärzteführer, leader of National Socialist physicians and radical racist) had already recommended the killing of persons with incurable diseases as early as 1935, and Hitler had expressed the opinion that such a program would be feasible only in case of war.[9] Many high-level functionaries were eager to earn Hitler's favor by participating in the T4 program, a code name that stood for the abbreviated office address of the enterprise (Tiergartenstraße 4). Hitler chose Professor Karl Brandt and a top administrator, Dr. Philip Bouhler, to head it up.[10] Bouhler delegated actual operations to Victor Brack, his deputy. The men were charged to proceed with speed and secrecy. However, the program was an open secret, not only within party and government circles, but also among the German population, where word spread rather quickly.[11] The lack of secrecy was enhanced by educational programs that tried to convince school children as well as adults that it was immoral to waste resources on the unproductive and the chronically ill. A widely read book by a National Socialist physician and author, Dr. Helmut Unger, entitled *Sendung und Gewissen* (Mission and Conscience),[12] and films such as *Ich klage an* (I Accuse) emphasized the "morality" of the program. Hitler knew both the book and films. He received running reports about the program from Dr. Brandt regarding its execution. He also was aware of publications from the pre-National Socialist era recommending such killing programs, such as *Die Freigabe der Vernichtung lebensunwerten Lebens* (The Destruction of Life that is Unworthy of Living), the "black bible" of euthanasia, coauthored by the psychiatrist Professor Alfred Hoche and the jurist Professor Karl Binding.[13] In fact, the elimination of some extremely sick and deformed patients had been practiced before National Socialism rose to power in Germany, and in many other countries as well—including the United States—though never to the extent that it was done in Nazi Germany.

Before the outbreak of the war, conferences were held to discuss the organization and procedure of both contemplated programs, for children and adults. Hitler received a petition from the father of a congenitally malformed and severely retarded blind child, "*the child Knauer*," and dispatched Brandt to examine the child. After Brandt's consultation with the child's physician, the Knauer child was granted the "death of mercy" and was killed by a lethal injection of a barbiturate solution given by a physician. The father expressed his gratitude after Hitler had given consent to kill his child. The organizations that handled the killing of children and adults were similar in principle. Physicians in children's hospitals and psychiatrists had to fill out elaborate questionnaires. Under the supervision of high-ranking experts, the Reich Committee for Scientific Determination of Hereditary and Constitutional Severe Illness determined who would live and who would die. Because in some documents a cross after the name indicated the death sentence, the bureaucrats of the program were called "cross-writers." The second major organization involved in the program was the Charitable Service Transport

Division for the Sick, which brought patients to the special institutions where they would be killed by carbon monoxide gas or phenobarbital injection (children were often killed by starvation).

The program, which was very important to Hitler, became known as the euthanasia program. The word euthanasia designates a beautiful death for patients who are about to die. However, even its most innocuous form, euthanasia, the withholding of heroic medical intervention, is considered controversial. One absolute condition of acceptance in practicing euthanasia is the voluntary permission of the patient or a person who is legally responsible (such as a parent or spouse). Without such consent, the killing of any patient is considered murder. In National Socialist practice, however, the destruction of life that was not worthy of living (*lebensunwertes Leben*) was radically different. There was no consent, and the motivation was not the desire to grant the patient easy relief from extreme and hopeless suffering, but rather the intent to eliminate a "useless" being who would consume and waste resources, thus making the survival of the stronger members of the race less likely.

In practice, the evaluation of patients to be killed was anything but thorough. Dr. Hermann Pfannmüller, one of the most notorious killers, evaluated thousands of child patients from November 1939 to April 1941. Like the other examiners, Dr. Pfannmüller received extra pay for these services, in addition to payment for his other duties as hospital director. The relatives of killed patients were deceived and given false death certificates. However, in spite of such deceit, the program became widely known throughout Germany. Protests from victims' families and friends became loud and strong. Some physicians protected their patients by altering the diagnoses they listed on reports that were turned over to the agencies in charge of the killing program. Few physicians, however, had the courage to protest. Even after the war, only a few of the culprits were brought to justice, and Alexander Mitscherlich was vilified for exposing the program.[14] Furthermore, relatively few of those convicted received long-term sentences. The Nuremberg Military Court found Dr. Karl Brandt guilty for his deeds in connection with the T4 project as well as for his role in organizing criminal experiments in the concentration camps, and sentenced him to death by hanging. His close collaborator, Dr. Victor Brack, also was executed. Philip Bouhler, Professor Werner Heyde, and Dr. Hermann Pfannmüller committed suicide in captivity. Few protests came from the medical community, although in some psychiatric clinics official orders were sabotaged to a degree. The effective protests were the work of some courageous eminent churchmen. The petitions of Pastors Paul Gerhard Braune and Fritz von Bodelschwingh and the sermons of Bishop Clemens von Galen and Cardinal Michael Faulhaber accusing the NSDAP of murder infuriated Hitler, but induced him to halt the murderous actions officially on 24 April 1941. In reality, however, the killing went on in the concentration camps, under the code name T14-13, becoming part of the larger genocide program. Martin Bormann recommended that Bishop Galen be hanged, and Hitler indicated that he would reckon with the Catholic Church after his victory.[15]

Hitler's Western and Northern Campaigns

Little happened on the western front after the Polish campaign was concluded. Hitler tried to abort the "phony war" through an unacceptable peace offer to Great Britain and France. When it was rejected, he was eager to press for a quick start of the western campaign. The chief commander of the army, General Walther von Brauchitsch, and his chief of staff, General Franz Halder, were reluctant because they felt the German army was not ready to fight such a war. For the first time, Hitler encountered resistance from his top army officers in military matters. He subsequently developed a strong dislike for von Brauchitsch, called him a coward, and humiliated him in front of members of the general staff. However, it took Hitler two years to retire von Brauchitsch. In spite of Hitler's eagerness for an early start, the northern and western campaigns did not begin until the spring of 1940, due to unfavorable weather conditions.

Without any formal declaration of war, the German army quickly overran Holland and Belgium in May 1940 and moved without military resistance into Denmark. To Hitler's annoyance, the Danes, from King Christian X down, were adamantly opposed to Nazification and protected their Jews more than any other nation. Norway was subdued after heavy fighting against the Norwegian resistance and British expeditionary naval units. According to General Jodl, the Norwegian campaign was the only one that Hitler did not plan personally. He was unfamiliar with the crucial naval operations. It was one of the few situations where Hitler was in favor of retreating from the northern port of Narvik. General Jodl had to reassure a panicked Führer, writing in his diary, "The hysteria is frightful."[16] In this case, the opinion of the general staff prevailed, and Narvik was held. The Norwegian campaign was concluded on 9 June 1940, when the western campaign against Great Britain and France was already in full swing. Hitler was unable to win the cooperation of King Haakon or the Norwegian people, and the resistance of Denmark and Norway deeply vexed him. He could not understand why these "Nordic" people, whom he treated so well, would not accept him as the champion of racial superiority. Norway was treated as a conquered nation and governed by the collaborator Vidkun Quisling. National Socialism's highly honored anthropological guru, Professor Hans Friedrich K. Günther, considered Quisling the ideal Nordic type, in contrast to Hitler, about whom he reached—after the war, of course—an unfavorable judgment.[17]

With limited manpower and material resources, Hitler had to conduct a blitzkrieg against France. He relied on innovative motorized warfare designed by Generals Erich Manstein and Heinz Guderian, much against the advice of the conservative general staff. On 24 May 1940, the British expeditionary force was pushed against the sea at Dunkirk, when, to the surprise of some of his generals, Hitler halted his tanks. The Britons were able to evacuate their army in a spectacular sea rescue. To this day, no convincing explanation as to why Hitler stopped the tank advance has been found. Perhaps

Hitler did it to avoid humiliating the British in a crushing defeat, thus making them more amenable to becoming his allies in a future war against Russia. Another explanation is that Hitler simply wanted to preserve his tanks for his campaign against France.

After the British expeditionary force was evacuated, it was easy for the German armies to attack the "impregnable" Maginot Line from the rear, destroy it, and then triumphantly enter a defeated Paris, on 14 June 1940. Mussolini declared war on France four days before its collapse and earned more ridicule than spoils for his participation. The northern part of France remained occupied by the Germans. The southern part, Vichy France, became a German satellite state under the aging World War I hero, Marshall Henri Pétain. The mild terms of armistice were quickly accepted by the French. Hitler attempted to induce Pétain to join him in his fight against the British. Although he was not successful in this, he received substantial collaboration until General de Gaulle was able to organize the military and civilian Free French Resistance. Peace between Germany and France, however, was never established.

The German lightning victory over the French was an extraordinary triumph for the former lance corporal of the Imperial Army defeated in World War I, and never was Hitler's prestige greater with the Germans and European satellites than at that moment. On receiving the news on 17 June 1940, an ecstatic Hitler was photographed slapping his thighs.[18] He entered Paris as a conquering tourist with artistic interests, accompanied by three of his architects. He visited Napoleon's tomb, the grave of the unknown soldier, and the Paris Opera, where he stunned his entourage by reciting architectural details that he had memorized. The signing of the armistice was dramatically staged in the forest of Compiègne, where the "Shame of Versailles" was wiped out in the same dining car in which it had been established in 1919. Speer reported that, on the eve of the armistice, Hitler sat silently in a darkened room of a peasant house and was heard to say, "What a responsibility."[19]

After the Victory

Hitler had become the most powerful man on the European continent, but major problems remained unsolved. He received food and raw materials from Russia in exchange for industrial and military supplies, but he felt this was only a short-term solution. Stalin felt reasonably satisfied with the Soviet–German trade agreement, but Hitler wanted autarky, not trade. The "Jewish problem" had not become smaller, but bigger. Hitler faced complex political problems with his satellites—the "shitty states" (*Dreckstaaten*), as he called them.[20] The main problem, however, was how to defeat the British or induce them to make peace on the Führer's terms. On 17 July 1940, in a long speech at the Reichstag reviewing his successes and rewarding military leaders with promotions and decorations, Hitler enjoined the British Prime Minister Winston Churchill:

. . . perhaps, for once, you believe me when I prophesy that a great empire will be destroyed. An empire that it was never my intention to destroy or even harm. . . . In this hour I feel it to be my duty before my conscience to appeal once more to reason and common sense in Great Britain. I consider myself in a position to make this appeal, since I am not the vanquished begging favors, but the victor speaking in the name of reason. I can see no reason why this war must go on.[21]

Churchill rejected any negotiations and insisted that only the total defeat of Germany would be acceptable to him.

Hitler responded by planning an invasion of England that was code named Operation Sea Lion. However, the difficulties were formidable. The leadership of the German navy believed that an invasion could not be carried out without strong support from the Luftwaffe, no longer a match for the British air force. Hitler decided to postpone the invasion until the next spring, but in fact the plan was given up and replaced by an intensive air war and a naval blockade. According to General Jodl, this was the only time when Hitler was persuaded by his top commanders to change a major military plan.[22]

The air war started with the bombing of military targets. When the British air force, which at the beginning of the conflict was inferior to the Germans, gained sufficient strength to defend the British Isles and attack German targets, the air war escalated on both sides to include the cruel strategic bombing of cities and cultural sites (the so-called Baedecker bombings). The first target was the undefended historical city of Coventry. One of the last major raids was the brutal, devastating, and unnecessary Allied firebombing of Dresden. When the British air force, later reinforced by the formidable American air force, became superior, the devastation of German cities was far greater than that of British targets. Not until 1942 did the Germans threaten the British Isles with rockets. In the last two years of the war, a helpless Hitler responded to the devastating Allied bombing with impotent rage and considered killing British parachutists.[23] Ultimately, the Germans outdid the Allies in human destruction, but the Allies led in material destruction. On the high seas, Hitler was more successful. The Germans were almost able to cut off Allied shipments of supplies and troops, until modern radar detection devices by the Allies forced the Germans to stop the U-boat war. Hitler strongly favored the U-boat war and had no use for large surface ships, the "dinosaurs of the sea." After the Germans had lost several battleships, Grand Admiral Raeder was replaced by a U-boat specialist, Karl Doenitz, a trusted National Socialist whom Hitler appointed Grand Admiral. Admiral Raeder's advice to concentrate efforts on defeating the British in the Mediterranean theater of operations was rejected. Hitler always considered the Mediterranean a secondary show and only sent troops to assist the Italians when they got into trouble.

When Hitler failed in his attempt to persuade the British to make peace on his terms, he tried other political means. In a meeting at Hendaye on 13

September 1940, his attempt to persuade General Francisco Franco and his minister of foreign affairs Ramon S. Suñer to let German troops pass through Spain and chase the British out of Gibraltar was unsuccessful. The Spaniards turned him down, as Franco already had doubts about Hitler's ultimate victory. Hitler also was unsuccessful with Marshal Henri Pétain in a meeting at Montoire, when the old Marshal decided on a course of neutrality, as far as military operations were concerned. Marshal Pétain felt little inclination to join the Germans, who had not yet concluded a peace treaty with France and had released only half of their French prisoners of war. Nevertheless, Marshal Pétain collaborated with the SD and the Gestapo to the detriment of Jews as well as Gentiles in France.

Although communiques about the exchanges between Hitler and Mussolini and his associates always stressed friendship and cooperation, in reality much personal and private irritation existed, particularly at the level of the foreign ministers, Ciano and von Ribbentrop. Both men were secretive about their plans and had little trust in cooperative endeavors. Hitler was privately annoyed and alarmed over the military incompetence of the Italians, although he expressed such thoughts only much later in the Bormann papers, when he blamed Mussolini's Balkan operation for his failure in Russia.[24] Hitler had become the dominant partner and could afford to be rather forgiving. When Mussolini's military operations in North Africa and Greece went badly, the Italian dictator absolutely depended on Hitler to rescue him. Historians have wondered whether these operations or the partisan warfare in Yugoslavia delayed Hitler's number one war aim of invading Russia. Actually, however, there was little delay, because the Russian spring rains would not have permitted an invasion much before the middle of June.

While Hitler was sufficiently motivated to see Franco and Pétain on their own turf, the rulers of the satellite countries had to come to see him to get their orders. Hitler did best with the Rumanians. The Rumanian oil fields were very important to his war efforts, and General Ion Antonescu, one of Hitler's staunch supporters, cooperated fully. With King Boris of Bulgaria, in spite of his sympathies for National Socialism, the going was more difficult because of the King's national affinity to Russia. Hitler could move troops through Bulgaria to fight Greece, but Bulgaria would not declare war against Russia. The Finns, on the other hand, sharing Hitler's anti-Russian sentiments, were willing to declare war on their old enemy. Hitler found it difficult to deal with the Hungarian Regent Miklos Horthy because of a deep mutual dislike between himself and Horthy, a conservative Catholic. Even the anti-Semitism of the "Grandseigneur of the old Austro–Hungarian Monarchy," as the interpreter Paul Schmidt called him, was radically different from Hitler's. It was a religious anti-Semitism, and the restrictions Horthy imposed on Hungarian Jews were relatively mild. Yet for a long time the Hungarian leader cooperated in military matters and benefited from the disappearance of an independent Yugoslavia, Czechoslovakia, and Poland. Altogether, Hitler, who thought it proper to bully the little *Dreckstaaten*, had his hands full in getting their cooperation. Until Germany invaded Russia,

Hitler remained neutral in the Russian–Finnish War, which he and his military advisors monitored with great care. Watching the ineptitude of the Russian armies against brave little Finland strongly encouraged Hitler's attempt to defeat Russia in a blitzkrieg. The alliance with Italy and Japan, which Hungary and Rumania—already under Hitler's thumb—were forced to join, was not too meaningful, because Japan concluded its own nonaggression pact with Russia. In his endeavor to bring Yugoslavia into the Tripartite Act, Hitler was able to pressure the Yugoslavian Prince Regent Paul to join the Tripartite Act countries in a treaty, but, in a coup engineered by anti-German forces in Yugoslavia, Prince Paul was forced to resign in favor of the Crown Prince, who became young King Peter II. Furious about this Yugoslav action, which disturbed his grand strategy of preparing an attack on Russia, Hitler ordered an immediate invasion of Yugoslavia. In a punitive action he ordered the destruction of undefended Belgrade by aerial bombardment, resulting in a loss of 17,000 lives. This was another flagrant example of Hitler reacting with fury and vengeance when his own plans were crossed. It had happened before in Austria, Czechoslovakia, and Poland.

While he did not want any interference in the Balkan region, Hitler considered the Mediterranean Sea (*mare nostrum*) Mussolini's domain. He did not want any meddling in the Balkans, as the Rumanian oil wells were too important to him. Mussolini surprised him with the occupation of Albania in April of 1939. The move made little sense, because Albania was already under Italy's complete control. Obviously, Mussolini did it to show the Italians that he also was capable of conquering countries. Hitler was far more disturbed about Mussolini's intention to attack Greece in October 1940. Greece, he correctly assumed, would ask Great Britain for assistance, and British airplanes could bomb Rumanian airfields. He tried to dissuade Mussolini from such a move, but his objection came too late. The vainglorious Mussolini told him proudly that his troops had already marched from Albania into Greece. Greece indeed asked for British military assistance, and succeeded in pushing the Italian troops back into Albania. Hitler was forced to enter the Greek campaign. German troops reinforced the Italians and quickly occupied Greece and the Greek islands. The British expeditionary forces had to withdraw, not reentering Greece until the fall of 1944. Hitler later maintained that the Greek campaign forced him to postpone the Russian campaign. Military historians debating the issue have concluded that the Greek campaign was calculated into the plan to conquer Russia, but that the occupation of Yugoslavia against partisan resistance delayed the Russian campaign.

Hitler concurred with Mussolini's plans to extend his possession in North Africa and start an offensive against British forces in Cyrenaica, with the ultimate goal of conquering Egypt and the Suez Canal. The Italian armies had to retreat, however, before a numerically weak British force. The Italians were reluctant to ask for German help, rightly assuming that the more efficient, arrogant Germans might dominate them. When the situation became very threatening, they were forced to invite the Germans for a rescue operation. Hitler sent an armored division under his best commander, General Erwin Rommel, who combined boldness and imaginative flair in battle with concern for his soldiers, which endeared him to the Germans and, for some time, to Hitler. In seesaw operations, Rommel advanced rapidly, preventing an Italian rout, but had to retreat before the British as quickly as he advanced. Supplies could not reach him because of Italian naval defeats and the British possession of Malta, which Hitler had not attacked after his severe losses in Crete. It did not bother Hitler greatly because his main interest at that time clearly had shifted to a campaign against Russia.

Rudolf Hess

On the evening of 10 May 1941, Hitler's deputy Rudolf Hess flew a Messerschmidt MEno, the best German pursuit plane, from Augsburg to the castle of Dungavel in northern Scotland, where he hoped to discuss the end of hostilities with his acquaintance the Duke of Hamilton. It was his fourth attempt to reach Scotland to carry out this dangerous mission. His high status within the Party had enabled him to procure the airplane. An experienced pilot, Hess successfully maneuvered the plane in a night flight to a spot within 20 kilometers of the castle, where he parachuted and was found, with minor injuries, by local farmers. It is likely that Hess first tried to convince his captors that Germany would win the war, that Hitler would be willing to make peace with Great Britain, and that such a peace would be desirable for Germany and the Western Allies before they jointly began a holy war against Russia. On Churchill's orders Hess, who flew the mission in a Luftwaffe uniform, was considered a prisoner of war and remained in Great Britain until the end of the war, when he was transferred to Nuremberg to be tried by the International Military Court. On 1 October 1945, Hess was sentenced to life imprisonment for conspiracy and crimes against world peace. The sentence by the International Court was not unexpected, but what followed was another matter. While most of the other top Nazis were released after serving full or shortened sentences, Hess, in spite of many petitions and protests in the West, remained the only prisoner in the Spandau Prison until his death on 26 April 1987, at the age of ninety-one. Stalin was convinced that Hess's real mission was to persuade the British to join Hitler in his crusade against the Soviet Union. This would explain Russia's intransigent attitude about Hess's possible release, which changed only after Mikhail Gorbachev became head of the Russian government.

To this day, it is uncertain what Hitler knew about Hess's flight. According to the official German story, Hitler knew nothing about it. He learned about it in a letter that Hess's adjutant, Karl Heinz Piutsch, brought to him. The letter allegedly began, ". . . My Führer, when you receive this letter I will be in England." It ended, ". . . and should this endeavor, which admittedly has little chance of success, fail and thus fate decides against me, it will not have any bad consequences for you or Germany. You can distance yourself from me. Declare me mad."[25] Whether Hitler plotted together with Hess or not, Hess followed Hitler's advice. Hess behaved like a madman, and Hitler acted surprised, embarrassed, and furious; worried that the flight would be interpreted as a sign of German weakness; and denied any knowledge of it. According to Ciano, the Hess affair had a tinge of tabloid news but was a serious calamity for Germany.[26] A joke circulated that the Reich of a Thousand Years had become a Hundred-Year Reich, "one zero less." Hitler summoned von Ribbentrop and Göring to the Berghof, and von Ribbentrop was dispatched to reassure Mussolini. While von Ribbentrop visited with Mussolini, he learned from an English informant that Hess had actually landed in Scotland. Goebbels, who heard about the incident on 12 May, thought that Hess's act was a calamity of the first order. Hitler's first communique, on 11 May 1941, stated:

> Party member Hess, who was strictly forbidden by the Führer to fly because of progressive illness, against such an order was able to obtain possession of an airplane.
>
> On Saturday, 10 May, at 6:00 p.m., Party member Hess started in Augsburg again on a flight from which he has not returned. A letter that he left behind shows, in its confusion, unfortunate evidence of mental derangement, which gives rise to the fear that Party member Hess is the victim of a delusion. Under such circumstances, the National Socialist movement must assume that Party member Hess has accidentally crashed somewhere.[27]

In a second news release the NSDAP announced on 12 May 1941:

> As far as letters left behind by Rudolf Hess indicate, Hess has lived in the delusion that through a personal step with acquaintances from England could result in a rapprochement between Germany and England. A report from England confirmed that he parachuted in Scotland near the place he wanted to reach and was found suffering from injuries.
>
> Rudolf Hess, as was known in Party circles, suffered gravely from illnesses, and in the recent past reported to all kinds of remedies, magnetisms, astrology, etc. An attempt is made to examine whether such persons can be blamed for the confusion which induced him to take this step. It is possible, however, that Hess was lured into a trap by the British. The whole procedure confirms the assumption of the first communique that he suffered from delusions. He knew the most sincere efforts of the Führer to establish peace better than anybody else. Obviously, he developed the idea that through personal sacrifice, he would be able to stop a development that only could end in the complete destruction of the British Empire. Everybody knew that Hess's field of competence, which was entirely within the Party, had, as one can assume from his notes, no clear idea about the achievement or the consequences of such a step.
>
> The National Socialist Party regrets that this idealist became the victim of such a fateful delusion. Nothing will change in the pursuit of the war Germany has been forced to wage against England. It will be continued—as

the Führer declared in his last speech—until the British power mongers are crushed or are ready to make peace.[28]

On Bormann's orders, most of Hess's adjutants, secretaries, and chauffeurs were arrested. The powerful Director of the Aviation Works, Professor Willy Messerschmidt, who had provided Hess with the MEno, remained free. Professor Karl Haushofer was arrested, released on Hitler's orders, and then rearrested; after the assassination attempt on 20 July 1944, he was executed. Hess's wife, Ilse, was given a small pension. For the Third Reich Hess had become an unperson.

In British captivity, during the Nuremberg trial, and also during his long imprisonment, Hess acted "mad" at times, stating that his captors wanted to poison him, while at other times he acted as normal as the quixotic man was able to behave. A team of British psychiatrists, under the leadership of Dr. Jack Reese, examined Hess and diagnosed him as a paranoid-schizoid personality who malingered at times and other times seemed amnesic. They declared him mentally competent and fit to stand trial. In the author's opinion, Hess feigned mental illness when his mission failed. His symptomatology came very close to a Ganser Syndrome, which occurs in prisoners and is characterized by pseudo-demented behavior in which such patients give silly answers to obvious questions (e.g., "snow is black" or "two and two make five"). It occurs in hysterical personalities, and Hess certainly fell into this diagnostic category.

On 17 August 1987, shortly before his scheduled release, Hess, then the last and only prisoner in the Spandau prison, guarded by soldiers from the four Allied powers, died, allegedly by hanging himself. As Hess would have had no obvious motivation to commit suicide before his impending release, rumors arose that he was murdered by British or Russian agents. Rumors also circulated that an expert on forensic medicine who conducted an autopsy excluded the possibility of suicide, which reinforced the hypothesis of foul play.

Barbarossa

Hitler never believed that the Russian–German political and trade treaty would last. Stalin did not believe it either, but the views of the two dictators as to when the treaty would be broken differed. Hitler wanted autarky at the earliest possible moment, but Stalin banked on a longer trade agreement. Even after getting convincing evidence of German preparation for war from his own and Western intelligence sources, Stalin stubbornly refused to accept reports about the German military buildup near the Russian border. Difficulties developed in 1940 after the Russians annexed Bessarabia and Germany guaranteed Rumanian boundaries to protect its oil supplies. The Russians were annoyed by Germany's negotiations with Finland for nickel and lumber. Germany complained about unreasonable demands from the Russians in their trade agreements. W. M. Molotov, the Russian foreign minister, came to Berlin in November 1940 to review the problems. The skeptical Russian was told by von Ribbentrop that the war was nearly over (yet Molotov noted that the conference had to be interrupted because of British bombing raids). Molotov listened to vague promises about how the world would be carved up—Germany would dominate Europe, Russia would gain access to the Indian Ocean, and Japan would rule Southeast Asia. The shrewd Molotov was amused to be asked to join the Tripartite Alliance, but before Russia could even consider the proposal it was dropped. While Molotov was in Berlin, Hitler already ordered the construction of an eastern military headquarters. Hitler's intention to attack Russia had been expressed in the Second Book and *Mein Kampf*. His clear aim always had been to conquer land in eastern Europe to feed Germany and supply it with raw materials, as well as to enslave the populations west of the Urals. He was seriously concerned that Russia intended to dominate Germany and all of Europe and saw himself as the only person who was protecting European interests. The code word "Barbarossa," chosen by Hitler, referred to a red-bearded German emperor in the Middle Ages, Friedrich, who, according to folk myth, is asleep in the Unterberg near Salzburg and someday will awaken to conquer the world. The preparations for "Barbarossa" were carried out in maximum secrecy. Hitler did not even inform his own ambassador, Count Friedrich Werner von Schulenberg, about his intentions. Von Schulenberg learned of the operations only after the Germans had crossed the Russian border.

Already before the Polish campaign, Hitler made it clear to his generals that the war would be fought in a merciless fashion. "Close your hearts to pity," he said.[29] On 6 June 1941 he issued the Kommissar order to kill captured political prisoners. The mild protest from some general staff members did not stop the order. Hitler set the stage for extraordinarily harsh treatment of Russian prisoners by his infamous statement that Soviet prisoners of war were not comrades: "You must give up the concept of soldierly camaraderie. The communist was never a comrade and is not a comrade now. We are dealing with a war of destruction."[30] The grim reality was that 58 percent of the Soviet POWs did not survive. Hitler's plan for the domination of the conquered eastern territories was expressed quite explicitly in his monologues. On 17 October 1941 he stated:

> The natives? We'll sieve them. The Jews we'll take out completely [*setzen sie ganz heraus*]. We won't go into the Russian cities, they have to perish completely. We don't need to have any pangs of conscience. We won't assume the role of nursemaids, we have no such obligations. To improve their dwellings, to catch lice, German teachers, newspapers, no! . . . If they just know traffic signs so they can't run into our cars. Under freedom I understand that they hope to wash only on a holiday. . . . Moscow will be leveled.[31]

On 22 June 1941, three army groups (152 divisions) invaded Russia: The northern group, under Field Marshal von Leeb, advanced toward Leningrad;

the central group, under Field Marshal von Bock, advanced toward Moscow; and the southern group, under Field Marshal von Rundstedt, moved toward Kiev. To conduct a two-front war, west and east, was an enormous decision; a keen student of military history, Hitler was well aware of Napoleon's fate and the risks. The initial reaction by the German population was mixed. The German population was first worried about prolonging the war but also relieved that the phony friendship with Russia had ended and that Hitler was "defending European culture." Pope Pius XII praised Germany's "high-minded gallantry in defense of the Foundations of Christian culture."[32] After one month of fighting, the German armies rapidly advanced 500 kilometers along a 1500-kilometer front. General Halder, noting that the Russian troops had been surprised by the attack, expressed the optimistic view that the campaign would be over very quickly.[33] Similar views were held at that time by the military staffs of many nations. In spite of the rapid advance, only the center army group had destroyed large Russian contingents—according to orthodox military strategy, the crucial mission. Hitler was interested in the northern advance because he hoped to join up with the Finns to secure the Baltic and conquer Leningrad (he always called it Petersburg), which he considered the ideological center of Soviet Russia. The southern advance was most important to him in order to gain the Ukraine's wheat fields and mines, and eventually the oil fields of the Caspian region. After weeks of uncertainty, on 18 September 1941 Hitler rejected the plan by the army general staff to concentrate the attack on Moscow. This was an extreme example of his difficulty in making decisions: He favored attacks on all three fronts. It was one of the crucial decisions in the eastern campaign, and it was Hitler's and not the generals' decision. He knew his supplies were short, and he wanted to bring the war to a quick end, but an early winter slowed down his troops and tanks first by mud, then by snow and grim cold. The Germans reached the outskirts of Moscow, but then were stopped by well-equipped Russian forces. Hitler insisted on holding the position at all costs. Generals who wanted to retreat, such as one of the ablest tank commanders, General Erich Hoepner, were relieved of their command. (Hoepner was later executed after the 20 July plot.) With great losses in manpower and equipment, Hitler was able to stabilize the front. It also became apparent that his armies were not equipped for a prolonged war and the aggravations of a very severe winter.

Hitler and His Generals

While Hitler had been almost subservient to the generals during the first year of his regime, his attitude began to change after the generals played a willing and disgraceful role in the massacre of the SA. Hitler's recognition of cowardice and moral decay was uncanny. His feeling of superiority was enhanced after he was able to sack Generals von Blomberg and von Fritsch. When it came to decisions about whether or not to wage war, most of the generals opted for peace until the German armed forces were ready. In any case, it was Hitler's sole decision to start the war in September 1939. During the campaign against Poland, Hitler rarely interfered with the conduct of the war. The first conflicts emerged over when to start the western campaign. Hitler postponed the campaign only because weather conditions would not have permitted an earlier start. In the western campaign, Hitler's convictions about motorized operations and a blitzkrieg strategy ran counter to the views of the older generals, particularly General von Brauchitsch and the Chief of Staff, General Halder. The outcome of the western campaign strongly enhanced Hitler's supremacy, and Field Marshal Keitel called him the greatest military leader of all times (*größter Feldherr aller Zeiten*—abbreviated "*Gröfaz*"). Most of the generals agreed that Hitler had an astounding knowledge of military matters. He drew on his experience as an infantry man during World War I, but also acquired impressive knowledge about modern warfare from voracious reading—including the innovative book on tank warfare by General de Gaulle. Hitler was disinclined to stick to established clichés in battle strategy and tactics. As long as Hitler was victorious, the conflicts between him and his generals did not amount to much. He always had his way, because the German generals' belief in authority was stronger than their critique. Some of Hitler's best generals, such as Alfred Jodl and Wolfram von Richthofen, admired his intuition. However, when the fortunes of war changed in the winter of 1940/41, the disagreements became open. The first victim was Field Marshal von Brauchitsch, whom Hitler called a conceited coward. Altogether, Hitler fired half of his field marshals and generals during the course of the war. General Jodl wondered about the nature of such antagonism and weighed the question of whether it was caused by social class differences.[34] In fact, this may well have been a factor, though Hitler's sensitivity to criticism and skepticism might have been more important. Hitler required support and unflinching loyalty under all circumstances, victory or defeat. The antagonism between the Führer and many generals gradually became fierce, even though open disagreement was rare. Occasionally, when generals such as Heinz Guderian or von Richthofen stood up to him, Hitler yielded. First and foremost, Hitler expected his generals to be good National Socialists. General von Halder, his Chief of Staff, cited: "Anybody can carry out operations and military tasks. What is required of the Supreme Commander of the Army is the qualification to educate troops in the spirit of National Socialism."[35]

Hitler's Genocide of Jews

In the fall of 1940, when Hitler was planning the Barbarossa campaign, he also began to hatch ominous schemes concerning European Jewry. The experience with Poland's Jews was a general rehearsal for the ghastliest slaughter in modern European history. Before the war, the Jews in countries under German control were harassed, humiliated, deprived of their citizen's and human rights, and robbed of their property. The escape was emigration or suicide. After the beginning of the war, their fate grew worse. Jews were virtually excluded from gainful occupations and not permitted to attend theaters or cinemas or seek recreation in parks or public swimming pools. They could use public transportation only with special permits. They were not permitted to send their children to public schools. Their food rations were far below the German minimum. Males had to use the middle name Israel, females Sarah. Jews were forced to wear the yellow star of David on their clothing. In Poland after the German invasion, Jews met a fate even worse. They were crowded into urban ghettos where they lived under deprived, unhygienic conditions. Diseases of epidemic proportions ravaged the ghettos. Adults and children alike were forced into slave labor. Pogroms were incited. The first individual killing actions (*Einzelaktionen*) by SD commandos took place in conquered Poland.

After the takeover of Austria, the invasion of Czechoslovakia, and the defeat of Poland, the number of Jews under German domination had increased by nearly four million. The Nazi leadership entertained different options about how to deal with the Jews. One was to set up a Jewish reservation in the general government (the Nisko plan). Another plan, in which Hitler was very interested, was to send the Jews to Madagascar. In the spring of 1941, however, after the armistice with France, the plan to establish a "devil's island" for Jews under SS supervision was discarded because the French were unwilling to turn over Madagascar without a peace treaty. A long time after the plan had been given up (as late as 24 July 1942), for unknown reasons Hitler continued to talk about the Madagascar plan,[36] possibly just because he liked the plan, or to mislead his followers and the world.

On 31 July 1941, with Hitler's consent, Göring commissioned Heydrich to plan a program for solution of the Jewish problem.

> I hereby charge you with making all necessary preparations with regard to organizational and financial matters for bringing about a complete solution of the Jewish question in the German sphere of influence in Europe.
>
> Wherever other governmental agencies are involved, they are to cooperate with you.
>
> I request, furthermore, that you send me before long an overall plan concerning the organizational, factual, and material measures necessary for accomplishment of the desired solution to the Jewish question.[37]

This put Heydrich and his superior, Himmler, in charge of working out a program that shifted its focus from deportation to outright killing. It is not exactly known when concrete plans to kill the Jews rather than deport them emerged. Most likely, it occurred in the spring of 1941, when the Commissar order emerged, to kill Jews who held political offices in the Soviet army. After a conference with Hitler, Rosenberg entered in his diary the sinister remark, "What I do not want to jot down, but will never forget."[38] In November 1941, Heydrich called for an informational and coordinating conference that took place on 20 January 1942 in Wannsee near Berlin. Participants included members of all of the ministries that were concerned with the final solution. Their task was referred to in the following summary statement:

Under appropriate guidance the Jews will enter a work program. In large work units, under separation of sexes, Jews who are capable of working will work building roads leading into these territories; undoubtedly a large portion will disappear through natural diminution. The remaining part will have to receive appropriate treatment because, if freed, due to natural selection it would become the germ cell of a new Jewish buildup.[39]

At the time the high bureaucrats met at Wannsee, the destruction was already well under way. On 3 March 1941, ten months before the Wannsee conference and three months before the invasion of Russia, General Jodl transmitted directives from Hitler to the supreme command of the army indicating that the Reichsführer SS be charged with elimination of the Jewish Bolshevik leadership. The army was expected to provide logistical support. The SS actions were directed not only against commissars, but against all partisans and, finally, against the general Jewish population—men, women, and children within the conquered territories—and carried out with the assistance of recruited auxiliary executioners from the Eastern countries, mostly Latvians and Ukrainians.[40] Hitler personally insisted on including Gypsies because these alien migrants resisted the work patterns of the Nazi German world.[41] It has been estimated that, ultimately, the program resulted in the deaths of five to six million Jews, 250,000 Gypsies, and an undetermined number of Russian, Polish, Yugoslavian, and Czechoslovakian civilians. Statistics, however, only trivialize the nameless horror of the mass murder.[42] Apart from dying from overwork, starvation, and disease, Jews were killed outright through two principal measures: shooting by mobile SS commandos and gassing in extermination and concentration camps. The killing took place on a large scale until the fall of 1944, when Himmler, sensing defeat, stopped it to gain bargaining chips with the Allies.

The orders for the murderous work of the SS special units were given implicitly and explicitly through directives issued between 3 March 1941 and the invasion of Russia.[43] Hitler acknowledged the work of the Einsatztruppen in a vague remark during one of his nightly monologues: "We will make a raid, square meter by square meter, and always hang them. This will be a real Indian war. In Estonia and Latvia the gang or guerilla warfare has almost stopped. But this one must know. If one does not exterminate Jewry—in Jewry they have the telephone communications —nothing will work." In a non sequitur he added: "It is interesting that this little priest [Josef Tiso, President of the Slovak Republic, executed in 1947 for crimes against humanity] sends us the Jews."[44]

Before the Wannsee conference, some extermination camps were already under construction, while others had already begun operations. The first extermination camp was Chelmno, followed in the spring of 1942 by Sobibor, Belzec, and Treblinka. The large camps, Maydanek and Auschwitz-Birkenau, functioned both as concentration camps and extermination camps. In extermination camps, the victims were killed on arrival; in some concentration camps physicians selected who died. One faction of the SS favored direct killing; the other preferred that inmates die from overwork and starvation, thus creating an SS industrial empire in cooperation with major German industries. Some personnel and equipment were transferred to the camps from the euthanasia actions. At first, carbon monoxide gas was used in vans, but later this was replaced by the quicker-acting potassium cyanide gas (Cyclon B) used in specially constructed gas chambers. Some victims were murdered with phenol and barbiturate injections. Hitler spoke about the "humane" method used to exterminate Jews.[45]

In addition to shooting and gassing, a large number of inmates lost their lives and health in medical experiments undertaken in the concentration camps. The experiments, conducted without the subjects' consent, had the specific approval of the Reichsführer SS.[46] Considering his high interest in medical matters, it is very likely that Hitler heard about the experiments from Himmler and Brandt, and approved of them. They were in full agreement with his philosophy of extreme social Darwinism. The experiments fell under three categories: (1) experiments to enhance the war effort, such as cooling, underpressure experiments, and ingestion of sea water with deliberate designs to produce death; (2) experiments to explore the pathology of typhus, malaria, and hepatitis after deliberate infection, and to explore therapy for fractures after experimental fracturing of subjects' bones; and (3) experiments to explore mass sterilization and the infamous experiments on twins conducted by Dr. Josef Mengele.

No written order by Hitler for the genocidal actions has been found. Relevant data in his speeches, in the monologues, and in the Bormann documents, reports of discussions with associates and foreign statesmen, and testimony by the executors of the actions are cited to document Hitler's role in the genocide.

The Genocide in Hitler's Speeches and in the Monologues

On 30 January 1942, Hitler stated before the Reichstag:

> We must be clear that the war can only end either with the destruction of Aryan peoples or that Jewry disappears from Europe. I expressed this already on 30 September 1939 [the correct date was 30 January 1939], and I am careful about premature prophesies that the war will not end as the Jews imagine—that is, that the European–Aryan peoples will be exterminated— but that the result of this war will be the destruction of Jewry.[47]

On 24 February 1942, the birthday of the Party, he stated:

> My prophesy will be fulfilled, that in this war not Aryan humanity but the Jew will be exterminated. No matter how long the fight lasts, the Jew will be exterminated. . . . And only then, after the elimination of this parasite, there will a long period of understanding and true peace for the world.[48]

On 8 November 1942, before old Party members, Hitler repeated his threat while the extermination program was already taking place in a sinister prophecy:

> Also another power which once was very present in Germany, in the meantime has experienced that National Socialist prophesies are not phrases. It is the main power to whom we owe our misfortune: international Jewry. You will remember the session of the Reichstag during which I declared: If Jewry imagines to start an international world war to produce the extermination of the European races, the result will not be the extermination of the European races, but the extermination of Europe's Jews. One always laughed about me as a prophet. . . . Many of those who laughed then do not laugh anymore today, and those who still laugh today won't do it anymore after a little while. This knowledge will spread over the whole world. International Jewry in its whole demonic danger will be recognized. We National Socialists will see to it. In Europe this demon is recognized, and state after state joins us in their legislation.[49]

In the monologues, Hitler referred to the genocide of Jews thirteen times. The term "extermination," or "*Ausrottung*" (literally, "to root out"), which he used frequently, is precise and unequivocal. A few samples include the following.

> 17 October 1941: We will put out the Jews completely [*den Juden setzen wir ganz hinaus*]. Hatred? No, that we don't have. . . . I am ice cold in tackling this matter. I feel like the executioner of a historical will. Whatever people think of me leaves me completely indifferent. I never heard that a German who eats a piece of bread has qualms about whether the soil on which it grew had to be conquered by the sword. We also eat Canadian wheat and don't think about the Indians. . . .[50]

In several statements, Hitler complained about German sensitivity regarding the destruction of the Jews. In the cluster of monologues between 8 and 11 August 1941, Hitler stated, "How sensitive we are can be recognized when it seems to be an extreme of brutality to free our land from 600,000 Jews, while the evacuation of our own people is taken for granted."[51] In the same monologue, Hitler made the significant statement that the destruction of the Jews was part of his great task of the future, a planned racial policy to meet the problem of inbreeding that was taking place.

> 25 October 1941: . . . Before the Reichstag I prophesied to the Jews that the Jew would disappear from Europe if the war was not avoided. This race of criminals has two million dead on its conscience, now again hundreds of thousands. Nobody should tell me we can't send them into the morass. Who cares about our people? It is good if terror precedes us (*wenn uns der Schrecken vorangeht*), that we exterminate the Jews. To establish a Jewish state will be a failure. If some citizens cried that Jews had to emigrate, then this is typical for

those creatures. One would have to ask them about when hundreds of thousands of Germans had to leave Germany year after year. [Hitler deliberately confused voluntary emigration with compulsory expulsion in this monologue.] These Germans had no relatives in the world. They were completely on their own, while the Jews have enough relatives all over the world. Pity for them is most inappropriate. When I take the Jews out, our bourgeoisie becomes unhappy. What happens to them? [a good question, which Hitler left unanswered in his rhetoric] Did the same [people] care what happened to the Germans who had [!] to emigrate? One has to do it speedily. It is not better when I extract a tooth every three months for a few centuries. When it is extracted the pain is gone. The Jew must get out of Europe. Otherwise, there will be no accord. He agitates everywhere. In the end, I am enormously human. At the time of the papal reign in Rome, Jews were mistreated. Until 1830 eight Jews were driven through the streets every year. I only say he must be eliminated. When he perishes then I can't help it. I only see: absolute extermination [*Ausrottung*] if they don't leave voluntarily. . . .[52]

These statements were made when the Wannsee Conference was in preparation and the mass killing in the extermination camps had already begun. It was absurd for Hitler to speak of voluntary emigration, because Jewish emigration had been forbidden since the fall of 1940. Some of the statements are ambiguous and confusing, quite typical for Hitler.

27 January 1942 [just before the surrender at Stalingrad]: The Jews must get out of Europe. It would be best if they would go to Russia. They always will be an element which incites peoples against each other. They do the same thing they do in relation to peoples that they do privately. They have to be taken out of Sweden and Switzerland. Where they are few they are most dangerous. Five thousand Jews will be in a short time in all positions. It will be easier to pull them out. We have enough reasons. It's like a vessel with communicating pipes.[53]

On 22 February 1942, in the presence of Himmler, Hitler expressed one of his favorite comparisons, equating Jews with bacilli:

It is one of the greatest revolutions of the world. The Jew will be recognized. The same fight that Koch and Pasteur had to fight will be waged by us. Innumerable illnesses have been caused by this bacillus: the Jew. Japan would have gotten it, too, if it had been open to Jews. We will recover when we eliminate the Jew. Everything has a cause. Nothing is due to chance. The cause of these illnesses is a racial nucleus that is so devastating in the mixture of blood it makes people insecure. Probably physical illness has been caused by the mixture of different blood groups.[54]

Hitler expressed his extreme anti-Semitism and determination to eradicate the Jews quite explicitly throughout the Bormann documents and in his political testament, the last expression of his hatred of Jews.

Associates' Statements regarding Hitler's Role in the Genocide

Assessing the statements made by Hitler's major helpers in the genocidal actions of the Third Reich with respect to Hitler's role is difficult. The accused were fighting for their lives and liberty in the postwar trials, and truth was not a priority. In general, one can state that the accused in the trial of the International Court at Nuremberg tried to distance themselves from the genocide, while the accused of the second echelon, amongst them the actual murderers, tried to assert that they acted on higher orders. About Hitler's role in the genocide, Göring stated: "In my opinion, the Führer was not informed about the details in the concentration camps, about . . . the cruelties . . . was not informed; as I know him, I don't believe that."[55] Speer visited concentration camps and so-called out-camps (often mines) but claimed to be ignorant of murders within the camps.[56] In his remarks at the Nuremberg trials, Joachim von Ribbentrop presented himself as a moderate anti-Semite: "Until 22 April 1945, when I saw him for the last time, he did not mention the killing of the Jews with one word. Therefore, I can't believe today that Hitler ordered the murder of the Jews, but assume that he was faced with accomplished facts by Himmler."[57] Von Ribbentrop obviously "forgot" his and Hitler's statements in the discussion about the killing of Hungarian Jews with Horthy on 17 April 1943. The Chief of the Reich Security Service of the SS, Ernst Kaltenbrunner, a preposterous liar, denied killing actions that he had ordered over his own signature. The abominable Streicher was more honest. He considered Hitler's genocidal actions humanity's greatest deed.[58] In his diary entry of 27 February 1942, Goebbels made the following statement:

> Starting with Lublin, the deportation of Jews in the general government to the East has been set in action. It is pretty barbarous business. One would not want to go into detail, and there are not many Jews left. I think one could reckon that about 60% have been liquidated and about 40% taken for forced labor. One simply cannot be sentimental about these things. The Führer is the moving spirit behind the racial solution, both in word and deed.[59]

Many statements implicating Hitler as the ultimate architect in the genocide were made by lower-echelon killers during the postwar trials. Rudolph Höß, the commandant of Auschwitz, and Adolf Eichmann, the major administrator of the death transports, tried to save their lives by stating that they had acted under orders. A statistical report about the genocidal actions, compiled by the SS statistical officer Richard Korherr, was typed on the Führer-typewriter (with extra large letters) and submitted to Hitler.[60]

Himmler and Heydrich were the chief organizers of the genocide. Heydrich became the most destructive force in the killing program. He was not a sadist but an ambitious, cold, and amoral technocrat, and a devoted servant to Himmler.[61] He recognized Himmler as his supervisor, never competed with him, and carried out his wishes and orders, just as Himmler carried out

Hitler's wishes and orders.[62] Himmler met frequently with Hitler, but no records of their conversations have been found, and probably none existed. One transaction was a recorded telephone order. On 30 November 1941, Himmler called Heydrich from the Führer's headquarters, "Transport of Jews from Berlin. No liquidation."[63] For historian David Irving, this was proof of Hitler's lack of involvement in the liquidation. For Martin Broszat, who dealt with Irving's revisionism in a long article, it was proof that Hitler knew, because otherwise Himmler would not have found it necessary to stop the killing.[64] Werner Maser provided a plausible explanation: Hitler was absent from the headquarters on that day, and Himmler would have ordered an execution only with Hitler's approval.[65] Hitler's and Himmler's views about the Jewish situation were similar. Both talked about the need to exterminate the Jews in many speeches and monologues. Both used linguistic disguises (*Tarnsprache*) to deceive the public, possibly also deceiving themselves. Both considered the Jews a criminal race that was determined to destroy the Germans. Both used the "declaration of war" by Chaim Weizmann, President of the Jewish World Congress, as a justification for retaliation[66]—although it is obvious that Hitler and von Ribbentrop knew that a private individual such as Weizmann cannot declare war.* Hitler and Himmler both stressed that the Jews had started the war and must be punished for this. Both used medical metaphors (Jewish poison, Jewish cancer) in their rhetoric. They justified their actions as necessary to protect humanity. In his speech on 24 April 1943, Himmler compared anti-Semitism to a delousing program: "It is not a question of belief [*Weltanschauungsfrage*] that lice should be removed. It is a question of cleanliness. For us anti-Semitism is not a belief system, it is a question of cleanliness. It is almost solved."[67] The following extraordinary remark, from the same speech, accurately expressed Himmler's—as well as Hitler's—beliefs: "To have remained decent fellows, that is what made us tough. That is a page of glory in our history." Himmler spent considerable time explaining why Jewish women and children had to be murdered: "It is in accord with Hitler's concern for a long-term solution. . . . We will not, notwithstanding our deep emotion coming from our hearts, let the hateful avengers grow up and leave it to our children and grandchildren to deal with them, while we, the fathers and grandfathers, are too weak and cowardly to act." Both Hitler and Himmler denied harboring any hatred against the Jews, at least in some of their writings. Both were incensed by Germans who defended the Jews.[68] Himmler's remarks about the genocide in his speeches in Posen and Sonthoven (1943–44) and Hitler's remarks in numerous speeches and conversations are so similar that one would almost think they had been written by the same speech writer; however, neither man used speech writers. Their speeches were the products of a shared ideology. Apart from all similarity, there is one difference between their speeches. Himmler's statements were

* This view of the declaration of war by the Jewish World Congress was widely held by Nazis.

precise and consistent (except when he spoke to Count Bernadotte and maintained that the Jews died in epidemics), while Hitler's were not. He spoke vaguely about evacuations to the East and left it unclear whether Jews would be killed, die of starvation, or be worked to death. In his speech on 5 May 1944, Himmler was remarkably frank: "You can imagine how I felt executing this soldierly order issued to me, but I obediently completed and carried it out to the best of my convictions." In other speeches he stated that "the Jewish question was executed according to order and rational analysis [*nach Befehl und verständnismäßiger Erkenntnis*]," or he spoke of the most terrible task and the most terrible directive. According to SS General Berger, Himmler twice mentioned that the mass liquidations were carried out on orders from Hitler.[69] Karl Wolff, Himmler's adjutant, quoted Himmler: "You can't imagine what a burden it is to silently relieve the Führer so he can be the messiah of the next 2000 years and can remain absolutely free."[70] During the last war years, Hitler did not tolerate any discussion about Jews unless he initiated it. Henriette Hoffmann-Schirach told the story that, after raising a question about a transport of Jews from Amsterdam to Auschwitz, she received no answer and fell into disgrace with her Führer.[71]

Statements Made to Foreign Statesmen about the Genocide

The Croatian minister of defense, Marshal Slavko Kvaternick, stated that on 21 June 1941 Hitler told him:

> . . . if only one state for whatever reasons would tolerate one Jewish family, it would become the bacillary focus for a new decomposition. If there were no Jews in Europe, the unity of European peoples would no longer be disturbed. Where the Jews are sent, to Siberia or Madagascar, does not matter. He [Hitler] will approach each state with this request. The last state in which Jews can maintain themselves will be Hungary. One has to send this State an inter-European request that it comply with the iron will of Europe.[72]

In two tense exchanges between Hitler and Horthy on 16 and 17 April 1943, in the presence of von Ribbentrop, an important topic was Horthy's attitude toward the Hungarian Jews. Hitler criticized Horthy because two Jews (*Volljuden*) had been elected to the upper house. Horthy replied that, for constitutional reasons, nothing could be done about it and that there were many baptized Jews living in Hungary, amongst them many valuable persons. He also stated that he had done everything that could be decently done against the Jews, but he couldn't murder or otherwise kill them (*ermorden oder sonstwie umbringen*). The Führer replied that this was not necessary. Hungary, like Czechoslovakia, could put Jews into concentration camps. Hitler then explained what opportunities would open up if the positions now held by Jews could be freed. If one were to speak of murder, Hitler argued, it is only the Jew who murders and starts wars. "The opportunity exists to let them work in mines. In any case, their influence in the host country must be eliminated. . . ." Horthy stated that he had to blush admitting that 36,000 Jews had been sent in working battalions to the front, of whom most perished in the Russian advance. The Führer replied that Horthy need not blush, because the Jews had started the war and therefore one need not pity them, even though the war had serious consequences for them. He said he also was convinced that the Jews had not been killed, but rather that they had deserted to the enemy. During this conference, von Ribbentrop (in Hitler's presence) stated that the Jews must be annihilated (*vernichtet*) or put into concentration camps, and during the continuing discussion Hitler talked about the destructive role of Jewry in the history of Germany.

Hitler also felt hatred and contempt for Gypsies.[73] In addition to the millions of Jewish, Polish, Russian, and Serbian civilians, about 200,000 members of the Gypsy tribes Sinti and Roma found their deaths in concentration camps through starvation, epidemic illness, overwork, medical experiments, and, in some cases, gassing. Hatred and mistrust of these nomadic tribes can be traced to the early Middle Ages, when Gypsies migrated to Europe. Like Jews, they were accused of ghastly crimes—murder and abduction of children, poisoning of wells, and so on. The regime was particularly concerned with half-breed Gypsies and their racial threat to Aryan Germans. It happened that, in some Gypsy families, one member served in the German army and another was killed in a concentration camp. In contrast to Himmler, Hitler did not talk about Gypsies in public. He did not have to do so, because many Germans and other Central Europeans shared his hatred and fear of these nomads.

The evidence for Hitler's crucial role in the genocide of Jews and others is massive, even though no direct order has been found. Probably, the lack of such an order has contributed to the interpretation that the genocide originated in a haphazard fashion—that it was the result of "accumulative radicalization," but did not follow a central plan. There was, however, a central plan, developed by Hitler. He never tried to halt the murder, which continued until the Allied armies were at the gates of the concentration camps. And only Hitler could have stopped the destruction.

The Monologues[74]

Citations from the monologues have been used throughout this text, specifically containing Hitler's statements about the genocide. The monologues were Hitler's statements to his intimates during lunches, dinners, and nightly teas at the Führer's headquarters, made with some interruptions, between 5 July 1941 and 7 September 1942. Martin Bormann instructed his adjutant Heinrich Heim to record these conversations. In Heim's absence the monologues were recorded by Henri Picker. Between 13 June 1943 and 30 November 1944, Bormann himself recorded later sessions. The records were produced from memory immediately after the talks. Some of the notes are followed by annotations like, "the Chief expressed in essence as follows . . . ," or, when Hitler was joking, the recorder noted, "in jest." Bormann believed that the monologues, which covered a wide variety of subjects, would be of great value in implementing the policies of the Führer, and even sent pertinent transcripts to Rosenberg to guide him in the governance of Russia. Bormann also wanted these soliloquies to be relaxing and to take Hitler's mind off the military problems that plagued him during the critical war years. Indeed, Hitler talked about virtually anything under the sun. His captive audience listened in silence. He was rarely interrupted or asked a question. The transcripts were confiscated from Bormann's wife after the war and finally surfaced in the Swiss publishing house of Genoud. At first the monologues appeared only in French translation, then in English; later they were retranslated into German and also appeared in English.

For an understanding of Hitler's complex mind, the monologues are invaluable. He never ceased to be an orator talking to an audience, even in the intimate atmosphere of the *Tischgespräche*, but the dictator felt freer, more relaxed than in his written statements and public speeches. Some of his thoughts were expressed previously in *Mein Kampf*, the Second Book, and various articles and speeches, but much was new. Often Hitler's statements addressed the concerns of visitors (e.g., Himmler, who was a frequent guest). The talks ranged from the sublime (e.g., his talk on 2 January 1942 concerning God—"one can't get around the concept") to the trivial (e.g., discussions about his fare of Tyrolean meat and potato hash during the pre-vegetarian days, plus lengthy tales of his youth, military service in World War I, and the "Party history"). Frequent topics were his world view, his extreme anti-Semitic and ethnocentric views, attacks on the churches and religion, the colonization of Russia, critique of the Allies and other opponents, and art. Nowhere else did Hitler express his hatred of the churches and his ethnocentricity more succinctly. At times he was remarkably frank in talking about personal matters (e.g., his relationships with women and personal idiosyncrasies such as his dislike of lawyers and teachers) but hardly talked about the course of the war. Systemic analyses of the monologues, mainly of political topics, exist, but psychological topics have received less attention in the relevant publications. Yet the monologues convey aspects of Hitler's grasp of many areas of modern life and technology, education and culture, and in many instances indicate a strong, synthesizing mind. Even in the ruminations about religion, the monologues convey a certain kernel of truth. Characteristically, Hitler treated many topics, even his radical anti-Semitism, in such a duplicitous manner that the monologues have been used to present Hitler as a man of peace and a genuine friend of the arts. Apart from any analysis of content, the monologues are remarkable because in them Hitler at times showed disturbances of thought. In some of the monologues, his thought processes were in varying degrees incoherent and uncontrolled. Hitler's flight of ideas was mirrored by a pressure of speech, and his speech was often rambling. This disturbance, even more than the content, justifies the assumption that Hitler at times might have spoken under the influence of drugs or toxic conditions such as severe sleep deprivation. This hypothesis will be discussed fully in Chapter 8.

The Fortunes of War Change

On 11 December 1941, in the midst of the troublesome winter campaign in Russia, Germany and Italy declared war on the United States following the devastating Japanese attack on the American fleet at Pearl Harbor on 7 December. Germany's treaty with Japan did not obligate Hitler to take this step. He took it against the advice of his foreign minister, without even trying to induce Japan to declare war on Russia. Hitler was delighted when he heard of the attack on Pearl Harbor. In his speech before the Reichstag on 11 December 1941, Hitler emphasized that he was already virtually in a state of war with the United States, which, through its naval patrols and the lend-lease agreement, had immensely helped Great Britain and Russia.[75] President Roosevelt, he said, was mentally ill and a pawn of the Jews.[76] He told the Japanese ambassador, General Hiroshi Oshima, that he empathized with the Japanese, who, like himself, had tried very hard to arrive at a solution and were rejected, but finally struck a hard blow.[77] In fact, Hitler gained one ally with limited strength while mobilizing the enormous potential of the United States against Germany.

Hitler welcomed spring in 1942: "Sunday is the first of March. Children, you don't know what this means for me. How these three months sapped my nervous energy."[78] He felt ready for the huge offensives on the Russian front at Leningrad, in the Southern Russian front, and in North Africa. The most important was the offensive in Southern Russia, aimed at occupying the bread basket of the Ukraine and Crimea, the industrial and mining region of the Donets basin, the communication center of Stalingrad, and, above all, the oil wells east and west of the Caucasus mountains. Two army groups moved with spectacular speed toward the Caucasus. In a surprise directive, Hitler ordered Army Group A, with support from Rumanian, Hungarian, and Italian divisions, to capture Stalingrad, and Army Group B to continue their march to the Caucasus and Caspian Sea. Army Group B reached the Caucasus but was unable to conquer the oil fields of Baku and Grozny. An angry Hitler relieved Field Marshal Wilhelm List from his command of Group B and berated General Jodl for defending him. From that point on, Hitler refused to eat with the generals and insisted on the presence of stenographers at staff conferences. The conflict between Hitler and his Chief of Staff, General Halder, who advised against the Stalingrad venture, became unbearable. Halder noted in his war diary, "The ever-present underestimation of the potential of the enemy reaches ever more grotesque proportions and becomes dangerous. Serious work is out of the question. . . . a complete lack of judgement . . . rage attacks if mistakes and their consequences are pointed out."[79] On 24 September 1942, Halder was "permitted" to resign and jotted down in his diary, "My nerves are used up; his nerves also are not fresh anymore. We must separate. Necessity of education of general staff to fanatical belief in the idea. Determination also in the Army to absolutely have his will."[80] Besides Field Marshal List, Field Marshals Gerd von Rundstedt and Fedor von Bock were replaced. Halder's successor was a tank commander, General Kurt Zeitzler—who lasted until July 1944. General Friedrich Paulus, commanding the Sixth Army at Stalingrad, was promoted to Field Marshal. In bitter fighting the Germans conquered most of Stalingrad. Exposed on both flanks, however, they were virtually encircled in a pocket with very limited supplies. Göring promised air supplies but was unable to deliver, especially after the last nearby German airport was captured. In this situation, Paulus asked Hitler for permission to fight out of the Stalingrad pocket, which Hitler refused. Threatened with the destruction of his Sixth Army, Paulus surrendered. Hitler expressed his anger and dismay both to General Jodl and his new Chief of Staff, Kurt Zeitzler:

> The man [Field Marshal Paulus] was to kill himself, as generals used to throw themselves into their swords when they saw the cause was lost. That's a matter of course. . . . What will he do now? He will be brought to Moscow. Imagine that rat cage [the Lublianka prison in Moscow]. He will sign anything, he will make confessions. You see, this will reach the bottom of infamy. . . . In this war, nobody will become field marshal anymore.[81]

The destruction of the Sixth Army was a major disaster for Germany. Some 146,000 men were killed in action; 90,000 became prisoners of war, 6,000 of whom returned home. Historians consider it a turning point in the history of Hitler's war. It was the end of the invincibility myth. The summer of 1942 marked Hitler's greatest expansion. German soldiers were at the Caucasus, 100 miles from Alexandria, and a serious threat was posed by the Japanese to capture India and Australia. The Allies had reason to worry. The fortunes of war, however, changed radically during this time, not only in Russia but in North Africa and the Pacific. The German front in Russia reached from the Arctic Ocean to the Black Sea, and supply routes were overextended. The German air force was no longer equal to the Allied air force. The U-boat war had become less of a threat due to the Allied radar detection devices, and, most of all, the United States potential in manpower and supplies began to be felt.

In the summer of 1942, General Rommel started another surprise offensive, succeeded in capturing the fortress of Tobruk, and was promoted to Field Marshal. He quickly moved to the Egyptian frontier, to be halted only 100 kilometers from Cairo. Mussolini was ready to enter the city on a white horse. Hitler began to consider conquering the middle-eastern oil wells.[82] He ordered Rommel to hold out at El Alamein: "The choice is victory or death."[83] It has not been established whether Rommel withdrew before or after he received Hitler's communication, but he withdrew after a crucial loss of men and weapons. Hitler was furious but did not sack General Rommel, who at the time enjoyed the highest prestige, built up by Goebbels's propaganda machine. Shortly afterward, Rommel left the North African theater of operations and developed headaches and insomnia, a condition the Allies called combat fatigue or combat neurosis—terms that were not in the medical vocabulary of the German armed forces. Rommel was not given another top command. He held lesser posts and, implicated in a plot to kill Hitler, was forced to commit suicide. The German and Italian troops in North Africa were rapidly pushed back by British forces. In November 1942 the Allies landed in Morocco and Algiers. Eisenhower moved toward Tunis and eventually made contact with General Montgomery's English army in Tripolitania. Strong German and Italian reinforcements that had landed earlier in Tripolitania on Hitler's insistence were captured. This made the landing in Sicily and Italy, the soft underbelly of Europe, possible. Hitler was clearly on the defensive, sensing treachery by the Vichy French, and occupied all of France.

From 9 to 26 January 1943, Roosevelt and Churchill met in Casablanca to discuss global war strategy; Stalin was absent. Roosevelt favored an invasion in the north of France, Churchill in the Mediterranean area. At the end of the conference, Roosevelt brought up the condition of unconditional surrender, which was accepted by Churchill and later also by Stalin. Hitler's response was a stereotypical, "I don't know the word capitulation." Goebbels's answer to the Allies' concept of unconditional surrender was to shake up German morale and commitment to total war. In an eloquent speech after the defeat at Stalingrad on 18 February 1943, he propagated total mobilization; the bringing of personal sacrifices; closing bars, luxury restaurants, theaters, and opera houses; and, most of all, mobilizing German manpower, and also woman-power, which until then had remained largely unutilized. Even after such restrictions were imposed, however, they were frequently circumvented. Dr. Morell, for instance, achieved the reopening of a favorite restaurant in Vienna, and Eva Braun influenced Hitler not to close all the beauty salons. Hitler's support of restrictions was lukewarm. He always spoke about sacrifices but was reluctant to ask for too much lest the population become disgruntled as they had been during the First World War. It also went against his grain to use women in war jobs in any significant way. The degree of German mobilization had always remained below that of the Western and Russian Allies. Only the production of war materials increased sharply under the new Armament Minister, Albert Speer. His predecessor, Fritz Todt, just before his death in an airplane accident, had felt quite pessimistic about German armament production.

Except for isolated successes, such as reconquering Kharkov, the Germans were forced to retreat along the entire Russian front. Hitler banked on a badly needed victory in Operation Citadel, a huge tank battle at the Russian salient of Kursk. To build up a larger force, Hitler hesitated to attack. The Russians beat him to the punch, counterattacked, and inflicted a costly defeat on the Germans with a huge loss of manpower and tanks. Hitler's chiefs of staff and his generals had to wrestle with him constantly over permission to withdraw. Retreat remained anathema to Hitler, manifested by his "breakwater" doctrine.[84] His rigidity during the last war years cost hundreds of thousands of lives. Hitler's style of command had changed; instead of issuing broad directives, he became preoccupied with micromanagement. Able military leaders like Field Marshals Manstein, von Kleist, and Rommel, were relieved of their commands, to the detriment of the German conduct of war. The collapse of the Italian Empire in Africa and the invasion of Italy heralded the fall of Mussolini. On 25 July 1943, at the recommendation of the Fascist Supreme Council, King Victor Emanuel ordered Mussolini's arrest. Field Marshal Pietro Badoglio formed a new government and started peace negotiations with the Allies. Hitler had Mussolini liberated in an audacious act of Waffen SS troops under Colonel Otto Skorzeny from a secret hideout in a mountain hotel in the Apennines on 12 September 1943. Hitler forced the depressed, sick, and reluctant Mussolini to become head of a fascist puppet state, the Republic of Salo, covering the territory of the northern half of the Appenine Peninsula. Hitler was proud of the daring rescue and believed it would impress the British that he stood by a friend.[85] Increasingly, Stalin was annoyed with the delay of the invasion across the Channel and assumed that the western Allies wanted an endless struggle in which Germany and Russia would bleed each other to death. Hitler sent out vague and ambivalent peace feelers to Russia through his Stockholm embassy, without success. Nothing came of Hitler's peace feelers to the western Allies, who were convinced that their victory was not far off.

The Fall of the Fortress Europe

Plans for the invasion of the Channel Coast were slow, and preparations were difficult. Hitler realized that the success or failure of these landings might decide the outcome of the war. Finally, after painstaking preparations, the Allied invasion of Normandy took place on 6 June 1944. The Germans believed they were prepared but held differing opinions about where the Allies would land. Hitler's intuitions about the place were right, but not about the date. Based on German meteorological reports, an invasion on 6 June 1944 was considered unlikely. Goebbels, who was visiting at the Berghof, wrote in his diary that he and Hitler spent a cozy evening together on 5 June 1944: "We sit together before the fireplace until 2:00 a.m. and reminisce and feel happy about the many beautiful days and weeks which we experienced together. In short, the atmosphere was like in the good old days. . . ."[86] As usual, Hitler slept late, and General Jodl, who received the news of the invasion first, did not want to wake up the chief. The German war conference dealing with the invasion, which had begun before dawn, took place nine hours later. Hitler actually believed the invasion would offer Germany a chance to inflict serious harm to the Allies by entrapping them. When Goebbels asked Hitler how he would do this in detail, he did not get an answer, but consoled himself that Hitler always knew what to do.[87] An important reason why the invasion succeeded so quickly was the breakdown of the Luftwaffe. Hitler blamed the generals of the army and the air force for their failure to restrict the Allies' entry into Normandy and throw them back into the sea. Once the Allies broke out of the Normandy pocket at Avranches, they advanced quickly toward Paris. Against Hitler's orders, the commandant of Paris, General Dietrich von Choltitz, surrendered, and General Charles de Gaulle triumphantly entered the city at the head of the Allied armies. On 25 August 1944, Allied troops landed at the Mediterranean coast of France. Converging armies liberated all of France, and on 21 October the Allies conquered the first German city, Aachen.

Throughout 1944, superior Russian forces pushed the Germans back. In spite of Hitler's desperate attempt to hold out in the Crimea, the Germans had to evacuate the peninsula with heavy losses. The collapse at the Army Group Center was a greater catastrophe for Germany than the surrender at Stalingrad. After the breakdown of the northern front, Finland asked for peace with Russia. The Russian armies entered East Prussia and Memelland in November 1944 and forced the evacuation of a very large German civilian population who were afraid of brutal retaliations. Hitler moved from his East Prussian headquarters to the bunker of the Berlin Reichskanzlei, which he later regretted because it set a bad example. The loss of Rumania meant the loss of the Ploesti oil fields. The Rumanian dictator, Antonescu, was captured and executed. To prevent the surrender of Hungary, Admiral Horthy was arrested and replaced by a German minion, Ferencz Szalasi. The Germans started a difficult retreat from Greece through Yugoslavia, where most of the German troops were captured. In the Pacific, the Allies were on the offensive since the battle of Midway in 1942, though it would take five months longer to defeat the Japanese after the Germans were overthrown. When the Germans capitulated, the Japanese considered it a breach of contract.

One front where Allied advances were slow was in Italy. After Mussolini had become the puppet ruler of the Republic of Salo, the country was ravaged by a civil war between fascists and partisans and by fighting between German and Allied troops. The Allies were not able to reach the Po Valley until the spring of 1945. After this, however, the end of the German and Italian troops came fast, in bloody fighting and massacres. For a short time, Goebbels touted the *Vergeltungswaffen*, the rockets V1 and flying rockets V2, as decisive for the outcome of the war. No defense existed against the flying rockets, which for some time caused havoc in British cities. When the launching sites were destroyed, however, this danger ceased to exist. In contrast to Göring, Hitler had limited understanding of the "Jewish" nuclear weapons; their production never got off the ground in Germany. German submarines no longer prowled the seas. The new, faster U-boats were never deployed. Hitler also lacked understanding of the development of advanced jet bombers and aircraft detection devices. In spite of a temporary remarkable increase in war production under Speer, the Germans were running short of oil, rubber, and heavy metals. The Germans possessed the deadly nerve gases Sarin and Tabun, but Hitler never used them, perhaps because he remembered his own combat gas injury.

Hitler and the Resistance

The term "resistance" is broad and covers activities ranging from expressions of displeasure, dissent, and critique to highly organized political, military, and paramilitary activities against the National Socialist regime. A widespread and often underrated form of resistance consisted of helping persons persecuted by the regime, a dangerous activity that was severely punished. Hitler always had a very low tolerance for dissent. On many occasions, he expressed his irritation with dissent, particularly on the part of intellectuals. This was accurately perceived by persons in his environment, who, afraid to incur the displeasure of the Führer, avoided disagreement. Even powerful persons such as Göring, Goebbels, and Himmler found it difficult to raise objections before Hitler. Himmler, for instance, told Count Bernadotte that he found it impossible to take a course of action to which Hitler might object.[88] Hitler was incensed when he felt that high-ranking officers meddled in politics, such as Rommel, who suggested to Hitler that he end the war. Hitler was infuriated by the resistance of churchmen, particularly Bishop Clemens von Galen, to the so-called euthanasia program.

Before the war, Hitler saw no reason to be alarmed over resistance. The former political parties were in shambles, and whatever opposition was expressed was ineffective. Most of the time, Hitler was convinced through direct encounters and SD reports that the vast majority of Germans were behind him. A small group of generals (Ludwig Beck, Hans Oster, and others) had vague plans to overthrow Hitler at the time of the Sudeten crisis, but they gave up any such plans after the occupation of Czechoslovakia and the complete lack of encouragement and support by the Western Allies. Most of all, Hitler could be certain that Himmler, through the brutal and efficient police system of SD and Gestapo, could check whatever little resistance there was. Dissidence meant arrest, death, or indefinite incarceration in concentration camps without trial for the isolated idealist, religious, and political opponents of the regime. The "police dogs" read their master's mind very well, and faithfully carried out his wishes.

The resistance changed radically with the onset of the war. From the beginning, partisan activities sprang up in all theaters of operation and in occupied countries, such as the second uprising in the Warsaw ghetto in 1944. The terror that was used in combating such partisan activities has been well documented and can be traced to highest authority. The order to kill Russian political commissars, the White Flag orders to kill civilians hoisting the flag of surrender, the orders to demolish entire cities such as Warsaw without any military justification, and the orders to kill the male populations of entire villages—such as occurred in Lidice, Czechoslovakia, in Duradour, France, and in Kalavrita, Greece—prove this point.

Until 1943, little organized resistance existed in Germany. The attempt to blow Hitler up in his airplane on 13 March 1943, led by Major General Henning von Tresckow, was unsuccessful. The students and professors of the White Rose action, a Catholic resistance group, who protested in 1942 and 1943 with pamphlets against the immorality of the regime, were arrested and executed. The rather disorganized youth protestors known as Edelweiss Pirates were harshly punished—eleven of them were executed. The conservative Kreisauer Circle (named after the estate of Kreisau owned by the leader of the group, James Count von Moltke) included members of the nobility, high public servants, diplomats, and industrialists. This group was not concerned with the overthrow of the National Socialist regime, but rather with the evolution of a broad and rather vague program for a postwar Germany. Count Moltke was opposed to the assassination of Hitler. His group cooperated with the so-called Solf Circle, another conservative group of opponents. Count Moltke was arrested on 25 January 1944, together with members of the Solf Circle, and executed one year later. The lack of organization and coordination among the German Resistance made the job of the Gestapo easy, and reassured Hitler. Until the assassination attempt on 20 July, the security measures used to protect the Führer were remarkably lax and inefficient (in spite of forty two attempts to assassinate him). What made Hitler feel so secure was his conviction that Providence had chosen him to lead the German people to victory and greatness. Yet even within the SS, faint resistance existed. The duplicitous Walter Schellenberg favored negotiations and tried to induce Himmler to bypass Hitler. Himmler maintained Hitler was suffering from general paresis but was torn between his loyalty to his Führer and the completely unrealistic notion that the Allies might negotiate with him.

The Assassination Attempt of 20 July 1944 and its Aftermath

The most significant conspiracy against Hitler and his regime was organized by a small group of high-ranking officers under the leadership of Colonel Count Klaus von Stauffenberg. In this group were some of the earlier conspirators, such as General Beck and Field Marshal Erich von Witzleben; a few conservative politicians, such as Karl Friedrich Goerdeler, mayor of Leipzig; and even fewer social democrats, such as the former Reichstag deputy Julius Leber. Count von Stauffenberg, a highly decorated officer and one-time National Socialist, became bitterly opposed to National Socialism on patriotic and ethical grounds and was convinced that Hitler would bring about the doom of Germany. He was committed to the assassination of Hitler. Count von Stauffenberg had been forced to abandon two previous attempts. On 20 July 1944 he was under pressure of time when he attended Hitler's war conference. He felt observed when he defused the first bomb in his briefcase and was unable to ready a second bomb. The conference, which took place at Hitler's headquarters in Rastenburg, had been scheduled earlier than usual because of a pending visit from Mussolini. It did not take place in the concrete bunker where all previous conferences had been held, but rather in a wooden barracks room with windows. If it had been held in the principal war room, all would have been killed. Von Stauffenberg placed the bomb under a heavy conference table near Hitler, then left the room and hurried back to Berlin for Project Walkyrie, the takeover of key governmental posts. A conference participant inadvertently pushed the bomb away from Hitler. A staff officer, Colonel Heinz Brandt, was killed instantly; four other persons were severely injured, and one, Hitler's military adjutant General Rudolf Schmundt, died from his wounds. All twenty persons in the room were wounded—all had their hair singed, and all but Field Marshal Keitel had ruptured ear drums. At the moment of the explosion Hitler had leaned over the table, which protected him from more severe injuries. He and all of the others who were capable rushed out of the room to avoid being crushed in the event that the concrete ceiling came crashing down. Hitler received first aid from the accompanying surgeon, Professor Hasselbach, and later from Dr. Morell (see section 2 of this chapter). He recovered quickly from the initial shock and was almost cheerful going to the railroad platform to greet Mussolini, who had just arrived for a conference. When he took Mussolini to the wrecked room, Hitler remarked, "After today's miraculous escape, I am more convinced than ever that I am destined to bring our great task to a happy ending."[89] Mussolini, stunned and terrified by what he saw, agreed. Shortly afterward, Hitler and his paladins met over tea to discuss the responsibility for the event. They quarreled and reproached each other with accusations of inefficiency.

After General von Stauffenberg left the Führer headquarters, he sped to the military headquarters in Berlin. He informed his co-conspirators that Hitler was dead. When it became known that Hitler was alive, the commanding officer of the home army, General Friedrich Fromm (who knew about the conspiracy), ordered Major Otto Ernst Remer to cordon off the military and government headquarters. Von Stauffenberg and his fellow conspirators, Field Marshal von Witzleben, General Friedrich Olbricht, General Erich Hoepner, and Stauffenberg's Adjutant Lieutenant Werner von Haeften, were arrested and executed after a summary court martial ordered by General Fromm, who wanted the witnesses of his own involvement rapidly eliminated. It did not help him. Shortly afterward he was sentenced to death by the People's Court for cowardice. All resistance activities ended in Berlin, and shortly afterward in Paris, Vienna, and Prague, when Hitler made a terse announcement about the plot and his survival on all German radio stations. Hitler wanted the German people to hear his voice as he told them the details of "a crime unparalleled in German history: A very small clique of ambitious, unscrupulous, criminal, stupid officers conspired to eliminate me and eradicate German military leadership. . . . A number of dear co-workers have been seriously injured." One (at that time) had died, and one died later. "I am free of injuries except for very small excoriations, contusions, and burns. The circle of usurpers is very small. It has nothing to do with the German armed forces, nor with the German army. This small gang of criminal elements will be exterminated without any pity. . . . While hundreds of thousands and millions of decent men give their last, this small group of ambitious, pitiful creatures tried to circumvent this. This time there will be the reckoning to which we are accustomed to as National Socialists."[90]

Hitler appointed a special military court, with Field Marshal Keitel as presiding officer, which expelled the accused from the army and turned them over to the People's Court under the notorious Judge Roland Freisler, whom Hitler called "our Vishinsky," referring to the infamous judge appointed by Stalin. Hitler expected Freisler to proceed speedily, without dramatics, and not to let the accused hold speeches. Six hundred persons were arrested, interrogated, many of them tortured, and 200 condemned to be hanged by Freisler's People's Court. Himmler also ordered mass arrests of the families of the accused and promised their elimination.[91] Startling was Hitler's alleged recommendation to pay pensions to the surviving widows.[92] If true, this would be another expression of Hitler's unpredictable ambivalence. More likely, however, Hitler wanted cruel revenge, because, at Himmler's insistence, many of the kin of the condemned were in fact imprisoned and mistreated. Some of the condemned were hanged on hooks on an iron girder in the execution room of the Ploetzensee Prison; some of them were slowly strangled. Films and photographs taken of the executions showed the bodies of the victims. Some pictures were left on Hitler's desk by SS adjutant Hermann Fegelein, but it is unknown what Hitler felt when he saw the gruesome pictures. He was not prone to engage in overt cruelty; he just ordered it. In carrying out the dirty work after 20 July, the division of labor was similar to Himmler's and Hitler's collusion in executing the genocide of the Jews and Gypsies. The failure on 20 July set back the effort to free Germany from tyranny. The majority of the German people still supported Hitler and National Socialism. Yet the statements of the condemned at the time of their executions or suicides were powerful expressions of hope and courage, such as Henning von Tresckow's farewell message: "Hitler is not only the arch enemy of Germany, but of the whole world. . . . The worth of a man is certain only if he is prepared to sacrifice his life for his convictions."[93] The event of 20 July had a deep impact on Hitler. He was gratified by his ability to crush the revolt and consoled himself that a small clique was behind the putsch, but to his physician he admitted that he suffered greatly.[94]

Field Marshal Erwin Rommel watched Hitler's measures against the conspirators with concern. He had good reason, because he had been involved in the conspiracy, as Hitler learned from the confession of a conspirator. Hitler requested that Field Marshal Keitel write a letter ordering Rommel to appear before the Führer. This letter was brought by Generals Burgdorf and Maisel to Rommel at his home near Ulm, where he was convalescing after a head injury. The letter gave Rommel the option of obeying Hitler's order, with the prospect of a trial and a likely death sentence, or of committing suicide by poisoning himself, but with the promise of a hero's funeral and a pension for his widow. Rommel opted for the latter and committed suicide in a staff car in the presence of the two generals. The corpse was brought to a military hospital in Ulm, where an autopsy was not permitted. It was maintained that the cause of death had been a brain embolism as a sequel to Rommel's head injury. After his most popular general's self-execution, Hitler merely remarked, "There goes another one of the Old Guard."[95]

Field Marshal Hans Günther von Kluge, one of Hitler's ablest generals, was implicated in the 20 July plot. Hitler became suspicious during von Kluge's temporary absence on the Normandy Front, assuming that the field marshal had made contact with the enemy. When von Kluge found out that he was under surveillance and was expected to report to Berlin, he committed suicide with potassium cyanide. In his farewell letter, von Kluge explained his suicide over guilt for having failed in the Normandy invasion.[96] As he had not been accused of such a failure, it is much more likely that he committed suicide because he feared arrest, prosecution, and dishonor. Hitler's response was: "I advanced him twice, gave him the highest decorations, a large donation, a large bonus in addition to his pay as a field marshal. It is most bitter and disappointing."[97]

The Last Attempt: The Ardennes Offensive

In the late fall of 1944, Hitler realized that the situation was very serious. Negotiations to preserve his empire and position would be possible only if he could demonstrate some military successes. He resolved to create more favorable conditions by a desperate counterattack. In late October 1944, in great secrecy and without an advance consultation with his western commanders, Field Marshals Walter Model and Gerd von Rundstedt, Hitler conceived an offensive through the Ardennes, with the goal of reconquering Antwerp. He believed that, through a partial victory, he could create favorable conditions to induce the western Allies to side with him against the Russians. In November 1944 he told his generals at the headquarters in Ziegenberg:

> Our enemies present the greatest extremes that are imaginable on earth: ultra-capitalist states on one side and ultra-Marxist states on the other side; on one side a dying empire, Great Britain, and on the other side a colony that is eager to inherit, the U.S.A. These are states that are incompatible in their goals even now, day by day. And he who will sit like a spider, I'd like to say in its net, and follow this development can watch how these conflicts develop hour to hour. If a few heavy blows follow, it can happen at any moment that the artificially maintained common front will collapse in a clap of thunder.[98]

The attack on 16 December 1944 took the Allies by surprise, but soon after initial successes the German assault weakened and was called off one month after it began. The western Allies' resolution to fight to unconditional surrender remained firm. Henry Morgenthau, Jr., Roosevelt's Secretary of the Treasury, recommended that Germany be made into an agricultural country, a plan rejected by the Allied leaders. In his propaganda to motivate the German people, Goebbels used the Morgenthau plan and the threat of Russian brutalities to encourage the Germans to fight to the bitter end at all costs.

The Inner Circle in the Last Phase of the Regime

Trevor Roper's words about Hitler's court are apt: "It was in its capacity for intrigue incalculable as any Oriental Sultanate."[99] The courtiers knew they were doomed, which hardly diminished the deep antagonisms among them. During the last year of Hitler's regime, considerable changes occurred in the power constellation. Never had the inner circle been so important for the Führer than during the last phase of the regime, when Hitler's relations with the leadership of the armed forces was troublesome and his contact with the population had decreased. Martin Bormann had become his most powerful vassal. Speer, as armament czar, was threatened and bothered by Himmler's SS industrial empire and deeply mistrusted by Martin Bormann. The status of the ineffective Reichsmarschall Göring had clearly declined. Baldur von Schirach, former Chief of the Hitler Youth, Gauleiter of Vienna, and at one time considered a possible successor to Hitler, was bounced from the inner circle because he had become too "Viennese."[100] The status of Himmler, who during the war years had become the most powerful man after Hitler, declined because of his poor performance as leader of the middle-aged reserve troops, the so-called Volkssturm. Goebbels, on the other hand, was now closer to Hitler. As Minister of Propaganda during the days of total destruction and disintegration, Goebbels undoubtedly had a strong influence on Hitler's staging of the *Götterdämmerung*. Hitler's need for devoted disciples who viewed him as a master, prophet, and genius had become ever stronger.

Albert Speer, then the armament czar, had become an important member of the inner circle. Speer's statement that, if Hitler had been capable of having a friend, he (Speer) would have been his friend,[101] contains a kernel of truth. During the early days of his career, the able and energetic young architect benefitted greatly from Hitler's favor, admired his sponsor, and worked for him with devotion. Later, Speer's relationship with Hitler became ambivalent, although he did not express severe criticism openly until after the fall of the Third Reich. It is very unlikely that Speer was ignorant, as he claimed, about the mass murders in the concentration camps. In fact, large numbers of inmates from these camps worked in the industrial empire that he controlled. The question as to whether Speer suppressed or repressed what he knew has been the main topic of a book by Gitta Sereny.[102] Hitler recognized and even tolerated Speer's ambivalence, but did not include him in a proposed postmortem cabinet. Von Ribbentrop, Hitler's "Bismarck," was disliked by nearly all other vassals and lost Hitler's confidence during the final years. Ley's alcoholism made him quite ineffective in the last stage of the regime, but his loyalty to Hitler did not change.

Martin Bormann, a fanatical National Socialist who was absolutely loyal to Hitler, had become a party member relatively late, in 1927. He served a one-year prison sentence for participation in a political assassination, then became

Hess's secretary and, later, Reichsleiter, a very powerful and influential position. Bormann was a brutal realist who sensed when and to what extent he
could influence the Führer. Although Hitler became very hostile to the
churches, he never accepted Bormann's radical rejection of them or his ideas
regarding polygamy as a means of increasing the German population. Bormann exercised great power through his intelligence, ruthlessness, incorrupt-
ibility, industry, and reliability, and by handling large and small matters in ways
he interpreted as representing the Führer's wishes. He adjusted his own
timetable to correspond with Hitler's strange schedule. No appointment was
made and no document was ever signed or even read by Hitler without Bormann's knowledge. In his testament, Hitler referred to Bormann as his most
loyal follower. To the last moment, Hitler remained the unquestioned leader of
his inner circle. Disobedience by some of the generals, such as SS General Felix
Steiner, occurred only at a considerable distance from the power center. One
person became increasingly important for Hitler during the last phase: Eva
Braun. At the end of March 1945, she left the Berghof and joined Hitler at the
Führerbunker. Allegedly, she came to the bunker on her own, but it is unlikely
that she could have come without Hitler's consent. Actually, Hitler felt comforted that she was with him. Hitler's final reactions to his trusted paladins,
Göring and Himmler, will be described later.

The So-Called Bormann Documents

In February and March, 1945, Martin Bormann allegedly wrote down the
content of talks he had with Hitler. The documents, lost for a while, were
acquired by the publishing house of Genoud and appeared first in French
translation under the title, *Le Testament politique de Hitler*. They were translated into English and re-translated into German, but the original text was
never found. It is not certain whether these documents are genuine, or
whether they accurately convey Hitler's thinking. The style is distinctly different from Hitler's, and it is possible that not only Bormann but also Goebbels
may have had a hand in writing or editing them.[103] In spite of these reservations, however, the Bormann documents are fundamental to our understanding of Hitler's political behavior. Written at a time when defeat was certain,
they provide explanations, critiques of both opponents and allies, analysis of
mistakes, and the penultimate expression of Hitler's anti-Semitism (the last
was expressed in his real political testament).

In the Bormann papers, Hitler asserted that his aim was a European
Monroe Doctrine, under German hegemony, but Europe was impervious to
his persuasion and charm; it had to be taken by violence. He felt condemned
to wage war because Germany's enemies did not want Germany to be
exalted.[104] Unfortunately, the Germans had no pride of race, were spiritually
unprepared, and Hitler started the war too late—he should have begun it in
1938, but he had been dissuaded from doing this by the deceptive Chamberlain. What he might have accomplished if the British had accepted all of his
demands! Hitler realized that the invasion of Czech lands had changed world

opinion. The enemies of the Third Reich wanted his hide. After the defeat of Poland, the British could have shed a few crocodile tears for the Poles and then left the Germans to take over the country at their leisure.[105] Churchill had another chance to make peace when the British defended the skies over England and inflicted a humiliating defeat on the Italians, but the Jews would have none of it. Hitler had underestimated the power of Jewish domination over England. Never before had there been a war that was so typically and yet so exclusively Jewish. The English preferred to perish by default rather than to admit National Socialism. Yet according to Hitler, National Socialism was not for export.[106]

The entire fifth section of the Bormann documents is devoted to the "Jewish problem." Hitler's views as presented in these documents are more radical and also more "sophisticated" than in earlier statements. Nowhere did Hitler talk more frequently and with more passion about Jewish poison and the role that the Jew-ridden, half-American drunkard Churchill played in pursuing a pro-Jewish policy. The "disgusting Jew" claimed all rights of citizenship, but at the same time remained a Jew. National Socialism was determined to purge the German world of the Jewish poison. It was a process of disinfection that was pursued to the ultimate limit, without which Germany would have been asphyxiated. The malady itself must disappear. Hitler stated that he was quite free of racial hatred, although he believed it undesirable for races to mix with one another. In the Bormann papers, contradicting previous and future statements in the testament, Hitler declared that the Jews were not a race, but rather a spiritually homogenous group (*Volksgemeinschaft*), to which all Jews throughout the world adhered. The Jewish race was an abstract race of the mind. Jewry was in no sense a religious entity, nor did Jews possess the characteristics that would stamp them as a homogenous race. But then Hitler again regressed to old crude nonsense. Every Jew in the world had a drop of Jewish blood in him, and this explained the presence of certain characteristics—the offensive nose, the cruel, vicious nostrils; and so on. Hitler stated, "For us this has been an essential process of disinfection, which we have prosecuted to its ultimate limit and without which we should ourselves have been asphyxiated and destroyed."[107] A few pages later, he said:

> I have always been absolutely fair in my dealing with the Jews. On the eve of war, I gave them one final warning. I told them that, if they precipitated another war, I would exterminate the vermin throughout Europe, and this time once and for all. To this warning they retorted with a declaration of war and affirmed that wherever in the world there was a Jew, there, too, was an implacable enemy of National Socialist Germany. . . . Well, we have lanced the Jewish abscess; and the world of the future will be eternally grateful to us.[108]

In the Bormann documents, Hitler dealt with past tactical and strategic military and political mistakes, but nowhere is any doubt or guilt expressed regarding his political doctrines and beliefs, nor is there evidence of any true regret over a war in which 50 million persons were killed. The mistakes that are mentioned include halting his tank attack at Dunkirk, caused by his unwillingness to humiliate the British and his desire to create a conciliatory atmosphere; his decision not to attack Gibraltar in spite of Franco's reluctance to cooperate; and the greatest mistake of all, which was to delay the Russian campaign for about three weeks because his friend Mussolini needed assistance in his precipitous and disastrous Balkan campaign.[109] In the Bormann papers, Hitler freely expressed his hatred of the French and his contempt for all Latin races. He still spoke of victory, but it is obvious that he did not believe his own words. Referring to Roosevelt's death, he noted how his great role model, Frederick the Great, won the war after the death of Catherine the Great. The Bormann documents consider the possibility of defeat: "If fate has decreed that we go down—that we should be crushed by forces superior to our own—then let us go down with our heads high and secure in the knowledge that the honor remains without blemish."[110] Hitler referred to the proud stand of Leonidas and the three hundred Spartans. In a revealing allusion to the passivity of the Jewish Holocaust victims, he said, "In any case we are not of the stuff that goes tamely to the slaughterhouse like sheep. They may well exterminate us, but they will never lead us to the slaughterhouse."[111]

Behavioral Changes in the Last Phase

Since 1944, witnesses of Hitler's behavior and appearance reported not only the decline of his health, but also changes in his habits. Speer noticed that his uniform, which previously had been immaculately clean, was spotted with food stains and crumbs.[112] To some extent, this can be explained by deteriorations in the living conditions in the bunker and by Hitler's tremors. The emotionally labile Hitler was given to occasional expressions of despair, such as during the war conference of 23 April 1945, when he sobbed. It is known, however, that such behavior had occurred before, in the "good days." Rages became more frequent. In the war conference of 23 April, according to the stenographer, Hitler had ten outbursts of anger. General Guderian described a rage attack in the spring of 1945, illustrating that Hitler was able to control his rage. Guderian, then Hitler's Chief of Staff, recommended that General Wenck be attached to Himmler's staff, supposedly because Himmler would have been incapable of mastering the situation without the General. Hitler recommended waiting. The argument reportedly proceeded as follows:

> HITLER: "I forbid you to reproach me for waiting."
> GUDERIAN: "I don't make any reproaches, but it makes no sense to wait and miss the right time for an attack."
> HITLER: "I just told you that I forbid you to make reproaches to me for waiting."

This reportedly went on for two hours, with undiminished intensity, flushed cheeks, and raised fists. Hitler was beside himself and beyond control, his entire body trembling. Guderian reported:

> After each outburst of rage, he ran up and down along the edge of the rug, stopped in front of me, made the next reproach. He screamed, his eyes bulged out, and the arteries at his temples were swollen. . . . Suddenly, Hitler stopped in front of Himmler and said, 'Himmler, General Wenck joins your staff tonight and leads the attack.' Then he sat down next to me and said, 'Continue your report. Today the general staff has won a battle.' He smiled his most charming smile.[113]

One witness, Hitler's adjutant Otto Günsche, considered this description exaggerated.[114]

According to Hitler's secretary Christa Schroeder, Hitler, who had always been very proper in his relationships with his secretaries, had become uninhibited. Once, lying on his couch, he said to Schroeder how wonderful it was to make love. Another time he said that one of the secretaries would look wonderful as a nude, with a wide-brimmed red hat and gloves.[115] Another secretary, Gerda Christian, however, maintained that she never heard such remarks.[116] Schroeder mentioned that Hitler's conversation had become uninteresting. According to Schroeder, Hitler also complained about the failure of his memory, though it should be remembered that Hitler wrote a concise and clear testament, and, most of all, in the fall of 1944 he was able to design and direct the complex Battle of the Bulge. From some of Hitler's remarks, one could conclude that his political and military judgement suffered. Almost to the last days of his life, he stated he could win the battle of Berlin.[117] He was correct in perceiving the potential antagonism between his Western and Eastern enemies, though he misguessed that this antagonism, would cause the Western Allies to shift to his side in order to fight against Bolshevism. According to some contemporary witnesses, Hitler functioned quite well mentally. Field Marshal Kesselring commented that Hitler was mentally alert, in striking contrast to his physical condition.[118] In Goebbels's opinion, the Führer never fully recovered from the trauma of 20 July; he appeared tired and abnormal, and only his iron will kept him going.[119] General Guderian aptly described the changes during the last year:

> When, after the Stalingrad disaster, I first saw him again following an interval of fourteen months, I noticed the change in his condition. His right hand trembled, he stooped, he stared fixedly, his eyes had a tendency to bulge and were dull and lusterless, there were hectic red spots on his cheeks. He was more excitable than ever. When angered he lost all self-control and then both what he would say and do became unpredictable. The external symptoms of his malady grew ever more pronounced, though the change was barely perceptible to his closer circle who saw him every day. Finally, after the assassination attempt of 20 July, 1944, it was no longer simply his

left hand but the whole left side of his body that trembled. He would place his right hand on his left and cross his right leg over the left one so that, when he was seated, this trembling might be less noticeable. He now walked awkwardly, he stooped more than ever, and his gestures were both jerky and slow. He had to have a chair pushed beneath him when he wished to sit down. His mind, it is true, remained active; but this very activity was itself unhealthy, since its mainsprings were his distrust of humanity and his anxiety to conceal his physical, spiritual, political, and military bankruptcy. Thus he attempted continually to deceive both himself and others in his efforts to keep his edifice standing, for he really knew what was the true state of himself as well as of his cause.[120]

The End of the Reich of a Thousand Years

After the failure of the Ardennes Offensive, Hitler suffered setbacks on all fronts. It was not a retreat but a disorganized rout. A crucial decision was to fight the Western Allies and abandon the German population in the East. Hitler's orders did not always reach the troops, and at times the troops for whom the orders were intended did not exist. The chaos was enhanced by the frequent changes of top commanders. Chief of Staff General Zeitzler was replaced by General Guderian, and General Guderian by General Burgdorf. Proposals by the general staff to strengthen the Eastern defense and let Germany be overrun by the Allies were rejected. Many times, the orders of top commanders were rescinded without their knowledge. A major offensive was started by the Russians in mid-January 1945. By the end of January, they stood at the Oder, only 100 kilometers from Berlin. On 13 February 1945, the Russians took Budapest, and on 16 March 1945 Vienna. The Western Allies crossed the Rhine at Remagen on 7 March 1945. In six weeks, they had overrun Western and Southern Germany. On 25 April 1945, Allied and Russian soldiers met at Thorgau on the Elbe. The German armies in Italy capitulated later, on 29 April 1945.

Himmler's White Flag Order demanded instant execution of any person who hoisted the white flag of surrender. In the action "Thunderstorm," newly established summary courts carried out innumerable executions of soldiers who did not resist the Allies or who surrendered. The general staff was barely able to resist Hitler's wish to execute captured Allied airmen in retaliation for the devastating strategic bombing that had killed German civilians. Hitler forbade the surrender of concentration camps, which, during this phase of the war, resulted in starvation and death for inmates who were forced to go on death marches or remain in abandoned camps without food. It was not the controlled rage that Hitler had been so apt to display, but an impotent fury. Some of the anger was directed particularly at the generals, whom he held responsible for his defeats, and the Jews, the "wire-pullers" behind the Allied commanders and politicians. On the day of Hitler's death, executions of the men behind the 20th of July plot were still taking place.

The final Russian offensive against beleaguered Berlin started on 17 April 1945. Against 2,500,000 Russian troops under Marshals Ivan Konev and Georgi Zhukov, Hitler commanded about 100,000 troops, many of them older men of the *Volkssturm* and over 3000 members of the Hitler Youth. Half of them had no weapons. By any account, Germany's military situation was hopeless. On 20 April 1945, Hitler's fifty-sixth birthday, the leadership of the army and the Party gathered once more in the bunker of the Reichskanzlei and offered congratulations to their Führer. In turn, Hitler spoke words of encouragement. The group sat, sipping champagne, milk, or fruit juice, and everybody, including Hitler, knew that the war was lost and that the end was very near, yet no one openly talked about it. Berlin was completely encircled. The first Soviet artillery shells exploded in the inner city. Hitler's hopes for a counterattack were wishful thinking. He permitted the exodus of high-ranking aides, secretaries, and other personnel—amongst them Dr. Morell—by air. Evaluations of the military situation had become totally unrealistic by the end of April. His hope for relief by General Steiner's army was sheer fantasy. Some of the most absurd remarks were cited by General Koller: "You will see the Russian suffer the greatest, the bloodiest defeat of his history before the gates of Berlin."[121] Did he really believe this? Was he trying to bolster the spirits of his men? Was it auto-suggestion? Did he deceive himself? Actually, Hitler warned against self-deception to a degree. In the war conference of 27 January 1945, in which he warned of suggestion and auto-suggestion, Hitler said: "It makes no sense, that one hypnotizes one's self (*sich hinein hypnotisiert*) and says, 'I need it, so it must happen.' In the end one has to deal with things as they are."[122] A stark difference between words and deeds was apparent.

Fragments of the war conferences on 23, 25, and 27 April 1945 were published almost verbatim by *Der Spiegel*[123] and reflect Hitler's emotional swings between optimism and despair. According to the stenographer Hergesell, Hitler had many fits of rage but was able to control himself quickly. "If one thinks about all of it, why continue to live? The dismal leadership of some generals resulted in catastrophic mistakes." A short time after, he stated: "The enemy knows I am here; it can be the last chance if obedient and decent work is done—in four days everything must be decided." "Only I can succeed here, . . . the battle has reached its height. I, and only I, the Party and the state are able to stop the communist colossus." He still expressed his conviction that the differences between the Western powers and the Russians would result in the breakdown of the Alliance. He was quite concerned about his personal role: "I can't leave like a coward. I can't disappear from the parquet of world history as an inglorious fugitive. . . ." He also expressed fear that, through some trick by the Russians, he could be extricated from the bunker. After the war conference on 27 April 1945, when the first shells had already exploded in the garden of the Reichskanzlei, Hitler calmed down. ". . . I will go to bed more quietly today and don't want to be awakened unless a Russian tank is in front of my bedroom, in order to have time to make my preparations." Field Marshal Keitel, Grand Admiral Doenitz, Bormann, and Speer advised Hitler to leave for the Berghof. Hitler rejected their pleas and, following Goebbels's advice, stayed. On 23 April a report of Hitler's despair seemingly reached Göring, who politely inquired as to whether Hitler would want him to take charge in case Hitler was unable to rule from Berlin. It was easy for Bormann and Goebbels, bitter enemies of Göring, to convince Hitler that Göring's offer was high treason. Hitler called Göring a morphine addict, accused him of incompetence and laziness, stripped him of his office, expelled him from the Party, and appointed General Greim as Göring's successor in the Luftwaffe.

The news of Himmler's negotiations with Count Bernadotte, which were conducted without Hitler's knowledge, caused a more severe reaction. Hanna Reitsch, then General Greim's pilot, stated that Hitler acted like a madman. His face became deep red and distorted.[124] The betrayal by faithful Heinrich was a devastating blow for the Führer. He stripped Himmler of his rank and office, and asked General Greim to attempt to arrest the traitor. During the last week of April, Hermann Fegelein, Hitler's SS adjutant, who had married Eva Braun's sister Gretl, absented himself from the bunker and was found, in civilian clothes, in a Berlin apartment. Hitler sentenced him to death for desertion but also connected his absence with Himmler's betrayal.

Hitler's Marriage and Last Will

Not until the last days of April 1944 did Hitler seriously consider a plan for a double suicide of himself and Eva Braun, preceded by marriage, thus fulfilling Eva Braun's ardent wish. Hitler probably had no problem accepting her offer to die with him; surviving she would have become an embarrassing witness to their intimate relationship. On 28 April, Hitler married Eva Braun in a simple civil ceremony performed by a magistrate who was quickly rounded up. The bride and groom stated they were of Aryan descent and had no hereditary illnesses. Like many brides before her, in signing the marriage document, Braun started to write her maiden name, then corrected it. A small party of adjutants and secretaries, and Hitler's dietician, joined the couple to celebrate the union, prelude to a double suicide.

On 29 April Hitler dictated a personal and a political will.[125] He expressed himself clearly, and there can be no doubt about his testatory capacity. In a preamble, Hitler stated:

> . . . I and my wife choose death to avoid the disgrace of flight or capitulation. It is our will to be cremated instantly on the spot where I rendered the largest part of my service to my people.

The final personal will is very similar to the will Hitler had written on 2 May 1938. Almost apologetically, he stated that the pictures he had collected (or stolen) had never been gathered for private purposes, but rather for a gallery in his home town of Linz. He continued:

> Furthermore, my most faithful party member, Martin Bormann, has per-
> mission to give possessions of a personal nature or anything that makes a
> small bourgeois life possible for my siblings, and the mother of my wife, the
> old secretaries, and Frau Winter [Hitler's housekeeper in Munich].

In one part of his political will, Hitler appointed a cabinet, rather than letting his successor, Grand Admiral Karl Doenitz, appoint it after his death.
The other part of the political testament consists of justifications and accusations; the second contains binding recommendations about the continuation
of the regime. The entire statement can be reduced to five major points.
First, Hitler reasserted that he was not responsible for starting the war that
he had lost; rather, the war had been started by statesmen who were of Jewish descent or who were fighting for Jewish interests. Second, Hitler left no
one in doubt that for the hundreds of thousands of women and children
burned to death in the bombing of cities, and the millions of men who had
died, the real culprit (e.g., the Jew) would have to pay for his guilt. Third,
Hitler blamed unprincipled or beguiled characters for the defeat. He
described his suicide as a happy and heroic act, although he admitted that he
did not wish to fall into the hands of his enemies, who, for the amusement of
their masses, would need a new spectacle, arranged by the Jews. Fourth, he
thanked Germany's soldiers, workers, and farmers for their fight and
expressed his belief that the rebirth of a National Socialist movement would
rise from their sacrifice. Fifth, Hitler once again appealed to the honor of
officers not to surrender until death. In the last sentence, he obligated the
leadership and his followers to the meticulous observation of racial laws and
pitiless resistance against the poisoner of all peoples, international Jewry.
Hitler's last message was a message of hate and doom. Suicide was the inexorable next step—Hitler's suicide and postmortem will be described in Section 2 of this chapter.

Section II: Hitler's Illnesses, Injuries, and Suicide

Dr. Morell's diaries during the war convey a vivid picture of Hitler's medical
regimen and the interactions between physician and patient.[126] The notes
are honest reflections of Morell's thinking, but often they do not convey
an accurate picture of the complex biomedical processes because Morell was
not a good medical examiner, did not always know what to examine, and
was defensive. Nonetheless, they provide a good picture of Morell's principal activities. To appreciate these notes, certain facts about Morell's medical
program need to be considered. First, Morell made extensive use of dysbacteria cures (Mutaflor and Enterofagos) and basic medications (10% glucose, Glyconorm, tonophosphan, calcium and iodine preparations, various
hormones, vitamins, and organ extracts, to name the most important ones),
most of which were administered by injection (see Appendix 4, List of
Significant Medications). These cures and medications were not necessarily

directed against specific illnesses, but against all illnesses. Morell was an extreme polypharmacist. Second, Morell considered Hitler's moderately elevated blood pressure and some evidence of ischemic heart disease alarming symptoms and monitored his patient's blood pressure on a very frequent basis. Third, Morell was virtually obsessed with the examination of Hitler's feces by his consultant, Professor Nissle, in connection with the dysbacteria cures. Fourth, in his diagnostic and therapeutic deliberations Morell considered both somatic and psychological factors—a distinct merit. Unfortunately, however, Morell often was unable to make up his mind about what was somatic and what was psychological. As Hitler's illnesses were extremely complex, this is not surprising.

One can be certain that before the war Hitler's illnesses were sporadic and not severe. He also was quite well during the first two years of the war. Morell spent time with Hitler during the Polish and French campaigns, but no notes about any treatment have been found. On 9 May 1940, Morell jotted down the results of laboratory tests, all roughly within normal limits: a measurement of systolic blood pressure at 140, and a negative Wassermann reaction, for syphilis (see Appendix 5). In a letter to his wife Johanna on 26 May 1940, Morell wrote: "Hardly any medical work. Asked the Führer if he had any complaints. He feels well, except for one big complaint: that his appetite is too big. He is brisk and happy."

In early August 1941, the clinical situation changed drastically. Morell recorded an acute episode that alarmed both the doctor and his patient. After that time, with rare intervals during which he was symptom-free, Hitler was either moderately or severely ill. The complex illnesses and injuries are best presented in four segments: (1) the illnesses of early August 1941 until the assassination attempt of 20 July 1944; (2) the injuries and recovery following the assassination attempt on 20 July 1944; (3) the serious illness of fall 1944; and (4) the final phase of illness from 1 January 1945 until Hitler's suicide.

Illnesses from Early August 1941 to 20 July 1944

Vascular Spasms with Plethora in the Temporal Region after Various Causes

On 7 August 1941, an illness developed that alarmed Dr. Morell and his patient. According to Morell's notes:

> 7.VIII.41: At 13:30, F. suddenly became dizzy while sitting in the map room. 3 x 3 hours in airplane round trip. Called by Junge [manservant], shall come to Führer immediately. He became suddenly dizzy. Is in the bunker. Went there with Junge. . . . Face pale. "I feel very badly, like never before. I became suddenly dizzy over there. I don't know what it is. Here, close to the temple, it is a peculiar feeling. During the flight there was a draft towards it, also I was recently extremely upset and haven't felt well since. Also my stomach has been upset for some time."
>
> Physical findings: temp. (axillary) 37.4 (centigrade), pulse 90.

Morell found that Hitler's face and temple area, innervated by the trigeminal nerve and, particularly, its supraorbital branch, were very sensitive to touch. The most significant findings Morell noted were an elevated blood pressure of 170mm Hg and an enlarged and somewhat "harder" liver. About the latter finding—in itself quite alarming—one cannot be sure. Morell also learned that Hitler had been having soft stools for three days. The soft stools and liver enlargement probably made Morell think that Hitler might have been suffering from amebic dysentery, and prescribed Yatren, a specific drug against amebic dysentery. At the same time, Morell was impressed with what he called, unconventionally, "vascular spasms with plethora in the temporal region after different causes." In other words, he assumed that the symptoms were caused by some blockage of arteries in the temporal region. Hitler also continued to complain of buzzing in his ears, but Morell learned that the otologist, Professor von Eicken, had diagnosed tinnitus of no definitive origin ten years earlier.

Hitler felt extremely miserable, not only because of his illness but because an infection following an injection added much to his discomfort. Morell complained that Hitler was cross with him even though he had been successful in reducing the dictator's elevated blood pressure, which was Morell's greatest concern. Hitler told Morell that he was a bad patient because, since his combat gas poisoning, he had never spent a day in bed. Indeed, from a physician's point of view, Hitler was a bad patient, because he constantly changed Morell's orders and did not adhere to his prescribed diet. Morell accepted this stolidly, probably reflecting that this was simply the way dictators behave as patients.

Hitler must have felt better on 8 August, because he got up and went to the map room again; however, his tinnitus and severe headaches continued, particularly on 10 August. For a day he complained of constipation, and Morell prescribed his favorite drastic purgative, Calomel, resulting in five explosive, watery bowel movements. When Hitler's systolic blood pressure continued to hover in the high 150s, Morell recorded an electrocardiogram and sent it to a well-known cardiologist, Professor A. Weber, in Bad Nauheim, under the pseudonym "Patient A," a gentleman from the Foreign Office. When he scrutinized the tracing by himself, Morell noted a flattened T-wave, usually taken as a sign of myocardial damage. Weber confirmed this suspicion (see Appendix 6 for interpretations and correspondence), suggesting that "Patient A" might suffer from an early coronary sclerosis, unless the damage had been caused by an infection or cardiac therapy. Morell was not reassured. He ruminated that Hitler, like himself, might simply have "rheumo", caused by the humidity, drafts, and bad air in the bunker, which he believed did not allow the red blood cells to take up enough oxygen. He tried to induce Hitler to go outdoors as much as possible, to make excursions by car or boat, or to walk—all to no avail. As a therapy against hypertension, Morell prescribed leeches—still used by many practicioners at the time. Hitler liked the treatment and watched the little bloodsuckers with interest.

In the last third of August, the headaches stopped and tinnitus became very rare; Morell stated on 29 August that Hitler had recovered from the episode.

Undoubtedly, the episode of illness in August 1941 was more than Dr. Morell bargained for. He was puzzled and upset. The "injection master" bent a needle during the injection and also caused a painful perivenous infiltration at the injection site. Most of all, he did not know what ailed his patient. Intuitively, he assumed vascular and intestinal problems, and pointed to the temporal area as a possible locus of trouble. The ECG, although only mildly abnormal, greatly worried Morell and induced him to focus on cardiovascular illness. It was no small matter that the Führer, in the middle of a war, had electrocardiographic signs of a beginning coronary sclerosis. Although he did not know what ailed Hitler, Morell treated Hitler for amoebic dysentery—a disease from which Hitler certainly did not suffer. The diarrhea was short-lasting and mild, aggravated by the cathartic that Morell had prescribed. David Irving assumed that it was because of Hitler's illness in August 1941 that the generals so easily had their way and launched the main attack in the central sector, whereas Hitler originally had wanted to attack in the northern and southern sectors. However, there is no evidence that Hitler was unable to function as commander in chief during this period of illness. Even at the height of the illness he went to the map room. Although Hitler's prolonged discussions with his staff resulted in a delay and compromise to simultaneously attack the central and southern sectors, this cannot be attributed to illness.

In his notes, Morell mentioned an acute vascular crisis in December 1941, when Hitler's systolic blood pressure rose to 200. In late spring 1942, von Ribbentrop reported a fainting episode after an argument he had with Hitler,[127] after which Hitler reproached von Ribbentrop for endangering him through his opposition. Based on the scant description, it is not possible to determine the cause of this episode.

Headaches and Impairment of Vision

A significant illness episode occurred on 22 July 1942 while Hitler was at his headquarters at Winniza in southern Ukraine. At 2 p.m. Morell was urgently called by Hitler, who complained about severe headaches, impairment of vision in his right eye, and insomnia. Hitler attributed his complaints to overwork. Aside from a systolic blood pressure of 170mm Hg, the physical findings were normal. Morell diagnosed vascular spasms of the head, prescribed Thrombovil, an anticoagulant, and advised bed rest and cold head compresses in addition to his routine therapy of 20% glucose, Septoiod and vitamin calcium injections. A few hours later Hitler's blood pressure fell to 150mm Hg, and the headaches and eye symptoms disappeared temporarily. From Morell's notes one can deduce that some complaints persisted, because he continued his attempt to reduce the blood pressure and treat Hitler's headaches by blood-letting and leeches, one of them placed in the area of the right temple.

Again, Morell was perplexed by this episode of illness. He noted a marked light and sun sensitivity, which had already appeared the previous summer when, after a day at the front, Hitler's face was badly sunburnt. Hitler had no such complaints before 1941. After the summer of 1942, Hitler stayed in his bunker, with artificial light, most of the time and was out in sunlight only for short periods of time. He also wore a specially designed military cap with an oversized visor to protect him. Morell recorded Hitler's subjective visual deficiency but the ophthalmological consultation took place 19 months later. Not until he was a prisoner of war did he begin to connect the Winniza episode with Hitler's Parkinson's disease. The idea that the episode might have been an encephalitis that could produce a Parkinsonian syndrome, similar to Economo's encephalitis, was suggested to Morell either by Hitler's opthamologist, Professor Löhlein, or by his Allied medical interrogators in 1945.

The next entry in Morell's diary was dated 9 December 1942, when Hitler complained about intestinal gases, foul breath, and malaise, which Morell treated with Calomel, later followed by Mutaflor and Enterofagos cures. On 21 December 1942 Morell reiterated in his diary the diagnosis of coronary sclerosis, vascular spasm (head and intestines), dysbacteria of the intestines, and liver enlargement. (Morell believed that he could palpate the left liver lobe, which is not possible unless the liver is extremely enlarged.)

In the spring of 1943—following the annihilation of the Sixth German Army in Stalingrad and beginning defeats on all fronts—Hitler's illnesses became more serious and disabling. Days during which Hitler felt well became rare. Based on his notes, one can distinguish the following complaints after 1943 and until Hitler's death: headaches, gastrointestinal complaints, cardiovascular complaints, ophthalmic complaints, neurological complaints, and a general decline.

Headaches and Head Pressure

Thirteen episodes of moderate to severe headaches and head pressure recurred after the illnesses in August 1941 and July 1942. No headaches were recorded after 7 November 1944. Most of the time, the headaches were unilateral, at times bilateral, primarily in the frontal and temporal areas, or they occurred as pressure behind the eyes. They were described as aches, feelings of pressure, or peculiar feelings. They were not preceded by premonitory symptoms or followed by nausea and vomiting. A prominent episode occurred during the evening of 24 March 1943.

After Hitler and Morell arrived at the Berghof, Hitler complained about very severe headache and head pressure; he felt tired and looked worn out. Morell considered worries as a cause, but primarily he thought the symptoms were caused by the *Föhn*, a warm southerly wind blowing down from the mountains causing in some people headaches, lassitude, and insomnia. The physical findings were not contributory except for a systolic blood pressure of 170mm Hg and another significant finding: the temporal artery (Morell did not state whether right, left or both) was 'badly swollen.' Morell prescribed his routine therapy of 20% glucose and Septopiod injections. When the headaches did not disappear but became stronger he added Brom Nervacit to calm Hitler. Early bed rest and massage were rejected by Hitler and an addition of egg yolks in wine to his diet was accepted. Gradually during the following two weeks the headaches diminished while Morell continued administration of Brom Nervacit and started another Mutaflor cure. Two weeks after the onset of this episode Hitler felt well. While Morell thought the episode was caused by the *Föhn*—and it is possible that the Alpine wind aggravated or precipitated the symptom—Hitler had different ideas. On 26 March 1943, Morell recorded Hitler's opinion: ". . . when the worries diminish, he'll improve."

Abdominal Spasms

Even more troublesome than the headaches were Hitler's intestinal symptoms. They were qualitatively and quantitatively different from his earlier dyspeptic complaints. During the winter of 1942/1943, Morell diagnosed a Roemheld syndrome, a German diagnosis not used in English-speaking countries. It refers to a feeling of fullness with epigastric and thoracic pain, caused, according to Roemheld, by a high diaphragm that presses against the heart. In May 1943, the gastrointestinal symptomatology became quite troublesome. Hitler complained of increasingly severe pains, first in the region of the transverse colon, later all over the abdomen. Pains were felt as cramps associated with constipation. After bowel movements, the pain lessened or disappeared. The pains occurred both day and night, but often started at nighttime. At times, they were triggered by bulky, gas-producing foods (salads, vegetables, leguminous foods); many times, however, dietary indiscretions were not followed by pain. Some attacks lasted for days. Hitler and Morell strongly believed that the gastrointestinal symptoms were caused by adverse events and upsets, particularly with Hitler's general staff. Morell mentioned particularly the bombing of the Möhntal dam on 17 May 1943 and the bombing of Hamburg on 24 July 1943. After many events that could be considered catastrophic for the Germans, however, no gastrointestinal symptoms occurred. The typical attack started with two or more days of constipation, a feeling of distention, and accumulation of gases. Morell responded, possibly on Hitler's request, by prescribing laxatives—first relatively mild cathartics, later ricinus oil, and finally the now obsolete, vicious purgative Calomel. At the same time, Morell prescribed relaxing medications such as belladonna obstinol—an anticholinergic and cathartic that also contains belladonna. A favorite drug was Papaverin, a smooth muscle relaxant that was given first intramuscularly and later intravenously. Finally, Morell added the narcotic substance Eucodal (oxycodone; American trade name: Percodan), which also was given intramuscularly and later intravenously. It is possible that Hitler received the controlled drug oxycodone without his knowledge. The drugs combined with the powerful laxatives was potentially quite dangerous. Until 20 July 1944, Hitler had ten attacks, altogether at least 24 until the end of December 1944.

One severe attack shortly before an important meeting with Mussolini at Venice is described in detail in Morell's diary. On 18 July 1943 in Wolf's Lair Headquaters at 10:30 a.m. Morell was called because Hitler had developed very severe abdominal pains at 3:30 a.m. and could not close an eye. Morell found that the abdomen was tight as a board and full of gas. He repeated his earlier diagnoses of cardio-gastric Roemheld complex and spastic constipation. Treatment: Ample laxatives such as Luizym, Euflat, and Leo pills and also abdominal massage. He administered only Eupaverine subcutaneously, because the conferences necessitated the avoidance of narcotics. At 3:30 pm before departure by air to the Berghof Hitler looked very pale and felt dizzy. Morell changed his mind and presribed the narcotic oxycodone. After arrival at the Berghof Hitler felt better. He received more laxatives and sedatives (phanodorm and quadronox). He slept well for four hours and departed for Italy at 6:30 a.m. Morell advised Hitler to take a Vitamultin tablet during the conference.

During the conference with the Duce, Hitler's associates noted, with some embarrassment, that Hitler was hyperactive, extremely talkative, and could not be interrupted by Mussolini. They wondered what drug Morell had injected. Was it oxycodone, Vitamultin tablets, amphetamine, or a placebo? The latter is the least likely—Morell gave Hitler ineffective medications, but not placebos. During the return flight Hitler remarked that Morell must be given credit for the success of the conference.

The gastrointestinal symptoms bothered Hitler greatly, but his and his physician's greatest worry was his cardiovascular status. On 11 April 1943, Morell took another ECG and sent it to Professor Weber. The electrocardiographic tracings indicated a deterioration of Hitler's heart condition. Professor Weber made some stringent but unrealistic recommendations, which Morell did not follow. (See Appendix 6 for a copy of the report and Weber's letter.) Suggested but not accepted by Hitler were massage, more sleep at night and more rest during the day, and reduced fluid intake. Hitler liked the recommended oxygen inhalations and a Strophanthin cure, and Morell obliged.

On 17 December 1942 Morell and his patient finally had a candid discussion about Hitler's cardiovascular status:

> Führer wants to be told by me whether his conditions would be very bad, because he would have to make important decisions regarding Germany. He does not fear death. It would be a relief for him. He only has continuing irritations and no time for himself. He lives only for the Fatherland, for Germany. There is no cure for death; he knows that. But in impending danger I have to tell him. I reminded him of the day last December, when I did not consult anybody because I said to myself, nobody can do anything better and something might get a little loused up. I'd rather have the responsibility completely and all to myself, even it were difficult. I reminded him also of the cerebral edema in Winniza and that, if there would have been no improvement after one day, I would have resorted to more intensive mea-

sures. He has full and complete confidence in me, and in such situations I should be sure to treat all by myself. Concerning his wish always to be informed about his condition, I referred to the existing coronary sclerosis, for which I have been giving iodine for a long time. Through the later ECG my assumption proved to be right. In human beings, faster calcification begins at 45. Through narrowing of the blood vessels of the coronary arteries, it could come to conditions of angina pectoris. For this I always carry a drug. And in case I might not be here—nitroglycerin and Esdesan cum nitro are left here. Through glucose I take care to keep the heart strong and to dehydrate the system. . . .

Hitler's and Morell's concerns continued. Morell noted light edemas over the shinbones on finger pressure, which he interpreted as a residual of the edema of 1936 and not as a cardiological symptom of decompensation. In the fall of 1943, Hitler urged Morell to obtain another electrocardiogram, but it was not until May 1944 that it finally was recorded, when Morell was able—not without difficulties—to obtain a new ECG apparatus. The ECG, which he personally recorded, was useless. But Morell took steps to improve Hitler's cardiological treatment, such as having an oxygen apparatus installed in Hitler's sleeping quarters, a measure Hitler liked although there was no objective reason for it, nor for the Strophanthin cure, which Hitler also appreciated. It seems Hitler liked the cure well enough (and perhaps it helped him) to ask for another Strophanthin cure in the winter of 1945. When Hitler wasn't feeling well, Morell suggested that he should not hesitate to take a little coffee or 10 to 15 drops Metrazol. Obviously reassuring himself, Morell recorded that anginal symptoms didn't exist; hence the short-term prognosis was favorable. Fortunately, smoking and alcohol consumption were not problems for the Führer.

In February 1944 Hitler again demanded an eye examination, which took place on 2 March 1944 [see report in Appendix 7]. The result of the eye examination was inconclusive. Hitler had a mild, unequal hypermetropia, the left eye being the leading eye. The only abnormality that the opthamologist, Professor Löhlein, could detect was a turbidity of the vitreous humor, which produced a light veil caused by delicate, faintly mobile, diffuse particles. No turbidity of the lens could be detected. The retina was normal, and the retinal vessels did not indicate any evidence of arteriosclerosis. No hemorrhages were noted. Professor Löhlein was unable or unwilling to make a definite diagnosis, but suspected that the objective and subjective eye findings might be the result of transitory variation in blood pressure, caused by a vascular spasm. The therapeutic measures of a heat lamp and medication with iodine were innocuous but not helpful, and the recommendation of rest impractical. Löhlein also prescribed bifocal lenses, which Hitler did not use. He used eyeglasses only rarely, and never in public, and when reading maps and printed materials he used a huge magnifying glass (the so-called *Führerlupe*). Löhlein cautioned against frequent reexaminations. Morell did not see fit to follow Löhlein's recommendations.

Before 20 July 1944, Morell mentioned Hitler's tremor only rarely and did not describe changes in posture or difficulties with walking. He noted fluctuations in intensity of the tremor that reinforced his belief that it was psychogenic. Certainly during the spring of 1944, however, Hitler was bothered by troublesome tremors of the upper extremities, a stooped posture, and a dragging gait. His great relief after the temporary disappearance of the tremor following the assassination attempt proves his prior discomfort. He tried to hide the tremor of the left hand by covering it with his right hand, or by anchoring it in his belt. The tremors had been noted already in 1943 by Hitler's valet Linge, his secretary Schroeder, General Guderian, and Goebbels—the most ardent Hitler watcher.

While Morell recorded fluctuations of all symptoms and related them to external events, such as military setbacks and upsets, he did not notice a general decline in the Führer. Other observers saw it clearly. W. Best, a particularly good observer, noted on 30 December 1943: ". . . when Hitler appeared, I was shocked about his appearance. . . . He made the impression of a tired, broken old man. He had a dragging gait and was stooped over, so he appeared hunchbacked. His face was sunken and lined."[128] After a visit on 20 February 1943, General Guderian reported:

> When I saw him for the first time after 13 months' separation, I noted the change in his condition. The left hand trembled, his posture was stooped, his gaze rigid, the eyes bulged lightly [slightly?] and were dull, the cheeks had red spots. His irritability had increased. He lost control when angry and then was unpredictable in words and evaluations. The external signs of illness increased steadily but were not noticed by his constant entourage, accustomed to seeing him daily.[129]

In early June 1944, Hitler was a rather sick person—even though he rarely spent a day in bed or reduced his workload.

Hitler's Injuries and Recovery after the Assassination Attempt

During the assassination attempt on 20 July 1944, Hitler had leaned over the conference table when the bomb exploded, which protected him from the full blast of the explosion. His wounds were not severe, but also not as insignificant as he maintained in his public statements. Both ear drums were ruptured. He had a contusion of the right elbow, a large excoriation of his lower back, and his legs were full of splinters, which Dr. von Hasselbach removed. His pants were in shreds. Later, he sent his bloody uniform to Eva Braun as "a souvenir."

After the explosion, Morell assisted von Hasselbach in giving first aid and recorded:

> *Evening, 20:00*: Pulse 100, regular, strong. Blood pressure 185–170. Wound treatment: penicillin powder. Right forearm badly swollen. Aluminum

acetate dressing [which was ordered by Morell and criticized by Professor von Hasselbach after Hitler developed a superficial infection]. Hemorrhage right calf. Third and fourth finger, left hand dorsal, large blister bandaged. Hair in the occipital region singed. On thigh, blister after burn the size of a hand and a lot of contusions and excoriations. Left arm: internal hemorrhage, is badly swollen and quite immobile. Immediately 2 Optalidon and 2 tbsp. Bromnervacit before retiring.

Hitler's otologist, Prof. Carl von Eicken, could not be reached. As a substitute, Dr. Erwin Giesing, an otorhinolaryngologist at the nearby station hospital in Lötzen, was summoned to treat the Führer. On 21 July 1944, Giesing made the following initial report:

> Right ear: large kidney-shaped central rupture lower front and rear. Bleeding badly. Whispering perceived only immediately into ear. Pronounced combined deafness of middle and inner ear. Indications of nystagmus to the right. Left ear: slit-shaped central rupture 3 mm long, lower rear. Whispered speech perceived at 4 meters. Slight combined deafness. Treatment: various coagulants to stop bleeding.

Hitler's recovery from his general injuries proceeded quite rapidly. On 21 July 1944, Morell was invited to Hitler's tea and rewarded with a gold watch for the first aid. On 28 and 29 July, two notations by Morell indicate that the leg tremor had disappeared. Hitler was delighted over this improvement, and Morell became more convinced than ever that the tremor was psychogenic. By the middle of September, Hitler had recovered completely from the injuries, but his tremor had returned.

The 20 July plot was taxing for Hitler. Privately, he complained to Morell: ". . . The weeks since 20 July have been the worst of my life. I mastered it with a heroism no German could dream of." In an undated entry, presumably in early October, Morell also gave Hitler credit for a spirited recovery: "In spite of hours of dizziness and malaise, about which he never spoke, in spite of questioning, he kept upright and fought against it with all his energy. Often there was danger of collapse, but through his energy he mastered the situation." But Morell had ideas of his own about what had happened. He considered the restlessness of Hitler's left leg and hands the result of a small nervous breakdown following 20 July and not, as Brandt believed, the result of strychnine poisoning. Specifically, Morell believed that Hitler had a traumatic lesion of a cerebral convolution of the right side (a very odd, unscientific interpretation).

Activities of the Otological Consultant, Dr. Erwin Giesing[130]

Dr. Erwin Giesing (1907–1977) studied medicine at the Universities of Düsseldorf, Innsbruck, and Vienna, and graduated from the University of Cologne in 1932. After a short period in sports medicine, Dr. Giesing had specialty training in ear, nose, and throat diseases from 1935 to 1936 under

Professor Eicken at the University Clinic of Berlin. He became the Chief of Otorhinolaryngology at the Rudolf Hospital in Berlin in 1936, and entered private practice in Berlin in 1938. He joined the NSDAP and SA in 1932.

Dr. Giesing's treatment of Hitler's injuries using cauterization, topical medications, irrigations, and massage followed the rules of the art. According to Professor von Eicken, Hitler's ears had healed by 18 August 1944, but according to Giesing the left ear did not heal until 10 September, 1944, and the right ear until 8 October, two days before Giesing was dismissed as Hitler's otological consultant. It can be safely assumed that, after 18 August, Hitler required little otological attention. Dr. Giesing, who liked the exciting atmosphere of the headquarters and access to his Führer, found another field of activity. He noted that Hitler had frequent colds and complained of periodic headaches. Giesing reported headaches that Hitler described as dull pressure, especially on the left side. He elicited slight pain over the left maxillary sinus and started to treat Hitler for sinusitis with 1% cocaine solution one month before the first X-ray of Hitler's sinuses was taken. Daubing the mucosa of upper respiratory pathways with cocaine solution was not an unusual treatment at the time, although many otolaryngologists refrained from using the addictive drug. Hitler enjoyed the treatment, and remembered that it made his head free. Once he warned Giesing in jest, ". . . I hope you don't make a cocaine addict out of me." After Giesing's departure, Hitler did not ask for cocaine treatments. Only once, shortly before his death, Dr. Morell gave him cocaine–adrenalin eye drops for a dust conjunctivitis. Giesing claimed that he carried out a complete physical and neurological examination of Hitler on 3 October 1944, at a time when Hitler was under intense treatment by Morell. According to Giesing, Hitler permitted him to carry out such an examination in order to find out whether the Führer suffered from any gall bladder disease. Giesing then described this examination in minute detail, including trivia about whether Hitler pulled his shirt up or down. Apart from lively reflexes (biceps, triceps, patellar, and ankle jerks), Giesing found Hitler's neurological status normal. In his account, Giesing further stated, "I could not see any anomalies of the genitalia. The prepuce was pulled back, and the glans penis was not over-sensitive." In an interview with John Toland, Professor von Hasselbach expressed the opinion that such an examination by an otologist was not only uncalled-for, but that it was also impossible that Hitler would have permitted it.

After the war Giesing described a cocaine collapse while he was alone with Hitler. The pulse was fast and weak, and Hitler did not respond. Giesing then realized that the mighty and powerful man was in his hands and decided that he did not want Hitler, who had started and nearly lost the war, to live. Following an inner compulsion, Giesing swabbed Hitler's throat with cocaine once again. At that moment, Linge returned. Hitler's face changed, and he drew up his legs. Linge remarked that Hitler was getting his intestinal cramps. Giesing packed his instruments and returned to his local military hospital. That evening, with von Hasselbach's permission, he went to Berlin to check on some bomb damage to his office. He learned through a telephone call to Linge that Hitler was alive. It is inconceivable that a loyal National Socialist, who tried to protect his Führer from the machinations of Dr. Morell, would want to assassinate his patient. It was nothing more than a ridiculous attempt to impress his captors after the end of the war. In another incredible tale, Giesing stated that he gave Hitler a brief intelligence test. What head of state—not to mention the suspicious Hitler—would ever permit such an examination?

The Illnesses of Fall 1944

By mid-September, Hitler was sicker than ever. On 8 September, he complained about pressure over the right eye, on 15 September about dizziness and head pressure. The tremors were worse than before. Morell believed that the bad military situation was responsible for the downturn. The Allies west and east were coming dangerously close to the German borders. Hitler felt he had been let down by his generals and betrayed by some, such as his counterespionage chief Admiral Wilhelm Canaris ("that slimy Greek"). On a more personal level, he seemed depressed because his former valet Hans Junge, the husband of his favorite secretary, Traudl Junge, had been killed in action. On 15 September, Morell also noted a swelling of Hitler's ankles (right 26 cm, left 28 cm) and intensified his cardiologic treatment. At that time, in addition to his basic treatment, Hitler was receiving massive injections of male and female sex hormones and an extract of the cortex of the suprarenal gland—a precursor to modern cortisone. Furthermore, at Giesing's suggestion an X-ray of the sinuses had been carried out and showed an opaqueness of the left maxillary sinus.

On 23 September 1944, Hitler developed severe intestinal spasms after an upset about the military situation. The spasms did not respond to routine spasmolytic therapy (oxycodone 0.02 and Eupaverine 0.03 i.v.). On 24 September Morell, by himself, obtained two electrocardiograms, one after physical exercise. He did not state why he decided on this procedure at that particular time. It is also unknown why Professor Weber did not receive the electrocardiograms until 2 December 1944 and sent his report to Morell on 4 December.

The Icterus

On 27 September an alarmed Morell noted when he made a call in Hitler's bunker that the dictator had a slight yellowish discoloration of the skin. Giesing claimed that he had noted the icterus two days earlier in daylight. Whether or not they notified Morell, all of Hitler's physicians and some staff members, amongst them Bormann, knew of Hitler's icterus. Morell also noted that Hitler's urine was beer brown, but no urinalysis was recorded. Clearly, Morell was worried about Hitler's jaundice, but he did not undertake even a minimal examination as to the cause of it. He speculated that it might have been brought on by a blockage of the gall bladder duct by the spasms. He also considered an inflammation of the gallbladder or gall duct, but at that time opted against it. On 28 or 29 September, Hitler felt extremely sick and exhausted. His body temperature was 37.2 centigrades pulse somewhat accelerated (90/minute). Morell described a very taut abdomen. The stomach region was sensitive to touch, less so the gall bladder region. To ease the painful spasms Morell administered oxycodone and Eupaverine, with little relief. For Hitler's constipation he prescribed first ricinus oil, later Calomel, without results. He then recommended an oil enema in bed, but Hitler preferred to administer it by himself in his toilet, while Morell had to wait in front of the locked door. Finally, Hitler happily told Morell that he had four explosive bowel movements. In vain, Morell again urged Hitler to obtain an X-ray examination of his stomach, intestines, and gall bladder.

On 1 October, Morell noted that Hitler's appearance had improved. His temperature was subfebrile 37.1 C, he felt very weak, and strict bed rest was advised, but the yellowish discoloration of the skin had almost disappeared. His abdomen was no longer tense, with a slight sensitivity on the left side, not in the gall bladder region. His appetite was poor, and he ate barley soup and apples. Routine therapy was prescribed, plus Progynon B. oleosum forte. Morell urged a change of location:

> Again urgently proposed a change of location, 2–3 days in Berlin, 8–14 days on the mountain. Declined completely. Berlin unsuitable, because he always would have to go into the shelter and can't walk now; he is too weak. I pointed out the unsuitability of the new bunker for him, small living room and small bedroom, in spite of ventilation not enough oxygen, much too modest for first man and Führer of the Reich. He promised to walk more. You won't do it, I replied, and I consider the creation of body reserves and much oxygen, hence better metabolic combustion, important on account of great demands in future months. When I was leaving, lifted himself up sideways. Probably gases and pressure toward the heart.

On 2 October, Morell noted further improvement. Hitler got out of bed for a war conference held in the Führer's quarters, but Morell commented that he made a very weak impression on the military gentlemen. Hitler's appetite was better. He wanted five oranges, which Morell promised to procure. Routine therapy was administered, plus Vitamultin forte, and self-administered chamomile enemas continued. On 3 October, Morell noted that the yellow discoloration of the skin had disappeared. He gave Hitler an injection of Scophedal (a potent narcotic) for sleep. Urinalysis on 3 and 10 October, after the crisis, was normal, with an acid specific gravity of 1019, traces of albumin, negative sugar, sediment, many bacteria, a few leucocytes, and moderate amounts of urate, oxalate, and epithelial cells. (Notable is the fact that there was no statement about bilirubin, urobilin, or urobilungen.) An Indican test (for fecal decomposed blood) was not carried out because the necessary chemical agents were not available. No blood bilirubin test was carried out. On 4 October, Morell noted that Hitler's abdominal symptoms were minimal, but Hitler complained about "dizziness in the head." From 5 to 8 October, Morell was sick, and his assistant, Dr. Weber, replaced him. Hitler confronted Morell: "You must take a break for several months." On 10 October, Hitler felt well; he had lost thirteen pounds in two weeks, which pleased him.

The Doctors' Feud

On 23 September, while waiting to treat Hitler, Dr. Giesing discovered several black pills on Hitler's breakfast tray. He was able to obtain the pills from Hitler's manservant, Linge, and soon afterwards determined that they were Koester's anti-gas pills, which contain extract of strychnine and belladonna. Giesing became greatly concerned that Hitler, who at the time had developed a slight icterus, was being endangered by Morell's therapy, and told Drs. Brandt and von Hasselbach about his findings. The discovery alarmed the attending surgeons and the highest members of Hitler's court— and last Dr. Morell—leading to what became known as the Doctors' Feud.

The doctors assumed that Morell, either deliberately or out of ignorance, was poisoning Hitler. They misinterpreted the composition of the Koester's pills and concluded that Hitler had received toxic amounts. Dr. Brandt saw Hitler, who stated that he was unaware of any toxicity in the pills that he had been taking off and on for some time, daily in the last two months, occasionally up to sixteen pills. After his discussion with Hitler, Brandt intimidated Morell, as Morell recorded on 4 October:

> Do you think that anyone would believe you that you did not order this prescription? Do you think that Himmler would treat you differently than anybody else? So many are being hanged now that the matter would be dealt with coldly. If anything happens to the Führer, you can imagine what would happen. One would not blame Hasselbach but you and probably me. It would be best if I always knew what goes on. . . .

Soon, however, both Hitler and Morell were reassured by the result of a chemical analysis of the Koester's pills by the SS laboratory, indicating that the Koester's pills, in the amounts that Hitler swallowed, were not toxic. Furthermore, Hitler never had the classic symptoms of strychnine or atropine poisoning. Giesing's assertion that he had tried out the Koester's pills on himself and that they produced symptoms similar to Hitler's was either a hysterical response or a lie. Hitler concluded that hostility among the physicians would not be in his best interest and dismissed Drs. Brandt, von Hasselbach, and Giesing. For a while, Brandt kept his post as Reichskommissar for Health. Hasselbach asked for front service, which turned out to be a life-saving move, because his successor, Dr. Ludwig Stumpfegger, was killed when he tried to escape from the bunker after Hitler's death. Giesing allegedly received a donation of 100,000 Reichsmark. Morell had won a clear victory over his critics. On 4 October 1944, Hitler addressed Morell affably, and condescendingly, as "*Doktorchen*" (little doctor). Morell reinstated his demand to be informed about all physician-prescribed and self-prescribed medications.

More Illnesses in Late Fall 1944

As soon as Hitler recovered from the hepatic–intestinal illness episode, he began to complain vigorously about upper respiratory symptoms. In contrast to the legitimacy of his cardiological, gastrointestinal, hepatic, and neurological complaints, his complaints about upper respiratory illness were vastly exaggerated, which was recognized by both Morell and the more conservative and reluctant ear, nose, and throat consultant Professor von Eicken. Hitler complained about symptoms of a mild chronic tonsillitis, a mild chronic sinusitis of the left maxillary sinus, and a hoarseness which, of course, bothered the orator Hitler greatly. The last complaint was legitimate, and eventually resulted in the removal of a singer's node by von Eicken.

Hitler was critical of Morell's treatment of his sore throat, because he believed that Morell did not treat the cause—bacteria that cause the infections—but rather tried to soothe the symptoms by applying different lotions and paraffin packs. Part of their argument dealt with what sulfonamide should be used, Morell's inferior Ultraseptyl or Tibatin, made by I. G. Farben. Morell recorded:

27.October.44, 13:30: [Hitler] In bad mood. Voice not good. In such condition, could not talk to the German people even over a microphone. I should be able to hear how bad his voice is. The voice is a little rough, but not very much. I pointed to the small irritation by the new nose irrigation, which is applied in cases of chronic laryngitis, according to Frank [Morell referred to his vade mecum, *Moderne Therapie* by R. Frank (Berlin, 1939)]. As camphor and menthol were present, temporary irritation would be possible, which, however, has a good effect by causing hyperemia, then producing more immune substances. [Hitler] How does the hyperemia help if the bacteria are not killed? That's what counts! Replied: It need not be bacteria that cause the roughness, but the mechanical irritation that the vocal cords have to endure. During examination of pharynx, the left side of the pharynx is normally colored and the right tonsil is normal. The left tonsil has a few light spots in the lacuna. In the upper part redness. No swelling of the neck. Daubed both tonsils with Neopyocyanase in the lacunae (no expression of pain).

Before this treatment I injected 10 cc 20% glucose i.v., Tonophosphan f. i.v., Vitamin Ca, and Glyconorm i.m. The patient started again about the killing of bacteria. He is in medical treatment since 20 July and the voice is worse than before. I pointed out that it is only a short time (1-1/2 weeks) since I treated the airways and that I follow the best procedure and that everything except the voice irritation has healed. "Yes, but this is the most important matter. You should have, then, when you used Ultraseptyl, used a bigger shock dose and not only singular applications." "Mein F., I have made Ultraseptyl injections for two days in a row." "Probably this is too little. You should have continued." "Starting today at noon, in the afternoon you will get a sulfonamide shock—actually Tibatin, because it is excreted most quickly—that is, in 24 hours. At the same time, I want to insert a paraffin pack into the nostrils, which will make the voice more supple." "This does not help, either. The bacteria must be killed. This is the same as with other insertions into the nose, which did not produce any recovery." "Mein Führer, camphor and menthol hurt a sore mucosa and irritate, but they also disinfect. The irritation is reduced by paraffin, the mucosa relaxes and heals. Can I begin with the treatment this afternoon?" "No, tomorrow. Besides, I went for a walk yesterday and did not get better."

It was a little more difficult to persuade Professor von Eicken to treat it vigorously. He first considered the slight opacity of the maxillary sinus insignificant. He did, however, remove a small singer's node (officially called a polyp) on 18 November 1944. The blood and urine examinations carried out on 26 November did not point to any acute infection of the sinuses, except for a moderately elevated erythrocyte sedimentation rate, which, however, in all likelihood resulted from other causes (see laboratory report in Appendix 5). Hitler recovered completely from his hoarseness, yet von Eicken continued to treat his sinuses and occasionally was able to squeeze out a drop of purulent secretion. Hitler's insistence on treatment prevailed. Hitler's preoccupation with upper respiratory infections had two other consequences. As Hitler insisted that he acquired these infections from his barber, and the unfortunate barber was forced to undergo a Tibatin cure. Also connected with Hitler's dread of dangerous bacteria was a remark that Morell recorded on 25 October 1944:

> . . . Conversation about the local water hard and full of nonpathogenic bacteria that disturb metabolism. Urine is certain not to contain bacteria. Conversation about hypospadia, spina bifida, cystopyelitis with pathogenic coli bacteria, main focus in the prostate. The latter has to be examined by me in the near future. . . .

It is surprising that Morell, who had considerable experience in the treatment of male urinary diseases, never carried out the examination, either before or after this conversation. Even more amazing is the conversation itself. Hypospadia and spina bifida are rare diseases. What induced Hitler to mention them? Morell did not comment. This strange remark will be scrutinized in the interpretive chapters.

On 30 October 1944, severe gastrointestinal symptoms reappeared. Morell believed they were caused by the tense military situation. Hitler was upset about the infidelity of one of his generals (Rommel or von Kluge): "F. worked through the night and had to make a very difficult decision [the Ardennes offensive] until quite suddenly, like always after great upsets, the spasm occurred. . . ." On 7 November, Hitler was unable to fall asleep until morning. He felt a dull pressure in the head, an oppressive sensation, and no desire to work. On 8 November he had sudden spasms in the region of the sternum with strong gas distention. As always, Morell administered oxycodone and Eupaverine, supplemented by cathartics. Another bout of gastrointestinal spasms also occurred on 8 November.

In mid-November, Morell changed his mind about the cause of the spasms. While he previously considered but rejected the possibility that the spasms could have been caused by cholecystitis or cholelithiasis, he now accepted the suggestion of his assistant Dr. Richard Weber, who substituted for him and began to treat Hitler as a case of cholecystitis with a nostrum Gallestol, which was suppose to increase gall flow. On 2 December, Morell finally received Professor Alfred Weber's report about the electrocardiograms, which had been mailed to him six weeks before. The cardiologist not only addressed the heart disease of "Patient A," but also of Morell, who at the time was sicker than his patient (see Appendix 6 for report). Again Morell felt the cardiologist's advice was not practical and did not see fit to follow his recommendations.

What bothered Hitler more than any other symptom in late fall 1944 was the tremor of his hands and difficulty in locomotion. A chair had to be pushed under him when he wanted to sit down. Morell was completely at a loss about what troubled his patient. Until June he believed that Hitler trembled because he was upset over his lost battles and mounting military problems. In November, however, Morell heard somewhere that placenta extract (Homoseran) might be helpful. He prescribed it, together with electric muscle stimulation, without any therapeutic benefit. He also was unable to give Hitler any satisfactory explanation about the cause of the tremor. This failure contributed to Hitler's loss of trust in Morell. There were, however, other reasons as well. Hitler was rightly critical of Morell's insufficient cleaning of injection sites, which resulted in minor infections. Morell's silly reply was that the infections were caused by staying in the bunker, with its lack of sunlight and bad air. Thus, according to Morell, Hitler's blood was low in oxygen, could not coagulate, and thus remained red. Hitler replied, however, that the infections were caused by bacteria that entered his body through the injection. Shortly before, Hitler had praised Morell highly. Morell jotted down with a glow:

> F. is very happy and told me these idiots [the dismissed surgeons] had no idea about what they would have done to me. I would have been without a physician, and these people must have known that during the eight years you [Morell] have been with me you have repeatedly saved my life. And how was it all before. All physicians who were dragged in failed. I am not an ungrateful person, my dear doctor. When both of us luckily get through this war, then you shall see how generously I will reward you. . . .

A marked change occurred in mid-November, after Morell's absence for four days to attend his brother's funeral. When Morell returned, he found Hitler cold and very unfriendly. There were no questions about the brother's demise, and even though he had left for the funeral with the patient's permission, Morell was criticized by Hitler and his camarilla for leaving.

Still, within a few days Hitler urged Morell to take a few days off to take care of himself. In early December, to Morell's consternation, Hitler wanted to talk with Dr. Stumpfegger about his illness alone, not in Morell's presence.

The intestinal spasms became more troublesome during December, and interfered with Hitler's work. Morell viewed this by now as gall bladder pathology, although on repeated examinations the gall bladder region was at most slightly sensitive. On 11 December Morell again observed slight jaundice and noted that the urine was beer brown. Urinalysis on 12 December revealed bilirubin 1+, a sign of liver pathology. On 19 December 1944 Morell made a strange entry in the diary:

> "Basic treatment. F. very well. On request 20 cc glucose solution i.v. Vita-multin forte. Liver and "Perand" i.m. (on account of work overload). Daily one-hour walk. Appetite very good."

What did the scribbled word "Perand" mean? It could have been the brand name, Perandran, for a male sex hormone, which, however, was not on Morell's list of "house medications." It also could have been a code word for Pervitin, the German name for amphetamine, but it is unlikely that Morell would inject amphetamine intramuscularly.

On 30 December 1944, Morell recorded the last gastrointestinal spasm: "Supposedly after eating green pea soup, in my opinion after excitement about coming events: (1) composition of speech and speech, (2) seemingly big military event [the failure of the Ardennes Offensive]." Morell's therapy was an intramuscular injection of 20% glucose, liver, and Vitamultin forte, along with oxycodone, Eupaverine, and Progynon B. oleosum forte intravenously. Besides the spasm, Morell recorded a very strong tremor of the left leg. What had become very obvious to many in Hitler's entourage, but kept from the general public, was his progressive general decline. Naval Captain H. Assmann described: ". . . He is a psychic wreck that moves slowly, slouching, step by step with a shaking head, bent over."[131]

The Final Phase of Illness (1 January 1945 to 30 April 1945)

Morell's notes from 1 January 1945 to 22 April, when he was flown from the bunker to Munich, are relatively short compared with earlier parts of the diary. This may have been a consequence of Morell's illness; perhaps it also was caused by the severity of the military and political problems, during a period when doom was close and unavoidable, requiring his energy and time to be spent on health concerns. Hitler also might have felt better subjectively, because the painful gastrointestinal spasms and the headaches were not bothering him anymore. Nevertheless, on his own he continued some palliative medications against a recurrence of the gastrointestinal symptoms. The relationship between Hitler and Morell was less close, less friendly. At times, Hitler's anger flared when he could not ignore the fact that Morell was unable to help him. During this last phase, Hitler became more directive. He demanded another Strophanthin cure, because he believed that it had helped him before. He requested and received bloodletting, although Morell felt it was unnecessary. Actually, the systolic blood pressure readings during this phase were never higher than 156 mm Hg. Clearly, Hitler never ceased to worry about his cardiovascular illness. He also was concerned lest he receive too much sedation during this calamitous military and political period, even refusing luminalettes with a low dose of phenobarbiturate (0.015 gm). One phenomenon that was barely reflected in Morell's notes was Hitler's general decline, which was so massive that a number of lay persons commented on it.

An eloquent description of Hitler's general decline was provided by Gauleiter Karl Wahl in the last meeting Hitler had with the Gauleiter, his most trusted paladins, on 24 February 1945:

> Hitler talked, sitting at a table, for about an hour and a half. His voice was not very loud. Sitting very close in the second or third row, I could observe him in minute detail. Then I really perceived what a bad state of health he was in. His left hand, or rather his left arm, shook so badly and constantly that the whole body began to vibrate. This was not trembling, these were strong and regular shaking movements, which disquieted me greatly during the speech. Whatever he undertook to suppress these movements, which were apparently embarrassing for him, he did not succeed. When he crossed his arms over his chest it got worse, the whole upper torso started to move.[132]

For many months, Hitler had complained about diminished vision in his left eye. Finally, an eye examination by Professor Löhlein took place on 7 April 1945 (see Appendix 7 for report and interpretation). Löhlein's findings and recommendations were meager. The report is very similar to the previous one, except for the notation of a mild conjunctivitis and a chalazion, transient findings that contribute nothing to an understanding of Hitler's ophthalmic pathology. The external eye, except for the chalazion, was normal. The refraction revealed the same inequality of farsightedness in both eyes (isohypermetropia) that had been found in 1943. In the vitreous body a slight turbidity was noted, caused by sluggishly moving minute particles, not enough to explain the impairment of vision. The retina was normal, and the retinal vessels did not show arteriosclerotic changes. Löhlein assumed that Hitler at one time might have had a hemorrhage in the vitreous body. The therapeutic recommendations dealt only with the chalazion: application of heat for fifteen minutes three times a day, and application of a mercury ophthalmic ointment.

At the end, the tremor and impairment of motility bothered Hitler more than any other symptoms. In vain, he quizzed Morell about these symptoms, but Morell could offer neither a satisfactory explanation nor an effective therapy. In all likelihood, Hitler became painfully aware that Morell—in spite of all attempts to reassure both Hitler and himself—did not understand the neurological syndrome and really did not know what to do about it, at least not until the last two weeks of Hitler's life.

At the time of the eye consultation in 1944, Professor Löhlein suggested to Morell that Hitler might have Parkinson's syndrome. He probably learned about it from Professor De Crinis, who was one of his colleagues in the medical faculty of the University of Berlin. Until 12 April 1945, Morell still used electrotherapy to treat the tremor. He switched to the so-called Bulgarian cure, the customary treatment of Parkinson's syndrome, on 15 April 1945, writing confidently: ". . . as the tremor is a variety of paralysis agitans, I am trying to influence it temporarily by subcutaneous injections of Harmine and Homburg 680." At the time, Harmine (a drug made from the Rauwolfia plant) and Homburg 680 were the best available therapies for all types of Parkinson's syndrome (the active substances were atropine and hyoscine). Morell followed the standard formula of increasing the dose of Homburg 680 by one drop a day.

On 21 April, Morell was dismissed as Hitler's personal physician. Dr. Stumpfegger took over Morell's responsibilities and continued the Bulgarian treatment schedule. Hitler also received adrenaline-cocaine eye drops for his conjunctivitis. According to Irving[133] and Katz,[134] Hitler spoke harshly with Morell on 21 April 1944, telling him to take off his uniform and return to the "Damm" (his practice at the Kurfürstendamm). It is quite likely that Hitler was irritable and upset, but actually he had done Morell a favor by permitting him and a few others to leave Berlin, which was doomed and just about to be conquered by the Russians. Morell allegedly was upset, too, but a letter he wrote to his wife shortly after his departure indicates that he recovered quickly after his arrival in Bavaria.[135] His correspondence indicates that he believed, quite unrealistically, that he could still pursue his business enterprises, as if nothing had happened. It must be kept in mind that Morell suffered from some cerebral impairment. Shortly before, he was seen by an American war correspondent, who described him as a confused and scared old man.[136] On 1 May 1945, the ailing Morell was admitted to the City Hospital of Bad Reichenhall. He was arrested by American troops on 17 June, and then detained in various prisons and prison hospitals. His physical and mental condition declined rapidly. Undoubtedly, he was depressed and demented. To Dr. Brandt, during the time they shared a prison cell, Morell once said, "I wish that I were not I."[137] He developed multiple cerebral infarcts, with a right hemiparesis and transient aphasia and was transferred from the Allied prison hospital in Dachau on 29 June 1947 to a German hospital in Tegernsee. He was not accused of any war crimes, and it is unlikely that Hitler discussed the genocide with him. The terminal diagnosis was arteriosclerosis with damage to the myocardial areas. The advanced chronic nephritis and cerebral impairment were not mentioned. When Morell died in March 1948, he was a demented, lonely, and destitute man.

Hitler's Suicide

The decision to commit suicide was not an easy decision, notwithstanding Hitler's remark after the surrender of Field Marshal Paulus in Stalingrad regarding how easy it was to die. To Hitler's thinking, suicide in Berlin would be a heroic act, while an escape to the mountain retreat appeared cowardly. Four different motivations probably played a role in this decision. First, how he would be remembered by posterity was most important: as a hero who never capitulated or as a coward who surrendered or escaped. Second, the Russians were almost at the gates of the Reichskanzlei, and Hitler did not want to fall into their hands, dead or alive. Whether or not he actually said that he did not wish to be exhibited in a Moscow zoo is uncertain, but there is no doubt about Hitler's fear of humiliation and the mutilation of his dead body. He knew about the gruesome assassination of Mussolini and his last mistress, Clara Petacci, by partisans, as well as about the desecration of their bodies after they were shot—they were stoned and hanged upside down from rafters in a filling station in Milan. According to Professor Schenck, who worked as a surgeon in the Führerbunker, everybody in the bunker knew about this, and Hitler must have been terrified by it.[138] Third, Hitler had finally abandoned his hope that the Western Allies would join him in the fight against Bolshevism and realized that the war was lost. Fourth, he was devastated by the "treachery" of Göring, Himmler, and others of his military staff, the SS, and the civilian administration. He was determined to die as a courageous leader. Nothing was left but to die and predict that National Socialism would rise out of its ashes. He ordered everybody who was capable to break out of the bunker and, if possible, join the troops who were still fighting. Only a small number of prominent persons, amongst them Joseph Goebbels and his wife, Magda, insisted on staying. The Goebbelses later committed suicide with potassium cyanide after they had poisoned their six children—the oldest daughter was thirteen years old—to protect them from "sadistic vengeance and disgrace" by the enemy.[139]

The 29th and 30th of April 1945 were busy days for Hitler. He slept little during the last days of his life. In the early morning of the 29th, Linge found him fully dressed. Hitler dictated his wills; he sent final dispatches to field commanders and secretaries. He consulted Professor Haase about a fail-safe method of suicide. Prof. Haase told Professor Schenck, who worked in the lazarett of the Reichskanzlei, about his advice to Hitler: To shoot himself through the temple and at the same time bite down on an ampule of potassium cyanide. First the poison was tested on Hitler's dog, Blondi, whom Hitler also did not want to live in a non-Nazi world! Finally, he instructed his staff to procure gasoline and to burn his and his wife's bodies immediately after their suicide.

Hitler had his last meal of spaghetti and tomato sauce—he was a consistent vegetarian. Then, at 3 p.m., he and Eva Braun said good-bye to Joseph Goebbels, Martin Bormann, and some of the members of his staff. Somewhat to his annoyance, Magda Goebbels succeeded in seeing him one more time. From this point on, reports contradict each other. Some heard a shot; others did not. When Linge first opened the foreroom to Hitler's private quarters, he smelled bitter almonds. He withdrew and quickly returned with Bormann. Hitler's face was bloody from a head wound. He had collapsed over a coffee table. Two revolvers and a puddle of blood were seen on the rug. Eva, still perched on the sofa, had died from potassium cyanide poisoning.

Immediately afterwards, the bodies were carried into the garden of the Reichskanzlei by Bormann, Linge, and Kempka and doused with gasoline that Hitler's driver had procured. At first the gasoline could not be lit because of heavy bombardment and a firestorm. Finally, a lighted rag was thrown over the bodies, which immediately ignited. Members of the small group watched the spectacle and rendered their final Hitler salute. The bodies burned until eleven o'clock that night. Then, during a pause in artillery fire, troops of the elite guard buried the bodies of Hitler, Eva Braun, and two dogs in two shallow bomb craters. The event was watched by chance by two SS men. A last mendacious communiqué was published, stating that "this afternoon in his command post in the Reichskanzlei, fighting to his last breath against Bolshevism, our Führer Adolf Hitler was killed in action for Germany."[140]

Postmortem

On 2 May 1945, officers and soldiers of the Soviet Counterintelligence (SMERSH) entered the Reichskanzlei and found a number of shallow graves in the garden. In one of these graves, they found the corpses of a man, a woman, and two dogs. Assuming these were the bodies of Hitler, Eva Braun, and their pets, they exhumed them. One corpse had darned socks on his feet and clearly was not Hitler. On 4 May, the SMERSH soldiers and officers reentered the Reichskanzlei and exhumed two other human corpses and the canine cadavers and brought them, together with the bodies of General Krebs, Joseph and Magda Goebbels, and their six children, to a morgue in the Military Hospital at Berlin-Buch, where they were autopsied. Hitler's corpse was designated number twelve, Eva Braun's number thirteen. The autopsies were carried out on 8 May 1945, and the report was written on 11 May by a commission of pathologists and specialists in forensic medicine who subsequently issued a report (Appendix 8). The chairman, Professor Faust Josefovitch Shklaravski, was a specialist in forensic medicine; his deputy Professor Nikolai Alexandrovitch Krajevski, a specialist in pathology. Although their credentials were impressive, their competence was doubted not only by German forensic medical experts, but also later by Russian experts. The autopsy report—the only one ever seen by Western observers—is short, one might say skimpy. See Appendix 8.

At Stalin's orders, the reports were designated top secret and stored in a Russian archive, not to be seen for another twenty years. The autopsy reports of the Russian commission came to the attention of the Western world in a book written by the Russian journalist Lev Bezymenski and published in English translation in 1968,[141] and in an expanded version in German in 1982.[142] Before the Bezymenski publication, a short article by Elena Rshevskaya-Kagan appeared in Russia in 1967.[143] Thus, the West learned about the finding of the corpses and the autopsies only from the publications of Rshevskaya and Bezymenski twenty years after Hitler died. Western historians and journalists knew only from German witnesses that Hitler had committed suicide. Their response to Russian secrecy was anger and mistrust, Bezymenski defended the Russian's delay in the second version, stating that a thirty-year waiting period in top secret matters is customary. But why the secrecy about an autopsy? Bezymenski offered strange explanations. By not publishing, the rise of usurpers could be prevented, and more of Hitler's henchmen could be caught (one could assume the opposite). A third explanation made a little more sense. The Russians—and particularly Stalin—were not sure that Hitler was dead. Stalin received the autopsy reports and ordered them buried in Russian archives. At the Yalta conference in July 1945, he declared that Hitler escaped, and he also repeated this to his top-ranking officer, Field Marshal Grigori K. Zhukhov. For a while, even General Eisenhower believed Stalin's story.

The Russian reports were supposed to provide information about the following matters: (1) Did the Russians correctly identify the corpse? (2) What was the cause of Hitler's death? (3) Did the autopsy contribute to knowledge about Hitler's illnesses? A Russian pathologist identified Hitler by his teeth. A jawbone with teeth was preserved and photographed by the Russian pathologists and compared with statements obtained in prolonged interrogations (lasting ten years) of prisoners Käthe Heusserman and Fritz Echtermann, assistants of Hitler's dentist, Professor Blaschke. Their descriptions matched what was found in the autopsy. Suspicious Western scholars were not satisfied with this proof. The quarrel over Hitler's teeth ended only when definitive proof was furnished by Western experts in forensic dentistry, Reidar F. Sognnaess and Ferdinand Strom.[144] Comparing Russian reports and Russian photographs of Hitler's teeth and bridges with the radiological pictures of Hitler's skull in the Washington National Archives, they came to the definitive conclusion that the corpse the Russian commission autopsied was in fact Adolf Hitler's. The lower left six-tooth bridge, in combination with the upper nine-tooth bridge, would be an absolute identification. In addition, there was a very unique bridge on the lower right, involving three teeth, numbers 27, 29, and 30: This was designed with an arm that attached numbers 27 to numbers 29 and 30, while avoiding or going around number 28. This is a very unique and peculiar design. The identification of this bridge, in addition to the other two bridges, leaves no room for doubt.[145]

What was not established with a high degree of probability was how Hitler died. In his earlier publication, Bezymenski cited the commission's conclusion that Hitler poisoned himself with potassium cyanide. Crushed glass ampules were found in his mouth. No evidence was reported by the

Russians in their first report indicating that Hitler had shot himself as Hitler's staff had claimed. In the second version, Bezymenski reported that skull fragments—parts of the parietal and occipital bones—with an opening caused by an exiting bullet were found. The Russians still insisted that Hitler poisoned himself and received a *coup de grace* from Linge. The new evidence makes it likely, however, that Hitler followed the recommendation by Professor Haase, which Schenck witnessed when he fled from the Chancellory together with Ambassador Walther Hewel. When they were caught by the Russians, Hewel committed suicide by biting down on a glass ampule containing potassium cyanide and at the same moment pressing the trigger of a revolver pointing at his temple. This, according to Hewel and Schenck, was the recommended fail-safe SS procedure. The question can be raised as to whether Hitler's Parkinson's tremor would have allowed him to follow this procedure. As the Parkinson's tremor is a tremor at rest, this is possible.

The postmortem findings by the Russian commission were inadequate and left much more to be desired. The descriptions of heart, lungs, liver, and kidneys were superficial. The gall bladder was not even mentioned. No reference was made to histopathological or toxicological findings. The only remarkable finding was the absence of the left testicle in the scrotal sac. The report states, "genital member is scorched. In the scrotum, which was singed but preserved, only the right testicle was found. The left testicle could not be found in the inguinal canal." It is almost amusing how Maser and Waite argued about this finding. Maser did not believe the Russians because they maintained that Hitler had only one testicle;[146] Waite believed them because of the very same reason.[147] Hans Ulrich Wehler sarcastically remarked that perhaps Hitler had three![148] Waite maintained that the members of the commission would not have risked their reputations by writing a fraudulent report. However, it is now proven—and this refers to the method of suicide—that their report was fraudulent. If they had written a truthful report, provided they were capable of doing so, that might have cost them more than their reputations. Sexual denunciation and degradation of an enemy is common, and it is possible that the report is nothing more than such a degradation. Rumors about Hitler's sexual malfunction were widespread. Allied soldiers sang a song belittling the sexual prowess of Hitler and other National Socialist leaders, and the Russians knew about that.

After the collapse of the Soviet Regime, new data about Hitler's corpse and autopsy came to light.[149] His charred and rotting remains were transferred nine times, from one burial site to another, until they reached the Lefortovo prison in Moscow, where they were cremated, with the exception of a fragment of Hitler's lower jawbone that remains in a Russian archive. Perhaps someday new reports and a correction of previous lies will be published. Lev Bezymenski admitted that the published reports were false because he did not want to lose the cooperation of Russian authorities or risk repercussions. This only confirms what Western historians and forensic experts suspected: that the Soviet investigation was fraught with deceit, secrecy, and incompetence. Today, it is certain that Hitler, who at present would be over 100 years old, is dead, and that he died by suicide. No serious student of history maintains that he escaped with the help of his paladins. General Jodl considered suicide justified because Hitler was too sick to fight.[150] General Koller believed he should have had the guts to stand trial.[151] If he had committed suicide earlier, millions of lives could have been saved, but this was not on his mind.

Many were disturbed or puzzled by Hitler's baby picture; however, most babies, unless seriously ill, look like little angels. (*Courtesy of the Bundesarchiv, Koblenz*)

The Veit branch of the Schickelgruber family, in which several psychotic and mentally retarded individuals were found. (*Courtesy of the Library of Congress, Washington, D.C.*)

Hitler's father, Alois
Hitler. The "super customs
official first class" was a
pompous authoritarian.
(*Courtesy of the Library of
Congress, Washington, D.C.*)

Hitler's mother, Clara. The
most sympathetic member of
the Hitler clan; she became a
depressed, burdened woman.
(*Courtesy of the Library of
Congress, Washington, D.C.*)

A caricature of one of young Adolf's professors. One interpreter asserts that the professor is masturbating; actually, he is eating candy or nuts from a coniform paper bag. Not a bad drawing for the eleven-year-old artist. (*Courtesy of the Bundesarchiv, Berlin*)

Dr. Eduard Bloch, as an émigré in the United States. The Jewish physician of Hitler's mother was falsely accused of causing her death and Hitler's deadly anti-Semitism. (*Courtesy of Lily Kren née Bloch, Brooklyn, New York*)

War enthusiast Hitler in Munich at Germany's declaration of World War I. (*Courtesy of the Bundesarchiv, Koblenz*)

During the *Kampfzeit*, Hitler often dressed in traditional alpine garb; later, he reminisced about the happy days when he was an unknown, nameless person. (*Courtesy of the Bilderdienst Süddeutscher Verlag, Munich*)

Hitler rehearses a speech before the mirror, 1926. Photograph by Heinrich Hoffmann. (*Courtesy of the Bildarchiv Preussischer Kulturbesitz, Berlin*)

Adolf Hitler campaigning in northern Germany on April 19, 1932. (*Courtesy of the Bildarchiv Preussischer Kulturbesitz, Berlin*)

Hitler and SA Chief Franz Ferdinand Pfeffer von Solomon, 1927. Note the dog whip and body distance, indicating a high level of aggression. (*Courtesy of the Bildarchiv Preussischer Kulturbesitz, Berlin*)

Hitler in formal clothes which made him look like an animal trainer or magician in a circus. He disliked it because it was not compatible with his revolutionary self-image. (*Courtesy of the Bilderdienst Süddeutscher Verlag, Munich*)

Hitler napping and Eva Braun on the terrace of the Berghof. The neglected mistress became Hitler's wife one day before their double suicide. (*Courtesy of the Bildarchiv Preussischer Kulturbesitz, Berlin*)

Sculpture of Hitler's half-niece Angela (Geli) Raubal by Ferdinand Liebermann. Hitler had an avuncular crush on the unfortunate young woman, who died under mysterious circumstances. (*Courtesy of the Bildarchiv Preussischer Kulturbesitz, Berlin*)

An absurd example of the Hitler myth; Hitler never mounted a horse. (*Courtesy of the Bildarchiv Preussischer Kulturbesitz, Berlin*)

Since 1942, Hitler complained about serious visual impairment. He used a large magnifying glass and reading glasses, but never in public. No definitive diagnosis of his visual impairment has been made. (*Courtesy of the Bildarchiv Bayerisches Staatsbibliothek, Munich*)

Professor Dr. Theodor Morell received the highest decoration in science and medicine. Only Reichsmarschall Hermann Göring equaled Morell's appetite for decorations and food. (*Courtesy of the Süddeutscher Verlag, Munich*)

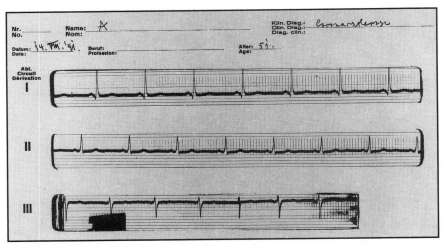

Hitler's electrocardiogram, August 14, 1941. (*Courtesy of the National Archives, Washington, D.C.*)

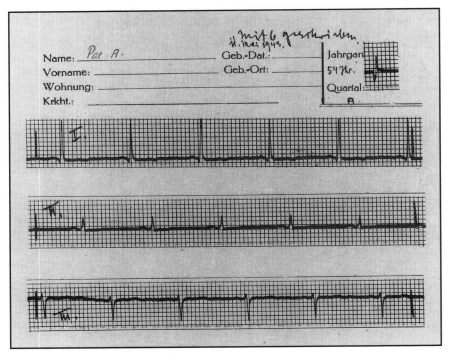

Hitler's electrocardiogram, May 11, 1943. (*Courtesy of the National Archives, Washington, D.C.*)

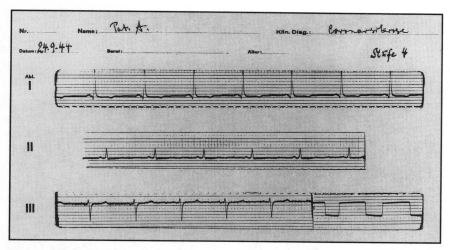

Hitler's electrocardiogram, September 24, 1944, *before* exercise. (*Courtesy of the National Archives, Washington, D.C.*)

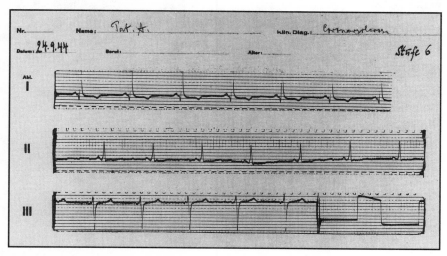

Hitler's electrocardiogram, September 24, 1944, *after* exercise. Hitler's electrocardiograms consistent with mild to moderate progressive ischemic myocardial disease. (*Courtesy of the National Archives, Washington, D.C.*)

A sick Hitler in front of a model of the Linz Art Gallery a few months before the German capitulation. Photograph by Heinrich Hoffmann. (*Courtesy of Ingrid Lauck, Munich*)

II

REVIEW,
COMMENTS, AND
INTERPRETATIONS

8

Medical Review

Biological Family History

HITLER'S FATHER died suddenly at the age of sixty-three (in 1903, when Adolf was fourteen), from an uncertain cause. Striking had been his early retirement (at the age of fifty-eight) for health-related reasons, without a specific diagnosis. The entry in the death registry states that he died from a pulmonary hemorrhage, but it also has been assumed that he died of a cerebral hemorrhage or cardiac arrest. According to an unsubstantiated story, he had suffered a pulmonary hemorrhage years or months before his death. Whether he actually had a life-threatening pulmonary hemoptysis or possibly a ruptured aneurysm of the aorta is unknown. Varices of the esophagus (occurring in severe alcoholism) ought to be considered because Alois Sr., in all likelihood, was an alcoholic. No evidence of a syphilitic infection or treatment has been documented. It is likely that Adolf Hitler was concerned about "hereditary syphilis" in his family and possibly alluded to it in *Mein Kampf* when he wrote about a "horned Siegfried" who infected his young and innocent wife. It could be a reference to his father, either fantasy or fact.[1] In my opinion, it is likely that Hitler suspected that some of his forebears had the disease. The cause of Hitler's mother's death at the age of forty-seven was a carcinoma of the breast. His sister Paula died of unknown causes at the age of sixty. Hitler's other siblings died at an early age: Gustav in infancy, cause unknown; Ida in infancy, from diphtheria; Otto two days after birth, cause unknown; and Edmund at the age of seven, from measles.

The Gestapo discovered information about mental illness in the so-called Veit branch of the Schickelgruber family. Josef Veit, the son of Maria Schickelgruber's sister Josefa (i.e., a cousin of Hitler's father), had several descendants who were mentally ill: One twenty-one-year-old son committed suicide, one daughter was a patient in an insane asylum, a second daughter was semi-retarded, and a third was mentally retarded.[2] It is very likely that Hitler was aware of mental illness in his family and was preoccupied with questions of heredity, miscegenation, and degeneration. In reality, having a psychotic relative in the family closet would not be such an issue; it occurs frequently. Hitler's often-expressed concern about mental illness and degeneration, however, mattered greatly. It is also likely that Hitler had some congenital anomalies (hypospadia and spina bifida occulta—discussed below). One minor congenital anomaly ascertained by visual refraction tests was an anisohypermetropia. In my opinion, Hitler's preoccupation with heredity and degeneration has been grossly underestimated. Together with his anti-Semitism, concern about degeneration and mental illness became a pillar of his Weltanschauung.

Cardiovascular Diseases

Beyond any doubt, Hitler suffered from a labile moderate hypertension. From 1941 to 1945, the average systolic blood pressure was 150 mm Hg (ranging from 200 to 110), average diastolic pressure (rarely measured) 95 mm Hg (ranging from 117 to 85). He never had a cerebral vascular accident; the fainting attack that occurred in the presence of his foreign minister von Ribbentrop was not a stroke but in all likelihood a dramatized syncope.[3] Professor Gibbels assumed that Hitler's headache attacks were caused by his hypertension.[4] Although a few headaches occurred when the pressure was high, others occurred when the pressure was low. No definite correlation between blood pressure fluctuations and headaches can be established. Dr. Morell and his consulting cardiologist, Professor Weber, established clinically and by electrocardiogram that Hitler suffered from a progressive left ventricular hypertrophy and a mild asymptomatic myocardial ischemia. This was later confirmed by Professor Schenck and his cardiologic consultant, Dr. Dietrich Pillen.[5] The American cardiologic consultant Richard Pasternak, M. D. concurred in general. He considered the first electrocardiogram (of August 1941), as revealing a small myocardial infarction. The small Q wave in Lead I as well as minor diffuse non-specific ST-T or repolarization abnormalities are compatible with a myocardial infarct and its clinical manifestation of occasional mild chest pressure. The second electrocardiogram (of May 1943) showed a worsening of the repolarization abnormality, compatible with either an increase of the left ventricular hypertrophy or of the myocardial ischemia. The final two electrocardiograms (of September 1944) were recordings made while the patient stepped on and off a two-step stool, known as a "Master Step Test." The ECGs showed worsening of the repolarization abnormalities, suggesting an increase of the myocardial ischemia. If this is correct, it would be strongly suggestive of coronary heart disease in the presence of left ventricular hypertrophy, and the repolarization abnormalities could have been due to the left hypertrophy alone. Thus, Dr. Pasternak concluded that the cause of the ischemia was, in all likelihood, atherosclerosis of the coronary arteries.[6] Cardiologist Professor Ian Tillish M. D. agreed.[7] In a minority opinion, Joseph Perloff accepted the diagnosis only of a left cardiac hypertrophy.[8] Nevertheless, Morell's and his patient's concern about serious heart disease runs like a red thread through the clinical history from the summer of 1942 to Hitler's death.

Gastrointestinal Diseases

During much of his adult life, Hitler suffered from gastrointestinal symptoms. According to the unreliable Müllern-Schönhausen, Hitler complained in a letter he wrote as an adolescent about stomach upsets and the ignorance of doctors who couldn't help him.[9] Later, Hitler stated to a circle of secretaries and Dr. Morell that his gastrointestinal troubles began in 1929.[10] In the mid-thirties Hitler remarked to Speer that he frequently suffered from periodic post-prandial pains, belching, bloatedness, and constipation.[11] He was not specific about which foods elicited the pains but complained that he could not eat anything without serious discomfort. In addition, Hitler as well as Morell and other persons in his environment were bothered by his flatulence.[12] The gastrointestinal symptoms were an important reason to consult Dr. Morell in 1936. Morell prescribed his universal remedy, the Mutaflor cure, which seemed to help Hitler's dyspepsia. The intestinal symptoms during the episode in August 1941—abdominal tension and mild diarrhea—were not prominent. Hitler recovered and had no further significant gastric complaints until the spring of 1943, when he developed attacks of severe diurnal and nocturnal abdominal spasms, during which the abdomen became "hard as a board" without any specific localization of pain or tenderness on pressure. At times, the spasms occurred after eating bulky or fatty foods. Altogether, Hitler had twenty-four or more attacks between January 1943 and December 1944. Most of the time Hitler was constipated; no fresh or occult blood was found in the stools. Loose or watery stools occurred only after medication with laxatives. Both Hitler and Morell considered the spasms psychogenic in origin. Hitler expressed the opinion that there was nothing wrong with his bowels because no blood had been found, and that the spasms were caused by annoyance with his generals.[13]

Professor Schenck refrained from making a diagnosis of Hitler's intestinal disease without the availability of radiological examinations and laboratory tests.[14] He retained Morell's diagnosis of a cardio-gastric syndrome (Roemheld's syndrome, a diagnosis not made in the U.S.) and added the diagnosis of gastritis. American gastroenterologists do not diagnose gastritis unless inflammatory changes in the gastric mucosa can be demonstrated. American consultants in gastroenterology (Drs. Dennis M. Jenson,[15] Sherman M. Mellinkoff,[16] and, with some reservations, Howard Spiro[17]) made the diagnosis of an irritable bowel syndrome, essentially identical with

Morell's diagnosis of spastic colon. What is difficult to understand is why, if these disturbances were psychogenic or psychosomatic in origin, the symptoms would last for years and then not recur after 31 December 1944, a time when Hitler was under the greatest stress—playing his last card for victory. Schenck correctly assumed that Hitler's gastrointestinal symptoms were aggravated by his dental pathology.[18] I find the idea convincing, expressed by Professor Schenck and the American consultant Dr. Art Schwabe,[19] that Dr. Morell's combination of medications—uppers (laxatives) and downers (opiates)—contributed to Hitler's gastrointestinal complaints.

While the gastrointestinal symptoms do not permit a definitive diagnosis, the hepatic symptoms are even more complex. The Hestons diagnosed gallbladder calculus with chronic cholecystitis and cholidocholelithiasis[20] and Bert Park cholecystitis.[21] Experienced gastroenterologists and hepatologists have felt skeptical about these diagnoses of Hitler.[22] According to Spiro, both diagnoses are much abused and should not be made unless the chronic state is preceded by an acute episode. Mellinkoff cautioned that many individuals with gallstones are free of symptoms.[23] At present, diagnoses of cholelithiasis and cholecystitis are confirmed on the basis of radiographic and nuclear tests, the latter of which were not available in Hitler's time. Hitler staunchly refused even a simple X-ray of chest and abdomen. Schenck assumed that Hitler had a mild case of hepatitis A, which was prevalent amongst the German troops in the Russian theater of operations.[24] However, why Hitler should have suffered two short icteric episodes six to eight weeks apart, and why bile metabolites in Hitler's urine should have disappeared in two days, is unclear. A laboratory error is one possibility. However, I propose another explanation later in this chapter, a tentative diagnosis of giant cell/temporal arteritis (see below).

Ear, Nose, Throat, and Respiratory Illnesses

In *Mein Kampf,* Hitler stated that he suffered from a serious lung illness (alleged to be tuberculosis) in 1905, which convinced his mother—at the advice of a physician, Dr. Keiss, in Weitra—to take him out of middle school.[25] No specific evidence of any treatment or medical consultation by Dr. Keiss exists.[26] No symptoms indicating active tuberculosis (fever, weight loss, expectoration, copious positive sputum after hemoptysis) were recorded. Dr. Eduard Bloch, Hitler's mother's physician, stated that he never saw or heard of any evidence indicating pulmonary tuberculosis.[27] The statement made by Hitler's uncle, Anton Schmidt, that Hitler recovered from his illness so quickly with the aid of milk, vegetables, and fresh air, also casts doubt on the claim of tuberculosis. It is more likely that Hitler suffered from an upper respiratory viral infection. In my opinion, it is likely that he consciously and/or unconsciously exaggerated his complaints to achieve his secondary gain of avoiding school.[28] Whether the illness was hysterical play-acting, conscious malingering, or both cannot be determined.

Hitler frequently complained about colds, which he dreaded. It is unlikely that he suffered colds any more often than anyone else, or that his colds were particularly severe. When he was under Morell's care, Hitler demanded and received drastic treatment with sulfonamides, particularly Morell's own inferior Ultraseptyl, manufactured in Morell's pharmacological plants. At one time, in the fall of 1944, Hitler traced an infection to his barber, who was forced to undergo a series of sulfonamide injections as treatment. In late August, when Hitler's ear injury was almost healed, the otologist Dr. Erwin Giesing diagnosed tonsillitis and sinusitis of the left maxillary sinus. The first radiological examination of the sinuses revealed a slight opacity in the left maxillary sinus, but no fluid levels. Professor von Eicken considered the radiological change insignificant, but Giesing diagnosed a chronic infection of the maxillary sinus. After initial doubts, von Eicken accepted this diagnosis and occasionally squeezed a few specks of pus from the sinus. No evidence of any preceding acute sinusitis could be found. The clinical picture was confusing, because Hitler also had liver disease at the time, which would account for the temporary slightly elevated temperature and an increased erythrocyte sedimentation rate, while blood cell counts were normal. In the opinion of the American ear, nose, and throat specialist Irwin Harris, Hitler at most may have had a mild chronic sinusitis, not unusual after frequent colds. Giesing treated the sinusitis with swabs of a 1 percent cocaine solution, a treatment that was acceptable but criticized by some physicians even then.

In the bomb explosion on 20 July 1944, both of Hitler's eardrums were ruptured and he suffered hemorrhages of both middle ears. His hearing was temporarily impaired, and he had a transient disturbance of his equilibrium. The ear injuries were treated by Giesing, using cauterization of the ear drums and anesthesia with 1 percent cocaine solution, and Hitler recovered promptly and fully from these injuries. Since the mid-thirties, Hitler had had repeated attacks of ringing and buzzing in his ears (tinnitus), without any impairment of hearing. He complained about it to Professsor von Eicken, who noted on 20 May 1935: "For several days, buzzing and high metallic ringing left. Ears normal, hearing normal."[29] Von Eicken remembered that such buzzing had already occurred at the time of the Röhm putsch and considered the symptoms psychogenic. Hitler was advised by Winifred Wagner to take lecithin and benefited from it. Tinnitus occurred again during the episode of illness in August 1941, when Morell assumed a vascular etiology. No evidence of a vascular cause in 1934 or 1936 existed, and no blood pressure reading taken at those times have been preserved. Thus, Hitler's tinnitus remains unexplained, like most cases of tinnitus.

In May 1935, Hitler complained of increasing hoarseness.[30] Professor von Eicken diagnosed a laryngeal polyp and removed it under local anesthesia (Pentocaine spray and morphine). For a short time after the operation, he received voice training from Professor Nadolesny. The pathological report by Professor Roessle revealed a polyp (also called a singer's or screamer's node) of one millimeter in size on the right vocal cord. Such polyps are neither inflammatory nor neoplastic, but are caused by over-strain of the vocal cord. Laryngologists compare them to the calloused hands of a farm worker. The orator Hitler recovered fully within two months in 1935 and after a second episode and operation by Professor von Eicken in 1944.

Eye Diseases

Almost at the end of World War I, a mustard gas injury caused painful swelling of Hitler's eyelids, photophobia, and blepharospasm. He recovered from this mild mustard gas poisoning in several weeks. He interpreted the above symptoms as blindness and referred to himself as a blind cripple but was discharged as fit for full military service.[31] The diagnosis of mustard gas poisoning was confirmed by Dr. Martin Dresse, who saw the medical record in the Pasewalk Hospital. According to Dresse, Hitler suffered from blepharospasm and conjunctivitis but not blindness.[32] He had a second episode of "blindness" after he received the news that Germany had surrendered. Hitler's dramatic description of the second episode establishes the diagnosis of a hysterical act of blindness.[33]

On 28 August 1941, Morell noticed that Hitler had a severe, painful sunburn. No mention was made of light sensitivity, but it had been noted since 1941 that Hitler avoided bright sunlight, began wearing a cap with a wide visor, and kept the lights dim in his working and sleeping quarters. Morell did not offer any explanations. In the thirties, Hitler prematurely developed presbyopia. He wore corrective lenses, but not in public, and used a huge magnifying glass for reading maps and fine print. Memoranda for him were printed using a special, large 1 Führer-type. During two eye examinations by Professor Löhlein, under unsatisfactory lighting conditions, Hitler was found to be farsighted. Professor Helmuth Fanta drew my attention to his slight anisohypermetropia,[34] a congenital symptom that in severe cases is associated with other congenital anomalies. The subjective complaints about a serious impairment were, at the time of Hitler's eye examinations, not corroborated by objective findings.

It is known, however, that persons with anisometropia experience impairment of vision when corrective lenses are used for the first time (anisometric amblyopia). This may well be the reason for Hitler's complaints; another is the possible impairment of vision caused by the temporal arteritis. Finally, a hysterical component cannot be completely excluded. The inadequate eye examinations do not permit a differential diagnosis.

During the episode of illness in July 1942, Hitler complained about haziness of vision, as if he was viewing objects through a thin veil, and of some eye pain. Nineteen months later, Löhlein carried out an eye examination in March 1944, during which he found a very delicate, faintly mobile, diffuse turbidity of the vitreous humor in the right eye, caused by infinitesimal particles. No turbidity of the lens could be observed, and no pathology of the fundus or the blood vessels of the fundus was noted. The left eye was normal. Löhlein thought that the particles caused the misty vision and interpreted this as minute hemorrhages into the vitreous humor, not originating in the blood vessels of the retina, but caused by variations in blood pressure and blood vessel spasm. The therapeutic recommendation of prolonged rest was completely unrealistic. Hitler continued to complain of diminished vision. Speer remembered in his memoirs that Hitler in 1943 expressed fears that he would go blind.[35] In fall 1944, the complaints became more vehement, but it was early April 1945 before Löhlein conducted another examination. The findings were a chalazion of the left upper eyelid and a mild conjunctivitis, caused by dust. Löhlein did not describe arteriosclerotic changes of the retinal vessels, but he did not think that the particles in the vitreous fluid could explain the decreased vision. He prescribed instillation of zinc drops against the conjunctivitis and possibly excision of the chalazion. I gained the impression that Löhlein knew more than he stated, suspecting an unexplained vascular cause for Hitler's amblyopia. One of my consultants, Bradley Straatsma, M.D., agreed with Löhlein about the vascular etiology and considered the small particles to be microhemorrages.[36] Another American ophthalmologist, Edwin Hill, M.D., referred to the clouding of the vitreous humor as stellar or asteroid hyalitis, a harmless condition of uncertain etiology that does not explain the diminished vision.[37] In my opinion a thorough re-evaluation of the eye findings by a competent specialist is indicated. More about a possible vascular cause will be mentioned later.

Genitourinary System

It has been vehemently maintained and denied that Hitler had a congenital malformation of his sex organs. The assertion that he had only one testicle is based on the Russian autopsy report and circumstantial evidence reported while he was alive. Weighing the pros and cons, it is likely that Hitler had a genital defect. According to the autopsy report ". . . the left testicle could not be found in either the scrotum or on the spermatic cord inside the inguinal canal, nor in the small pelvis."[38] Some historians (e.g., Waite) have believed this finding, while others (e.g., Maser) have denied it. Over the course of time, it has been revealed that the Russian pathologists falsified data in their report, maintaining that Hitler did not shoot but poisoned himself and giving credence to the assumption that the Bolsheviks wanted to present Hitler as a coward with a sexual defect. Amongst the opponents of the monorchism thesis, Hitler's valet Linge claimed he observed that Hitler's genitals were normal when they both urinated in the woods.[39] It is obvious that such a claim is plain nonsense.[40] Giesing claimed he found Hitler's genitalia to be normal during a physical examination. According to von Hasselbach, it is out of question that Giesing ever examined Hitler's abdomen.[41] Schenck is undecided whether Morell was permitted to examine Hitler's genitalia, even though Morell answered in a medical questionnaire that the cremaster reflexes were normal.[42] Morell, however, had no reason to examine the cremaster reflexes, and probably never did. When author John Toland asked Professor von Hasselbach about the alleged monorchism, von Hasselbach replied that Hitler did not have monorchism but some other deformity, about which Emil Maurice (Hitler's bodyguard) could furnish information;[43] Toland, however, was unable to contact Maurice. His widow, Dr. Hermine Maurice, told me in a personal interview that her husband never spoke about any genital malformation of Hitler in his family circle.[44] An important clue was provided in a conversation between Hitler and Morell on 28 October 1940, regarding urinary coli infections, spina bifida, and hypospadia.[45] Morell simply recorded this but did not comment, mentioning only that he intended to examine Hitler's prostate—which he never did, which is amazing, considering that Morell was a self-appointed specialist in male urological diseases. Why would Hitler have made such a remark? It is possible that he was talking about his own afflictions. Spina bifida is a developmental defect of the lumbar region in which the vertebral arches and meninges do not close. In its severest form, the meninges and spinal cord protrude, causing paralysis and anesthesia of the legs, and partial or total inability to control anal and urethral sphincters. Schenck correctly stated that it is impossible that Hitler suffered from a spina bifida. In contrast, spina bifida occulta is a relatively common anomaly in which the vertebral arches do not close but the meninges and spinal cord do not protrude. It can be asymptomatic but in many cases causes urethral sphincter dysfunctions and bladder infections, may be associated with other congenital defects such as hypospadia, epispadias, and monorchism in males, and anomalies of the urethral and rectal sphincter. It is easy to establish the diagnosis of spina bifida occulta by radiological examination. In my view, it is possible that Hitler suffered from such an anomaly, discovered by a radiological examination after which Hitler probably decided not to undergo another X-ray of his trunk, while he did not object to a radiological examination of skull, sinuses, and teeth. The previously described meeting between Henriette Hoffmann and Professor Kielleuthner—in which the old professor remarked that if Hitler would have come to him earlier, he would have been able to help him—lends credence to the hypothesis that Hitler had a spina bifida occulta and hypospadia, because patients with hypospadia benefit from operations during childhood. Hypospadia may contribute to sexual problems in adulthood, although many patients have neither coital nor urinary problems. In my opinion, it is possible that Hitler had some slight leakage after urination, which would explain his excessive changing of underwear and bathing, often several times a day. I favor this interpretation over the assumption that Hitler had a washing compulsion. It is possible that he believed such a lesion was caused by "hereditary" syphilis. I assume that Hitler would have been worried that the deformity might be discovered. Other implications are that perhaps this was one of his great secrets, which the "intellectual brain parasites" must not discover! Perhaps the idea of preventing degeneration in other Germans led him to his vulgar Darwinism, eventually to the cruel and inhuman legislation on sterilization, and, ultimately, to euthanasia and elimination of the inferior by genocide. Hitler saw himself as a redeemer (there is a bit of Wagner and, more specifically, Parsifal in this) who would deliver his people through his own suffering.

The Alleged Syphilis

Hitler's ruminations in *Mein Kampf* about syphilis and prostitution are intense and highly personal, as can be seen in his remarks, "Who can know whether he is sick or healthy? Are there not numerous cases in which a [syphilitic] patient [who was] apparently cured relapses and causes frightful mischief without himself suspecting it at first?"[46] No wonder the rumor arose that, between 1909 and 1910 (when Hitler was in the Viennese Männerheim), he acquired a syphilitic infection from—of all possible partners—a Jewish prostitute.[47] This "fact" is supposed to explain Hitler's fear of syphilis and prostitutes. The lack of any documentation does not seem to matter, nor does the lack of evidence indicate that Hitler was ever treated for syphilis. According to Dr. Edmund Ronald, who invoked a Dr. Anwyl Davies, Hitler was treated by Dr. Odo Spiethoff, professor of dermatology and venereal diseases, in Jena. Spiethoff had to surrender his medical records to the Chief of the Führerkanzlei Bühler. Spiethoff's son, an attorney in Munich, cannot affirm this.[48] Twelve years after Hitler's and Himmler's deaths, it was learned from the memoirs of Felix Kersten that, according to conversations between Kersten and Himmler, the latter believed that Hitler suffered from general paresis and that, in Himmler's opinion, it was very dangerous for Germany to have a ruler with such a serious illness.[49] According to Kersten, Dr. Brandt also knew about this, but Brandt did not mention it in any of his written statements. Kersten was a controversial figure. He presented himself as a "Medizinalrat," clearly a medical title, although he was only a successful masseur with a lucrative practice serving influential patients. If the designations of quack and charlatan fit anybody, they fit Kersten. Trevor Roper, who roundly condemned Dr. Morell for being a quack and a charlatan, praised Kersten highly, in part because he helped endangered Scandinavians, Dutch, and Jews[50]—the latter of which has been staunchly denied by the Dutch historian Louis de Jong.[51] What Himmler really stated and assumed is unknown. Did he arrive at his conclusions after listening to Hitler's confused statements about syphilis? Was he really concerned about certain mad acts on the part of his sick leader, or did he just want to do Hitler in and assume leadership himself? We do not know the answers to these questions and probably never will. It is certain, however, (and I rarely use this word) that Hitler did not suffer from general paresis, a severe meta-syphilitic illness with easily diagnosed signs and symptoms, including rapid mental deterioration, psychotic and usually absurdly grandiose behavior, characteristic and easily recognized neurologic signs (such as irregular pupils that do not react to light, a severe dysarthria), and, in untreated cases, positive tests for syphilis in serum and spinal fluid. Hitler's Wassermann reaction and related tests were negative. The untreated illness is always fatal. In Hitler's time the only treatment was malaria inoculation, introduced by the Nobel Laureate Julius Wagner-Jauregg, later replaced by penicillin treatment. Neither method cures; they only arrest the disease process in some cases. In my opinion, Hitler had a severe syphilophobia and believed that syphilis was an illness transmitted through many generations that destroyed races and nations and, ultimately, mankind. As previously stated, he possibly believed that syphilis existed in his family—more specifically, he might have believed that his father was syphilitic, that he himself suffered from "hereditary" syphilis (which he confused with syphilis in a newborn infant who acquires the disease in the womb of an infected mother), and that this might have produced in him degenerative changes. Combating this plague, particularly among the Germans, Hitler considered one of his most important tasks. Additionally, he irrationally believed that syphilis was a "Jewish" disease,[52] which enhanced his radical racist views.

Parkinson's Syndrome

Observations of a tremor and impairment of motility were made by persons in Hitler's environment in 1942. Morell had already noted a fine hand tremor in August 1941, which was different from the tremors that were reported later.[53] Linge stated, "At the end of 1942 as the battle of Stalingrad entered a dangerous phase, Hitler's left hand began to tremble again. He had great trouble suppressing this in the presence of visitors. The left hand was pressed to the body—or held with the right hand. He crossed his legs when his left leg developed jerking movements."[54] More observers noted neurological changes in 1943 and 1944. It was noted that, when Hitler stretched out on a sofa, his servant had to elevate his legs[55]—indicating increased muscular rigor. Morell accepted the diagnosis of a Parkinson's syndrome only a few weeks before Hitler's death. Some of the lay observers, such as General Guderian, were quite perceptive, noticing his trembling, stoop, and awkward gait. Hitler had to have a chair pushed beneath him when he wished to sit down.[56] Immediately after the assassination attempt of 20 July 1944, Hitler's neurological condition improved remarkably, only to relapse in mid-August. From that point on, the symptoms steadily got worse. The brief remission, known to occur in cases of severe somatic or psychological trauma, only contributed to Morell's assumption that the illness was psychogenic.

The diagnosis of a Parkinson's syndrome was first made on the basis of weekly newsreels by Professor Max de Crinis, Chairman of the Departments of Psychiatry and Neurology at the University of Berlin. He communicated his findings through his friend in the SS, Walter Schellenberg, to Himmler, who forbade any further discussion. The symptoms also were observed by Professor Schenck, who originally diagnosed Bechterew's disease because of Hitler's stooped posture, but later made the diagnosis of Parkinson's disease.[57] After Hitler's death, the diagnosis of Parkinsonism was first published by von Braunmühl, but most commentators remained skeptical.[58] Maser insisted that the tremors were the result of a hysterical post-traumatic reaction in World War I, wrongly considering the Parkinson's tremors symptoms of a *Kriegszitterer* (war trembler, a combat neurosis).[59] The Hestons rejected the diagnosis of Parkinson's disease and considered Hitler's tremors the result of amphetamine abuse[60]; however, tremors resulting from amphetamine abuse are fine tremors, while Hitler's tremors were coarse. The diagnosis of a Parkinson's syndrome can be made on visual inspection of a patient or films of the patient. The definitive proof of a Parkinson's syndrome was the result of a painstaking motility analysis in newsreels made by Ellen Gibbels.[61] Gibbels concluded that Hitler had a hypomotility of the left upper extremity in 1941, a hypomotility of the left leg in 1942, a hypomotility of both upper extremities in 1943, a marked disturbance of gait in 1944, and four-per-second tremors at rest in 1945. These observations clinched the diagnosis of a Parkinson's syndrome. Not knowing of Professor Gibbels's investigation at the time, I viewed the final newsreels depicting Hitler and also arrived at same diagnosis. In these newsreels, Hitler showed hypomotility of the face, tremors of the upper extremities, and a shuffling gait. In still photographs, a kyphosis could be observed.

Parkinson's syndromes are differentiated into primary or idiopathic Parkinsonism (without identifiable antecedents) and secondary Parkinsonism (in which a definite cause produces the damage). The syndrome and others similar to it occur after medication with certain psychoactive drugs (chlorpromazine and reserpine), after chemical trauma (carbon monoxide poisoning), and after vascular changes (arteriosclerosis, possibly other vascular damage) and infectious diseases. Röhrs speculated that Morell secretly administered psychoactive drugs to Hitler, but these medications (such as chlorpromazine and reserpine, the earliest psychopharmaceuticals) were not available in Germany until the post–World War II period.[62] Park's idea that Hitler's Parkinsonism was the result of his mustard gas poisoning (which occurred about twenty years earlier) is far-fetched.[63] Park did not heed his own warning, "Don't diagnose zebras when you hear hoofs!" Hitler's combat gas poisoning was mild and followed by a quick recovery. Cerebral arteriosclerosis is often considered a cause of Parkinsonism. Although experts in the field increasingly doubt this, one eminent Parkinson expert, the late Walther Birkmayer, considered it a legitimate entity.[64] No good evidence exists, however, to indicate that Hitler had general or cerebral arteriosclerosis. In Hitler's case, it has not even been demonstrated conclusively that arteriosclerosis caused his coronary artery disease.

One of the most important forms of secondary Parkinson's syndrome is postencephalitic Parkinsonism. The best-known postencephalitic Parkinsonism was a sequela of the disease described by Economo after the worldwide epidemic of encephalitis ("encephalitis lethargica" or "sleeping disease") in 1919 and 1920. This Parkinson's syndrome has characteristics that differentiate it from idiopathic Parkinsonism, such as lack of a pupillary reaction in convergence of the eyes, gazing spasms (oculogyric crises), jerking and twitching movements (myoclonus), sleep disturbances, vegetative syndromes (such as excessive seborrhea of the face), and psychotic manic–depressive or schizophreniform episodes. These manifestations may occur years after the encephalitis, and, in some cases, the encephalitis is not remembered or recorded. As the typical symptoms of postencephalitic Parkinsonism were not present in Hitler, the diagnosis of idiopathic Parkinsonism is favored. Johann Recktenwald assumed that Hitler's encephalitis occurred in 1900, when he was eleven and his brother Edmund died of measles (possibly a measles encephalitis), from which Hitler, according to Recktenwald, also suffered when he was twelve.[65] Two very severe and usually fatal forms of encephalitis after measles are known. The first is a subacute sclerosing encephalitis that occurs in very young measles patients, six to eight years after measles. Symptoms include convulsive seizures, myoclonus, chorioretinitis, and rapid intellectual deterioration. The second form, an encephalitis associated with immunosuppression, occurs within months after measles with a fulminant course and fatal outcome. It is virtually certain that Hitler was not afflicted with these severe forms of encephalitis.

Recktenwald believed that Hitler's behavioral changes in puberty (learning difficulties, increased aggression, and hyposexuality) were the result of encephalitis. He described Hitler clinically as a postencephalitic monster (*Unhold*), reminiscent of the old English diagnosis of moral insanity. It strains one's imagination to follow Recktenwald's argument that Hitler's moral insanity developed in Linz, disappeared in the benign atmosphere of Munich and World War I, and reemerged in the postwar period when his political career began. Recktenwald asserted that Hitler was similar to the asocial postencephalitic patients described by Engerth and Hoff,[66] but no evidence for the postencephalitic *Unhold* theory exists. If Hitler were to have a work-up by contemporary neurologists, other diagnostic entities such as Jacob Kreutzfeld's disease and, even more remotely, hepatico-ventricular degeneration (Wilson's disease) might be considered. Without adequate clinical data, however, these are idle speculations. In conclusion, the diagnosis of a Parkinson's syndrome with its characteristic symptoms of hypomotility of the face and upper extremities, a festinating gait, muscular rigor, and typical four-per-second tremors has been clearly established. Intellectual deterioration and depression resulting from Parkinsonism cannot be assumed. In Hitler's case, the Parkinson's syndrome was of low to moderate severity. Morell's treatment of Hitler's Parkinson's syndrome was a hodgepodge of suggestion, Homoseran treatment, and electrotherapy, until he resorted to the Bulgarian Rauwolfia cure—the best treatment of its kind at the time—only weeks before Hitler's death.

Diagnostic Loose Ends

Hitler's diagnostic assessment leaves many questions unanswered. This is in part the result of Dr. Morell's limited knowledge as well as Hitler's uncooperative attitude, which did not permit Dr. Morell to carry out necessary procedures such as an X-ray of the chest and abdomen. The etiology of many of Hitler's symptoms is unclear, with explanations ranging from pure psychogenesis to serious somatic diagnoses. The simple medical dictum that this is rarely an either-or question has been overlooked—though not by Morell, who accepted the coexistence of psychological and somatic etiological factors. Oddly, the only diagnosis that is reasonably certain is the one that has been most contested: the Parkinson's syndrome, yet the etiology of the syndrome is not certain. The Russian pathologists did an incompetent job in conducting an autopsy of Hitler's charred body, failing to obtain important pathological, histopathological, and chemical evidence. Fairly good agreement exists about the cardiological diagnosis of mild hypertensive heart disease and obstruction of the coronary arteries. The etiology of the underlying vascular changes is undetermined. Evidence for arteriosclerotic changes of peripheral, coronary, cerebral, or retinal arteries is lacking. The gastrointestinal diagnostic picture is quite inconclusive. Early complaints point both to a non-ulcer dyspepsia and to a later diagnosis of irritable bowel—not altogether satisfactory diagnoses. The hepatic pathology, with atypical findings and three diagnoses (infectious hepatitis A, cholecystitis, and cholelithiasis) is even more puzzling. An inadequate work-up contributed to the confusion. The ophthalmological examinations under difficult conditions and the lack of such examinations at critical times make a satisfactory evaluation difficult. The etiology of tinnitus is rarely established, and Hitler's tinnitus was no exception. The photosensitivity of skin and eyes also has not been satisfactorily explained. Finally, the two episodes of acute illness, in August 1941 and July 1942, have remained unexplained.

Giant Cell Arteritis/Temporal Arteritis

To tie up loose ends, a tentative diagnosis of giant cell arteritis (GCA) or, in broader terms, an autoimmune disease, is offered.[67] GCA is a chronic inflammatory disease of medium and large arteries. It rarely occurs in patients before age fifty. When primary cranial arteries are involved, the disease is called by its old name, temporal arteritis. At one time it was considered a rare disease, but since more ambulatory patients have been seen in modern medical practice, its prevalence has been estimated at 1 to 1000. It is self-limited but can be fatal when complications such as myocardial infarct occur. The arteries show a granulatomous inflammation of the intima, with an invasion of lymphocytes, epithelial cells, and the characteristic giant cells. GCA and its close relatives, Tayasaku disease and polymyalgia rheumatica, are considered to be diseases of the immune system, but no specific etiology has yet been found. The clinical manifestations are varied, depending on which arteries are affected. Most frequently extra-cranial and particularly the temporal arteries are affected. The temporal arteries become thickened and tender to pressure. The most common symptoms are attacks of headaches and head pressure. Pathology of ophthalmic arteries can cause the most dreaded complication, permanent or temporary blindness and misty vision at an early stage, various degrees of ischemia, and atrophy of the optic artery. Eye muscle paralyses are seen. Frequently, patients complain of tinnitus and dizziness, and pain attacks in the jaw. GCA has been called the cardiological blind spot, because it has been overlooked as a cause of coronary heart disease. The frequency of cardiac complications in patients with GCA, however, is not greater than in the general population. Hepatic complications with mild and transient icterus have been observed, as well. Gastrointestinal symptoms such as spastic pain, constipation, or diarrhea have been reported in the literature. Patients with GCA usually look sicker than expected. Weight loss and a mild anemia are often noted. Many patients are mildly depressed. Typically, the erythrocyte sedimentation rate (ESR) is elevated.[68] GCA patients often look older than they are—in some cases, pre-senile and decrepit.

Hitler's symptoms and signs fit GCA fairly well. He was younger than most GCA patients, but still falls within the expected age range. Morell, who undoubtedly never heard of the diagnosis, described the symptoms of moderate to severe headaches and head pressure. Hitler also had episodes of misty vision, an early visual symptom of GCA.[69] Richard Pasternak expressed the opinion that Hitler's coronary sclerosis could be explained by an obstructing cause such as giant cell arteritis—and not by arteriosclerosis, from which Hitler in all likelihood did not suffer.[70] Whether Hitler's severe intestinal spasms were caused by GCA of the mesenteric arteries is doubted by gastroenterologists with whom I consulted—with the exception of Howard Spiro, M.D.[71]—because these symptoms were not severe enough; however, these clinicians had not seen patients who were diagnosed by biopsy as having GCA. Hunder, who has seen a large number of GCA cases, thinks this etiology is entirely possible.[72] I also consider it possible that the two short icteric episodes were caused by GCA rather than by cholelithiasis or cholecystitis. Circulatory hepatitis B surface immune complexes have been found in cases of vasculitis.[73] In the older German literature, two cases with a Parkinson's syndrome were attributed to GCA,[74] but without pathological verification it would be imprudent to make this assumption. In a review of more than 1000 autopsied cases of Parkinson's syndrome, no vasculitis was found, but the pathologists did not look for it.[75] Hunder told me that it is conceivable that the occlusion of basal ganglia arteritis could cause vasculitis[76]; yet, based on available evidence, I do not assume that Hitler's Parkinson's syndrome was caused by vasculitis. Hitler's ESR was moderately elevated in two measurements in 1944; in rare cases GCA occurs without elevated ESR.[77] No other convincing cause for the elevated ESR has been detected; the mild chronic tonsillitis and sinusitis Hitler had in the fall of 1944 would not account for it. Hitler's general symptoms of weight loss and mild normochromic anemia are also known to be frequent symptoms of GCA. His marked decrepitude in the mid forties would fit the clinical picture of the unusually sick appearance of GCA patients as well. Frequently, GCA is the cause of tinnitus and vertigo. Hitler, however, suffered from tinnitus in 1936, when no other signs of GCA existed. His over-sensitivity of skin and eyes to light, first observed in 1941, remain unexplained. No toxic factors can be ascertained. No evidence points to the two disease categories with photosensitivity, such as porphyria and systemic lupus erythematosus. Thus, Hitler's symptoms of headache attacks, visual impairment, hepatic and cardiac symptoms, elevated ESR, weight loss, mild anemia, and wasted appearance all point to a diagnosis of GCA. A definitive diagnosis would require confirmation by biopsy, which was not carried out for any of Hitler's diseases, with the exception of the laryngeal polyps. Even the well-established Parkinson's syndrome has not been confirmed by pathological findings.

Citron and colleagues have reported cases of necrotizing arteritis of brain, heart, liver, and pancreas in moribund patients who injected street drugs containing impure amphetamines.[78] In controlled experiments, amphetamines do not cause such pathological changes.[79] One needs to consider, however, whether the frequent injections of glucose might have caused vasculitis. This has been assumed, as a variant of the "medical stab in the back" legend, to be part of a plot to assassinate Hitler.[80] One can be certain that Morell had no intention of murdering Hitler, but he probably injected contaminated substances at times. Glucose was injected after January 1945, which would make the infection hypothesis untenable. Hitler's clinical symptoms—such as the swollen temporal artery, headaches, slight elevation of temperature, and weight loss, and perhaps also the ophthalmic, cardiologic, and hepatic symptoms as well as the elevated erythrocyte sedimentation rate and pre-senile appearance—however, are suggestive of the diagnosis, and it is surprising that the diagnosis was not even thought of. The clinical data are convincing enough to warrant serious consideration of the diagnosis without pathological verification. Two eminent investigators of the disease, Gene Hunder and Paul Beeson, have encouraged me in the tentative diagnosis of Giant Cell Arteritis.

The Question of Drug Dependence

The question as to whether Hitler was drug-dependent or abused drugs and whether Morell prescribed addictive drugs injudiciously has been much debated.[81] The drugs in question are opiates (morphine, oxycodone), barbiturates, cocaine, and amphetamines. Hitler also received bromides, which are not addictive but can augment the effect of barbiturates and opiates. Dependence implies (1) that a drug is taken in excess of normal doses over prolonged periods of time, with impairment of psychosocial and/or physical functions, and that (2) discontinuation of the drug leads to craving for the drug (psychological dependence) and to characteristic physical symptoms (physical dependence due to neuroadaptive changes). Tolerance refers to the need to increase the dosage to obtain the desired effects. Abuse and misuse denote the taking of drugs in spite of undesirable and hazardous psychosocial and occupational consequences. To establish drug use and abuse, one needs to know how much, how often, and over what period of time a drug was taken. The only objective method is an assay of serum, urine, or other body fluids—a method that was not available in the forties. Second best is to rely on reports of the consumer or provider. If no reliable reports of drug consumption are available, one needs to resort to the assessment of signs and symptoms of drug use, which may or may not provide circumstantial evidence. In general, apart from the obvious evidence of needle marks, the rule of thumb applies that the more severe the signs and symptoms, the more likely a diagnosis can be made.

Opiates

The drugs of the opioid group are powerfully analgesic, euphoriant, highly addictive, and subject to narcotic laws in most countries. The principal opiate Hitler received between March 1943 and December 1944 was oxycodone (American trade name Percodan; German trade name Eukodal), prescribed for his severe intestinal spasms. In injecting oxycodone intravenously and intramuscularly, Morell took considerable risk. It is likely that Morell did not tell Hitler he was receiving opiates.[82] On one occasion—on 3 October 1944—Hitler received a combination of a morphine derivative and scopolamine (German trade name Scophedal), a powerful sedative substance, after which he immediately fell asleep. He also received morphine sulfate injections before his polyp operations, a routine procedure. After 31 December 1944, Hitler had no more intestinal spasms, and oxycodone was discontinued. It is likely that some symptoms of opiate misuse, such as constipation and occasional euphoria after injections, existed. Other symptoms, such as drowsiness, bradycardia, respiratory depression, and hypotension, were not noted. None of the usual abstinence symptoms (psychological craving, general malaise, restlessness, perspiration, lachrymation, rhinorrhea, muscular twitching) were observed. In conclusion, one can assume that Hitler was not addicted to drugs of the opioid group.

Barbiturates and Bromides

In the forties, barbiturates were used extensively against insomnia. They were used less extensively after sleep research in the sixties established that these drugs are not only dangerous but inefficient in the treatment of persistent insomnia. They can produce—even in doses only slightly higher than the initial therapeutic dose—somnolence, depression, difficulty in thinking, emotional lability, and a variety of neurological symptoms including slurred speech, nystagmus, ataxia, and, in high doses, stupor, coma, and death. Barbiturates produce an abstinence syndrome (restlessness, tremors, and anxiety), and prolonged abuse in higher doses can produce hypotension, convulsions, and a delirium-like syndrome. Morell frequently prescribed barbiturates for Hitler's persistent insomnia, but both Morell and his patient were aware of the need to stay alert; thus, Morell used them with care. These sedatives often were given on demand, although at times Hitler declined sedation. In conclusion, no tolerance or abstinence syndromes were noted. Hitler did not become dependent on barbiturates.

Bromides, hardly used at present, have a sedative effect, augmenting the action of barbiturates. These drugs are not addictive, but can produce a variety of toxic symptoms ranging from dullness and apathy to severe dementia, hallucinations, delusions, and delirium. Physical symptoms include foul breath, gastritis, and acne. Morell prescribed these drugs in moderate quantities. It is possible that the acne, pustules, and bad breath about which Hitler complained were caused or aggravated by bromides, but otherwise no serious sequelae of bromide prescriptions can be detected.

Cocaine

Cocaine is an anaesthetic for skin and mucous membranes, and also a powerful euphoriant, subject to narcotic laws in most countries. It is used externally in powder solutions, and in its synthetic forms by injection. Cocaine produces a short, intensive burst of euphoria, a subjective feeling of power, and, in some users, a state of sexual excitement. In toxic doses it produces tachycardia, hypertension, restlessness, insomnia, convulsive seizures, myoclonus, and permanent myocardial damage. Symptoms of delirium and hallucinations are frequent, and transitory collapse as well as coma and death have been observed. Cocaine addicts usually need to increase their doses to obtain and extend the short-lasting euphoria. Hitler received nasal applications of a 1 percent cocaine solution from Giesing in daily sessions from the end of August until the end of September and beginning of October 1944, for an alleged inflammation of his maxillary sinus. According to Giesing, Hitler experienced these treatments with pleasure. Giesing also reported cocaine collapses with muscular twitching. When Giesing departed from the Führer headquarters on 4 October 1944, no withdrawal symptoms were noted. Hitler received ophthalmic drops of a 1 percent cocaine solution in 1944 due to mild conjunctivitis caused by a hair tonic, and the same solution again for dust conjunctivitis shortly before his death. There is no evidence that Hitler was dependent on cocaine.

Amphetamines

Whether Hitler was dependent on amphetamines or abused them is under dispute. The properties of drugs of the amphetamine group were recognized and scientifically explored in the mid-thirties. Amphetamines are sympathomimetic neuroleptics with very limited therapeutic usefulness. They are highly addictive and used only in the treatment of narcolepsy. The German amphetamine (trade name Pervitin, phenyl-$_2$-methyl-amino-propanol) is chemically only slightly different from the American amphetamine (trade name Dexedrine, $_\beta$-Phenylisopropylamine), with identical pharmacological effects. In most persons, an initial dose of 5 milligrams produces a reduction of fatigue as well as wakefulness, a feeling of alertness and energy, and decreased appetite. Mild undesirable symptoms are jitteriness, restlessness, excessive speech, tension, and headaches. Moderate to severe symptoms are increased anger and anxiety, as well as transient visual, auditory, and tactile hallucinations, paranoid delusions, stereotyped behavior (such as assembling and disassembling objects like clocks and radios, preoccupation with ultimate religious and philosophical themes (eureka complex), and a sense of cleverness. Some patients have episodes that resemble fits in temporal lobe epilepsy.[83] Severe symptoms are schizophrenia-like psychotic episodes with dangerously violent behavior. Physical symptoms are loss of appetite and weight, head scratching, skin picking (at times with delusions of parasites), grinding of the teeth (bruxism), elevated blood pressure, cardiac arrhythmia, chest pains, and convulsions. Psychological dependence is marked, tolerance high, and withdrawal symptoms variable, but prolonged sleep and depression are frequently observed. Addicts recover quickly, even from psychotic episodes. In the United States, amphetamines have been taken orally, with and without prescription, since the mid-thirties by students cramming for examinations, truck drivers, pilots, and others, to ban sleepiness and fatigue. After the United States entered the war, combat troops, particularly in the Air Force, used amphetamines, as well. Only gradually were the ill effects noted; concerns increased when epidemics of psychoses broke out in Japan after World War II following intravenous injections of surplus amphetamine tablets. At present, amphetamines are under strict legislative control worldwide.

The German pharmaceutical industry and occupational medicine in the mid-thirties became highly interested in the American experience. German laboratory and clinical trials took place between 1936 and 1938, before the pharmaceutical firm Temmler rigorously marketed its amphetamine under the name of Pervitin. It was first widely used by civilians and military personnel without prescription. When its psychological and physical ill effects were noted, an acrimonious debate developed as to whether the drug should be restricted. The opposition to restriction came mostly from the German armed forces. After November 1939, amphetamines could be obtained only with medical prescription, and on 1 June 1941, amphetamines fell under the regulations of the German Narcotics Law. However, the application of these regulations was much less strict in the military than in the civilian sector. In the German armed forces, just about anyone from general to private knew about Pervitin, and it can be assumed with certainty that Hitler not only knew of the energy-enhancing properties of the drug but was interested in it. In 1942 or 1943 Professor E. G. Schenck, amongst others, became concerned about the drugs Morell was prescribing for Hitler. He obtained one of the gold-wrapped "Vitamultin" tablets prepared especially for the Führer, labeled "SVF" (*Sonderverpackung Führer*), and had it analyzed in a Wehrmacht laboratory. He found that the pill contained Pervitin and caffeine in concentrations that ten years later he could not remember.84 Unfortunately, when Schenck returned from ten years of imprisonment in Russia, he could not remember who carried out the examination, but he repeated his statements in court under oath. Schenck reported his findings to Himmler through his superior, SS Gruppenführer Oswald Pohl, but was ordered in unmistakable terms not to pursue the matter. Leonard and Renate Heston learned about this finding from Professor Schenck and developed their thesis that Hitler's main medical problem was an amphetamine addiction, causing his decline and downfall. Their findings and conclusions were published in *The Medical Casebook of Adolf Hitler*, with an introduction by Albert Speer. When the Hestons wrote their book, the Morell diaries were not available, which explains some of their omissions and errors. In his introduction to the Hestons' book, Speer described Hitler both as inscrutable, insincere, cruel, unjust, unapproachable, cold, intemperate, self-pitying, as well as solicitous, forbearing, amiable, self-controlled, proud, and enthusiastically responsive to beauty and grandeur. According to Speer, Hitler never truly loved anyone but himself. Obstinacy paired with a skill at dissimulation, a compelling need to deceive others—what Napoleon once said about Robespierre could also be applied to Hitler. According to Speer, Hitler was a fanatic, a monster, but incorrupt-ible. As far as amphetamine abuse was concerned, Speer was interested in the Hestons' explanation of his Führer's behavior, but he clearly stated that some of Hitler's monstrous, evil deeds occurred before amphetamine abuse. Speer wondered what sort of disruptive energy was in the man that found its outlet in destruction. He considered it a mistake to portray Hitler as the unfortu-nate victim of addiction. Speer believed that Hitler's true addiction was to power and to the applause of his entourage and the masses. When these "stimulants" began to fail, he attempted to replace them with amphetamines. Speer said, "I certainly would not want to see anyone excusing Hitler on grounds of health and saying, 'You see, he was a sick man; otherwise every-thing might have turned out well.'"[85]

The Hestons assumed that Morell administered large amounts of amphetamines at frequent intervals in standard Vitamultin in the gold-wrapped packages (Sonderverpackung Führer), and by injections of Vita-multin forte. The Hestons held some startling views about Hitler. According to them, before he began taking amphetamines Hitler was normal, relaxed, and friendly.[86] They described him as extremely efficient, one of the first pro-fessional politicians. They conceded that "he held some false beliefs from time to time, as everyone does," and that he had an utter faith in his convic-tions. They recognized that Hitler's anti-Semitism antedated his drug use, but anti-Semitism, in their view, was the European norm.[87] Then Hitler—in collusion with Morell—began to take amphetamines and everything changed. The Hestons stated that Hitler began to take amphetamines in 1938, possibly earlier, and that he showed definite amphetamine toxicity in the winter of 1941 and in 1942. He developed morbid rages and was indecisive, suspicious, and preoccupied with detail. The severe rage attack that occurred after mountain troops climbed Mt. Elbrus was ascribed by the Hestons to amphetamine abuse.[88] Hitler, however, had rages throughout his life.[89] According to most observers, these rages became more severe and more fre-quent after the setbacks in Russia and North Africa, with severe disagree-ments with his general staff. The rage attack over the mountain troops' con-quest of Mt. Elbrus could be explained by Hitler's wish to reach the Transcaucasian oil fields and not to celebrate a sportive achievement. He was furious with Field Marshal List for not accomplishing his goal and displaced his emotions on the mountain troops after they climbed Mt. Elbrus and hoisted the swastika flag.

The Hestons listed a number of physical symptoms observed in psy-chotic and non-psychotic amphetamine addicts (such as itching, scratching, nail-biting), but none of them are pathognomonic for amphetamine addic-tion. Itching can be produced by many drugs, and nail-biting, which was noted in Hitler, is a sign of excitement and restlessness. According to Winifred Wagner, who saw Hitler frequently at her parents' home, Hitler had been a nail-biter in the twenties.[90] Amphetamine abuse might have increased the symptoms. In Hitler's case, some of the symptoms preceded any possible amphetamine abuse.[91] Scratching, particularly of the head, as observed by Best,[92] could well be a symptom of amphetamine toxicity, yet it also could be an allergic reaction to many other medications. Bromide, for example, often causes acne and other minor skin infections. Hitler's insomnia—or, rather, the alteration of his sleep rhythm—had existed since his adolescence.[93] While these observations weaken the case for a toxic amphetamine reaction, other observations make it very likely that Hitler abused amphetamines. They are found in certain utterances in the monologues, which abound with extraordinary triviality, crudeness, cruelty, and megalomania. These traits also appear in other statements by Hitler, however, particularly during the *Kampfzeit*. It would be wrong to explain this solely as the result of amphetamine toxicity, but it is likely that amphetamines enhanced such expressions. In a crude assessment, I found that about one-quarter of the night monologues and about 10 percent of the dialogues at noon show thought disturbances such as those often seen in amphetamine addicts. These include vague philosophical statements, similar to what Ellingwood calls "eureka statements." Many of the monologues show what almost amounts to a flight of ideas. In the monologue of 5 May 1942, Hitler rapidly changed subjects from talking about table neighbors to food chefs, Switzerland, the Finns, the port of Aden as the hottest spot on earth, Prince Arenberg, Mercedes cars, and Russia. Some of these statements could be called witty remarks, but many fall into a category that Ellingwood would call a sense of cleverness, one symptom of amphetamine abuse.[94] Several examples follow.

> On 24 August 1942 he made two absurd statements, especially in light of the fact that Hitler had, at most, only a rudimentary understanding of English, "Eden speaks a disgusting English . . . Lloyd George's English sounds marvelous." On 10 January 1942: "the abolition of the burning of widows and of hunger towers in India by England originated in the desire to increase the labor force and perhaps to save wood." On 12/13 January 1942, in response to a remark by Reichsleiter Bormann to the effect that Hitler had always been very religious, he stated, "I will become clerical [*kirchlich*]. I will become the chief of the Tartars. The Arabs and Moroccans pray to me today. Of the Tartars I'll become Khan. The only thing I cannot do, when a sheik stuffs a piece of mutton steak in my mouth. If they do it soon I'll stick to the harem."

I first considered Hitler's strange behavior in his conversations with Dahlerus before the invasion of Poland to be symptoms of temporal lobe epilepsy,[95] but changed my mind when I learned of Ellingwood's observation of such behavior in amphetamine addicts. It is very likely that the strange behavior Dahlerus noted during his talks with Hitler before the onset of war was produced by amphetamines. Shirer's observation on 28 November 1939 corroborates this point.[96]

Bert Park also considered the possibility that Hitler suffered from temporal lobe epilepsy and then changed his mind. Reports that Hitler had epileptic seizures are fiction. He told Giesing that, at one time in youth, he believed that a teacher's head grew larger and his voice became louder. This sounds more like a depersonalization experience than temporal lobe epilepsy.[97]

It has been established by Professor Schenck that Morell had amphetamines in his house pharmacy and that the director of his laboratory, Kurt Mulli, supplied him with small amounts of amphetamines. Morell denied in his interrogations by American military personnel that he ever administered amphetamines to Hitler.[98] In his interview with an American reporter, Tania Long, he also denied that he had prescribed amphetamines.[99] In a private letter to an acquaintance, he denounced the use of amphetamines, stating that it was a whip and not a fodder.[100] On 16 December 1944, Morell recorded an abbreviation in his diary, using the word "Perand" to indicate a substance he had administered. It is conceivable that Morell wanted to camouflage the use of Pervitin by mentioning a drug with a similar name. It is also possible that "Perand" stood for the sex hormone Perandran—which, however, was not one of the male sex hormones Morell regularly used. It is unlikely that amphetamine was added to the frequent glucose injections that Hitler received. The stimulating effect of these injections of 10 percent glucose was a placebo effect. Moreover, as noted above, injections of amphetamines were not customary in the forties, and in any case injections of Vitamultin forte were administered only after March 1944. It is also unlikely that the standard Vitamultin powder contained amphetamines. In his book, *Patient Hitler*, Schenck stuck to his thesis that Hitler abused amphetamines, but thought it likely that doses prescribed by Morell varied. In my opinion, it is likely that Hitler self-administered amphetamines just as he self-administered other substances, such as the Koester pills, Dalman-Cola tablets, and so on, without his doctor's knowledge. Such self-medication with amphetamines would have been easy, even though they fell under the drug law, although dosage and frequency of such abuse remain unknown. Hitler actually was afraid of harming himself, which makes me think that the amounts of amphetamines he took were rarely excessive. Usually, he stopped self-medications when he learned of possible ill effects. It should be remembered, too, that at the beginning of World War II thousands, or more likely tens of thousands, of German soldiers and civilians took amphetamines, but also discontinued such abuse without becoming addicts. Without definitive proof, I assume that Hitler abused amphetamines, particularly between 1939 and 1943, was temporarily impaired by such abuse, and discontinued it—either on his own or at the advice of Dr. Morell.

What were the effects of such abuse, if any? Some of the symptoms were described previously. Could some of Hitler's major tactical or strategic errors, such as impulsive military decisions, or enormous, multi-causal decisions such as declaration of war, be ascribed to amphetamine abuse? Existing evidence does not permit this conclusion beyond any reasonable doubt. It is possible that amphetamines increased Hitler's aggression and recklessness in

late August 1939 just at the time when he made the momentous decision to
attack Poland (see end of Chapter 6). No convincing evidence exists to consider the amphetamine abuse directly responsible for Hitler's colossal crimes
against humanity—except perhaps in the sense that it might have contributed
to characterological changes, such as increased cruelty. Yet during the last two
war years, when Hitler was extremely embittered and cruel, amphetamine
abuse was in all likelihood not prominent.

Alcohol and Nicotine

Hitler was a teetotaler and roundly rejected nicotine. He had tremendous
cravings for pastries, but for a native Austrian, that can hardly be called an
addiction. After becoming Chancellor, he barely consumed alcohol in any
form unless it was prescribed as a medication. He found beer too bitter, wine
too sour.[101] Before he became Chancellor, he had consumed beer, but in
small quantities by Bavarian standards. Occasionally, however, he would
drink some to help him fall asleep. He condemned alcoholism, pointing to its
victims—Dietrich Eckart and Robert Ley. He felt even more strongly about
smoking. He told his round-table that he at times had smoked twenty to
forty cigarettes a day in his youth and even during his early adult years. But
after the assumption of power, he condemned it in the strongest terms and
blamed nicotine for many illnesses: "There is nothing more disgusting than
smoking."[102] He went so far as to say that the German people owed their salvation to his anti-alcoholism and anti-nicotinism.[103] Smoking was strictly
forbidden in his company—unusual behavior in Hitler's time. He expressed
the opinion that smoking might cause cancer.

An Appraisal of Hitler's Physicians and Their Therapies

Dr. Theodor Morell

During his tenure as Hitler's personal physician, Dr. Morell had more admirers than critics and enemies. After the war, with few exceptions, he was
severely criticized. Amongst contemporary physicians, his most severe critics
were Drs. Brandt and von Hasselbach. Brandt believed that Hitler was
unduly impressed by Morell's ability to improve and maintain his patient's
stamina, that Morell's medical knowledge was abysmally low, and that
Morell adhered to unproven fads. He and his colleague, Dr. von Hasselbach,
considered Morell a disgusting and exploitative person. The American physicians who interrogated Morell concurred.[104] Echoing their opinions, Hugh
Trevor Roper, with his characteristic eloquence, called Morell a quack:

> Those who saw him, after his internment by the American forces, a gross
> but deflated old man, of cringing manners, inarticulate speech, and the
> hygienic habits of a pig, could not conceive how a man so utterly devoid of
> self-respect could ever have been selected as a personal physician by anyone
> who had even a limited possibility of choice. But Hitler not only chose him;

he kept him for nine years, in constant attendance, preferring him above all other doctors, and, in the end, surrendering his person, against unanimous advice, to the disastrous experiments of a charlatan. From 1936 to 1945, Morell, in his own words, was Hitler's "constant companion"; and yet the health of his patient was to him only a secondary consideration. From all the evidence, it is perfectly clear that Morell's god was mammon. He was totally indifferent to science or truth. Rather than study the slow methods of patient research, he preferred to play with quick drugs and fancy nostrums; and when critics hinted at the inadequacy of his qualifications, he merely extended his claims in the empire of lies.[105]

Such critique has been widely accepted by most biographers and historians. One of Morell's bitter enemies, Dr. H. Fikentscher, went even further and believed that Morell and Bormann were Stalin's agents, trying to destroy Hitler.[106] In fact, Bormann had very little use for Morell. O. Katz, at the other end of the scale, describes Morell throughout his book as an exemplary physician.[107] Gibbels also tended to rehabilitate Morell by stating that he had the limitations of a general practitioner but kept Hitler functioning.[108] Schenck, though critical of some of Morell's medical and commercial practices and procedures, stated that Morell was aware of his historical mission, acted in good faith, and was a good doctor although he exploited Hitler.[109]

My Views of Dr. Morell

Morell's medical school training was broader than average, because he attended both German and French medical colleges. What he did not learn in medical school or later was critical medical thinking, the ability to evaluate techniques and therapies. He had no post-graduate hospital training before he became a general practitioner and no specialty training in the fields in which he claimed to be an expert. It is very likely that his odd choice of specialty, combining the treatment of urinary diseases and electrotherapy, was motivated by a desire to earn a high income without completing a prolonged course of specialty training. In his defense, one could state that, in the early twenties, training in medical specialties was not regulated. On many occasions, Morell expressed unsound opinions. For instance, he believed that the confinement to bunkers had caused Hitler's mild anemia; he thought a medication made from placental tissue would cause an elevated ESR; and he believed that Hitler felt weak because there was too little blood in his veins. Some of Morell's statements about his physical findings are absurd, indicating that he was not a good examiner. He stated, for instance, that he could palpate the margin of the left liver lobe, which can be palpated only in case of extreme liver enlargement. He continually emphasized the finding of an accentuated second aortic tone, which is not significant. When some of Hitler's physicians were prisoners of war, they had to fill out medical questionnaires, a procedure to which the captive German physicians were unaccustomed. In these forms, Morell stated that he examined normal and pathological reflexes such as Oppenheim's reflex and the cremaster reflex, which would be quite unlikely for a general practitioner. The general practitioner's knowledge is broad rather than deep, yet even given this proviso, I find Morell shockingly ignorant. It is not known what medical treatises or journals he read. He never referred to any, but it is known that he relied heavily on Frank's *Moderne Therapie*,[110] a simplistic book that cannot be compared with a modern vade mecum such as *The Merck Manual*. Yet Morell was superior to many other practitioners in considering social and psychological factors in his patients' lives and in relating to his patients. It is important to bear in mind that Hitler never gave a complete and truthful medical history and could never be thoroughly and completely examined. It is very unlikely that Morell ever examined Hitler's genitalia and he ever performed a rectal examination. At one time Morell, the "urologist," intended to examine Hitler's prostate gland, but never did. Hitler even preferred to carry out an enema by himself, while Morell stood behind a closed door.

As a diagnostician, Morell earns a mixed report. I get the impression that, notwithstanding his lack of medical knowledge, Morell had an intuitive flair both in diagnosis and treatment, similar to some experienced nurses. The diagnoses of the gastrointestinal diseases such as spastic colon, although not uncontested, have stood up quite well over time. About cardiological illnesses Morell was relatively well informed because he suffered from cardiac and renal illness himself. Morell came closer to an appreciation of a hypothetical diagnosis of a vasculitis than all later reviewers. Except for the consultation with cardiologist Professor Alfred Weber, Morell avoided consulting with other specialists in internal medicine—such as the eminent liver specialist, Professor Hans Eppinger, an ardent Nazi who would have gladly responded. Morell missed the diagnosis of Parkinson's disease, however, until it was brought to his attention by a consulting ophthalmologist, Professor Walter Löhlein, a few weeks before Hitler's death. He did not thoroughly explore the episodes of serious illness in August 1941 and July 1942. An expert eye consultation in the Winniza episode would have been mandatory. Based on his notes and the remarks he made during his captivity, one gets the impression that Dr. Morell was never quite sure how sick Hitler was. He vacillated between assuming that Hitler's symptoms were psychogenic and concluding that Hitler was seriously ill. However, in spite of his insecurity, Morell would state his diagnoses with great conviction, probably to impress his gullible patients with his understanding of their illness and to reassure them that he was in firm control. Morell was a physician who would pronounce patients with self-limited illnesses as seriously ill, treat them with cures, polypharmacy, and suggestion, and consider any improvement the result of such treatment. I wonder whether Morell knew the fundamental truth that many diseases are self-limited. He did, however, believe in his therapies, as he used them on his own person.

Morell was an enthusiastic therapist. He used cures and practiced extreme, indeed unsurpassed polypharmacy. Altogether, Hitler received over ninety drugs (see Appendix 3). Morell also supplied Hitler with scores of vitamins, hormones, and metabolites. Many of Morell's patients, including

Hitler, were subjected to the Mutaflor cure, which was supposed to heal infections, dyspepsia, constipation, cholecystitis, stomach and duodenal ulcers, dysmenorrhea, anemia, migraines, ischias, depression, insomnia, and even coronary sclerosis and carcinoma of the colon. Morell firmly believed in the value of this treatment, and so did Hitler after the eczema of his left leg and his gastrointestinal symptoms improved. Evidence of the cure's effectiveness was never presented, but it was used by a considerable number of practitioners in Morell's time and continues to be used by some believers today. While most academic physicians rejected the cure, one exception was the reputable Professor Erwin Becher, whom Morell expected to become his successor. After Morell developed the production of coli-bacilli cultures in his own pharmaceutical factories, his relationship with Nissle soured. In my opinion, the cure has no value whatsoever.

Morell believed that all patients needed supplementation of vitamins, hormones, enzymes, and metabolites such as glucose, calcium, and iodine compounds. During the late twenties and thirties, great strides in the understanding of metabolic and deficiency diseases (diabetes, scurvy, pellagra, etc.), and of endocrine diseases were made. When some of the complex findings about these vitamins and first-generation hormones filtered down to Morell through Frank's *Moderne Therapie* and advertisements from pharmaceutical firms, he enthusiastically adopted them into his therapeutic regime. Simplifying as much as his patient and master Adolf Hitler, he assumed that all patients suffered from some deficiency and needed vitamins, hormones, and metabolites. Morell used vitamins abundantly and without any evidence as to whether his patients showed signs and symptoms of avitaminosis. He indiscriminately prescribed all vitamins known at the time. Some were given as simple vitamins, such as Betabion and Benerva forte (containing vitamin B_I), and others as vitamin cocktails. The most frequently prescribed vitamin mixture was Vitamultin, containing vitamins B, C, and nicotinic acid nicotinamide. This was administered in the form of tablets, which he prescribed for Hitler in considerable quantities. The drug was produced in Morell's pharmaceutical factories and dispensed in large volume to the German armed forces. A special Vitamultin concoction in silver wrapping was supplied to the Nazi elite, and the notorious Vitamultin forte in gold wrapping (*sonderverpackung Führer*, abbreviated SVF, and possibly containing varying doses of amphetamine) was reserved especially for Hitler. Morell also injected water-soluble Vitamultin forte intramuscularly. He prescribed several sex hormones, including Testoviron, a male sex hormone. During his interrogation he also stated that Hitler received the female sex hormones Progynon B oleosum, and progesterone. In all likelihood, testosterone was administered not to augment his sexual function, but as a tonic. Morell frequently administered Tonophosphan, an ineffective, now obsolete, drug used in sports medicine to increase energy levels. Besides sex hormones, Hitler received organ extracts from the placenta (Homoseran), the heart (*Herzpreßsaft*), and liver extract in horse serum. Another medication administered frequently was Glyconorm, also produced within Morell's pharmaceutical empire. The compound was supposed to cure diseases of absorption, anacidity, and gallbladder problems. One commonly used drug, Omnadin, was prescribed by Morell in the treatment of colds. It was supposed to change the patient's immune status. The substance was a mixture of proteins produced by I. G. Farben. The most frequently administered substance was glucose, injected intravenously as a 20 percent solution, usually in quantities of 20 cc. According to Schenck, Morell gave Hitler at least 350 injections between 1942 and 1945.[111] Morell held the belief that glucose would provide energy. The nutritional value of 20-cc injections would provide only 20 calories. Morell also assumed that glucose injections would be beneficial in Hitler's coronary disease. This assumption was based on an opinion put forth by Dr. Theodor Büdingen,[112] who recommended glucose injections as a brief treatment, but not as a continuous regimen over a period of years. Omnadin, Glyconorm, and Tonophosphan landed in the large cemetery of obsolete, ineffective drugs. A medication of limited value that Morell used frequently was intravenous injection of 10 percent calcium gluconate to benefit Hitler's heart disease. He often used an iodine preparation, "Septoform," a drug that was recommended for arteriosclerosis, now also discarded. Both Morell and his patient were preoccupied with constipation, which was treated drastically with dozens of laxatives, amongst them the vicious and now obsolete Calomel.

Typical for Morell's therapeutic fervor was his treatment of colds. Morell clearly did not acknowledge the old adage that an untreated cold lasts three days, while a treated cold lasts seventy-two hours. As noted before, Hitler dreaded colds, believing they were caused by bacteria, and encouraged Morell to treat them drastically. Obviously, the money-minded Morell preferentially prescribed drugs that were manufactured in his own factories. When Hitler refused to take the dangerous and ineffective sulfonamide Ultraseptyl, Morell reluctantly replaced it with Tibatin, produced by I. G. Farben. Morell also falsely claimed to have introduced penicillin in the German pharmaceutical market. For a while, he produced an inferior penicillin in his own factory, which was never used. Morell was able to convince Hitler that he was not only a superior practitioner but also an eminent scientist. In recognition of his merits, Hitler gave Morell a professorial title and the highest medical decoration. Morell was almost as eager to collect medals and other honors as the other fat man in Hitler's inner circle, Göring. Even though he had no understanding of the scientific method, Morell wanted to be seen as an original investigator.

One peculiarity of Morell's therapeutic endeavors was his preference for intravenous and intramuscular injections. Actually, very few drugs needed to be given intravenously. Morell—always concerned with image and prestige—chose this method to impress his patient. One other explanation for this unwarranted method of application might have been Hitler's impatience. Hitler wanted immediate results. Morell prided himself in giving injections skillfully, and Göring referred to him as the *Reichsspritzenmeister*

(Reich Injection Master). As previously noted, however, there were a few occurrences when infections occurred, and Hitler complained of pain and criticized Morell for not sufficiently cleaning the injection site with alcohol. Morell had no sterilization apparatus, nor did he use disposable needles or syringes; he cleaned needles and syringes with alcohol. I considered but then rejected the possibility that certain symptoms I tentatively diagnosed as vasculitis were caused by infections.

In 1936, when Morell became the Führer's personal physician, Hitler was a rather strict vegetarian. Like most physicians, Morell knew little about diets but put Hitler on a very restricted diet during the later war years. In addition to the self-imposed vegetarian diet, Hitler was forbidden to eat bread and rolls with crusts, toast, hard cheeses, cottage cheese, margarine, egg yolk, farina, most kinds of flour, oatmeal, beets, cauliflower, lentils, walnuts, lingonberries. In small quantities, he was permitted to eat graham bread, bacon, butter, lard, egg whites, buttermilk, heavy cream, macaroni noodles, green peas, hazelnuts, and cocoa. Without restriction were potatoes and other vegetables, with the restrictions listed above, and fruit juices as beverages. Hitler's diet certainly was not tasty,[113] but its caloric supply was adequate. In reality, he did not follow Morell's regime and transgressed frequently. Morell and Hitler's dietitians were often desperate when he ate pea soup, for instance, which he liked, followed by severe abdominal pain, distention, and flatulence. Morell tried to convince Hitler to use physical therapeutic measures, but Hitler only rarely permitted the use of galvanic or faradic electricity—much used at the time—and rejected common folk medicine such as poultices or woolen scarves. Morell tried unsuccessfully to induce Hitler to exercise, although the paunchy doctor was not an inspiring example. Morell was also unsuccessful in interesting Hitler in massage. With rare exceptions, Hitler did not permit it, particularly not the deep and painful massage practiced by Himmler's masseur, Felix Kersten.

A physician is ethically and legally bound to consider medical information about patients confidential. This rule is particularly stringent if the patient is a national leader. Morell lived up to this responsibility reasonably well. He was badgered by Göring, and particularly by von Ribbentrop (who was also a patient of Dr. Morell), who suggested medications and exercise for the Führer, but Morell did not reveal any more to the inquisitive von Ribbentrop than the fact that Hitler was a difficult patient. Morell was accused of breaking the vow of confidence by revealing that his patient Heinrich Hoffmann had gonorrhea. However, this information was given to a United States Army interrogation officer by Giesing.[114] Ultimately, of course, it must have come from Morell, but conversations between physicians travel easily and can become the source of a leak. More serious were Morell's remarks to friends that Hitler was in good health in the fall of 1944. Possibly, Morell wanted to brag and reassure the Germans that their Führer was in good shape. However, the information was false in the first place, and in any case such a disclosure would not have been justified unless authorized by the patient.

Harm or Help?

One of the gravest mistakes Morell made was to prescribe potent laxatives simultaneously with opiates (uppers and downers) for an unrecognized intestinal disease. It was sheer luck for Hitler and Morell that no serious harm resulted. Most physicians would tend to avoid the prescription of oxycodone, but Morell undoubtedly was under great pressure to provide relief. A second mistake was the Strophanthin cure. The administration of Strophanthin, one of the most powerful glycosides—far more potent than digitalis—was at the time of Hitler's treatment indicated only in cases of severe myocardial and valvular pathology, from which Hitler did not suffer. One could object to the prescription of Metrazol, an unnecessary cardiac stimulant, as well. The only drugs Hitler really needed at times were aspirin, anticholinergic medications, and nitroglycerine as a standby against angina pectoris. Most of Morell's polypharmacy was unnecessary and, to a physician who believes in parsimonious pharmacy, unacceptable but not necessarily dangerous. The use of sulfonamides, and particularly inferior sulfonamides for colds, was also a mistake, even though Hitler pressured Morell to use these drugs. The injudicious use of addictive substances has been noted before. Another mistake was the abundance of injections, particularly intravenous injections, under unsterile conditions that were harmful and potentially dangerous. One of the more serious reproaches against Morell was his unwillingness to use a consultant in internal medicine. He defended himself against this by telling Hitler that this would lead only to confusion. The real explanation for this omission was Morell's insecurity; for obvious reasons, he kept his cards close to his chest.

It is my impression that even a well-informed physician could hardly have helped Hitler in the forties with his complex and obscure diseases. Morell had to take care of a very difficult and often uncooperative patient. He faithfully supported his patient and did the best within his limited biomedical abilities to keep Hitler as fit as possible. He cared for Hitler, he was aware of his task in treating the leader of a country, and it seems he even liked Hitler and put up with his lack of cooperation, mistrust, and, at times, outright abuse. Hitler, in turn, liked and trusted Morell as much as he trusted and liked anybody. Only in the fall of 1944 did Hitler begin to realize that his physician was sicker than the patient and unable to help him. It is possible to discern in the Hitler–Morell patient–physician relationship elements of transference—Morell was for Hitler not an authoritarian father figure, but a mother figure. He praised him at times in an exaggerated manner. At other times he criticized him (at times realistically), got angry, and felt neglected. Essentially, Hitler vastly overestimated Morell as a clinician, investigator, and person. While Morell was "patient blind," because he saw his patient constantly and did not perceive changes, Hitler was blind for a long time to the deficiencies of his physician.[115]

Medical Criminal, Quack, or Charlatan?

To describe Morell as a criminal who deliberately harmed Hitler is a variant of the "medical stab in the back" legend. Morell never deliberately harmed Hitler, as some of his Nazi critics implied. He was proud of his historical role as Hitler's personal physician; he also exploited this role to the hilt. To call him a quack—that is, a healer who uses unconventional medicine—is also not justified, because all of Morell's remedies and cures, effective or not, were legitimate and approved in official listings. I would consider him, however, a charlatan—that is, a healer who pretends to know more than he does, and who also promises to cure when this is impossible. It is not easy to describe precisely what charlatanry is, because a trace of it is found in some of the best physicians. Morell, however, exhibited extraordinary pretentiousness. He was not a swindler, because he believed in his therapy, and proof of this is the fact that he employed the same treatments for himself when he was ill. Perhaps Morell had to be a charlatan in his dealings with Hitler's complex illnesses because he knew so little and could admit this to neither Hitler nor himself. To some extent, his belief in his therapies also explains his successes. Wasn't there a similarity between the eager doctor, in whom many believed as a miracle doctor, and his charismatic patient? As an academic physician who adheres to frugal medicine, based on clinical and basic science, I do not esteem Morell. As a matter of fact, I find him repulsive, but his charismatic quality is undeniable. At the same time, I concede that Morell was the right physician, probably the only physician, for Hitler. In a sensitive manner, he alleviated Hitler's dependency needs (the only other person who was able to do this, in the late phase of their relationship, was Eva Braun). It also should be remembered that, as Gibbels noted, Morell kept Hitler on his feet most of the time.[116] Finally, Hitler could not have tolerated a scientific physician but needed the guru Morell.

When Morell became Hitler's personal physician, he continued the employment of his assistants, Drs. Wohlgemuth and Weber, to run his regular practice. Considerable sums of money still accrued to Morell from this lucrative practice, and Morell's wife, Johanna, warily watched over the practice to ensure that the Morells got their share in the deal. Schenck stated to me that Morell was the only person capable of exploiting Hitler.[117] Morell was eager to socialize with affluent and influential patients, and often such associations had tangible advantages for him. He and his wife were frequent guests at Hitler's mountain retreat, and Morell had no compunctions about exploiting his professional and personal relationship with his Führer. Morell's close contact enabled him to obtain small as well as big favors from Hitler, both for himself and for certain persons who helped him. Morell even had Hitler's backing in protecting his employees from the wrath of the powerful Martin Bormann. Morell was apolitical and not an anti-Semite, closing his eyes to all the anti-Semitic activities he witnessed as well as the euthanasia program. His lack of anti-Semitic views, however, did not prevent him from profiteering by the "aryanization" of pharmaceutical firms owned by Jews. To facilitate these acquisitions and obtain key posts on boards, Morell used the prestige he gained as Hitler's physician, but he also obtained the Führer's active backing. Through shrewd manipulations, the greedy doctor acquired a significant share of the Hamma Works in Hamburg. He garnered huge profits from factories in Olmütz, in the Czech protectorate, where large quantities of Vitamultin were produced for the Labor Front. In the Milo Works, also in Olmütz, the inferior Russla lice powder was manufactured and palmed off to the army. In the Kosolup Works, Morell manufactured a liver extract, Perhepar, with materials obtained from Ukrainian slaughterhouses. A major coup was Morell's acquisition of the Farmacija Riga Works and the monopoly on utilization of animal glands for the production of insulin and other "first-generation" hormones at the Endocrinological Institute in Kharkov and the Ukrainian Pharmo, which later was evacuated to Nuremberg. Another major financial success occurred when Morell scored a windfall and became the highly paid director and controlling stockholder of the Hungarian Chinoin Works after they were "aryanized." Hitler closed his eyes to such profiteering. An ordinary citizen who engaged in such activities might have been considered a war profiteer and imprisoned or executed. If Germany had won the war, Dr. Morell would have been a very rich man, but his end was very different. Last but not least, a great merit was Morell's historical contribution in the form of his diary. Apart from some defensive assertions, stupidities, and Morell's need to cover his rear, the diary was honest and supplies the most pertinent data for a historical analysis of Hitler's illnesses.

Consulting Physicians

Attending surgeons and consultants played a small role in Hitler's treatment. Dr. Brandt, the senior attending surgeon, never treated Hitler. When he, Dr. von Hasselbach, and Dr. Giesing stepped out of their passive role of watching Morell's activities in dismay, they met with disaster and were dismissed. In matters of health policy, however, Brandt played a major role, implementing Hitler's convictions regarding who should be treated and who should be sterilized or killed. Von Hasselbach treated Hitler only once in the surgical emergency of the bombing plot on 20 July 1944. Even during the Allied interrogations, von Hasselbach never changed his mind in believing that Morell seriously endangered Hitler by letting him take the harmless Koester pills. After his dismissal, von Hasselbach transferred to the Russian front. Following his discharge from internment, he worked as a private practitioner in surgery. Dr. Stumpfegger, who replaced the Brandt–Hasselbach team, did not treat Hitler, except for substituting for Morell for a short period of time. Stumpfegger was killed during his escape from the Reichskanzlei. The cardiological consultant, Professor Alfred Weber, whom Morell consulted both for himself and for Hitler, was a competent specialist. Giesing treated Hitler efficiently for his ruptured ear drums. His treatment of a possible chronic sinusitis using swabs soaked in cocaine solution, acceptable at the time, would now be considered an unwise and unnecessary treatment. In contrast to Brandt and von Hasselbach, Giesing was a totally unreliable reporter, except when strictly otological matters were concerned. After the war he entered private practice. I gained the impression that competent specialists, such as the otorhinolaryngologist Professor von Eicken and the ophthalmologist Professor Löhlein, were somewhat reluctant to be involved in Hitler's treatment. To treat the Führer was a great honor, but also risky business, and the professors did not feel comfortable in their role as consulting physicians and surgeons. Although von Eicken performed the polyp operations successfully, he was not completely convinced that Hitler had significant ear, nose, and throat diseases. Löhlein could carry out his ophthalmological examinations only under adverse circumstances. His diagnoses remained vague, and his recommendation of weeks of absolute rest (during the late phases of the war) were unrealistic. My impression is that he knew more than he wanted to say. He was the physician who suggested to Morell that Hitler was suffering from Parkinson's syndrome. Professor Blaschke, Hitler's dentist, treated Hitler skillfully for his rotten teeth.

The Impact of Physical Illness on Hitler's Mistakes and Crimes

Physical and/or mental impairment and addiction in political leaders are not rare occurrences. Post and Robins explored the topic in depth and listed many sick historical personalities and leaders. They also described the conspiracy among leaders, their personal physicians, and associates that may result in the continued tenure or the fall of such leaders. In most cases, particularly in the past, the public has been kept in the dark about the illnesses of leaders. Certainly, this was true in Hitler's case, when only a few observers in the dictator's immediate environment had some vague knowledge. Such lack of knowledge is not limited to dictatorships. Actually, two of Hitler's great adversaries were impaired, and knowledge of these impairments was kept from the public. President Roosevelt was seriously ill during his third term in office, and Churchill was impaired by alcohol abuse and, after the war, by illness. The salient question in Hitler's case is whether illness contributed to his mistakes and crimes. All of his major illnesses—the neurological, cardiovascular, and digestive illnesses, and the vasculitis (tentatively diagnosed with hindsight)—were of moderate severity. As such illnesses always do, they caused lassitude and fatigue, as well as impairment through pain. A high-ranking private executive or public servant in a democratic society who had similar symptoms would be retired. For a leader of a nation, however, this is often not the case. As Post and Robins have shown, the ailing leader, the leader's physician, and his associates often conspire to keep the leader in office, usually to the country's detriment. Certainly this happened in Hitler's case.[118] One can also assume that, under such circumstances, Hitler did not function optimally, although no serious dysfunction can be detected because he was so highly motivated to pursue his mission. Even the episode of illness in the summer of 1941 cannot account for the mistakes of the winter campaign. Hitler's crimes and errors were not caused by illness. Moderate and even mild illness can cause impairment; this is the justification for excusing persons from their ordinary social and occupational duties during periods of illness. What such impairment might have been during the periods when Hitler was bedfast or in severe pain cannot be succinctly stated. It is my impression that it did not result in any definite alteration in his behavior or motives or, more specifically, in serious mistakes or errors. Undeniably, Hitler was highly motivated to carry out his plans, and this kept him going when other persons might have slowed down or given up. One possible indirect association between illnesses and crimes and errors, however, was Hitler's *Zeitangst*—the fear that he would not live long enough to fulfill his mission and hence his rush to destructive action. Any possible association between drug abuse and crimes and errors is more complex. It is well known and accepted that certain psychoactive substances—in Hitler's case, amphetamines—do not cause but facilitate criminal activity by lowering inhibitions, and potentially contribute to errors by alteration of perception and judgment. To connect Hitler's crimes with abuse of amphetamines would require precise knowledge about when the misuse occurred and the specific quantities of substances used. This remains unknown. All we know is that Hitler's greatest crimes and errors occurred between 1939 and 1945—the invasion of Poland, the attack on Russia, the declaration of war against the United States, the Holocaust, and—undoubtedly—a general increase in aggressiveness and cruelty. This, however, is not sufficient evidence to assume that Hitler's deeds were the result of amphetamine abuse.

9

A Psychopathological Profile

THIS CHAPTER contains a psychopathological review and critical interpretation of Hitler's behavior. I wish I could portray him as an artist or poet would, but if I were a poet I would not be a psychiatrist. My consolation is the knowledge that intuitive descriptions of Hitler by great writers like Thomas Mann provide intriguing pictures but do not pretend to be accurate, reliable, valid, or complete. I hope my pathography of Hitler comes closer to such an ideal. Influenced by John Dollard's *Criteria for a Life History*,[1] I present: (1) an assessment of Hitler's family history; (2) a brief longitudinal assessment of Hitler's personal and political life data; (3) a cross-sectional psychopathological assessment of personal and political data concerning Hitler as Führer, chancellor, and warlord; (4) Hitler's social system; (5) Hitler's values; and (6) the problem of a psychiatric diagnosis. An assessment of Hitler's physical health data—one of Dollard's criteria—is found in Chapter 8.

The Hitler Clan

Rudolf Koppensteiner, a distant relative of Adolf Hitler who recorded Hitler's family tree,[2] did not find any outstanding or mentally ill person among seven generations of peasants of the Waldviertel who were Hitler's ancestors. Koppensteiner did not state that, in the Veit branch of the family—descendants of Josef Veit, a nephew of Hitler's paternal grandmother, Maria Schickelgruber, and a cousin of Hitler's father—several individuals were psychotic and mentally retarded. Hitler's maternal aunt Johanna was an odd, ill-humored, hunchbacked woman whom observers called crazy and whom the family physician at the time diagnosed as a schizophrenic. Such facts are not unusual; but they are significant, because of Hitler's preoccupation with degeneration and mental illness, not only in the general population but, more specifically, in his family. The preoccupation with degeneration and hereditary physical and mental illness in my opinion played a greater role in the evolution of Hitler's political beliefs than previously has been assumed.[3] Hitler also was obsessed with the possibility that his paternal grandfather might have been a Jew, and he a quarter Jew. The origin of this belief can be traced to personal statements made by Hitler and to the investigation, undertaken at Hitler's request, by his attorney Hans Frank.[4] No concrete evidence that Hitler had a Jewish grandfather was uncovered. Hitler's concern that his father was a half Jew persisted, and had consequences for his identity and political beliefs.

Adolf Hitler's Nuclear Family

Hitler's father was an ambitious, restless, intelligent, and robust individual. His social mobility was impressive and enabled him to reach the highest rank in the Imperial Customs Service that his limited education would permit. He was a hard, disciplined worker, considered by his colleagues to be authoritarian, righteous, and pompous. He demanded strict discipline in the service and in his family. His political orientation remains uncertain, but he probably was a Schönerian. He talked a lot, and expressed his opinion with authority. He was sexually very active, unlike his son, was married three times, and had at least two illegitimate children. His first wife, Anna Glassl, an affluent lady, was fourteen years his senior and divorced him, which was rare at the time. Alois Sr. was a good provider for his family but certainly not an affectionate or sensitive father or husband. He retired early, for unknown health reasons, but felt unhappy without a job and tyrannized the family, particularly his sons. To escape irritation, he spent considerable time in the village pub, where he died of unknown causes. It is very likely that Hitler's father was an alcoholic.

Clara had hoped for a good life when she joined her uncle and later husband, but her lot was not easy. She had to put up with her bossy husband and take care of her stepchildren, and she lost four of the six children she had with Alois Sr. Although burdened and depressed, she was deeply devoted to her family. Alois Sr. clearly adhered to the German principle for women of KKK (*Kinder, Küche und Kirche*—children, kitchen, and church), which means that the woman's lot is to bear and raise children, spend her days in the kitchen, and go to church. Clara accepted this maxim, as well, and later Adolf, too, in essence approved it. Like his great model, Richard Wagner, Hitler wanted women to serve. My formulation about Adolf's relationship with his parents: He loved and hated his father, who, however, to Adolf's sorrow, did not love his son. Adolf loved his mother, but felt that her love for him, which he had to share with his father, was not enough. According to Erikson, security and faith in later life are based on a trustful relationship with the parents, and particularly with the mother. In my opinion Hitler did not trust his mother nor any women, and always remained a mistrustful person.

Adolf had no use for his half-brother, Alois Jr., who became a petty criminal. He avoided him in childhood, and even more so in adulthood. Later, Adolf became greatly annoyed with Alois Jr.'s son Patrick when he began to generate newspaper articles about the Hitler family. Adolf had little regard for his sisters, whom he called stupid geese. As a youngster, his half-sister, Angela, was quite attractive and seductive, and it is no coincidence that Hitler later became interested in Angela's older daughter, Angela (called Geli). Adolf lost contact with Angela after he moved to Munich, but in the late twenties, Angela joined him and ran his household. She was abruptly dismissed when she became critical of his love affair with Eva Braun. For his younger sister, Paula, according to her testimony, Hitler showed a certain affection. Why she chose to live in solitude and obscurity in Vienna, under the name Wolf (Hitler's pet name), while her brother was Germany's leader remains unknown.

Hitler's ties to his clan were never close. The last time he visited his relatives in the Waldviertel was during military leave in World War I. The fact that the ancestral village of Döllersheim became an artillery range before World War II—which could not have happened without Hitler's knowledge and consent—could hardly be interpreted as a sign of love and respect for his family and ancestors. At the end, as revealed in the monologues, Hitler denied any knowledge of his family and ethnic origin,[5] and this at a time when millions of Jews, Slavs, and Gypsies were being killed and mistreated because of their ethnic background. To add to contradictions, in his personal testament Hitler bestowed a small sum of money to each member of his family.

Infancy and Early Childhood

Significant data about Hitler's infancy and childhood are sparse, and statements are often contradictory. Maser considered the conditions during Hitler's infancy and early childhood almost ideal (such as having a strong father and a caring mother).[6] Psychohistorians assume that the child had troublesome, deep conflicts (including ambivalent feelings about his mother and father) that were significant for his later life. I am more impressed with the fact that useful data about eating habits, sleep disorders, and toilet training are lacking. No evidence exists for Bromberg's and Small's hypothesis that young Adolf was unable to fuse the good and bad mother images,[7] or for Binion's assumption that young Adolf was overindulged because his mother breast-fed him for four years.[8] Actually, it has not even been established whether the infant Hitler was breast- or bottle-fed. Hitler's later indulgences in sweets and rich Austrian desserts, his food fads, gastrointestinal illnesses, and even his loquaciousness point to a significant oral frustration, but definitive proof for this assumption does not exist. Stierlin's hypothesis that Hitler's mother set him up as a bound delegate against the tyrannical pater familias is an interesting interpretation but would require more evidence to support it.[9] Some conclusions can be drawn from the "ugly family" fantasy in

Mein Kampf.[10] Some historians have looked at this as another meaningless fantasy, but to psychoanalytically trained clinicians it has significance.[11] It is a so-called screen memory, almost a real memory: a slightly disguised recall of parental intercourse—what analysts call the "primal scene." Based on my own clinical experience, I fully support this view. Waite cited ten reasons why the passage in *Mein Kampf* was not a meaningless fantasy but a recall of the primal scene, the most convincing one being the fact that not even the busiest clinician could have seen hundreds of such cases.[12] The significance of the experience has been exaggerated by psychoanalysts, but its emphasis on sexuality as ugly and dangerous is of interest. It may be viewed as an omen of later sexual difficulty. Even more significant is the depiction of the father as an ugly aggressor and the woman, and also the child, as victim. Some of Hitler's political acts may be viewed as acts of vengeance, rescue, and redemption.

In his outstanding book on Hitler's childhood, Bradley F. Smith assumed that young Adolf's difficulties started when his father retired and his brother Edmund and sister Paula were born.[13] Before that, Adolf was the only infant in Clara's care. Paradise was lost when the new siblings arrived and the father retired and spent much time at home. Still, there are no reports indicating major problems. Adolf was a very active child and a leader in war games, which—like most boys—he loved. He received good marks in the undemanding country schools that he attended. No evidence of destructive aggression or cruelty can be found, with the exception of the dubious Leonding billy goat story. Serious difficulties began when young Adolf entered puberty and became enrolled in a middle school in Linz.[14]

Puberty, Adolescence, and Early Adulthood

In Hitler's own words, his puberty was especially painful.[15] As nearly always happens during this developmental period, the antagonism between the father and his sons increased. It came to severe clashes between the father and the provocative boys. Alois Jr. either left the parental home or was thrown out by his angry father. The fact that he became a petty criminal and Adolf a gigantic political criminal deserves attention. It is quite likely that both Alois Jr. and Adolf received more than the customary physical punishment. Hitler later bragged that he accepted it stoically. It is probable that he was more hurt by humiliation and lack of love. Alice Miller linked the beatings and humiliations to Hitler's manifest cruelty as an adult.[16]

The intelligent boy did miserably in middle school and had to repeat grades. He later explained his failure as a deliberate act of protest against his father, who wanted him to become a bureaucrat. It is doubtful that Hitler's father insisted on such a career, but the disgraceful failure in school could be explained at least in part as an act of rebellion. After his father's death in 1903, however, the bad school performance continued. Finally, after respiratory illness in the summer of 1904, Adolf was able to persuade his mother to take him out of school. In my opinion, his difficult puberty was more likely due to his budding sexuality associated with a puritanical attitude and deep anxieties about a likely genital defect. After his father's death, Hitler was the only "man" in a small household with three females—an atmosphere that was both seductive and prohibitive. Adolf's sexual turmoil revealed itself in his puritanism (the "flame of life" fantasies in Vienna, the den of iniquity) and his distant love for Stefanie. Three traumatic events occurred during his puberty and adolescence: (1) the genital deformity (if it was present it could not be overlooked during and after puberty); (2) the death of his father in 1903 and his mother in 1907; and (3) the failed entrance examination for the Viennese Academy of Art. No evidence of a long-term reaction to his father's death has been found. His immediate overt reaction to the death of his father and mother was vehement grief. Grief on the anniversary of his mother's death was observed. After his parents' deaths, the Hitler household was dissolved and Adolf moved to Vienna, where he first enjoyed the grandeur and beauty of the city. After he failed the Academy entrance examination for the second time and ran out of the money he had inherited, he went into a serious downward social spin, being forced to live in a shelter and later a workmen's hotel.

According to Hitler's account in *Mein Kampf*, he became a rabid anti-Semite in Vienna. He was already an anti-Semite in Linz, like many of his schoolmates and teachers. In Vienna, as Hitler stated in *Mein Kampf* about fifteen years later, Hitler was enraged with the immorality of the "dirty Jew" and expressed deep resentment over the Jewish domination of Viennese cultural life. Yet in reality he had stable business relations with Jewish art merchants and frame makers, was close to some Jewish acquaintances in the Männerheim, and even accompanied his friend Gustl on a visit to the wealthy Jewish Jahoda family. He liked the composers Felix Mendelssohn and Gustaf Mahler. He did not even hint at being cheated or humiliated by Jews. In the high treason trial in 1924, he maintained that he had become an anti-Semite in World War I after an encounter with a Jewish military surgeon, Dr. Stettiner, whose pacifist views annoyed him[17]—not exactly a convincing explanation. My conclusion is that Hitler found building blocks in Vienna for his later extreme anti-Semitism. For anybody so inclined, it was easy to become an anti-Semite in Vienna, but Adolf was not a politically active anti-Semite at that time. Vienna provided other important insights. Hitler learned about the misery of the lower classes and became aware of the political skills and limitations of Vienna's mayor and the Nationalist deputies. After attending a few parliamentary sessions he became very critical of the parliamentary process. When he felt better, he realized that the Männerheim was a dead end and moved to Munich, a "German city." One of the reasons for moving was to escape the Austrian military draft. When the authorities caught up with him, the draft commission found him unfit to bear arms. The cause of his rejection remains unknown. He probably had mixed feelings about it: humiliation about being too weak to serve, and happiness about not having to fight the Austro–Hungarian army.

Eight months later, Hitler enlisted and served with enthusiasm in the German army during World War I. After his years as a bohemian and vagrant, he acquired a new identity as a brave and patriotic soldier. As a front soldier, Hitler participated in many major battles and was wounded twice, first by a shrapnel wound of his thigh and second by a mild combat gas injury that later enabled him to adopt and exploit the myth of the patriotic blind cripple. Hitler was highly decorated but never rose beyond the rank of lance corporal, presumably because he was still too depressed and lacked self-confidence. The war was a time of recovery from his depression—a moratorium. Germany's defeat enraged and depressed him again, and he was at a loss about what occupation to pursue, falsely maintaining that the combat gas injury of his eye would make painting and draftsmanship impossible.

The Major Transformation

Historians and biographers have tried to understand Hitler's crucial transformation from an inconspicuous soldier to a charismatic politician. The turning point in his career did not occur at the end of the war in November 1918, but during the summer and fall of 1919, after he had the luck of becoming an "educational officer" of the defeated German army and later star speaker and chairman of the tiny German Workers Party. Hitler sensed and shared the angry feelings many Germans had about the injustice and humiliation of the Treaty of Versailles. Along with many Germans he blamed Jews and Bolsheviks for Germany's plight, and he expressed these feelings in fiery and crude words. Partly because of political calculation and partly because of an inner need, he made the international Jew the Giant Scapegoat[18] and in his earliest anti-Semitic document (the "Gemlich letter") demanded the removal of the Jew from Germany. Hitler maintained that the transformation happened during a meeting in the Hofbräukeller on 16 October 1919, in which he electrified the listeners and afterward exclaimed, "I could speak!"[19] Fest commented that it was the hammer-stroke of fate that shattered the shell of everyday life.[20] Tyrell, in a careful analysis of events, concluded that it took longer, that Hitler first viewed himself as a forerunner or messenger, a St. John figure.[21] At other times somewhat defensively, Hitler referred to himself as a drummer who preceded the leader.[22] Probably for a short time he envisaged General Ludendorff for the leadership role.

The transition invites speculations about what might have happened. Perhaps Hitler thought for the first time that he was superior to his father and that his mother would be proud of him. Perhaps in fantasy his humble mother had become Germania, whom he could serve, avenge, and save. And more explanatory speculations can be traced to bits of evidence. I add that it is likely that, in 1919, Hitler consulted Professor Kielleuthner for his likely hypospadia, a congenital lesion of the genitalia, which Hitler casually mentioned in a conversation with Dr. Morell and that Professor Kielleuthner might have ordered a radiological examination that revealed a spina bifida occulta. Afterward, Hitler did not permit any more radiological examinations of his trunk, no matter how urgently they were needed. Hitler might have considered these congenital lesions degenerative symptoms caused by syphilis, which he considered a Jewish disease and one of the two great scourges of humanity (the other was Christianity, the issue of Judaism).

Hypothetically, when Hitler was told by the urologist that he could not be helped as an individual, he may have decided preconsciously or consciously to save Germany from the deadly Jewish disease by forbidding miscegenation and expelling the Jews. This may sound like a far-fetched idea, yet it can be traced to data and could contribute to an understanding of Hitler's extraordinary sense of mission to save Germany.

It was a profound transformation. Yet it must be assumed that Hitler brought with him experiences he had during childhood and in Vienna, Munich, and World War I—and behavioral traits such as high intelligence, extraordinary fantasy, passionate convictions, contentiousness, stubbornness, resilience, a pervasive ambivalence, and, most of all, a restless mind searching for simple solutions. Inferiority became superiority, weakness strength. One could speak of a major satori that destined him to move inexorably to great heights as a leader and prophet, and finally to his and his country's doom. The fall of 1919 was a crucial period in Hitler's life.

Milestones, Turning Points, and Crises

During his assignment as an army "educational officer," in the summer of 1919, Hitler became a member of an insignificant political splinter party, the German Workers Party (DAP), which he transformed into the National Socialist German Workers Party (NSDAP). Hitler developed into an extraordinarily effective speaker, agitator, and recruiter; attracted followers in ever larger numbers; and assembled a cadre of men who, like himself, hated the Weimar Republic. His program was simple: cancellation of the Peace Treaty of Versailles and punishment of the traitors who were responsible for it—namely Jews, Bolsheviks, and supporters of the Weimar Republic. Racist themes were strong, but social and economic issues of the time played a minor role in his program. After unifying the militant splinter parties, Hitler saw himself first as a forerunner or drummer for the coming leader. Pushed by his aggressive followers and threatened by a possible move on the part of the conservative Bavarians, under the leadership of Ritter von Kahr, to march on Berlin, Hitler decided on a putsch, which failed. Accused of high treason, he was able to cast his accusers into a defensive role and emerged from the trial as a martyr, with a five-year prison sentence. In prison, he established himself as a definite leader of his fellow prisoners. He read a lot and boasted that he obtained "a university education at the state's expense." He also wrote *Mein Kampf*, in which he outlined his philosophy and a program that never changed: establishment of a strong German state, autarky by expansion to the east, deprivation of the Jews of their citizenship rights, and their eventual removal. When he left prison, paroled after serving only nine months, his party was in a shambles, which he did not mind. It gave him the opportunity to rebuild it. He learned from Mussolini, who became a model for Hitler, and much of National Socialism was—externally at least—an imitation of the fascist movement. Over the years, the two men had a love-hate relationship, with more love than hate on Hitler's side. Gradually, Hitler became the dominant partner. At the end, the Italian was a hapless puppet—indeed, a victim.

Hitler learned from mistakes. First, to attain power he needed the military and the workers on his side. He despised democratic and parliamentary methods but realized that a putsch for a weak politician was not a suitable method and embarked on a course of "pseudo-legality." With his remarkable rhetoric and grasp of propaganda, he was able to attract the German masses. Together with a gifted disciple, Joseph Goebbels, Hitler generated a cult of personality, the Führer myth, to which he eventually succumbed himself, viewing himself as the savior of Germany. Third, he grasped that he had to be in complete charge. He viewed himself and wanted to be recognized as Germany's man of destiny. Non-believers were expelled from his inner court—two of his most important associates, Ernst Röhm and Gregor Strasser, eventually were murdered.

Hitler was not only a persuasive orator and propagandist, but also a very skillful politician, who, in his consistent drive for power, outmaneuvered all of his adversaries and competitors, amongst them wily politicians such as von Papen, von Hugenberg, and General Schleicher. Turner reflected that, if General Schleicher had been as effective a chancellor as he was in the role of the "Field Gray Eminence," Hitler might not have become chancellor.[23] Hitler was fully aware of that fact that, in politics and warfare, luck is essential. In his contacts with what he considered a degenerate aristocracy and the upper and lower bourgeosie, Hitler became contemptuous of their cowardice and unprincipled character. In the end game before his appointment, the fanatic Hitler was determined not to compromise—even at a time when the Nazi party temporarily lost votes. Hitler received great help from the old and demented President von Hindenburg, who appointed Hitler as *Reichskanzler* of a nationalistic cabinet. Hitler's handling of von Hindenburg, who disliked "the Bohemian corporal," was remarkably skillful.

For Hitler and his men, his appointment as chancellor was an incredible triumph that emboldened him to realize his far-reaching dreams. He purged the bureaucracy of Jews and opponents of the regime and even inactivated his own cabinet. The only opposition left was the masses of disgruntled SA men under Röhm, who believed that the SA had not been adequately rewarded for their share in seizure of power. Hitler, threatened by Röhm and his lieutenants, responded with the massacre of the SA leaders, other dissidents, and opponents. President von Hindenburg, the leadership of the armed forces, and his followers approved of Hitler's act and condoned immorality.

After 1934, a year of crises when much dissatisfaction among all classes over unkept promises prevailed, Hitler initiated economic, social, and military changes that the Germans considered major achievements. First was the abolition of unemployment and stabilization of the economy. The "economic miracle" was based on the ingenious concepts of Hitler's finance minister, Hjalmar Schacht. It enabled Hitler not only to provide work, income, and social benefits for the German people, but also to build up his armed forces. In fact, much of the procured work served the military buildup. All of this improved morale and signaled a new nationalistic pride. To Hitler, these changes were not only necessary but instrumental to what he really wanted: to obtain needed resources with the goal of economic autarky and, most of all, to create a strong racial Germany that would not be threatened by foreign (i.e., Jewish) contamination. Hitler's revolution was a racial revolution, rather than a social or economic one. He did not want to eliminate private capital but wanted a Germany ruled by a racial elite—the Party—and guided by the Führer. Hitler pursued his goal by instituting negative measures, sterilization and later euthanasia for German undesirables, and deportation and genocide for Jews. A milestone in legislation was the Nuremberg Racial Laws, enacted in 1935. To many German Jews, they looked like a modus vivendi; to Hitler and the Nazi leadership, they were merely a first step leading inexorably to the final solution. It would not have been possible for Hitler to accomplish this in peace time, which certainly was another reason for his shift in emphasis from domestic concerns to foreign policy and war. Hitler wanted a quick solution, and sterilization and euthanasia would have provided only a slow solution. This was another manifestation of Hitler's *Zeitangst,* his fear of being unable to carry out his plans during his lifetime, and his compulsion to rush forward into ever riskier enterprises.

In the mid-thirties, Hitler's interest shifted to foreign policy and preparation for war. He scored spectacular bloodless successes in his foreign policy: the occupation of the Rhineland, Saar, and Memel, and, most of all, the triumph of incorporating Austria into the Reich and the takeover of the rich bounty of the Sudetenland. This was not enough, and Hitler made his first foreign policy mistake. When Hitler invaded Czechoslovakia he lost the last bit of trust of the Western Allies. He demanded that a corridor to East Prussia be established through Polish territory, and that Danzig become part of the Reich. The Poles balked, strengthened by promises from the British and French. Actually, Hitler was less interested in Danzig than in Polish cooperation in an eventual attack on Russia. To the world's surprise, Hitler's countermove was a treaty with Russia—the pact with the devil. Neither Hitler nor Stalin assumed that the pact would last, although Stalin did not expect that Hitler would break it as soon as he did. Hitler was convinced that war was unavoidable; he just was not certain about when and where he would start it. When he finally attacked Poland, he was surprised that England and France stood behind their treaties. He had gambled himself into an enterprise of enormous consequences.

After Poland was conquered by Hitler and Stalin, Hitler occupied Holland, Belgium, Denmark, Norway, Yugoslavia, and northern France and was clearly the master of continental Europe. For a while, he considered invading England, but then, on the advice of his naval and air force commanders, changed his mind—according to General Jodl, this was the only time this happened. Hitler had become the undisputed master of continental Europe, but huge problems remained unsolved. He had not gained control of Russia's resources, and he had more Jews under his control than before the war. Attempts to induce England to join him in a war against Russia were turned down. Then, in the fall of 1940, Hitler made a fatal decision. Fully aware of

Napoleon's fate in starting a two-front war, Hitler decided to attack Russia on his own. He also made the fateful decision to kill the Jews under his control through outright murder or overwork. Hitler felt certain he could defeat Russia in a blitzkrieg, and the military staffs of the Western Allies and Japan shared this opinion. He was wrong. He had an abysmally low opinion of the Russians but ambivalently admired Stalin, in contrast to his views concerning the Western Allied leaders, Roosevelt and Churchill, for whom he felt only hatred and contempt. Then he made another mistake: After the Japanese bombed Pearl Harbor, Germany and Italy declared war on the United States and Great Britain. After a lightning advance into Russia in the summer and fall of 1941, Hitler was bogged down in mud and snow. His troops were not prepared for a long war under adverse climactic conditions. At that time, Hitler began to wonder whether he could win the war. In the spring of 1942, he made another impressive attempt to emerge as the victor. When his troops reached the Caucasus and were a hundred miles from Alexandria, and Japan for a short time controlled the Pacific, the prospect for the Allies looked grim. Hitler, however, by then lacked the material resources and manpower to win. After Stalingrad and further major defeats in Russia, it was clear that the war was lost. The rout in Africa, the invasion of continental Europe north and south sealed his fate. For a while, through his emissaries, Hitler tried to induce the Allies to negotiate with him on his conditions. The Allies insisted on an unconditional surrender, for Hitler an unacceptable demand.

On 20 July 1944, a courageous but weak resistance movement of his own generals tried to topple his regime. After their defeat, Hitler became angrier and more cruel. He felt not only betrayed by his generals, but also let down by what he considered the weakness of the German people, although the majority of Germans remained loyal to him. During this last phase, Hitler showed a deterioration of his reality sense. He hoped for a miracle — a quarrel that would break out between the Eastern and the Western Allies — saving him and the Third Reich. Yet Hitler was unwilling to give up his role as a charismatic leader. Because he was desperate, which revealed itself in the brutal and destructive Nero order, he finally decided to commit suicide, together with his faithful companion Eva Braun, a short time after their marriage. He did not want to be caught, humiliated, or to have his body mutilated as happened to his brother-in-arms Mussolini. Fifty million people died in Hitler's war. Many could have been saved by an early surrender, but that did not interest Hitler. In his political will, he uttered a last cry of hatred against the Jews.[24]

Several authors have expressed the opinion that, beginning with the ill-fated invasion of Russia and perhaps earlier, at the time of the Dunkirk evacuation, some of Hitler's military and political acts were self-destructive. I am rather of the assumption that Hitler made mistakes that were not caused by self-destructiveness. At certain critical periods he took unnecessary risks. He was a reckless gambler, and risk-taking can be self-destructive, but did he ever feel guilty and want to punish himself? Although there are some cues that Hitler occasionally was very defensive about his evil deeds, I cannot detect any real guilt. His conviction about saving the world through his acts was not defensive but genuine, and more will be stated below in the section on shame, guilt, and depression.

Psychopathological Assessment

Appearance

Psychiatric diagnostic assessments routinely start with the description of a person's appearance. Hitler was of average height (175 cm, or 5' 9") but in the last three years of his life became shorter because of his marked scoliosis. No reliable figures regarding his weight exist, but during his chancellorship he was slightly overweight. After he developed a Parkinson's syndrome, he compensated for his stooped posture by forcing himself to stand and walk erect, though he never managed to strut and posture like Mussolini. He did not belong to a definite constitutional body type. Hitler's tall mother was an ectomorphic type, his shorter father a mixture of endomorphic and meso-morphic types.[25] Probably, Hitler did not care much about his constitutional type, but it upset him that he was, according to Hans Friedrich Karl Günther, the Nazi guru of anthropology, a mixed racial and definitely not a Nordic type.[26] It was widely noted and joked about that Hitler and his intimates, Goebbels and Himmler, were anything but Nordic knights. Professor Max von Gruber, teacher of the prominent National Socialist racial hygienist Fritz Lenz (as an education officer Hitler attended von Gruber's lectures), commented on Hitler's appearance:

> For the first time I saw Hitler at close quarters. Face and head, bad race, crossbreed. Low retreating forehead, ugly nose, broad cheek bones, small eyes, dark hair; facial expression not that of a man in full command of himself, but of one frantically excited.[27]

No matter how carefully Hitler's skull was measured, it could not be validated as a dolichocephalic, or "Nordic" skull. In one point Professor von Gruber was wrong. Hitler's eyes were not small, but bulging like his mother's eyes. According to Hanfstaengl, Hitler once compared his mother's protruding eyes and uncomfortable gaze to a portrait of Medusa by one of his favorite painters, Franz von Stuck.[28] After 1942 Hitler's exophthalmos became more prominent and his gaze uncomfortable, as if he were looking through people.[29] It is known, however, that Hitler purposefully used his eyes to create desired impressions. His eyes could look kind or cruel, mostly according to the viewer's interpretations. He told Christa Schroeder that he tried to give each person who passed his review stand in a parade the feeling that he was looking specifically and straight at that individual.[30] He also deliberately fixed his gaze on people to stare them down. Hitler did not like his plump nose, with its large nostrils. According to Waite, Hitler believed he had a "Jewish" nose.[31] During the First World War, Hitler sported a handle-bar moustache and even, according to some photographs, a Wilhelminian moustache (tips upward). It is possible that Hitler was trying to camouflage his broad nose with his "fly moustache." At any rate, it is fairly certain that he wanted to look more masculine. I once scratched off the moustache in one of Hitler's photographs and found that the face looked quite bland, like many faces one sees in the Austrian and Bavarian provinces. Of course, during Hitler's rise, many men sported such moustaches. One of his earliest followers, Hermann Esser, bore a striking resemblance to Hitler and could have posed as a double. In fact, there was much talk about doubles, although there is no real evidence of their existence.

In his youth—as long as he could afford it—Hitler dressed like a dandy. As a politician, however, he chose to dress simply. He clearly and deliberately felt he did not need medals or fancy uniforms like the generals and diplomats in his following. During the twenties, he loved to wear leather shorts (lederhosen), the peasant garb of the Austrian and Bavarian Alps, as well as breeches, a field jacket or a trench coat, a fedora hat, and occasionally a knapsack, replaced later by the SA uniform—a brown shirt and breeches with Jack boots. At home he liked to change into civilian clothes. He disliked wearing formal clothes and looked uncomfortable in a morning coat or top hat. During the *Kampfzeit* Hitler carried a rhino whip, with which he was photographed as late as 1940 after the defeat of the French. He occasionally used the whip to discipline his dogs. There are only two interpretations of a person who routinely displays whips: He either is or wants to appear hard, cruel, and possibly sadistic. When war broke out, Hitler replaced his civilian clothes with a special army uniform (a simple gray jacket without insignia, the iron cross pinned to it, and black pants) that he swore not to take off until victory or death.

To contemporary observers, particularly children, Hitler looks odd, unreal, and almost funny. But to many Germans, especially women, the Führer looked divine, proud, superior—the quintessence of masculinity. With his mini-moustache and wild shock of hair, Hitler was an ideal subject for cartoonists all over the world. Heinrich Hoffmann, the court photographer and Hitler's confidante, followed Hitler's wishes in depicting him as a stern and grim superman—also in typical politician's poses with children— but rarely in a casual or relaxed posture.[32] One exception, showing a more natural demeanor, is shown in Eva Braun's home movies.[33] For many photographs, Hitler posed with his hands folded over his genitalia (like a soccer player expecting a free kick) or hid his lower torso behind a chair. It is a common pose, and no deep psychological explanation such as castration anxiety (which, however, probably was high) is required to explain it.

Hyperactivity

Hitler was an overactive person. He described himself as a lively child and a "little ringleader."[34] Kubizek described his indefatigable walking and, most of all, his incessant talking and rages.[35] In the trenches he stayed up at night to hunt rats, and his job as a dispatch runner required a high degree of activity. During the political years, he was constantly on the go, planning, organizing, and campaigning. As Reichskanzler he rapidly moved on from one major project to the next, at times before any real consolidation could occur. One gains the impression that Hitler tended to get bored or frustrated with a project and then aggressively—or, to use the National Socialist term, dynamically—moved on to the next task. Was Hitler's restlessness a feature of his temperament, due to nature rather than nurture—in other words, a constitutional trait? There is reason to assume that some persons by constitution are hypoactive, others hyperactive. It should be noted, however, that our knowledge of the essence of such constitutional predisposition is limited. Hitler's father was a restless man; Hitler's hyperactivity may have been genetic, by identification, or by pervasive anxieties—we do not know.

Shlomo Aronson directed my attention to the possibility that Hitler might have been a case of an attention-deficit hyperactivity disorder (ADHD) as a child and also as an adult. ADHD occurs frequently in childhood and can persist into adulthood. The main symptoms are inattention and increased non-purposeful activity. In children, the symptoms are fidgeting, squirming, inability to remain quiet, inability to await turns at games, blurting out answers, difficulty in following orders, unsustained attention in tasks, excessive talking, butting in, inability to listen, a tendency to lose things, and dangerous play. The onset usually occurs before school age and becomes most evident in prepuberty. About two-thirds of afflicted individuals outgrow their symptoms. Hitler was aware of his restlessness as a child and called himself a little Satan.[36] Whether he was aware of his talkativeness is not established. Nevertheless, he could also listen silently. In my opinion, Hitler cannot be diagnosed as having had ADHD. The essence of the disorder is attention deficit, but no evidence of diminished attention exists in Hitler's case, with the possible exception of a brief period when he attended middle school. Hitler's attention was not impaired at the time when he started to paint, nor when he served as a dispatch runner during World War I, and most of all not after he became a politician—when he had to plan, organize, compose, and deliver long and elaborate speeches and a complex political action program.

Speech and Language

Speech for Hitler was a most important political tool—or, rather, a weapon. He loved to talk, he loved to lecture. Young Kubizek was witness to Hitler's tirades in his youth.[37] The incessant flow of speech did not abate until the final phase of Hitler's life. It was apparent in innumerable speeches and nightly monologues. Only when the fortunes of war turned against him and his health deteriorated did Hitler talk less. He delivered his last speech on 24 February 1945. Count Ciano lamented, "Hitler talks, talks, talks . . . Mussolini suffers—he, who is in the habit of talking himself and instead practically has to keep quiet."[38] Recktenwald cited a prominent Munich resident, Lumnitzsch, who spoke of Hitler's terrible uninhibited garrulousness and believed his incessant talking overwhelmed both his opponents and his followers.[39] Hitler was described either as talking or, at times, as listening silently, but rarely as engaged in free discussion. What Poncet said about the three faces of Hitler can be extended to his speech. He was either detached, remote, and silent; a fiery and overwhelming speaker; or a rustic Bavarian type, garrulous and quite ordinary.[40] Hanfstaengl stated that he could play his voice like an instrument.[41] A common error in describing Hitler is to present him as a mad screamer. He screamed only when he decided to do so, either in public lectures or in private. In personal conversations he had an agreeable baritone voice[42]—unless he was irritated or consciously decided to intimidate his audience.

No comprehensive study of all aspects of Hitler's language exists.[43] Such a study would have to deal with the study of linguistic signs (semiotics), the study of sounds (prosodics), the study of the grammatical structures of language (syntactics), the study of the meaning of verbal and nonverbal signals (semantics), and the study of the transactions between senders and receivers of verbal and nonverbal behavior (pragmatics). Hitler's knowledge of German grammar and syntax was inadequate, a result of his lack of schooling and probably his disdain for all kinds of rules. He was quite eager to make up for his lack of school knowledge through autodidactic efforts, but his syntax remained poor. In his critique of Hitler's style in *Mein Kampf*, Maser cited pages of violations of syntax.[44] Notorious examples include Hitler's tendency to make nouns into adjectives and adverbs, such as "Manchesterly" (*Manchesterlich*)[45] and "lemonade-y" (*limonadig*),[46] and to invent awkward neologisms, such as "syphilization" (*Syphilisierung*).[47] Such verbal misconstructions might have escaped notice in spoken German, but not in written German. An example of one of Hitler's poor sentences occurred in the long speech he gave before the Reichstag after the massacre of the SA leadership: "I have given the order to shoot the main culprits and have given further orders to burn out the ulcers of the well poisoning to the raw flesh."[48] Yet however offensive such a sentence may be, the bad metaphor does convey threat and counter-threat to the audience in a very effective fashion. Hitler intended to frighten and to arouse, and he was effective in both. His disregard for syntax reflected his view of the relative unimportance of the written message. He stated that all great, world-shaking events had been brought about not by written matter, but through the spoken word.[49] Conveniently, he forgot about the Bible (which he knew fairly well).

Semantics have been popularized by Alfred Korzibsky[50] and S. I. Hayakawa,[51] who pointed out the basic abuse of language through the creation of false maps, faulty generalizations, and the use of loaded words. Hitler's racist policies of suppression, annihilation, and territorial expansion through war are based on what these semanticists call "false maps." Hitler excelled in such falsifications, both deliberately and unconsciously. The outstanding example was his use of the word Jew. It was not the individual Jew but the generic Jew who was exploitative, manipulative, evil, and destructive. Hitler was a master at using and misusing loaded words: Blood was not a body fluid, but a substance that determined the race—that is, the value of a person. The word soil was used to arouse patriotic feelings of belonging. Hitler's misuse of medical terminology was notorious: Bacillus, infection, ulceration, blood poisoning, and cancer were used not as medical terms, but as metaphors for social and political processes. One particular form of semantic abuse was what the National Socialist regime called regulation of language (*Sprachregelung*), the deliberate distortion and camouflage of concepts or procedures: Deportation (*Ausweisung*), for example, became relocation (*Umsiedlung*), or moving to a new address (*Wohnsitzverlegung*)—the word used when elderly Jews were moved to the "model camp" Theresienstadt. Hitler personally used this technique when he spoke of sending Jews into the morass (de facto, into extermination camps).[52] Both Erik Erikson and J. P. Stern spoke of Hitler's language as the language of the prophet—it was Delphic language, with the alternatives of salvation or doom.[53] His startling contradictions (e.g., describing the Jews as very dumb or very intelligent) and his inclination to speak in riddles fit the speaking patterns of prophets. The uncritical believers swallowed the whole message of the totem father.

As to pragmatics, or the study of how Hitler received and transmitted signals and how his signals were received, no systematic study or survey exists. Certainly, the majority of the German people had a distorted picture of their Führer, based not only on the deceptive messages Hitler sent out, but also on their own interpretations and misinterpretations, and, most of all, the unprecedented propaganda that produced the Hitler myth. It is difficult to make a general and simple statement about how Hitler processed the messages he received. He read security service reports and abstracts of national and international newspapers and received daily war reports. It is my impression that Hitler was adequately supplied with information. This did not change until 1945, shortly before his death, when a grossly distorted picture of reality emerged. On the other hand, he had not the slightest compunction about deceiving and misleading internal and external enemies, or even his associates, by use of false messages.

In his analysis of Hitler's speech, Cornelius Schnauber used concepts derived from the psychiatrist and psycholinguist Felix Trojan[54] to distinguish between ergotropic speech and trophotropic speech.[55] Ergotropic speech is the speech of aggression, used to make an impact on others, while trophotropic speech is used to enhance inner qualities, feelings, self-understanding, and empathy. Hitler's speech was clearly ergotropic. The most characteristic elements were rhythmic accentuations with changes in volume, tempo, and frequency. His voice had an unusually wide frequency range, and during rhythmic accentuations he moved toward the upper limits of his range, usually not with falsetto, but often with screaming. Schnauber believed that screaming was more acceptable during Hitler's time, particularly by the early followers, a rough crowd. Hitler's sharp rhythmic accentuations were particularly evident when he wanted to justify his claim to power; when he demanded submission and sacrifice; when he had to justify crimes, departures from policy, or major policy changes; and when he felt attacked, bypassed, or tricked. Another element of Schnauber's analysis was the so-called acueme, the state of voice determined by basic emotions such as anger, hatred, and disgust or joy, tenderness, and sympathy. Five acuemes can be distinguished in Hitler's speech, and, according to Schnauber, Hitler used predominantly the vocal correlate to anger, hatred, and defiance. It is also the acueme of rejection, of disgust related to the rejection of food. It would be interesting to understand the linguistic counterpart of Hitler's inclination to change roles, lie, and deceive. Unfortunately, no research on this topic has been undertaken. Hitler was interested in exerting a hypnotic effect on his public. It is likely that the high-pitched sequences had an irritating effect, possibly inducing listeners to tune out. The sedating portion of his speeches probably occurred during the opening section—the "slow movement." Schnauber's research was limited to the analysis of Hitler's speech, and specifically to orations during the seizure of power. Hitler's private voice was never analyzed.

Maser submitted Hitler's handwriting to a professional handwriting expert as a blind sample, resulting in a description of many of Hitler's traits. Essentially, Hitler emerges as a bright, aggressive, ruthless individual. Was it truly a blind analysis?[56] American psychologists are skeptical about handwriting analysis, with the exception of its use for forensic purposes to identify persons by their handwriting. In spite of promising beginnings by Klages,[57] hardly any scientific validation that would stand up to modern standards has been undertaken. This is regrettable, because handwriting—like speech, gestures, and mimicking—should be analyzed, and can potentially assist in understanding the writer. From a medical point of view, the deterioration of Hitler's handwriting after 1944 is of interest. No micrographia, characteristic of Parkinson's disease, has been found. After 1944 Hitler's handwriting became a scribble, caused by his tremor.

Intelligence

The term intelligence refers to the ability to solve problems and the capacity to learn. It requires the capacity to understand a problem and carry out the logical operations to solve it. Hitler's superior intelligence was attested by close associates, but many opponents underestimated him. Hitler made outrageous and at times stupid statements (the monologues are full of them), but prophets grant themselves license to make extraordinary statements. Grand Admiral Raeder recognized Hitler's ability to see the essence of a problem and present it clearly.[58] His naval adjutant, Captain Assmann, commented on Hitler's compelling logic and precision of thinking.[59] General Jodl stated that Hitler was an extraordinary leader whose knowledge, leadership, and will were triumphant at the end in every discussion with anyone. Jodl also praised Hitler's restless mind, which could throw light into the darkness of the future long before the eyes of his military associates could see anything tangible or threatening.[60] A more detached commentator—the historian Toynbee, not an admirer of Hitler—commented after a two-and-a-half-hour discussion with Hitler of topics ranging from world history to current politics, "I cannot think of any academic lecturer to whom I have ever listened who could have spoken continuously for that length of time without ever losing the thread of his argument."[61] Appropriately, the French journalist Bertrand de Jouvenel called him a *"simplificateur terrible."*[62] Hitler not only oversimplified, but all logic left him when his highly charged ethnic beliefs and prejudices were involved.

Hitler saw himself as a genius. In a revealing passage written early during the *Kampfzeit*, he stated:

> . . . in long periods of humanity it may happen once that the politician is wedded to the theoretician (*Programmatiker*). The more profound this fusion, however, the greater are the obstacles opposing the work of the politician. He no longer works for the necessities that will be understood by the shopkeepers, but for aims that only the fewest comprehend. Therefore, his life is torn by love and hate. The problem of the present, which does not understand the man, struggles with the recognition of posterity, for which he works.[63]

Success and the cult of personality melted all doubts in the minds of many Germans about Hitler's being a great leader and a genius. As in the case of Stalin, the personality cult credited Hitler with great inventions. He was called the originator of the Autobahn, although plans for the Italian Autostrada and U.S. superhighways existed when the first stretch of the Autobahn from Düsseldorf to Cologne was built in 1932. Hitler was highly motivated to be original. When he picked up new ideas he promoted them— only rarely giving credit to the inventors. An exception was the automotive engineer Ferdinand Porsche, whom he praised as the greatest German mind.[64] More than others, German authors still debate whether Hitler was a genius. Lange Eichbaum, Germany's lexicographer of geniuses, considered him one.[65] Even the critical De Boor devoted twenty pages to the genius debate.[66] In my view, a genius is a person who, through extraordinary gifts, makes outstanding contributions to the improvement of human existence. Hitler contributed to the modernization of the world. He helped change the world in a major way. But more than most he increased its misery and therefore does not merit the sublime designation of genius.

Memory

Hitler's associates were in full agreement that he possessed an exceptionally good memory. Christa Schroeder spoke of his memory as a "chest-of-drawers memory."[67] Speer remarked that Hitler's memory was the terror of his entourage.[68] He was able to store and retrieve a large body of knowledge. Hitler could cite figures of gun calibers and ship tonnage with great accuracy. He liked to display this ability quite frequently and thus impress or bluff his admiring audiences. It is possible that he prepared himself ahead of time for such exhibitions, but the performances were impressive. He complained to Christa Schroeder during the last war years that his memory had decreased, and Schroeder noted that he repeated himself in his stories and that his conversation was less entertaining during the last year of his life.[69]

Based on available anecdotes, one cannot assume that Hitler had an objective impairment of memory and recall. Dr. Erwin Giesing reported in a statement in February 1945 that Hitler's memory had decreased because he could not remember Giesing's home town or the fact that Giesing's wife had received a decoration for maternity.[70] This and similar trivial observations do not justify the assumption of a defective memory. Far more important than anecdotal observations is the fact that Hitler was able to compose and deliver long speeches until the spring of 1945—one of them a lengthy statement to his generals about the impending Ardennes campaign in the fall of 1944—and was coherent and relevant as cited in the Bormann documents and his political testament. My conclusion, in agreement with Ellen Gibbels,[71] is that Hitler did not suffer from memory defects. This is significant because memory impairment is an early and sensitive symptom of intellectual deterioration.

Knowledge and Half-Knowledge

Hitler was an eager and conceited autodidact. For formal school knowledge he had outright contempt, and as a dictator he proposed far-reaching changes in education. There was no subject under the sun about which he would not express an opinion, and the words "I don't know" were almost absent in his vocabulary. This was apparent to an appalling degree in the monologues between 1941 and 1944. Hitler's excellent memory enabled him to acquire a large body of knowledge. In his writings, speeches, and conversations he covered many areas of knowledge. He was an avid reader who devoured books, pamphlets, and digests, and his knowledge was in part the result of rapid and spotty reading. About his time in Vienna he wrote, "I read enormously and thoroughly,"[72] but in fact thorough reading was not his thing. As he was not restrained by traditional school knowledge, Hitler's views had an innovative and original quality at times—vastly overrated by his admirers—but he betrayed serious gaps in knowledge as well. His idiosyncratic views, in both youth and adult life, were reinforced by the striking lack of critique by his associates.

A gap in Hitler's knowledge was his ignorance of and lack of interest in novels and poetry. Eberhard Jäckel discovered that the poetry ascribed to him turned out to be a falsification.[73] His knowledge of the German classics, so cherished by educated Germans, was scant. He told Frank that he carried a pocketbook edition of Schopenhauer in his soldier's pack during the First World War,[74] but how much of Schopenhauer he actually read is another matter. He occasionally quoted Schopenhauer and Nietzsche, but one can safely assume that his understanding of these philosophers was quite limited. To understand the complexity of these texts requires considerable knowledge of philosophy and also much patience—neither of which Hitler possessed. He never even commented on Schopenhauer's anti-Semitism, nor on Nietzsche's rejection of anti-Semitism. He claimed he had read Marx thoroughly, but it is very doubtful that Hitler plowed through the turgid text of *Das Kapital*.

Christa Schroeder did not consider Hitler a *Menschenkenner* (a person who understands other human beings).[75] There is plenty of evidence that he was attuned to the motivations of his fellow men, to opponents as well as to people who served his goals. His perceptions were keen when it involved human weakness, deception, and bluffing, resulting in a basically cynical and mistrustful view of human beings. Hitler's insight was seriously limited by his suspiciousness and his need for loyalty. This need accounts for the tolerance he showed toward disgusting rogues such as Streicher, even though Streicher was condemned by Party courts for corruption and sexual immorality. Similarly, for a long time Hitler turned a blind eye to Röhm's homosexuality, as long as he viewed him as a faithful ally. It is difficult to assess how much insight Hitler had into his own actions, because he was concerned not to let anybody know what went on in his head. His physicians—Drs. Morell, Brandt, von Hasselbach, and Giesing—told their interrogators about Hitler's interest in medical matters, stating that his knowledge exceeded that of the average lay person.[76] Yet Morell's detailed diaries reveal that Hitler's medical knowledge was superficial and often erroneous. Hitler's inquisitiveness about medical matters was an expression of his hypochondriacal concerns and his inclination to second-guess physicians. He was familiar with the Bible and used his knowledge to denounce Judaism and Christianity. In the dialogue between Dietrich Eckart and Hitler, both men outdid themselves in finding damaging evidence about the "wicked" Jew.[77] It is almost amusing to note how he unknowingly cited the famous Jewish-German poet Heinrich Heine, whom he detested.[78]

Deficiencies in Knowledge

Hitler's half-knowledge was palpably present in areas of great importance to a leader, such as information about the character of other nations, economics, and history. Absurd statements about other nations—the Swiss, Hungarians, and Russians—in the monologues permit the conclusion that Hitler was less informed than he pretended about geography and ethnography. He admitted that some of his geographical knowledge about North America had been acquired through the reading of Karl May, not the best source.[79] Hitler's horizon did not extend beyond Europe and the colonies of European nations. He rarely mentioned South American or Asian nations, such as his ally Japan. Hitler was not only disinterested in economics but had a disdain for expertise in the field. He never paid much attention to his early associate Feder, an amateur economist who thundered against enslavement by interest (*Zinsknechtschaft*). He used scathing words to describe economists and their theories.[80] For a while he followed the advice of the knowledgeable and resourceful financier Hjalmar Schacht, but when Schacht became concerned about the extent of the increasing indebtedness, Hitler dropped him and replaced him with Göring, who admitted he knew little about economics— which probably was one of the reasons Hitler picked him.

Hitler considered knowledge of history to be extremely important. His history teacher, Professor Poetsch, was the only instructor to whom Hitler gave high praise,[81] although his class work earned him poor marks as a student.[82] Later however, he supplemented his meager school knowledge with extensive readings and acquired a vast and extremely biased store of historical knowledge. Strongly impressed by the thoughts of Dietrich Eckart, Alfred Rosenberg, and Houston Stewart Chamberlain (the son-in-law of Richard Wagner), Hitler came to view history as the struggle between races, in which the strong defeat, dominate, or destroy the weak—a vulgarized view of social Darwinism in which war plays a fundamental role. This notion became the center of Hitler's worldview and eventually contributed to unprecedented destruction.

Being knowledgeable about military matters was of the utmost importance to Hitler.[83] According to the generals who worked under him, as well as military historians, Hitler's knowledge of military sciences was impressive. Some of this knowledge can be traced back to his personal experience as a dispatch runner during the First World War, but much was derived from studies of military publications. Hitler rarely gave credit to his sources, such as to the eminent military analyst von Clausewitz. His decisions were based more on his intuition than expertise, but they led to impressive victories in the lightning campaigns of the early period of the war. In the later part of the war, however, his intuition failed him. Several military historians noted that Hitler overvalued the personal qualities of leadership and troops, such as the will to win and the assumption that nothing is impossible.[84] This—or his disdain and ignorance of military economics—led to an underestimation of the strength of his opponents, specifically, Russia and the United States. Another major deficiency was Hitler's reluctance to withdraw from conquered terrain and territory. His major mistakes, however, were not military but political—the initiation of a two-front war, the declaration of war against the United States, his disregard for the economic power of his enemies, and the brutal and inhumane treatment of the populations of conquered territories.

Hitler has been falsely credited for inventing an automatic rifle, new anti-tank guns, and super-tanks. In fact, he did not possess the technical knowledge to invent such military weapons, but he had an open mind concerning technical innovations. His major accomplishment was to promote and utilize motorized warfare, against the advice of his conservative general staff. On the other hand, Hitler had serious gaps in military knowledge. His knowledge of military aviation was inadequate, and he recognized the significance of jet propulsion quite late. He left matters in the hands of Göring, who let the Germans fall behind the Allies in military air power. His knowledge of naval warfare also was inadequate, but he took the advice of Admiral Doenitz, who replaced surface naval warfare with submarines and scored spectacular successes early in the war before the Allies developed effective detection devices. Hitler had some appreciation of the importance of rockets but little understanding of atomic warfare. At one time German physicists led the world in the theoretical work underlying nuclear warfare, but not after the emigration of European, mostly Jewish, nuclear scientists. The center of nuclear research shifted from Germany to laboratories in the United States. More than a mistake was Hitler's continuation of the war when he knew defeat was certain, and his decision to continue a war on the Eastern Front in 1944 and 1945, when he was convinced that the Russians would take vengeance on the Germans. He could have stabilized the Eastern Front and let himself be overrun by the Western Allies but didn't. This cannot be explained by ignorance. These decisions were made by a deeply embittered and vengeful man who felt betrayed by everybody and saw the only solution in a *Götterdämmerung* for himself and his country.

The Question of Cerebral Deterioration

The question of cerebral impairment is pertinent because Hitler suffered from Parkinson's syndrome. Some 35 to 50 percent of such patients show signs of intellectual deficit; older patients who have a long duration of illness and severe symptomatology are more likely to show deterioration. Hitler did not fall into this category, and his capacity for problem-solving and information processing was not impaired. Memory, retention, and recall are the most sensitive and early indicators of an organic deficit state.[85] These functions remained unchanged. Organic deterioration is characterized not only by intellectual deficit, but also by emotional changes and impaired social relations. Depressive changes have been noted in 40 to 60 percent of Parkinson's patients. A mild state of depression from January 1943 until the end of his life can be accounted for by a series of military and political setbacks, in addition to the discomfort of his illnesses. His statement to his foreign ministry adjutant, Walter Hewel, who urged him to look for a political solution in 1944—"I don't politick anymore; it nauseates me"[86]—can be interpreted as the sign of a justified depressive mood. At times, such dysphoria was counteracted by unwarranted optimism and euphoria. Emotional incontinence and compulsive crying are symptoms observed in elderly patients with a variety of cerebral lesions, particularly vascular lesions of the basal ganglia. Hitler was both brutal and sentimental and cried easily. His "emotional incontinence," however, predated any cerebral pathology. Schacht, for example, reported that Hitler cried "crocodile tears" when he tried to persuade him not to resign.[87]

According to many associates—such as Speer, Guderian, Koller—Hitler's rages became more severe and frequent over time. To explain this on the basis of organic or toxic cerebral impairment is tenuous. With his empire collapsing and his feeling of having been betrayed by his generals, it is not surprising that Hitler—who all his life had a tendency to choleric outbursts—felt easily enraged. Christa Schroeder's report of crude and tactless behavior[88] referred to one incident when Hitler reportedly made sexually provocative or seductive remarks, which were denied by Gerda Christian, another secretary.[89] In any case, the tactless remarks Schroeder reported would not justify the assumption of cerebral impairment. Observations of personal neglect—such as crumbs of food on his uniform—were mentioned by Speer,[90] but this could have been due to Hitler's tremors rather than to negligence. According to General Kesselring Hitler acted resolutely until the end of his life (examples are the execution of Eva Braun's brother-in-law, SS General Fegelein, and the expulsion of Himmler and Göring).[91]

Undeniable, however, was a loss of reality sense, which will be discussed more fully later. This was clearly manifested in Hitler's statement to General Karl Koller in April 1945 that "Ivan" (the Russian) would suffer the greatest defeat at the gates of Berlin when he issued orders to nonexistent armies.[92] In my opinion, the gradual impairment of Hitler's reality sense cannot be attributed to a permanent organic deficit state. The reality loss (i.e., Hitler's unwillingness and inability to accept the collapse of the Third Reich and the threat to his identity as a messianic leader) can be better explained psychologically. Thus, I do not see any convincing evidence during the last phase of Hitler's life for a cerebral deficit.

Drives and Affects

AGGRESSION

No trait was more prominent or has been better documented than Hitler's high aggression after he became established as a political and military leader. Aggression is attack behavior. It is the drive to overcome opposition forcefully. Hitler's aggression was directed against persons, institutions, and nations. It manifested itself in rages, hateful and angry words, and destructive acts. With rare exceptions (the incident when Hitler beat up his opponent Ballerstedt), it was not physical. Directly and implicitly, Hitler ordered murder and destruction on an enormous scale. He was a monstrous "desk murderer." He wanted brutal and disagreeable men to assist him, men with "cold dog snouts"[93] who would behave like butcher dogs and beat up their opponents both during the *Kampfzeit* and later—and he succeeded in selecting such men.[94] He shrewdly sized up the weaknesses of his opponents, then attacked and defeated them easily, one after the other, until he encountered the superior combined forces of Great Britain, Russia, and the United States, and was destroyed.

Hitler's aggressive drive was associated with a strong need for dominance, for absolute control of the political scene as well as his personal environment. The submission of the tough Göring was obvious when he stated before the Nuremberg court, "I tie my fate, for better or worse, to yours [Hitler's]. I don't exempt my head."[95] Such a relationship existed not only between Hitler and Göring, but also between Hitler and other vassals. Unanswered remains the question as to why Hitler, who undoubtedly also had strong passive needs, was always the dominant person in such interactions, or why he remained dominant and succeeded in subjugating others and inducing them to accept him unconditionally as their leader. He could not bear the idea of a rival. He had serious qualms about who should succeed him.[96] The other need associated with aggression and dominance was Hitler's need for autonomy. Independence, freedom, and resisting restriction—what Harry Murray called inviolacy[97]—had been guiding motivations since his adolescence. It was only after chronic illness and serious military setbacks that

Hitler more openly expressed the need for dependence on his physician and a yearning for the company of Eva Braun.

Animal psychologists distinguish between affective aggression and predatory aggression.[98] The animal responds to a threat by attacking, concomitant with autonomic arousal of the sympathetic nervous system (snarling, sounding off, pilo-erection, dilation of pupils), with the goal of frightening, but not necessarily killing, the opponent. In predatory aggression, the animal stalks its prey and attacks to kill and devour. Applying this concept to human behavior, Melroy found that in what he called psychopathic personalities, predatory aggression is dominant.[99] Hitler demonstrated both affective and predatory aggression. Affective aggression manifested itself first and foremost in his rage attacks. Schroeder, amongst others, described Hitler's autonomic responses: reddening of the skin, tension of the jaw muscles, and shouting accompanied by threatening gestures.[100] Manifestations of such affective aggression would appear even when he dictated threatening speeches. These rage attacks had been observed as early as during Hitler's adolescence, existed as temper tantrums even during adolescence, and continued throughout his life—even though such attack behavior has been exaggerated by memoirists and biographers. In general, Hitler was able to control his rages and use them to intimidate his environment or evoke submissive and compliant behaviors in others. According to Tyrell, during his early political career some of Hitler's rages were the expressions of helplessness.[101] It is my impression that many of Hitler's affective rages were play-acted. He learned to use them effectively, such as calling General Keitel to intimidate Chancellor Schuschnigg. While affective aggression was present, most of Hitler's aggressive acts fall into the category of predatory aggression. The purpose of Hitler's aggression was to destroy and to get bounty. The attacks were swift, but the deliberation preceding the aggression extended over considerable periods of time. The stimuli for many attacks were threats and sentiments of deprivation and injustice. Often they were vengeful and cruel acts, as in the case of the bombing of Belgrade. One of Hitler's favorite phrases, "in this case I am ice cold," is more than a manner of speaking; it expresses a basic mode of thinking. With the exception of specifics about his genocidal actions, Hitler was amazingly open about his cruel aggressiveness. He spoke without any qualms about his intention to destroy St. Petersburg and Moscow, but felt compelled to rationalize his intent:

> I can imagine that some people are clutching their heads: How can the Führer destroy a city like St. Petersburg? Certainly, basically I am of a different kind. I don't want to see anybody suffer, or hurt anyone, but when I recognize that the species is endangered, then ice-cold reason replaces feelings. I only see the sacrifices of the future if no sacrifice is brought today.[102]

Hitler was totally committed to war, and his love for it knew no bounds. He expressed this conviction in numerous statements, for example, ". . . basically I believe that a peace of longer than 25 years is harmful to any nation."[103] Whenever he made an opposite statement and talked of peace, it was, as he finally admitted, a lie or an attempt to deceive his opponents.[104] Hitler was amazingly frank about his aggression, for example, in his statement that he never would have achieved what he had accomplished without the utmost brutality.[105] One could compare Hitler to what veterinarians and animal trainers call "fear biters"— animals that, when they feel attacked or threatened, respond with aggressive behavior.

As has been noted, no severe aggression, destructive act, or cruelty is known in Hitler's early childhood, with the exception of the billy goat incident. The war games of his youth cannot be interpreted as evidence of unusual aggression. Eitner cited Kubizek as reporting that Hitler was opposed to the military,[106] but it was the Austrian military he opposed. Eitner also mentioned that, as a child, Hitler objected to the arming of airplanes. Hitler was quite apt, however, to make opposing statements because he was garrulous. Certainly he was not a pacifist. Any war facilitates major "legitimate" aggression, but still no reports of cruelty or particularly destructive behavior on the part of Hitler during World War I exist. The loss of World War I, which Hitler ascribed to betrayal, was a severe trauma not only for him, but also for millions of Germans. Hitler responded to it furiously, with profound aggression. After the putsch in November 1923, he felt he had been pushed into the failed uprising before he and his men were ready for it. He learned from the failure and for a while controlled his aggression, to a degree, during the phase of pseudo-legality. Hitler boasted that the takeover in 1933 had not been accompanied by aggressive acts, which even at the time of the takeover was untrue. Certainly, it took enormous skill and aggression—though little physical aggression—to abolish the parties and eliminate opposition. A major act of planned aggression was the radical elimination of opponents in the SA in 1934. It was another turning point; afterward, one aggressive action followed another, from the takeover of Austria and the Sudetenland to the destruction of the Czech state, the attack on Poland, and, finally, Russia. On the domestic front, a powerful police state kept opponents powerless and intimidated. A sharp escalation in the aggressive persecution of Jews occurred after the annexation of Austria, and particularly after the *Kristallnacht*. Hitler was rewarded for all his aggression by internal German approval and little resistance inside and outside Germany.

Hitler recognized that individuals suffered during war and genocide, but considered it a historic necessity. A remarkable increase in aggression associated with destructiveness can be noted in the Polish and Russian campaigns. In the monologues, Hitler expressed his brutality quite openly. Hitler's manifest extreme aggression and cruelty, however, developed in World War II— directed mostly against Poles, Serbs, Jews, and Gypsies, and culminating in his war against Russia and in the genocide—and was not related to setbacks. Gradually, the cruelty, fueled by a deep feeling of frustration and helplessness, went out of control when Hitler wanted prisoners of war executed in retaliation for Allied cruelties against civilians. He developed more than resentment—actually deep feelings of vengeance—even toward his own general staff. Toward the end, he felt let down by the German population, which was expressed in a statement the Germans learned about only years after his death: "Here, too, I am ice cold. If the German population is not ready to take a stand for self-determination, then it should disappear."[107] It is possible but not proven that cruelty and uncontrolled anger were associated with amphetamine abuse.

Erich Fromm, an eminent psychoanalyst and social scientist, considered Hitler a case of necrophilia.[108] He did not use the term in the customary sense, as a perversion in which a person engages in sexual relations with corpses, but rather defined it as extreme destructiveness and an attraction to dirt, decay, and foul matter in general. Fromm viewed whatever appeared constructive in Hitler as mere veneer. The fact that Hitler was compulsively clean did not deter Fromm; he considered Hitler's cleanliness a reaction formation. Fromm considered Hitler's syphilophobia and inability to form friendships necrophilic traits.

SELF-DESTRUCTIVENESS AND PASSIVITY

It is certainly true that Hitler and National Socialism had a strong affinity to death. It was a glorification of the dead, a Wagnerian apotheosis of death, salvation, and resurrection. The liturgy of National Socialism exalted in macabre and pompous funeral ceremonies, in torch parades for the dead and reverence for their heroism. National Socialism wanted to be remembered by gigantic monuments surpassing the pyramids of Egypt, scattered around the periphery of the conquered eastern territories. National Socialist glorification of death and the question of self-destructiveness raises the question as to whether Hitler was a self-destructive person. Certainly, Hitler's suicide seems to justify this question. His suicide, however, was not driven by murderous or self-destructive impulses, but was simply a way out of an insoluble problem, since capture and punishment were inevitable. Hitler found it easier to die than to live, which confirms Shneidman's fundamental hypothesis that persons are apt to commit suicide when death becomes more desirable than life.[109]

Loewenberg emphasized in his profile of Hitler a marked self-destructiveness during the last years of his life, pointing to mistakes such as the lack of pursuit of the British at Dunkirk and the declaration of war against the United States without forcing the Japanese to attack Russia.[110] Hitler made many political mistakes which started with the invasion of the Czech Republic. According to Hitler, the mistakes started earlier than Loewenberg assumed. Hitler's own explanations for his actions are not always valid, such as his explanation that he could not defeat Russia because he had to bail out the Italians after their defeat in Greece. In the case of stopping the tanks at Dunkirk rather than pursuing the British, historians are not certain whether Hitler was worried about risking his tanks or whether he did not want to humiliate the British, whom he saw as potential partners in his pending war against Russia. In the case of his declaration of war against the United States without forcing the Japanese to join him in his war against the Soviet Union, the situation also was complex. Hitler was happy about the Japanese attack on Pearl Harbor. His worry was that the Japanese might win a quick victory and quit. It also would have been impossible to force the Japanese into a war against Russia. In other words, unless the reality situation was very clear and Hitler's thought processes well known, it would not be prudent to assume self-destructiveness on Hitler's part. Self-destruction inevitably implies self-punishment, and I do not feel sanguine about the notion that Hitler had guilt feelings over his terrible deeds and preconsciously tried to punish himself. Hence, the assumption of self-destructiveness, in spite of Hitler's suicide, is tenuous.

In contrast to Hitler's enormous aggression and need to be dominant are the observations of several historians, particularly Maser, that Hitler was a passive person. Maser documented this in numerous examples of slow and reluctant decision-making.[111] The validity of some of these statements will be addressed in the discussion of whether Hitler was a strong or a weak leader. To a certain extent, passivity was expressed in Hitler's relationship with Dr. Morell, when illness provided a legitimate reason to be dependent and passive. Hitler was described as an effeminate person, and this characterization is not just an invention of hostile observers. When he described Richard Wagner in silk robes, one senses that he almost envied the man who could be so unabashedly effeminate.[112] His yearning for "retirement" during the last war year expresses as much a desire to escape from a hopeless situation, for which he was responsible, as a passive need for a quiet life. It is my impression, however, that Hitler's passivity has been exaggerated. After all, he made a large number of important decisions in a timely and efficient manner. The passive factor in Hitler's identity as an artist and some feminine traits, combined with his destructive aggression and cruelty, give Hitler a Neronic quality. Incidentally, Hitler believed that it was not Nero but the "communist" Christians who set Rome on fire.[113]

Sexuality

To understand Hitler or any person, some knowledge of sexuality is essential. Unfortunately, solid knowledge about Hitler's sexuality is sparse and uncertain. Sexual behavior is private, and with rare exceptions (such as in the monologues) Hitler did not talk about his erotic and sexual experiences. Reliable statements by persons who had sexual and erotic relations with him are rare; notable are the fragments of the diaries of Eva Braun and a statement by Maria Reiter.[114] Many statements are of questionable veracity and contain erroneous or deliberately false reports. Third-party statements abound and are even less valid and reliable. Hanfstaengl believed Hitler was impotent,[115] while Röhrs viewed him as hypersexual.[116] Linge eavesdropped in front of Hitler's bedroom and, after hearing orgasmic noises, maintained that the Führer was sexually normal.[117] This tells us little about the nature of his sexual performance, however. The proposition that Hitler was sexually normal has been expressed by Maser[118] and Schenck.[119] Otto Strasser, a bitter enemy, claimed in several contradictory statements that Hitler suffered from a severe perversion by which he obtained sexual gratification by having a woman urinate on him.[120] This belief was repeated by Langer,[121] Waite,[122] and Bromberg and Small,[123] and denied by others. What are the facts? Unfortunately, not many are known.

SEXUAL BEHAVIOR IN CHILDHOOD

Since Freud's epochal discoveries about sexual experiences during childhood, many students of human behavior assume that these experiences are of fundamental importance in determining a person's conscious and unconscious behavior. Of interest is that the Hitler family lived in a fairly tight spatial arrangement during Hitler's childhood and youth. Until brother Edmund arrived, Hitler shared the parents' bedroom, which was the custom of the land. From birth he was surrounded by two females, his mother and his older half-sister, Angela, and from his sixth year on also by his younger sister, Paula. It can be assumed that there was opportunity to observe sexual behavior between the parents and nudity in the family. It also can be assumed that an atmosphere of both temptations and taboos existed, which had its impact on Hitler's later sexual development. I concur with the interpretation of Hitler's narration of a boy's observation in the parental bedroom in *Mein Kampf* as a thinly disguised screen memory of his own observation of parental intercourse.[124] This view permits the conclusion that Hitler viewed sexuality, preconsciously, as violent, ugly, and dirty. A brutal, powerful man victimized a helpless woman. The little observer was frightened but also aroused. According to Hitler's story, the child was headed for further ugly and criminal experiences. From clinical practice, however, it is known that such common experiences may be overcome by later benign experiences and sexual enlightenment. In Hitler's case they apparently were not. For Hitler, sexuality remained dangerous. I noticed another bit of evidence indicating that the parental bedroom was important for young Adolf. At the age of ten, he drew a sketch of it. I wonder how many other budding young artists choose this particular topic for their drawings.

The account by Paula Hitler that Adolf was beaten frequently and severely by his father is credible.[125] These beatings and, more important, other humiliations probably exceeded the punishment generally meted out by hard German fathers.[126] In my opinion, humiliation was the critical factor. Such beatings and humiliations may lead to sadomasochistic character traits and symptoms. Alice Miller can be credited with pointing this out convincingly.[127] Cruelty often is the result of a malignant blend of pathological aggression or submission and the sexual drive. The Leonding prank, pissing into the billy goat's muzzle, would make psychoanalysts think of aggressive infantile oral sexuality, perhaps latent homosexuality. One cannot be certain that the incident actually occurred, however, and without the subject's associations, such an interpretation would be precarious.

Puberty and adolescence are difficult periods for any youngster. For Hitler, they were an especially painful process.[128] His difficulties included learning difficulties, a very taxing relationship with his father, and, presumably, sexual problems, ever-present in puberty even though Hitler did not mention them specifically. His distant crush on Stefanie was not an ordinary adolescent experience but indicates an unusual sexual inhibition. Kubizek never observed that Hitler masturbated and also believed that he was physically normal.[129] One would conclude either that Hitler did not masturbate, which could be considered unusual behavior, or else that he was hiding it because he was ashamed of it. He spoke of abstinence as the will to preserve the "flame of life"[130]—to consider the absence of masturbation a fear of sexuality is probably the correct interpretation. Hitler's defensive morality was also notable in the "Potiphar" story when he viewed himself as the chaste Joseph.[131] A morbid fear of dirty sexuality was most clearly expressed in Hitler's rantings about prostitution and syphilis. After he marched up and down the Spittelberggasse, a lower-class red-light district in Vienna, young Adolf lectured his friend Gustl about the immorality of that city.

Hitler pushed for very severe measures to eradicate prostitution.[132] Both street prostitution and prostitution in brothels were declared criminal activities in one of the earliest laws passed in the Third Reich (26 May 1933), and strict health controls were enforced for prostitutes. In the German armed forces, infection with venereal disease was punished as a crime.[133] The measures, however, did not result in a reduction of venereal disease, because prostitutes and pimps went underground and the incidence of venereal infection increased. When war broke out, prostitution was legalized and strictly controlled. Brothels existed even in some concentration camps—for Aryan inmates only. My tentative conclusion from these speculations is that Hitler's mission to create a healthy German master race may well have been related to his syphilophobia and a genital lesion.

Hitler was not a homosexual. Kubizek reported that he and Hitler once met a homosexual man in Vienna who invited the boys to dinner. Hitler recognized the man as a homosexual, while his naïve friend did not, but Hitler seemed not to feel threatened by the encounter.[134] Hitler knew that his SA chief of staff, Ernst Röhm, was bisexual and did not object until after the massacre of 30 July 1934, when he expressed extreme indignation and made political capital of it.[135] After 1934, punitive laws against homosexuals were strictly enforced in the Third Reich, with Hitler's full approval, and many homosexuals were imprisoned, sent to concentration camps, and some executed. Hitler falls into the category that Freud called latent or unconscious homosexuality.[136] The term latent male homosexuality designates a male with passive strivings who in childhood had the desire, later repressed, for sexual intimacy with his father. According to Freud it is a universal striving, the opposite of the Oedipus complex, in which the child's infantile sexual drive is directed toward the parent of the opposite sex. Freud considered the concept of latent homosexuality crucial for the development of passivity, a trait encountered to a degree in all men, and certainly in Hitler's case. Such infantile homosexuality may be repressed in varying degrees. It may manifest itself in passive dependent behavior, in bisexual behavior, or in a complete denial of homosexual inclination, often with outright disgust over anything that could be considered homosexual behavior or homosexual temptation. According to a friendly witness, H. S. Ziegler, Hitler could not look at male ballet dancers and had to avert his eyes.[137]

ADULT SEXUALITY

According to current information, Hitler had no lasting relationships with women in Vienna or Munich before the outbreak of the First World War. Wartime conditions provide sexual opportunities for many men who otherwise would have rather restricted and conventional sexual lives, but not for Hitler. Hitler postulated that the bravest soldier was the most desired by women; he was a brave soldier, but it seems he did not take sexual advantage of his prowess. His comrades in the war called him a monk. Jean Marie Loret maintained that he was the son of Hitler and a Mlle. Lobjoy,[138] but an anthropological examination of Loret in the Heidelberg Institute of Anthropology by C. V. Steffen and F. A. Vogel, requested by Maser, did not confirm such paternity.[139] During the *Kampfzeit*, Hitler bragged in the monologues that he knew many women.[140] At one time, he was actually criticized for associating unwisely with women.[141] According to Röhrs, Hitler had at least forty illegitimate children,[142] but evidence of this is lacking, and it can be dismissed as an overestimation of his Führer by an old Nazi. A different statement can be traced to Hitler's bodyguard and chauffeur, Emile Maurice, who stated he had to procure young women as social partners for Hitler in the evening after campaigning.[143] In the monologues, Hitler reminisced, "There is nothing more beautiful than to dine with a beautiful woman."[144] In a very illuminating statement, Gregor Strasser—at the time of the following citation still a follower—deplored:

> Hitler is suspicious and vain. It is dangerous to tell him something. . . . He is ignorant of the world. He works without knowledge of man, even without the ability to judge people. . . . He lives without any inner contact with others. He is only genius and body. And this body he castigates, one could cry. He does not smoke, he eats only greens, he does not touch a woman. Where can one start to explain other people to him?[145]

Yet Hitler was attracted to women, and scores of German women adored him. He received innumerable love letters. At the same time, he was an extreme male chauvinist. He had a low opinion of women's intellectual abilities, though he appreciated their intuition. He believed, as did his father, that the woman's task was to breed and devote herself to her husband and her children. Most of all, Hitler felt that women should not participate in politics. No woman must be a member of the Reichstag or play a significant role within the Party.[146] In his view, the woman's role was to serve, a Wagnerian idea; yet Hitler contradicted himself in his extraordinary remark, "Once we have a men's society (*Männerstaat*), humanity will be on a downhill course."[147] Intellectuals, and particularly intellectual women, were a horror for Hitler. Some women, mostly artists, he respected, such as the so-called parade women;[148] the actress and director Leni Riefenstahl; the widow of his architect, Gertrud Troost; most of all, his ardent admirer, Winifred Wagner; and, to a degree, Gertrud Scholtz Klink, the leader of the National Socialist women. Other exceptions were Walkyrie Mitford, sister of the British fascist leader Oswald Mosley, and the test pilot Hanna Reitsch. Hitler engaged in guarded relationships with two different groups of women. With mature women who were socially—and financially—helpful to him during the early *Kampfzeit*, the relationship was platonic, at times almost subservient. The other group of woman, with whom Hitler maintained safe and distant relationships, consisted of beautiful young actresses, dancers, and singers whose company he enjoyed. These women were frequently invited to receptions where Hitler felt stimulated and entertained. Amongst them was the daughter of the famous tenor Leo Slezak, Gretl Slezak, who was by National Socialist racial laws a quarter Jew. With a large number of women, ranging from sisters of chauffeurs to diplomats' daughters and wives of high party officials (such as Emma Hanfstaengl, Inge Ley, and Magda Goebbels), Hitler had friendly but presumably not intimate relationships. Clearly, he liked women—at a distance.

According to reliable reports, Hitler entertained close relationships with only three women: Angela (Geli) Raubal, Eva Braun, and Maria (Miezl) Reiter. The avuncular romance with Geli Raubal was the only adult passionate romantic relationship Hitler ever had.[149] Whereas Henriette Hoffmann, Gregor Strasser, and others stated that Geli radiated charm, Hanfstaengl thought she was a dull provincial maiden and considered her relationship with Hitler the repetition of earlier incestuous strivings toward his older half-sister.[150] Heinrich Hoffmann and his daughter Henriette Hoffmann-Schirach, who followed this relationship quite closely, assumed that no sexual relations occurred. Otto Strasser, on the other hand, claimed in his statements to OSS investigators that Hitler forced Raubal into an extremely perverse relationship, insisting that she urinate on him to provide him with an orgasm, referred to in the older literature as undinism.[151] Walter C. Langer, at that time working for the Office of Strategic Services, and other analysts such as Jenny Wälder-Hall and, later, Bromberg and Small,[152] accepted Strasser's views and considered such a perversion typical for Hitler.[153] Waite also maintained that a jealous Hitler forbade a flirtatious Geli from having contact with other men, had no intention of marrying her, and forced her into a perverse relationship that left her no way out but suicide.[154] Strasser was not consistent in his statements, later stating that Hitler made peculiar overtures—for example, that Geli squat over him in such a way that he could see everything,[155] that Hitler was an ascetic with a perverse fantasy, and that he was sadistic and masochistic.[156] So what was the perversion? After all, there is quite a difference between a scoptophilia and so-called undinism. In my opinion, Geli Raubal first enjoyed the attentions of her famous uncle but later felt trapped when a jealous Hitler drastically restricted her freedom to meet other men, which could have been the cause of her suicidal act. Geli Raubal's death and its possible causes remain a mystery, but there can be no question that Hitler in one way or another contributed to her tragic end.

I do not concur with the assumption of a severe perversion such as undinism and consider the inconsistent statements of Otto Strasser to be political denunciation by a bitter enemy. Strasser also told a similar story about Henriette Hoffmann—even maintaining that Henriette's father knew about and did not object to it because it helped further his career. Hanfstaengl also reported that he once found Hitler kneeling before Frau Hanfstaengl, burying his head in her lap—an act suggestive of desires for oral sexuality or perhaps maternal tenderness. Wagener's report that Hitler's radical vegetarianism started after Hitler watched Geli Raubal's autopsy is another specious story, as no autopsy occurred.

From fragments of diary notes, one can conclude that a sexual relationship between Hitler and Eva Braun existed,[157] but whether sexual intercourse took place cannot be ascertained. Henriette Schirach and her father, Heinrich Hoffmann, believe that no coitus took place between Hitler and Eva Braun.[158] Eva allegedly confided to her hairdresser that she and Hitler never had sexual intercourse. The same statement also allegedly was made by the wife of Martin Bormann's gynecologist, Dr. Scholten.[159] Although the hairdresser claimed she repeated this statement under oath before her Munich attorney Klaus von Schirach, the attorney replied to my personal inquiry that he never heard of such a statement.[160] Thus, the matter remains inconclusive. In the early part of the relationship, Braun was a mistress barred from official functions. She surfaced gradually—but even Hitler's second surgeon, Professor von Hasselbach, never even knew of her existence. After the assassination attempt in July 1944, Hitler began to show more regard and affection for her. In all likelihood, she resolved to die with Hitler of her own accord. Yet much of her life, spent with Europe's most powerful man, was far from happy.

Maria (Miezl) Reiter was more explicit in her account of a sexual encounter during a relationship:

> He pressed me to his body and kissed me. It was well past midnight. I leaned back more and more on his sofa. Wolf (A.H.) grabbed me even more firmly. I let anything happen to me. I was never as happy as during that night.[161]

It is impossible to make out what happened, but it seems it was a mutually satisfactory and not a grossly deviant relationship. Sexuality is a private matter, and except for extremely deviant relationships, it is difficult to define abnormality. From all accounts, in contrast to his friend Mussolini, Hitler was monogamous, and in the last few years of his life celibate. In the monologues he stated, ". . . there was nothing more beautiful than to train a young thing; a girl of 18 or 20 years is as flexible as wax. It must be possible for a man to press his imprint on her."[162] Whatever his imprint was remains unknown.

Regardless what occurred sexually between Hitler and these women, one fact stands out: Hitler wanted a mistress and not a marriage partner. He was quite explicit and talked about it bluntly with his staff in the monologues and granted himself, as an outstanding person, the right to have a mistress. He gave many, indeed, too many reasons why he refrained from marriage: He was too busy, his female voters would not like it, and he feared the offspring of a genius like him could be degenerate. Hitler also expressed thoughts to the effect that he had no luck with women, that they misunderstood him, that they interpreted the slightest interest on his part as a major commitment.[163] Eva Braun accepted Hitler's bidding and became his mistress. Maria Reiter did not, and separated from him. A desperate Geli Raubal died.

Hitler made contradictory statements about sexuality in the monologues. He advocated what one might call a healthy, conventional sexuality as serving the National Socialist goal of producing martial men and devoted women. "The sex drive must be in the service of propagation but also must grant man sexual pleasure to keep him fit for combat. . . ."[164] "A reasonable man can only smile when a saint like St. Anthony wants to deprive man of his greatest joy through self-castigation with a dog whip."[165] He also opposed the code that officers must not have premarital relations, especially when they resulted in pregnancy and thus became public knowledge.[166] From such remarks one might gain the impression that Hitler was sexually normal and happy. He certainly talked a good game. Yet some data—such as his conversations with Speer and the journalist Price—indicate sexual unhappiness. In the event that he had a hypospadia and/or monorchism, an impairment of his sexual functions would have been likely but not certain, because in some cases coital functions remain normal in these conditions. I have already stated my opinion that a severe perversion is very unlikely. Hitler was not an overt homosexual, but his latent or infantile homosexuality was high. His syphilophobia in all likelihood was associated with disturbances of potency, such as premature emission—the most frequent form of partial impotence associated with anxiety. This statement, however, is nothing more than what clinicians call a guesstimate. In summary, Hitler most likely was sexually impaired, but our knowledge about his sexuality is not secure.

Anxiety

Anxiety is an emotion associated with fear (avoidance behavior), a universal response of all human beings, and indeed of higher organisms, to danger. Anxiety results in flight behavior, attack behavior, or fusions of both. The worst anxieties occur when, in the face of danger, neither flight nor fight is possible. Anxiety can be diffuse or focused; it can follow a threat or anticipate it. The subjective anxiety response is associated with a host of muscular and vegetative responses, such as restlessness or freezing of motility, tachycardia, dyspnea, gastrointestinal or genitourinary symptoms, sweating, and insomnia. It is likely that Hitler's early gastrointestinal symptoms and his insomnia, though not his disturbance of sleep rhythm, were caused by anxiety. The borderline between normal and abnormal anxiety is difficult to draw. All one can say is that abnormal anxiety is intense, enduring, and unrealistic. Anxieties during infancy and childhood—a period of helplessness—can be powerful. Child-rearing is designed to overcome these anxieties, but often it makes them worse. Hitler talked about fear of darkness at the age of three (probably autobiographic), but this is also a universal experience.[167] His sexual anxieties during puberty were intense, which is not such a universal experience. When he compared a young soldier's first experience with a woman to the first experience in combat, Hitler was telling posterity as much about his sexual anxieties as about his anxiety in combat.[168] In lengthy and rather boring letters to his Munich landlords, the Popp family,[169] and to an acquaintance, Ernst Hepp,[170] Hitler did not mention anxiety in combat. In *Mein Kampf* he described how he mastered anxiety through the age-old approach used by drill sergeants: will power.

Thus it went on year after year; but the romance of battle had been replaced by horror. The enthusiasm gradually cooled and the exuberant joy was stifled by mortal fear. The time came when every man had to struggle between the instinct of self-preservation and the admonitions of duty. I, too, was not spared by this struggle. Always when Death was on the hunt, a vague something tried to revolt, strove to represent itself to the weak body as reason, yet it was only cowardice, which in such disguises tried to ensnare the individual. A grave tugging and warning set in, and often it was only the last remnant of conscience which decided the issue. Yet the more this voice admonished one to caution, the louder and more insistent its lures, the sharper resistance grew until at last, after a long inner struggle, consciousness of duty emerged victorious. By the winter of 1915–16, this struggle had for me been decided. At last my will was undisputed master. If in the first days I went over the top with rejoicing and laughter, I was now calm and determined. And this was enduring. Now Fate could bring the ultimate tests without my nerves shattering or my reason failing. The young volunteer had become an old soldier. And this transformation had occurred in the whole army. It had issued old and hard from the eternal battles, and as for those who could not stand up under the storm—well, they were broken.[171]

Clearly, Hitler believed that cowardice was a great sin, and courage a great virtue. It can be assumed that Hitler was quite anxious after the combat gas injury in 1917, as all gas-injured patients are. His brief "relapse," however, was a hysterical response after hearing about Germany's surrender. During the putsch in 1923, Hitler exhibited excited and overdramatic behavior that can be interpreted as anxiety. He was anxious and depressed when he fled after he was wounded while marching to the Feldherrenhalle. The putsch was ill-planned, and Hitler's high anxiety and depression can be related to the awareness of losing, the feeling that he had no control over events and had failed. His anxiety and depression gave way to anger about the unjust treatment of his comrades. During the following period of imprisonment and trial, he was remarkably cool and collected and behaved as the accuser rather than the accused.

Before the reoccupation of the Rhineland in 1936, a hazardous military venture, Hitler was very apprehensive. Before he marched into Austria, which was politically risky, according to one of the witnesses, he was outright "hysterical."[172] Another severe spell of anxiety occurred before Hitler decided not to withdraw from Narvik in the Norwegian confrontation. Yet these episodes were intense but isolated. After the extremely stressful assassination attempt of 20 July 1944, in which he suffered significant injuries, Hitler showed no overt anxiety. What remained after the attempt was dejection, cold anger, and the resolve to punish anyone who had the slightest connection with the plot. Hitler told his physician how much he had suffered: "the weeks since the 20th of July were the worst of his [Hitler's] life. Nobody, no German, could even dream of how heroic he was. In spite of the greatest infirmity, hours of dizziness, nausea (which he never communicated on questioning), he remained unbroken and fought on with iron energy. Often danger of collapse existed, but with iron energy he mastered the situation."[173] Waite considered Hitler's anxieties extreme. Yet he mastered extreme stresses quite effectively. Loewenberg drew attention to the expectation that a leader would reduce anxieties in his followers, and history bore this out after 1918 when Hitler reduced the Germans' anxieties following their defeat, deprivations, and humiliations.[174] He promised the Germans that they would be the strongest nation in the world.

Phobias

Phobias are preventive avoidance responses associated with objects or processes that arouse fear. What plagued Hitler most was a fear of infections, and specifically of syphilis. He was obsessed with measures to prevent infections, even of colds, for instance by frequent hand washing and once by quarantining his barber and also the photographer Hoffmann, who was accused of being a typhoid carrier. Occasionally, Hitler got into arguments with Morell over what he considered inadequate precautions against infection caused by injections.[175] The preoccupation with dangerous and destructive bacilli became generalized to non-medical topics. Hitler compared his enemies—particularly Jews—to bacilli and vermin that had to be exterminated— a view that was shared by other top Nazis such as Himmler. Possibly, Hitler's fear of infections can be traced back to early childhood experiences. Infections killed at least two of his siblings, and the danger of infection must have been considered within the family as a real and serious threat. Hitler also was temporarily concerned that he suffered from tuberculosis and cancer. The latter manifested itself twice, when he suffered hoarseness and the loss of his voice due to laryngeal polyps. The symptom was threatening to the orator Hitler, who thought of Emperor Friedrich III, who died of cancer of the larynx.[176] Christa Schroeder assumed that Hitler had a water phobia and could not swim.[177] Yet according to Kubizek, Hitler could swim and once rescued

Kubizek's mother.[178] At one time, Hitler nearly drowned swimming in the Danube.[179] Since that time, he perhaps was reluctant to get into a rowboat. Probably, his hesitation to swim at beach parties was caused not by a fear of water, but by his reluctance to be seen in bathing trunks. He criticized Mussolini, who was not plagued by such inhibitions, for such behavior. I also assume that Hitler's hesitation to mount a horse was not a phobia of horses, but rather a disinclination to look awkward and inelegant astride a horse. Hitler was never seen driving a car on a public road, and such avoidance of driving an automobile, for the auto fan Hitler, raises the question of whether he had a driving phobia. His explanation that he avoided driving because an accident could have resulted in his expulsion from Germany is not convincing.[180] As one can judge on the basis of some remarks, he definitely felt uneasy about flying; mild discomfort about flying, however, is so common that no particular significance should be attributed to this finding.

Hypochondriasis

The term hypochondriasis denotes an unrealistic preoccupation with illness and the treatment of illness. Bacteriophobia was not the only sign of hypochondriasis in Hitler. He had no imaginary illnesses, but he took illness very seriously. His dentist, Professor Blaschke, and otologist, Dr. Giesing, reported a stoic attitude when Hitler was under their care.[181] Hitler wanted to be seen as a patient who could endure pain and illness. Morell considered him a demanding, difficult, and argumentative patient.[182] It is likely that the patient–physician relationship provided Hitler's only opportunity to express infantile feelings of dependency without harming his reputation. To Morell, he felt free to complain—not only about his illness, but about his life situation.[183] Hitler was preoccupied with the idea of an early and premature death that would prevent the realization of his ideas: "Where others have eternity at their disposal, I have but a few short, miserable years. I have now reached the stage where I wonder whether among my immediate successors there will be found a man predestined to carry on the torch when it has slipped from my hand."[184] Most startling is a similar statement in the monologues: "I am sorry that, like Moses, I will see the Holy Land only from a distance."[185] He believed that the lack of time (German historians called it *Zeitangst*) threw off his planning. In the Bormann papers, he expressed the opinion that the Second World War had come too early because his disciples had not attained their full manhood; at other times he indicated that the war had come too late because he had been appeased at the Munich Conference. In essence, he believed he was condemned to wage war.[186] Hitler adjusted his time table of operations in accordance with his *Zeitangst*, a horrendous manifestation of his narcissism.

While Hitler was afraid of dying early, he was not afraid of death. On 17 December 1942, Morell, presumably after an unspecified cardiovascular crisis, recorded: "The Führer wants to be told if he were in a very bad condition, because then he would have to make some very important decisions relating to Germany. He is not afraid of death; it would be a salvation for him. He has only upsets and no time for himself. He lives only for his father-land, for Germany. There is no cure for death. We know that. But under dangerous circumstances I have to tell him." Death for Hitler was a heroic death, a Wagnerian departure for Valhalla. After the surrender of Stalingrad, Hitler was furious and incredulous that a German Feldmarschall would surrender and not commit suicide after being unable to fulfill his mission: "It is so easy with a pistol. What cowardice to shrink from this."[187] Hitler's Wagnerian thoughts about redemption through a pure, heroic death also negate Fromm's ideas about love of decay.

Shame and Guilt

Often anxiety is associated with other dysphoric experiences, such as shame, guilt, rage, and depression. Gerhard Piers differentiated guilt anxiety and shame anxiety.[188] Shame occurs when a person does not live up to external or internal ideals. Expectations about standards may be realistic or unrealistic. Psychoanalysts speak of the ego ideal, which is the internalization of the conscious and unconscious ideals of one's parents (in a man, mostly of his father), but also of other models. Shame is usually associated with unacceptable sexual behaviors, but it also can be associated with one's appearance, lack of vitality, loss of control, or lack of certain qualities such as courage or generosity.[189] In a culture in which he preached the virtues of beauty and strength, Hitler was ashamed and dissatisfied with his appearance, his unathletic physique, his plump nose, his body odor, his bad breath, and his flatulence. He talked with envy about the appearance of elite guards and about how women are attracted to strong men.[190] He hid his body, particularly his genitals, before his physician, not permitting medical examinations of his genital and anal regions. Morell was perplexed when Hitler refused his help with the administration of an enema.[191] Hitler's sensitivity about his body was also demonstrated in his order to have his corpse burned lest it fall into his enemies' hands, who would desecrate it.[192] This however, is not surprising, considering what happened to such rulers as Mussolini or Russia's last czar and his family.

It is more difficult to assess Hitler's guilt feelings. Guilt is the nagging feeling associated with acts that deviate from the prevailing morals and are punished by others and self as violations of the ethical or criminal code. Conscious guilt is synonymous with a bad conscience. Freud developed the concept of unconscious guilt: He assumed the existence of an unconscious psychological agency—the super ego—that punishes the transgressor through self-punitive acts.[193] I already expressed some doubt about whether Hitler should be viewed as a self-punitive and self-destructive person. It is often difficult to differentiate plain mistakes from self-destructive acts. At Stalingrad in January 1943, Hitler did not assess his opponent realistically, just as he failed to do in the putsch of 1923. The series of successes between these two events would militate against self-destruction. I would prefer to view this aspect of Hitler's psychopathology as an Icarus complex. Like Icarus, who got burned when he flew too close to the sun, Hitler did not properly assess the risk involved in his action and over-reached his capabilities. The notion, however, that Hitler was self-destructive because he may have been punishing himself for his horrendous crimes is a fascinating idea and should not be lightly dismissed. To prove it, however, more convincing evidence would be needed. The conscious moral code is learned by imitation from parental and other models. The super ego develops from an unconscious internalization or identification with the parental figure. From what we know about Hitler's father, one could consider him a man with a somewhat flexible conscience that permitted him to make false statements to obtain permission to marry a blood relative. He also made a little more money than a "customs super-inspector" would be expected to make. Perhaps Hitler identified with his cunning father. He felt little if any conscious guilt for his criminal acts and viewed himself as an ethical person who wanted nothing other than to save the world. Whether he felt any unconscious guilt is a question I am unable to answer.

In the pre-political era, Hitler's transgressions were minor, and in the political era they were horrendous. During his youth, Hitler showed no regrets over rudeness to his friend Gustl and to a schoolmate.[194] He was completely untouched by the disapproval of his mother, his half-sister Angela, and her husband over his loafing and self-indulgence after he quit school. He had no remorse about his draft-dodging or about not telling his real motivation for avoiding the draft. All he cared about was not getting punished. None of this is seriously deviant behavior. On the other side of the ledger is Hitler's concern about social injustice in Vienna, as expressed in *Mein Kampf* and in a report of Hitler's kind heartedness when he stood up for a mistreated person.[195] No evidence of cruel or unethical behavior during World War I has been found. The bottom line is that Hitler, up to this point, was not significantly unethical and had no major reasons to experience serious conscious guilt. A radical change took place when Hitler started his political career. Like tens of thousands of other soldiers, Hitler was in a state of rage over what had happened to him and, after Germany's surrender, was anxious about what his future would be. In this mood, and without any feeling of guilt, he continued his wartime morality: The destruction of one's enemies was approved behavior. The principal enemies were the traitors, Jews, and Bolsheviks. Friends were treated according to traditional morals as long as they were loyal. When they ceased to be loyal, they were destroyed, too. Hitler's cadre and a large number of Germans responded with approval and in time enabled Hitler to commit crimes with minimal guilt. Hitler showed shame after the failed putsch in 1923. He did not feel guilty, because he managed to portray his accusors as the guilty parties. After the bloody destruction of the oppositional SA leadership, he was visibly upset about killing his friends and associates, but he managed to convince the German people, President Hindenburg, and himself that he had taken the right action. He never felt any guilt over attacking and cruelly destroying Poland, or later over launching an unprecedented war of destruction against Russia. The Slavs and the Jews were enemies and sub-humans, "vermin," and no guilt was experienced over their murder. Actually, Hitler was furious about Germans who sympathized with the plight of the Jews.[196] In self-contradictory statements that are so typical of Hitler, he spoke of Himmler's reprehensible methods[197] but never stopped him. Even during the last phase of the regime Hitler never personally committed an act of destruction. When defeat followed defeat, Hitler became extremely vengeful. If he ever had felt any guilt, he lost it, and expressed this in scornful statements about Christian and Jewish morality, which he wanted to replace with the new morality of the Aryan superman.

Hitler also showed little regret about past mistakes.[198] He justified his decision not to pursue the British forces at Dunkirk by stating he wanted to win the British over as allies and did not want to shame them. He did not consider the cruelty of the Eastern Campaign or the declaration of war against the United States mistakes. Also, he felt he had been too permissive and trusting with the Latin races—the French, the Spaniards, and particularly the Italians, with the exception of Mussolini. In one of the last war conferences, he said: "One always regrets after being too good."[199] Hitler knew anxiety and shame, but hardly overt guilt in the Judeo–Christian tradition. In the following discussion of defenses, I will point to Hitler's enormous conscious and preconscious denial of guilt because he believed he was performing deeds that would be of great benefit to Germany and the world. It is of interest that the Germans—en masse—also denied any collective guilt. He knew the anxiety and shame of the German masses. Without such knowledge, he could not have seduced so many Germans to follow him.

Depression

Hitler's preoccupation with dying before completing his tasks was a manifestation neither of self-destructiveness nor of depression. At no time can a severe enduring or psychotic depression be detected, but Hitler suffered grief reactions after the deaths of his father and mother, Geli Raubal, and his favorite driver Julius Schreck; after the death in combat of a secretary's husband; and following the death of his army adjutant General Rudolf Schmund after 20 July. Even after Geli's death, however, Hitler bounced back quickly, returning to a very active political life within a week, but Geli's room became a shrine that only Hitler could enter. A more lasting period of mild depression occurred after Hitler moved to Vienna and probably lasted until the beginning of his political career in 1919. In addition to the grief reaction after his parents' deaths, precipitating causes were the rejection by the Academy of Arts and his dismal life situation after he had squandered his inheritance. The symptoms were depressed mood, low productivity (he painted relatively little and at times not at all), pessimism, and presumably low self-esteem. The psychiatrist Roland Henke and psychologist Klaus Steinbau pointed out that Hitler's paintings from that period were without people and done in brown or black, ordinarily considered signs of depression.[200] The depression reached its peak between 1907 and 1909, the azimuth of Hitler's life, improving already in Vienna when he found work, emotional support from friends and acquaintances, and financial help from Aunt Johanna. It improved further in Munich and almost vanished during the First World War. After the victory over France, Hitler was at a loss as to what his next step should be. He was rejected in his bids for peace by Great Britain, wavered about the idea of an invasion, and had annoying problems with Mussolini, Franco, and Pétain. One could call this "low" a mild dysphoria. He finally came out of it in 1940 when he hatched his plans to invade Russia. The invasion of Russia, particularly the early successes, buoyed him up. From early 1942, several remarks indicate another period of mild dysphoria, probably associated with the difficult military situation and the impairment due to his illness. On 3/4 January 1942, he stated, "Today I could not lecture every evening. The awareness of this depresses me."—adding, however, that it was most important to overcome such feelings.[201] On 13 May 1942, Hitler stated that he had to think two or three times about what he would have done without any ado ten years before.[202] Beginning in the fall of 1942, many persons noticed fatigue and attributed it to overwork and illness. Already in 1942, Goebbels, who followed Hitler's ups and downs closely, stated: "He is overworked. There is always the danger that, under the severe physical strain, he'll crack up."[203] After the 20th of July, Hitler's general condition had deteriorated further, noted again by Goebbels. Fatigue causes symptoms that are very similar to those of depression. It can be safely assumed that Hitler's general decline was the result of his physical illnesses, particularly his Parkinson's disease, but also due to his worry over the precarious military situation and the likely failure of his mission. These depressions were not cyclic psychotic depressions, but rather mild dysthymias, reactions to life events—perhaps, as Hitler also assumed, caused by innate dispositions. According to Hitler, one is born either a pessimist or an optimist.[204] Some improvement in the degree of mild depression was brought about by Morell's medications (either real or by suggestion) and by amphetamines, which, in all likelihood, Hitler used at that time.

Paranoid Delusions

Paranoid delusions were Hitler's most significant psychopathological complex. The attribute paranoid refers to persons who are extremely suspicious and believe that other persons or institutions are persecuting them, discriminating against them, and exploiting them. They bear grudges, are unwilling to forgive, and tend to retaliate in words and behavior. Paranoid individuals are experienced by others as unpleasant and difficult. They are secretive and guarded, and thus social relations are tenuous. Paranoid persons are apt to search for hidden meanings. They are usually jealous, and Hitler was quite jealous of Geli (not without justification) and his distant love Stefanie. Hitler used the defense of projection abundantly. He was hostile and paranoid toward enemies, but loyal to followers. He wanted loyal associates, and toward them his behavior was quite benign. When he felt betrayed by formerly loyal associates, such as Himmler, Göring, and Brandt during the last year of his life, Hitler's positive feelings turned into extreme hostility. The concept of the paranoid community, formulated by Norman Cameron,[205] throws some light on Hitler's behaviors. The paranoid pseudo-community consists of real or imaginary persons who have been made into enemies. They are persons whom the creator of the paranoid community does not understand and therefore assumes to be hostile towards him. In Hitler's case, these were Jews, Bolsheviks, and Western leaders such as Churchill and Roosevelt.

Hitler's suspiciousness probably originated in his infancy and childhood. One could assume that what Erikson called basic trust in infancy was lacking. I expressed tentative ideas about this when I discussed Hitler's ambivalent relations with both parents. If Kubizek's comment is valid, Hitler's remark after he failed the entrance examination for the Viennese Academy of Fine Arts that snares had been put out to get him is evidence that some suspiciousness existed in early adulthood. After Germany's defeat in the First World War, Hitler was convinced that the defeat had been caused by traitors, Jews, and Bolsheviks. From the time he assumed leadership, Hitler always worried about usurpers. Röhm was a victim of such fears. Most important, Hitler developed a strong tendency to blame others, particularly the Jew and, later, also his own generals. After the plot of 20 July 1944, Hitler was more convinced than ever that his suspicions were justified.

At one time or another, everybody is suspicious of another person or organization. The psychologically healthy person, however, checks out suspicions and drops them unless they are proven valid. Yet often it is not possible to establish a clear boundary between "normal" and pathological suspiciousness. A more fruitful approach is to investigate whether the topics of suspicion—in Hitler's case, his anti-Semitism and his concern that other powers wanted to keep Germany weak and poor—were delusions. In a classical definition, Carl Jaspers defined delusions as rigidly held false ideas or beliefs that are not accessible to correction by logic or empirical evidence.[206] Hitler's views about Jews would fall into this category. The content of the belief was totally unrealistic: World domination was not on the Jews' mind when they were struggling to establish a small state. To disagree with Hitler about this in a logical discussion was impossible, and only aroused his anger. Hitler's anti-Semitism, however, was widely shared, particularly in Germany, and shared delusions—for example, religious delusions—are evaluated differently by experts and laypersons than unshared delusions. Hitler's delusion that syphilis was one of the greatest threats to humanity, however, was essentially an individual, idiosyncratic delusion. The anti-Semitic idea that Jews are diseased and carry secret poisons has been shared by a few persons in the twentieth century, but Hitler's version—that syphilis is one of the two most serious world problems—has not been shared. Hitler regretted that he had expressed his syphilis complex in writing, but he did not change his beliefs.

De Boor brought us a step closer to understanding Hitler's paranoid delusions.[207] His deliberations rest on the work of Carl Wernicke (1848–1905), who called some delusions over-valued ideas and established that they do not only occur in schizophrenics, infections, toxic diseases, and dementia.[208] These delusions are usually complex belief systems of great intensity, with a high action potential. Wernicke also distinguished between benign and destructive over-valued ideas, and established the existence of a continuum between harmless *idées fixes* and destructive delusions. De Boor distinguished three classes of persons with over-valued ideas (actually, he described lifestyles): (1) over-valued ideas of positive social value, such as those of scientists and artists who subordinate their lives to these ideas; (2) dominant ideas of neutral value, such as those of fanatic collectors, athletes, and persons who pursue hobbies and fads; and (3) dominant ideas of negative social value, which are destructive, such as those of terrorists and members of certain cults. Hitler's principal over-valued ethnic delusion of Germanic constructiveness and Jewish destructiveness would fall into the third category. Other pursuits would fall into the first category—for example, Hitler as a passionate collector of art (for Germany, of course—not for himself!)—and some into the second category—for example, his being a vegetarian. De Boor went further in his thinking and linked Hitler's dominant idea with other psychopathology, such as infantile feelings of omnipotence, high aggression potential, chronic identity crisis, narcissism and egocentricity, hostility to science, disturbed social relations, and strong repressive defenses. The new concept he called monoperceptosis. More about the validity of the concept of paranoia and its implications will be discussed in the section on diagnosis.

Since C. Lasegue and J. Falret published a description of the *folie à deux*,[209] psychiatrists have become aware of shared delusions. The dominant person induces delusions in one or more passive recipients. For example, shared delusions can be held by families, as T. Lidz and S. Fleck established in studying families of schizophrenics as compared with healthy control families.[210] Less is known about large groups, such as cults, in which delusions are shared by leaders and followers. The Nazi movement has some characteristics of a cult—such as the dominance of the leader and his extraordinary acceptance by his followers—but it is too large and too diversified to be considered a cult. Shared religious and ideological delusions, however, are appraised differently than individual delusions, and persons with very weird beliefs are not necessarily considered paranoid within their own cultures. To give one example among many, the Indian guru Ramakrishna was considered a wise man and saint by many Hindus, while Westerners considered him psychotic. If comparisons can be made, National Socialism bears some resemblance to large historical fanatic movements such as the Crusades. The Crusades started with a delusion pronounced by Pope Urban II that God willed that Christ's burial site should be in Christian hands. I would like to emphasize, however, that this does not explain or define the Crusades, a movement that had complex political, social, and historical antecedents and consequences, just as Hitler's delusions have only limited explanatory value in understanding the historical event of National Socialism.

Robert S. Robins and Jarrold L. Post used the concept of paranoia in their analysis of Hitler's leadership.[211] They described three types of paranoid leadership. The first is the eccentric paranoid who does not interact with supporters or opponents. The second is the interactive paranoid who overreacts to a hostile environment and oversteps norms in an escalating manner. The interactive paranoid lacks charismatic leadership qualities and does not propose major changes. Examples would be Idi Amin in Uganda and the older and younger Duvaliers in Haiti. All these leaders wanted to achieve was enhancement of their own power. The third type of paranoid leadership Post and Robins described is the charismatic destructive paranoid leader. The major dictators of the twentieth century fall into this category. They visualized a millennial change. Combined with great political skill, these leaders tried to change mankind and society. They produced historical changes at the cost of enormous destruction. Hitler was a charismatic leader who conveyed a providential message based on his misunderstanding of history and the nature of man. The destructive content of the message outweighed all constructive aspects. It was a millennial message, promising to fundamentally change followers who believed in it. Robins also showed that paranoid behavior, though pathological, can have adaptive functions, especially if the paranoid leader has charismatic characteristics. Such charismatic leaders can impart to their followers the message that they possess an important truth. They believe their opponents are evil and describe these evil qualities in an exaggerated manner. By their own hostility, they create self-fulfilling counter-hostility in the target.[212] Clearly, the shared and unshared delusions in Hitler's worldview imply a distortion of reality.

Reality Sense and Judgment

Judgment, roughly synonymous with reality sense, is the capacity to assess options for practical action. Judgment requires intelligence and knowledge as well as motivation. Psychiatrists have little trouble assessing the lack of judgment in psychotic or demented patients. In persons with personality disorders and in the normal population, however, it is more difficult, especially if the tasks to be performed are complex. Assessing the moves of a champion chess player requires extraordinary knowledge of the game, and this is true for the assessment of military or political acts, as well. Assessment of past historical personalities is easier because the outcomes of their actions are known. A flat statement that Hitler's judgment and reality sense were poor is inadequate, and a more searching analysis is required. First, the destructive paranoid aspects were embedded like a poisonous pill in a stew of ardent nationalism and a trace of socialism that appealed to many Germans. A relatively small core group of fanatic Nazis was clearly aware of Hitler's ultimate aims. The bulk of his followers, however, and even antagonists either could not read Hitler's crucial messages or discounted them. Hence, Hitler was not viewed by the German majority as a destructive paranoid leader—except for a few overt and covert opponents. The majority did not see the unrealistic core of the system, least of all in times of war. The second reason why Hitler's lack of reality sense was not obvious was his conduct as a political and military leader during the long years of successful operations. During these years, Hitler made few mistakes—in any case, fewer than the Allies, who, until 1940, underestimated him. Hitler could point to remarkable economic and military successes. His ultimate, radical goals of creating a German superman, destroying his opponents, and implementing a new morality were, to the average German and even to Hitler himself, so unrealistic that he used *Zeitangst* as a major alibi. In the Bormann papers, Hitler, and presumably Bormann and Goebbels, analyzed mistakes—which, incidentally, were not identical with the mistakes historians, with the gift of hindsight, list. The Bormann papers are more an alibi than a true post factum analysis. What was lacking in the phase of Hitler's decline was any acknowledgment of Allied superiority, perhaps with the exception of his angry accusation that the Germans should perish if they couldn't stand up against the stronger "Eastern People."[213]

Amongst others, Hitler offered the following explanations in the Bormann papers: (1) The putsch had not succeeded because he had no choice but to act. (2) He did not think that the destruction of the Czech state, which cost him the last bit of trust from his opponents, was a mistake. Instead, he believed he had acted too late. (3) He did not pursue the British at Dunkirk because he was afraid of risking his tanks and did not want to humiliate the British, who he hoped would join him in his fight against the Bolsheviks. (4) He did not think the attack on Russia had been a mistake because he believed Russia would collapse quickly in a blitzkrieg (an opinion that was shared by Allied military staffs) and because the conquest of Russian soil and mineral treasures was of the utmost importance. The mistakes in Russia—the three-pronged attack with much delay, the debacle at Stalingrad, the late withdrawal in the Crimea—Hitler blamed on the lack of fighting spirit and betrayal on the part of his general staff. (5) A major misjudgment was his declaration of war against the United States, especially when he had failed to persuade Japan to open a front against Russia in Manchuria. President Roosevelt, hampered by U.S. isolationism, felt Hitler did him a favor. Hitler, however, was tremendously relieved by the Japanese actions, saying, "A millstone was lifted from my heart."[214] Only at the very end was Hitler grossly unrealistic. Until March 1944 he still spoke in a war conference about being on guard against self-hypnosis,[215] but at the end he was not. War conferences and reports by different commanders (e.g., General Koller) testify to this. He gave orders to imaginary armies and was deeply convinced that he had been betrayed by his generals. Some of this final lack of realism was caused by disease and exhaustion, but, in essence, it was the grim disappointment that his actions had failed and that he and Nazi Germany were doomed.

Defenses

When faced with stress and conflict, human beings respond with fight, flight, or problem-solving responses. When anxiety impairs problem-solving, other psychological processes, referred to as defenses, occur. The understanding of unconscious and preconscious defenses is one of the great contributions of psychoanalysis, notably of Anna Freud.[216] The purpose of defenses is to reduce the impact of unpleasant emotions—primarily anxiety, anger, guilt, shame, and grief. In most cases these defenses are not adaptive—one could call them an unsuccessful inner flight—and do not solve the problem. They are barred in varying degrees from consciousness. Usually, the individual is unaware or only partly aware of what he is defending himself against. Psychoanalysts list scores of defenses. Some of them can be adaptive, such as some forms of humor, but most are not adaptive and do not solve problems. Some defenses, such as rationalizing, can become part of the character structure.

Hitler's defenses could serve as examples in a psychopathology course. Persons with pervasive defenses usually impress others as ingenuine. The fact that many followers considered the defensive Hitler a genuine and sincere person is puzzling; it probably resulted from a far-reaching identification with Hitler by his followers. The fundamental defense is repression. It may be partial, just a dimming of consciousness, or total, such as in hysterical conversion symptoms. Hitler had hysterical symptoms during the second case of blindness in 1918. He fits quite well, however, into what older psychiatry called a hysterical character (a dramatic, exhibitionistic, infantile, egocentric, emotionally labile, and suggestible person). Examples of partial repression are what Lifton calls numbing and doubling.[217] Numbing refers to the emotional detachment that is employed to make aggressive acts possible. Lifton described it in Nazi physicians working in concentration camps, enabling them to carry out their inhuman work. Yet numbing need not be pathological: All generals leading their troops into battle or surgeons performing destructive operations show numbing. Hitler showed numbing in many situations, ordering and discussing cruel deeds against internal and external enemies. Doubling refers to the assumption of split roles—being kind to children and animals in family settings and merciless and cruel to inmates of concentration camps.

Suppression is a conscious or near-conscious inhibition of psychological processes. The general observation is that Hitler was more likely to suppress (and also repress) sexual conflicts and stresses than conflicts over aggressive acts. One aspect of what Hitler referred to as his strong will was his suppression of behavior that he found uncomfortable and unacceptable. A startling example is his remark to Robert Wagener that he "overcame the urge for the physical possession of a woman."[218] In a classic study, Sigmund Freud showed how humor and wit can reduce anxiety, make a harsh reality more acceptable, and reduce conflicts over aggressive, dependent, and sexual needs.[219] Schroeder did not describe Hitler as humorless, but guarded; she quoted the adage that the ridiculous is only one step away from the sublime.[220] Actually, Hitler often laughed at jokes, and had a sense of humor. Christa Schroeder described his laugh as a strident cackle. He liked popular local comedians, such as Karl Valentin, and considered them superior to American "grotesque clowns."[221] He had a strong aversion to sexual jokes. They upset him, and he forbade them to be told in his presence.[222] There is no doubt about Hitler's sarcasm. It is clearly evident in some of the famous speeches, particularly in his reply to President Roosevelt, which abounded in offensive sarcasm.[223] He could be mercilessly critical of associates and acquaintances, usually applauded by his audiences. The crippled Max Amann, publisher of Hitler's books, was the frequent butt of his impersonations. Another target of Hitler's sarcasm was Mathilde von Kemnitz, General Ludendorff's odd wife. Hitler's propensity for sarcasm also showed in some of his doodling and in caricatures he drew of people. A sample of the youthful caricaturist's work is Hitler's drawing of a professor holding a cone of seeds or candies.[224] Yet Hitler was as sensitive about people criticizing him as he was caustic about others when it suited him. Even adoring Severus Ziegler stated that one had to be very respectful in expressing a contrary view.[225] Least of all could he stand being ridiculed. In an infamous speech on 8 November 1942, Hitler complained that the Jews had been laughing about him as a prophet but now weren't laughing anymore.[226] The complexity of Hitler's personality and his capacity to be self-critical in a humorous fashion is shown in the following statement he made in a secret speech: "Once a man said to me, 'Listen, if you do that, Germany will perish in six weeks.' I say, 'The German people survived the wars with the Romans. The German people survived the mass migration. The German people survived the great battles of the early and late Middle Ages. The German people survived the religious wars. They survived the Napoleonic Wars; they survived the First World War and a revolution. They also will survive me.'"[227]

Projection is a defense mechanism whereby a person places his thoughts, emotions, and drives into another person. It occurs in cases of severe psychopathology, such as in paranoid schizophrenia, but also in normal persons. Without projection, no creative art or appreciation of art would exist, and one person could not understand another or fall in love. A crucial difference between normal and abnormal projection is the normal projector's ability to check and correct his projections. Both loving and hostile affects can be projected. One can distinguish types of pathological projection: simple projection[228] and projective identification in which a person projects fantasies on another person and then identifies with this individual. Hitler was a projector who had little control over his hostile projections. This was already evident during his young adulthood when he assumed that trip wires had been laid out to defeat him after he failed his entrance examination for the Academy. One of his main political concepts was the assumption that Germany was surrounded by enemies. He attacked Russia because he assumed, incorrectly at that time, that Stalin would attack Germany. At the time of Hitler's invasion, Stalin had no such plans. Bromberg and Small furnished an interesting analysis of projective identification. Hitler wrote in Mein Kampf: "... with satanic joy in his face, the black-haired Jewish youth lurks in wait for hours for the unsuspecting girl whom he defiles with his blood, thus stealing her from her people."[229] Bromberg and Small assumed that young Adolf was the black-haired Jewish youth, who not only projects his sexual wishes for Stefanie, but identifies with the Jewish rapist.[230]

The defense of displacement is related to projection: The subject does not project his experiences on another person, but displaces them from one person or topic to another person or topic. When Hitler was infuriated over the Mountain Troops planting a flag on Mt. Ebrus, he displaced his anger with his generals over a calamitous military situation onto innocent soldiers. Splitting refers to the subject's dividing of persons into all good and all bad persons, and also to reversals from one extreme to the other. It is a pathological mechanism, allegedly caused by psychological trauma in infancy, either overindulgence or frustration by the mother. Bromberg and Small assumed that this defense was very prominent in Hitler, who experienced the world in extremes of all good (the Aryans) and all bad (the Jews). As we do not possess adequate data about Hitler's early infancy, speculations about the cause of splitting are futile. In my view, Hitler had ambivalent views about many persons and many problems, and I consider his tendency toward polarization a defense against his ambivalence. More will be said about this in the section on identity.

Reaction formation refers to the changing of an unacceptable trait into the opposite. I have already discussed Hitler's bravado as a defense against his anxiety. Using the concept of reaction formation with reference to a dead historical personality, however, can easily lead to errors and facile explanations. An example is Binion's explanation of Hitler's anti-Semitism as a hostile reaction against Dr. Bloch, who, according to Binion, killed Hitler's mother.[231] In reality, Hitler was grateful to Dr. Bloch and treated him leniently compared with other Jews. It is well known that some patients are unconsciously angry with their physicians when they are unable to help. To show this to be the case with Hitler's attitude toward Dr. Bloch, however, would require specific detailed and convincing data that we do not possess. Another example of questionable use of the concept of reaction formation is Erich Fromm's assumption that Hitler was attracted to dirt and decay. According to Fromm, Hitler's excessive cleanliness was just proof that he loved dirt. More important, however, is to consider—as a partial explanation, at least—Hitler's aggression as a reaction formation to his passivity. The "*macho*" reaction of a passive man (or woman)—what Alfred Adler called male protest—is a common phenomenon.

Regression, a universal defense, is the return to earlier patterns of behavior. It is not clear whether regression should be considered a defense or a symptom of stress. It can occur in a chaotic or an orderly fashion. Ernst Kris referred to the latter as regression in service of the ego, such as regression to art and play. This was particularly evident toward the end of Hitler's life when he wished to escape from a hopeless military and political situation and make Linz into a world art center. National Socialism had a strong tendency to regress to primitive modes of living, evidenced in its myth of blood and soil and the primitive rituals of its monster meetings. Hitler partook in this, but at the same time he ridiculed the mythology of the old Germanic cults and rituals that Himmler and Rosenberg espoused and opposed a Wotan cult.[232] The exalted regression of Wagnerian drama—to heroism, lust, murder, and incest—was enough for him. Hitler's propensity for primitive vengeance and cruel punishment, replacing conventional justice, might also be considered a form of regression. The historian Otto Hintze told his colleague Friedrich Meinecke, "This man does not actually belong to our race. There is something very foreign in him—something like in an extinct primitive race that is completely amoral."[233] Related to regression is Freud's concept of repetition compulsion. Under stress, persons not only regress to earlier periods, but actually to traumatic events—fixations—and are prone to repeat reactions to the earlier traumas. Hitler probably repeated in his infatuation with Geli his earlier incestuous fantasies about his half-sister Angela and his mother.

More a character trait than a defense was Hitler's extreme righteousness. He was always right, and the others were always wrong. He always had good reasons to act, as he acted for the benefit of Germany and the world, no matter what he did. If he was destructive, it was either because he was defending his or Germany's or the world's best interest, or because he had to protect future generations. This basic attitude manifested itself in facile explanations, self-exculpation, and an enormous overt exaggeration of his abilities and importance. Hitler always had an answer, and whoever opposed him was wrong.

Hitler's Narcissism and Human Relations

Narcissism is one of the most widely used and abused concepts of psychoanalysis, psychiatry, and populist psychology. Sigmund Freud, the first to use the term extensively, was well aware of its looseness and ambiguity.[234] It refers not to selfishness or egotism, but to self-love and feeling of self-worth and also to self-hatred, excessive preoccupation with one's self, exaggeration of one's own importance, and denial of the importance of others. It is used as a descriptive term, a diagnostic label, and a developmental concept, and it also designates a psychotherapeutic relationship. One of the confusing aspects of the concept is the fact that it designates a healthy feeling of worth but also can refer to a destructive and self-destructive narcissism. In this section, narcissism is discussed as a descriptive trait. Hitler can be considered a narcissistic person. This assertion is based primarily on: (1) his tenuous human relations; (2) his convictions of grandeur about himself and his tasks; (3) his unusual risk-taking behaviors; (4) his high sensitivity to criticism, experiencing even justified critiques as slights (narcissistic mortification); and (5) his potential for rage reactions (narcissistic rages following real and imaginary slights). One caveat must be kept in mind: Narcissism is a characteristic trait of nearly all outstanding persons, political leaders, creative scientists, artists, and even great moralists and "saints" who emphasize their humility.

Many of Hitler's associates and other contemporary observers commented on his limitations in human relations. Speer spoke of Hitler as being unable to establish or maintain contact,[235] stating, "If Hitler would have had friends, I would have been his friend."[236] He also stated that Hitler adored himself.[237] Manstein's statement that Hitler felt no loyalty to the German soldier is surprising, but probably was shared by some members of his upper military staff.[238] General Keitel remarked that he felt as if he was in a permanent state of hypnosis around Hitler and felt no close relationship. Hitler's relationship with his general staff was always distant and wary, and degenerated even further after the 20th of July plot. According to von Ribbentrop, Hitler did not want people to get too close to him.[239] His relationship with Mussolini, although always ambivalent, was the closest he ever had with a major political figure. Of course, a relationship with a governing person, and particularly with a dictator, is not apt to be close. With his lower staff—his secretaries, drivers, and servants—Hitler was friendly in a distant way. The ambivalence to his father and mother are described elsewhere. No warm friendships existed; even with Gustl Kubizek, the friendship lasted only for a short period of time. Apart from the avuncular romance with Geli Raubal and the relationship with Eva Braun—which was close only in the last year of Hitler's life when he was sick and desperate—Hitler did not feel close to other human beings. All his life, Hitler was extremely sensitive to real or imaginary slights, in psychoanalytic terms, narcissistic mortification. Above all, he did not want to be belittled, ridiculed, criticized, humiliated, or neglected. Many of Hitler's rages were narcissistic rages in response to slights.

This does not necessarily mean that Hitler was incapable of forming a relationship. Best reported human warmth and sympathy in his early contacts with Hitler; he called Hitler during the *Kampfzeit* a seductive prophet, during the years of peace an angry prophet, and during the war a mad prophet.[240] Hitler's enemy, Otto Strasser, noted that Hitler had a good antenna for the feelings of others and knew what was going on in the Germans' minds.[241] Carl G. Jung called him the loudspeaker that magnified the inaudible whispers of the German soul.[242] Clearly, Hitler could be sensitive and responsive when he wanted to be. He felt comfortable with children and liked them. Richard Wagner's granddaughter, Friedelinde Wagner, the black sheep of the Wagner family, a critic, confirmed this from her own experience,[243] and it is corroborated by Eva Braun's home movies, which show that children were at ease with "Uncle Adi."[244] Hitler liked animals, particularly German shepherd dogs (but not boxers, which he considered degenerate). Toward the end of his life, he reportedly remarked that he could rely only on Blondi (his dog) and Fräulein Braun.[245]

A prominent feature of Hitler's narcissism was his grandiosity. As Germany's Führer, Hitler developed extreme ideas of grandiosity and omnipotence. He saw himself as a messianic leader whom Providence had chosen to make Germany into the greatest nation on earth and free the world from the Jewish peril. What Hitler wanted that no other secular leader had expressed so succinctly, however, was to change man and create a new man. He had the political sense not to compare himself in public to Jesus, but he implied similarities by characterizing Jesus as a revolutionary leader whom he "aryanized." Hitler told his secretaries he would be considered the greatest German after the Czech President Hacha consented to the invasion of his country.[246] In a secret speech to the top commander of the Wehrmacht in Flenstein on 23 November 1939, Hitler referred to himself as "irreplaceable": "I am convinced of the power of my brain and decisiveness; I have the greatest experience in all questions of armament; I will not shy away from anything and will destroy anybody who is against me."[247] In the beginning of the Russian campaign, before setbacks occurred, he spoke of Germans as superior *Herrenmenschen* destined to rule inferior races. In the monologues he frequently spoke about world events in lofty, cosmic terms. Hitler's grandiosity was clearly expressed in his desire to erect gigantic buildings. The cupola of the Great Hall in Berlin was supposed to be nearly 900 feet high—twice as high as the tallest cathedral towers. Clearly, the enormity of these buildings was supposed to impress the world with Hitler's might: "Whoever enters the Reichskanzlei must have the feeling of standing before the master of the world, and the path to it must take away one's breath."[248] This grandiosity applied not only to buildings, but also to weapons—there was a gigantic Tiger tank, too large to be effective, and even railroads in Russia with tracks twice as wide as those of standard trains. Waite interprets Hitler's interest in enormous buildings as a reaction not only to feelings of general and sexual inadequacy, but to the putative monorchism.[249]

Hitler's Will

The concept of will has almost disappeared from the psychological literature, although it has remained important in ethical, philosophical, and religious discourse. For Hitler it was of fundamental importance.[250] Erikson maintained that will develops when a child is taught to control his excretory functions and one day decides to withhold or let go.[251] In Hitler's case, we know nothing about toilet training. Some of his ideas about will can be traced to populist interpretations of Schopenhauer and Nietzsche, but essentially his views about will were his own. Will had two meanings for Hitler: impressing his will on others, and never giving up. He considered it essential that the men who worked for him, in both the civilian and the military spheres, submit to him and carry out his will. He endeavored to achieve this through coercion, seduction, and persuasion, complaining once in the monologues, "My entire life has been nothing but a continuous persuasion."[252] He also believed he had the ability hypnotize people. Hitler's coworkers as well as the German masses complied and submitted to the Führer's will, which supposedly is characteristic of Germans although identical phenomena have been observed in other dictatorships. Not only during the "drummer" period, but also at the height of his power, Hitler claimed that he acted on higher authority, naming fate, Providence, history, and occasionally the Almighty. The second manifestation of Hitler's will was his stubbornness, his complete unwillingness to give up or surrender. His fanaticism was a fundamental trait. In the Stalingrad disaster, his stubbornness led to the loss of an entire army. To give up meant weakness. Hitler's emphasis on an iron will was a defense against such weakness. It also was a defense against his ambivalence. Again proving his point, Hitler quoted the Old Testament : "What is not hot and not cold shall be spit out of the mouth.[253] In the final analysis, a strong will meant strength and power to Hitler, and lack of will meant weakness, impotence, inferiority.

Hitler's Lies

In the fall of 1944, Field Marshal Rommel angrily accused Hitler of being a pathological liar.[254] Although Hitler does not fit the diagnostic picture of a pathological liar who, like the fabulous Baron von Münchausen, senselessly tells fantastic stories, Rommel had good reasons to accuse Hitler of breaking promises and misleading the German people. One idea that Hitler carried over from his pre-political years was his understanding of Allied propaganda during World War I. Already before the war, he elaborated on it, refined it, and used his knowledge to create a myth about himself as well as to restrict and modify public information to a degree equal to what Bolshevik Russia did, and by far exceeding the Allied propaganda of World War I. Hitler became the father of the big lie. He was a Machiavellian politician par excellence, and it is likely but not certain that he read Machiavelli's *The Prince* or a popular version of the opus. A crucial question is whether or not Hitler was sincere about his belief system. He misled friendly reporters in saying he had no intention of annexing Austria. In 1934, he told von Wiegand he had no intention of curtailing the privileges of Jews.[255] To Ward Price in 1934, Hitler announced that Germany had no interest in occupying Russian territory.[256] Experienced politicians, such as Neville Chamberlain, believed him for a long time. Most of all, the majority of the German people believed him. After Hitler did not keep his promise of 26 November 1939 about the annexation of the Sudetenland being his last territorial demand, the British, French, and Americans did not believe him anymore. A shrewd maneuver was his declaration to the German people on 8 November 1938, in which he admitted that he had had to lie to them about pretending to seek peace. This was at a time when Hitler could no longer hide the buildup of the German armed forces. Only after Hitler's death did the majority of Germans recognize the seductive and broken promises that Hitler had made to his bride, *Germania*. It became widely recognized that Hitler was a prolific liar: Lies, half-lies, broken promises and pacts, and self-deceit all were in his repertory. At the same time, he emphasized his commitment to truth and his dislike of liars.[257] He attacked ministers from all churches, as well as Marxists and intellectuals, for poisoning people's minds with lies. Hitler's angriest accusations, however, were leveled against Jews, "the greatest of all liars and deceivers."

It remains unknown whether Hitler lied much during his childhood. A child with a lively imagination, he was apt to invent tales. Hitler once said that the customs service was corrupt,[258] and although he did not specifically state that his father was dishonest, it is possible that he had the old man in mind when he made this remark. Hitler probably was aware that his father had made false statements about the degree of relationship to his bride, and he had doubts about his father's descent. Justifiably, Hitler did not trust his half-brother Alois Jr. Overall in families with little trust, lying is bound to occur. Hitler certainly was deceitful when he was summoned by the Austrian Consul in 1914 to explain his avoidance of the military draft. He also was a tax swindler, which was not unusual in Germany at the time. He was anything but truthful in his statements about his own illnesses, both before and after he became a politician. To what extent the tuberculosis story was consciously distorted remains unknown. Hitler certainly exaggerated in the story of his "blindness" after the gas attack, and he never gave a clear account of his fall in the Feldherrenhalle march to Morell, who complained about not being properly informed about his patient's history of illness. In general, such medical misinformation is not rare, and the aforementioned personal swindles, however, do not compare in significance with Hitler's political falsehoods.

Hitler emphasized his commitment to personal truthfulness as well as his dislike for liars. He fired his valet, Karl Krause, for instance, for telling tall tales—something Hitler did himself.[259] Guarding and not sharing secrets was very important to Hitler, and he was furious about the "brain parasites" who knew what was going on in his brain (referring to Jewish émigré journalists).[260] Undoubtedly, he and his sympathizers would have looked at an investigator such as myself as a "brain parasite." During the political years, he repeatedly talked about the necessity of guarding secrets. Certainly, all politicians and military leaders guard their secret policies, especially during wartime, but Hitler's preoccupation with secrets seemed greater than that of other contemporary leaders. On the other hand, he was remarkably open about his program and such major points as his conquests and elimination of the Jews. One other distinction was Hitler's extraordinary record of breaking pacts and formal agreements. When faced head-on with a statement by Birger Dahlerus that he could not be trusted, Hitler angrily asserted that he never lied.[261] Did he lie or deceive himself? In Hitler's statement to Ambassador Hewel that he would never tell a lie on his own behalf, but that there was no falsehood he would not tell for Germany,[262] the second part is significant because Hitler's lies, deceptions, and breaches of contract were directed against his enemies. As Hitler had many enemies, such falsehoods were numerous. His political lies were applications of his principle that whatever was useful to himself and to Germany was justified. Ethicists concede that lies on the part of politicians who can demonstrate that the falsehoods serve a "good" purpose, such as lies during war designed to deceive the enemy, are more acceptable than other lies.[263] Many of Hitler's lies fall into this category.

The question of whether Hitler was sincere in his fundamental beliefs or whether he was a power-hungry demagogue who deceived both the Germans and the world has been debated by two eminent British historians, Alan Bullock and H. R. Trevor Roper, who held opposing views.[264] Bullock originally viewed Hitler as a demagogue, while Trevor Roper argued that Hitler was sincere—a proposition that earned him angry attacks. In an interview with Ron Rosenbaum, Bullock presented a modification of his original position, asserting that the demagogue Hitler gradually came to believe his own lies.[265] Bullock's analysis is intriguing. He cites Nietzsche, who described a hypnotizer and seducer, who, in turn, becomes hypnotized and seduced. A similar process was described by Alvar Nuñez Cabeza de la Vaca, a Spanish explorer who was shipwrecked in Florida in 1528.[266] When the Indians found him, they demanded that he cure their sick through prayers. After he succeeded, he became convinced of his own supernatural powers. In my opinion, however, there is a deeper well that feeds Hitler's fanatic and false belief—essentially a delusion that the Jew harmed him and the world. Hitler was not just a hysterical fanatic. He was a paranoid fanatic.

Hitler's Complex Identity and Ambivalence

I conclude the psychogram with a discussion of Hitler's complex identity and pervasive ambivalence. The concept of identity is vague and complex; yet for an understanding of Hitler, it is useful. Erikson—to whom we owe much for elegantly describing although never satisfactorily defining the concept of ego identity—readily admits this.[267] Identity answers the questions "What am I?," "What do I want to be and what can I be?," and "How do I want to be seen by others?" It also is shaped by "How am I seen by others?" It is more than self-understanding or a sense of self worth—it contains an active component of shaping one's transactional roles. A person's identity is shaped by identifications—an unconscious process—and by the conscious imitation of role models. Erikson emphasized that adolescence is the crucial period during which the adult identity is established and previous identifications are integrated. However, later identifications and imitations of role models occur and can be significant. Identity is positively reinforced by successes and achievements, and negatively by the lack of them. In Hitler's case, propaganda shaped not only how he viewed himself and his sense of worth, but also how he was seen and regarded by his followers, the indifferent masses, and even his opponents. I distinguish three phases in Hitler's identity: the pre-political identity and two identities after he became a politician.

There is no better description of Hitler's failure to assume a definite identity during adolescence and early adulthood than the words of Thomas Mann describing the frustrated young artist.[268] After the failed entrance examination at the Academy of Fine Arts, Hitler came close to a malignant identity diffusion during the low of his Viennese existence. It took him a long time— a moratorium of four years as a soldier in the First World War—to overcome this phase. At the end of World War I, a new trauma hit Hitler as it hit millions of Germans: the loss of the war, a humiliating peace, and the dashing of any hopes he might have had of establishing an orderly bourgeois existence. At this time, aided by a unique constellation of events, Hitler was able to assume his new identity. With a fanatic message, accepted by a small group of followers who gave him a new and until then unknown feeling of worth, he came to view himself as a forerunner, a drummer, a prophet, a Saint John figure for a reborn Germany. Defensively, he stated that being the drummer was the most difficult job, but the truth was that he lacked the inner confidence to be more than a drummer, although this was a role for which he was extremely well suited. In 1924, after a major failure—the disastrous putsch and the subsequent trial and imprisonment—Hitler assumed his final identity: that of the Führer. One step in this transition was his emerging conviction that no other leader—specifically, Generals Ludendorff and Hindenburg—could provide the leadership required for the rebirth of Germany. In the late twenties, this new identity of the charismatic leader was established. In my opinion, Hitler was a charismatic prophet in both stages: as a drummer and Führer. My use of charismatic leadership follows Max Weber's definition:[269] It refers to an extraordinary quality of a person, regardless whether this quality is actual, alleged, or presumed. Charismatic leaders were viewed by Weber as transitional revolutionaries who appear in times of crisis and great need for political and social change. A charismatic leader can enhance life, such as Mahatma Gandhi, Pope John XXIII, and Albert Schweitzer, or destroy life, such as Hitler. Even though he viewed himself as constructive, Hitler was, notwithstanding some constructive deeds, a destructive charismatic leader with paranoid delusions.[270] One implication of Hitler's mercurial identity is that many persons, even devoted followers, stated that it was difficult to understand him—and there are also some doubts among historians as to whether Hitler was a strong or a weak leader. Hitler was a prophet, and prophets can remain mysterious and still be followed, regardless of whether they appear strong or weak, rational or irrational. They also can make contradictory statements, speak to their followers in riddles, and, to use a Zen term, present koans or impossible tasks and questions.

Maintaining the identity of a messianic leader is at best a very difficult task. For Hitler, the identity of the "drummer" was already quite taxing, and the loftier task of being a prophetic leader was even more difficult. At the Parteitag on 13 September 1936, Hitler exclaimed jubilantly, "It is the miracle of our times: That you found me amongst many millions. And that I found you is Germany's fortune."[271] It is my impression that, notwithstanding all the talk about Providence selecting him, Hitler was never quite sure of the "miracle." To maintain this belief, he needed constant reaffirmation through his achievements and successes, and beyond that he needed confirmation through the approval of the masses. Hitler was quite amenable to suggestion, and the veneration manifested in the Führer myth maintained his identity. When successes turned into failures, when the Führer myth eroded, Hitler's identity was threatened. Preserving the Führer identity, however, was so important to him that he maintained it desperately with the utmost determination, finally at the cost of his perception of political reality.

Hitler's complex identity, which was rigid but also shifting and full of contradictions, can be described only by taking into account his deep ambivalence. Another condition that impinged upon a strong and clear identity was his inclination to play-act. When Hitler quoted from the Bible, "So then because thou art lukewarm and neither cold nor hot, I will spit thee out of my mouth,"[272] he was defending not only against the ambivalence of his followers, but against his own, which extended back to his early childhood when he formed ambivalent images of his parents. He both loved and hated his father. Even when he praised his father, referring to him as the "old gentleman" (as he also did President von Hindenburg), there was a trace of condescension in it. Hitler adored his mother but at the same time was angry and suspicious of her because she submitted to his father and did not side with and protect her son. All of Hitler's relationships with his siblings were distant, yet he remembered them in his will. For Eva Braun he expressed affection, but also callous disregard. His beloved Geli had to suffer under his avuncular tyranny. Hitler maintained ambivalent relationships with many important allies and foes, such as Mussolini and Stalin. Once more, I cite the important statement in *Mein Kampf* about being torn by love and hate.[273] Even about the Jews, Hitler was ambivalent; he overestimated and at the same time despised them,[274] even asserting that there was something good in all races. Hitler was a consummate actor, and persons in his environment often could not tell whether he was bluffing or acting seriously. He prided himself on hiding his motives and never letting other persons discern what he intended to do. This, incidentally, is in stark contrast to the fact that rarely, if ever, has a political leader announced his program in such detail as Hitler did in *Mein Kampf* and the Second Book so many years before the execution of it. To some extent, this can be explained by the fact that Hitler was willing and even eager to explain his program but was secretive about tactics. Hitler stated many times that the Jews must be destroyed, while the killing actions were prepared and executed in secrecy. What else could one call this but confused ambivalence, notwithstanding the dreadful fate that befell the Jews? Ambivalence is a universal human trait, but Hitler's ambivalence was extreme. One of the great puzzles is the fact that a near majority of Germans made such an ambivalent person their leader.

Little is known about persons with whom Hitler identified or whom he imitated. Just as he rarely gave credit to others for ideas, he was loathe to acknowledge models or to admit any identification with other individuals. Every human being identifies to a degree with parental figures. It is my impression that Hitler identified ambivalently with both parents. Perhaps he identified with the cruelty of his father and passivity of his mother. Two persons whom he placed above all others could be considered models: Richard Wagner and Frederick, King of Prussia. As a teenager, Hitler tried to imitate (and surpass) Wagner by attempting to compose an opera. During adulthood, however, Wagner was not a model whom Hitler wanted or was able to imitate but a source of inspiration, the greatest German composer and dramatist, a genius whom Hitler admired and protected. He identified, however, with some of Wagner's operatic figures. His favorite opera was *Tristan and Isolde*, in which Tristan falls in love with Isolde, King Marke's wife, and the two lovers die in atonement for their sin. Hitler particularly identified with Parsifal, the pure fool who cured the ailing (syphilitic?) King Amfortas, and with Lohengrin, the hero of secret origins. He was intrigued by the *Ring* cycle, and he deeply appreciated this story of murder, greed, deceit, incest, and also social justice. Probably, this led Waite to assume that what Hitler appreciated most in Wagner's works was the incest motif. Indeed, both Hitler and Wagner (especially in *The Valkyre*) were preoccupied with incest motifs.

Frederick the Great, the martial King of Prussia, aesthete, philosopher, and in his personal relations a rather disagreeable and arrogant man, was

Hitler's all-time hero and a definitive model. He was impressed that, against great odds, King Frederick won victories against superior adversaries, Russia and Austria. Hitler admired the king's courage and ruthless determination. In difficult days, he found solace in thinking of the Prussian king, whose picture hung in his workroom. Hitler put Frederick the Great high above Napoleon, whom he respected as a unique military genius[275] but criticized him for his nepotism and because he abandoned the Jacobins who helped him to power.[276] It is understandable that Hitler praised populist revolutionary leaders like Garibaldi and Cromwell, more remote models. Surprising was that he had only faint praise for Martin Luther. Although he saw Luther as a revolutionary leader who rebelled against the Pope, and gave him credit for translating the Bible, which established modern German, he also deplored the translation of this "Jewish hair-splitting tome."[277] It is understandable that Hitler viewed Jesus, the revolutionary leader fighting against the Hebrew high priests, as a model. Mind-boggling, however, was Hitler's previously mentioned remark that, like Moses, he would not see the Promised Land.[278] Is it some clue about his preoccupation with possible Jewish ancestry?

After trying to make a case that Hitler, in his core identity, was a prophet, I would be less than candid not to cite a statement in which he rejected the identity of a prophet: "If some persons, in their enthusiasm about the resurrection of our people, want to forcibly make a prophet of me, a second Mohammed or Messiah, I can only declare that I feel no talent to appear as a prophet or messiah."[279] As a twentieth-century secular leader, Hitler could not possibly admit openly that he was or wanted to be a prophet or messiah. He was too sensitive about what would enhance or diminish himself in the public view, and clearly an unabashed statement about being a messianic figure would offend some sensibilities, just as it at one time had offended Dietrich Eckart.

The Social System

Social Class and Social Mobility

Hitler's parents' strong upward mobility was evident. After Alois Sr. left his native village and joined the Imperial Customs Service, he climbed to the highest position his education would permit. Clara Hitler helped her husband establish a solid lower-middle-class home. It is impossible to ascribe Adolf Hitler to any social class, because his social mobility was phenomenal. In his downward social descent in Vienna, Hitler became acquainted with the lowest social strata, and during his spectacular rise after World War I, with the highest class. While he despised and feared the *Lumpenproletariat*, he loved and appreciated the skilled German worker and almost pathetically considered himself to have been such a worker in the past. In fact, Hitler was forced to do manual labor, as an unskilled worker, during a short period of time. He considered the lower middle class weak, constantly threatened by the danger of descent and fearful of the classes above, but most of all the upper and upper middle classes—professionals and executives in business and industry—as cowards and weaklings. The aristocracy, for whom he had no good words, he called degenerate. Hereditary aristocracy was not fit to rule, and he thought monarchies—particularly the Austrian monarchy—deserved to be abolished.[280] One of Hitler's strong convictions was to provide the opportunity for optimal development to every German. He falsely stated that he himself had not had such an opportunity because his parents had been poor.[281] Opportunity for personal development for German citizens was one of Hitler's important social concepts. In *Mein Kampf* and in his speeches, he used the slogan, "a free path for the able," copied from U.S. slogans about America being the land of unlimited opportunity. Clearly, such a chance was reserved for the German nationals and nobody else. Education should be provided for the best, but not to make half-apes into lawyers.[282]

Hitler believed in a unified society of Führer, party members, and masses. He completely rejected the Marxist concept of class struggle. It was very important to him to win over German workers and destroy the two existing workers' parties. He cherished the idea of uniting "workers of the fist and brain." All workers would receive their just dues. Indeed, fringe benefits for workers under National Socialism were considerable, though they were accompanied by a lack of self-determination. In Hitler's view, antagonism between social strata must be adjudicated by rational and just leadership. He felt contempt for the Social Democrats. Only once he praised them, giving them credit for toppling the Hohenzollern dynasty.[283] For German Communists and Bolsheviks he had more respect, but viewed them as bitter enemies.

Leadership in Large and Small Groups

Hitler's understanding of large groups (masses) and his exceptional ability to handle them were described earlier. In all likelihood, personal experiences and a natural talent for understanding and handling the masses were more important to him than the study of books about mass psychology. The responses of large groups of people—in huge meetings and at the national congresses—contributed more than any other factor to Hitler's identity as a charismatic leader. His contact with the masses was through large and eventually enormous meetings such as the party congresses. During the later war years, Hitler's speeches were held less frequently, and when his rendering became less eloquent and convincing, he was worried that the responses of the masses would change, too. Hitler was worried about a loss of popularity, but also angry when the masses didn't respond, believing they were not worthy of him. One could almost speak of an "Antaeus" syndrome (in reference to Antaeus, the mythical giant who lost his strength when he could not touch the earth and was strangled by Hercules in midair): Hitler was losing his strength because he could no longer touch the masses. In his last words, Hitler expressed the hope that a new flame of hatred would rise again from the ashes. Fortunately, a new spirit of democracy and liberty arose in Germany and Austria.

Less is known about Hitler's relationship with small groups. In his early endeavors to recruit a cadre, he attracted aggressive men who shared his ideology. He expected the men who formed his cadre to be absolutely loyal to him—he told General Halder that loyalty to him and National Socialist beliefs was more important than military ability. Men who were suspected of disloyalty were quickly expelled by Hitler. Loyalty meant more than personal loyalty; it meant adherence to Hitler's ideas. In his governance of the Reich, Hitler followed the traditional pyramidal structure of the military. The commander-in-chief is advised by a general staff and gives orders to line officers below him, who, in turn, adhere to the same principle. A problem arose, however, in that Hitler's civilian sub-leaders—ministers as well as Gauleiter—were also extremely aggressive men who established their own fiefdoms. Cooperation among these competing men was poor and resulted in lack of coordination and, at times, chaos. Hitler had an extraordinary need to be and to remain the top person. Hitler's remark about the poppy heads that stick out and have to be cut down illustrates this.[284] He demonstrated this trait from the earliest days of his political career, culminating in the murder of his comrade Röhm and the SA leadership. He expected his orders to be followed, and nearly always they were. Severe sanctions followed disobedience in both war and peace. His charismatic leadership was questioned only by few, and then mostly after massive defeats during the war. Dissent troubled Hitler greatly, and he was particularly sensitive to real or imaginary dissent on the part of some generals, whom he suspected and accused of not being good National Socialists. Hitler had a profound dislike for democracy and parliamentary procedures, which originated after he had been a spectator in the Austro–Hungarian parliament in Vienna. He asked for debate when he felt it was necessary, and it had to be submitted in a reverent but not obsequious manner. Throughout his book Peterson emphasized that any limitation of Hitler's power was caused less by the government structure than by his helplessness—which, of course, could never be admitted.[285]

Of explanatory value for the functioning of groups are the theories of W. R. Bion.[286] Bion found that group leaders and members have anxieties about their positions in the group and their transactions with each other that interfere with the group's tasks. Defending against these anxieties, group members develop what Bion called basic assumptions about the group and group leadership. In the dependency assumption, groups become inactive and over-dependent on the leader, or else hostile to the leader if he does not fulfill the dependency need. In the fight–flight assumption, group members want action at all costs, fight with each other and the leader, and also turn against real or imaginary outside enemies. In the pairing assumption, members conspire to produce a messianic leader. These descriptions of dysfunctional groups are reminiscent of Hitler's groups. All three of Bion's basic assumptions can be observed in Hitler's transactions with groups. Helmut Stierlin reaffirmed the applicability of Bion's theories to Hitler's performance in groups.[287] The most important is the pairing assumption, leading to the birth of a messianic or charismatic leader. Many historians (e.g., M. Broszat and H. Mommsen) have considered Hitler's groups dysfunctional and referred to the organizational chaos in the Third Reich. However, Hitler's groups also functioned very well, for a while all too well. Broszat explained this on the basis of the fanaticism of both the leader and his followers.[288]

Hitler was a charismatic leader. He believed that his mission was dictated by Providence, and a very large number of Germans—in all likelihood during the war a majority—believed him. Early successes and achievements reinforced this belief, both in the masses and in Hitler. Even at the time of his defeats, his followers stuck with him. The Third Reich was not defeated by inner collapse or insurrection, but by the victory of the Allies. As always occurs with charismatic personalities, Hitler's followers believed in him fervently, while others either remained untouched or hated him. Hitler was keenly aware of this and was infuriated by individuals who remained indifferent to him. No satisfactory answer exists as to why groups and individuals join and believe such a leader. It often happens in times of great distress. What is the propensity of a group or nation to do this? The phenomenon has been studied in cults, but National Socialism was too varied to be considered a cult—although it had similarities. Alexander Mitscherlich spoke of a compulsion to submit (*Unterwerfungsdrang*),[289] Peter Hofstätter of addiction to a leader (*Führersucht*).[290] Both believed that the Germans have a propensity for such behavior. Mitscherlich in particular believed that the Germans have a tendency to simultaneously submit and revolt. T. W. Adorno and colleagues established a certain personality type that they called the authoritarian personality.[291] This type, they assumed, was typical for Hitler's followers. The characteristics are conviction of superiority, conservatism, a view of the world as threatening and unfriendly, use of projection, and sharp differentiations between the strong and the weak, and the leader and the led. Hofstätter could not confirm these findings and remarked that this type also would fit the Puritan settlers who became the spiritual fathers of the United States.

A Strong or a Weak Leader?

Historians differ as to whether Hitler was a strong or weak leader. The intentionalist faction, amongst them Eberhard Jäckel and Karl Dietrich Bracher, believed that Hitler was the central person determining National Socialist policy and action. According to them, the basic National Socialist policies were derived from Hitler's personality and philosophy. In the extreme, National Socialism is equated with Hitlerism. Opposing this view are other eminent Hitler scholars, such as Martin Broszat and Hans Mommsen, presenting the structuralist school that views Hitler as a weak dictator. They maintain that the actions of National Socialism were largely dependent on other centers of power, resulting in the previously mentioned chaotic National Socialist power structure. Broszat assumed the chaos was the result not of Hitler's deliberate divide-and-conquer strategy, but of his inability to manage his dysfunctional and rambunctious vassals. Mommsen saw in Hitler a weak dictator, more a propagandist than a leader, a man eager to protect his prestige and reputation, unable to make realistic and incisive decisions.[292] Amongst others, Maser referred to Hitler's passivity and unwillingness to commit himself and make decisions, citing many examples of indecisiveness. Reading Maser, one almost gets the impression that Hitler could not decide in the morning whether he should first step into the right or the left leg of his trousers. A thorough psychosocial analysis of Hitler's major decisions, such as Irving Janis has conducted on other leading politicians, still needs to be done on Hitler.[293] Hitler's decisions would often fit Janis's category of seat-of-the-pants decisions. Indecisiveness and unwillingness to commit himself, however, were real. Hitler had a great need to keep everything in flux. With surprise and admiration, Goebbels described throughout his diaries how Hitler would let events come up to him and then make the "right" decision at the very last moment.[294] In agreement with Kershaw, I do not view Hitler as a weak or indecisive leader.[295] He alone made the important decisions. General Jodl remarked that only Hitler could unleash a world war.[296] His example of the spider (in the German language, a female symbol of aggression) that rushes in once its helpless prey is caught in its web does not convey weakness. Last but not least, a charismatic leader need not be a strong leader, as long as his followers believe he is strong.

Hitler's Value System

Ethnocentricity and art were supreme in Hitler's value system. He viewed himself as an artist–politician, which fit his charismatic leadership style. In the monologues, he stated that the power he obtained was justified only because he would make culture the foundation of German governance.[297] Many times he asserted that he wanted to be an artist and had become a politician against his will; perhaps he believed it. In the monologues he expressed the wish to retire after victory to the company of artists and philosophers.[298] Under Hitler's leadership, the arts received greater support in Germany than in other nations; however, it was art as Hitler defined it. It had to enhance what he viewed as the German spirit and, particularly in architecture, German power. He built for eternity, or in any case for a Reich of a thousand years. Art forms since the beginning of expressionism he viewed as deceitful, ugly, deformed, degenerate, and sick. This included some of the greatest painters of all time, such as Van Gogh. Eliminating such art was his task, and Hitler went about it with all his might. Because of these acts he will be remembered not as a friend but as a destroyer of art and culture.

Hitler was a fanatic aggressive nationalist. This conviction grew in Vienna, the capital of a multiethnic empire, and during World War I, in which he fought with enthusiasm for a greater, more powerful Germany. The defeat of Germany while its armies were still fighting on foreign soil and the Peace of Versailles created in Hitler and millions of Germans a sense of deep humiliation and betrayal, and a fervent desire to overcome it. When Hitler promised to reckon with inner as well as outer enemies, restore German power, and conquer space to provide Germany with needed resources, many Germans listened and joined him. He built his message into a theory of social Darwinism that was rampant at the time.

Sociopsychological Implications of Hitler's Worldview (Hitler's Vulgar Darwinism)

It was most important to Hitler that National Socialism should be based on a scientific worldview. In the eleventh chapter of *Mein Kampf*, he gave a succinct description of the underlying theory of his worldview, which he preached as early as 1920.[299] It is derived from misunderstood and popularized concepts of Charles Darwin, Jean-Baptiste Lamarck, and Ernst Haeckel, whom he never quoted. According to Hitler, life is an eternal struggle in which the strong races, nations, or individuals conquer, subdue, enslave, or kill the weak.[300] This parallels events in the animal kingdom, where strong animals kill weaker animals—at the end, however, "to be devoured by the sole survivors, bacteria."[301] It is a depressing view, counteracted only by Hitler's conviction that, under his leadership, the German race would dominate the other nations, create a Germanic paradise, and rule the world: "Germany today, and tomorrow the world." According to Hitler, the roots of the National Socialist philosophy "followed the eternal laws of life."[302]

One tenet was to improve the race, which Hitler proposed to accomplish through selective breeding and the elimination of genetically unworthy and undesirable genetic material. Selective breeding—in which individuals who fulfilled Nazi racial standards would breed racially desirable issue—was never of any practical significance; neither was Himmler's idea of forced separation of "Nordic" children from their parents in the conquered Eastern territories.[303] The other approach to prevent the propagation of "defective human beings" was recommended by Hitler first as sterilization, and later, after the outbreak of World War II, as euthanasia, de facto a killing procedure. Some 90,000 mentally and physically ill people were murdered. He defended such actions as the most humane measure, a phrase also used in connection with the genocide.[304] Hitler had no difficulty obtaining approval from many German anthropologists, racial hygienists, and physicians, and was enraged by pressure against it from the churches.

Hitler believed that the worst crime against race was the mixing of higher and lower races. He wrote: "A foreign racial fragment has entered our people. It must yield." At the bottom of that same page, he, as the great healer, recommended: "It must be done quickly. It is not better to extract a tooth by a few centimeters every three months. When it's out, the pain is gone."[305] Mixing races would inevitably lead to the physical and mental decline of the higher race.[306] It was a sin against the will of the Creator. Hitler pointed to the "Germanic immigrant" in North America who remained the master of the continent, contrary to the bastardized South American.[307] The worst and most disastrous "bastardization" was the miscegenation of Aryans and Jews, which the Jews wanted to bring about in order to destroy the Aryans.[308]

Hitler's Conquest of Living Space (*Lebensraum*) and Lust for War

Hitler was convinced that he had to conquer land in the East. It was not just the need for food, but the need for industrial raw materials—metals, oil, and rubber. In a lucid treatise, Jäckel described this need, which guided Hitler's foreign policy.[309] Binion explained Hitler's appetite for territory and resources on the basis of his infantile oral frustration following a four-year period of breast-feeding.[310] I have expressed my doubt about such data before. Furthermore, Hitler's views were not unconscious and not unrealistic. Yet space in the East could have been obtained by peaceful trade agreements. This would have suited Stalin—for the time being—but Hitler wanted to conquer space because he did not trust Stalin and loved war.[311]

Hitler's lust for war was consciously motivated but goes back to his childhood.[312] He expressed his love for war in numerous statements, such as "I became more enthusiastic about everything that was connected to war or, for that matter, with soldiers."[313] On one occasion, he asserted that a country needs a war every twenty years lest it degenerate,[314] but hypocritically added that, as an ex-soldier, he could not be in favor of war.[315] Hitler's early belligerence was reactivated by rage and revenge over humiliating and "undeserved" losses and reinforced by the Free Corps members, ex-soldiers who held similar sentiments.

Since his adolescence, Hitler had seen himself as an ardent German patriot. He hated and despised the Austro–Hungarian monarchy because it was a multinational state. He felt an extreme pride in all that was German, considering Germans superior to any other nation at times to an absurd degree, claiming for instance, that only the Germans could perform Shakespeare and that the Germans had played a crucial role in establishing the United States.[316] Was Hitler's world view typically German? Was he a German prototype—and Mussolini a typical Italian, Stalin a typical Georgian? In general, I am reluctant to come to such a simple conclusion. Yet Karl Bracher, one of the most eminent political scientists of the Third Reich, entertained the idea that Hitler, with his principles, rigors, and perfectionism, was "typically" German.[317] On the lighter side, the Austrians called Hitler a German, but Beethoven an Austrian. I am reluctant to accept national stereotypes, yet Hitler's social Darwinism, his attraction to martial matters, and even his sense of inferiority—which he vigorously denied—have a German tint.[318] For other nations in varying degrees, Hitler had little understanding or liking. He intensely disliked the French,[319] had contempt for all Slavs,[320] belittled southern Italians,[321] strongly disliked Americans,[322] despised the Swiss,[323] and called Sweden and Denmark lousy states.[324] He had very little understanding of nearly all races outside of Europe—notwithstanding some superficial friendly words for Arab nations and for Japan. Yet he was aware of the threat to "the white race" of Japan's possible military expansion into Southeast Asia and Indonesia.[325] Fantasies and thoughts about changing Germany's plight, about revising and, in good time, expanding its frontiers in a new war, a new reckoning, occurred to Hitler early after the defeat of the First World War.[326] He would destroy Germany's enemies. France and Russia were high on his list, but most of all Hitler wanted to destroy the eternal enemy: international Jewry.

Hitler's Fanatic Anti-Semitism

The archenemy who had to be eliminated, "one way or another" (*so oder so*), was the international Jew. Haffner mockingly stated that, according to Hitler, all nationalities engage in fierce but clean fights, except for the Jew, the eternal spoiler, who wants to destroy everybody.[327] Hitler's anti-Semitism was not the ordinary German anti-Semitism.[328] Beginning with the Gemlich letter and ending with his political testament, Hitler described Jews not as defined by their religion, but as a race, and later as a nation or national community that was the enemy of mankind and wanted to dominate or destroy Aryans and pollute their blood. Hence, the Jews must be removed. His fear and hatred of Jews was reflected in endless hateful diatribes in which he used metaphors derived from bacteriology, parasitology, toxicology, and oncology. Although as an adult Hitler did not believe in a corporeal devil, he ascribed qualities to Jews that depicted them as the devil. Like the devil of German folklore, he saw the Jew-devil as both cunning and dumb.[329] He saw himself performing the work of the Lord by destroying this devil. A statement in the Bormann documents illustrates the paranoid character of Hitler's destructive anti-Semitism:

> I have always been absolutely fair in my dealings with the Jews. On the eve of war, I gave them one final warning. I told them that, if they precipitated another war, they would not be spared and that I would exterminate the vermin throughout Europe, and this time once and for all. To this warning they retorted with a declaration of war and affirmed that wherever in the world there was a Jew, there, too, was an implacable enemy of National Socialist Germany.
>
> Well, we have lanced the Jewish abscess; and the world of the future will be eternally grateful to us.[330]

At times, Hitler proposed less radical measures than other National Socialist anti-Semites such as Himmler, Heydrich, and Streicher. At other times, he stated that the Jew was more satanic and bloodthirsty than Streicher imagined.[331] In any case, Hitler was the most important anti-Semite. Only he had the stature to unleash the forces, with or without an order, that resulted in the genocide. He needed and had helpers, sympathizers, and passive bystanders to support him and execute his wishes, and became quite angry when some Germans did not support his anti-Semitism.[332] A minority did; the majority looked the other way. Hardly anybody resisted.

Goldhagen asserted that Hitler found willing executioners among the Germans.[333] This cannot be doubted, but the number of actual executioners was relatively small and had to be supplemented by executioners from other nations, notably Latvians and Ukrainians.[334] As far as the participation, knowledge, and approval of the wider German population is concerned, more needs to be learned. The cooperation of vocational groups—such as the clergy helping to identify who was a Jew, the railroad workers transporting the victims to their deaths, and physicians organizing or carrying out killing procedures—certainly existed. Much of the murder remained a secret for a long time. My impression, based on interviews with individuals such as Dr. Ella Lingens (who worked as an Aryan physician prisoner in Auschwitz), friends, and family members, is that the secret was fairly well kept. More accurately, perhaps—and this is also based on interviews (e.g., with Professor Hans Strotzka, who served in the German army at the Eastern front)—many persons were not eager to know or to inquire, because it was dangerous and upsetting knowledge or because they admired and loved Hitler and, like Winifred Wagner, did not want to see "the dark side" of Hitler and National Socialism. Some knew, such as Dr. Erich Bielka (a childhood friend, later foreign minister in the second Austrian Republic), who also served in the German army and saw evidence such as abandoned Jewish villages and was told by superiors not to inquire further.

The Five Phases of Hitler's Anti-Semitism

How did Hitler's anti-Semitism develop? Five phases can be distinguished: (1) the ethnophobic anti-Semitism of the Linz period; (2) the resentful anti-Semitism of the Vienna period; (3) the racist (political) anti-Semitism of the period following Germany's defeat in World War I; and (4) the implementation of Hitler's anti-Semitism after the seizure of power, leading to (5) the genocide during World War II.

PHASE I: ANTI-SEMITISM DURING THE LINZ PERIOD

In Linz, young Hitler demonstrated hardly more than the prevalent xenophobia and ethnocentricity. Considerable anti-Semitism existed in the Austrian provinces, but according to Hitler, who described himself as an ardent nationalist, none existed in his family.[335] Almost mockingly (and probably wrongly), he described his father as a cosmopolitan person without any prejudices. It is more likely that Alois Sr. sympathized with Schönerer's party and was not only anticlerical but also anti-Semitic. Few Jewish students attended Hitler's middle-school classes, and no hostile encounter was ever reported, yet there was considerable anti-Semitism in the population, particularly among the professors and students. Kubizek reported a remark by Hitler that the local synagogue did "not belong here." One Jew with whom Hitler had contact at that time was Dr. Eduard Bloch, who treated Hitler's mother during her terminal illness. Hitler's anti-Semitism in Linz was the prevailing anti-Semitism. He was an anti-Semite before he came to Vienna.[336]

PHASE II: ANTI-SEMITISM IN VIENNA

A short time after his arrival in Vienna, according to the accounts in *Mein Kampf* (written seventeen years later), Hitler had become extremely anti-

Semitic. In angry and crude words, he stated that Jews dominated and degraded the cultural and economic life of the city, from which he, after being rejected by the Academy of Arts, felt excluded. One of the frustrated young man's major grievances was that Jews corrupted sexual life of Vienna and were responsible for the spread of syphilis, a Jewish disease and a scourge of humanity. Hitler described the Jews of Vienna as materialistic, dishonest, dirty, and corrupting sexual mores.[337] No accounts exist to indicate that Hitler suffered any humiliation or harm from Jews, notwithstanding Paula Hitler's claim that he was cheated by Jewish art merchants.[338] Actually, he was never cheated by Jewish merchants, but by his Aryan buddy Hanisch, whom he promptly denounced to the police. He reported his dislike of Jewish music, but while in Vienna he liked the composers Mendelssohn and Mahler. The social and sexual misery of Hitler's Vienna years, his resentment over the social injustice he observed in Vienna, and the need to find the most readily available scapegoat explain Hitler's relatively unpolitical anti-Semitism of envy and resentment. He approved of but also criticized two major anti-Semitic politicians of this period, Karl Lueger and Georg von Schönerer, and was not inclined to join their parties. It has been clearly proven that Hitler had not only sold his pictures to Jewish merchants, with whom he was on friendly terms, but also entertained social relations with Jews in the Männerheim and even visited the wealthy art-loving Jahoda family.[339] In Vienna he did not become a member of the Antisemitenbund, because the Antisemitenbund did not exist at that time. His reading of anti-Semitic literature was restricted to pamphlets and daily papers. Wilfried Daim's claim that the fantastic writings of Jörg Lanz von Liebenfels profoundly influenced him seems exaggerated.[340] He later distanced himself from Liebenfels's fantasies. The question arises as to why Hitler emphasized the Viennese origin of his anti-Semitic Weltanschauung so strongly. One simple explanation is his misery and resentment about his failure and his need for an alibi. A second explanation is that he wanted his followers to believe that the source of his anti-Semitism was based on real experiences and not on book knowledge or dialogues with his tutors in Munich. His anti-Semitism in Vienna could be called an anti-Semitism of anger, frustration, and envy. It was not the extreme, organized anti-Semitism that developed after the war.

PHASE III: ANTI-SEMITISM DURING THE KAMPFJAHRE

The third period of Hitler's anti-Semitism started at the end of the First World War. In preparation for his assignment to "educate" soldiers before their discharge, he attended classes in which anti-Semitic lecturers talked about the role the Jews and Bolsheviks had played in Germany's defeat. Like many Bavarian burghers, Hitler was horrified by the Communist *Räterepublik* and its Jewish leadership. His principal tutors were Dietrich Eckart and Alfred Rosenberg, who showed him how vicious and destructive Jews could be. Together, Eckart and Hitler found evidence in the anti-Semitic literature, notably the Bible and by anti-Semitic authors such as Theodor Fritzsch,[341] as well as Jewish self-accusations such as those of the philosopher Otto

Weininger.[342] Information about a Jewish conspiracy came from the German Baltic party philosopher Rosenberg.[343] Rosenberg drew Hitler's attention to the vicious and fraudulent *Protocols of the Elders of Zion*, which Hitler considered valid and truthful.[344] The *Protocols* matched his own view regarding the existence of a Jewish world conspiracy. Soon afterward, Hitler absorbed some of the anti-Semitic writings of Richard Wagner's son-in-law, Houston Stewart Chamberlain, although he never quoted Wagner's own anti-Semitic writings.

Already in September 1919, Hitler expressed his new ideas in a letter to another *V-Mann*, Adolf Gemlich: Jews are not a religious community, and the interests of this alien group—money and dominance—are opposed to the interests of Germans. Hitler declared Jews to be a serious threat. For the first time he spoke of a racial tuberculosis. He opposed an emotional anti-Semitism that found its expression in pogroms and proposed a political racist anti-Semitism with the elimination of civic privileges for the Jews and their ultimate removal.[345] Until the *Machtergreifung*, Hitler's statements were inflammatory propaganda statements made in numerous lectures in the 1920s, amongst them the important lecture, "Why Are We Anti-Semites?"[346] and the so-called hate speech.[347] The rabble-rousing propaganda was successful. Ever-increasing masses streamed into the lecture halls, and Hitler was personally rewarded by the applause and confirmation he received from German anti-Semites who adopted and shared his values. Making the Jew a major scapegoat had paid off. It did not escape Hitler's attention that later the international community protested only weakly against his aggressive anti-Semitism, and showed appalling reluctance to help with Jewish emigration. An extremely vicious statement was made in a private conversation with Josef Hell. The eight-page, single-spaced report by Hell—deposited under oath—describes an extremely angry statement followed by a coldly rational explanation made by Hitler in 1922:

> Once I am really in power, then the annihilation of Jews will be my first and foremost task. When I have power, for instance, I will have gallows erected on the Marienplatz in Munich, as much as traffic permits. Then Jews will be hanged, one after the next, and they will remain hanging until they stink. They will remain hanging as long as hygienic considerations permit. After they are cut off, the next group will be hanged, until the last Jew in Munich is extinguished. The same will happen in other cities until the German is at last freed from the Jew.[348]

Hell asked Hitler why he wanted to annihilate this intelligent nation, to whom the world owed so much in the areas of art and science. Hitler calmed down quickly and described his reasons in a sober and dispassionate manner. He asked himself against what part of the nation a hate propaganda would be most likely to succeed. A victim had to be found against whom the fight would also be financially advantageous. He discovered that there were few Germans who, at one time or another, had not been annoyed with the Jews.

A small number of Jews owned a large portion of national wealth. If the hatred against the Jews was triggered properly, the resistance to radical action would quickly break down. They couldn't protect themselves, and nobody would want to be their protector. This statement was made twenty years before the Jews were murdered. Hitler made ferocious anti-Semitic statements in *Mein Kampf*. Angered by his combat gas injury, he recommended putting 12,000 or 15,000 Hebrews under gas.[349] Such early statements have been interpreted as indications of Hitler's intent to eradicate the Jews even before the seizure of power. In my opinion they were fantasies, but these fantasies became a terrible reality after he gained power. They also indicate a high degree of outright opportunism in his anti-Semitic agitation.

PHASE IV: ANTI-SEMITISM AFTER THE SEIZURE OF POWER

Anti-Semitic actions against German Jews were initiated under Hitler's tight control immediately following the *Machtergreifung*. He reluctantly curtailed some pogroms fomented by the SA at the entreaty of his Finance Minister, Schacht, who feared repercussions from the international finance world, and he put anti-Semitic actions on the back burner during the Olympic Games in 1936. Yet except for such tactical reasons, the pursuit of his anti-Semitic goals was relentless and merciless. The earliest anti-Semitic act was the removal of Jewish officials in the Reich bureaucracy. It was a program that could be accomplished easily, without resistance, and it ensured a "cleansed" and cooperative bureaucracy for the Führer. A most important step in Hitler's anti-Semitic program was the implementation of the Nuremberg Racial Laws in 1935, in which he took a strong interest. The Nuremberg Laws may be considered the most crucial decision in his program to destroy the German Jews. It opened the door to all further acts by depriving Jews of their citizenship rights. The Nuremberg Laws were comprised of three laws, the German Citizenship Law, the Law to Protect German Blood, and the German Flag Law. The Nuremberg Laws stipulated: (1) that Jews became second-class citizens—not Reichsbürger but unwanted Staatsbürger—which opened the door to unlimited discrimination, deprivation, and expropriation; (2) that "German blood" must not be contaminated with Jewish blood through marriage or extramarital intercourse (a crime called *Rassenschande*, or racial defilement) and, at Hitler's specific request, that employment of domestics under the age of forty-five in Jewish households be forbidden (possibly motivated by Hitler's concern that his paternal grandmother was impregnated by a Jew when she worked in a Jewish household); and (3) that Jews were not permitted to display the German flag (or, more important in everyday life, to wear swastika pins). Within the context of these laws, Jews and persons of mixed Jewish blood (*Mischlinge*, i.e., half Jews, quarter Jews) were never satisfactorily defined. Actually, many Jews took comfort in the Nuremberg Laws, hoping they would enable Jews, as second-class citizens, to have a relatively orderly existence and pursue their livelihoods in business and industry.

Anti-Semitic measures rose to new heights after the annexation of Austria. In Austria, the Nazis were able to achieve more in a few months than they had been able to accomplish in Germany in years. It was not just a cold and "rational" approach that Hitler advocated. During the *Kristallnacht* a wild, planned program of humiliation took place, with the vicious aftermath of forcing the Jews to pay for the damage that had been inflicted upon them.[350] Before the beginning of the Second World War, Hitler warned world Jewry not to start a war—likely a projection of his intentions.[351] He was most concerned about blaming the Jews for the war, and not himself.

PHASE V: THE GENOCIDE

After the onset of World War II, a new situation evolved. The brutality of war made it possible to replace forced emigration and expropriation with deportation and murder. From his experience with the euthanasia program, which was initiated on Hitler's order but had to be concealed because of protest by the churches, he had learned not to give direct orders and to let others—primarily Himmler, Heydrich, and their underlings—do the dirty work in carrying out the Führer's wishes. The existence of the genocide or holocaust is accepted by all respected historians; only malignant cranks deny it.[352] Serious controversy exists only about the extent of the genocide and its causes. At the beginning of World War II, the persecution of the Jews took on catastrophic proportions. During times of war, ethical codes change, and conduct that cannot be imagined in times of peace—murder, mutilation, destruction—becomes celebrated. Hitler was keenly aware of this. Just as he waited with the euthanasia program, he waited with the destruction of the European Jews.[353] One can safely assume that without the war the genocide could not have occurred. This does not mean that the war caused the genocide any more than the darkness of night produces crimes. Certain crimes occur more easily in wartime, and are less likely to be punished. Furthermore, Hitler stated a number of times that the Jews were responsible for the war and had to be punished. This conviction was strengthened when he became worried that he would not win the war, leading to extreme embitterment and vengeance. It was Hitler's firm belief that, without the "drunken Churchill" and the "insane Roosevelt," both servants of the Jews, the British never would have declared war. One can also assume that Hitler had to project whatever guilt he felt about the war onto the Jews.

No direct order by Hitler for the genocide has been found. This has led to different interpretations by historians. Tim Mason distinguished two groups: the intentionalists and the functionalists.[354] The intentionalists assume that Hitler made the important decisions derived from his extreme anti-Semitic ideology. The functionalists assume that the genocide was the result of many local actions and a cumulative radicalization inherent in National Socialist politics. Some historians, such as Martin Broszat, Christopher R. Browning, and, most convincingly, Saul Friedländer, found that these divisions have not furthered genocide research. Browning did not accept the concept of Final Solution as a fixed goal before the war, but recognized Hitler's fierce anti-Semitism as a driving force that made the genocide possible.[355] For Hitler, the constellation was right when the number of Jews in the Third Reich and its occupied territories had increased greatly, when it became easier to kill than to create reservations, when the chance to deport them to Madagascar or "the East" disappeared, and when the choice was narrowed to outright killing or letting Jews die as slave laborers from disease and exhaustion. Hitler was quite explicit about this in the monologues, and also in statements to Admiral Horthy.

On the basis of existing documents, it is evident that Hitler knew about the genocide; with his eagerness to know details, he probably even knew some operational details. David Irving was wrong when he maintained that Hitler was uninformed and only learned about the genocide in 1943. Hitler stated in 1941 that he was the only one who could have decided whether Jews had to be marked by the Star of David. If he assumed responsibility for this detail, it is unlikely that the murderous actions occurred without his consent.[356] Secret orders or even hints of the Führer's wishes would have been enough for Himmler and Heydrich to implement actions. Lack of secrecy about the euthanasia also induced Hitler to stop a program that was close to his heart, and he did not want to repeat this mistake. He also felt that the broader German population was not ready for outright genocide. Based on some hints contained in Himmler's statements, it is possible that Hitler preferred that Himmler go down in history as the executioner of Jews, while he (Hitler) would be the future messiah.[357] It is not known, and never will be known, what Hitler and Himmler discussed when they were alone. We only know that the two men's reasoning was strikingly similar.

One more important consideration is the following: Although no Hitler order mandating the genocide has been found, no Hitler order for stopping the genocide has been found, either. Obviously, only he could have issued such an order. It is evident that Hitler never stopped the terrible events, which he could have done had he so desired. This, in my opinion, establishes his intent and guilt as much as if he had issued an order in writing. Even when defeat was inevitable, Hitler did not relent and did not stop the genocidal actions. According to Aronson, Hitler wanted revenge for the bombing terror, the Jews had lost their value as possible hostages, and he probably assumed that Churchill and Roosevelt would not bomb concentration camps or the railroad tracks leading to them because they did not want a "Jewish war."[358] At the end, Hitler expressed his satisfaction that he could avenge the misdeeds of the war, for which the Jews were responsible, and he admonished his followers never to forget the racial laws.

During the editing of this manuscript, I read Saul Friedländer's new book about the Jews in Nazi Germany, in which he defined Hitler's anti-Semitism as redemptive anti-Semitism, different from other brands of anti-Semitism.[359] Friedländer referred to Hitler's view of Jews as evil and destructive and his idea that he—the redeemer—had the task of protecting the world from such evil by removing and killing the Jews. I arrived at a similar view, not through historical but psychological analysis, which induced me to consider Hitler a destructive and paranoid prophet. Furthermore, I offer a hypothesis about how Hitler's redemptive anti-Semitism might have been shaped by certain personal experiences—such as his concern over personal and national degeneracy.

Psychodynamic Theories about Hitler's Anti-Semitism

Philosophers, historians, sociologists, anthropologists, theologians, and psychoanalysts have tried to explain, justify, or condemn anti-Semitism. Psychoanalysts have searched for unconscious roots for the hatred of Jews. According to psychoanalyst Rudolf Lowenstein, anti-Semitism is often caused by unconscious hatred of a paternal authority figure in the Oedipal triangle.[360] Such hatred also is noted in non-anti-Semites, which renders the explanation unsatisfactory. Nevertheless, several other psychoanalysts have used it as a central explanation in their attempts to explain Hitler's anti-Semitism. Gertrud Kurth stated that young Adolf felt guilty about his Oedipal fixation on his mother and his hatred of his father.[361] He later displaced this unconscious hatred to his mother's physician, Dr. Eduard Bloch. Consciously he respected and felt gratitude toward Dr. Bloch, but unconsciously he was jealous of the intimate contact between the physician and his mother. In addition, according to Kurth, Hitler was resentful of Dr. Bloch's inability to cure his mother. Kurth, however, did not point to any malpractice on the part of Dr. Bloch. Hitler's reaction was simply an unconscious reaction of patients and family members toward a physician who was unable to help. I find this interpretation too general and insufficiently backed up by specific data.

Another attempt to explain Hitler's anti-Semitism was made by psychohistorian Rudolf Binion, who assumed that Clara Hitler suffered from a "psychogenic" cancer and received a lethal dose of iodoform from Dr. Bloch, who in addition charged his patient rather steep fees. Binion's assumptions are based on billing notes written by Dr. Bloch's wife and on rather odd calculations of how much iodoform powder and iodoform gauze were used in the treatment of Clara Hitler's purulent post-operative wound.[362] No medical evidence has been found to indicate that Clara Hitler died from either of the two lethal types of iodoform poisoning—an idiosyncratic reaction or severe hepatic damage. Rather, it appears that she died from the metabolic breakdown caused by her breast cancer. Hitler also acknowledged that no cure for cancer existed. Of course, it still could be possible that Adolf believed, consciously or unconsciously, that Dr. Bloch was responsible for his mother's death, but evidence for this is lacking. Consciously, he was grateful to his mother's physician, sending him hand-painted postcards and, after the annexation of Austria, protecting him until he emigrated, quite late in 1941. Dr. Bloch's daughter even mentioned that the grateful son kissed Dr. Bloch's hand—at the time not an unusual sign of gratitude and respect.[363] Peter Loewenberg also objected to Binion's quantum leaps from the odor of iodoform gauze to the combat gas poisoning incident in 1919, and then to the gassing of the Jews during the later part of the Second World War.[364]

Another set of explanations was presented by R. L. Waite.[365] He started out with the assumption that Hitler was uncertain as to whether his father was an Aryan or half Jew, making Hitler possibly a quarter Jew. The principal source for this is Hitler's private request to his lawyer, Hans Frank, to investigate Hitler's family tree. Frank maintained that he discovered a sexual liaison between Hitler's paternal grandmother, Maria Schickelgruber, and a young Jew in Graz, in whose house she worked. Although evidence for such a liaison was never found, Hitler remained uncertain about his ancestry. Waite also pointed to Hitler's dislike of his "large nose" and his body odor—which are stereotypes of the "ugly Jew." More evidence about Hitler's doubt and concern comes from strange statements about his ancestors and lineage in the monologues[366] and in another statement: "Clearly, everybody has ancestors. No one is alive without ancestors. It is just a chance that one person's books are burnt while for another person one has found them."[367] Waite, however, went further and postulated that: (1) Hitler wanted to kill his father but instead killed the Jews; (2) Hitler felt guilty about incest and perversion and shifted his own guilt to the Jewish scapegoat, and thus felt justified in killing them; and (3) the more Hitler hated the scapegoat, the more he hated himself.[368] Waite's interpretation I find unconvincing. I believe that Hitler's thought processes and feelings in the area of anti-Semitism were much closer to the surface. Hitler recognized the value of the Jewish scapegoat and consciously used it to the hilt. The time when he recognized the value of making the Jews a scapegoat was in 1919, when the Jews were accused by many of being cowardly shirkers (actually, 120,000 Jews were killed in action during World War I), and of being responsible for the capitulation (when, in fact, Kaiser Wilhelm, General Ludendorff, and other leaders were). Additionally, the Russian Bolshevik Jews in Bavaria (actually very few in number) were perceived as an enormous threat. This does not deny that unconscious factors in the construction of the scapegoat thesis (which essentially is a form of projection and displacement) played a major role in Hitler's anti-Semitism. Irrational factors play an important role in the etiology of anti-Semitism, which is what makes it so inaccessible to exploration, logic, and reason. Certainly, this was the case in Hitler's anti-Semitism, as well, but to view Hitler's beliefs as predominantly unconsciously motivated is wrong. Hitler was keenly aware that making the Jews a scapegoat had enormous advantages for the unification of the Party. In a well-known, though not necessarily authentic citation, Rauschning asked Hitler whether the Jew should be destroyed. "No," answered Hitler. "Then one would have to invent him."[369] Waite raised the question, and also David Irving,[370] about whether killing the Jews was counterproductive to Hitler's war efforts, because he had to use important resources to kill the Jews rather than his enemies at the battle fronts.[371] In my opinion, it proves only that the destruction of the Jews was most important to Hitler. Even at the end, when the war was lost, Hitler expressed satisfaction that at least he had killed the Jews. Harold Laswell postulated that a leader's private neurosis can become his public policy.[372] One application of this hypothesis is my attempt to link his mission to eliminate the Jews to his conclusions about syphilis, which threatens Germany and the world with destruction.

Syphilis, a Jewish Disease and the Degeneration and Salvation Hypothesis

From the previous pages, it is clear that I consider the genital lesion hypothesis too unspecific to explain Hitler's anti-Semitism. Instead, I offer the degeneration–salvation hypothesis, which is better suited for explaining his mission. The ten pages devoted to syphilis in *Mein Kampf* are irrational.[373] Hitler expressed the same views eighteen years later, when he spoke of syphilis and Christianity (an offshoot of Judaism) as humanity's greatest problems. In a conversation with his lawyer H. Frank, Hitler mentioned that the only thing he would have omitted from *Mein Kampf* was his statement on syphilis.[374] It was not a change of mind, but rather the realization that these pages were too revealing and quite private. The statement reveals an association between his views of syphilis and anti-Semitism (e.g., Hitler wrote in one sentence about the mammonification (a Hitler neologism) of the human mating instinct and the Jewification (another neologism) of spiritual life, which enhanced syphilis).[375] He stated that syphilis was a Jewish disease. It is uncertain whether he meant that Jews were carriers of the disease,[376] or whether he referred to the role of the Jews in moral corruption and their alleged prominent role in the white slave trade.[377] According to Hitler, syphilis was one of the most vile problems of the nation, ignored by the authorities. He was deeply concerned that there was no effective treatment and that the cases of disease were not properly reported.

Hitler had highly idiosyncratic ideas about syphilis. He mistook syphilitic infections passed on from mother to child during pregnancy as hereditary syphilis in his tribulations, dwelling mostly on what syphilis would do to future generations: "The most visible results of mass contamination will be found in insane asylums and unfortunately in our children."[378] In his pages on syphilis, for the first time Hitler proposed that ruthless decisions be made to assure that defective offspring were not permitted to propagate, and that the incurable be pitilessly segregated to prevent the spread of disease. At the time, Hitler considered this a barbaric measure but nonetheless a blessing for posterity.[379] "The sins of the father are avenged down to the tenth generation. This applies to blood and race. Blood sin and desecration of the race (i.e., cross-breeding between Aryans and Jews) are the original sin in this world and the end of humanity which surrenders to it."[380]

Two questions come to mind. Is there any evidence that Hitler or his father had syphilis? Was Hitler referring to the degenerative malformation of his genitals from which, in my opinion, he suffered? In Chapter 8 I cite evidence that Hitler did not suffer from syphilis, in spite of Himmler's assertions. No concrete evidence exists to indicate that Hitler's father had syphilis or died from it, although such a cause of death is possible. It is worth noting that Hitler made allusions to an older, sexually promiscous husband (horny Siegfried) who infected an innocent and defenseless young wife.[381] The second question, whether Hitler thought his own putative congenital lesion of his genitalia—a stigma and manifestation of degeneration—had been caused by syphilis, is even more difficult to answer, but I offer the following speculations. In the event that Hitler had such a deformity and believed that it had been caused by syphilis, it would have resulted in increased hatred of his father and the Jews. I assume that Hitler became possessed with the idea of saving the Germans, and eventually all of humanity, from the great scourges—syphilis, Judaism, and its offspring Christianity—and that this contributed to his extraordinary sense of mission. One could imagine the following scenario: During his puberty and until the end of World War I, Hitler was depressed about his genital deformity. In Munich, after the end of the war, I assume he consulted a urologist—probably Professor Kielleuthner—who told him he could have been helped at an earlier age, but not as an adult. Kielleuthner possibly recommended a radiological examination of the lower back that revealed a spina bifida occulta. After that, Hitler steadfastly refused further X-rays of his trunk, even though they were strongly recommended by his physician and he did not mind having X-rays taken of his skull. He accepted his fate but resolved to help future generations through a program of prevention of syphilis and by elimination of the Jews. Immediately after the seizure of power, a law permitting very strict measures against prostitution was passed. When it drove prostitutes underground, and the incidence of venereal diseases increased, supervised prostitution was reinstated, particularly in the armed forces and in concentration camps, for Aryan prisoners. Of some interest is the fact that, within the German armed forces, a venereal infection was a punishable crime.[382] Hitler's other major remedy was early marriage, again raising the question as to whether his father was the "dehorned Siegfried who had sown his wild oats" and infected his young and innocent wife, as described in *Mein Kampf*.[383] Clearly, my statement is speculative, but it pulls together startling data and enables us to understand Hitler's emerging sense of mission. It is offered as one piece of the jigsaw puzzle.

Hitler's Ethics

When Christa Schroeder briefly encountered Hitler's surgeon, Dr. Carl Brandt, during a prisoner transport, she asked him, "Was Hitler a good person or a bad person?" Brandt replied: "He was a devil."[384] The concept of moral badness or evil has been debated for thousands of years by theologians, philosophers, and lawyers, and, quite recently, by psychiatrists and behavioral scientists. In the seventies I was strongly interested in medical ethics and read a tiny fraction of the enormous literature. Unfortunately, it left me more confused than enlightened; hence I offer my own, admittedly naïve, proposition. It may be difficult to define evil, but it is possible to state what an evil act is. It is an act of destruction carried out intentionally and not in self-defense. Ergo: Hitler was one of the most evil persons in the history of mankind.

Before the First World War, Hitler's ethics were not exactly ordinary, but also not remarkable. He worked to live but did not live to work. With the exception of Gustl Kubizek, he had no friends, but he socialized with people; one of them remarked that he had a good heart and a sense of social justice.[385] In sexual matters as a teenager and young adult he was a frightened Puritan. No antisocial act, marked selfishness, brutality, or crime or misdemeanor are known—except possibly some pranks, including the dubious goat prank, and a marked egocentricity and rigidity. His draft evasion and deceitful statement to the Austrian authorities cannot be considered severely unethical because Hitler was evading the draft out of conviction. He was a tax evader, but this was not unusual in Germany at Hitler's time. During World War I Hitler was a brave and conscientious soldier, a good comrade; no cruel acts are known to have occurred during this period. His buddies thought he was a loner and a prude, perhaps obnoxious, but not cruel or antisocial. In all civilians who become combat soldiers, however, a major ethical change is mandatory. A soldier is required to destroy the enemy, to capture, injure, or kill him and take his arms and possessions as booty. In modern times, warfare is regulated by rules and conventions that are obeyed to varying degrees. During the two world wars, as the fighting became desperate, these rules were often disregarded by leadership and soldiers on both sides. Certainly during the last phase of the war, Hitler was disinclined to follow the rules of the Geneva Convention, for example. A soldier is required to show loyalty and obedience to the superior officer and, ultimately, the commander-in-chief, as well as fidelity to fellow soldiers, a Spartan attitude, and a willingness to bring sacrifices and to put the common interest above individual interests. The common interest of the brotherhood of Germans (women had a supportive role) was to win battles and wars and to destroy or enslave the enemy (most of all, Jews, Bolsheviks, and Slavs). It was the doctrine of a radical social Darwinism. Hitler did not have to read about social Darwinism; he lived it. In *Mein Kampf* he stated: "[Nature] confers the master's right on her favorite child, the strongest in courage and industry."[386] He also wrote that the most aggressive fighting is the most humane.[387] During the *Kampfjahre*, Hitler expressed his views in shrill rhetoric, or in fantasies (e.g., when he told Josef Hell how he would hang the jews on the Marienplatz). Occasionally, he muted his views, particularly during the years of pseudolegality. After the seizure of power, the fantasies became dreadful realities. A milestone in the deterioration of conventional ethics was the murder of his own men: Ernst Röhm and the leadership of the SA. The approval of this act by President von Hindenburg and many Germans emboldened Hitler to proceed to worse deeds, including euthanasia and genocide. Hitler was quite aware of his deviations from conventional ethics and justified them by maintaining that he committed certain acts to safeguard the interest of Germany and National Socialism. At one time he even offered a cost–benefit explanation: "If one charges me that one hundred or two hundred thousand men lost their lives I reply: Through my activity so far the German nation has gained two and one-half million [author's comment: through the increased birth rate] if I demand ten percent as a sacrifice and have given ninety percent."[388] Hitler also remarked that Himmler did not shrink from using reprehensible methods, although that did not stop Hitler from using him.[389] These statements express a crucial aspect of Hitler's ethics: The ends justify the means.

Historians agree that Hitler as a ruler and warlord was extremely destructive and cruel. Even revisionists such as David Irving have conceded that Hitler was "a man of the radical act."[390] The list of cruelties is long, including orders such as the Commissar Order, the White Flag Order, the Night and Fog Order, and the Nero Order. Some of Hitler's orders were expressions of a reactive rage, such as the order to shoot prisoners of war after the Allied destruction of German cities, or to shoot survivors after torpedo attacks on Allied ships. Hitler stopped certain orders, such as the Commissar Order, after remonstrations by his general staff, particularly when he knew the war was lost. His tendency to react to what he considered betrayals and humiliations already existed before the war. It was manifested during the *Kampfzeit* when he chose "A Reckoning" as the subtitle for *Mein Kampf*. Early in the war, Hitler destroyed Belgrade after he felt betrayed by the Yugoslavian government. Cruel acts of retaliation included the killing of hostages and the burning of villages in response to crimes against Germans. Yet the worst cruelties were levied against the innocent victims in the genocide of civilians: Jews and Gypsies.

One specific aspect of Hitler's value system was his severity with criminals. With rare exceptions, no judgment was too harsh in punishing those convicted of crimes. Many times, Hitler overturned the judgments of legitimate courts. This spirit of extreme punishment was reflected both in traditional justice and particularly in the extralegal system of the concentration camps. Prison sentences were often changed into death sentences. Hitler often procrastinated, which was more an expression of his dilatory work habits than of mercy. Hitler's hardness in matters of criminal law was a deep conviction and exhibited itself in years of feuding with the conventional justice system, which he wanted to abolish. The severity of sentences was associated with a reduction in crime, although other factors (such as reduction of unemployment) also contributed to lower crime rates. Many citizens applauded it, but the price was horrendous—a heretofore unheard-of loss of freedom and human rights in modern Europe. A pertinent remark can be found in the monologues:

> Here [in a prison] a crook is fed at the expense of the community. After ten years in the penitentiary, he is already lost for the community. Who would give him work? Such a subject either should be put in a concentration camp for a lifetime or be executed. In this time [during the war], the latter is more important: An example should be created for all like him.[391]

In summary, one facet of Hitler's ethical code was the code of a vulgar social Darwinism. He postulated that goals justify the means. He exhibited exceptional cruelty. To understand this, it is essential to understand that Hitler wanted to overcome conventional ethics, such as the ethics of major Western religions, and replace them with the new ethics of a new National

Socialist man and a new master race. As so often was the case, Hitler was inconsistent and at one point even acknowledged that the Ten Commandments were valuable laws of order. It also must be kept in mind that Hitler saw himself as a highly ethical person. His closest and most prominent helpers—for example, Himmler and Goebbels—viewed themselves and each other as pure men. Hitler ultimately wanted to create a new man, one guided not by Judeo-Christian ethics but by new beliefs. His increasing fury with churches and traditional religions, discussed in the following section, can be understood in part as frustration about not reaching this goal.

Religion

As an adult, Hitler adopted a pantheistic belief, assuming a creative force that could not be fathomed.[392] At times, he referred to it as the law of nature. He believed that he and National Socialism simply reverently followed the laws of nature and the intent of the creator. He recommended such a faith to those he considered the best of his followers. He was opposed to atheism—to believe was better than not to believe.[393] He wanted to distance himself from Bolshevism and its doctrine that religion is opium for the people, although he later came close to such a view. Until his thirteenth year, Hitler was a practicing Catholic. His father did not believe in the teachings of Catholicism, but expected his children to be raised as Catholics by his pious wife.[394] In his childhood, Hitler was enthralled by the pomp and ritual of the Catholic Church. Allegedly, for a while he even considered becoming a priest. During middle school he made the life of his teacher of religion, Father Salo Schwarz, miserable with his provocative questions about God and creation.[395] While many teenagers raise such questions, and later calm down, Hitler never did. In essence, he adhered to his father's view that religion was for the stupid and old women.[396] During the war, in another context, he stated that the Russian peasants could be kept in a state of slavery, superstition, and ignorance by the Russian Orthodox Church.[397]

Hitler's attitude toward church and religion underwent marked changes, though essentially he always showed ambivalence. During the *Kampfjahre*, he insisted that religion remain inviolate, and that only fools and criminals would attack it. He opposed the Away from Rome movement.[398] Hess called Hitler a good Catholic—obviously a false statement—but perhaps Hess gained the impression that Hitler was an admirer of Catholicism. Indeed, he expressed admiration for the discipline of the Catholic Church and its ability to recruit priests from the people, and spoke positively of celibacy. Twenty years later, Hitler made very different statements. He castigated the Catholic Church—and even more the besotted Protestant churches—for the denial of earthly pleasures, saying "the Catholic paradise is so boring."[399] He also was highly critical of the self-serving business interests of the churches. In contrast to the Christian denominations, Hitler expressed some praise for Islam and Shinto, because they were heroic beliefs.[400] Judaism he considered the ultimate evil, which he was eager to prove using citations of biblical text. But even about Judaism Hitler was ambivalent, praising the Ten Commandments as good laws of order.

A milestone in Hitler's relationship with the Catholic Church was the Concordat, which he concluded in order to neutralize the church, while Pope Pius XII was motivated by his preference of National Socialism over atheistic communism. After the war began, both parties regretted the Concordat. A definite change in Hitler's attitude toward religion occurred in 1941, when he was effectively opposed by Catholic and Protestant theologians to give up the euthanasia program. His anger increased when he attacked the oppositional church leaders, Bishop Clemens August Count von Galen and Bishop Konrad Count Preysing. In due time, he would reckon with them, as he did with the Jews.[401] Christianity was the heaviest blow that humanity had to endure. Bolshevism was the illegitimate son of Christianity. Both were the miscegenation of Judaism. It was through Christianity that the conscious lie in questions of religion originated. In the ancient world, a glow of reverence could be surmised. It's work was tolerance. It was reserved for Christianity to kill uncounted numbers in the name of love. Its mark was intolerance.[402] Hitler lecturing about intolerance—quite startling! At different times, Hitler obsessed about what he could do about the church, concluding that it would be wrong to precipitate a fight with the church:

> It would be best to let Christianity fade away. . . . If we forcefully eliminate the church, the whole people will scream: Where is the substitute? . . . We will see to it that the churches do not profess any doctrines that are not in accord with our doctrine. We will push our doctrines and our youth will only hear the truth.[403]

In the summer of 1942, Hitler's anger with the churches increased:

> I will let the priests [Hitler used the derogatory term *Pfaffen* whenever he was attacking Catholic or Protestant clergymen] feel the power of the state, that they'll be stunned. Now I am just watching this. When I think they have become dangerous, I will have them shot. This reptile always rises when the state's power becomes weak. Therefore, it must be crushed under one's foot like a reptile.[404]

Friedrich Heer described Hitler as a preacher, prophet, and crusader who wanted to save the occident from a barbaric Eastern invasion. He also clearly recognized Hitler's ambivalence toward Catholicism. According to Heer, Hitler was a misguided Catholic who formed a counter-belief to his Catholic faith.[405]

Even though I consider Heer one of the most sensitive Hitler scholars, I disagree with him about the motivations for Hitler's ambivalence to the Christian Churches and religions and more specifically to catholicism. It was not a love-hate relationship but rather an impotent rage, that the Churches were a formidable power which he was unable to replace by what he called science and reason.

HITLER'S VIEW OF JESUS

Hitler had a strong interest in the life of Jesus Christ. Although he did not specifically mention any similarity with Jesus, Hitler viewed Christ and himself as revolutionary leaders. He stated, "The dear God uses a virgin to give birth to a human being, who delivers humanity through his death," "Christianity is the craziest thing a human brain in its madness could produce, a derision of the Divine. A Negro with his fetish is sky high above anyone who seriously believes in the miracle of transubstantiation."[406] In *Mein Kampf* he stated:

> [Christ] made no secret of his attitude toward the Jewish people, and, if necessary, he even took to the whip to drive from the temple of the Lord this adversary of all humanity, who then, as always, saw religion as nothing but an instrument for his business existence. In return, Christ was nailed to the cross.[407]

In the monologues Hitler was eager to assert that Jesus Christ was not a Jew:

> The Galilean, who later was called Christ, . . . was a people's leader who took a stand against Jewry. Galilee was a colony in which Roman legionnaires settled, and Jesus was certainly not a Jew. The Jews called him the son of a whore and a Roman soldier.[408]

Hitler maintained that Paulus trickily changed the teaching of the Galilean, who had the idea of freeing the land of Galilee from the Jews and was killed for it by the Jews. Hitler maintained that Paulus was one of the meanest "commissars." When Paulus noted that many people were willing to suffer death for the doctrine of the Galilean, Paulus had what he called his "inspiration"—that one can, if one does it properly, topple the Roman Empire, which the Jews hated. Paulus had the insight that one could topple it only by professing the equality of all people before one God, by elevating divine laws over secular laws, and by establishing one deputy of God on earth who would be above all secular laws. The declaration of war against Jewish materialism (by Jesus) was turned into the fundamental idea of equality of the inferior, the slaves. The religion of Paulus was nothing but a form of pre-Bolshevism.[409]

Many Germans saw Hitler as a messianic figure, but much of the rest of the world viewed him not as a savior but as a devil, the incarnation of evil. What kind of devil was he? I will not indulge in a theological differential diagnosis but rather turn to Goethe's greatest work, *Faust*. Mephisto appears in Goethe's study:

> FAUST: Who art thou?
> MEPHISTO: Part of that force which would do evil evermore, and yet creates the good.[410]

Hitler was the opposite; he maintained that he willed good, but he produced immense evil.

Hitler's Psychiatric Diagnoses

The difficulties in arriving at a medical diagnosis of Hitler were described in the previous chapter. To obtain a meaningful and concise psychiatric diagnosis of Hitler poses far greater obstacles. The variables of behavior are greater than the variables of biological systems, and the technology of biological assessment is more advanced than that of psychosocial assessment. During the last twenty years, committees of American psychiatrists devised a system of classification that was published as the *Diagnostic and Statistical Manual of Mental Disorders*, now in its fourth edition (DSM-IV).[411] The manual's operational definitions have reduced the linguistic confusion in the psychiatric Tower of Babel. It has been widely used in the regulation of psychiatric practice and is of some value in the classification of psychotic disorders, but it has had limited impact in solving the taxonomic problem of overlapping personality diagnoses that refer not to classes but to types. As Hempel put it, personality diagnoses are not mutually exclusive and exhaustive.[412] In my opinion, the manual is not a useful instrument in psychiatric research, and specifically not in pathographic research. Only Ellen Gibbels has used the DSM manual in describing Hitler;[413] the Hestons referred to a similar, older system of classification, the International Classification of Diseases, that includes both medical diseases and psychiatric disorders.[414] Using the DSM-IV classifications of personality diagnoses, not only in the case of Adolf Hitler, I often feel as if I were in a cheap clothing store: Nothing fits, and everything fits. I will henceforth discuss and critique some of the older diagnoses made by various authors in the past, particularly the diagnoses of antisocial personality disorder and borderline disorder, and finally support a politological diagnosis offered by Robert C. Robins and Jerrold M. Post.[415]

Diagnoses in Childhood and Adolescence

It is almost certain that Hitler in his early childhood suffered from temper tantrums, nightmares, eating problems, and perhaps—considering his excitability—nocturnal bedwetting, but no reports or observations to this effect exist. As I consider it likely that Hitler had a hypospadia, infantile nocturnal enuresis is likely, as well. A mild urinary incontinence might have existed in adulthood. Hitler's incessant bathing and hand-washing strengthen this assumption. Real proof, however, does not exist. With the onset of puberty, Hitler developed distinct difficulties. The highly intelligent boy failed miserably in school. In the contemporary culture of the Western nations, a learning disorder would have been diagnosed and the child brought to the attention of a school psychologist. During Hitler's childhood, this type of care was nonexistent. In Chapter 8 the diagnosis of attention deficit hyperactivity disorder was considered and rejected. Hitler explained his failure in school as the result of his opposition to his father. Naturally, the simplistic, descriptive diagnosis of oppositional conduct disorder suggests itself. Hitler's behavior persisted beyond his father's death, however, making such a diagnosis untenable. In my opinion, the sexual problems that are so common in puberty and the possible painful experience of becoming aware of a genital deformity at this stage of life might have increased his anxieties and learning difficulties.

Diagnoses in Adulthood

Psychiatrists possessed by a furor diagnosticus have enumerated quite a few diagnoses of Hitler: multiple phobias, anxiety states, hypochondria, hysterical reactions, neurotic oppression, sexual dysfunctions, psychosomatic illnesses, psychopathic personality disorder, hysterical personality disorder, narcissistic personality disorder, antisocial personality disorder (the most frequent Hitler diagnosis), and the catch-all borderline personality disorder. On the other end of the scale is the Hestons' statement that, until he became an amphetamine addict, Hitler was normal except for a few quirks.[416] It has been established that Hitler did not suffer from any of the major psychotic disorders (schizophrenic disorder, manic-depressive disorder, psychoses caused by psychiatric substances, or dementia caused by brain disease, such as his Parkinson's syndrome). Wolfgang Treher was the only clinician who made the diagnosis of schizophrenia.[417] He based this diagnosis on Hitler's "messianic delusion" and believed it began during late adolescence, in Vienna, at which time he considered Hitler completely demented. Profound disturbances of thinking and affect, characteristic for schizophrenia, however, did not exist. Regardless of whether one follows the classical descriptions by Emil Kraepelin and Eugen Bleuler or the information listed in the DSM-IV, criteria for schizophrenia are absent. No evidence exists to support Johann Recktenwald's assumption of a "moral insanity" as a late sequela of measles encephalitis or Economo's encephalitis lethargica.[418]

Fairly good agreement exists that Hitler suffered from a fairly large number of psychiatric symptoms: phobias, periods of anxiety states, hypochondriacal concerns, and a likely mild sexual dysfunction. Hitler's bacteriophobia and syphilophobia are significant for a historical assessment, while other symptom complexes contribute little. Many psychiatrists are inclined to elevate such symptoms to diagnostic terms if they are of a certain intensity, duration, and frequency. An enduring fear of syphilis, for example, becomes the diagnosis of syphilophobia. This is a simplistic way of thinking, not much different from bestowing on a person who habitually arrives late the diagnosis of latecomer, or labeling a person who has red hair a redhead. The two most frequent diagnosis of Hitler are antisocial personality disorder and borderline personality disorder.

ANTISOCIAL PERSONALITY DISORDER

The diagnosis of psychopathic personality was favored by the older generation of German psychiatrists. Oswald Bumke named Hitler an hysterical psychopath.[419] Hans Strotzka refined this diagnosis and called Hitler a fanatic psychopath with hysterical features.[420] Ernst Kretschmer, before the seizure of power, simply remarked: "In normal times we diagnose them; in disturbed times they govern us."[421] In the United States during the past decades, the term psychopathy has been replaced by the term sociopathy, and more recently by antisocial personality disorder—old wine in new bottles. This diagnosis is nothing more than a simple description of an asocial or antisocial person. The essence of the diagnosis is aggressive behavior unmitigated by guilt or regard for the concerns of other human beings. Its main aspects are a high level of aggression (including sexual aggressiveness), cruelty, and mendacity. The psychopath can be described like a two- or three-year-old who lives according to the pleasure principle, with little regard for others, reality, and ethical codes. Such persons do not learn new, unoffensive behavior or change their behavioral patterns after punishment. The long list of DSM-IV diagnostic criteria for antisocial personality disorder does not fit Hitler well. It is a list of terms more suited for the lower-class patient who violates the criminal code than for a political leader. Once when Hitler's secretary, Christa Schroeder, accused him in jest of stealing her flashlight, he responded: "I don't steal flashlights, I steal countries."[422] Hitler did not lie about trivia but broke all major treaties and pacts and deceived his enemies as well as the German people on a grand scale. Psychopathic persons are said to be incapable of close and loving relationships. Hitler claimed, credibly, that he experienced both intense hatred and love. Even though many persons may doubt that he could love, Hitler ambivalently loved his father and mother and also had close relationships with Geli Raubal, Eva Braun, and Dietrich Eckart, as well as fairly good but not close relationships with some of his helpers (amongst them Speer, Hess, his driver Schreck, and some secretaries). This is different from the ordinary behaviors of sociopathic personalities. Furthermore, the crucial psychopathology did not appear in childhood or adolescence but after he reached maturity, after the age of thirty. Yet although I believe little knowledge is added by calling Hitler a sociopathic personality, the diagnosis is of interest because, like no other, it focuses on the problem of differentiation between sick and evil. Furthermore, this behavior pattern emerged after the age of thirty, when Hitler became a politician. Except for the dubious goat incident, no cruelty to animals is known to have taken place in Hitler's childhood. It also must be kept in mind that Hitler not only committed horrendous crimes, but also wanted to be, and was, in a limited way, constructive. In his fashion, he tried to enhance German culture and improve social conditions for the Germans and related races—though not for others. One other objection to this diagnosis is that, more than any other psychiatric diagnosis, it exemplifies the dictum of my teacher, Professor Otto Pötzl, that many psychiatric diagnoses are forms of slander and abuse. Undoubtedly many have the desire to abuse or curse Hitler, but I object to doing this by abusing psychiatric terminology.

BORDERLINE DISORDER AND NARCISSISTIC DISORDER

Since the mid-fifties, the diagnosis of borderline personality disorder has become fashionable in the United States. It is a favorite diagnosis among psychoanalysts and psychiatrists with a psychodynamic orientation. Robert Knight used it first when he felt the need for a separate diagnostic category between schizophrenia and neurosis.[423] Since then, particularly through the work of Grinker,[424] Kernberg,[425] Kohut,[426] Mack,[427] and Masterson,[428] the concept has become popular. The diagnosis has been used differently by various authors, and any diagnostician would have to state whether he was using the description of the above-named authors, the approach of Wilhelm Reich (who used the term severe character neurosis),[429] or the definition (301.81) in the DSM-IV. It is really quite bewildering, but with some pushing and shoving Hitler could be fit into the Procrustes bed of 301.81. Little is gained by it, however, because Perry and Klerman[430] and Guze[431] established that the diagnosis cannot be reliably differentiated from other personality disorders, especially not from the antisocial, narcissistic, histrionic, and identity personality disorders. Still, Bromberg and Small made a major effort toward establishing this diagnosis.[432] Influenced by Kernberg's theories, they combined the diagnosis of a borderline personality and a narcissistic personality, and listed twenty-four items that are supposed to clinch the diagnosis. These can be divided into two groups: (1) simple and complex symptoms (general anxiety, poor human relationships, anger, hatred, cruelty, grandiosity, omnipotence, megalomanic self-image, risk-taking, hunger for praise, control and manipulation, demandingness, envy, apparent kindness, lack of enjoyment, self-contradictions and reversals, poor human relationships, ego weakness, ambivalence without warmth, defective conscience); and (2) complex symptoms (exhibitionism and voyeurism, neurotic symptoms, hypochondriasis, paranoia, and polymorphous perversions). It is impossible to handle such a laundry list unless one specifies what items are essential and necessary to arrive at a diagnosis.

DIAGNOSIS: A DESTRUCTIVE AND PARANOID PROPHET

While the diagnoses of antisocial disorder, borderline disorder, narcissistic disorder, and hysterical disorder are inadequate, they touch on important traits that Hitler displayed. The picture drawn by Robins and Post comes closer to the core of Hitler's psychopathology. These authors viewed Hitler as a destructive and paranoid charismatic leader, elaborating on his charismatic qualities. Hitler was loved by his fanatic followers and by a gullible population, not only in Germany and Austria, and, in turn, they felt certain that he loved them. This created the charisma of nurturance and dependence. Hitler was a powerful demonic figure who could do what his followers did not dare to do: the charisma of the outrageous, the redeemer. He had the charisma of the teacher who guided his followers and the masses toward his ideas, which he presented with a moralistic certainty. Robins and Post represented this complex under the heading of political paranoia, the title of their book, which describes the anti-governmental paranoid behavior of militia groups in the United States as well as that of paranoid charismatic leaders, amongst them—predominantly—Adolf Hitler.[433] For those who like short labels, political paranoia is the diagnosis. My own label is very similar: Hitler was a destructive and paranoid prophet. Usually one associates the word prophet with a good person—Mahatma Gandhi comes to mind. Yet there are bad prophets, such as Hitler, whose visions are apt to guide others to evil and destructive deeds. In the subtitle I spoke only of a destructive prophet, for brevity's sake. The destructive quality of Hitler, however, implies the paranoid quality. He created enemies, and had enemies in fantasy as well as in reality.

Normality/Abnormality

In the preceding pages I expressed my reservations about psychiatric diagnoses of Adolf Hitler. Precise and subtle description is superior to the inaccurate generalizations implied in the above-mentioned personality diagnoses. Nothing is gained by such diagnoses but a false sense of knowledge. While it is problematic to tag Hitler with a psychiatric diagnosis, it is easier to answer the question as to whether he was normal or abnormal. Within the psychiatric literature, the concept of normality is used in three contexts: statistical, normative, and clinical.[434] Using a statistical approach, a determination is made as to whether an act, trait, symptom, or diagnostic entity in a certain person deviates from the statistical average within a certain population. This approach presumes that characteristics can be measured or at least counted. All too often, however, they cannot, and hence we cannot say that certain traits of Hitler were or were not average. Leaders sui generis are statistically abnormal, and about Hitler as a person, one can say that he was unique, hence statistically abnormal. Thus, the statistical approach yields little useful information. Clinical abnormality means that organs, systems, tissues, cells, or subcellular structures do not function according to their design. This usually can be determined in biological medicine; in behavioral systems, which are more complex, it is often difficult or impossible. Gross abnormality can be discerned more easily, whereas subtle changes are difficult to delineate. The clinical boundaries are fuzzy between normal and abnormal behavior. It is difficult enough to determine psychological normality in ordinary persons; in leaders, it is particularly difficult. In ordinary persons, we try to assess whether an individual's needs were fulfilled or frustrated, whether the individual achieved or failed, and whether or not the individual follows prevalent ethical standards. In any innovative leader, this is difficult, perhaps impossible. Another difficulty in evaluating a leader is that, in the average patient, we assess according to minimal standards. In a leader, maximal standards need to be considered, which is very difficult at best. These include, for example, the leader's contribution to prosperity, cultural enrichment, and peace. Still, Hitler's terrifying destructiveness would justify calling him clinically extremely abnormal. Most persons in free societies would arrive at this same evaluation by using common sense; however, this is not a value-free judgment. In fact, most statements about normality have value connotations. Medicine is not a value-free system, and this is particularly true within psychiatric parameters. It is undeniable that our judgments about what is normal and abnormal are normative or value judgments. Although Hitler adhered to some traditional values (love for his country, beauty, and animals, and an appreciation of martial virtues such as courage), the main theses of his social Darwinism (the right of the strong to enslave or kill the weak) were fundamentally opposed not only to the teachings of Christianity and Judaism, but to the teachings of all major religions and ethical belief systems. Nevertheless, Hitler and some of his close associates, such as Bormann, Goebbels, and Himmler, thought of themselves as highly ethical persons, but, along with an uncounted number of lesser followers, they held the views of a primordial culture. And this happened in Germany, which until 1933 had ethical and legal standards neither better nor worse than the rest of the civilized world.

Another way of looking at the slippery problem of normality is to consider the so-called psychiatric sick role. The medical sick role and its implications for the physician–patient relationship were described in Chapter 8. Two psychiatric sick roles may be distinguished: the sick role of the severely disturbed person suffering from psychotic disorders, severe character disorders, or severe degrees of mental retardation; and the sick role of the mildly disordered person who suffers so-called neurotic symptoms, mild character disorders, psychosomatic illnesses, or what Harry Stack Sullivan called the headaches of living.[435] In the severe group, the patient not only is entitled to care, but is often forced by legal means to submit to treatment or detention. (In 1938, high-ranking military officers led by General von Beck and Colonel Oster tried, naïvely and unsuccessfully, to induce Professor Bonhoeffer, head of the Berlin University Psychiatric Clinic, to commit Hitler to a mental institution.) In the mild to moderate group, the assumption of the sick role is voluntary. Only a percentage of such persons assume this sick role by turning to psychiatrists and other mental health workers, physicians, clergymen, or para-medical healers. Treatments encompass a wide range of goals from attempting self-fulfillment to mere removal of symptoms. Hitler chose his personal physician, a general practitioner of medicine, Dr. Theodor Morell, to help him with both his physical ailments and his psychological needs (particularly his need for dependency). Hitler did not consider himself a psychiatric patient and never would have considered assuming any psychiatric sick role. Georg Groddeck, a free spirit amongst psychoanalysts, believed that Hitler could have benefitted from psychoanalysis.[436] In my opinion, Hitler had insights into preconscious processes but never would have considered any outright psychotherapy. Most politicians shun psychiatric help. In my view, psychiatrists and psychoanalysts who treat major politicians holding state secrets enter a relationship fraught with insoluble conflicts. Hitler never consulted a psychiatrist and was never examined by a psychiatrist. The "psychiatric report" by Dr. Joseph Brinsteiner, a general practitioner, was naïve and cannot be considered an expert professional statement. It is unlikely that Professor Foster treated Hitler in the last days of World War I. The only documented encounter, with Professor K. Schneider, a famous German psychiatrist, was not a professional encounter. Professor De Crinis made the diagnosis of a Parkinson's syndrome based on weekly newsreels but did not examine Hitler. Professor Wilmans got into serious trouble over diagnosing Hitler as hysterical, also without examining the patient. The book by Krueger, *Hitler Was My Patient; or, Inside Adolf Hitler*, is a fraud.[437] Ella Lingens heard from Prince Loewenstein that Freud refused to make a diagnosis of Hitler, stating that he would not render a diagnosis of a living person whom he had not seen.[438]

Responsibility for the Crimes

I already expressed my opinion that Hitler's paranoia was associated with his evil deeds. Before discussing the question of Hitler's responsibility for his crimes, it can be stated with some conviction that, if he had come to trial before the International Military Court for conspiracy to wage war, war crimes, and crimes against humanity, Hitler would not have entered an insanity plea. Hitler was convinced that he was not a criminal but a genius and a benefactor of humanity. Lawyers, historians, and psychiatrists have examined the question as to whether Hitler was responsible for his misdeeds. De Boor, an eminent forensic expert, considered Hitler clearly responsible.[439] Certainly, Hitler would have been competent to stand trial. His political and personal will, written hours before his suicide, is evidence of his mental competence. The insanity defense is based on the assumption of free will and postulates that a sane person may choose between good and evil behavior (defined by the criminal code). Most jurisdictions essentially accept what the grandfather of all insanity tests, the M'Naghten test, asserts, that a person is considered sane unless a defense on the ground of insanity proves that, at the time of committing the act, the party accused was laboring under such a defect of reason from disease of the mind, as not to know the nature and quality of the act he was doing; or if he did know it, that he did not know that what he was doing was wrong.[440] The Nuremberg Military Court, had it tried Hitler, would have used a similar test. Some jurisdictions in the United States have used other tests because the M'Naghten test over-emphasizes cognitive over affective criteria. One of the newer tests, developed by the American Law Institute, became known as the appreciation test and states that a person is not responsible for criminal conduct if, at the time of such conduct, as a result of mental disease or defect, he lacks the essential capacity either to appreciate his conduct or to conform his conduct to the requirements of law.[441] Hitler clearly was able to appreciate the nature of his conduct, even though he did not consider it criminal. He was responsible for his deeds. No court would acquit Robin Hood because he robbed from the rich to help the poor, and even less the desk murderer Hitler because he wanted to save the world from an imaginary Jewish Bolshevik peril or its destruction by syphilis. In some European countries and in some states in the United States, the concept of diminished responsibility or irresistible impulse has been used to obtain milder sentences. This would not apply to Hitler because, in his major decisions, he was under full control and even bragged about the rationality of his acts. De Boor raised the question as to whether amphetamine abuse could have contributed to Hitler's criminal behavior. As it is unknown how often, how frequently, and during what period of time Hitler took addictive drugs, the amphetamine factor's contribution to his crimes cannot be assessed. However, all of this is academic discussion. By committing suicide, Hitler deprived the judges of the Nuremberg International Military Court from trying and punishing him. Beyond any doubt the Nuremberg judges would have sent him to the gallows. Hitler's delusional destructive paranoid syndrome could be viewed as a symptom of mental disorder, but most of the personality functioned more than adequately. He knew what he was doing and he chose to do it with pride and enthusiasm. One could conjure up a scenario in which clever lawyers and hired expert witnesses argue whether Hitler was sane or insane, or a borderline case. I prefer to follow Hannah Arendt's formulation: Hitler believed he could decide what nations or races should inhabit this earth.[442] But nobody has this right. He was too dangerous to remain a member of human society.

Epilogue

MY WIFE, HERTA, once asked me what kind of a person Hitler was and what made him tick. I hedged; it is impossible to make a succinct statement. He deliberately misled people about himself and his motivations. At times he lied, and at other times he was shockingly truthful; often it was uncertain what he elected to do. Even the persons closest to him, such as Albert Speer and General Alfred Jodl, stated that they could not understand him. Others, like Winston Churchill and Dr. Karl Brandt, changed their minds, first praising, then condemning him. My wife did not give up, and asked me to describe Hitler's cardinal traits in a few sentences. I started out with a little lecture: He was a highly intelligent man with a large store of knowledge—much of it, and in critical areas, half-knowledge. The centerpiece of his *Weltanschauung* was his social Darwinism and anti-Semitism. He was a fanatic, but at the same time often ambivalent and defensive. His defenses, and particularly his projections could fill a psychiatry textbook. He clung to a paranoid belief in a Jewish world conspiracy against Germany. When his military and political programs failed, he became rigid and extremely vindictive. His destructiveness by far exceeded his constructive programs, which made him one of the world's greatest criminals.

Nobody who knew Hitler before 1919 would have predicted an extraordinary career. In 1919, however, a fundamental change occurred. The mildly depressed man discovered that he could speak and announced a world view and a program in fiery speeches. It would be naive to assume that Hitler had such an impact because he was an effective orator. He changed Germany and the world because he had a message and carried out a program—although, fortunately, the change did not follow his intentions. He promised that he would overcome Germany's defeat and humiliation, and make it the most powerful nation in Europe. He would destroy internal as well as external enemies, and, most of all, the archenemy, the international Jew. He promised to create a proud, nationalistic Germay, to restore the German army to its old glory, and to create employment and prosperity. He succeeded in these endeavors to a degree, but he wanted more. The charismatic leader was a prophet with a millennial goal. He wanted to create a German-Aryan super-man who would dominate Europe, and perhaps the world. To achieve this, he considered it justifiable to plunge the world into a war and to endlessly harass Europe's Jews, finally killing half of them. I have tried to contribute to the understanding of this process by offering what I call the degeneration-salvation theory.

I described the moderately severe somatic and psychosomatic complex illnesses during the last years of Hitler's life and concluded that they did not have any decisive impact on his political or military actions, except insofar as they accelerated his operations due to his fear that he would run out of time. In all likelihood Hitler abused amphetamines but was not addicted to them, like his great antagonist, Sigmund Freud, who used cocaine for a time but did not become addicted. No solid evidence can be cited indicating that Hitler's amphetamine abuse caused his crimes, but it might have played a role in lowering his inhibitions and in his committing such grave mistakes as declaring war on the United States. Ultimate proof for this assumption does not exist.

In much of this book, I have focused on Hitler's intrapsychic processes and the biological aspects of his health, touching only lightly on the social aspects of his activities. A prophet needs followers, however; without them he would be a lone crank. To study the psychosocial transactions between Hitler and his followers is a crucial task, perhaps also more feasible than solving the riddle of the inner man in Hitler. It would be important to know why some became willing executioners, why a few heroes resisted him, and, most of all, why the great majority of Germans closed their eyes and ears to the genocide. It would be important to know why some strong men and women, amongst them some good men, found it impossible to resist and contradict Hitler. Fortunately, these questions are being studied by social historians, and the answers might contribute to the task of prevention.

At this point, my wife interrupted my speech and asked, "Was he mentally ill?" "Yes, he was, in a way," I replied. "And what was the diagnosis?" she wanted to know. I mumbled something like political paranoia. For a while she sat quietly and thoughtfully, then said, *"Er war ein schlechter Mensch"*—he was an evil person.

Appendix 1

Chronology of Hitler's Illnesses and Treatments

Year	Event
20 April 1889	Normal birth; no anomalies reported, but, based on indirect evidence, it is likely that Hitler had a hypospadia and spina bifida occulta.
1897	Scarlet fever.
1900	Brother Edmund died of measles encephalitis.
1904	According to Hitler, acute pulmonary tuberculosis infection (very unlikely) during the summer.
1913	Rejection by the Austro-Hungarian military draft board: "too weak, unfit to bear arms."
1916	Shrapnel wound, left thigh and calf.
1918	Mild combat gas (mustard gas) injury.
1924	Medical examination in Landsberg prison. Hitler in good health except for dislocation of left shoulder joint.
1936	Consultation with Dr. Theodor Morell for skin disease of both calves (diagnosed eczema) and dyspepsia. Treatment: Mutaflor cure; "cured" after one year; Dr. Morell becomes Hitler's personal physician.
World War II	No significant illnesses reported during the first two war years. After 7 August 1941, detailed data about Hitler's illnesses and therapies are available from Morell's diary.

7–28 August 1941	Sudden onset severe malaise, dizziness, tinnitus, head pressure, and headache. Nausea, peculiar feeling in left temporal region. Temperature 38°C for two days, pulse 72–76, blood pressure 172 mm Hg. Enlarged liver; soft stools. Diagnosis: vascular spasms, head and intestines. Treatment: cold compresses to temples, laxatives, Yatren, bloodletting with leeches, later Mutaflor cure. Some improvement after two to three days, but headaches and tinnitus persist.
14 August 1941	Electrocardiogram report by Professor Weber: hypertension, question of initial coronary sclerosis.
30 August 1941	Free of symptoms. After this episode, Morell applied basic medication (20% glucose, Tonophosphan, calcium injections, vitamins) every two to four days. After mid-1943, treatment with first-generation male and female sex hormones, precursor of cortisone, organ extracts of heart and liver. Mutaflor and Enterofagos cures every one to three months. Three prominent features of Morell's regime were numerous blood pressure measurements, extreme polypharmacy, and the continuous examination of feces in connection with the Mutaflor and Enterofagos cures.
22–30 March 1942	Strong headaches and diminished vision in right eye. Blood pressure 170; pulse 66. Diagnosis: vascular spasms of head and intestines, dysbacteria of intestines, liver enlargement. Treatment: bloodletting with leeches, barbiturates, Brom-Nervacit, Optalidon.
9 December 1942	Intestinal gases, halitosis, malaise. Treatment: basic medications, Calomel, Enterofagos cure.
15 December 1942	Insomnia. (Hitler suffered from chronic insomnia.) Treatment: barbiturates in moderate doses, and bromides.
21 December 1942	Mutaflor cure.
3 January 1943	Bilateral head pressure.
13 January 1943	Head pressure, poor sleep.
22–30 March 1943	Very strong headaches, head pressure, tiredness, strong swelling of temporal arteries. (Morell ascribed the symptoms to the *Föhn*, a southern wind blowing from the mountains.) Blood pressure 154–156.
20 April 1943	Treatment: Enterofagos cure.
11 May 1943	Second electrocardiogram. Report by Professor Weber: progressive coronary sclerosis.
17 May 1943	Severe insomnia (Allied bombing of Möhntal Dam), abdominal pains. Treatment: laxatives, including Calomel; Enterofagos cure.

25–28 May 1943	Severe abdominal spasms lasting for days, extreme excitability. Treatment: laxatives, Eukodal 0.02, Eupaverin 0.015 (intravenous injection). Spasms ended after bowel movement.
11 June 1943	Complaints about intestinal gas. Pulse 72–78. Blood pressure 144.
17 June 1943	Treatment: Mutaflor cure.
3 July 1943	Head pressure following stress, only two hours' sleep.
18 July 1943	Severe abdominal pains, lack of sleep, dizziness after overwork and dietary indiscretion, much excitement. Diagnosis: spastic constipation, gastro-cardial complex. Because of pending conference with Mussolini, no strong sedative. Treatment: Euflat, olive oil, laxative, light abdominal massage, Eupaverin and Eukodal (intramuscular injection).
1 August 1943	Strong head pressure in right frontal area.
9 August 1943	Installation of oxygen inhaler apparatus in Hitler's sleeping quarters.
23 September 1943	Strong abdominal distention. Treatment: Eukodal, Eupaverin (intramuscular injection). Pain at injection site.
27 September 1943	Pain at injection site. Swollen forearm. Treatment: heat application.
3 October 1943	Continued pain in upper arm.
7 October 1943	Swollen arm (infection after injection).
14 October 1943	Poor sleep, much excitement.
17 October 1943	Called at 0600: Intestinal spasm. Treatment: Eupaverin and Eukodal (intravenous injection), which provided prompt relief.
19 October 1943	Treatment: Vitamultin forte.
27 October 1943	Abdominal distention, much excitement.
5 November 1943	Intestinal gas pains. Treatment: laxatives.
26 November 1943	Treatment: Mutaflor cure.
1 December 1943	Abdominal distention. Treatment: Eupaverin, Eukodal.
4 January 1944	Intestinal spasm. Treatment: Eupaverin and Eukodal (intravenous injection), drastic cathartics (Calomel).
10 January 1944	Intestinal spasm. Treatment: same.
29 January 1944	Tremor of left leg noted by Morell (general decline and tremor had been noted by others earlier, though not by Morell).

2 February 1944	Upper respiratory infection, tremor of left leg.
12 February 1944	Intestinal spasm for several days. Treatment: Eupaverin and Eukodal, drastic catharsis.
13 February 1944	Strong spasm, severe constipation, vomiting. Treatment: Eupaverin, Eukodal, Calomel, ricinus oil, other laxatives.
15 February 1944	Intestinal spasm, no sleep. Treatment: Eukodal, Eupaverin, heat application to abdomen, massage declined, chamomile tea.
22 February 1944	Jerkiness of leg, hand tremor.
3 March 1944	Eye examination: subjective diminished vision of right eye, mild anisohypermetropia, clouding of vitreous humor; no definitive ophthalmological diagnosis.
8 March 1944	Intestinal pain and constipation. Diagnosis: spastic constipation.
14 March 1944	Treatment: Vitamultin forte (intramuscular injection, for fatigue).
23 March 1944	Intestinal gases.
26 March 1944	Treatment: Vitamultin forte.
10, 20, 24 April 1944	Treatment: Vitamultin forte.
30 April 1944	Slight cold.
4 May 1944	Treatment: Euflat, anti-gas pills, heart muscle extract, oxygen inhalation.
5 May 1944	Electrocardiogram taken (not fit for evaluation). Slight ankle edema, head cold. Treatment: Strophanthin cure, Ultraseptyl, reduction of fluid intake.
9 May 1944	Head pressure (left side), tremor of legs. Treatment: Vitamultin forte.
28 May 1944	Treatment: Vitamultin forte.
14 July 1944	Influenza, conjunctivitis (after irritation by hair tonic).
20 July 1944	Bomb explosion caused multiple contusions, abrasions, burns on back and extremities, bilateral perforation of ear drums. Blood pressure 150. Healing of injuries after the assassination attempt took about 6 weeks (8 weeks for ear drums), tremor disappeared for 4 weeks. Otologist Dr. Giesing treated Hitler for chronic sinusitis of right maxillary sinus until early October; healed in mid-August.
2 August 1944	Pressure over eye. Treatment: venal section, 200 cc.
Mid-August	Recovery from head injuries, except for ear symptoms (which disappeared in mid-September). The leg tremor, which disappeared on 20 July, returned in mid-August.
8 September 1944	Pressure around right eye.

14 September 1944	Treatment: Vitamultin forte.
15 September 1944	Vertigo, head pressure, reappearance of tremor of hands and legs.
16, 20 September 1944	Treatment: Vitamultin forte.
24 September 1944	Icterus episode, 24 September to 10 October 1944. After two days of severe spasms, which were not alleviated by Eukodal/Eupaverin injections, Hitler developed a slight yellowish discoloration of the skin that lasted from 26 September to 2 October 1944. Severe spasms and constipation continued. Subjectively, Hitler felt very ill until 2 October; then gradual improvement. Urinalysis negative. No serum determination of bilirubin or liver function tests carried out. Treatment: drastic cathartics, fasting, Eukodal, Eupaverin, Scophedal 0.6, routine medication.
2 October 1944	Treatment: Vitamultin forte.
10 October 1944	Recovery from episode. Loss of 13 pounds.
14 October 1944	Symptoms of upper respiratory infection, lasting for the next six weeks. Treatment: first Ultraseptyl, later replaced by Tibatin.
15 October 1944	Insomnia. Treatment: Brom-Nervacit.
27 October 1944	Complaints of hoarseness.
30 October 1944	Intestinal spasm. Treatment: Eukodal, Eupaverin (intravenous injection).
3 November 1944	Increasing complaints about tremor of upper and lower extremities. Treatment: faradic currents, placenta extract (Homoseran).
6 November 1944	Insomnia, pressure across head.
7–10 November 1944	Intestinal spasms. Treatment: Eupaverin, Eukodal.
10 November 1944	Urinalysis: urobilin, urobilinogen positive.
12 November 1944	Urinalysis: normal.
13 November 1944	Intestinal spasm, slight sensitivity in gall bladder region. Treatment: Eupaverin, Eukodal. Diagnosis: cholecystitis (new diagnosis suggested by Morell's assistant, Dr. R. Weber).
16 November 1944	Treatment: Vitamultin forte.
22 November 1944	Glottis polyp. Treatment: removal by Professor von Eicken. Pathological report: singer's node. Good recovery.
8 December 1944	Intestinal spasms after great annoyance and disobedience of military officers. Treatment: Eupaverin, Eukodal (intravenous injection).

10 December 1944	Intestinal spasm. Treatment: Eupaverin, Eukodal (intravenous injection).
11 December 1944	Second icterus episode. Urine beer-brown, slight yellow discoloration of face (disappeared after one to two days).
16 December 1944	Strong tremor of left hand.
25 December 1944	Increased tremor. Treatment: placenta extract.
30–31 December 1944	Intestinal spasm. Treatment: Eupaverin, Eukodal.
2 January 1945	Great tension about Ardennes offensive.
5 January 1945	Treatment: calcium sandoz (intravenous injection), glucose, galvanization (for tremor). Both Morell and Hitler avoid sedatives to maintain alertness.
7 January 1945	Treatment: calcium sandoz (intravenous injection), glucose.
13 January 1945	Treatment: calcium sandoz (intravenous injection), glucose.
16 January 1945	Head cold (mild upper respiratory infection?). Treatment: glucose.
18 January 1945	Treatment: glucose (intravenous injection), Omnadin, Vitamultin forte.
20 January 1945	Treatment: calcium sandoz.
22 January 1945	Good appetite, ability to sleep with minimal sedation. Treatment: calcium sandoz, glucose (intravenous injection), liver extract (intramuscular injection), Vitamultin forte.
24 January 1945	Treatment: glucose, calcium sandoz (intravenous injection), Vitamultin forte (intramuscular injection), liver extract (intramuscular injection), Testoviron.
25 January 1945	Treatment: phenobarbital.
27 January 1945	Treatment: phenobarbital (refused), glucose, calcium sandoz (intramuscular injection).
1 February 1945	Treatment: glucose, calcium sandoz (intravenous injection), Vitamultin forte and liver extract (intramuscular injection)
3 February 1945	Treatment: glucose and calcium sandoz (intravenous injection), Vitamultin forte and liver extract (intramuscular injection), Betabion forte.
5, 7 February 1945	Treatment: glucose and calcium sandoz (intravenous injection), Vitamultin forte and liver extract (intramuscular injection).

10 February 1945	Treatment: venal section (on Hitler's request, unsuccessful). Blood pressure 154. Treatment: glucose, Gallestol, Pepsin wine, Brom-Nervacit, acidol pepsin (self-medication).
12 February 1945	Strong tremor. Treatment: venal section (at Hitler's insistence, considered unnecessary by Morell).
17 February 1945	Treatment: Strophanthin cure (on Hitler's demand).
6 March 1945	Tremors. Treatment: massage (declined). (Hitler believed the tremor was psychogenic.)
23 March 1945	Complaints about impaired vision.
7 April 1945	Ophthalmological consultation.
15 April 1945	Morell accepts diagnosis of Parkinson's syndrome. Treatment: Bulgarian belladonna cure, Harmin.
21 April 1945	Dismissal of Dr. Morell. Dr. Stumpfegger takes over. Treatment: Bulgarian belladonna cure (continued almost to the last day of Hitler's life).
30 April 1945	Suicide of Adolf Hitler (gunshot and potassium cyanide poisoning) and Eva Braun Hitler (potassium cyanide poisoning).

Appendix 2 *Hitler's Extended Family*

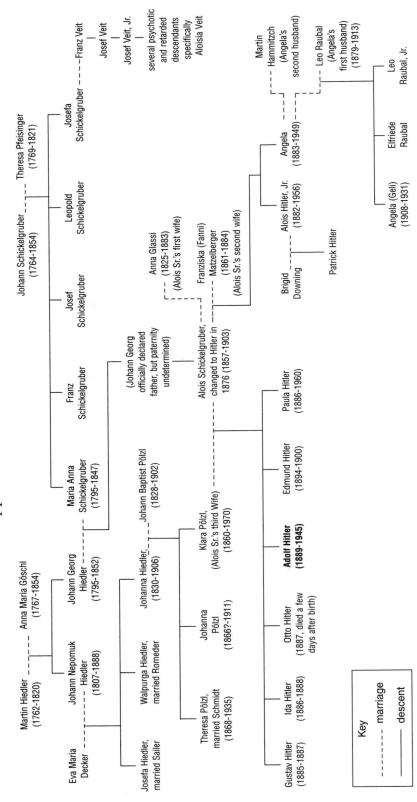

Key

- – – – – marriage
- ——— descent

Appendix 3

*Glossary of Medical Terms**

Albumin: Protein component of blood, abnormal component of urine.

Amblyopia: Impairment of vision without somatic signs.

Amoebic dysentery: A tropical infection of the gut caused by amoebae.

Anacidity: Lack of gastric acid in the stomach.

Analeptic (drug): Restorative, stimulating, exciting.

Analgesic: Pain-relieving substance.

Anemia: Reduction of red blood cells or hemoglobin.

Aneurysm: Ballooning of a blood vessel (e.g., of the aorta), formed by weakness in the wall of a blood vessel.

Angina pectoris: Attack of chest pain caused by diminished blood supply to the heart muscle.

Anisohypermetropia: Unequal degrees of farsightedness in the eyes.

Anticholinergic: An action by substances that block the parasympathetic system (such as increased intestinal activity).

Aphasia: Loss of expressive language or comprehension of language caused by brain lesions.

Arteriosclerosis: Common disease of old age; thickening of the artery walls and narrowing of arteries resulting in a variety of dysfunctions of different organs, especially the brain and heart.

Ataxia: Inability to coordinate muscular movements, caused by brain disease.

Atherosclerosis: A form of arteriosclerosis characterized by plaques of cholesterol and lipoids inside the artery lining, with effects similar to those of arteriosclerosis.

* The author is indebted to the W. B. Saunders Company for the perusal of *Dorland's Illustrated Medical Dictionary* (Philadelphia, 1994) which helped in many definitions.

Atrophy: Wasting of cells, tissues, or organs.

Attention deficit hyperactivity disorder (ADHD): A common brain disease of unknown etiology that occurs in children and adults, characterized by marked restlessness and inability to concentrate.

Autoimmune: Immune reaction to one's own body tissue.

B. (bacillus) coli: *Escherichia coli*—normal inhabitant of the large intestines, which can also produce pathological effects.

Babinski reflex: Pathological reflex indicating central nervous system lesions of the motility centers and pathways.

Bacteriophobia: Fear of bacteria.

Basal ganglia: Deep areas of the brain regulating motility and vegetative functions.

Bechterev's disease: Inflammatory degenerative disease of the vertebral column resulting in deformity and stiffness of the vertebral column, pain, and impairment of motility.

Bilirubin: Gall pigment found in urine or serum in liver and gall bladder pathology.

Blepharospasm: Involuntary cramps of the eyelids after trauma to the eye and covering membranes.

Blood pressure, diastolic: Measurement of blood pressure at dilation of the heart.

Blood pressure, systolic: Measurement of blood pressure at contraction of the heart.

Brachial plexus: Nerve bundle innervating arms and hands.

Bradycardia: Slowing in frequency of heart rate.

Bruxism: Involuntary grinding of the teeth.

Bulgarian cure: Obsolete treatment of Parkinson's disease with extract of nightshade, later synthetic drugs containing atropine and hyoscine.

Carcinogenic: Causing cancer.

Carcinoma pectoris: Cancer of the mammary gland. (Clara Hitler's surgeon used the term "sarcoma pectoris.")

Cerebral vascular accident: Destruction of brain tissue caused by a blood clot or gradual occlusion of the artery supplying blood (e.g., arteriosclerosis).

Cerebral deficit: Reduction of intellectual, emotional, and willing functions caused by brain disease. *See also* Deterioration, cerebral.

Chalazion: Inflammation of sebaceous gland of the eyelid.

Chlorpromazine: A psychoactive drug, not available in Hitler's time.

Cholecystitis: Acute and chronic inflammation of the gall bladder.

Cholelithiasis: Acute and chronic inflammation of the gall bladder and gall duct, associated with gallstones.

Chordee (tethered chord): Variant of spina bifida occulta.

Chronic alcoholism: Generic, imprecise term for enduring abuse of alcohol, with personality impairment.

Coma: Total loss of consciousness.

Convulsive seizure: Violent muscular contraction with loss of consciousness.

Coronary sclerosis: Old-fashioned term referring to reduction of lumen of coronary arteries, by arteriosclerosis or other causes.

Cremaster reflex: Normal reflex elicited by stroking the skin of the upper leg near the scrotum, resulting in upward movement of the scrotum; absence may indicate lesions of the lower spine.

Cystopelitis: Inflammation of the bladder and pelvis of kidney.

Depression: Generic term covering everything from normal and abnormal reactions to losses, to lifelong low mood and vitality, and specific major psychotic conditions with feelings of dejection, guilt, and inactivity.

Deterioration, cerebral (*see also* Cerebral deficit): Denotes deterioration caused by brain disease.

Deterioration: Reduction of intellectual, emotional, and willing functions.

Dysarthria: Impairment of articulation of speech, caused by diseases of the central or peripheral nervous system.

Dysbacteria: Idiosyncratic expression by Dr. Morell, referring to diseases caused by degeneration of *Escherichia coli* bacteria.

Dyspareunia: Painful coitus.

Dyspepsia: Gastrointestinal symptoms without demonstrable organic pathology.

Dysphoria: Pathological change of mood.

Ectomorphic (asthenic): Constitutional type.

Edema: Swelling caused by fluid in tissue.

Edema, cerebral: Abnormal amounts of fluid in the tissue of the brain.

Ejaculation praecox: Premature ejaculation.

Electrocardiogram: Tracing of electrical activity in the heart muscle. (The terms used in electrocardiographic reports in Appendix 6 are not defined because they are of interest only to the medically informed reader.)

Encephalitis after measles: Severe, fatal brain disease.

Encephalitis lethargica (also Economo's encephalitis): Pandemic viral brain disease in the twenties, followed by late symptoms such as Parkinson's syndrome, sleep disturbance, and psychosis.

Endomorphic (pyknic): Constitutional type.

Eosinophile: A type of white blood cell.

Erythrocyte sedimentation rate (ESR): A test measuring the rate of sinking of red blood cells in plasma; useful in the diagnosis of infections, coronary infarct, and liver and vascular disease.

Erythrocytes: Red blood cells.

Euthanasia (National Socialist definition): Killing of undesirable, physically sick, or mentally ill persons.

Faradic current: Alternating electric current used to stimulate nerves.

Festinating gait: Short decelerating steps, seen in Parkinson's Syndrome.

Galvanic current: Unidirectional electric current used to stimulate nerves.

Gastritis: Inflammation of the stomach lining.

General paresis: Malignant psychosis and deterioration in the late stage of syphilis infection, fatal without treatment.

Giant cell arteritis (GCA): Chronic inflammation of blood vessels, especially the temporal artery, with headaches and visual symptoms. *See also* temporal arteritis.

Glottis polyp: Benign growth near vocal cords.

Granuloma: Aggregation of normal and abnormal white blood cells and epithelial cells in tissues forming nodes.

Hallucination: A false, incorrigible perception.

Hemi-paresis: Paralysis of one-half of the body.

Hemoglobin: Pigment in red blood cells that transports oxygen.

Hemoptysis: Coughing up of blood.

Hepatitis: Inflammation of the liver caused by viral and other infections, and also chemical agents (e.g., alcohol, other drugs). The most frequent forms of hepatitis are: (1) hepatitis A (transmitted by fecal route), (2) hepatitis B (transmitted by blood route), and (3) cholestatic hepatitis (probably an autoimmune disease).

Huntington's disease: Severe genetic brain disease characterized by impairment of motility and deterioration.

Hyalitis (asteroid or stellar): Disease of the vitreous body of the eye.

Hypertrophy, ventricular: Enlargement of the muscle of the lower heart cavity.

Hypnotic (hypnotica): Generic term for a drug (or drugs) producing or facilitating sleep.

Hypospadia: A congenital anomaly in which the opening of the urethra is located on the underside of the penis.

Icterus: Jaundiced skin and mucous membranes (such as the membranes covering the eyes), occurring in a large number of liver, gall bladder, and other diseases.

Immunosuppression: Inhibition of immune responses.

Impotence (male): Impairment of erection, ejaculation, and sexual desire in males.

Infarction: Death of tissue (necrosis) caused by insufficient blood supply. (A myocardial infarction is necrosis of the heart muscle.)

Intima: Innermost layer of a blood vessel.

Iritis: Inflammation of the iris.

Irritable bowel syndrome (Morell called it spastic colon): Disease of the large intestine characterized by painful diurnal intestinal spasms and constipation.

Ischemia: Symptoms produced by insufficient blood supply (e.g., myocardial ischemia, which causes symptoms ranging from angina pectoris to sudden cardiac death).

Jacob Kreutzfeld's disease: Chronic viral brain disease.

Kahn test: A test for syphilis.

Keratitis: Inflammation of the cornea.

Kyphosis: Increased convexity of the thoracic spine (hunchback).

Lachrymation: Excessive secretion of tears.

Leucocytes: Blood cells, differentiated by type into segmentophiles, rod cells, eosinophiles, monocytes, lymphocytes, and basophiles.

Logorrhea: Abnormal increase of output of spoken words.

Lupus erythematosus: Chronic systemic disease of the immune system, with dermatological and other lesions.

Manic-depressive psychosis: Major mental illness characterized by alternating manic and depressed behavior.

Maxillary sinus: One of the paranasal cavities.

Mental retardation (also called mental deficiency): Subnormal intellectual and emotional development caused by an acquired or genetic brain disease.

Meteorism: Accumulation of large amounts of gas in the intestines.

Micrographia: Diminution of size of handwriting, occurring in certain central nervous system diseases (e.g., Parkinson's Syndrome).

Monocytes: White blood cells.

Monorchism: Absence of one testicle in the scrotal sac.

Muscular rigor: Pathological rigidity of muscles in Parkinson's disease.

Mustard gas (yellow cross gas): Combat gas causing burns of the respiratory tract, eyes, and skin.

Myocardial ischemia: Diminuation of blood supply to the heart muscle.

Myocardial infarction: Damage to the heart muscle caused by obstruction of the blood flow in the coronary arteries.

Myoclonus: Involuntary contraction (jerking and twitching) of muscles occurring in some neurological diseases.

Narcotic: Generic term for drugs that reduce sensibility to pain, often impair consciousness and may produce personality changes.

Necrosis (necrotic, necrotizing): Decay or death of tissue.

Neuroleptic drugs: Generic name for drugs used in modern treatment of psychosis.

Nieden-refraction test: Obsolete German method of measuring refraction of close vision.

Normochromic: Relating to the normal color of red blood cells.

Nystagmus: Involuntary oscillating movements of the eye muscles.

Occult blood: Presence of blood in the intestinal tract that can be detected only by tests.

Oculogyric crisis: Attack of involuntary eye-rolling, occurring in encephalitis.

Oppenheim reflex: Reflex with lesions of motor tracks in the spinal cord and brain.

Optic papilla: Disc at the entrance of the optic nerve into the retina.

Optic atrophy: Atrophy of the optic nerve.

Papilloma: Benign tumor.

Parkinson's disease (paralysis agitans, also called Parkinsonism): Chronic brain disease, of unknown etiology, with characteristic motor and mental vegetative disorders described by James Parkinson.

Parkinson's syndrome: The main characteristics of Parkinson's disease; may have various causes, such as infections, drugs, vascular damage, chemical agents.

Parkinsonism, postencephalitic: Parkinsonism as a sequela of Economo's encephalitis.

Pathognomic: Characteristic for a specific disease.

Pellagra: Chronic disease caused by deficiency of niacin, vitamin B complex.

Photophobia: Over-sensitivity of skin or eyes to sunlight.

Placebo: Prescription of an inert substance that may relieve symptoms psychologically and not by specific pharmaceutical action.

Polymyalgia rheumatica: Immune pathological joint disease, part of giant cell arteritis.

Polyp: Benign growth of tissue.

Polypharmacy: Excessive medication with many drugs.

Porphyria: Chronic metabolic-hematological disease with neurological and skin symptoms.

Presbyopia: Diminished vision in old age, usually caused by loss of accomodation of inelastic lens.

Psychoactive drugs: Drugs used in the treatment of behavior disorders.

Rhinorrhea: Excessive mucous secretion from the nose.

Rigor: Increase of muscle tone, occuring in certain central nervous system diseases (e.g., Parkinson's syndrome) and resulting in stiffness and impairment of motility.

Rosolimo reflex: Pathological reflex indicating central nervous system dysfunction of the motility centers and pathways.

Sarcoma pectoris: Term falsely used at the beginning of the twentieth century, indicating carcinoma of the breast (in case of Hitler's mother).

Schizoid: Vague term denoting closeness to schizophrenic processes, though not necessarily abnormal.

Schizoid personality: Personality characterized by avoidance of close contacts. (Ernst Kretschmer placed schizoid personality between schizophrenia and normal schizothymic persons.)

Schizophrenia: A major mental illness with profound alterations of cognitive, emotive, and drive functions, often associated with delusions, hallucinations, and misjudgment of reality.

Scurvy: Disease caused by vitamin C deficiency.

Seborrhea: Extreme secretion of sebum (fat and epithelial debris from sebaceous glands).

Sedative: A drug that reduces excitement and anxiety and/or produces sleep (confused with hypnotics, substances used to produce sleep).

Sinusitis: Acute and chronic inflammation of bony (cranial) cavities such as the ethmoid, frontal, and maxillary sinuses.

Somnolence: Sleepiness.

Spastic colon: *See* Irritable bowel syndrome.

Spina bifida: A developmental anomaly of absence of closure of the spinal canal, with protrusion of the meninges and cord, causing paralysis of the legs and incontinence.

Spina bifida occulta: Incomplete occlusion of the vertebral canal not affecting the cord and meninges, with mild or no symptoms.

Stupor: A state of lowered or absent responses.

Supraorbital region: The area above the eyeball, innervated by the supraorbital nerve, a branch of the trigeminus nerve, which is responsible for sensory innervation of the face.

Sympathomimetic: Drugs producing adrenaline-like effects.

Syncope: A temporary loss of consciousness.

Syndrome: A cluster of signs and symptoms.

Tachycardia: Increase of heart frequency rate.

Tayasaku disease: Immune-pathological illness similar to giant cell arteritis.

Temporal: Region over the temples.

Temporal arteritis (TA): Chronic immune-pathological vasculitis of temporal and other medium-sized arteries; more frequently referred to as giant cell arteritis. *See also* Giant cell arteritis.

Temporal lobe epilepsy: Epileptic seizures caused by a lesion of the temporal lobe.

Tinnitus: Noise in the ears, such as buzzing or ringing, without external stimuli.

Tremor: Involuntary trembling. (Hitler had a 4/sec. tremor at rest, which is characteristic for Parkinson's syndrome.)

Upper respiratory infection: Includes common colds, laryngitis, pharyngitis, bronchitis; usually caused by viral infection.

Urobilin, urobilinogen: Substances that occur in abnormal quantities in the urine of persons with some liver diseases.

Varices: Dilations of veins; varices of the esophagus are a symptom of severe liver disease, often seen in chronic alcoholics.

Varices esophagus: Widening of the veins of the esophagus.

Vasculitis: Inflammation of the arteries.

Venal section (venesection): Originally, draining of blood.

Vertigo: Rotary form of dizziness.

Vitreous humor: Glassy liquid in the inner eye.

Wassermann reaction: Original, most widely used diagnostic test for syphilis.

Wilson's disease: Chronic disease of the liver and brain (basal ganglia).

Appendix 4 *List of Significant Medications*

Name	Composition	Indication (according to Dr. Morell)	Method of Application	Remarks
Acidol-Pepsin (also pepsin wine)	Digestive pepsin	Dyspepsia, lack of appetite	Oral	
Belladonna Obstinol	Laxative, anticholinergic	Constipation, intestinal spasms	Oral	
Benerva-forte	Vitamin B complex	Vitamin B deficiency, sciatica, circulatory disorders	Oral	
Betabion-forte	Vitamin B complex	Vitamin deficiency	Oral	
Boxberger pills	Laxative	Constipation	Oral	
Brom-Nervacit	4% potassium bromide, 0.1% sodium phosphate, 1% nephrodyl, diethylbarbiturate acid, phenyldimethylpyrazolon, alcohol	Insomnia, psychological tension	Oral	Obsolete
Calcium sandoz	Calcium gluconal actobional	Cardiac medication	Intravenous	Frequently used
Calomel	Subchloride of mercury (drastic laxative)	Constipation	Oral	Dangerous medication; obsolete
Cardiazol (Metrazol)	Pentamethylenetetrazol	Cardiac stimulant	Intramuscular and oral	
Chineurin	Low dose of Quinine	Medication for colds	Oral	Obsolete

Name	Composition	Indication (according to Dr. Morell)	Method of Application	Remarks
Cocaine	1% solution	Conjunctivitis	Eye drops	Not recommended at present; addictive
Cortioron	Extract of adrenal cortex	Strengthening of organism	Intramuscular	First generation of cortisone
Dalman Cola pills	Cola extract (minimum dosage)	Stimulant	Oral	Available without prescription
Detoxified *Escherichia coli*		General cure (like Mutaflor, Enterofagos cures)	Oral	Routine care
Dolantin	Opiate	Narcotic	Oral	Addictive
Dr. Koester's Anti-Gas Pills	Per pill extr. of strychnin 4.2 mgm; extr. belladonna 4.2 mgm	Dyspepsia	Oral, available without prescription	Obsolete; amounts Hitler used not toxic
Enterofagos cure	Detoxified *Eschericia coli*	Many illnesses	Oral	Frequently used
Euflat	Laxative	Constipation		
Eukodal (U.S. Percodan)	Oxycodone (synthetic morphine derivative)	Severe pain	Intramuscular, intravenous	Addictive, frequently used
Eupaverin	Synthetic alkaloid	Constipation, intestinal spasms	Intramuscular, intravenous	Frequently used
Glucose, 20%		Hypoglycemia, nutritional supplement, cardiacum	Intravenous	Routine therapy

Name	Composition	Indication (according to Dr. Morell)	Method of Application	Remarks
Glyconorm	Mixture of organ extracts (heart, liver, adrenal cortex) plus vitamins	Dietary supplement, used for nutritional deficiency; immunity modifier (?)	Intramuscular	Routine therapy
Glycovarin	20% glucose solution	Nutrient, cardiac support	Intravenous	Frequently used
Homoseran	Placenta extract	Idiosyncratic use for Parkinson's disease, tremor	Intramuscular	Obsolete
Intelan	Vitamins A & D, plus glucose	Avitaminosis	Oral (Intramuscular?)	
Leo-Pillen	Laxative	Constipation		
Liver Extract (Hamma)	Extr. from pig and bovine livers	Strengthening of organism	Intramuscular	
Luizym	Enzyme preparation	Cardiac complaints	Oral	
Luminal	Sedative, phenyl-ethyl-barbiturate	Insomnia	Oral	Addictive
Luminalette	Sedative, phenobarbital 0.015 gm	Insomnia	Oral	
Morphium sulfate solution		Narcotic; used preoperatively twice	Subcutaneous	Addictive
Mutaflor cure	Detoxified *Eschericia coli*	Routine	Oral	Frequently used
Neo-Pyocyanase		Upper respiratory inflammation	External (on mucous membranes)	
Nitroglycerine (Esdesan)	Glycerial trinitrate	Angina pectoris	Sublingual	Never used

Name	Composition	Indication (according to Dr. Morell)	Method of Application	Remarks
Obstinol	Laxative	Acute and chronic constipation	Oral	
Omnadin	Proteins, lipoid substances	Infections (to change immune status)	Intramuscular	Obsolete
Optalidon	Amidopyrine and barbiturate	Analgesic	Oral	
Orchikrin	Male sex hormones	Fatigue and depression		
Pervitin	Amphetamine	Stimulant (see text)	Oral	Addictive
Phanodorm	Cyclobarbital	Insomnia		Addictive
Progynon B Oleosum forte	Female sex hormone	General stimulation	Intramuscular	
Quadronox	Sedative	Insomnia	Oral	
Scophedal	Oxycodone scopolamine	Extreme sedative	Intramuscular	Obsolete
Septoiod	3% iodine (iodine salts)	Respiratory infection	Intravenous	
Strophanthus	Glycoside cardiacum	Myocardial damage	Intravenous	Three cures; risky
Sympathol	Para-oxyphenyl-ethanol-methylamine	Cardiac stimulant	Intramuscular plus oral	
Tempidorm	Barbiturate	Insomnia	Suppository	
Testoviron	Male sex hormone	Stimulant	Intramuscular	
Tibatin	Sulfonamide	Infections	Intramuscular	

Name	Composition	Indication (according to Dr. Morell)	Method of Application	Remarks
Tonophosphan	Sodium salt of dimethyl-amino-methyl-phenyl-phosphinic acid	Stimulant	Intramuscular (Subcutaneous?)	Routine therapy
Trocken-Koli-Hamma cure	Coli preparation	Many illnesses; not specific	Oral	Frequent cures
Ultraseptyl	Sulfonamide	Infections	Oral, intramuscular	Inferior drug; obsolete
Vitamultin-Calcium	Multiple vitamin plus calcium	Dietary supplement	Intravenous (Oral?)	Frequently used
Vitamultin-forte	Multiple vitamin	Prevention of fatigue	Intramuscular	Frequently used
Yatren	Chinoiforum iodoxychinolinsulphate	Amoebic dysentery	Oral	

Appendix 5

Significant Laboratory Reports

9 January 1940
Blood pressure: 140/100 (age 50)
Pulse: 72
Blood group: A
Hemoglobin: 97%
Red corpuscles: 4.7 Mill.
Color index: 1.03
White blood cells: 5000
Blood sugar: 110 mg%
Blood sedimentation rate: 4.9
   Average value: 6.5

15 January 1940
   Wassermann: negative
   Meinicke (MKRII): negative
   Kahn: negative
Pallida reaction:
Complement test for gonorrhea:
Complement test for tuberculosis:
Meinicke-tuberculosis-reaction:
       (signed) E. Brinkmann

10 October 1944 (Urinalysis)
Normal findings.
Specific gravity: 1.013
Albumen: negative

Sugar: negative
Urobilinogen: no increase
Sediment: Very sporadic leucocytes, one or two in field of view. Otherwise normal.
  No bacteria.
              (signed) Weber

24 November 1944
Sedimentation Rate of Blood Corpuscles
Westergreen Method
1st hour = 33 mm   Normal value: up to 10 mm
2nd hour = 66 mm
  Average rate mm: 33
Blood sedimentation: 33/66 mm
Hemoglobin: 88%
Blood count
  Leucocytes   5-600
  Erythrocytes   4,380,000
  Color index   1.01
White blood corpuscle differential
  Segment nuclei 56%
  Lymphocytes   30%
  Eosinophils   3%
  Monocytes   4%
  Neutrophils   4%
  Staff nuclei   3%

Urine:
  Specific gravity 1.017
  Albumen   0
  Sugar   0
  Urobilinogen   0
Sediment: Inconclusive.
  Very small amount of calcium carbonate and a few epithelia.

26 November 1944
Blood sugar: 80 mg%
  Nonprotein nitrogen: 22 mg%
Cholesterin (undifferentiated): 182 mg%
Bilirubin: direct, negative; indirect, under 0.3 mg%
Hence all normal.

Appendix 6

Electrocardiographic Reports and Recommendations

Electrocardiogram I
Balneological University Institute
Director: Prof. Dr. A. Weber

Bad Nauheim
August 14, 1941

Date: August 14, 1941
Age: 51
Auricular Rate: 88
Ventricular Rate: 88
Rhythm: Pacemaker apparently
    originates in the uppermost
    portion of Tawara node

Clinical Diagnosis: Coronary Sclerosis
P-QRS Interval: 0.10.11
ORS Complex: 0.08
Axis deviation: Left

Lead I: Slight slurring of Q+R, voltage of T (0.20 mm), slight depression of R-T
    segment, slight notching of P, small Q-wave present (1.2 mm), R-wave (12 mm),
    P-wave (0.-0.5 mm).
Lead II: slight slurring of R, voltage of T (0.5 mm), low take off of S-T segment,
    R-wave 5 mm, P-wave 0.3-0.4 mm.
Lead III: slight slurring of R+S, diphasic P, R-wave 1.8 mm, S-wave 5-6 mm, slight
    arrhythmia.

Note: Standardization present
    Horizontal spacing: 0.04 sec. Vertical sp. 1 mm.
    Actual square spacing: 0.075"

Professor Weber's Reply
Balneological University Institute   Bad Nauheim
Director: Prof. Dr. A. Weber   20 August 1941

Dear Colleague Morell:
    I was glad to hear that you are in good health despite what must be very great
responsibility. Let us hope that things progress far enough for us all to enjoy real
peace soon.
    The electrocardiogram you submitted showed: sinus rhythm, left type. Transition
to left retardation. Beginning depression of S-T and S-T$_I$. Considerable flattening of
S-T$_I$ and S-T$_{II}$. If these are not the consequence of digitalis or an infection, we must
assume primarily that the cause is coronary sclerosis. I recommend making further
electrocardiograms at fourteen-day intervals.
    In the hope that things continue to go well for you I remain, with best wishes,
                              and Heil Hitler!
                              your obedient
                              A. Weber

Electrocardiogram II
Balneological University Institute   Bad Nauheim
Director: Prof. Dr. A. Weber   May 11, 1943

Date: May 11, 1943
Age: 54   Clinical Diagnosis: Coronary Sclerosis
Auricular Rate: 85-90   P-QRS Interval: 0.12
Ventricular Rate: 85-90   QRS Complex: 0.08
Rhythm: Pacemaker apparently origi-
    nating in the uppermost region
    of Tawara node or in the lower
    most region of Sinus node.   Axis deviation: Left

Lead I: Slight notching of base of R, low-inverted T, very slight low take-off of RT
    segment, P-wave 3 mm, R-wave 9.5 mm, Q-wave 0.75 mm.
Lead II: slurring of R, practically isoelectric T, low take-off of RS-T segment, voltage
    of P 3 mm, voltage of R 3 mm.
Lead III: slight slurring of R+S, low voltage; nearly isoelectric T, voltage of R~1
    mm, voltage of S 5.5 mm.

Note: Standardization is not present
    Horizontal spacing: 0.04 sec. Vertical sp. 1 mm.
    Actual square-spacing: 0.075"

Dear Colleague Morell,
    The two ECGs of 11 May 1943 show: sinus rhythm, left type, possibly also incipient
left retardation, slight depression of ST$_I$ and ST$_{II}$. T$_I$ beginning negative, T$_{II}$ on the
base line. Compared with the 1941 take, an unquestionable deterioration has taken
place inasmuch as the ST depression has become clearer and the T$_I$, then clearly positive, is now negative. The T$_{II}$, then clearly positive, now virtually coincides with the
base line. The electrocardiogram of 11 May this year reinforces my earlier diagnosis:
Coronary Sclerosis, and this is evidently a progressive case.

I would urgently recommend three or four weeks' complete rest. One cannot make a definitive prognosis in such cases, but the probability is not a very favorable course, while to give more definite data is not possible. I recommend ECG controls at quarterly intervals and repeated cures with Teominal or Deriphyllin or iodine-calcium-diuretin. Three weeks of each compound, then three weeks and so on several times. Stop, absolutely, any use of nicotine abuse, diet reduction of fluids and salt, if possible one fruit a day, also fasting and no drinking in these [?] 24 hours, and reduce professional work to the most necessary. Regular siesta of one hour, and as much night sleep as possible.

I can see that these measures, which are absolutely indicated, are difficult to carry out, or may not be carried out at all with a gentleman in such a responsible position, but as much as possible should be carried out for the preservation of working ability.

> Heil Hitler, cordial greetings
> Your Prof. A. Weber

Electrocardiogram III

Balneological University Institute   Bad Nauheim
Director: Prof. Dr. A. Weber

Electrocardiogram A
Date: 24 September 1944
Age: Disease: Switch on A.
Auricular Rate: 85-90   P-QRS
Interval: 0.10-11
Ventricular Rate: 85-90

Rhythm: Pacemaker apparently originates   Axis deviation: Left
  in the uppermost portion of Tawara node.
  (Conduction time: 0.10-11.)

Lead I: low-inverted T_I, slight low take off of R-T segment, notching of P 0.3 mm, small Q-wave (1 mm), voltage of R 8.5 mm.
Lead II: slight slurring of P, isoelectric T, low take off of R-T segment, voltage of P 0.3 mm, voltage of R 3 mm.
Lead Ill: slight slurring of base of R, voltage of R 1.3 mm, voltage of S 6 mm.

Note: Standardization present
  Horizontal spacing: 0.04 sec. Vertical sp. 1 mm.
  Actual square-spacing: 0.075"

Electrocardiogram Interpreted

Balneological University Institute   Bad Nauheim
Director: Prof. Dr. A. Weber   September 24, 1944

Electrocardiogram D
Date: September 24, 1944   Clinical diagnosis: Coronary sclerosis
Age: Disease: Switch on No.6,
                                        apparently affect standardization.
Auricular rate: 85-90   P-QRS Interval: 0.10-11
Ventricular rate: 85-90   QRS Complex: 0.08

Rhythm: Pacemaker apparently   Axis deviation: left
    originates in the uppermost
    portion of Tawara node. (Conduction
    time 0.10-11.)
Lead I: notching of P, low take off of R-T segment
Lead II: slight slurring of R, isoelectric T, low take off of R-T segment
Lead Ill: very slight slurring of R + S

Note: Standardization present
    Horizontal spacing: 0.04 sec. Vertical sp. 1 mm.
    Actual square-spacing: 0.075"

Cardiologist's Reply
Balneological University Institute   Bad Nauheim
Director: Prof. Dr. A. Weber   4 December 1944

Dear Professor Morell,
    I am replying to your courteous letter from my cellar while hordes of enemy
bombers thunder overhead. Please accept my heartfelt condolences on the death of
your brother. I would be interested to learn whether it was an apoplexy or a sudden
cardiac failure, as he had been suffering from angina for a number of years.
    As far as your own electrocardiogram is concerned—and I am not pulling any
punches—compared with 1941 the signs of a coronary insufficiency have become
clearer. Between 28 July 1944 and 9 October 1944, there was a noticeable improvement, namely in II. S-T is showing an increasing tendency again. I can well understand that your present way of life is not actually good for your coronary arteries. But
all of us are wishing that in the foreseeable future there may be a change for the better
which also will have a favorable effect on your health. May I suggest adopting a philosophical attitude toward all the petty intrigues that are bound to occur given the position that you occupy. Can't you make one day completely free each week? Taking a
day off like that often does more good than all the drugs. I would continue to take the
Iodine-Calcium-Diuretin but avoid any kind of sudden physical strain, even if it is
only a brief muscular exertion like lifting a piece of heavy furniture, for instance.
    And now to the graphs of Patient A [Hitler]: Interpretation of 14 August 1941:
sinus rhythm, left type. Flattening of T in all three Leads. A very slight depression of
S-T in I and II. Initial complex lasting about 0.09". Interpretation of May 1943: sinus
rhythm, left type. Somewhat more clearly denoted than two years earlier, as is the
depression of S-T in I and II. T in I is barely negative. QRS lasting 0.08-0.09". Interpretation of 24 September 1944: left type, even more clearly marked. Depression of
S-T in I, which commencing now is showing a track that is convex upward. T in I is
clearly negative. S-T in II is also clearly more strongly depressed. QRS cannot be measured with certainty but apparently lasts longer than in 1943.
    There are slowly progressive symptoms of left coronary insufficiency, and probably
also of left retardation. In view of everything you set out in your covering letter, these
changes for the worse should not surprise us.
    I recommend primarily that he should if at all possible take complete days of rest
and eat a low-salt diet. The vegetarian diet must not be allowed to result in albumin
deficiency. From time to time he should test his weight at morning and night; losing
about two pounds or more weight during the day would indicate a disturbed water
balance, which can easily occur if there is an albumen deficiency. If Iodine-Calcium-

Diuretin does not agree with this patient, then please try administering Deriphyllin, one or two tablets to be taken daily. Of course there is no drug that can make up for the harm done by an unhealthy way of life, but that is just another cost of this war.

I hope it may prove possible for you to come here in the foreseeable future. With the best wishes for your good health, and Heil Hitler, I remain your obedient
[Signed] A. Weber

Appendix 7

Eye Examinations

2 March 1944
The Director of the University Clinic for Eye Diseases
Berlin NW 7
Ziegelstraße 5–9

I. Findings of Examination
The Führer complained that he had been seeing everything as through a thin veil over his right eye for about two weeks. On closer questioning he mentioned that he had experienced a light stabbing pain, of transitory nature, in his right eye recently. He reads, of course, a good deal—especially before falling asleep—and the presbyopic glasses prescribed in 1935 are hardly enough for this purpose now.

Visual acuity was tested under rather unfavorable lighting conditions. Results were as follows:

Right	3/12 (+1.5 sph) 5/6
Left	5/6, glasses rejected

Close vision:

Right	(+4.0) Nieden II in 25–30cm
Left	(+3.0) Nieden I in 5–30cm

Lid function normal. No fibrillation in orbicularis, incidentally no strong defensive reaction to instilling drops or to tonometry. Motility normal. Anterior eye in good order on both sides in every respect. Pupils of equal diameter, round, and of normal reaction. Anterior chamber shows normal depth. Color of the iris on both sides equally dark blue-gray. After determination of normal inner pressure by palpation, mydriasis of pupils was induced, right with Homatropin, left (currently the eye with better vision) only with Veritol.

Ophthalmoscopy after about thirty minutes gave following results:
Left: Refractive media exceptionally clear. Eye background entirely clear and with-

out pathological findings. Papilla of normal color, exhibiting well-defined physiological excavation. The retinal blood vessels were of normal width and extent. The choroid vessels could not be diagnosed because of the dark shade of epithelial pigment. Posterior pole and periphery also without pathological manifestation.

Right: Background was obscured by a delicate veil. With the use of a magnifying mirror, a very delicate, faintly mobile, diffuse turbidity of the vitreous humor could be observed, obviously composed of infinitesimal particles. No turbidity of the lens could be observed. The picture of the eye background was therefore not as clear as in the left eye, but still permitted all details to be distinguished: Papilla showed no evidence of pathology. Retinal blood vessels exhibited no noticeable peculiarities, especially no varices of veins or caliber irregularity of arteries. No hemorrhages or white degenerative foci were observed. A foveolar reflex was not distinctly discernible. Periphery showed no pathological conditions.

The tonometric examination (under Psicain) which was performed immediately following resulted in a reading of 8 on both sides with a weight of 7.5, that is to say, a completely normal inner-eye pressure.

Diagnosis: The misty perception with the right eye is explained by a very delicate but diffuse turbidity of the vitreous humor which, since no inflammatory processes can be observed, is to be attributed to minute hemorrhages into the vitreous humor. These hemorrhages do not seem to originate with the blood vessels of the retina. At least no pathological retinal conditions can be observed on either side. Probably a transitory variation in pressure possibly caused by a vessel spasm — the explanation of the presence of blood.

Proposal:
In order to assist in clearing up the turbidity, local application of heat is recommended, perhaps quarter-hour treatments twice a day with electrothermopor or Sollux lamp. Further recommendation is instillation of one percent JK [potassium iodide] solution into right eye.

A discussion with Professor Morell was held in the presence of the Führer, during which means of preventing the recurrence of such hemorrhages were evident. Everything contributing to the avoidance of unnecessary excitement, particularly during the period immediately before the night's rest, such as diversion in light reading, was recommended. The use of sedatives is naturally narrowly restricted. Some consideration was given to the use of Luminal tablets.

In addition a change of glasses was prescribed: continuous use of glasses for distant vision is not necessary, but occasional use might be convenient. Therefore, the following prescription was made for distant vision: Right +1.5 diopter spher., left plane. The glasses for near vision must be strengthened. Right +4.0 diopter spher., left +3.0 diopter spher. Bifocal glasses of the same strength are also to be provided.

[Signed] Dr. W. Löhlein

March 2, 1944
To Prof. Dr. Morell

My dear Professor,
As arranged I am sending you (encl.) . . . the result of my examination, which fortunately appears to be comparatively favorable, though it of course indicates the existing danger to the vessel system. I would like in addition to make a few explanatory remarks.

Application of heat twice a day for some 15–20 minutes will surely help to clear up the turbidity of the right eye more quickly. At the same time, I feel that the period of quiet which it makes necessary—even though only twice a day for twenty minutes—offers an opportunity for relaxation which is supplemented by the influence of the heat. Would a similar effect be achieved by very moderate body massage once a day?

Regarding the use of glasses I should like to say the following: The glasses for distant vision will hardly ever be necessary. The bifocal glasses, on the other hand, would be very convenient whenever it is necessary to shift the eyes quickly between near and distant objects, for example, during a conference in which an individual must be seen clearly while at the same time a letter must be glanced at or followed. The wearer of the glasses thus does not have to put them on and take them off, but looks at distant objects through the upper section of the glasses and at objects near at hand, a document for instance, through the lower.

I consider frequent reexamination of the eyes unnecessary, for psychological reasons undesirable. I do think it advisable, however, to recheck my findings after six or eight weeks, particularly in order to keep current on the conditions of the retinal blood vessels.

I would like to take the opportunity afforded by this letter to express again my sincere thanks for the friendly reception which you have accorded me, and for your advice. It has been a deeply impressive experience for me to be able to have a glimpse into the manifold aspects of your highly responsible activity.

>With best wishes,
>Heil Hitler!
>Your obedient
>[Signed] W. Löhlein

April 7, 1945
The Director of the University Clinic for Eye Diseases
Berlin NW 7
Ziegelstraße 5-9

Eye Examination of the Führer on April 7, 1945
According to the Führer the vision of the right eye has gradually grown worse rather than better, while that of the left is as good as ever. The left eye is impeded by a swelling on the left upper lid which is tender and causes him to rub it. There is a secretion from both eyes of late, which is understandable in view of the dusty atmosphere in the center of Berlin. The Führer generally leaves the well-ventilated and illuminated bunker only for short periods, for half an hour or two hours daily, and then goes into the Reich Chancery's garden, which is not badly damaged but is of course quite dusty, particularly when windy. He finds himself then very sensitive both to light and the dust-laden wind. It is difficult to arrange a regular treatment in view of the irregularity of his life-style and the need for him to be constantly available for reports, et cetera.

Results:
Close vision: right (with lens +4.5)
                   Nieden II in 25 cm
                   left (with lens +3.0)
                   Nieden I in 25 cm

Distant visual acuity:

Right: (+1.5 diopter sph) 5/10. As he hardly ever wears his spectacles he is disproportionately inconvenienced by the bad vision of his right eye.

Left: 5/5 + glasses rejected.

There is a moderate chronic conjunctivitis on both sides without involvement of the conjunctive bulbi. Secretion very slight. No indications of lachrymal sac involvement.

Quite a large insipid chalazion on left upper eyelid, which provokes rubbing and is bothersome.

Pale conjunctiva on both eyeballs, clear cornea. Anterior chamber shows normal depth, well-shaped iris with prompt reaction by the pupils to light.

Ophthalmoscopy right (after Homatropine): lens clear. In vitreous humor slight delicate turbidity, sluggishly mobile; probably not enough to explain the reduction of vision by itself. Papilla well defined, of adequate color, not paler temporally than on the left where the central vision is good.

But no fovea reflex in contrast to the left. Posterior pole otherwise without pathological manifestation, and in particular no hemorrhages. The retinal blood vessels were not blocked. While the arteries were perhaps a bit thin, there were no marked irregularities. Periphery without pathological manifestation.

Ophthalmoscopy right: (after Veritol): Vitreous humor and lens clear. Eye background without pathological manifestation. Perfect macula reflex.

Diagnosis: Moderate chronic conjunctivitis on both sides. Chalazion on upper left eyelid. Right: The residue of a hemorrhage in the vitreous humor. Lack of macular reflex.

Treatment: On account of the conjunctivitis on both sides: instillation of zinc suprac. drops three times a day on each side. On account of the chalazion left: heat application to left eye for fifteen minutes three times daily (interpose some gauze). In addition before going to bed gently rub two percent yellow mercury ointment into left eye.

If a rapid reduction and amelioration of the chalazion on the left upper lid does not result, it should be excised in an early operation.

Further examination in one week's time, possibly with excision of the chalazion from the left upper lid at the same time.

[Signed] Dr. W. Löhlein

Appendix 8

*Autopsy Report**

Document No. 12

Concerning the forensic examination of a male corpse disfigured by fire (Hitler's body)

Berlin-Buch, 8.V., 1945
Mortuary CAFS** No. 496

The Commission consisting of Chief Expert, Forensic Medicine, 1st Byelorussian Front, Medical Service, Lieutenant Colonel F. I. Shkaravski; Chief Anatomist, Red Army, Medical Service, Lieutenant Colonel N. A. Krayevski; Acting Chief Anatomical Pathologist, 1st Byelorussian Front, Medical Service, Major A. Y. Marants; Army Expert, Forensic Medicine, 3rd Shock Army, Medical Service, Major Y. I. Boguslavski; and Army Anatomical Pathologist, 3rd Shock Army, Medical Service, Major Y. V. Gulkevich, on orders of the member of the Military Council 1st Byelorussian Front, Lieutenant General Telegrin, performed the forensic-medical examination of a male corpse presumably the corpse of Hitler).

Results of the examination:

A. External Examination
The remains of a male corpse disfigured by fire were delivered in a wooden box (Length 163 cm., Width 55 cm., Height 53 cm.). On the body was found a piece of yellow jersey, 25 x 8 cm., charred around the edges, resembling a knitted undervest.

---

* From Lev Bezymenski, *The Death of Adolf Hitler* (New York, 1968).
** Abbreviation for *Chirugisches Armeefeldlazarett*.

In view of the fact that the corpse is greatly damaged, it is difficult to gauge the age of the deceased. Presumably it lies between 50 and 60 years. The dead man's height is 165 cm. (The measurements are approximate since the tissue is charred), the right shinbone measures 39 cm. The corpse is severely charred and smells of burned flesh.

Part of the cranium is missing.*

Parts of the occipital bone, the left temporal bone, the lower cheekbones, the nasal bones, and the upper and lower jaws are preserved. The burns are more pronounced on the right side of the cranium than on the left. In the brain cavity parts of the fire-damaged brain and of the dura mater are visible. On face and body the skin is completely missing; only remnants of charred muscles are preserved. There are many small cracks in the nasal bone and upper jawbones. The tongue is charred, its tip is firmly locked between the teeth of the upper and lower jaws.

In the upper jaw there are nine teeth connected by a bridge of yellow metal (gold). The bridge is anchored by pins on the second left and the second right incisor. This bridge consists of 4 upper incisors (2(1((1 (2), 2 canine teeth (3((3), the first left bicuspid ((4), and the first and second right bicuspids (4(5(), as indicated in the sketch. The first left incisor ((1) consists of a white platelet, with cracks and a black spot in the porcelain (enamel) at the bottom. This platelet is inset into the visible side of the metal (gold) tooth. The second incisor, the canine tooth, and the left bicuspid, as well as the first and second incisors and the first bicuspid on the right, are the usual porcelain (enamel) dental plates, their posterior parts fastened to the bridge. The right canine tooth is fully capped by yellow metal (gold). The maxillary bridge is vertically sawed off behind the second bicuspid ((5). The lower jawbone lies loose in the singed oral cavity The alveolar processes are broken in the back and have ragged edges. The front surface and the lower edge of the mandibula are scorched. On the front surface the charred prongs of dental roots are recognizable. The lower jaw consists of fifteen teeth, ten of which are artificial. The incisors (2(1((1(2) and the first right bicuspid (4( ) are natural, exhibiting considerable wear on the masticating surface and considerably exposed necks. The dental enamel has a bluish shimmer and a dirty yellow coloration around the necks. The teeth to the left ((4, (5, (7, and (8) are artificial, of yellow metal (gold), and consist of a bridge of gold crowns. The bridge is fastened to the third, the fifth (in the bridge, the sixth tooth), and the eighth tooth (in the bridge, the ninth tooth). The second bicuspid to the right (5() is topped by a crown of yellow metal (gold) which is linked to the right canine tooth by an arching plate. Part of the masticating surface and the posterior surface of the right canine tooth is capped by a yellow metal (gold) plate as part of the bridge. The first right molar is artificial, white, and secured by a gold clip connected with the bridge of the second bicuspid and the right incisor.

Splinters of glass, parts of the wall and bottom of a thin-walled ampule, were found in the mouth.

The neck muscles are charred, the ribs on the right side are missing, they are burned. The right side of the thorax and the abdomen are completely burned, creating a hole through which the right lung, the liver, and the intestines are open to view. The genital member is scorched. In the scrotum, which is singed but preserved, only the right testicle was found. The left testicle could not be found in the inguinal canal.

---

* At a somewhat later date occipital parts of a cranium were found, quite probably belonging to Hitler's corpse.

The right arm is severely burned, the ends of the bone of the upper arm and the bones of the lower arm are broken and charred. The dry muscles are black and partially brown; they disintegrate into separate fibers when touched. The remnants of the burned part (about two thirds) of the left upper arm are preserved. The exposed end of the bone of the upper arm is charred and protrudes from the dry tissue. Both legs, too, are charred. The soft tissue has in many places disappeared; it is burned and has fallen off. The bones are partially burned and have crumbled. A fracture in the right thighbone and the right shinbone were noted. The left foot is missing.

B. Internal Examination
The position of the internal organs is normal. The lungs are black on the surface, dark red on the cut surface, and of fairly firm consistence. The mucous membrane of the upper respiratory tracts is dark red. The cardiac ventricles are filled with coagulated reddish-brown blood. The heart muscle is tough and looks like boiled meat. The liver is black on the surface and shows burns; it is of fairly firm consistence and yellowish-brown on the cut surface. The kidneys are somewhat shrunken and measure 9 x 5 x 3.5 cm. Their capsule is easily detachable; the surface of the kidneys is smooth, the pattern effaced; they appear as if boiled. The bladder contains 5 cc. yellowish urine, its mucous membrane is gray. Spleen, stomach, and intestines show severe burns and are nearly black in parts.

Note: 1. The following objects taken from the corpse were handed over to the SMERSH Section of the 3rd Shock Army on May 8, 1945: a) a maxillary bridge of yellow metal, consisting of 9 teeth; b) a singed lower jaw, consisting of 15 teeth.
2. According to the record of the interrogation of Frau Kathe Heusermann it may be presumed that the teeth as well as the bridge described in the document are those of Chancellor Hitler.
3. In her talk with Chief Expert of Forensic Medicine, Lieutenant Colonel Shkaravski, which took place on May 11, '45,* in the offices of CAFS No.496, Frau Käthe Heusermann described the state of Hitler's teeth in every detail. Her description tallies with the anatomical data pertaining to the oral cavity of the unknown man whose burned corpse we dissected.

Appended: A test tube with glass splinters from an ampule which were found in the body.

signed (Shkaravski) Chief Expert, Forensic Medicine,
1st Byelorussian Front, Medical Service,
Lieutenant Colonel

signed (Krayevski)
Chief Anatomical Pathologist, Medical Service, Red Army,
Lieutenant Colonel

---

* I asked N. Krayevski how it was possible for this date to appear in an autopsy report that had been written on May 8. He explained that the report had originally been written by hand; only later was it decided to add the statements of Heusermann. As was mentioned above, the delay between evidence and conclusion is absolutely normal.

signed (Marants)
Acting Chief Anatomical Pathologist,
1st Byelorussian Front, Medical Service,
Major

signed (Boguslavski) Army Expert, Forensic Medicine,
3rd Shock Army, Medical Service,
Major

signed (Gulkevich)
Army Anatomical Pathologist,
3rd Shock Army, Medical Service,
Major

2. Conclusion

Based on the forensic-medical examination of the partially burned corpse of an unknown man and the examination of other corpses from the same group (Documents Nos. 1–11), the Commission reaches the following conclusions:

1 . Anatomical characteristics of the body:
Since the body parts are heavily charred, it is impossible to describe the features of the dead man. But the following could be established:

a) Stature: about 165 cm. (one hundred sixty-five).

b) Age (based on general development, size of organs, state of lower incisors and of the right bicuspid), somewhere between 50 and 60 years (fifty to sixty).

c) The left testicle could not be found either in the scrotum or on the spermatic cord inside the inguinal canal, nor in the small pelvis.

d) The most important anatomical finding for identification of the person are the teeth, with much bridgework, artificial teeth, crowns, and fillings (see documents) .

2. Cause of death:
On the body, considerably damaged by fire, no visible signs of severe lethal injuries or illnesses could be detected.

The presence in the oral cavity of the remnants of a crushed glass ampule and of similar ampules in the oral cavity of other bodies (see Documents Nos. 1, 2, 3, 5, 6, 8, 9, 10, 11, and 13), the marked smell of bitter almonds emanating from the bodies (Documents Nos. 1, 2, 3, 5, 8, 9, 10, 11), and the forensic-chemical test of internal organs which established the presence of cyanide compounds (Documents Nos. 1, 2, 3, 4, 5, 6, 7, 8, 9, 10, 11) permit the Commission to arrive at the conclusion that death in this instance was caused by poisoning with cyanide compounds.

signed (Shkaravski)
Chief Expert, Forensic Medicine,
1st Byelorussian Front, Medical Service,
Lieutenant Colonel

signed (Krayevski)
Chief Anatomical Pathologist, Medical Service, Red Army,
Lieutenant Colonel

signed (Marants)
Acting Chief Anatomical Pathologist,
1st Byelorussian Front, Medical Service,
Major

signed (Boguslavski)
Army Expert, Forensic Medicine,
3rd Shock Army, Medical Service,
Major

signed (Gulkevich)
Army Anatomical Pathologist, 3rd Shock Army, Medical Service,
Major

Thus far the contents of Document No.12. Before entering into the question of what corpse was being examined—a question left in abeyance in the document—let us consider Document No.13, which records the results of the forensic-medical examination of a female corpse.* The Commission came to the following conclusions:

1. Anatomical characteristics of the body:
In view of the fact that the body parts are extensively charred, it is impossible to describe the features of the dead woman. The following, however, could be established:
   a) The age of the dead woman lies between 30 and 40 years, evidence of which is also the only slightly worn masticating surface of the teeth.
   b) Stature: about 150 cm.
   c) The most important anatomical finding for identification of the person are the gold bridge of the lower jaw and its four front teeth.

2. Cause of death:
On the extensively charred corpse there were found traces of a splinter injury to the thorax with hemothorax, injuries to one lung and to the pericardium, as well as six small metal fragments.
   Further, remnants of a crushed glass ampule were found in the oral cavity.
   In view of the fact that similar ampules were present in other corpses—Documents Nos. 1, 2, 3, 4, 5, 6, 7, 8, 9, 10, 11—that a smell of bitter almonds developed upon dissection—Documents Nos. 1, 2, 3, 4, 5, 6, 7, 8, 9, 10, 11—and based on the forensic-chemical tests of the internal organs of these bodies in which the presence of cyanide compounds was established—Documents Nos. 1, 2, 3, 4, 5, 6, 7, 8, 9, 10, 11—the Commission reaches the conclusion that notwithstanding the severe injuries to the thorax the immediate cause of death was poisoning by cyanide compounds.

In both cases the experts were faced with the most seriously disfigured of all thirteen corpses. Because of this obstacle to the examination two sentences need to be particularly stressed: "Splinters of glass, parts of the wall and bottom of a thin-walled ampule, were found in the mouth" (Document No. 12)—and "In the oral cavity . . . yellowish glass splinters . . . of a thin-walled ampule were found" (Document No.13

---

* This is not the complete text of Document 13.

[Appendix]). These findings permitted the Commission to come in their summary in both cases to analogous conclusions: Death was caused by poisoning with cyanide compounds.

This conclusion is in no way contradicted by the splinter injuries in Eva Braun's body. These could not possibly have been inflicted on her in the bunker. Most probably they occurred during the burning in the garden, which was under artillery fire. Only shell splinters could have caused the injuries and the hemorrhage in the pleura.

Notes

Preface

1. Adolf Hitler, *Mein Kampf* (Boston, 1943), 224; translated by Ralph Manheim from the German *Mein Kampf* (Munich, 1927). The statement reads, "I was numbered amongst the nameless" (*"Da ich nun einmal zu den namenlosen zählte"*).

2. Gordon A. Craig, *The Germans* (New York, 1982).

3. It is gratifying that eminent scholars and political leaders have become aware of the importance of prevention. Witness the recent report of the Carnegie Foundation: *Preventing Deadly Conflict*, prepared by a comission chaired by David Hamburg in collaboration with Cyrus Vance, Washington, D.C., 1997.

4. The most important sources are the medical diaries of Dr. Theodor Morell, Rolls T253-62 and T1270-31, Modern Wars section, National Archives, Washington, D.C. These diaries were published by David Irving as *The Secret Diaries of Hitler's Doctor* (New York, 1976). They were not secret, however, at the time of publication. The most important and authoritative work about Hitler's illnesses is Ernst Günther Schenk's *Patient Hitler* (Düsseldorf, 1989). I have used it extensively but ultimately came to some new and different conclusions. Ellen Gibbels made original contributions about Hitler's Parkinson's syndrome and the question of cerebral deficit. See Ellen Gibbels, "Hitlers Nervenkrankheit," *Vierteljahresheft für Zeitgeschichte* 42 (1994): 155–219; "Hitlers Nervenleiden: Differentialdiagnose des Parkinson Syndroms," *Fortschritte der Neurologie und Psychiatrie* 57 (1989): 505–19; "Hitlers Parkinson Syndrom," *Nervenarzt* 59 (1988): 521–28; and *Hitlers Parkinsonkrankheit: Zur Frage eines hirnorganischen Psychosyndroms* (Berlin, 1990). Ottmar Katz's *Prof. Dr. Med. Theodor Morell: Hitlers Leibarzt* (Bayreuth, 1982) is a lively account in which the author underestimated the seriousness of Hitler's illnesses and overestimated the abilities of the physician. Leonard L. Heston and Renate Heston, *The Medical Case Book of Adolf*

Hitler (New York, 1979), presents Hitler's medical as well as some other troubles as the result of amphetamine addiction. Other works in which a chapter is devoted to Hitler's illnesses are Bert Edward Park, *The Impact of Illness on World Leaders* (Philadelphia, 1986); and Anton Neumayr, *Diktatoren im Spiegel der Medizin* (Vienna, 1995).

5. Alan Bullock, *A Study in Tyranny*, revised ed. (London, 1964); Joachim Fest, *Hitler* (New York, 1978), translated by Richard Winston and Clara Winston from the German *Hitler* (Frankfurt, 1973); Werner Maser, *Hitler: Legend, Myth, and Reality* (New York, 1973), translated by Peter Ross and Betty Ross from the German *Hitler: Legende, Mythos, Wirklichkeit* (Munich, 1971); Hans Ulrich Thamer, *Verführung und Gewalt: Deutschland 1933–1945* (Berlin, 1986); John Toland, *Adolf Hitler* (New York, 1976); and, last but not least, one of the oldest Hitler biographies by Konrad Heiden (New York, 1936). Monographs are: Rudolf Binion, *Hitler amongst the Germans* (New York, 1976); Norbert Bromberg and Verna Volz Small, *Hitler's Psychopathology* (New York, 1983); William Carr, *Adolf Hitler* (London, 1980); Wolfgang de Boor, *Hitler: Mensch, Übermensch, Untermensch: Eine kriminalpsychologische Studie* (Frankfurt, 1985); Hans Jurgen Eitner, *Der Führer* (Munich, 1981); Erik H. Erikson, "The Legend of Hitler's Childhood," chapter 9 in *Childhood and Society* (New York, 1950); Erich Fromm, "Malignant Aggression: Adolf Hitler, A Clinical Case of Necrophilia," chapter 13 in *Anatomy of Human Destructiveness* (New York, 1973); Peter Loewenberg, "Nixon, Hitler, and Power: An Ego–Psychological Study," *Psychoanalytic Inquiry* 6 (1986): 27–48; Wilhelm Reich, *Mass Psychology of Fascism* (New York, 1970); Bradley F. Smith, *Adolf Hitler: His Family, Childhood, and Youth* (Stanford, 1967); Helmut Stierlin, *Adolf Hitler: Familienperspektiven* (Frankfurt, 1975); Robert G. L. Waite, *The Psychopathic God: Adolf Hitler* (New York, 1977). One day before mailing the manuscript to Oxford University Press, I received an important book by Robert S. Robins and Jarrold L. Post, *Political Paranoia: The Psychopolitics of Hatred* (New Haven, 1997). I have cited many ideas presented in previous publications by these authors throughout this book, and feel gratified by the congruence of our ideas, which ultimately can be traced to the genius of Max Weber. Through the kindness of Mrs. H. A. (Nina) Murray, I obtained a sketch by her late husband, the Harvard University psychologist Harry A. Murray, concerning Adolf Hitler, written between 1940 and 1944. It contains important ideas about Hitler's complex character—the politics of believing and his ambivalence, and also the prediction that he would commit suicide. In a later publication—*The Mind of Adolf Hitler* (New York, 1972)—Walter C. Langer, who not only knew about this work but collaborated with Murray, did not cite him. Professor Hans W. Gatzke also commented on this in his article, "Hitler and Psychohistory," *American Historical Review* 78 (1973): 394–401. Murray's biographer, Forrest A. Robinson, commented in *Love's Story Told* (Cambridge, Mass., 1994), "Harry's original suspicions were confirmed. Langer had taken the best of his ideas without a word of acknowledgment."

6. Irving Bernstein, personal communication.

7. Ron Rosenbaum, "Explaining Hitler," *The New Yorker*, 1 May 1995, 50–70.

8. Sigmund Freud, "The Disposition to Observational Neurosis: A Contribution to the Problem of Choice of Neurosis" (vol. 12, p. 320), "The Unconscious" (vol. 14, p. 194), and "Recommendations to Physicians Practicing Psychoanalysis" (vol. 12, pp. 115–16), in James Strachey, ed., *Standard Edition of the Complete Psychological Works* (London, 1974).

9. Adolf Hitler, *Mein Kampf*; Adolf Hitler, numerous articles from *Illustrierter Beobachter* (1926–44); *Hitlers zweites Buch: Ein Dokument aus dem Jahre 1928*, with introduction and comments by Gerhard L. Weinberg (Stuttgart, 1961); Eber-

hard Jäckel with Axel Kuhn, eds., *Adolf Hitler: Sämtliche Aufzeichnungen 1905–1924* (Stuttgart, 1980); Max Domarus, ed., *Adolf Hitler: Reden und Proklamationen 1932–1945* (Würzburg, 1962) (for the period from 21 March to 31 July 1942); Werner Jochmann, ed., *Adolf Hitler: Monologe im Führerhauptquartier 1941–1944. Die Aufzeichnungen Heinrich Heims* (Hamburg, 1980); Henry Picker, ed., *Hitlers Tischgespräche im Führerhauptquartier* (Stuttgart, 1976); Helmut Heiber, ed., *Hitlers Lagebesprechungen* (Stuttgart, 1962); *The Testament of Adolf Hitler: The Hitler–Bormann Documents,* with an introduction by Hugh R. Trevor Roper (London, 1961).

10. Otto Dietrich, *Zwölf Jahre mit Hitler* (Munich, 1955); Hans Bernd Gisevius, *Adolf Hitler: Versuch einer Deutung* (Munich, 1963); Joseph Goebbels, *Die Tagebücher von Joseph Goebbels,* vols. 1–5 (Munich, 1986–95); Heinz Guderian, *Panzer Leader* (London, 1953), translated from the German *Erinnerungen eines Soldaten* (Heidelberg, 1951); Franz Halder, *Kriegstagebuch* (Stuttgart, 1962); Ernst Hanfstaengl, *Zwischen weißem und braunem Haus* (Munich, 1970); Albert Kesselring, *Soldat bis zum letzten Tag* (Bonn, 1953); Heinz Linge, *Bis zum Untergang,* ed. Werner Maser (Munich, 1980); Erich von Manstein, *Verlorene Siege* (Frankfurt, 1963); Joachim von Ribbentrop, *Zwischen London und Moskau* (Leoni, 1954); Hjalmar Schacht, *Account Settled* (London, 1949), translated by Edward Fitzgerald from the German *Abrechnung mit Hitler* (Hamburg, 1948); Christa Schroeder, *Er war mein Chef: Aus dem Nachlaß der Sekretärin von Adolf Hitler,* ed. Anton Joachimsthaler (Munich, 1985) [see also Albert Zoller, *Hitler Privat: Erlebnisbericht einer Geheimsekretärin* (Düsseldorf, 1949)]; J. L. Schwerin-von Krosigk, *Es geschah in Deutschland* (Stuttgart, 1951); Albert Speer, *Inside the Third Reich: Memoirs* (New York, 1970), translated from the German *Erinnerungen* (Berlin, 1969); Otto Wagener's notes as recorded in H. A. Turner, ed., *Hitler aus nächster Nähe: Aufzeichnungen eines Vertrauten* (Frankfurt, 1978).

11. Riefenstahl and other memoirists often have lifted statements from other publications (e.g., Hitler's monologues) and presented them as their own. This certainly diminishes authenticity. More detached and more useful are the observations of Hitler's French ambassador André François-Poncet, *The Fateful Years: The Memoirs of a French Ambassador, Berlin 1931–1938* (New York, 1949) and the American journalist William L. Shirer, *The Rise and Fall of the Third Reich* (New York, 1959)

12. Peter Loewenberg, *Decoding the Past: The Psychohistorical Approach* (Los Angeles, 1969), 4–5.

13. Percy W. Bridgman, *The Logic of Modern Physics* (London, 1927).

14. Several authors described Hitler as a prophet: Erik H. Erikson, *The Legend of Hitler's Childhood* (New York, 1965); Friedrich Heer, *Der Glaube des Adolf Hitler* (Munich, 1968); J. P. Stern, *The Führer and the People* (Los Angeles, 1975); Robins and Post, *Political Paranoia.* These authors as well as I have extensively used Max Weber's concept of charismatic leadership, which is related to the prophet role. In this opus I have referred frequently to the work of Robins and Post prior to their publication of *Political Paranoia.*

15. Speer, *Inside the Third Reich.*

16. Percy Ernst Schramm, *Hitler als militärischer Führer* (Frankfurt, 1965).

Chapter 1: Family and Childhood

1. Nobody was more sensitive to Hitler's propensity for creating legends than Erikson; see Erik H. Erikson, *The Legend of Hitler's Childhood* (New York, 1950), 26–257. Note also J. P. Stern, *The Führer and His People* (Los Angeles, 1975), 75–85.

2. Adolf Hitler, *Mein Kampf* (Boston, 1943), 3, translated by Ralph Manheim from the German *Mein Kampf*, vols. 1 and 2 (Munich, 1925, 1927).

3. The description of the Hitler clan is based on the NSDAP Hauptarchiv, mostly reel 17; August Kubizek, *Adolf Hitler: Mein Jugendfreund* (Graz, 1953), translated by E. K. Anderson, with a foreword by H.R. Trevor Roper, *Young Hitler* (Maidstone, 1954). In this book, the third edition of Kubizek's book was cited, although Brigitte Hamann pointed out that this edition was heavily changed by Kubizek's editor; unfortunately the early versions were not available to me); Franz Jetzinger, *Hitlers Jugend: Phastasien, Lügen und die Warheit* (Vienna, 1956). An important recent publication is Brigitte Hamann, *Hitler in Wien: Die Lehrjahre eines Diktatoren* (Munich, 1996).

4. The spelling varied in the church book entries.

5. Rudolf Koppensteiner, *Die Ahnentafel des Führers* (Leipzig, 1937). A distant relative of Hitler, Koppensteiner traced back his ancestors to the seventeenth century.

6. Werner Maser, *Hitler: Legend, Myth, and Reality* (New York, 1973), 19, translated by Peter Ross and Betty Ross from the German *Hitler: Legende, Mythos, Wirklichkeit* (Munich, 1971). The most judicious information about Hitler's family and youth is provided in Bradley F. Smith, *Adolf Hitler: His Family, Childhood, and Youth* (Stanford, 1976).

7. *Mein Kampf*, 51.

8. Franz Jetzinger, *Hitlers Jugend*, 59.

9. Ibid., 77.

10. For more on Alois's financial circumstances, see Smith, *Adolf Hitler*, 46–49.

11. *Mein Kampf*, 17.

12. *Freisinnige Zeitung* (Linz), 8 Jan. 1903.

13. Smith, *Adolf Hitler*, 33. Once again, I consider Smith's work the best description and interpretation of the young Hitler.

14. See the reproduction of signatures in Jetzinger, *Hitlers Jugend*, 136.

15. Monologues, 29 August 1942, evening soliloquy. Hitler's monologues are stated by dates rather than by title and page, because many authors have published annotated versions of the monologues. The original notes can be found in the Bundesarchiv Koblenz. My principal source is Werner Jochmann, ed., *Adolf Hitler: Monologe im Führerhauptquartier 1941–1944. Die Aufzeichnungen Heinrich Heims* (Hamburg, 1980).

16. *NSDAP Hauptarchiv*, Reel 1, File 17.

17. *Mein Kampf*, 18.

18. Patrick Hitler, "Mon Oncle Adolphe," *Paris Soir*, 21 August 1938.

19. Prof. Hanskarl von Hasselbach, *Consolidated Interrogation Reports*, "Hitler as Seen by his Doctors," nos. 2 and 4, 15 and 29, October 1945, National Archives, Washington, D.C.

20. Adolf Hitler, Personal Testament, Documents of the International Military Trials (IMT), Nuremberg ND3569-PS.

21. John Toland, *Adolf Hitler* (New York, 1976), 365.

22. Jetzinger, *Hitlers Jugend*, 226.

23. Monologues, 8/9 January 1942.

24. Interrogation of Paula Hitler, 26 May 1945, Berlin Document Center. See also *New York Times*, 5 March 1959.

25. Christa Schroeder, *Er war mein Chef: Aus dem Nachlaß der Sekretärin von Adolf Hitler*, ed. Anton Joachimsthaler (Munich, 1985), 63.

26. Statement by Rosalie Hörl, NSDAP Hauptarchiv, Reel 1, File 17.

27. Ben E. Swearingen, "Hitler's Family Secret," *Civilization*, March/April 1995, 54–55.

28. Koppensteiner, *Die Ahnentafel.*

29. Jean Marie Loret and R. Mathot, *Mon père s'appellait Hitler* (Paris, 1957).

30. C. V. Steffen and F. A. Vogel, "Ein Sohn Hitlers?," *Homo,* 29 (1976):145–58.

31. Christa Schroeder, as cited by Albert Zoller, *Hitler Privat: Erlebnisbericht einer Geheimsekretärin* (Düsseldorf, 1949), 115.

32. Robert G. L. Waite, *The Psychopathic God: Adolf Hitler* (New York, 1977), 30.

33. Maser, *Hitler*, 22.

34. Toland, *Adolf Hitler*, 247.

35. Gestapo Report, NSDAP Hauptarchiv, Reel 1, File MA.

36. Hans Frank, *Im Angesicht des Galgens* (Munich, 1953), 330–31.

37. Nikolaus Preradowicz in *Der Spiegel* 31 (1967):42.

38. Cornelius Schnauber, personal communication.

39. Jetzinger, *Hitlers Jugend*, 16.

40. Smith, *Adolph Hitler*, plate V.

41. Monologues, 21 August 1942, noon.

42. Bernhard Loesener, Nürnberg IMT, NG 1944-A. Also *Vierteljahresheft für Zeitgeschichte* (1961); 261–311.

43. Billy F. Price, *Adolf Hitler: The Unknown Artist* (Houston, 1984), 95.

44. *Mein Kampf*, 5.

45. Otto Dietrich, *Zwölf Jahre mit Hitler* (Munich, 1955), 164.

46. Paula Hitler, U.S. Army Intelligence Service Interrogation Report, Berchtesgaden, 26 May 1945, National Archives, Washington, D.C.

47. Joseph Mayrhofer, NSDAP Hauptarchiv, Reel I, File 17.

48. Alice Miller, *For Your Own Good: Hidden Cruelty in Child-Rearing and the Roots of Violence* (New York, 1984), 142–95, translated by Hildegarde Hannum and Hunter Hannum from the German *Am Anfang war die Erziehung* (Frankfurt, 1980).

49. Toland, *Adolf Hitler*, p.12.

50. Jetzinger maintained that, if Hitler's father had wanted a governmental career for his son, he would have enrolled Hitler in the *Gymnasium*. However, the *Realschule* was preferable for governmental careers in the technical professions, and a supplemental year after the *Realschule* would have opened up any career option.

51. *Mein Kampf*, 8.

52. Ibid. See also Monologues, March 1942, noon.

53. Jetzinger, *Hitlers Jugend*, 100–103.

54. Monologues, 29 August 1942.

55. NSDAP Hauptarchiv, File 17, Reel 1. After Hitler's ascent to power, Professor Huemer changed his evaluation into an obsequious eulogy.

56. August Kubizek, *Adolf Hitler: Mein Jugendfreund* (Graz, 1953), 60. This is hearsay, because Kubizek did not know Hitler in 1903 when his father died. August Kubizek (Gustl), Hitler's only childhood friend, was an important source. Not everything he remembered was true, however. Jetzinger criticized him for his imagination, even though in the process added a few fantasies of his own.

57. Jetzinger, *Hitlers Jugend*, 105.

58. Monologues, 8/9 January 1942.

59. *Mein Kampf*, 18.

60. Johann Schmidt, statement in NSDAP Hauptarchiv Reel 1, File 17.

61. *Mein Kampf*, 18.

62. Eduard Bloch, "My Patient Adolf Hitler," *Colliers* 107, 15 March 1941, 35–39; 22 March 1941, 69–73.

63. Ibid., 17.

64. Johann Recktenwald, *Woran hat Hitler gelitten?* (Munich, 1963).

65. D. Güstrow, *Tödlicher Alltag: Strafverteidiger im Dritten Reich* (Berlin, 1981).

66. *Mein Kampf,* 21. "The hollowness of comfortable life" was an expression Hitler used to describe this phase of his life. He also called it the happiest period of his life. Actually, he used the superlative attribute frequently and in many contexts, such as describing "the most beautiful experience."

67. Kubizek, *Adolf Hitler,* 20.

68. Ibid., 21.

69. *Mein Kampf,* 21.

70. Kubizek, *Adolf Hitler,* 110.

71. Ibid., 241.

72. Ibid.

73. Ibid., 19.

74. Ibid., 72.

75. Paula Hitler, U.S. Army Intelligence Service Interrogation Report.

76. *Mein Kampf,* 51.

77. Ibid., 52.

78. Kubizek, *Adolf Hitler,* 107.

79. Ibid., 187.

80. Hamann, *Hitler in Wien,* 83.

81. Bloch, "My Patient."

82. Ernst Günther Schenck, *Patient Hitler* (Düsseldorf, 1989), 525. Professor Schenck refuted Binion's claims that Dr. Bloch was responsible for Clara's death.

83. Smith, *Adolf Hitler,* 111.

84. Rudolf Binion, *Hitler amongst the Germans* (New York, 1976), 1–35 and 138–42.

85. NSDAP Hauptarchiv, Reel 1, File 17.

86. Ibid.; Mrs. Gertrud Kren, personal communication.

87. Comparison of handwriting of Dr. Eduard Bloch and Mrs. Lily Bloch by court-approved graphological expert Felix Lehmann, New York, 1986.

88. Binion, *Hitler amongst the Germans,* 138–42.

89. *Mein Kampf,* 18.

90. Report of Admissions Test of Adolf Hitler, Vienna Academy of Fine Arts.

91. *Mein Kampf,* 20.

92. Ibid., 20.

93. Monologues, 27/28 Sept. 1941.

94. Kubizek, *Adolf Hitler,* 159.

95. Binion, *Hitler amongst the Germans,* 140.

96. Kubizek, *Adolf Hitler,* 158.

97. Bloch, "My Patient."

Chapter 2: Vienna

1. Adolf Hitler, *Mein Kampf* (Boston, 1943), 21, translated by Ralph Manheim from the German *Mein Kampf,* vols. 1 and 2 (Munich, 1925, 1927).

2. August Kubizek, *Adolf Hitler: Mein Jugendfreund* (Graz, 1953), 178.

3. Monologues, 1 Sept. 1942. Hitler's monologues are stated by dates rather than by title and page, because many authors have published annotated versions of the

monologues. The original notes can be found in the Bundesarchiv Koblenz. My principal source is Werner Jochmann, ed., *Adolf Hitler: Monologe im Führerhauptquartier 1941–1944. Die Aufzeichnungen Heinrich Heims* (Hamburg, 1980).

4. Kubizek, *Adolf Hitler*, 186.

5. Ibid., 179.

6. Ibid., 182. Hitler mixed up Potiphar, an officer of the pharaoh, with Potiphar's wife.

7. NSDAP Hauptarchiv, Reel I, File 17.

8. Kubizek, *Adolf Hitler*, 285.

9. Monologues, 24/25 January 1942.

10. Kubizek, *Adolf Hitler*, 243.

11. Ibid., 231.

12. NSDAP Hauptarchiv, Reel I, File 17.

13. Kubizek, *Adolf Hitler*, 216.

14. *Mein Kampf*, 22.

15. Wilfried Daim, *Der Mann, der Hitler die Ideen gab* (Munich, 1958; 1991).

16. Adolf Hitler, secret speech (*Geheimrede*), 23 November 1937, in Sonthofen.

17. Kubizek, *Adolf Hitler*, 195.

18. Ibid., 209.

19. Ibid., 192.

20. Ibid., 209.

21. *Mein Kampf*, 20.

22. Kubizek, *Adolf Hitler*, 188.

23. Ibid., 312. Not only Kubizek but also Hitler felt awkward. Hitler ended his letters formally, like business letters.

24. Ibid., 134.

25. *Mein Kampf*, 361.

26. Ibid., 40.

27. Ibid., 41. Also Kubizek, 178.

28. It is uncertain whether Hitler had such thoughts when he was in Vienna, or later when he wrote *Mein Kampf*.

29. *Mein Kampf*, 41.

30. Ibid., 75.

31. Ibid., 56–58.

32. Ibid., 57.

33. Ibid., 56–58.

34. Ibid., 59.

35. Brigitte Hamann, *Hitler in Wien: Die Lehrjahre eines Diktatoren* (Munich, 1996), 504; Kubizek, 285.

36. Reinhold Hanisch, "I Was Hitler's Buddy," *New Republic* 98 (5, 12, and 19 April 1939).

37. Hamann, *Hitler in Wien*, 496.

38. Kubizek, *Adolf Hitler*, 263.

39. Ibid., 85–99.

40. Ibid., 274.

41. Ibid., 273.

42. At the time when my manuscript was virtually finished, I read Hamann's newly published *Hitler in Wien* (Munich, 1996) and was deeply impressed with her scholarship and ideas, which independently affirmed my own. The book also vividly describes lower class Vienna before World War I; it was not the Vienna of the philoso-

pher Wittgenstein, who was a student at Hitler's *Realschule* almost at the same time Hitler was there.

43. With the exception of one move in the fall of 1909, Hitler's moves in Vienna can be followed through the obligatory registrations that are recorded in the NSDAP Hauptarchiv, Reel I, File 17.

44. Kubizek, *Adolf Hitler*, 154.

45. Ibid., 106.

46. A good description of the Meidling shelter for the homeless, as well as of the men's hostel in the Meldemannstraße, is contained in William Jenck's *Vienna and the Young Hitler* (New York, 1961).

47. Josef Greiner, *Das Ende des Hitler Mythos* (Vienna, 1947). Greiner is considered an unreliable informant.

48. Statement by Prof. Grassberger, NSDAP Hauptarchiv, Reel 86, File 1714.

49. Thomas Mann, "That Man Was My Brother," *Esquire*, March 1939, 131–32. Translated from German "Bruder Hitler," *Gesammelte Werke*, vol. XII (Frankfurt, 1960), 845–52.

Chapter 3: To Munich and World War I

1. Adolf Hitler, *Mein Kampf* (Boston, 1943), 126, translated by Ralph Manheim from the German *Mein Kampf*, vols. 1 and 2 (Munich, 1927).

2. Ibid.

3. Werner Maser, *Hitler: Legend, Myth, and Reality* (New York, 1973), 362, translated by Peter Ross and Betty Ross from the German *Hitler: Legende, Mythos, Wirklichkeit* (Munich, 1971). Maser obtained his data during personal interviews with the Popps.

4. *Mein Kampf*, 163.

5. Maser, *Hitler*, 54.

6. Adolf Hitler's letter to the Magistrate of the City of Linz, reprinted in Franz Jetzinger, *Hitlers Jugend: Phantasien, Lügen und die Wahrheit* (Vienna, 1956), 262. Jetzinger called it the "justification letter"; in modern American military jargon, it could be called a TS ("tough shit") letter.

7. Letter from the Austrian–Hungarian Consul in Munich to the Magistrate of the City of Linz, reprinted in Jetzinger, *Hitler's Jugend*, 257.

8. Adolf Hitler's letter to the Magistrate of the City of Linz, reprinted in Jetzinger, *Hitlers Jugend*, 262.

9. *Mein Kampf*, 128.

10. Copy (not original) of report of 5 February 1914, at Salzburg; now at the Österreichisches Kriegsarchiv, Vienna.

11. *Mein Kampf*, 161.

12. Ibid., 163.

13. Maser, *Hitler*, 86. Maser summarized laudatory comments by Hitler's superior officers.

14. Hans Mend, *Adolf Hitler im Felde* (Munich, 1931). See also B. Brandmayer, *Mit Hitler Meldegänger* (Überlinger, 1940).

15. Jean Michel Charlier and Jacques Launay, *Eva Hitler née Braun* (Paris, 1978), 32–35. See also Jean Marie Loret and R. Mathot, *Mon père s'appellait Hitler* (Paris, 1957), chapter 1.

16. Fritz Wiedemann, *Der Mann, der Feldherr werden wollte* (Berlin, 1964), 29.

17. Ibid.

18. Ibid.

19. Hitler's letters to Josef Popp and Ernst Hepp, reprinted in Eberhard Jäckel with Axel Kuhn, eds., *Adolf Hitler: Sämtliche Aufzeichnungen 1905–1924* (Stuttgart, 1980), 58–69.

20. Letter to Hepp, reprinted in ibid., 67.

21. *Mein Kampf*, 165.

22. Monologues, 10/11 November 1941. Hitler's monologues are stated by dates rather than by title and page, because many authors have published annotated versions of the monologues. The original notes can be found in the Bundesarchiv Koblenz. My principal source is Werner Jochmann, ed., *Adolf Hitler: Monologe im Führerhauptquartier 1941–1944. Die Aufzeichnungen Heinrich Heims* (Hamburg, 1980).

23. *Mein Kampf*, chapter 6.

24. Wiedemann, *Der Mann*, 26.

25. *Mein Kampf*, 201.

26. Archiv Dr. Georg Franz-Willing, cited in Ernst Günther Schenck, *Patient Hitler* (Düsseldorf, 1989), 307.

27. Jäckel and Kuhn, *Adolf Hitler*, 1062.

28. *Mein Kampf*, 204.

29. According to his daughter Dr. Ruth Wilmans Lidz, in 1932 Wilmans told medical students who doubted the occurrence of hysteria in men that Hitler suffered from hysteria. Wilmans had never examined Hitler, but he learned of Hitler's case history from trusted colleagues. After Hitler became Chancellor, Professor Wilmans was temporarily detained in "protective custody" and lost his job.

30. Ernst Weiss, *Der Augenzeuge* (Munich, 1963).

31. Ottmar Katz, *Prof. Dr. Med. Theodor Morell: Hitlers Leibarzt* (Bayreuth, 1982), 69.

32. Jäckel and Kuhn, *Adolf Hitler*, 1062.

33. Ibid.

34. Katz, *Prof. Dr. Med. Morell*, 72.

35. Karl von Wiegand, "Hitler Foresees His End," *Cosmopolitan*, 28/29 April 1939, 152–55.

36. *Mein Kampf*, 175.

37. Ibid., 207.

Chapter 4: Entry into Politics

1. An excellent account of Hitler's early evolution to Führer is found in Albrecht Tyrell, *Vom Trommler zum Führer* (Munich, 1975). Other important works about this period include: Ernst Deuerlin, "Hitlers Eintritt in die Politik und die Reichswehr," *Vierteljahreshefte für Zeitgeschichte* 7 (1959), 177–226; Werner Maser, *Der Sturm auf die Republik: Frühgeschichte der NSDAP* (Stuttgart, 1973); and Georg Franz Willig, *Die Hitler Bewegung* (Hamburg, 1962).

2. See Adolf Hitler, *Mein Kampf* (Boston, 1943); translated by Ralph Manheim from the German *Mein Kampf*, vols. 1 and 2 (Munich, 1925, 1927). In *Mein Kampf*, Hitler claimed he had already mentioned to comrades during the war his intention of becoming a *Werberedner*. In the English translation of *Mein Kampf* (p. 175), it is translated as speaker. Literally, it signifies a person who persuades, agitates, and recruits. (In modern times, this would come close to the talents of a radio or television evangelist.)

3. Tyrell, *Vom Trommler zum Führer*, 193.

4. Dietrich Eckart, *Der Bolshewismus von Moses bis Lenin: Zwiegespräche zwischen Adolf Hitler und mir* (Munich, 1925). The importance of this early manifestation of Hitler's anti-Semitism has been emphasized by Ernst Nolte.

5. Monologues, 1–2 December 1941. Hitler's monologues are stated by dates rather than by title and page, because many authors have published annotated versions of the monologues. The original notes can be found in the Bundesarchiv Koblenz. My principal source is Werner Jochmann, ed., *Adolf Hitler: Monologe im Führerhauptquartier 1941–1944. Die Aufzeichnungen Heinrich Heims* (Hamburg, 1980).

6. See N. Cohn, *Protocols of the Wise Men of Zion* (London, 1920).

7. Hitler speech of 7 August 1922, in Eberhard Jäckel with Axel Kuhn, eds., *Adolf Hitler: Sämtliche Aufzeichnungen 1905–1924* (Stuttgart, 1980), 677.

8. Alfred Rosenberg, *Der Mythos des zwanzigsten Jahrhunderts* (Munich, 1923).

9. Richard Wagner wrote widely about Jews, and his particular brand of anti-Semitism. More specifically, see "Das Judentum in der Musik," in *Gesammelte Schriften*, vol. 5 (Munich, 1977), 66.

10. Houston Stewart Chamberlain, *The Foundations of the Twentieth Century* (London, 1911); first published in German as *Die Grundlagen des Zwanzigsten Jahrhunderts* (Munich, 1906).

11. Hitler's letter to Alfred Gemlich, reprinted in Jäckel and Kuhn, *Adolf Hitler*, 88–90.

12. *Mein Kampf*, 219–20.

13. Joachim Fest, *Hitler* (New York, 1975), 120; translated by Richard Winston and Clara Winston from the German *Hitler*, pocketbook edition (Frankfurt, 1975).

14. *Mein Kampf*, 66.

15. Franz Willig, *Die Hitler Bewegung*, 66.

16. Anton Drexler, *Mein politisches Erwachen* (Munich, 1919).

17. *Mein Kampf*, 219.

18. Ibid., 222.

19. Hitler's letter to Captain Mayr, 4 October 1919, and letter to the DAP, 19 October 1919, cited in Jäckel and Kuhn, *Adolf Hitler*, 90–91.

20. Ibid.

21. *Mein Kampf*, 207.

22. The membership numbers started with 500; hence, at that time the DAP counted 55 members.

23. *Mein Kampf*, 224.

24. Ibid., 216.

25. Monologues, 10 May 1942.

26. Alan Bullock, *Hitler* (London, 1964), 61.

27. Monologues, 27 March 1942, evening.

28. Preface to *Mein Kampf*, 183. This paragraph summarizes Hitler's statements in chapter 6 of the first book and chapter 6 of the second book.

29. Ibid.

30. *Mein Kampf*, 471.

31. Ibid., 471.

32. Ibid., 469.

33. Ibid., 535.

34. Ibid., 477.

35. Ibid., 370.

36. Ibid., 533.

37. Ibid., 479.

38. Max Domarus, ed., *Adolf Hitler: Reden und Proklamationen 1932–1945* (Würzburg, 1962), vols. 1 and 2.

39. *Mein Kampf*, 533.

40. Werner Maser, *Mein Schüler Hitler: Das Tagebuch seines Lehrers Paul Devrient* (Pfaffenhofen, 1975).

41. Christa Schroeder, *Er war mein Chef: Aus dem Nachlaß der Sekretärin von Adolf Hitler*, ed. Anton Joachimsthaler (Munich, 1985), 53.

42. Hans Jürgen Eitner, *Der Führer* (Munich, 1981), 146.

43. André François-Poncet, *The Fateful Years: The Memoirs of a French Ambassador, Berlin 1931–1938* (New York, 1949), 356.

44. Kurt G. W. Lüdecke, *I Knew Hitler* (New York, 1937), 22.

45. Elias Canetti, *Masse und Macht* (Hamburg, 1984), 207.

46. *Mein Kampf*, 496–97.

47. Monologues, 3/4 January 1942. In this particular statement, Hitler did not talk about the word Führer itself, which derived from Mussolini's title, Duce, but of the address "my Führer" (*mein Führer*), which he particularly liked and which only Germans could use. He believed it had been used first by women.

48. In Georg Schott, *Das Volkbuch von Hitler*, cited by Albrecht Tyrell, *Vom Trommler zum Führer* (Munich, 1975), 272, n. 122.

49. Hitler's speech before the National Klub, 29 May 1922, in Jäckel and Kuhn, eds., *Adolf Hitler*, 642.

50. *Der Hitler Prozess vor dem Volksgericht in München: Erster Teil. Auszüge aus den Verhandlungsberichten* (Munich, 1924), 29.

51. Cited in Tyrell, *Vom Trommler zum Führer*, 153 and 271 (documents in Bundesarchiv Koblenz, NS26-49).

52. Hitler's speech at party rally, 11 November 1936, in Domarus, ed., *Adolf Hitler*, 611.

53. Hitler's speech of 13 November 1936, in ibid.

54. Cited in Philip W. Fabry, *Mutmaßungen über Hitler* (Düsseldorf, 1969), 91. See also Heinrich Brüning, *Memoiren* (Stuttgart, 1970), 650.

55. *Mein Kampf*, 441.

56. Monologues, 3/4 February 1942, night.

57. Henry Ashby Turner Jr., *German Big Business and the Rise of Adolf Hitler* (New York, 1985).

58. Monologues, 16 August 1942.

59. Oren Hale, "Adolf Hitler: Taxpayer," *American Historical Review* 55 (1960): 830–42.

60. Statement by Dr. Brinsteiner cited in Otto Lurker, *Hitler hinter Festungsmauern* (Berlin, 1933). See also Ernst Günther Schenck, *Patient Hitler* (Düsseldorf, 1989), 300.

61. *Hitler Prozess*, 28. See also Jäckel and Kuhn, *Adolf Hitler*, 1001.

62. Ernst Hanfstaengl, *Zwischen weißem und braunem Haus* (Munich, 1970), 149.

Chapter 5: Ascent to Power

1. Harold Gordon, *Der Hitler Prozess* (Munich, 1928), 28.

2. Otto Lurker, *Hitler hinter Festungsmauern* (Berlin, 1933), 68. The statement by Dr. Brinsteiner was translated by the author.

3. Ibid., 60.

4. For an overview, see Harold Gordon, *Hitler and the Beer Hall Putsch* (Princeton, 1974); and *Der Hitler Prozess: Auszüge aus den Verhandlungsberichten* (Munich, 1924).

5. Eberhard Jäckel with Axel Kuhn, eds., *Adolf Hitler: Sämtliche Aufzeichnungen 1905–1924* (Stuttgart, 1980), 1210.

6. Gordon, *Hitler and the Beer Hall Putsch*, 264.

7. Hans Frank, *Im Angesicht des Galgens* (Neuhaus, 1955), 38.

8. Monologues, 20 August 1942, evening. Hitler's monologues are stated by dates rather than by title and page, because many authors have published annotated versions of the monologues. The original notes can be found in the Bundesarchiv Koblenz. My principal source is Werner Jochmann, ed., *Adolf Hitler: Monologe im Führerhauptquartier 1941–1944. Die Aufzeichnungen Heinrich Heims* (Hamburg, 1980); translated by the author.

9. Adolf Hitler, *Mein Kampf*, vols. 1 and 2 (Leipzig, 1925, 1927). For citations and interpretations in this book, the revised English edition (1943; Boston, 1971) and translated by Ralph Manheim has been used.

10. Lurker, *Hitler*, 56.

11. Werner Maser, foreword to *Mein Kampf* (Munich, 1966), 32.

12. Preface to *Mein Kampf*, 32.

13. Karl Lange, *Unbeachtete Maximen: Mein Kampf und die Öffentlichkeit* (Stuttgart, 1968), 30.

14. Joseph Goebbels, entry for 10 June 1931 in *Die Tagebücher des Joseph Goebbels*, vol. 1 (Munich, 1987), 62.

15. *Mein Kampf*, 203.

16. Ibid., 21.

17. Conclusion to *Mein Kampf*, 688.

18. Max Domarus, ed., *Adolf Hitler: Reden und Proklamationen 1932–1945* (Würzburg, 1963); translated by the author. The term *Parteigeschichte* is used in many citations.

19. Hitler's Letter to an Unknown Person, in Jäckel and Kuhn, eds., *Adolf Hitler*, 525.

20. In spite of his excellent memory, Hitler was casual and at times misleading about dates. The errors in this version, however, are so gross that one might assume it was a fraudulent document.

21. Amongst others, for example, Robert G. L. Waite, *The Psychopathic God: Adolf Hitler* (New York, 1977), 163–64. Psychohistorian Peter Loewenberg told me once that *Mein Kampf* could be viewed as a fantasy that warrants interpretation. I hope that he or one of his students will pursue this project.

22. Hans Gatzke, "Hitler and Psychohistory," *American Historical Review* 78 (1973): 394–401; Hans Ulrich Wehler, " Psychoanalysis and History," *Social Research* 47 (1980): 53, "Kritiken und kritische Antikritiken," *Historische Zeitschrift* 225 (1977): 347–84.

23. *Mein Kampf*, 31–33.

24. Ibid., 28–29.

25. Ibid., 26.

26. Ibid., 246–51, 254–57, 439.

27. Ibid., 255.

28. Frank, *Im Angesicht*, 45.

29. Monologues, 9 October 1941, night.

30. Adolf Hitler, *Hitler's Secret Book* (New York, 1962); translated from the German *Hitlers zweites Buch* (Stuttgart, 1961).

31. Werner Best in Archiv Schenck, private possession of Ernst Günther Schenck, Aachen, Germany.

32. *Völkischer Beobachter*, 7 March 1925.

33. Carl G.W. Luedecke, *I Knew Hitler* (New York, 1937), 217–18.

34. *Völkischer Beobachter*, 27 February 1925.

35. Peter Bucher, *Der Reichswehrprozess 1929/30* (Boppard, 1967), 237.

36. Henry Ashley Turner Jr., *German Big Business and the Rise of Hitler* (Oxford, 1985) p. 341.

37. Joseph Goebbels, entry of 15 February 1926 in *Die Tagebücher des Joseph Goebbels*, vol. 1, 162.

38. Elke Fröhlich, "Hitler und Goebbels im Krisenjahr 1944," *Vierteljahresheft für Zeitgeschichte* 32 (1990): 195–224.

39. Ottmar Katz, *Prof. Dr. Med. Theodor Morell: Hitlers Leibarzt* (Bayreuth, 1982), 87.

40. Johannes von Müllern-Schönhausen, *Die Lösung des Rätsel Adolf Hitler* (Vienna, 1971). Müllern-Schönhausen is considered a controversial and unreliable author.

41. August Kubizek, *Adolf Hitler: Mein Jugendfreund* (Graz, 1953), 180.

42. Henry Ashley Turner Jr., ed., *Hitler aus nächster Nähe: Aufzeichnungen eines Vertrauten* (Frankfurt, 1987), 362.

43. The best data on Hitler's nutrition is provided by Schenck, an internist who sub-specialized in nutrition. See Ernst Günther Schenck, *Patient Hitler* (Düsseldorf, 1989), 27–60.

44. Ward Price, *I Know These Dictators* (London, 1938) p. 21.

45. Leni Riefenstahl, *A Memoir* (New York, 1992), 229; translated from the German, *Memoiren* (Munich, 1987).

46. Monologues, 26 January 1942, evening.

47. The citation is from Syberberg's film of Winifred Wagner.

48. Monologues, 26 January 1942.

49. Riefenstahl, *A Memoir*, 100.

50. Eva Braun, fragments of a diary, 26 February 1935 to 28 May 1935, special documents, Library of Congress, Washington, D.C.

51. Günther Peiss, "Die unbekannte Geliebte," *Stern* 24 (1959): 24–35; 62–65.

52. Ibid.

53. Turner, *Hitler*, 59.

54. Henriette Hoffmann von Schirach (based upon notes), *Frauen um Hitler* (Munich, 1983), 44–80.

55. Heinrich Hoffmann, *Hitler: Wie ich ihn sah* (Munich, 1974), 123.

56. Ernst Hanfstaengl, *Zwischen weißem und braunem Haus* (Munich, 1970), 233.

57. Henriette Hoffmann von Schirach, personal communication.

58. Based on inspection of a reproduction of a private letter and information provided by Maurice's widow, Dr. Hermine Maurice, Hitler and Geli were engaged, but Geli's mother objected to it. According to a widely circulated story, Hitler once bodily threw Maurice out when he found him in an embrace with Geli. Hitler also refused to pay Maurice his salary, although after a lawsuit Hitler paid him again. As it became evident during a postwar trial in which Maurice received a four-year sentence for his NS activities, a Jewish ancestor had been discovered in the SS man Maurice's history, and Himmler allegedly wanted him thrown out of the SS. Eventually, Maurice was reinstated in the SS and became reconciled with Hitler. Professor von Hasselbach

assumed that Maurice had some knowledge about Hitler's genital abnormality. Perhaps this knowledge saved his hide.

59. Heinrich Hoffmann, 127.

60. Ibid., 131.

61. A police report signed by a Dr. Müller—and cited in H. Horvath, "Das Grab von Onkel Adolphs Nichte," *Der Spiegel* 24 (1987): 83–99—was never found, nor is it clear which Dr. Müller signed the report. Perhaps Heinrich Müller, who became chief of the Gestapo, was in charge of the investigation, or rather obfuscation.

62. Turner, *Hitler*, 357.

63. Ibid.

64. Interview of Otto Strasser by OSS investigators, OSS file, National Archives, Washington, D.C. See also Otto Strasser, *Hitler und Ich* (Buenos Aires, 1940), 202–3.

65. OSS file, 922.

66. Strasser, *Hitler und Ich*, 129.

67. Cited in Turner, ed., *Hitler*, 128.

68. Reproductions of paintings fraudulently attributed to Hitler, as well as of all known Hitler paintings, drawings, and sketches, are included in Billy F. Price, *Hitler: The Unknown Artist* (Houston, 1985). (Of 740 paintings, drawings, and caricatures reproduced in this book, about twenty percent are fake reproductions.)

69. Hanfstaengl, *Zwischen weißem und braunem Haus*, 233.

70. When asked about this matter in a personal interview, Henriette Hoffmann von Schirach pointed out that it would be absurd to assume that her father, who had a very good business relationship with Hitler, would want to promote a very perverse relationship between Hitler and his adolescent daughter. She added during the interview, "For us young girls, he was an old man."

71. OSS report, 222.

72. In her passport, Eva Braun called herself a private secretary.

73. Jean Michel Charlier and Jacques de Launey, *Eva Hitler geborene Braun* (Stuttgart, 1979), 90; translated from the French *Eva Hitler née Braun* (Paris, 1978).

74. Albert Speer, *Inside the Third Reich,* (New York, Collier's edition, 1981), 93.

75. Nerin Gun, *Eva Braun* (New York, 1969). See also Charlier and de Launey, *Eva Hitler*; and Werner Maser, *Hitler: Legend, Myth, and Reality* (New York, 1973), translated by Peter Ross and Betty Ross from the German *Hitler: Legende, Mythos, Wirklichkeit* (Munich, 1971).

76. David Irving, *Führer und Reichskanzler* (Munich, 1989), 19.

77. Monologues, 25/26 January 1942, night.

78. Speer, *Inside the Third Reich*, 104.

79. For the hairdresser's alleged statement before attorney Klaus von Schirach in Munich, see Christa Schroeder, *Er war mein Chef: Aus dem Nachlaß der Sekretärin von Adolf Hitler,* ed. Anton Joachimsthaler (Munich, 1985), 156.

80. Gun, *Eva Braun*, 203.

81. Heinz Linge, *Bis zum Untergang* (Munich, 1980), 68, 93–94.

82. Dietmar Petnia, ed., *Sozialgeschichtliches Arbeitsbuch*, vol. 3 (Munich, 1978).

83. William L. Shirer, *The Rise and the Fall of the Third Reich* (New York, 1960), 136.

84. Ploetz, *Das dritte Reich* (Freiburg, 1983), 87.

85. Henry Ashley Turner Jr., *Thirty Days to Power* (New York, 1996).

86. Bennett Wheeler, *The Wooden Titan* (London, 1967).

87. The German word *einrahmen* does not denote framing, but rather being corralled.

Chapter 6: Führer and Chancellor

1. Joseph Goebbels, diary entry of 30 Jan. 1933, *Die Tagebücher von Joseph Goebbels*, vol. 2 (Munich, 1986), 357.

2. Hitler's *"Erste Proklamation als Regierungschef,"* 1 Feb. 1933, in Max Domarus, ed., *Adolf Hitler: Reden und Proklamationen 1932–1945* (Würzburg, 1962). vol. 1, 194.

3. Based on General Liebmann's notes, *Institut für Zeitgeschichte*, Munich, no. 167/51, folder 39.

4. "Wolfs Telegraphisches Büro (WTB)," in Domarus, ed., *Adolf Hitler*, vol. 1, 199.

5. *Völkischer Beobachter*, 18 May 1933, in ibid., 270.

6. Hitler's speech of 10 Nov. 1938, in ibid., 974.

7. Hans Mommsen, "The Reichstag Fire and its Political Consequences," in Hajo Holborn, ed., *From Republic to Reich* (New York, 1972), 129.

8. Hitler's speech before the Reichstag on 12 March 1933, in Domarus, ed., *Adolf Hitler*, vol. 1, 225.

9. Monologues, 12/13 January 1942. Hitler's monologues are stated by dates rather than by title and page, because many authors have published annotated versions of the monologues. The original notes can be found in the Bundesarchiv Koblenz. My principal source is Werner Jochmann, ed., *Adolf Hitler: Monologe im Führerhauptquartier 1941–1944. Die Aufzeichnungen Heinrich Heims* (Hamburg, 1980).

10. Saul Friedländer, *Pius XII and the Third Reich* (New York, 1966), 32.

11. Hitler's speech at the Reichsparteitag on 13 July 1934, in Domarus, ed., *Adolf Hitler*, vol. 1, 411.

12. Norbert Frei, *Der Führerstaat: Nationalsozialistische Herrschaft 1933 bis 1945* (Munich, 1987), 9.

13. Adolf Hitler, quoted in Peter Hayes, "Polycracy and Policy in the Third Reich: The Case of the Economy," in Thomas Childers and Jane Caplan, eds., *Reevaluating the Third Reich* (New York, 1993), 198, 208n. 48.

14. Henry Ashley Turner Jr., *German Big Business and the Rise of Adolf Hitler* (New York, 1985), 355.

15. Rainer Zitelmann, *Hitler: Selbstverständnis eines Revolutionärs* (Stuttgart, 1987).

16. Monologues, 5 Aug. 1942, evening.

17. Monologues, 19 Nov. 1941.

18. Hitler's speech of 4 July 1944, in Domarus, ed., *Adolf Hitler*, vol. 2, 2113.

19. Hitler's speech to the Gauleiter on 24 February 1945, in Domarus, ed., *Adolf Hitler*, vol. 2, 2203.

20. Norbert Frei provides a concise description of the Führerstaat in his book, *Der Führerstaat*.

21. Adolf Hitler, *Mein Kampf* (Boston, 1943), 443; translated by Ralph Manheim from the German *Mein Kampf*, vols 1 and 2 (Munich, 1925, 1927).

22. Ibid., 476.

23. Ibid., 449.

24. Ibid., 449–50.

25. Monologues, 9 Aug. 1942.

26. Ernst Fraenkel, *The Dual State* (New York, 1941).

27. *Mein Kampf*, 439.

28. Frei, *Der Führerstaat*, 107.

29. Hermann Göring, cited in Hjalmar Schacht, *Account Settled* (London, 1949), 216.

30. Monologues, 13 March 1944.

31. Hans Severus Ziegler, *Adolf Hitler aus dem Erleben dargestellt* (Göttingen, 1964), 114.

32. Edward N. Peterson, *The Limits of Hitler's Power* (Princeton, 1968).

33. Zitelmann, *Hitler*, 499.

34. *Mein Kampf*, 8.

35. Monologues, 13 March 1944.

36. Albert Zoller, *Hitler Privat: Erlebnisbericht einer Geheimsekretärin* (Düsseldorf, 1949), 149.

37. Hitler's speech of 16 March 1936, in Domarus, ed., *Adolf Hitler*, 606. This remark ("I am as secure as a somnambulist") allegedly was made at the time of the occupation of the Rhineland, when Hitler was very "nervous" about the outcome of his venture. (Incidentally, somnambulists are anything but secure.)

38. Monologues, 17 Sept. 1941.

39. Ibid.

40. Frei, *Der Führerstaat*, 128.

41. Monologues, 2 Nov. 1941.

42. Monologues, 17/18 Jan. 1942.

43. Monologues, 1/2 Aug. 1941.

44. Monologues, 16 Nov. 1941.

45. Monologues, 1/2 November 1941. See also the long discussion of judges in the monologue of 20 August 1942.

46. Peter Loewenberg, "The Unsuccessful Adolescence of Heinrich Himmler," *American Historical Review* 76 (1971):612–41.

47. Felix Kersten, *The Kersten Memoirs, 1940–1945* (London, 1956).

48. Christa Schroeder, *Er war mein Chef: Aus dem Nachlaß der Sekretärin von Adolf Hitler*, ed. Anton Joachimsthaler (Munich, 1985), 329.

49. Hans Ulrich Thamer, *Deutschland 1933–1945: Verführung und Gewalt* (Berlin, 1986).

50. Basic work on the Führer myth has been done by Ian Kershaw in *Der Hitler Mythos* (Stuttgart, 1980).

51. Monologues, 21/22 October 1941, night.

52. Monologues, 20 May 1942, noon.

53. Kershaw, *Der Hitler Mythos*, 25.

54. Leni Riefenstahl's film *Triumph of the Will* is commercially available on videotape.

55. Monologues, 20 May 1942, noon.

56. Sebastian Haffner, *The Meaning of Hitler* (New York, 1979), 84; translated from the German, *Anmerkungen zu Hitler* (Munich, 1976).

57. Gerhard Wagner, cited in Norbert Frei, ed., *Medizin und Gesundheitspolitik* (Munich, 1991), 17.

58. Michael Burleigh and Wolfgang Wippermann, *The Racial State: Germany, 1933–1945* (New York, 1991), 253.

59. Monologues, 5 September 1942.

60. Important works are: Benno Müller Hill, *Tödliche Wissenschaft* (Reinbeck, 1984); Robert J. Lifton, *The Nazi Doctors* (New York, 1983), 29; Alexander Mitscherlich and Fred Mielke, *Doctors of Infamy* (New York, 1949), translated from the German *Medizin ohne Menschlichkeit* (Frankfurt, 1947), and republished as *The Death Doctor* (London, 1962); and Robert N. Proctor, *Racial Hygiene: Medicine under the Nazis* (Cambridge, MA, 1988).

61. Erwin Baur, Eugen Fischer, and Fritz Lenz, *Grundriß der menschlichen Erblichkeitslehre und Rassenhygiene* (Munich, 1927).

62. Konrad Lorenz, "Domestikation verursachte Störungen arteigenen Verhaltens," *Zeitschrift für Angewandte Psychologie* 59 (1940):2–81. See also Norbert Bischof, *Gescheiter als alle die Laffen: Ein Psychogram von Konrad Lorenz* (Munich, 1993), 35.

63. Konrad Lorenz, personal communication.

64. The phrase was attributed to Hess by Martin Bormann.

65. *Mein Kampf*, 255.

66. Ibid., 402.

67. Ibid., 404.

68. Hitler's speech of 30 January 1934, as reported in the *Völkischer Beobachter*, 31 January 1934, cited in Domarus, ed., *Adolf Hitler*, vol. 1, 355.

69. Nuremberg Military Tribunals, Medical Case, vol. 2, 2414.

70. Ernst Klee, ed., *Dokumente zur Euthanasie* (Frankfurt, 1985), document no. 22; declaration by Viktor Brack, 86.

71. Bernhard Loesener, "Als Rassereferent im Reichsministerium des Inneren," *Vierteljahresheft für Zeitgeschichte* 9 (1961): 537.

72. See Hitler's remark in the monologues, 1/2 December 1941. Did Hitler think of his maternal grandmother Maria Schickel Gruber?

73. For a description and analysis of this event, see Hermann Graml, *Der 9. November 1938: Kristallnacht* (Bonn, 1957); and Peter Loewenberg, "The Kristallnacht as a Public Degradation Ritual," *Leo Baeck Institute Yearbook* XXXII (1987): 309–23.

74. Otto Dietrich, *Zwölf Jahre mit Hitler* (Munich, 1955), 55.

75. Goebbels, *Die Tagebücher*, vol. 3, 639.

76. Hitler's speech before the Reichstag on 30 January 1939, in Domarus, vol. 2, 1058.

77. Gregor Strasser, *Kampf um Deutschland* (Munich, 1932), 171.

78. *Mein Kampf*, 407–14.

79. Ibid., 413.

80. Burleigh and Wippermann, *Racial State*, 201.

81. Monologues, 3 April 1942.

82. Ziegler, *Adolf Hitler*, 57.

83. *Mein Kampf*, 414.

84. Felix Dahn (1834–1912), a German author of moderate fame, now virtually unread.

85. Monologues, 29 August 1942.

86. *Mein Kampf*, 14.

87. Ibid., 414.

88. Ibid., 403–4.

89. Ibid., 430.

90. Frei, *Der Führerstaat*, 117.

91. Monologues, 20/21 February 1942.

92. Burleigh and Wippermann, 204–06.

93. Hitler's speech in Reichenberg, 2 December 1938, in *Ursachen und Folgen*, ed. H. Michalis and E. Schraepeler, vol. 2, 138.

94. Monologues, 1 Sept. 1940.

95. Monologues, 25 Dec. 1941, evening.

96. *Mein Kampf*, 258.

97. Henry Picker, *Hitlers Tischgespräche im Führerhauptquartier* (Stuttgart, 1976), 221.

98. Hildegard Brenner, *Die Kunstpolitik des Nationalsozialismus* (Reinbeck bei Hamburg, 1963), 142–45.

99. Heinz Linge, *Bis zum Untergang*, ed. Werner Maser (Munich, 1987), 87.

100. Monologues, 17 Feb. 1942, evening.

101. Ibid. It is not certain whether he read these books.

102. Ibid.

103. Monologues, 25 June 1943.

104. Ernst Hanfstaengl, *Zwischen weißem und braunem Haus* (Munich, 1970), 55.

105. Intelligence Service Center OI Consolidated Interrogation Report no. 2, 15 October 1945; also no. 4, 29 Nov. 1945, National Archives, Washington, D.C.

106. Monologues, 30 April 1942.

107. Dr. Frederic Hacker, personal communication. (Dr. Hacker was a psychoanalyst who had good contacts with German refugee actors and directors in Hollywood.)

108. Monologues, 21 Aug. 1942.

109. Ziegler, *Adolf Hitler*, 60.

110. Hitler's speech before the Reichsparteitag, 1936, cited in Zitelmann, *Hitler*, 261, 518n.

111. Hitler's speech of 13 July 1934, in Domarus, ed., *Adolf Hitler*, vol. 1, 412.

112. Hitler's speech before the Reichsparteitag, 7 September 1937 in Domarus, ed., *Adolph Hitler*, vol. 1, 717.

113. Monologues, 26 Jan. 1942, evening.

114. Turner, *German Big Business*, 117.

115. Monologues, 3 April 1942.

116. Monologues, 22 Feb. 1942, evening.

117. Monologues, 24/25 January 1942.

118. Ibid., night.

119. Monologues, 20 August 1942.

120. Photograph of Hitler instructing his niece, Geli Raubal, on how to drive, (Preussischer Kulturbesitz: Bildarchiv), in Henry Picker, *Hitlers Tischgespräche im Führerhauptquartier* (Stuttgart, 1976), 32.

121. Monologues, 3/4 February 1942, night.

122. Werner Best, in Archiv Schenck, private collection of Ernst Günther Schenck, Aachen, Germany.

123. Monologues, 10/11 March 1942, night.

124. Monologues, 31 Jan. 1942, evening.

125. Goebbels, diary entry of 26 April 1942, *Die Tagebücher*.

126. Monologues, 22 Jan. 1942.

127. Monologues, 5 Nov. 1942.

128. Monologues, 28/29 Jan. 1942.

129. Monologues, 28/29 Dec. 1943.

130. Monologues, 5 Nov. 1942.

131. Albert Speer, introduction to Leonard L. Heston and Renate Heston, *The Medical Case Book of Adolf Hitler* (New York, 1979), 11–20.

132. Ernst Günther Schenck, *Patient Hitler* (Düsseldorf, 1989), 513.

133. Schroeder, *Er war mein Chef*, 152; personal communication with Henriette Hoffmann von Schirach, who verified Schroeder's account.

134. Dr. Gabriel Mayer, a former assistant of Professor Kielleuthner, told me in a

telephone conversation that he is "certain" that Hitler was not Kielleuthner's patient. In spite of Dr. Mayer's denial, I find Henriette Hoffmann's statement credible; Dr. Mayer may not have known about a private consultation that took place in 1919 or 1920.

135. Kurt Krueger, *Inside Adolf Hitler* (New York, 1941).

136. Diary notes by Dr. Theodor Morell on microfilm T253, referred to as Morell Diary and Correspondence of Dr. Morell on Microfilm 1270. National Archives, Washington, D.C.

137. It is not known who started Hitler's medication with Koester's pills. Morell did not mention them in his diary before September 1944.

138. Schenck, *Patient Hitler*, 315.

139. Karl Brandt, Consolidated Medical Interrogation Report of Hitler, CIR 201-CIR2, 15 Dec. 1945.

140. Lifton, *Nazi Doctors*, 114.

141. Headquarters U.S. Forces European, Military Intelligence Service Center, OI Consolidated Interrogation Report, CIR No. 4, 29 Nov. 1945: Hitler as seen by his doctors (henceforth referred to as Consolidated Medical Interrogation Reports of Hitler), National Archives of Modern Wars, Washington, D.C.

142. Albert Speer, *Inside the Third Reich: Memoirs* (New York, 1970), 104; translated from the German *Erinnerungen* (Berlin, 1969).

143. I am indebted to Kevin Frawley, D.D.S., for summarizing Hitler's dental pathology.

144. Ottmar Katz, *Prof. Dr. Med. Theodor Morell: Hitlers Leibarzt* (Bayreuth, 1982), 101.

145. Ibid., 34.

146. Joachim von Ribbentrop, *Zwischen London und Moskau* (Leoni am Starhemberger See, 1954), 64.

147. Mme. Titayna, cited in Domarus, ed., *Adolf Hitler*, 565; reported also in the *Völkischer Beobachter*, 26 Jan. 1936.

148. Monologues, 21/22 Dec. 1941.

149. *Mein Kampf*, 681.

150. Ernst Nolte, *Three Faces of Fascism* (New York, 1966).

151. Benito Mussolini, in *Encyclopedia Italiana*, vol. 32, cited in *Encyclopedia Britannica*, vol. 27, 465.

152. Monologues, 21/22 July 1941.

153. Ivone Kirkpatrick, *Mussolini* (New York, 1964), 189.

154. Ernest Jones, *The Life and Work of Sigmund Freud* (London, 1955), vol. 3, 113.

155. Monologues, 13 Dec. 1941, noon.

156. Monologues, 31 Jan. 1946, evening.

157. Rüdiger von Starhemberg, *Between Hitler and Mussolini* (London, 1942), 150.

158. *The Ciano Diaries* (New York, 1946), 364–65.

159. Adolf Hitler, interview with Mme. Titayna, journalist for the *Paris Soir*, on 26 January 1936, cited in Domarus, ed., *Adolf Hitler*, vol. 1, 565.

160. Hitler's speech before the Reichstag on 30 January 1937, in Domarus, ed., *Adolf Hitler*, vol. 1, 666.

161. *Mein Kampf*, 3.

162. These events are quite accurately described in Kurt von Schuschnigg, *The Brutal Takeover* (London, 1971) .

163. International Military Tribunal, 949-PS (hereafter referred to as IMT).

164. Cited in Schenck, *Patient Hitler*, 78. See also B. Brehm, *Am Rande des Abgrundes von Lenin bis Truman* (Vienna, 1950), 190.

165. Hitler's speech cited in the *Völkischer Beobachter*, 16 March 1938.

166. *Völkischer Beobachter*, 15 March 1938.

167. Monologues, 1 Sept. 1942, evening.

168. Domarus, ed., *Adolf Hitler*, vol. 1, 851.

169. Monologues, 1 Nov. 1941.

170. Speech of 12 Sept. 1938, in Domarus, ed., *Adolf Hitler*, vol. 1, 987.

171. Monologues, 1 November 1941, evening.

172. Domarus, ed., *Adolf Hitler*, vol. 1, 927.

173. William L. Shirer, *The Rise and Fall of the Third Reich*, paperback ed. (New York, 1960), 538.

174. Winston Churchill, 5 Oct. 1938, cited in Alan Bullock, *Hitler* (London, 1964), 430–31.

175. *The Testament of Adolf Hitler: The Hitler–Bormann Documents*, with an introduction by Hugh R. Trevor Roper (London, 1961), 84 (henceforth referred to as Bormann Documents).

176. IMT, XIII, 4, cited in Alan Bullock, *A Study in Tyranny* (New York, 1952), 431.

177. Bormann Documents, 84.

178. Monologues, 13 Jan. 1942, evening.

179. Zoller, *Hitler Privat*, 84.

180. Galleazo Ciano, *The Ciano Diaries, 1939–1943* (Garden City, 1945), 47.

181. Hitler, cited in Domarus, ed., *Adolf Hitler*, vol. 2, 1237.

182. Neville Chamberlain speech, *Times*, 18 March 1938.

183. Ernst von Weizsäcker, *Memoirs*, 27 March 1939 (Freiburg, 1950), 154.

184. Hitler's speech at Wilhelmshaven on 1 April 1939, cited in Domarus, ed., *Adolf Hitler*, vol. 2, 1119.

185. Adolf Hitler, *Akten zur deutschen Auswärtigen Politik*, VI, 574, Bundesarchiv Koblenz.

186. Paul Schmidt, *Statist auf diplomatischer Bühne* (Bonn, 1950), 460.

187. Von Ribbentrop, *Zwischen London und Moskau*, 184.

188. Generaloberst Franz Halder, *Kriegstagebuch, I* (Stuttgart, 1962), 38.

189. Heinrich Hoffmann, "Hoffmanns Erzählungen," *Münchner Illustrierte*, 48, no. 6 (1954).

190. *Mein Kampf*, 158.

191. Monologues, 31 July 1941.

192. Hitler's speech of 23 Aug. 1939, in Domarus, ed., *Adolf Hitler*, 1197.

193. Hitler's speech before top military leadership on 22 Aug. 1939, in ibid., 1234–40.

194. "Documents Concerning German-Polish Relations and the Outbreak of Hostilities between Great Britain and Germany," *The British Blue Book* (London, 1939), no. 56. See also Bullock, *A Study in Tyranny*, 484.

195. Birger Dahlerus, *The Last Attempt* (London, 1948), 61–62, 119, translated from Swedish *Sista Forsoket* by Alexandra Dick, Stockholm, 1945.

196. William L. Shirer, 1960, 538.

197. Schmidt, *Statist auf diplomatischer Bühne*, 451.

198. Hitler's speech before the Reichstag on 1 Sept. 1939, in Domarus, ed., *Adolf Hitler*, vol. 2, 1316.

199. A. J. P. Taylor, *The Origins of the Second World War* (London, 1961).

Chapter 7: Warlord

1. Paul Schmidt, *Statist auf diplomatischer Bühne* (Bonn, 1950), 464.

2. Hitler's Manifest to the German People, 3 Sept.1939, in Max Domarus, ed., *Adolf Hitler: Reden und Proklamationen 1932–1945* (Würzburg, 1962), vol. 2, 1300.

3. Joseph Goebbels, diary entry of 5 Dec. 1939, *Die Tagebücher von Joseph Goebbels* (Munich, 1987), 658.

4. Monologues, 18 Sept. 1941. Hitler's monologues are stated by dates rather than by title and page, because many authors have published annotated versions of the monologues. The original notes can be found in the Bundesarchiv Koblenz. My principal source is Werner Jochmann, ed., *Adolf Hitler: Monologe im Führerhauptquartier 1941–1944. Die Aufzeichnungen Heinrich Heims* (Hamburg, 1980).

5. The high estimate is questionable.

6. Trials of Major War Criminals, International Military Tribunals, 630-PS Ex 330. (henceforth referred to as "IMT)."

7. Karl A. Schleunes, "Nationalsozialistische Entschlußbildung und die Aktion T4," 74, in Eberhard Jäckel and Jürgen Rohwers, eds., *Der Mord an den Juden im Zweiten Weltkrieg* (Stuttgart, 1985). F. K. Kaul, *Nazimordaktion T4* (Berlin, 1973), 54; Ernst Klee, ed., *Dokumente zur Euthanasie* (Frankfurt, 1983); and Robert J. Lifton, *The Nazi Doctors* (New York, 1983).

8. IMT, 2498.

9. IMT, 2413.

10. Klee, *Dokumente*, 76–81; 100.

11. Schleunes, "Nationalsozialistische Entslußbilduing," 74.

12. Helmut Unger, *Sendung und Gewissen* (Berlin, 1935).

13. Alfred Hoche and Karl Binding, *Die Freigabe der Vernichtunglebensunwerten Lebens* (Leipzig, 1920).

14. Alexander Mitscherlich and Fred Mielke, *Doctors of Infamy* (New York, 1949), translated by Heinz Norden from the German *Das Diktat der Menschenverachtung* (Heidelberg, 1947). The book was bought up by right-wing groups, reappeared under the title *The Death Doctors* (London, 1961).

15. Monologues, 25 Oct. 1941, evening.

16. General Alfred Jodl, cited by David Irving, *Hitler's War* (New York, 1977), 100.

17. Hans Friedrich K. Günther, *Mein Eindruck von Hitler* (Pähl, 1969), 4 and 133ff.

18. John Toland, *Hitler* (New York, 1976), 614. According to Toland, it was trick cinematic photography by the Allies that made the scene appear like a Bavarian folk dance, a *Schuhplattler*.

19. Albert Speer, *Inside the Third Reich: Memoirs* (New York, 1970), 171.

20. Adolf Hitler, remark made in an undated war conference, cited by Percy Ernst Schramm, *Hitler als militärischer Führer* (Frankfurt, 1965), 111.

21. Hitler's speech before the *Reichstag* on 17 July 1940, in Domarus, ed., *Adolf Hitler*, vol. 2, 1540–49.

22. Schramm, *Hitler als militärischer Führer*, 151.

23. Monologues, 6 Sept. 1942.

24. *The Testament of Adolf Hitler: The Hitler–Bormann Documents*, with an introduction by Hugh R. Trevor Roper (London, 1961), 65; translated from the French, *Le testament politique de Adolf Hitler* (Paris, 1959).

25. Wolf Rüdiger Hess, *Mein Vater Rudolf Hess* (Munich, 1984), 91.

26. Galleazo Ciano, *The Ciano Diaries, 1939–1943* (Garden City, 1945), 351.

27. Hitler, cited in Domarus, ed., *Adolf Hitler*, 1714.

28. Ibid., 1715.

29. Hitler's secret speech on 22 August 1939, in Domarus, ed., *Adolf Hitler*, 1239.

30. Hitler, cited in Domarus, ed., *Adolf Hitler*, 1582; see also C. Streit, *Keine Kameraden: Die Wehrmacht und die sowietischen Kriegsgefangenen* (Stuttgart, 1981).

31. Monologues, 17 October 1941.

32. Saul Friedländer, *Pius XII and the Third Reich: A Documentation* (Hamburg, 1965), 78.

33. Franz Halder, *Kriegstagebuch* (Stuttgart, 1964), vol. 3, 38.

34. Schramm, *Hitler als militärischer Führer*, 155.

35. Franz Halder, *Hitler als Feldherr* (Munich, 1949), 51.

36. Monologues, 24 July 1942. Possibly, Hitler wanted to mislead his audience about his intentions, or perhaps the remark was a Freudian slip because he felt some ambivalence about the terrible slaughter for which he would be charged before history.

37. IMT, PS 710, 31 July 1941.

38. Alfred Rosenberg, 2 April 1941, cited in Robert M. W. Kempner, *Eichmann und Komplizen* (Zurich, 1961), 97.

39. IMT, NG 2586.

40. Monologues, 11/12 July 1941.

41. Note of 2 May 1940 in Major Gerhard Engel, *Heeresadjutant bei Hitler* (Stuttgart, 1974). See also H. Katze, ed., *Aufzeichnungen des Majors Engel* (Stuttgart, 1974)

42. Norbert Frei, "Die Juden im SS Staat," in Plötz, *Das dritte Reich* (Würzburg, 1983), 185–95.

43. Helmut Krausnik, "Hitler und die Befehle an die Einsatztruppen im Sommer 1941," in Eberhard Jäckel and Jürgen Rohwers, eds., *Der Mord an den Juden im Zweiten Weltkrieg* (Stuttgart, 1985), 88–106.

44. Monologues, 30 Aug. 1942, evening.

45. Hitler's Political Testament, 29 April 1945, in IMT NB 3569-PS.

46. Mitscherlich and Mielke, *The Doctors of Infamy*, 5–6.

47. Hitler's speech before the Reichstag on 30 Jan. 1942, in Domarus, ed., *Adolf Hitler*, 1826.

48. Hitler's speech of 24 Feb. 1942, in ibid., 1842

49. Hitler's speech of 8 Nov. 1942, in ibid., 1937.

50. Monologues, 17 Oct. 1941.

51. Monologues, 8–11 Aug. 1941.

52. Monologues, 25 Oct. 1941.

53. Monologues, 27 Jan. 1942.

54. Monologues, 22 Feb. 1942.

55. IMT, vol. 9, 678.

56. Speer's conscious and unconscious denials are described in Gitta Sereny, *Albert Speer: His Battle with the Truth* (New York, 1995).

57. Joachim von Ribbentrop, *Zwischen London und Moskau* (Leoni, 1954), 275.

58. See Eugene Davidson, *The Trial of the Germans* (New York, 1966), 315.

59. Goebbels, entry of 27 Febr. 1942, *Die Tagebücher*.

60. Gerald Fleming, *Hitler and the Final Solution* (Berkeley, 1982), 88.

61. Shlomo Aronson, *Reinhard Heydrich und die Frühgeschichte der NSDAP* (Stuttgart, 1971), 254; personal communication from Ella Linge, who knew Mengele personally in Auschwitz.

62. Aronson, *Reinhard Heydrich*, 254.

63. David Irving, *Hitler's War* (New York, 1977), 504.

64. Martin Broszat, "Hitler und die Genesis der Endlösung aus Anlaß der Thesen von David Irving," *Vierteljahreshefte für Zeitgeschichte* 25 (1977): 739–75. See also W. H. Koch, ed., *Aspects of the Third Reich* (New York, 1985), 390–429.

65. Werner Maser, *Adolf Hitler: Das Ende der Führer-Legende* (Düsseldorf, 1980), 213.

66. Monologues, 24 July 1942.

67. Heinrich Himmler, speech of 24 April 1943, in Bradley Smith and Agnes F. Peterson eds., *Heinrich Himmler: Geheimreden 1933–1945* (Frankfurt, 1975), 162–83.

68. Monologues, 4 April 1942.

69. Gerald Fleming, *Hitler and the Final Solution* (Los Angeles, 1984), 52; Irving, *Hitler's War*, 392; Richard Breitman, *The Architect of Genocide* (London, 1992), 238.

70. The statement has been reproduced by Irving in *Hitler's War*, 79, and by Jochen von Lang in *Der Adjutant Karl Wolff: Der Mann zwischen Hitler und Himmler* (Munich, 1955), 179. Wolff made it when he was 76 years old. He was considered by many contemporaries and historians, amongst them von Lang, to be an unscrupulous liar.

71. Henriette Hoffmann von Schirach, personal communication. It is impossible to assess the veracity of this story.

72. Protocol by Ambassador Walter Hewel, Film #7/0119 BAK. Cited by Andreas Hillgruber, *Staatsmänner und Diplomaten bei Hitler*, vol. 1 (Frankfurt, 1967), 557.

73. J. S. Hohmann, *Geschichte der Zigeunerverfolgung in Deutschland* (Frankfurt, 1981).

74. I have used Werner Jochmann, ed., *Adolf Hitler: Monologe im Führerhauptquartier 1941–1944. Die Aufzeichnungen Heinrich Heims*. I have also referred to data from 21 March to 31 July 1942 recorded by Henry Picker, *Hitlers Tischgespräche im Führerhauptquartier* (Stuttgart, 1976). All documents have been acquired by the Bundesarchiv Koblenz.

75. Hillgruber, *Staatsmänner und Diplomaten*, vol. 2, 31.

76. Monologues, 4 May 1942, night.

77. Monologues, 4/5 Jan. 1942, night.

78. Monologues, 26/27 Feb. 1942, night.

79. General Franz Halder, *Kriegstagebuch*, vol. 3 (Stuttgart, 1964), 421.

80. Ibid., 528.

81. Helmut Heiber, ed., *Hitlers Lagebesprechungen* (Stuttgart, 1962), 126–27.

82. Monologues, 5 Jan. 1942.

83. Hitler, telegram, T84/R274 0891, National Archives, Washington, D.C.; cited in Irving, *Hitler's War*, 441.

84. Schramm, *Hitler als militärischer Führer*, 65.

85. Cited in Domarus, ed., *Adolf Hitler*, vol. 2, 2040. This report is based on a statement by Hitler's valet, Linge, not a reliable witness.

86. Goebbels, diary entry of 5 June 1944, in *Die Tagebücher*.

87. Elke Fröhlich, "Hitler und Goebbels im Krisenjahr 1944," *Vierteljahreshefte für Zeitgeschichte* 38 (1990): 195–224.

88. Count Falke Bernadotte, *The Fall of the Curtain* (New York, 1945), 22.

89. Schmidt, *Statist auf diplomatischer Bühne*, 583.

90. Hitler, cited in Domarus, ed., *Adolf Hitler*, vol. 2, 2128.

91. Heinrich Himmler, speech of 6 Aug. 1944, cited in the *Vierteljahreshefte für Zeitgeschichte* 4 (1953): 357–84.

92. Irving, *Hitler's War*, 695.

93. Henning von Tresckow, cited in Fabian von Schlabrendorff, *The War against Hitler* (New York, 1966), 294.

94. Morell's medical diary, undated entry made during the first week of October 1944.

95. Irving, *Hitler's War*, 714 and 892.

96. Christian Zentner, *Illustrierte Geschichte des 2. Weltkriegs* (Cologne, 1989), 510; Hans Kluge; File OCMH, File X-967 (National Archives, Washington, D.C.).

97. Irving, *Hitler's War*, 695.

98. Hitler, cited in Domarus, ed., *Adolf Hitler*, vol. 2, 2172.

99. Hugh R. Trevor Roper, *The Last Days of Hitler* (New York, 1947), 1.

100. Monologues, 1 September 1940.

101. Albert Speer, introduction to Leonard L. Heston and Renate Heston, *The Medical Casebook of Adolf Hitler* (New York, 1979), 11–20.

102. Gitta Sereny, *Albert Speer: His Battle with the Truth* (New York, 1995).

103. Joachim Fest, *Hitler* (New York, 1978), 1150; translated by Richard Winston and Clara Winston from the German *Hitler* (Frankfurt, 1973).

104. *The Testament of Adolf Hitler*, The Bormann Document, February–April 1945 translated from the German by R. H. Stevens (London, 1960) first published in French *Testament Politique de Hitler* (Paris, 1959).

105. Ibid., 35.

106. Ibid., 32–33.

107. Ibid., 51.

108. Ibid., 54.

109. Ibid., 51.

110. Ibid., 51.

111. Ibid., 40.

112. Speer, *Inside the Third Reich*, 472.

113. Heinz Guderian, *Panzer Leader* (London, 1952); translated from the German *Erinnerungen eines Soldaten* (Stuttgart, 1951), 375–77.

114. Ellen Gibbels, based on a statement by Hitler's adjutant Otto Günsche, considered Guderian's statement to be exaggerated (but not untruthful). See also Ellen Gibbels, *Hitlers Parkinsonkrankheit: Zur Frage eines hirnorganischen Psychosyndroms* (Heidelberg, 1990), 45.

115. Albert Zoller, *Hitler Privat: Erlebnisbericht einer Geheimsekretärin* (Düsseldorf, 1949), 232.

116. Gerda Christian, cited by Ellen Gibbels, *Hitlers Parkinsonkrankheit*, 67.

117. Karl Koller, *Der letzte Monat* (Mannheim, 1948), 31.

118. Albert Kesselring, *Soldat bis zum letzten Tag* (Bonn, 1953), 338.

119. Goebbels, diary entry of 16 April 1945, in *Die Tagebücher*, vol. 10. Goebbels was observant of the marked fluctuations in Hitler's appearance and physical condition.

120. Guderian, *Panzer Leader*, 402.

121. Diary notes of General Karl Koller, cited in Schramm, *Hitler als militärischer Führer*, 127. See also Karl Koller, *Der letzte Monat* (Mannheim, 1948), 19.

122. Heiber, ed., *Lagebesprechungen*, 824.

123. *Der Spiegel* 20: no. 3 (10 Jan. 1966): 30–46.

124. IMT, 3734-PS.

125. Hitler's Political and Personal Testaments, in IMT, NB 3569 PS.

126. Theodor Morell Papers, diary and correspondence microfilm T253-R34-44; National Archives, Washington, D.C. Citations, unless noted, from Morell Diary. Reader is also referred to Appendices 1, 3–8.

127. Joachim von Ribbentrop, *Zwischen weißem und braunem Haus* (Leoni am Starhemberger See, 1954), 256.

128. Werner Best, in Archiv Schenck, private collection of Ernst Günther Schenck, Aachen, Germany; also cited in Schenck, *Patient Hitler*, 390.

129. Heinz Guderian, *Erinnerungen eines Soldaten* (Stuttgart, 1979), 402.

130. The account of Hitler's treatments by Dr. Giesing is based on Giesing's notes, "My Treatment of Adolf Hitler," in the Archives of the Institut für Zeitgeschichte in Munich.

131. H. Assmann, "Some Personal Recollections of Adolf Hitler," *Naval Institute Proceedings* 79 (Dec. 1953): 1289–95.

132. K. Wahl, *Es ist das deutsche Herz: Erlebnisse und Erkenntnisse eines ehemaligen Gauleiters: Patrioten und Verbrecher* (Hensenstamm, 1979), 385–89.

133. David Irving, ed., *The Secret Diaries of Hitler's Doctor* (New York, 1976), 272.

134. Ottmar Katz, *Prof. Dr. Med. Theodor Morell: Hitlers Leibarzt* (Bayreuth, 1982), 348.

135. Morell, letter to his wife, cited in Schenck, *Patient Hitler* (Düsseldorf, 1989), 502.

136. Tania Long, "Doctor Describes Hitler's Injections," *New York Times*, 22 May 1945.

137. "Hitler as Seen by His Doctors" (Professor Karl Brandt), Consolidated Interrogation Report, 15 Oct. 1945, Modern Military Records Division, National Archives, Washington, D.C.

138. Schenck, *Patient Hitler*, 441. (Schenck was in the Reichskanzlei at the time of Mussolini's death.)

139. Ernst Günther Schenck, *Als Arzt in Hitlers Reichskanslei* (Stockach, 1985), 119.

140. H. Michaelis and E. Schraepler, *Ursachen und Folgen: Urkunden und Dokumentensammlung 1918–1945*, vol. 12 (Berlin, 1966), 225.

141. Lev Bezymenski, *The Death of Adolf Hitler* (New York, 1968).

142. Lev Bezymenski, *Der Tod des Adolf Hitler* (Munich, 1982).

143. Elena Rshevskaya-Kagan, *Hitlers Ende ohne Mythos* (Berlin, 1945). Cited by Bezymenski. Clearly, the Russian reporters were under pressure to make false statements.

144. Reidar F. Sognaess and Ferdinand Strom, "The Odontological Identification of Adolf Hitler," *Acta Odontologica Scandinavia* 31 (1973): 43–69.

145. Schenck, *Patient Hitler*, 440.

146. Werner Maser, *Adolf Hitler: Legend, Myth, and Reality* (New York, 1973), 525–27.

147. Robert G. Waite, *The Psychopathic God: Adolf Hitler* (New York, 1977), 420.

148. Hans Ulrich Wehler, "Zum Verhältnis von Geschichtswissenschaft und Psychoanalyse," *Historische Zeitschrift* 208 (1969): 524–54.

149. The new data are related by Ada Petrowa and Peter Watson, *The Death of Adolf Hitler: The Full Story with New Evidence from Secret Russian Archives* (New York, 1995); and also in "Hitlers letzte Reise," *Der Spiegel* 46 (1992): 110–16.

150. "Aufzeichnungen des General Obersten Alfred Jodl," in Percy Ernst Schramm, *Hitler als militärischer Führer*, 154.

151. Koller, *Der letze Monat*, 19.

Chapter 8: Medical Review

1. Adolf Hitler, *Mein Kampf* (Boston, 1943), translated by Ralph Manheim from the German *Mein Kampf*, vols. 1 and 2 (Munich, 1925, 1927) 251.

2. Gestapo report of 24 January 1944 (Library of Congress, Washington, D.C.).

(The report of January 1944, seemed important enough to Himmler that he sent it to Bormann.) See also Ben E. Swearingen, "Hitler's Family," *Civilization* (March/April 1995): 54–55.

3. Joachim von Ribbentrop, *Zwischen London und Moskau* (Leoni, 1954), 256.

4. Ellen Gibbels, *Hitlers Parkinsonkrankheit: Zur Frage eines hirnorganischen Psychosyndroms* (Berlin, 1990).

5. Ernst Günther Schenck, *Patient Hitler* (Düsseldorf, 1989), 325–343.

6. Richard Pasternak, M.D., personal communication.

7. Ian Tillish, M.D., personal communication.

8. Joseph Perloff, M.D., personal communication.

9. Johannes Müllern-Schönhausen, *Die Lösung des Rätsels Adolf Hitler* (Vienna, n.d., [probably between 1950–1960])

10. Diaries of Dr. Theodor Morell, National Archives (Modern Wars Section), Washington, D.C., Microfilms T253-R62 and T253-R34-44.

11. Albert Speer, *Inside the Third Reich* (New York, Collier's edition, 1970), 104; translated from the German *Erinnerungen* (Frankfurt, 1969).

12. Schenck, *Patient Hitler*, 374.

13. Monologues, 8 Dec. 1944. Hitler's monologues are stated by dates rather than by title and page, because many authors have published annotated versions of the monologues. The original notes can be found in the Bundesarchiv Koblenz. My principal source is Werner Jochmann, ed., *Adolf Hitler: Monologe im Führerhauptquartier 1941–1944. Die Aufzeichnungen Heinrich Heims* (Hamburg, 1980).

14. Schenck, *Patient Hitler*, 378; see also the annotations in the section on abdominal complaints, 344–81.

15. Dennis M. Jenson, M.D., personal communication.

16. Sherman M. Mellinkoff, M.D., personal communication.

17. Howard Spiro, M.D., personal communication.

18. Schenck, *Patient Hitler*, 309.

19. Art Schwabe, M.D., personal communication.

20. Leonard L. Heston and Renate Heston, *The Medical Casebook of Adolf Hitler* (New York, 1979), 124.

21. Bert Edward Park, *The Impact of Illness on World Leaders* (Philadelphia, 1986), 158.

22. Howard Spiro, M.D., personal communication.

23. Sherman M. Mellinkoff, M.D., personal communication.

24. Schenck, *Patient Hitler*, 377.

25. *Mein Kampf*, 17.

26. This is based on the author's personal search in the Niederösterreichisches Landesarchiv, Vienna, Austria.

27. Eduard Bloch, "My Patient Adolf Hitler," *Colliers* 107, 15 March 1941, 35–39; 22 March 1941, 69–73.

28. Schenck came to the identical conclusion, *Patient Hitler*, 296.

29. "Hitler as Seen by his Doctors," O.I. Consolidated Interrogation Report no.2, 15 October 1945, National Archives, Washington, D.C.

30. O.I. Consolidated Interrogation Report no. 4, 29 November 1945.

31. Eberhard Jäckel with Axel Kuhn, eds., *Adolf Hitler: Sämtliche Aufzeichnungen 1905–1924* (Stuttgart, 1980), 1064.

32. Schenck, *Patient Hitler*, 307.

33. *Mein Kampf*, 204.

34. Helmuth Fanta, personal communication.

35. Speer, *Inside the Third Reich*, 335.

36. Bradley R. Straatsma, M.D., personal communication.

37. Edwin Hill, M.D., personal communication.

38. Autopsy report no. 12 in Lev Bezymenski, *The Death of Adolf Hitler* (New York, 1968). A second, expanded edition is: Lev Bezymenski, *Der Tod des Adolf Hitler* (Munich, 1982). No reference to original Russian text is made.

39. Heinz Linge, *Bis zum Untergang* (Munich, 1980), 93.

40. Christa Schroeder, *Er war mein Chef: Aus dem Nachlaß der Sekretärin von Adolf Hitler*, Anton Joachimsthaler, ed. (Munich, 1985), 274.

41. John Toland interview of Professor von Hasselbach, in the Toland Collection, Library of Congress, Washington, D.C.

42. Schenck, *Patient Hitler*, 216. The prisoner physicians were required to answer medical questionnaires, and it is likely that the deteriorated Dr. Morell did not know what he answered.

43. John Toland interview of Professor von Hasselbach.

44. Dr. Hermine Maurice, personal communication.

45. Morell Diary, entry of 28 October 1940.

46. *Mein Kampf*, 257.

47. Such views were expressed by, amongst others, Simon Wiesenthal, cited in Ron Rosenbaum, "Explaining Hitler," *The New Yorker*, 1 May 1995, 50–70.

48. Letter to the editor of the *Frankfurter Zeitung*, 10 June 1975 (Archiv Franz Willing), cited in Schenck, *Patient Hitler*, 124.

49. Felix Kersten, *The Kersten Memoirs* (London, 1956), 165–71.

50. Ibid., introduction by Hugh R. Trevor Roper.

51. Cited in John Toland, *Adolf Hitler* (New York, 1976), 1007.

52. *Mein Kampf*, 253.

53. Ellen Gibbels believed this particular tremor was not caused by Parkinson's syndrome. See Ellen Gibbels, "Hitlers Nervenkrankheit," *Vierteljahreshefte für Zeitgeschichte*, 42 (1994): 155–219; and Ellen Gibbels, "Hitlers Parkinson Syndrom," *Nervenarzt* 59 (1988): 521–528.

54. Linge, *Bis zum Untergang*, 160.

55. Albert Zoller, *Hitler Privat: Erlebnisbericht einer Geheimsekretärin* (Düsseldorf, 1949), 69.

56. Heinz Guderian, *Panzer Leader* (London, 1952), 442–43; translated from the German *Erinnerungen eines Soldaten* (Heidelberg, 1951).

57. Ernst Günther Schenck, cited by Hans Dietrich Röhrs, *Hitlers Krankheit: Die Zerstörung einer Persönlichkeit* (Neckargemünd, 1966), 173.

58. A. von Braunmühl, "War Hitler Krank?" in *Stimmen der Zeit*, 154 (1953/54): 94–102.

59. Werner Maser, *Hitler: Legend, Myth, and Reality* (New York, 1973), 231; translated from the German *Hitler: Legende, Mythos und Realität* (Munich, 1971).

60. Heston and Heston, *Medical Casebook*, 122.

61. Gibbels, "Hitlers Nervenleiden: Differentialdiagnose des Parkinson Syndroms," *Fortschritte Neurol. Psychiat.* 57 (1989):505–19; "Hitlers Parkinson Syndrom."

62. Röhrs, *Hitlers Krankheit*, 174.

63. Park, *Impact of Illness*, 157.

64. Walter Birkmayer and Peter Riederer, *Die Parkinson Krankheit* (Vienna, 1980), 2; also Walter Birkmayer, personal communication.

65. Johann Recktenwald, *Woran hat Adolf Hitler gelitten?* (Munich, 1963), 101.

66. Gottfried Engerth and Hans Hoff, "Über das Schicksal von Patienten mit Charaktervänderungen nach Encephalitis epidemica," *Deutsche medizinische Wochenschrift* 55 (1929): 181–183. Whether encephalitis caused changes in these patients is not certain. All of them were socially neglected and abused, and some had severe premorbid personality behavioral problems. Ten years later, Professor Erwin Stengel and I saw some of these patients at the Neurological University Clinic in Vienna, and were not impressed with the conclusions reached by Engerth and Hoff.

67. The literature about GCA and its treatment is large. The disease was first described in B. T. Horton, T. B. Magath, and G. L. Brown, "Arteritis of the Temporal Vessels," *Proceedings of the Mayo Clinic* 12 (1937): 548–53. Recent review articles, amongst others, include: G. G. Hunder, "Giant Cell (Temporal) Arteritis," *Rheumatic Diseases Clinics North America* 16 (1990): 399–409, and L. A. Healey and K. R. Wilske, *The Systemic Manifestations of Temporal Arteritis* (New York, 1978). Author's Publication: F. C. Redlich, *A New Medical Diagnosis of Adolf Hitler: Giant Cell Arteritis–Temporal Arteritis.* Archives of Internal Medicine 153 (1993), 693–97.

68. J. W. Jundt and D. Mock, "Temporal Arteritis with Normal Erythrocyte Sedimentation Rates," *Arthritis and Rheumatism Review* 34 (1991): 217–219.

69. Howard Kraus, M.D., personal communication.

70. Richard Pasternak, M.D., personal communication.

71. Howard Spiro, M.D., personal communication.

72. Gene G. Hunder, M.D., personal communication.

73. S. M. Wolff, "The Vasculitic Syndromes," in J. B. Wyngaarden and L. H. Smith, eds., *Cecil's Textbook of Medicine* (Philadelphia, 1988), 1988–2025.

74. B. Gramberg-Danielson, "Die Bedeutung des Arteritis temporalis für die Neurologie," *Nervenarzt* 25 (1954): 296–301; P. Siegert, "Akute Ischemie der Papille," *Klinisches Monatsblatt der Augenheilkunde* 120 (1952): 254–260.

75. Walter Birkmayer, personal communication.

76. Gene G. Hunder, M.D., personal communication.

77. J. S. Sargent, "Giant Cell Arteritis," *Archives of Internal Medicine* 151 (1991): 378–380.

78. B. P. Citron et al., "Necrotizing Angiitis with Drug Abuse," *New England Journal of Medicine* 283 (1970): 1003–1011.

79. M. W. Fishman and C. R. Schuster, "Behavioral, Biochemical, and Morphological Effects of Methamphetamine in the Rhesus Monkey," in B. Weiss and V. G. Laties, eds., *Behavioral Toxicology* (New York, 1972), 375–94.

80. Röhrs, *Hitlers Krankheit*, 179. See also H. Fikentscher, *Prof. Dr. Med. Theodor Morell 1936–1945* (Neckargemünd, 1972).

81. Heston and Heston, *Medical Casebook*; Park, *Impact of Illness*; Schenck, *Patient Hitler*; also Bert Edward Park, *Ailing, Aging, Addicted* (Louisville, 1993).

82. Schenck, *Patient Hitler*, 447.

83. E. H. Ellingwood and S. Cohen, eds., *Current Concepts in Amphetamine Abuse* (Washington, D.C., 1972).

84. Schenck, *Patient Hitler*, 447. In a previous statement to H. D. Röhrs, a high medical officer of the SA, Schenck repeated the same assertion but added that the quantities of Pervitin and caffeine frightened him; cited in Röhrs, *Hitlers Krankheit*, 95.

85. Heston and Heston, *Medical Casebook*, introduction by Albert Speer, 11–20.

86. Ibid, 37.

87. Ibid., 49.

88. Ibid., 39.

89. August Kubizek, *Adolf Hitler: Mein Jugendfreund* (Graz, 1953), 328.

90. Winifred Wagner, *Heritage of Fire* (Bayreuth/New York, 1945), 86.

91. William Bayles, "Caesars in Goose Step: Lifetime Personal Observations, 1940," cited in OSS Report, 3, National Archives, Washington, D.C.

92. Werner Best, cited in Schenck, *Patient Hitler*, 384.

93. Kubizek, *Adolf Hitler*, 203.

94. E. H. Ellingwood, "Amphetamine Psychosis," *Journal of Neurological and Mental Diseases* 144 (1967): 273–83.

95. Bert Park first expressed the same opinion, then corrected himself.

96. William L. Shirer, *The Rise and Fall of the Third Reich* (New York, 1959), 538.

97. Morell papers, T253-R39 and T253-R43, from 3934–3941 (cited by Schenck).

98. O.I. Consolidated Interrogation Reports, OI Circ. 4, 29 November 1945, National Archives, Washington, D.C.

99. Tania Long, "Doctor Describes Hitler Injections," *New York Times*, 22 October 1945.

100. Dr. Theodor Morell correspondence T253-R37, National Archives, Washington, D.C.

101. Monologues, 22 Jan. 1942, evening.

102. Monologues, 1 Sept. 1942.

103. Monologues, 11/12 March 1942.

104. C. F. Enloe and H. H. Reese, "This Was Hitler's Mind," *Colliers*, 4 May 1946.

105. Hugh R. Trevor Roper, *The Last Days of Hitler* (New York, 1947), 60.

106. Fikentscher, *Prof. Dr. Med. Theodor Morell*, 44–46.

107. Ottmar Katz, *Prof. Dr. Med. Theodor Morell: Hitlers Leibarzt* (Bayreuth, 1982) .

108. Ellen Gibbels, "Hitlers Nervenkrankheit."

109. Schenck, personal communication.

110. R. Frank, *Moderne Therapie*, 9th ed. (Berlin, 1938).

111. Schenck, *Patient Hitler*, 204.

112. Ibid., 205.

113. When I described Hitler's meager diet to Professor H. A. Turner, Jr., his terse comment was, "Couldn't happen to a nicer guy."

114. O.I. Consolidated Interrogation Report No. 4. Hitler as seen by his Doctors, Military Section, National Archives (Modern Wars), Washington, D.C.

115. Schenck, *Patient Hitler*, 416.

116. Ellen Gibbels, "Hitlers Nervenkrankheit."

117. Schenck, personal communication.

118. Jerrold M. Post and Robert S. Robins, *When Illness Strikes the Leader* (New Haven, 1993).

Chapter 9: A Psychopathological Profile

1. John Dollard, *Criteria for a Life History* (New York, 1949).

2. Rudolf Koppensteiner, *Die Ahnentafel des Führers* (Leipzig, 1937).

3. Ben F. Swearingen, "Hitler's Family Secret," *Civilization* (March/April 1995): 54–55.

4. Hans Frank, *Im Angesicht des Galgens* (Munich, 1953), 330.

5. Monologues, 21 Aug. 1942, noon. Hitler's monologues are stated by dates rather than by title and page, because many authors have published annotated versions of the monologues. The original notes can be found in the Bundesarchiv Koblenz. My principal source is Werner Jochmann, ed., *Adolf Hitler: Monologe im Führerhauptquartier 1941–1944. Die Aufzeichnungen Heinrich Heims* (Hamburg, 1980).

6. Werner Maser, *Hitler: Legend, Myth, and Reality* (New York, 1973), 23; translated from the German *Hitler: Legende, Mythos und Realität* (Munich, 1971).

7. Norbert Bromberg and Verna Volz Small, *Hitler's Psychopathology* (New York, 1983), 14.

8. Rudolf Binion, *Hitler amongst the Germans* (New York, 1976), 143–46.

9. Helmut Stierlin, *Adolf Hitler: Familienperspektiven* (Frankfurt, 1975), 50–88.

10. Adolf Hitler, *Mein Kampf* (Boston, 1943), 31–33; translated by Ralph Manheim from the German *Mein Kampf*, vols. 1 and 2 (Munich, 1925, 1927).

11. The question is whether it is just another relatively unimportant experience—a notion entertained by Hans W. Gatzke, "Hitler and Psychohistory," *American Historical Review* 78 (1973): 394–401; or a screen memory, as stated by Robert G. L. Waite, *The Psychopathic God: Adolf Hitler* (New York, 1977), 163–64.

12. Ibid., 163ff.

13. Bradley F. Smith, *Adolf Hitler: His Family, Childhood, and Youth* (Stanford, 1967), 55ff.

14. Ibid., 75.

15. *Mein Kampf*, 212.

16. Alice Miller, *For Your Own Good: Hidden Cruelty in Childrearing and the Roots of Violence* (New York, 1984), 147–95; translated by Hildegard Hannum and Hunter Hannum from the German *Am Anfang war die Erziehung* (Frankfurt, 1983).

17. Eberhard Jäckel with Axel Kuhn, eds., *Adolf Hitler: Sämtliche Aufzeichnungen 1905–1924* (Stuttgart, 1980), 1063.

18. The expression is attributed to Rudolf Augstein, editor of *Der Spiegel*.

19. *Mein Kampf*, 215ff.

20. Joachim Fest, *Hitler*, Vintage Book edition (New York, 1974) 120; translated by Richard and Clara Winston from the German *Hitler* (Frankfurt, 1973).

21. Albrecht Tyrell, *Vom Trommler zum Führer* (Munich, 1975). 272, n.122.

22. Jäckel and Kuhn, eds., *Adolf Hitler*, 1200.

23. H. A. Turner, Jr., *Thirty Days to Power* (New York, 1996).

24. Peter Loewenberg, "Nixon, Hitler, and Power: An Egopsychological Study," *Psychoanalytic Inquiry* 6 (1986): 27–48; and Michael Nelken, *Hitler Unmasked* (Glastonbury, 1996).

25. Ernst Kretschmer, *Physique and Character* (New York, 1926); H. Sheldon, S. S. Stevens, and W. B. Tucker, *The Varieties of Human Physique* (New York, 1940). Sheldon's terms endomorphic, mesomorphic, and ectomorphic are synonymous with Kretschmer's old terms pyknic, athletic, and leptosomic (asthenic).

26. Hans Friedrich Karl Günther, *Mein Eindruck von Hitler* (Pfähl, 1969). Hitler was an avid believer in the theories of Professor Günther, who adored Hitler and benefitted greatly from his support. After the demise of National Socialism, the professor became critical of Hitler.

27. Max von Gruber (private letter), cited in Konrad Heiden, *Adolf Hitler: Das Zeitalter der Verantwortungslosigkeit: Eine Biographie* (Zürich, 1936), 298.

28. Waite, *Psychopathic God*, 157–60.

29. Werner Best, cited in Ernst Günther Schenck, *Patient Hitler* (Düsseldorf, 1989), 385. Original statement in Archiv Schenck, private collection of Ernst Günther Schenck, Aachen, Germany.

30. Christa Schroeder, *Er war mein Chef: Aus dem Nachlaß der Sekretärin von Adolf Hitler*, ed. Anton Joachimsthaler (Munich, 1985), 75.

31. Waite, *Psychopathic God*, 131.

32. The Hoffmann collection is deposited in the National Archives in Washington,

D.C., and in the Bayrische Staatsbibliothek in Munich. A large number of Hoffmann's photographs were exhibited in German museums and published in Rudolf
Herz, *Hoffmann und Hitler: Fotografie als Medium des Führer-Mythos* (Munich, 1994).

33. The movies are in the Bundesfilmarchiv Koblenz.

34. *Mein Kampf*, 6.

35. August Kubizek, *Adolf Hitler: Mein Jugendfreund* (Graz, 1953), 68.

36. Monologues, 3 March 1942, noon.

37. Kubizek, *Adolf Hitler*, 32.

38. Galleazo Ciano, *The Ciano Diaries, 1939–1943* (Garden City, 1945), entry of 30
April 1942, 478.

39. Cited in Johann Recktenwald, *Woran hat Hitler gelitten?* (Munich, 1963), 84.

40. André François-Poncet, *The Fateful Years: Memoirs of a French Ambassador in
Berlin 1931–1938* (New York, 1949).

41. Ernst Hanfstaengl, *Zwischen weißem und braunem Haus* (Munich, 1970), 36 and
84.

42. Ibid., 36.

43. Important contributions are contained in the literary study by J. P. Stern,
Hitler: The Führer and his People (Los Angeles, 1975), and the linguistic study by Cornelius Schnauber, *Wie Hitler sprach und schrieb* (Frankfurt, 1972).

44. Werner Maser, *Adolf Hitler: Mein Kampf* (Esslingen, 1974), 50–90.

45. *Mein Kampf*, 102.

46. Ibid., 116.

47. Ibid., 249.

48. Hitler's speech before the Reichstag on 13 July 1934, cited in Max Domarus
(editor), *Adolf Hitler: Reden und Proklamationen 1932–1945* (Würzburg, 1963), vol. 1,
411.

49. *Mein Kampf*, 469.

50. Alfred Korzibsky, *Science and Sanity: Introduction to Non-Aristotelian Systems and
General Semantics* (Lancaster, 1953).

51. S. I. Hayakawa, *Language in Action* (New York, 1941).

52. Monologues, 25 October 1941, evening.

53. See Erik Erikson, "The Legend of Hitler's Childhood" (chapter 9), in *Childhood
and Society* (New York, 1950); J. P. Stern, *Hitler: The Führer and the People*, paperback
edition (Los Angeles, 1975), 78–84.

54. Felix Trojan, *Sprachrythmus und Vegetatives Nervensystem* (Vienna, 1951).

55. Cornelius Schnauber, *Wie Hitler sprach und schrieb* (Frankfurt, 1972).

56. Werner Maser, *Adolf Hitler*, 8th (paperback) edition (Munich, 1983), 474. The
author published a "blind analysis" of Hitler's handwriting. Was it truly a blind analysis? In any case it did not provide any new information.

57. Ludwig Klages, *Handschrift und Charakter* (Leipzig, 1941).

58. Erich Raeder, *Mein Leben*, vol. 2 (Tübingen, 1956), 210.

59. Heinz Assmann, "Some Personal Recollections of Adolf Hitler," *U.S. Naval
Institute Proceedings*, vol. 79 (1953):1289–1295.

60. General Alfred Jodl, cited in Percy Ernst Schramm, *Hitler als militärischer
Führer* (Frankfurt, 1965), 150.

61. Arnold Toynbee, *Acquaintances* (London, 1967), 276.

62. Bertrand de Jouvenel (21 February 1936), cited in Domarus, ed., *Adolf Hitler*,
vol. 1, 80.

63. *Mein Kampf*, 212.

64. Monologues, 22 Feb. 1942, evening.

65. Wilhelm Lange Eichbaum and Wolfram Kurth, *Genie: Irrsinn und Ruhm* (Munich, 1967).

66. Wolfgang De Boor, *Hitler: Mensch, Übermensch, Untermensch. Eine kriminalpsychologische Studie* (Frankfurt, 1985), 340–61.

67. Christa Schroeder, cited in Albert Zoller, *Hitler Privat: Erlebnisbericht einer Geheimsekretärin* (Düsseldorf, 1949), 36.

68. Albert Speer, *Inside the Third Reich: Memoirs*, Collier's ed. (New York, 1970), 231; translated by Richard and Clara Winston from the German *Erinnerungen* (Frankfurt, 1969).

69. Christa Schroeder, cited in Zoller, *Hitler Privat*, 230 and 42.

70. Erwin Giesing, U.S. Interrogation Report of June 15, 1945, cited in Maser, *Adolf Hitler*, 395.

71. Ellen Gibbels, *Hitlers Parkinsonkrankheit: Zur Frage eines hirnorganischen Psychosyndroms* (Berlin, 1990), 16.

72. *Mein Kampf*, 22.

73. Jäckel and Kuhn, eds., *Adolf Hitler*, addendum.

74. Hans Frank, *Im Angesicht des Galgens* (Neuhaus, 1955), 46.

75. Zoller, *Hitler Privat*, 113.

76. Interrogation Reports of Hitler's Physicians, Headquarters U.S. Forces European Theater, Military Intelligence, O.I. Consolidated Interrogation Report no. 4, 29 November 1945, National Archives (Modern Wars), Washington, D.C.

77. Dietrich Eckart, *Der Bolschevismus von Moses bis Lenin* (Munich, 1925).

78. Monologues, 25/26 January 1942.

79. Monologues, 17 February 1942.

80. Monologues, 19 May 1944.

81. *Mein Kampf*, 10.

82. Franz Jetzinger, *Hitlers Jugend: Phantasien, Lügen und die Wahrheit* (Vienna, 1956), 107–08.

83. Percy Ernst Schramm, *Hitler als militärischer Führer: Aufzeichnungen des Generaloberst Jodl* (Bonn, 1965), 145.

84. See, amongst others: Gert Buchheil, *Hitler der Feldherr* (Rastatt, 1958); Lothar Gruchmann, *Der Zweite Weltkrieg* (Munich, 1967); B. H. Lidell Hart, *History of the Second World War* (London, 1970).

85. Jeffrey L. Cummings, *Dementia* (Boston, 1983), 33ff.

86. Schramm, *Hitler als militärischer Führer*, 137.

87. Hjalmar Schacht, *Account Settled* (London, 1949), 101; translated from the German *Abrechnung mit Hitler* (Hamburg, 1948).

88. Schroeder, *Er war mein Chef*, 207.

89. Gibbels, *Hitlers Parkinsonkrankheit*, 67.

90. Albert Speer, *Inside the Third Reich*, 472.

91. Albert Kesselring, *The Memories of Field Marshall Albert Kesselring* (London, 1954); translated from the German *Soldat bis zum Ende* (Bonn, 1953), 386.

92. Karl Koller, *Der letzte Monat* (Mannheim, 1948), 19.

93. Monologues, 2 Nov. 1941.

94. Monologues, 17/18 Jan. 1942.

95. Hermann Göring, International Military Tribunal, vol 9, 489.

96. Zoller, *Hitler Privat*, 203.

97. Harry Murray, *Explorations in Personality* (New York, 1938), 81.

98. John P. Flynn, "The Neural Basis for Aggression in Cats," in D. Glass, ed., *Neurophysiology and Emotion*, (New York, 1967), 40–59.

99. J. Reid Melroy, *The Psychopathic Mind* (Northvale, 1988), 185–242.

100. Schroeder, *Er war mein Chef*, 79.

101. Tyrell, *Vom Trommler zum Führer*, 109.

102. Monologues, 25/26 Sept. 1941.

103. Monologues, 26 Aug. 1942.

104. Hitler on 10 Nov. 1938, cited in Domarus, ed., *Adolf Hitler*, vol. 1, 974.

105. Monologues, 29 Aug. 1942.

106. Hans Jürgen Eitner, *Der Führer* (Munich, 1981), 49.

107. Monologues, 26 Jan. 1942, night.

108. Erich Fromm, *Anatomy of Destruction* (New York, 1973); also Petra Tauscher, *Nekrophilie und Faschismus* (Frankfurt, 1985).

109. Edwin Shneidman, *Suicide as Psychache* (Northvale, 1993), 15.

110. Peter Loewenberg, "Nixon, Hitler, and Power."

111. Werner Maser, *Hitler: Das Ende der Führerlegende* (Düsseldorf, 1980), Maser expounded on his passivity thesis in great detail in part 1, pp. 15–243.

112. Monologues, 28/29 Dec. 1941.

113. Monologues, 25 Oct. 1941, evening.

114. Fragments of Eva Braun's diaries can be found in the Special Collections of the Library of Congress, Washington, D.C. See also Günther Peis, "Die unbekannte Geliebte," *Stern* 24 (1959): 24–35, 62–65.

115. Hanfstaengl, *Zwischen weißem und braunem Haus*, 71.

116. Third-party communications from H. D. Röhrs to E. G. Schenck, cited in Schenck, *Patient Hitler*, 123.

117. Heinz Linge, *Bis zum Untergang: Als Chef des persönlichen Dienst bei Hitler*, Werner Maser, ed. (Munich, 1980), 69.

118. Werner Maser, *Adolf Hitler*, 8th (pocket) edition (Munich, 1977), 527.

119. Schenck, *Patient Hitler*, 122.

120. Otto Strasser, varying statements in OSS Report and in *Hitler und Ich* (Buenos Aires, 1940), 73.

121. Walter Langer, *The Mind of Adolf Hitler* (New York, 1972), 134 and 167.

122. Waite, *Psychopathic God*, 237.

123. Norbert Bromberg and Verna Volz Small, *Hitler's Psychopathology* (New York, 1983), 243.

124. The first comment was made by Gertrud Kurth, "The Jew and Adolf Hitler," *Psychoanalytic Quarterly* 16 (1947): 11–32.

125. Interrogation of Paula Hitler, National Archives (Modern Wars), Washington, D.C. See also Institut für Zeitgeschichte, David Irving Collection, Munich, Germany.

126. Alexander Mitscherlich, personal communication.

127. I once discussed this problem with Konrad Lorenz, who felt persuaded by Alice Miller's arguments.

128. *Mein Kampf*, 17.

129. Kubizek, *Adolf Hitler*, 274.

130. *Mein Kampf*, 270.

131. Ibid., 182.

132. Willi Baur, *Geschichte und Wesen der Prostitution im Dritten Reich* (Stuttgart, 1965).

133. This unusual measure is reminiscent of Samuel Butler's novel *Erewhon*, concerning a fantasy country where disease, but not crime, was punished.

134. Kubizek, *Adolf Hitler*, 273.

135. Hitler's speech before the Reichstag on 13 July 1934, cited in Domarus, ed., *Adolf Hitler*, vol. 1, 1308.

136. This was a central concept for Sigmund Freud, which he described in many articles, amongst others "Analysis of a Phobia of a Five-Year-Old Boy" (vol. 10, pp. 1–148) and "History of an Infantile Neurosis (vol. 17, 1–123), both in *Standard Edition of the Complete Psychological Works*, ed. James Strachey (London, 1974). Translated from the German "Analyse der Phobie eines fünfjährigen Knaben," *Gesammelte Werke* (1909).

137. Hans Severus Ziegler, *Hitler aus dem Erleben dargestellt* (Göttingen, 1964), 57.

138. J. M. Loret and R. Mathot, *Mon père s'appellait Adolf Hitler* (Paris, 1957). See also Werner Maser, "Adolf Hitler: Vater eines Sohnes," *Zeitgeschichte* 87 (1978): 200.

139. C. V. Steffen and F. A. Vogel, "Ein Sohn Hitlers," *Homo* 29 (1976): 145–58.

140. Monologues, 25/26 Jan. 1942.

141. Albrecht Tyrell, *Vom Trommler zum Führer* (Munich, 1975), 40.

142. Hans Dietrich Röhrs, cited in Schenck, *Patient Hitler*, 123.

143. Emile Maurice, cited in ibid., 153.

144. Monologues, 10/11 March 1942, night.

145. H. A. Turner Jr., ed., *Hitler aus nächster Nähe: Aufzeichnungen eines Vertrauten 1929–1932* (Frankfurt, 1978), 128.

146. Monologues, 26 Jan. 1942, night.

147. Monologues, 1 March 1942.

148. Monologues, 26 January 1942.

149. Henriette von Schirach, *Frauen um Hitler: Nach Materalien* (Munich, 1983), 44.

150. Hanfstaengl, *Zwischen weißem und braunem Haus*, 231. At the time, Hanfstaengl may have gotten ideas from Washington psychoanalysts.

151. OSS file, Adolf Hitler, National Archives, Washington, D.C. See also Strasser, *Hitler und Ich*, 285.

152. Bromberg and Small, *Hitler's Psychopathology*, 247.

153. Walter C. Langer, *The Mind of Adolf Hitler* (New York, 1972), 19. I wonder what "typical" means to these psychoanalysts who, by necessity, see only very few patients over a lifetime. No clear pattern can be discerned, except sadomasochistic traits, which occur frequently with or without such a perversion.

154. Waite, *Psychopathic God*, 226.

155. Strasser, *Hitler und ich*, 168.

156. Ibid., 74.

157. Eva Braun, *Tagebuch-Fragmente* Library of Congress (Special Collections), Washington, D.C.

158. Henriette Hoffmann, personal communication.

159. Schroeder, *Er war mein Chef*, 156.

160. Klaus von Schirach, personal communication.

161. Peis, "Die unbekannte Geliebte."

162. Monologues, 25/26 Jan. 1942.

163. Ibid., night.

164. Monologues, 23 April 1942.

165. Ibid.

166. Monologues, 14 May 1942.

167. Monologues, 9 April 1942.

168. Monologues, 25/26 Sept. 1941.

169. Letters to Popp Family in Jäckel and Kuhn, eds., *Hitler*, 58–60.

170. Hitler's letter to Ernst Hepp, 5 Feb. 1915, in Jäckel and Kuhn, eds., *Adolf Hitler*, 64–69.

171. *Mein Kampf*, 163–66.

172. B. Brehm, *Am Rande des Abgrunds* (Vienna, 1950), 190, cited by Schrenck, *Patient Hitler*, 78.

173. Morell diary entry, 3 Oct. 1944.

174. Peter Loewenberg, "Anxiety in History," *Journal of Preventive Psychiatry and Allied Disciplines* 4 (1990): 141–64.

175. Morell diary entries, 27 and 28 Oct. and 30 Dec. 1944.

176. Cited in Schenck, *Patient Hitler*, 316.

177. Schroeder, *Er war mein Chef*, 74.

178. August Kubizek, cited in Franz Jetzinger, *Hitlers Jugend* (Vienna, 1956), 159.

179. The OSS files contain a reference to a bathing accident of an unemployed man named Adolf H. who drifted into a strong current in the summer of 1911 and had to be rescued. It is not certain whether Adolf H. refers to Adolf Hitler.

180. Monologues, 20 July 1942, evening.

181. Enloe Cortez F., Report of an interrogation, from personal files T Forces, 12th Army Group, (Wiesbaden), 16 June 1946.

182. Morell diary entry, 6 June 1943. See also Schenck, *Patient Hitler*, 233.

183. Monologue of 31 Aug. 1944. See also Helmut Heiber, ed., *Hitlers Lagebesprechungen* (Stuttgart, 1962), 616.

184. *The Testament of Adolf Hitler: The Bormann Documents*, with an introduction by Hugh R. Trevor Roper (London, 1959), 94.

185. Monologues, 27 Feb. 1942.

186. *The Testament of Adolf Hitler: The Bormann Documents*, 36.

187. Helmut Heiber, ed., *Hitlers Lagebesprechungen*, (Stuttgart, 1962).

188. Gerhart Piers, *Shame and Guilt* (Springfield, MA, 1953).

189. Ibid.

190. Monologues, 3/4 Jan. 1942.

191. Morell diary entry of 30 September 1944, T253–62, National Archives (Modern Wars), Washington, D.C.

192. Adolf Hitler, *Testament*, in Nuremberg Documents, NB 3564-PS.

193. Freud, "The Ego and the Id" (vol. 19), *Standard Edition of the Complete Psychological Works*.

194. Kubizek, *Adolf Hitler*, 328.

195. NSDAP Hauptarchiv, Reel I/File 17.

196. Monologues, 19 Nov. 1941.

197. Adolf Hitler, cited in Heiber, ed., *Hitlers Lagebesprechungen*, 63.

198. *The Testament of Adolf Hitler: The Bormann Documents*, 54.

199. *Der Spiegel* 3 (1966): 42.

200. Cited in Werner Maser, *Das Ende der Führerlegende* (Düsseldorf, 1980), 401, n. 22.

201. Monologues, 3/4 Jan. 1942.

202. Monologues, 13 May 1942.

203. Joseph Goebbels, *Die Tagebücher des Joseph Goebbels* (Munich, 1987), entry of 27 April 1942.

204. Monologues, 3/4 Jan. 1942.

205. Norman Cameron, "The Paranoid Community Revisited," *American Journal of Sociology*, 14 (1959), 52–62.

206. Carl Jaspers, *Allgemenie Psychopathologie* (Heidelberg, 1946), 80.

207. De Boor, *Hitler*, 25–34 and 201–48.

208. Carl Wernicke, "Über fixe Ideen," *Deutsche medizinische Wochenschrift*, (1892): 581–82.

209. C. Lasegue and J. Falret, "La folie á deux ou folie communiqué," *Annals of Medical Psychology*, 18(1877): 321–35.

210. Theodore Lidz, Steven Fleck, and Alice Cornelius, *Schizophrenics and their Families* (New York, 1966). Lidz once casually defined the family as a social unit ruled by the sickest member.

211. Robert S. Robins, "Paranoid Ideation and Charismatic Leadership, *Psychohistory Review* 6 (1986): 15–55; Robert S. Robbins and Jerrold M. Post, "The Paranoid Political Actor," *Biography* 10 (1987): 1–19.

212. Robins, "Paranoid Ideation and Charismatic Leadership."

213. Monologues, 27 Jan. 1942, noon.

214. Monologues, 5 Jan. 1942, noon.

215. Helmut Heiber, ed., *Hitlers Lagebesprechungen*, 824.

216. Anna Freud, *The Ego and Mechanism of Defense* (New York, 1946).

217. Robert J. Lifton, *The Nazi Doctors* (New York, 1986), 443–47.

218. H. A. Turner, *Hitler aus nächster Nähe: Berichte eines Vertrauten* (Berlin, 1978), 358.

219. Sigmund Freud, "Jokes and their Relation to the Unconscious" (vol. 8, p. 1), *Standard Edition of the Complete Psychological Works*. Translated from the German, "Der Witz und seine Beziehung zum Unbewußten," *Gesammelte Werke*, 6 (1905).

220. Christa Schroeder, cited in Zoller, *Hitler Privat*, 126.

221. Monologues, 21 Aug. 1942, evening.

222. Henriette Hoffmann, personal communication.

223. Albert Krebs, *Tendenzen und Gestalten der NSDAP* (Stuttgart, 1948), 128.

224. According to Waite, Hitler assumed the professor masturbated, because ice cream cones did not exist at the time. The Austrians, however, used paper wafer cones filled with whipped cream, custard, nuts, or seeds long before ice cream cones became popular. In the picture, the word "pepper" is printed on the wrapper of the cone. See Waite, *Psychopathic God*, 158.

225. Hans Severus Ziegler, *Adolf Hitler aus dem Erleben dargestellt* (Göttingen, 1964), 78.

226. Hitler's speech of 8 Nov. 1942, cited in Domarus, ed., *Adolf Hitler*, 1531.

227. Hitler on 10 Nov. 1938, cited in Domarus, ed., *Adolf Hitler*, 1007.

228. Freud, "Psychoanalytic Notes on an Autobiographical Account of a Case of Paranoia (Dementia Paranoides)" (vol. 12, p. 11), *Standard Edition of the Complete Psychological Works*. Translated from the German "Psychoanalytische Bemerkungen eines autobiographisch beschriebenen Fall von Paranoia (Dementia paranoides)," *Gesammelte Werke* 3 (1911).

229. *Mein Kampf*, 325.

230. Bromberg and Small, *Hitler's Psychopathology*, 278.

231. Binion, *Hitler amongst the Germans*, 1–23.

232. Monologues, 14 October 1941. In a paper entitled "Wotan" in Zurich's *Neue Schweizer Rundschau* (3 March 1936): 657–59, Carl Gustav Jung, in his unique style, compared Hitler with a dangerous, stormy, seizing (*ergreifenden*) archetype.

233. Friedrich Meinecke, *Die deutsche Katastrophe* (Wiesbaden, 1946), 89. Cited by Hans Ulrich Thamer, *Verführung und Gewalt* (Berlin, 1986), 629.

234. Freud, "On Narcissism: An Introduction" (vol. 14, p. 69), *Standard Edition of*

the Complete Psychological Works. Translated from the German "Zur Einführung des Narzissismus," *Gesammelte Werke* 10 (1914).

235. Speer, *Inside the Third Reich*, 353.

236. Albert Speer, introduction to Leonard L. Heston and Renate Heston, *The Medical Casebook of Adolf Hitler* (New York, 1979).

237. Speer, *Inside the Third Reich*, 367.

238. Erich von Manstein, *Verlorene Siege* (Bonn, 1955), 317.

239. Joachim von Ribbentrop, *Zwischen London und Moskau* (Leoni am Starhembergersee, 1954), 45.

240. Walter Best, in Archiv Schenck (private possession of Ernst Günther Schenck).

241. Strasser, *Hitler und Ich*, 69.

242. Carl Gustav Jung, Oct. 1938, cited in Binion, *Hitler amongst the Germans*, 53.

243. Friedelinde Wagner, *Heritage of Fire* (New York, 1945), 31.

244. Home movies by Eva Braun, Filmarchiv, Bundesarchiv Koblenz.

245. Speer, *Inside the Third Reich*, 479.

246. Schroeder, *Er war mein Chef*, 88.

247. Domarus, ed., *Adolf Hitler*, vol. 1, 142.

248. Monologues, 21 and 22 Oct. 1941.

249. Waite, *Psychopathic God*, 155. Waite based his assertions on statements by Peter Blos, "Comments on the Psychological Consequences of Cryptorchism," *Psychoanalytic Study of the Child* 15 (1960 [1966]): 408–20.

250. J. P. Stern discussed Hitler's concept of will, from a literary point of view, in *The Führer and His People* (Berkeley, 1975).

251. Erik Erikson, *Identity and the Life Cycle* (New York, 1959).

252. Monologues, 18 Jan. 1942.

253. Hitler's speech of 10 April 1923 in Munich, in Jäckel and Kuhn, eds., *Adolf Hitler*, 873. The citation is from the Bible, Revelations 4: 16.

254. Field Marshal Rommel, cited in Hans Speidel, *Invasion* (Tübingen, 1961), 305.

255. Karl von Wiegand in *N.Y. American*, 5 January 1930.

256. Ward Price, *Führer und Duce* (Berlin, 1939), 206

257. Monologues, 24/25 Jan. 1942.

258. Monologues, 2 Nov. 1941, noon.

259. Monologues, 24/25 Jan. 1942

260. Hitler's speech of 1 May 1939, cited in Domarus, ed., *Adolf Hitler*, 1181.

261. Birger Dahlerus, *The Last Attempt* (London, 1948), 61.

262. Ambassador Hewel, cited in David Irving, *Hitler's War* (New York, 1977), xvi.

263. Sisela Bok, *Lying: Moral Choice in Public and Private Life* (New York, 1978).

264. Ron Rosenbaum, "Explaining Hitler," *New Yorker*, (11 May 1995): 50–70. Note citation of Nietzsche by A. Bullock, 67.

265. Ibid.

266. Nuñez Cabeza de la Vaca and Long Haniel, *The Power Within Us: Story of His Journey from Florida to the Pacific* (New York, 1944).

267. Erikson, *Identity and the Life Cycle*.

268. Thomas Mann, "Bruder Hitler," *Gesammelte Werke*, vol. 2.

269. Max Weber, *Essays in Sociology* (New York, 1948), 295.

270. This concept was stated first by Robert C. Robins in "Paranoid Ideation and Charismatic Leadership," *Psychohistory Review* 6 (1986), 15–55; and by Robbins and Post, "The Paranoid Political Actor."

271. Hitler's speech before the Parteitag on 12 Sept. 1936 in Domarus, ed., *Hitler*, vol. 1, 643.

272. Bible, King James version, Revelations 4:16.

273. *Mein Kampf*, 212.

274. Nobody was more sensitive to the inconsistencies and ambiguities of Hitler about religion and even race than Friedrich Heer, *Der Glaube des Adolph Hitler* (Munich, 1968). Werner Jochmann also focuses on this in Adolph Hitler, *Monologe in Führerhauptquartier 1941–1944* (Hamburg, 1980), 35.

275. Monologues, 5 April 1942.

276. Monologues, 31 March 1942.

277. Monologues, 21 July 1941 and 2 May 1942.

278. Monologues, 27 Feb. 1942.

279. Monologue of 5 July 1942.

280. Monologues, 11 Nov. 1941.

281. *Mein Kampf*, part II, chapter 2.

282. *Mein Kampf*, 430.

283. Monologues, 21 Sept. 1941.

284. Adolf Hitler, cited in Turner, *Hitler aus nächster Nähe: Aufzeichnungen eines Vertrauten 1929–1932*, 234.

285. Henry Peterson, *The Limits of Hitler's Power* (Princeton, 1968).

286. W. R. Bion, *Experiences in Groups* (New York, 1961).

287. Stierlin, *Adolf Hitler: Familienperspektiven*, 141.

288. Martin Broszat, "Soziale Motivation und Führerfindung des Nationalsozialismus," *Vierteljahreshefte für Zeitgeschichte* 18 (1970): 392–409.

289. Alexander Mitscherlich, preface to Stierlin, *Adolf Hitler*, 9.

290. Peter R. Hofstätter, *Einführung in die Sozialpsychologie* (Stuttgart, 1963), 359.

291. E. Frenkel, E. Brunswick, D. J. Levinson, and R. N. Sanford, *The Authoritarian Personality* (New York, 1950).

292. Hans Mommsen, *Adolf Hitler als Führer der Nation* (Tübingen, 1984).

293. Irving Janis, "Crucial Decisions: Leadership in Crisis" in *Policy Making and Crisis Management* (New York, 1989).

294. Goebbels, diary entry of 6 June 1944, *Die Tagebücher*.

295. Ian Kershaw, *Hitler* (New York, 1991).

296. General Jodl, cited in Schramm, *Hitler*, 145–55.

297. Monologues, 21/22 October 1941, night.

298. Monologues, 20/21 Feb. 1942.

299. See Jäckel and Kuhn, eds., *Adolf Hitler*; also numerous speeches and in the monologues (13 August 1920).

300. The most systematic exposition is in *Mein Kampf*, chapter 11; many references can be found in the monologues—e.g., a succinct statement in the monologues is, "The stronger prevails, that is the law of nature" (Monologues, 23 September 1941).

301. Monologues, 1 Dec. 1941, night.

302. *Mein Kampf*, conclusion.

303. Larry W. Thompson, "Lebensborn and the Eugenics of the Reichsführer SS," *Central European History* 4 (1971): 55–77.

304. *Mein Kampf*, 255.

305. Ibid., 310; many other statements to this point can be found in *Mein Kampf*. See also monologues, 25 Jan. 1942.

306. *Mein Kampf*, 286.

307. Ibid.

308. Ibid., 562.

309. Monologues, 17 Sept. 1941.

310. Binion, *Hitler amongst the Germans*, 143–46.

311. Monologues, 23 Sept. 1941, evening.

312. *Mein Kampf*, 6.

313. Ibid.

314. Monologues, 19/20 Aug. 1941.

315. Hitler's speech of 17 May 1933, cited in Domarus, ed., *Adolf Hitler*, 273.

316. Monologues, 22/23 July 1941, night.

317. Karl Dietrich Bracher, "Zeitgeschichte im Wandel der Interpretationen," *Historische Zeitschrift* 225 (1977): 635–55.

318. Adolf Hitler, secret speech to the leadership class at the Nazi academy (Ordensburg) at Sontofhen, 23 Nov. 1937, reproduced in Henry Picker, ed., *Hitlers Tischgespräche im Führerhauptquartier* (Stuttgart, 1976): 491–502.

319. From his earliest speeches in 1920 to the Bormann documents, Hitler expressed a dislike of the French—with the exception of ambivalent praise for Napoleon.

320. Since childhood, Hitler had a deep dislike and underestimation of all Slavs. In one statement in his monologue of 22 July 1942, he indicated that the Russians ought not to receive smallpox inoculations.

321. Hitler despised southern Italians and the Italian Court, a sentiment expressed in his monologue of 17 Feb. 1942.

322. Hitler believed the Americans had no culture and were poor soldiers. However, he admired American industry. See statements in the monologue of 7 Jan. 1942.

323. Monologues, 22 Jan. 1942.

324. Monologues, 26 Aug. 1942.

325. Adolf Hitler, "Der Weltkrieg und seine Macher" abstract of speech of 19 June 1920 in Rosenheim, cited in Jäckel and Kuhn, eds., *Adolf Hitler*, 147–48.

326. One can assume this on the basis of Hitler's speeches around 1922.

327. Sebastian Haffner, *The Meaning of Hitler* (Cambridge, 1979), 84; translated by Ewald Osers from the German *Anmerkungen zu Hitler* (Munich, 1978).

328. *Mein Kampf*, 57–8.

329. Monologues, 12/13 Jan. 1942, night.

330. *The Testament of Adolf Hitler: The Bormann Documents*, 57.

331. Monologues, 22 Feb. 1942, evening.

332. Monologues, 19 Nov. 1941.

333. Daniel Jonah Goldhagen, *Hitler's Willing Executioners* (New York, 1996).

334. Monologues, 11/12 July 1941.

335. *Mein Kampf*, 51.

336. Kubizek, *Adolf Hitler*, 107.

337. *Mein Kampf*, 56.

338. Paula Hitler, Military Interrogation, National Archives (Military Section), Washington, D.C. See also the David Irving Collection, Institut für Zeitgeschichte.

339. Brigitte Hamann, *Hitlers Wien: Lehrjahre eines Diktatoren* (Munich, 1996), 506.

340. Wilfried Daim, *Der Mann, der Hitler die Ideen gab* (Vienna, 1985).

341. Dietrich Eckart, *Der Bolschevismus von Moses bis Lenin: Zweigespräche zwischen Hitler und mir,* Hauptarchiv der NSDAP, no. 668. Theodor Fritzsch, *Handbuch der Judenfrage* (Hoover Library, Stamford), LEIPZIG 1936, 36th edition, was warmly recommended by Hitler as the catechism of anti-Semitism (see Jäckel and Kuhn, eds., *Adolf Hitler*, 219).

342. Monologues, 1/2 Dec. 1941.

343. Alfred Rosenberg expressed his ideas in rather turgid style in *Der Mythos des zwanzigsten Jahrhunderts* (Munich, 1923).

344. *Mein Kampf*, 307.

345. Hitler's letter to Adolf Gemlich, 18 Sept. 1919, cited in Jäckel and Kuhn, eds., *Adolf Hitler*, 88.

346. Hitler's "Why Are We Anti-Semites?" 13 August 1920, cited in ibid., 219.

347. Hitler's hate speech of 10 April 1923, ibid.,873.

348. Archives of the Institut für Zeitgeschichte, ZS 640 Hell, Josef.

349. *Mein Kampf*, 679.

350. Peter Loewenberg, *The Kristallnacht as a Public Degradation Ritual*. (Leo Baeck Institute: Year Book XXXII, 1987).

351. Hitler's speech of 30 Jan. 1939, in Domarus, ed., *Adolf Hitler*, vol. 1, 1058.

352. Michael R. Marrus, *The Holocaust in History* (New York, 1987), xii.

353. Monologues, 25 Oct. 1941, evening.

354. Tim Mason, "A Current Controversy about the Interpretation of National Socialism," in Gerhard Hirschfeld and Luther Kettenacker, eds., *Der Führerstaat: Mythos und Realität* (Stuttgart, 1981). A very informative summary statement about both theories is provided by Saul Friedländer in the book by Eberhard Jäckel and Jürgen Rohwer, *Der Mord an den Juden im Zweiten Weltkrieg: Vom Antisemitismus zur Judenvernichtung*; see particularly Saul Friedländer, "Von Antisemitismus zur Judenvernichtung: Eine histobiographische Studie zur nationalsozialistischen Judenpolitik und Versuch einer Interpretation," 18–70. The intentionalist position was presented by Lucie Dawidowiz, *The Holocaust and the Historians* (Cambridge, Mass., 1981); Gerald Fleming, *Hitler and the Final Solution* (Berkeley, 1982), and, particularly, Eberhard Jäckel, "Die Entschlussbildung als historisches Problem" in Eberhard Jäckel and Jürgen Rohwer, eds., *Der Mord an den Juden* (Stuttgart, 1985), 9–17. Examples of the functionalist approach are found in Hans Mommsen, "Der nationalsozialistische Polizeistaat und die Judenverfolgung," *Vierteljahreshefte für Zeitgeschichte*, 10 (1962), 76–100; and Martin Broszat, "Hitler und die Genesis der Endlösung," *Vierteljahreshefte für Zeitgeschichte*, 25 (1977): 752.

355. Christopher R. Browning, "Beyond Intentionalism and Functionalism: A Reassessment of Nazi Jewish Policy from 1939 to 1941," in *Reevaluating the Third Reich*, Thoma Childers and Jane Caplan, eds. (New York, 1993), 211–33.

356. Raul Hilberg, *The Destruction of the European Jews*, paperback edition (New York, 1961), 120.

357. This is based on a statement by Himmler to his adjutant Karl Wolff. See Jochen von Lang, *Der Adjutant* (Munich, 1985), 179.

358. Shlomo Aronson, "The Triple Threat," *Vierteljahreshefte für Zeitgeschichte* 32 (1984): 29–65.

359. Saul Friedländer, *Nazi Germany and the Jews: Years of Persecution, 1933–1939* (New York, 1997), 73–112.

360. Rudolf M. Lowenstein, *Christians and Jews* (New York, 1952).

361. Gertrud M. Kurth, "The Jew and Adolf Hitler," *Psychoanalytical Quarterly* 16 (1947): 11–2.

362. Binion, *Hitler amongst the Germans*, 138–43.

363. Gertrud Kren, personal communication.

364. Peter Loewenberg, "Psychohistorical Perspectives," *Journal of Modern History* 47:2 (1975).

365. Waite, *Psychopathic God*, 127–29.

366. Monologues, 21 Aug. 1942, noon.

367. Monologues, 21 Aug. 1942.

368. Waite, *Psychopathic God*, 365ff.

369. Hermann Rauschning, *Gespräche mit Hitler* (Zurich, 1970).

370. David Irving, introduction to *Hitler's War* (New York, 1977).

371. Waite, *Psychopathic God*, 391.

372. Harold D. Laswell, *Psychopathology and Politics* (New York, 1960), 261ff.

373. *Mein Kampf*, 246–51, 254–57, 439.

374. Frank, *Im Angesicht des Galgens*, 38.

375. *Mein Kampf*, 246–51, 254–57, 439.

376. Ibid., 253.

377. Ibid., 59.

378. Ibid., 252.

379. Ibid., 255.

380. Ibid., 249.

381. Ibid., 251.

382. Again, this is reminiscent of Samuel Butler's classic novel, *Erewhon*, about a state in which disease, but not crime, was punished.

383. *Mein Kampf*, 251.

384. Schroeder, *Er War mein Chef*, 9–10.

385. NSDAP Hauptarchiv, Reel I, file 17.

386. *Mein Kampf*, 134.

387. Ibid., 136.

388. Monologues, 19/20 Aug. 1941.

389. Cited in Fest, *Hitler*, 621.

390. Irving, *Hitler's War*, xv.

391. Monologues, 8 Feb. 1942.

392. Monologues, 11/12 July 1941.

393. "Adolf Hitler's Geheimrede vor dem militärischen Führernachwuchs vom 30. März 1942," cited in Henry Picker, *Hitlers Tischgespräche im Führerhauptquartier* (Stuttgart, 1976), 491–502.

394. Bradley F. Smith, *Adolph Hitler: His Family, Childhood, and Youth* (Stanford, 1967), 27.

395. Monologues, 8/9 Jan. 1942.

396. Monologues, 13 Dec. 1941, noon.

397. Monologues, 19/20 Aug. 1941.

398. *Mein Kampf*, 114.

399. Monologues, 13 Dec. 1941.

400. Monologues, 4 Apr. 1942.

401. Monologues, 25 Oct. 1941, evening.

402. Monologues, 11/12 July 1941.

403. Monologues, 14 Oct. 1941.

404. Monologues, 11 Aug. 1942.

405. Friedrich Heer, *Der Glaube des Adolph Hitler* (Munich, 1958).

406. Monologues, 13 Dec. 1941, noon.

407. *Mein Kampf*, 307; see also similar statement in a speech of 12 April 1921 cited by Jäckel and Kuhn, eds., *Adolf Hitler*, 623.

408. Monologues, 21 Oct. 1941, noon.

409. Monologues, 30 Nov. 1944.

410. Goethe's *Faust*, Part 1, In Faust's Study. Translation by Walter Kaufmann (New York, 1963) pp. 158–59.

411. *Diagnostic and Statistical Manual of Mental Disorders*, 4th ed. (Washington, D.C., 1994).

412. Carl G. Hempel, "Problems of Taxonomy and Their Application in Nosology and Nomenclature in the Mental Diseases," in Joseph Zubin, ed., *Field Studies in the Mental Disorders* (New York, 1961), 3–22.

413. Ellen Gibbels, *Hitlers Parkinsonkrankheit* (Berlin, 1990), 77.

414. Heston and Heston, *Medical Casebook*, 124.

415. Robert S. Robins, and Jerrold M. Post, "Political Paranoia," *The Psychopolitics of Hatred* (New Haven, 1997).

416. Heston and Heston, *Medical Casebook*, 72.

417. Wolfgang Treher, *Hitler, Steiner, Schreber* (Emmendingen, 1966).

418. Johann Recktenwald, *Woran hat Hitler gelitten: Eine neuropsychiatrische Deutung* (Munich, 1963), 81.

419. Oswald Bumke, *Erinnerungen und Betrachtungen* (Munich, 1952).

420. Hans Strotzka, personal communication.

421. Personal communication from one of my teachers, Professor Eugen Kahn, who attributed the statement to Ernst Kretschmer.

422. Schroeder, *Er war mein Chef*, 112.

423. Robert P. Knight, "Borderline States," *Bulletin of the Meininger Clinic* 17 (1953): 1–12.

424. R. R. Grinker and B. Werba, *The Borderline States* (New York, 1968).

425. O. F. Kernberg, *Severe Personality Disorders* (New Haven, 1984).

426. Heinz Kohut, *The Analysis of Self* (New York, 1971).

427. John E. Mack, introduction to *Borderline States* (New York, 1975).

428. J. Masterson, *Treatment of the Borderline Adolescent* (New York, 1972).

429. Wilhelm Reich, *Character Analysis* (New York, 1949).

430. J. C. Perry and G. L. Klerman, "The Borderline Patient: A Comparative Analysis of Four Sets of Criteria," *Archives of General Psychiatry* 35 (1978): 141–50.

431. Samuel Guze, "Differential Diagnosis of Borderline Syndrome," in John E. Mack, ed., *Borderline States*, 69–74.

432. Bromberg and Small, *Hitler's Psychopathology* 7–26, 157–202.

433. Robert S. Robins and Jerrold M. Post, "Political Paranoia," *The Psychopolitics of Hatred* (New Haven, 1997).

434. F. C. Redlich, "The Concept of Normality," *American Journal of Psychotherapy* 6 (1952): 551–56; F. C. Redlich, "The Concept of Health in Psychiatry," in Alexander Leighten, John A. Clausen, and Robert N. Wilson, eds., *Explorations in Social Psychiatry* (New York, 1957), 138–67.

435. Harry Stack Sullivan, *The Psychiatric Intereview* (New York, 1954).

436. Personal communication with psychoanalyst Ernst Kris, a friend of Georg W. Groddeck.

437. Kurt Krueger, *Hitler Was My Patient; or, Inside Adolph Hitler* (New York, 1941).

438. Dr. Ella Lingens, personal communication. Dr. Lingens received this information from Prince Loewenstein, an intimate acquaintance of Freud.

439. De Boor, *Hitler*, 403.

440. M'Naghten Test: M'Naghten's Case 1843/10 C&F 210-211 8 Eng. Rep. 722–23.

441. American Law Institute Model Penal Code, 1962.

442. Hannah Arendt, *Eichmann in Jerusalem: A Report on the Banality of Evil* (New York, 1963), 279.

Index